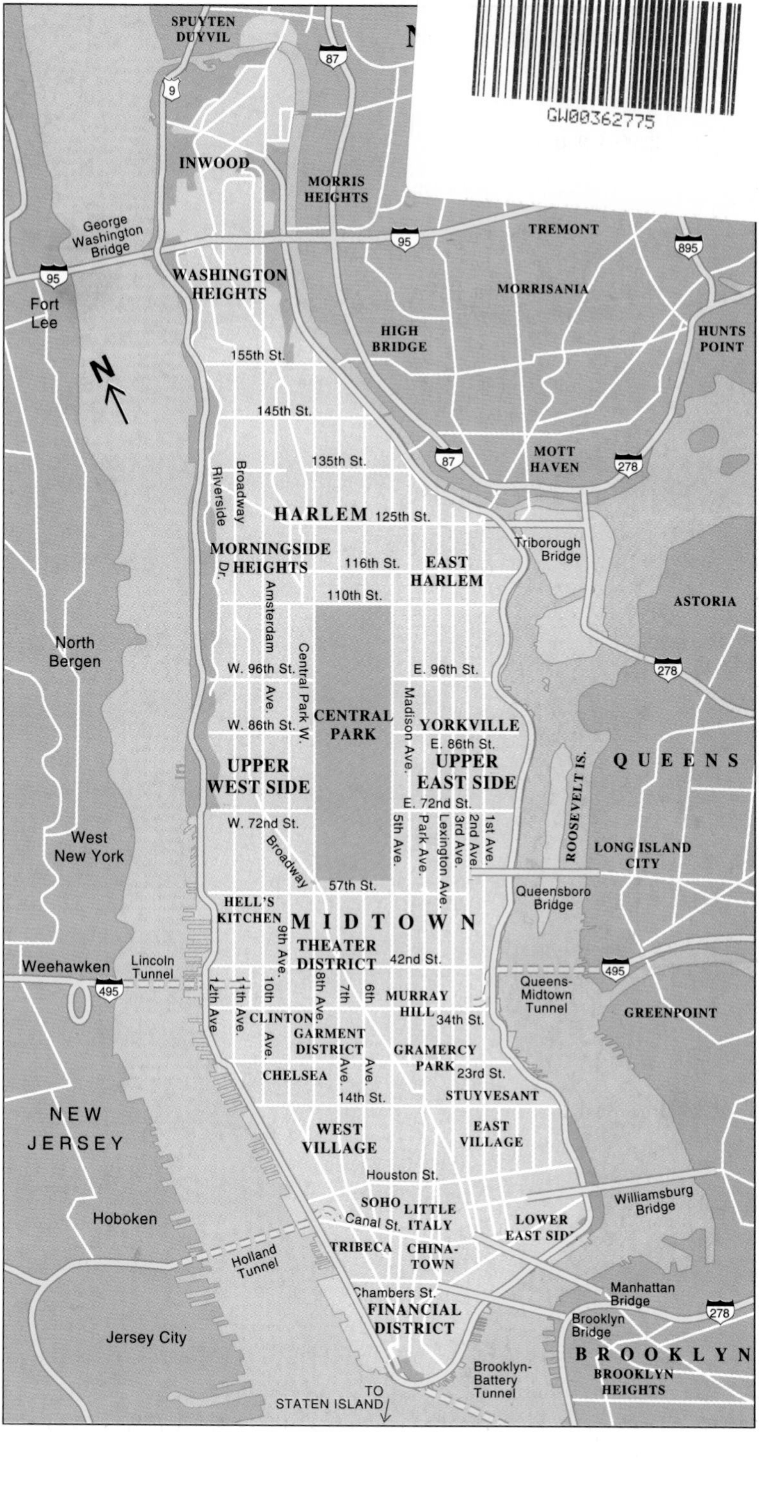
SPUYTEN DUYVIL
87
9
INWOOD
MORRIS HEIGHTS
George Washington Bridge
95
Fort Lee
WASHINGTON HEIGHTS
TREMONT
895
MORRISANIA
HIGH BRIDGE
HUNTS POINT
155th St.
145th St.
135th St.
MOTT HAVEN
278
Riverside Dr.
Broadway
HARLEM
125th St.
MORNINGSIDE HEIGHTS
116th St.
EAST HARLEM
Triborough Bridge
110th St.
ASTORIA
Amsterdam Ave.
North Bergen
Central Park W.
W. 96th St.
E. 96th St.
CENTRAL PARK
Madison Ave.
YORKVILLE
W. 86th St.
E. 86th St.
UPPER WEST SIDE
UPPER EAST SIDE
ROOSEVELT IS.
QUEENS
E. 72nd St.
W. 72nd St.
Broadway
5th Ave.
Park Ave.
Lexington Ave.
3rd Ave.
2nd Ave.
1st Ave.
West New York
LONG ISLAND CITY
57th St.
Queensboro Bridge
HELL'S KITCHEN
MIDTOWN
THEATER DISTRICT
9th Ave.
42nd St.
Weehawken
Lincoln Tunnel
495
12th Ave.
11th Ave.
10th Ave.
8th Ave.
7th Ave.
6th Ave.
MURRAY HILL
Queens-Midtown Tunnel
34th St.
GREENPOINT
CLINTON
GARMENT DISTRICT
GRAMERCY PARK
CHELSEA
23rd St.
14th St.
STUYVESANT
NEW JERSEY
WEST VILLAGE
EAST VILLAGE
Houston St.
SOHO
LITTLE ITALY
Williamsburg Bridge
Hoboken
Canal St.
LOWER EAST SIDE
TRIBECA
CHINA-TOWN
Holland Tunnel
Chambers St.
FINANCIAL DISTRICT
Manhattan Bridge
Brooklyn Bridge
Jersey City
BROOKLYN
Brooklyn-Battery Tunnel
BROOKLYN HEIGHTS
TO STATEN ISLAND

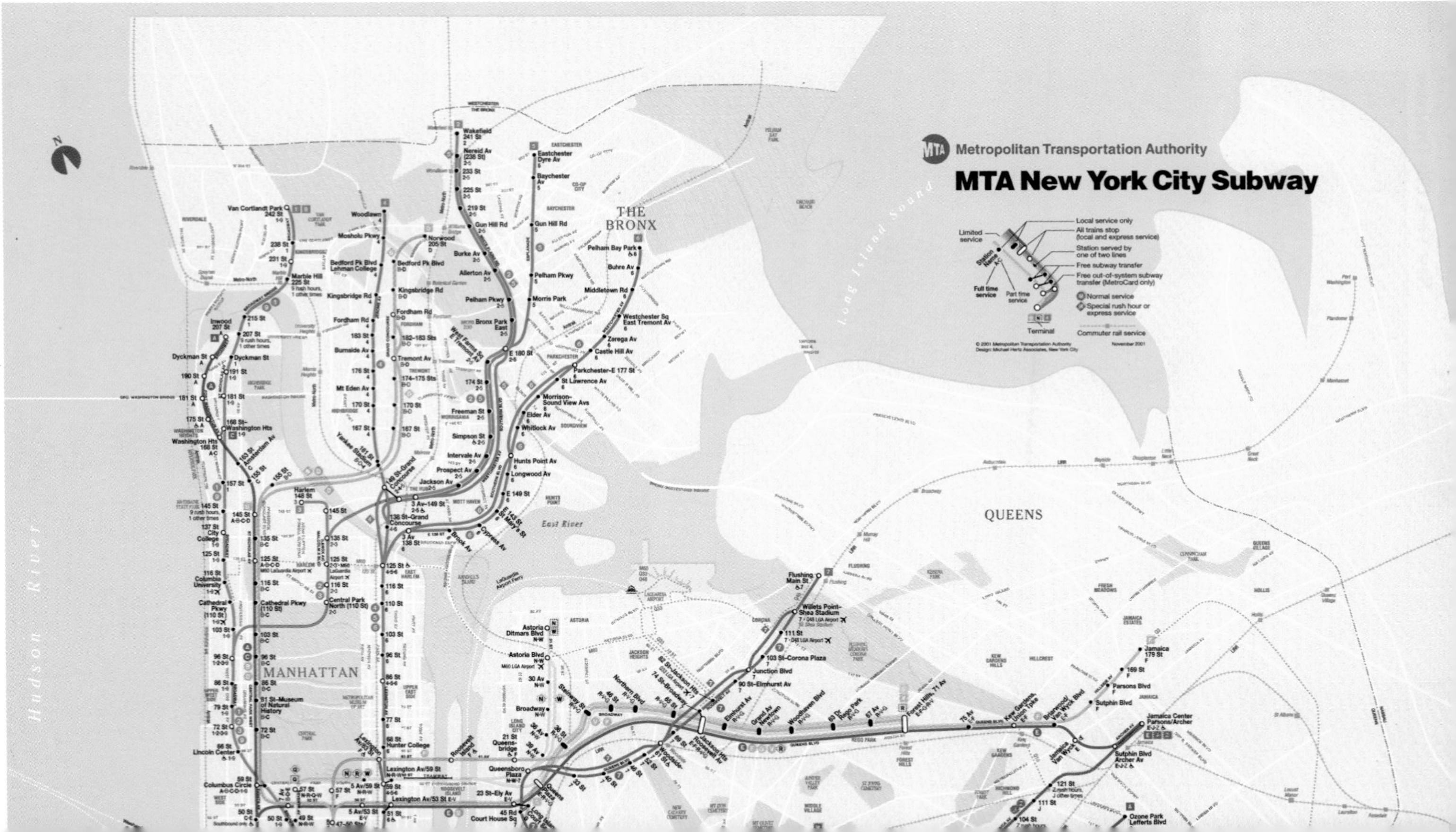
Metropolitan Transportation Authority
MTA New York City Subway
Limited service
Station Name
Full time service
Part time service
Terminal
Local service only
All trains stop (local and express service)
Station served by one of two lines
Free subway transfer
Free out-of-system subway transfer (MetroCard only)
Normal service
Special rush hour or express service
Commuter rail service
© 2001 Metropolitan Transportation Authority
Design: Michael Hertz Associates, New York City
November 2001
THE BRONX
MANHATTAN
QUEENS
Long Island Sound
East River
Hudson River

BROOKLYN
STATEN ISLAND
Jamaica Bay
Far Rockaway Mott Av
Beach 25 St
Beach 36 St
Beach 44 St
Beach 60 St
Beach 67 St
Broad Channel
Beach 90 St
Beach 98 St
Beach 105 St
Rockaway Park Beach 116 St
Canarsie Rockaway Pkwy
East 105 St
New Lots Av
Livonia Av
Pennsylvania Av
Van Siclen Av
Junius St
Rockaway Av
Saratoga Av
Sutter Av–Rutland Rd
Ralph Av
Utica Av
Crown Hts Utica Av
Kingston Av
Kingston-Throop Avs
Nostrand Av
President St
Sterling St
Winthrop St
Church Av
Beverly Rd
Newkirk Av
Flatbush Av Brooklyn College
Franklin Av
Botanic Garden
Prospect Park
Parkside Av
Beverley Rd
Cortelyou Rd
Avenue H
Avenue J
Avenue M
Kings Hwy
Avenue U
Neck Rd
Sheepshead Bay
Brighton Beach
Ocean Pkwy
West 8 St NY Aquarium
Coney Island Stillwell Av
Avenue X
Avenue P
Avenue N
Avenue I
Bay Pkwy
18 Av
20 Av
25 Av
86 St
Bay 50 St
New Utrecht Av
71 St
79 St
62 St
55 St
50 St
Fort Hamilton Pkwy
9 Av
Ditmas Av
Fort Hamilton Pkwy
15 St Prospect Park
7 Av
Grand Army Plaza
Eastern Pkwy Brooklyn Museum
Myrtle-Willoughby Avs
Bedford-Nostrand Avs
Classon Av
Clinton-Washington Avs
Fulton St
Lafayette Av
Atlantic Av
Bergen St
DeKalb Av
Nevins St
Hoyt-Schermerhorn
Hoyt St
Lawrence St
Jay St
Borough Hall
Court St
Clark St
High St
York St
Carroll St
Smith 9 Sts
4 Av–9 St
Union St
Prospect Av
25 St
36 St
45 St
53 St
59 St
Bay Ridge Av
77 St
86 St
Bay Ridge 95 St
East Broadway
Grand St
Bowery
Spring St
Canal St
Franklin St
Chambers St
City Hall
Brooklyn Bridge–City Hall
Fulton St
Park Place
World Trade Center
Cortlandt St
Rector St
Wall St
Broad St
Bowling Green
Whitehall St
South Ferry
Highlands Ferry
Atlantic Highlands Ferry
Staten Island Ferry
St. George
Ballpark Station
Tompkinsville
Stapleton
Clifton
Grasmere
MTA Staten Island Railway
Old Town
Dongan Hills
Jefferson Avenue
Grant City
New Dorp
Oakwood Heights
Bay Terrace
Great Kills
Eltingville
Annadale
Huguenot
Princes Bay
Pleasant Plains
Richmond Valley
Nassau
Atlantic
Tottenville

Downtown Manhattan

Downtown

Alternative Museum, 28
Anthology Film Archives, 33
Buddhist Temple, 27
Castle Clinton, 1
Cherry Lane Theatre, 34
Chinatown Fair, 26
Church of the Ascension, 44
Church of Our Lady of the Rosary, 8
City Hall, 24
Clocktower Gallery, 25
Cooper Union, 39
Downtown Heliport, 9
East Coast Memorial, 2
Federal Hall, 15
Federal Reserve Bank, 16
Forbes Magazine Galleries, 47
Forbidden Planet, 43
Fraunces Tavern, 10
Fulton Fish Market, 17
Grace Church, 41
Jefferson Market Library, 45
Joseph Papp Public Theater, 38
Morgan Guaranty Trust Company, 13
Museum of Holography, 29

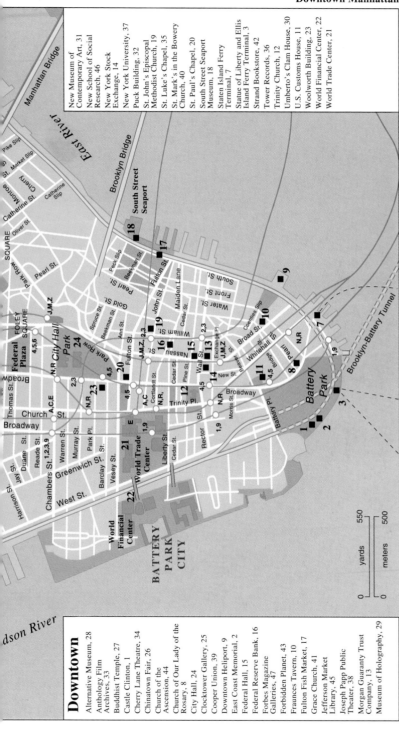

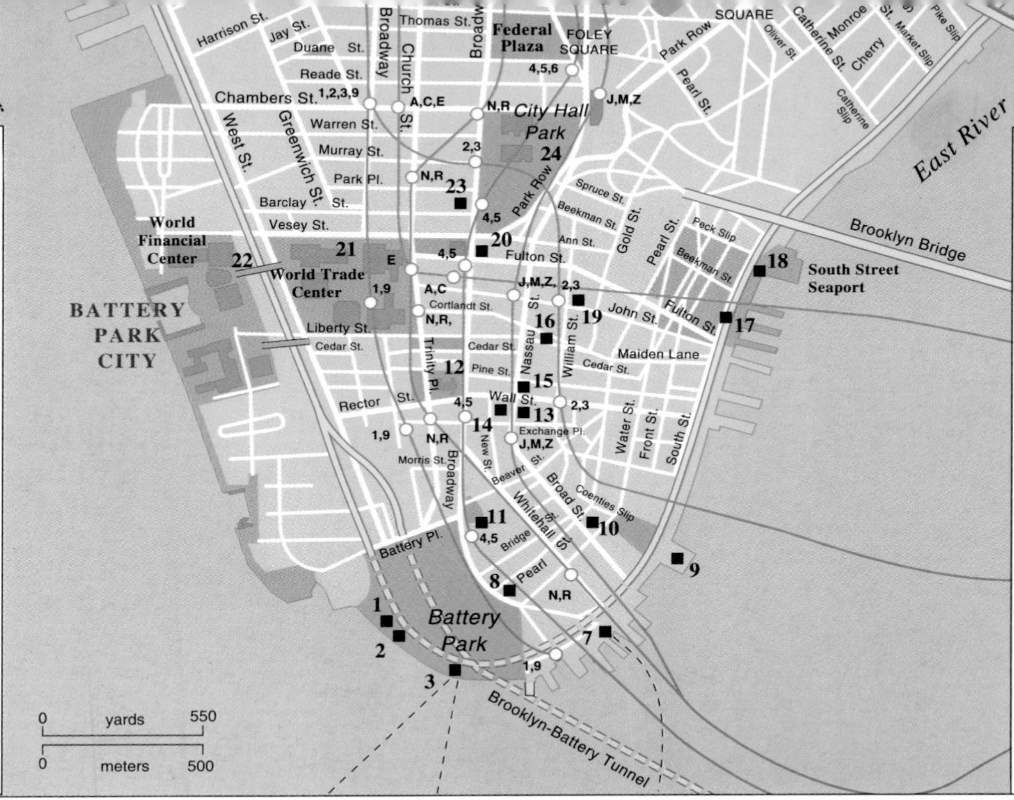

New Museum of Contemporary Art, 31
New School of Social Research, 46
New York Stock Exchange, 14
New York University, 37
Puck Building, 32
St. John's Episcopal Methodist Church, 19
St. Luke's Chapel, 35
St. Mark's in the Bowery Church, 40
St. Paul's Chapel, 20
South Street Seaport Museum, 18
Staten Island Ferry Terminal, 7
Statue of Liberty and Ellis Island Ferry Terminal, 3
Strand Bookstore, 42
Tower Records, 36
Trinity Church, 12
Umberto's Clam House, 30
U.S. Customs House, 11
Woolworth Building, 23
World Financial Center, 22
World Trade Center, 21

Midtown Manhattan

East River
Queens-Midtown Tunnel
FDR Dr.
Queensboro Bridge
United Nations
TURTLE BAY
First Ave.
Second Ave.
Third Ave.
Lexington Ave.
Park Ave.
Madison Ave.
Fifth Ave.
Seventh Ave.
Broadway
Eighth Ave.
Ninth Ave.
Dyer Ave.
Tenth Ave.
Eleventh Ave.
Twelfth Ave.
E. 60th St.
E. 59th St.
E. 58th St.
E. 57th St.
E. 56th St.
E. 55th St.
E. 54th St.
E. 53rd St.
E. 52nd St.
E. 51st St.
E. 50th St.
E. 49th St.
E. 48th St.
E. 47th St.
E. 46th St.
E. 45th St.
E. 44th St.
E. 43rd St.
E. 42nd St.
E. 41st St.
E. 40th St.
E. 39th St.
E. 38th St.
E. 37th St.
E. 36th St.
E. 35th St.
E. 34th St.
E. 33rd St.
E. 32nd St.
W. 60th St.
W. 59th St.
W. 58th St.
W. 57th St.
W. 56th St.
W. 55th St.
W. 54th St.
W. 53rd St.
W. 52nd St.
W. 51st St.
W. 50th St.
W. 49th St.
W. 48th St.
W. 47th St.
W. 46th St.
W. 45th St.
W. 44th St.
W. 43rd St.
W. 42nd St.
W. 41st St.
W. 40th St.
W. 39th St.
W. 38th St.
W. 37th St.
W. 36th St.
W. 35th St.
W. 34th St.
W. 33rd St.
Central Park South
Grand Army Plaza
Citicorp Center
Museum of Modern Art
Carnegie Hall
Rockefeller Center
Grand Central Terminal
New York Public Library
Bryant Park
TIMES SQUARE
COLUMBUS CIRCLE
New York Convention & Visitors Bureau
Port Authority Bus Terminal
MURRAY HILL
Empire State Building
HERALD SQUARE
GARMENT DISTRICT
General Post Office
HELL'S KITCHEN
Lincoln Tunnel

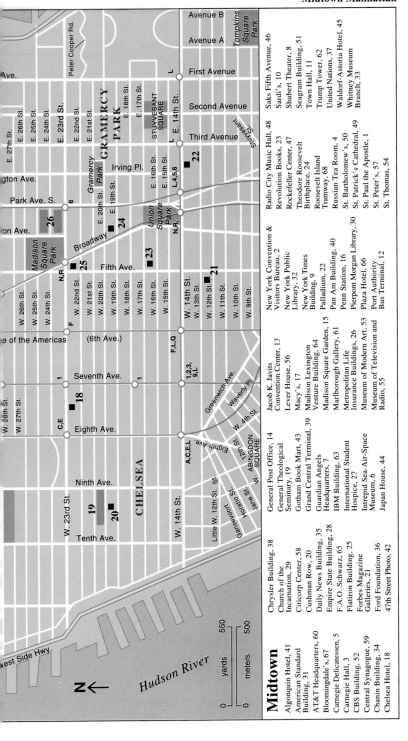

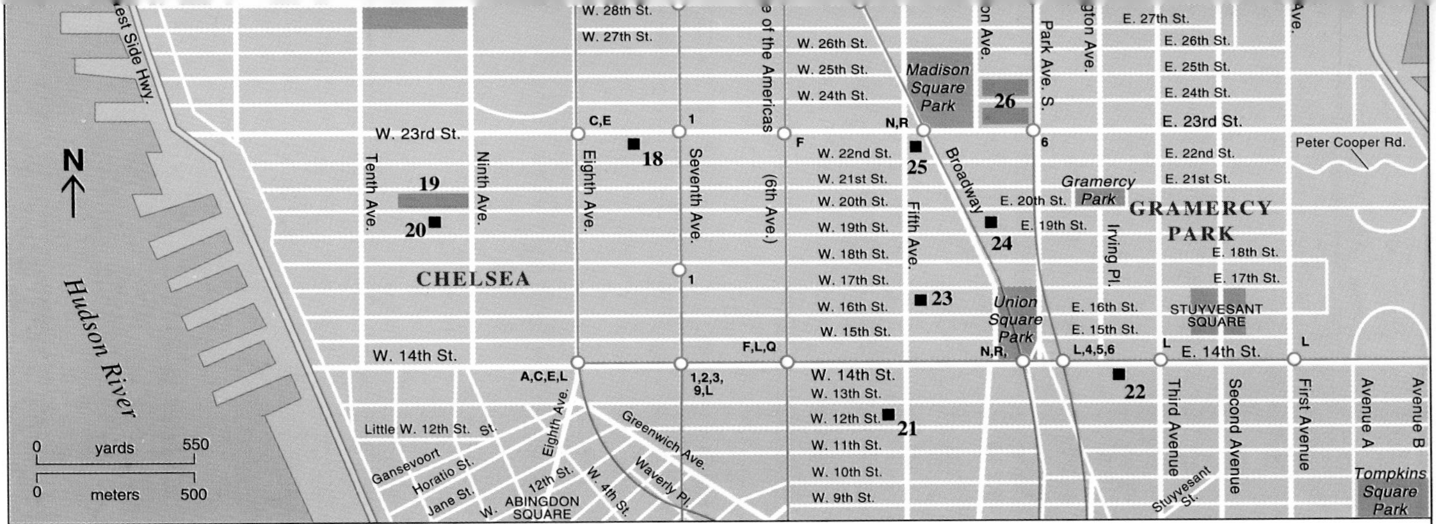

Midtown

Algonquin Hotel, 41
American Standard Building, 31
AT&T Headquarters, 60
Bloomingdale's, 67
Carnegie Delicatessen, 5
Carnegie Hall, 3
CBS Building, 52
Central Synagogue, 59
Chanin Building, 34
Chelsea Hotel, 18
Chrysler Building, 38
Church of the Incarnation, 29
Citicorp Center, 58
Cushman Row, 20
Daily News Building, 35
Empire State Building, 28
F.A.O. Schwarz, 65
Flatiron Building, 25
Forbes Magazine Galleries, 21
Ford Foundation, 36
47th Street Photo, 42
General Post Office, 14
General Theological Seminary, 19
Gotham Book Mart, 43
Grand Central Terminal, 39
Guardian Angels Headquarters, 7
IBM Building, 63
International Student Hospice, 27
Intrepid Sea-Air-Space Museum, 6
Japan House, 44
Jacob K. Javits Convention Center, 13
Lever House, 56
Macy's, 17
Madison Lexington Venture Building, 64
Madison Square Garden, 15
Marlborough Gallery, 61
Metropolitan Life Insurance Buildings, 26
Museum of Modern Art, 53
Museum of Television and Radio, 55
New York Convention & Visitors Bureau, 2
New York Public Library, 32
New York Times Building, 9
Palladium, 22
Pan Am Building, 40
Penn Station, 16
Pierpont Morgan Library, 30
Plaza Hotel, 66
Port Authority Bus Terminal, 12
Radio City Music Hall, 48
Revolution Books, 23
Rockefeller Center, 47
Theodore Roosevelt Birthplace, 24
Roosevelt Island Tramway, 68
Russian Tea Room, 4
St. Bartholomew's, 50
St. Patrick's Cathedral, 49
St. Paul the Apostle, 1
St. Peter's, 57
St. Thomas, 54
Saks Fifth Avenue, 46
Sardi's, 10
Shubert Theater, 8
Seagram Building, 51
Town Hall, 11
Trump Tower, 62
United Nations, 37
Waldorf-Astoria Hotel, 45
Whitney Museum Branch, 33

Uptown Manhattan

Uptown

- American Museum of Natural History, 53
- The Ansonia, 55
- The Arsenal, 25
- Asia Society, 14
- Belvedere Castle, 36
- Bethesda Fountain, 33
- Blockhouse No. 1, 42
- Bloomingdale's, 22
- Bridle Path, 30
- Cathedral of St. John the Divine, 47
- Central Park Zoo, 24
- Chess and Checkers House, 28
- Children's Museum of Manhattan, 51
- Children's Zoo, 26
- China House, 19
- Cleopatra's Needle, 38
- Columbia University, 46
- Conservatory Garden, 2
- Cooper-Hewitt Museum, 7
- The Dairy, 27
- Dakota Apartments, 56
- Delacorte Theater, 37
- El Museo del Barrio, 1
- Fordham University, 60
- Frick Museum, 13
- Gracie Mansion, 10
- Grant's Tomb, 45
- Great Lawn, 39
- Guggenheim Museum, 9
- Hayden Planetarium (at the American Museum of Natural History), 53
- Hector Memorial, 50
- Hotel des Artistes, 57
- Hunter College, 16
- International Center of Photography, 5
- Jewish Museum, 6
- The Juilliard School (at Lincoln Center), 59
- Lincoln Center, 59
- Loeb Boathouse, 34
- Masjid Malcolm Shabazz , 43
- Metropolitan Museum of Art, 11
- Mt. Sinai Hospital, 4
- Museum of American Folk Art, 58
- Museum of American Illustration, 21
- Museum of the City of New York, 3
- National Academy of Design, 8
- New York Convention & Visitors Bureau, 61
- New York Historical Society, 54
- New York Hospital, 15
- Plaza Hotel, 23
- Police Station (Central Park), 40
- Rockefeller University, 20
- 7th Regiment Armory, 17
- Shakespeare Garden, 35
- Soldiers and Sailors Monument, 49
- Strawberry Fields, 32
- Studio Museum in Harlem, 44
- Symphony Space, 48
- Tavern on the Green, 31
- Temple Emanu-El, 18
- Tennis Courts, 41
- Whitney Museum of American Art, 12
- Wollman Rink, 29
- Zabar's, 52

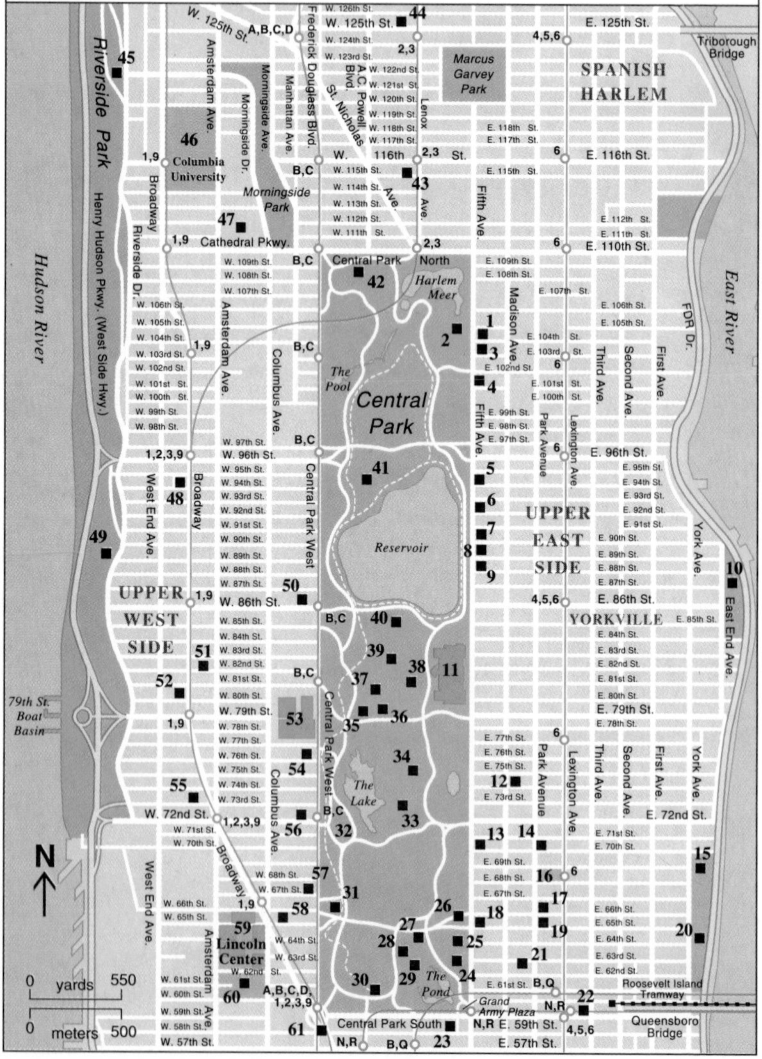

Let's Go Publications

Let's Go: Alaska & the Pacific Northwest 2002
Let's Go: Amsterdam 2002 **New Title!**
Let's Go: Australia 2002
Let's Go: Austria & Switzerland 2002
Let's Go: Barcelona 2002 **New Title!**
Let's Go: Boston 2002
Let's Go: Britain & Ireland 2002
Let's Go: California 2002
Let's Go: Central America 2002
Let's Go: China 2002
Let's Go: Eastern Europe 2002
Let's Go: Egypt 2002 **New Title!**
Let's Go: Europe 2002
Let's Go: France 2002
Let's Go: Germany 2002
Let's Go: Greece 2002
Let's Go: India & Nepal 2002
Let's Go: Ireland 2002
Let's Go: Israel 2002
Let's Go: Italy 2002
Let's Go: London 2002
Let's Go: Mexico 2002
Let's Go: Middle East 2002
Let's Go: New York City 2002
Let's Go: New Zealand 2002
Let's Go: Paris 2002
Let's Go: Peru, Ecuador & Bolivia 2002
Let's Go: Rome 2002
Let's Go: San Francisco 2002
Let's Go: South Africa with Southern Africa 2002
Let's Go: Southeast Asia 2002
Let's Go: Southwest USA 2002 **New Title!**
Let's Go: Spain & Portugal 2002
Let's Go: Turkey 2002
Let's Go: USA 2002
Let's Go: Washington, D.C. 2002
Let's Go: Western Europe 2002

Let's Go *Map Guides*

Amsterdam
Berlin
Boston
Chicago
Dublin
Florence
Hong Kong
London
Los Angeles
Madrid
New Orleans
New York City
Paris
Prague
Rome
San Francisco
Seattle
Sydney
Venice
Washington, D.C.

Let's Go

New York City

2002

Eric Todrys editor

researcher-writers

Seth Kleinerman

Daryl Sng

Avra van der Zee

Paul Guilianelli map editor

Rebecca L. Schoff managing editor

Luke Marion photographer

Macmillan

HELPING LET'S GO If you want to share your discoveries, suggestions, or corrections, please drop us a line. We read every piece of correspondence, whether a postcard, a 10-page email, or a coconut. Please note that mail received after May 2002 may be too late for the 2003 book, but will be kept for future editions. **Address mail to:**

Let's Go: New York City
67 Mount Auburn Street
Cambridge, MA 02138
USA

Visit Let's Go at **http://www.letsgo.com,** or send email to:

feedback@letsgo.com
Subject: "Let's Go: New York City"

In addition to the invaluable travel advice our readers share with us, many are kind enough to offer their services as researchers or editors. Unfortunately, our charter enables us to employ only currently enrolled Harvard students.

Published in Great Britain 2002 by Macmillan, an imprint of Pan Macmillan Ltd.
20 New Wharf Road, London N1 9RR
Basingstoke and Oxford
Associated companies throughout the world
www.panmacmillan.com

Published in the United States of America by St. Martin's Press.

ISBN: 0-333-90608-X
First edition
10 9 8 7 6 5 4 3 2 1

Let's Go: New York City is written by Let's Go Publications, 67 Mount Auburn Street, Cambridge, MA 02138, USA.

Printed in the USA on recycled paper with biodegradable soy ink.

ABOUT LET'S GO

FORTY-TWO YEARS OF WISDOM

For over four decades, travelers crisscrossing the continents have relied on *Let's Go* for inside information on the hippest backstreet cafes, the most pristine secluded beaches, and the best routes from border to border. *Let's Go: Europe*, now in its 42nd edition and translated into seven languages, reigns as the world's bestselling international travel guide. In the last 20 years, our rugged researchers have stretched the frontiers of backpacking and expanded our coverage into the Americas, Australia, Asia, and Africa (including the new *Let's Go: Egypt* and the more comprehensive, multi-country jaunt through *Let's Go: South Africa & Southern Africa*). Our new-and-improved City Guide series continues to grow with new guides to perennial European favorites Amsterdam and Barcelona. This year we are also unveiling *Let's Go: Southwest USA*, the flagship of our new outdoor Adventure Guide series, which is complete with special roadtripping tips and itineraries, more coverage of adventure activities like hiking and mountain biking, and first-person accounts of life on the road.

It all started in 1960 when a handful of well-traveled students at Harvard University handed out a 20-page mimeographed pamphlet offering a collection of their tips on budget travel to passengers on student charter flights to Europe. The following year, in response to the instant popularity of the first volume, students traveling to Europe researched the first full-fledged edition of *Let's Go: Europe*. Throughout the 60s and 70s, our guides reflected the times—in 1969, for example, we taught you how to get from Paris to Prague on "no dollars a day" by singing in the street. In the 90s we focused in on the world's most exciting urban areas to produce in-depth, fold-out map guides, now with 20 titles (from Hong Kong to Chicago) and counting. Our new guides bring the total number of titles to 57, each infused with the spirit of adventure and voice of opinion that travelers around the world have come to count on. But some things never change: our guides are still researched, written, and produced entirely by students who know first-hand how to see the world on the cheap.

HOW WE DO IT

Each guide is completely revised and thoroughly updated every year by a well-traveled set of nearly 300 students. Every spring, we recruit over 200 researchers and 90 editors to overhaul every book. After several months of training, researcher-writers hit the road for seven weeks of exploration, from Anchorage to Adelaide, Estonia to El Salvador, Iceland to Indonesia. Hired for their rare combination of budget travel sense, writing ability, stamina, and courage, these adventurous travelers know that train strikes, stolen luggage, food poisoning, and marriage proposals are all part of a day's work. Back at our offices, editors work from spring to fall, massaging copy written on Himalayan bus rides into witty, informative prose. A student staff of typesetters, cartographers, publicists, and managers keeps our lively team together. In September, the collected efforts of the summer are delivered to our printer, who turns them into books in record time, so that you have the most up-to-date information available for your vacation. Even as you read this, work on next year's editions is well underway.

WHY WE DO IT

We don't think of budget travel as the last recourse of the destitute; we believe that it's the only way to travel. Our books will ease your anxieties and answer your questions about the basics—so you can get off the beaten track and explore. Once you learn the ropes, we encourage you to put *Let's Go* down and strike out on your own. You know as well as we that the best discoveries are often those you make yourself. When you find something worth sharing, please drop us a line. We're Let's Go Publications, 67 Mount Auburn St., Cambridge, MA 02138, USA (feedback@letsgo.com). For more info, visit our website, www.letsgo.com.

Contents

shopping 201

daytripping 217

planning your trip 233

accommodations 247

living in nyc 269

service directory 279

index 285

maps

HOW TO USE THIS BOOK

Some said that you can't write *the book* on New York, but that didn't keep us from trying. This is the guide for those who want to wander both on and off the beaten path. For the tourist who wants to act like a savvy native and the local who secretly desires to be a flash-happy traveler.

BEFORE YOU GO. Start planning your jaunt to the big city with **Discover NYC,** which lists New York's top 25 sights along with suggested itineraries, themed tours, Let's Go Picks (the best—and strangest—of the Big Apple), and three great **walking tours** (complete with maps) if you need help strategizing your sightseeing. Thumb through **Life and Times** for a quick and easy-to-swallow survey of Gotham's history and culture, from the founding of New Amsterdam to the reign of Rudy Giuliani. For the nuts and bolts details of planning your urban sojourn, flip to the end of this guide, where you'll find **Planning Your Trip** (with advice about passports, plane tickets, insurance, and more), the **Accommodations** section for booking a room from home, and even a chapter on **Living in NYC,** which details everything from obtaining a visa to finding housing for those planning to spend months (or years) in New York.

ONCE THERE. When you touch down in New York, **Once in NYC** will be your best friend, dishing the dirt on the city's neighborhoods and offering tips on how to act like a true New Yawker. For easy navigating, the neighborhood breakdown here mirrors that found in the other chapters of the book. Manhattan comes first, with its neighborhoods listed from downtown to uptown; the outer boroughs—Brooklyn, Queens, the Bronx, and Staten Island—follow in kind. You'll spend most of your time in the city flipping through the chapters that follow: **Sights, Museums, Food & Drink, Nightlife, Entertainment,** and **Shopping.** Listings in these sections are oganized in the order of our preference within each neighborhood; if you want to know which restaurant we think is the best, just look at the top of the list. The Let's Go thumbs-up () next to a listing lets you know it's one of our favorites—those places that are either super cheap, super hip, or just plain super. **Gay New York** is a comprehensive guide for gay and lesbian travelers to New York, with information on resources, accommodations, hangouts, and the best parties. **Daytripping** will guide you around the greater metropolitan area, from the Historic Hudson Valley to Long Island.

MAPS AND MORE. All neighborhoods—complete with their hotels, museums, monuments, restaurants, bars, and subway stops—are plotted in the **map appendix** at the back of this book, marked off with a black strip running down the side. Right before the maps comes the **Index** and a useful **Service Directory,** listing all the different services you might require during your trip, from taxis to pharmacies.

THE INSIDE SCOOP. Tips on how best to explore New York are found in the black sidebars scattered throughout the guide. Those on a strict budget should peruse for On the Cheap sidebars, while those living in style will find The Big Splurge sidebars helpful. Kids in the City will help for travelers with children. The absolute essentials are highlighted in white **Essential Information** boxes.

A NOTE TO OUR READERS The information for this book was gathered by *Let's Go* researchers from May through August of 2001. Each listing is based on one researcher's opinion, formed during his or her visit at a particular time. Those traveling at other times may have different experiences since prices, dates, hours, and conditions are always subject to change. You are urged to check the facts presented in this book beforehand to avoid inconvenience and surprises.

RESEARCHER-WRITERS

Seth Kleinerman

A seasoned New Yorker, well-versed in the city's lore, Seth used his expertise to navigate Gotham's streets, reporting back eloquently and honestly. Always willing to take on whatever the city threw at him, Seth tirelessly roamed the sidewalks, scrutinizing which sights were worthy and which did not measure up. Seth braved the ferry to Staten Island and the tram to Roosevelt Island armed with a biting sense of humor, but was at his rhapsodical best while manning his own turf on the Upper East Side.

Daryl Sng

The Singapore army would just have to wait. Instead, Daryl would take his fourth tour of duty for Let's Go. An expert on just about everything from horticulture to baseball, from public transportation to DJing, Daryl channelled his vast knowledge into every copybatch. Relentlessly exploring the outer boroughs, he uncovered some of the city's gems. Neither the Chelsea club scene nor the bars of the East Village proved any match for Daryl. Maybe manning the artillery will prove more difficult, though my guess is not bloody likely.

Avra van der Zee

A fearless researcher who explored the grit of the city, Avra was a godsend to the bookteam. From writing the Daytripping chapter from scratch to fending off the advances of hopeful beaus in Harlem, Avra took on New York with bravado and courage. Her lucid copy was a joy to read, overflowing with enthusiasm and passion. Avra provided a steady stream of advice and always volunteered for more work when the opportunity arose. For her, it was truly a labor of love.

Arthur Koski-Karell *Atlantic City*

ACKNOWLEDGMENTS

The Let's Go 2002 series is dedicated to the memory of Haley Surti

Thank you to all who have shared their New York experiences with me. Barry Popik and Professor Gerald Cohen have helped uncover the truth behind the Big Apple. Gail and Michael Hochman gave pointed advice on the ins and outs of Park Slope.

All the folks in the basement provided moral support and laughs throughout the summer. Thanks to Jean, Joseph, Blazejewski, Angela, Sarah, Monica, Karen, Carla, Anne, Nikki, Nat, Cody, Ben, Steve, Nat, Tom, and Sarah. Especial thanks to Rebecca Schoff, who provided a sense of sanity in the midst of chaos, and Paul Guilianelli, whose maps are far clearer than my writing.

The New York City researchers went above and beyond the call of duty. Seth Kleinerman, Daryl Sng, and Avra van der Zee guided me throughout the writing of this book. Without them, of course, this book is nothing.

Thanks to my friends back in New York and at school, especially all the boys of K32/E102. Thanks to my family for their love, support, and the Red Sox tickets.

Thanks to Kate for not leaving me when I was working 15-hour days and to Mom, Dad, and Mark for the research, advice, and phone calls. I love all you guys.

INSIDE

Discover NYC

Immensity, diversity, and a tradition of defying tradition characterize the city known as the "Crossroads of the World." Since its earliest days, New York has scoffed at the timid offerings of other American cities. It boasts the most immigrants, the tallest skyscrapers, the biggest museum in the Western Hemisphere, and its plenty of large landfills. Even the vast blocks of concrete have their own gritty charm. Returning from a dull vacation in Westchester, talespinner O. Henry noted, "there was too much fresh scenery and fresh air. What I need is a steam-heated flat and no vacation or exercise."

New York City is full of folks. The stars are invisible behind the array of lights. The buildings soar, the subways scream, the people scramble. All is rushed. There may be grime, but for every inch of it, there's a yard of silver lining. Countless people mean countless pockets of culture—you can find every kind of ethnicity, food, art, language, attitude. It's possible to be alone, but that's not the point—plunge into the fray and you'll find eight million stories, curmudgeonly humor, innovative ideas, and a fair share of madness. Meanwhile, there's flamenco at an outdoor cafe, jazz in historic speakeasies, house and techno in a flashy club—whatever the question, New York has the answer.

WHEN TO GO

Tourists flock to New York year round, but the city teems with visitors in July and August. There is no true off season to avoid the crowds and save a few dollars; from January to mid-March is the closest New York gets to slowing down. New York's weather is the worst of both worlds: summers are hot and sticky, while winters compete with neighboring New England for cold and snow. Winter snowfalls are common, but the city clears streets immediately (sidewalks are a different matter). In spring and fall, frequent impromptu showers make carrying an umbrella a good idea. The city is most pleasant in

LET'S GO PICKS

Best nickname for the city: Gotham. Celebrates the city's bad guy image. Much cooler than the Big Apple.

Best place to plot a revolution: a tie between the Morris-Jumel Mansion (p. 88), where George Washington devised his plan for the Battle of the Harlem Heights and the bar KGB (p. 163) in the East Village.

Best place to enjoy the status quo: the Hamptons in Long Island (p. 221).

Best privy: Bar 89 (p. 159). Watch the glass doors fog from transparent to opaque. Rinse, repeat.

Best free sauna: a summer subway ride.

Best budget dining in Manhattan: Chinatown, East Village, Morningside Heights, Harlem.

Best places to fish drunk: The Bronx's City Island. Rowboats, bait, tackle, and accessories are available at The Boat Livery (p. 167).

Best place to catch a three-eyed fish: the East River, where many line-casters still set up shop.

Best place to play video games and still be cool: Fun (p. 158), on the Lower East Side, which hosts a weekly Playstation night.

Best place to imitate senior citizens and still be cool: Pete's Candy Store, (p. 166) in Williamsburg, which hosts a weekly Bingo night.

May and June and generally experiences an abrupt transition to autumn in early September.

The US uses the Fahrenheit temperature scale rather than Celsius. To convert Fahrenheit to Celsius temperatures, subtract 32, then multiply by 5 and divide the result by 9.

JANUARY	APRIL	JULY	OCTOBER
RAIN 3.4"	**RAIN** 4.2"	**RAIN** 4.4"	**RAIN** 3.6"
HIGH 37	**HIGH** 61	**HIGH** 85	**HIGH** 65
LOW 25	**LOW** 43	**LOW** 68	**LOW** 49

NEW YORK'S GHOSTS

NEW YORK PAST

Learn about Gotham's history at the **Museum of the City of New York** (p. 120). For more specific scholars, there's subway history at Brooklyn's **New York Transit Museum** (p. 122), criminal history at the **New York City Police Museum** (p. 122), and the history of immigration at the **Lower East Side Tenement Museum** (p. 119). But not all of the city's history is behind a glass case. Some of it is behind a bar. Try **Chumley's** (p. 60) in Greenwich Village, where many an author has lifted a frosty mug, or **McSorley's Old Ale House** (p. 161) in the East Village, where Abraham Lincoln once grabbed a beer.

NEW YORK PRESENT

There are no New Yorkers as attentive to the here-and-now as the traders on the **New York Stock Exchange** (p. 50), where a delay of minutes may cost investors millions. If your idea of being in the present doesn't jive with materialism, you might try the **Mahayana Buddhist Temple** (p. 56). Or head to the **Imagine Mosaic** (p. 79) in Central Park, which commemorates John Lennon's dream of "all the people living for today." If all else fails, dance your sorrows away at **Nowbar** (p. 197) in Greenwich Village.

NEW YORK FUTURE

The future happens in New York City. This is where new trends start, where slang originates, where new forms of art emerge. The **Knitting Factory** (p. 176) is home to avant-garde jazz and rock performances. Young artists emerge from the galleries of SoHo, Chelsea, and Williamsburg (p. 123). The future of baseball, not just art, is on display in the Big Apple. New York's major league baseball teams, the Mets and the Yankees, both have minor league clubs in the city, the Brooklyn Cyclones (p. 96) and the Staten Island Yankees.

Astor Place Hair Stylists

Rockefeller Center

Street Musicians

TOP 25 SIGHTS

25. City Hall. The mayor keeps his office in what might be the most beautiful building in New York (p. 53).

24. New York Stock Exchange. Billions of dollars are exchanged here every day. Watch other people make money (p. 50).

23. New York Botanical Garden. A feast for the eyes and nose. Unless you enjoy bees, don't wear perfume (p. 102).

22. Cathedral of St. John the Divine. The largest cathedral in the United States ... and it's still not completed (p. 85).

21. American Museum of Natural History. Dinosaurs and an overwhelming planetarium await you at this classic New York museum (p. 112).

20. Bloomingdale's. The finest department store in New York. Expensive clothing, but it's well worth experiencing (p. 213).

19. Yankee Stadium. A monumental ball park home to the world's greatest baseball team. Get out to the Stadium and watch a game (p. 101).

18. SoHo/Chelsea Galleries. Ground zero for the New York art scene. To be on the cutting edge, also head to Long Island City or Williamsburg (p. 123).

17. New York Public Library. A temple to reading. Even if you're not bookish, go inside and enjoy one of New York's greatest public institutions (p. 71).

16. The Cloisters. A museum devoted to antiquities. The tapestries will carry you to medieval Europe. You may even contemplate becoming a monk. Or not (p. 113).

15. Lincoln Center. Dress up and make like the cultured elite as you promenade through this arts complex; go at night, when the buildings and fountain glitter with lights (p. 83).

14. The Bronx Zoo. Lions, tigers, and bears? Of course. Try marmosets, lynx, and nyala. This zoo puts others to shame. It doesn't just display more animals, but re-creates their natural habitats, which might make viewing more challenging, but certainly more interesting (p. 102).

13. Chinatown. The only question is which one? New York has three. There's one in Manhattan that is traditionally known as Chinatown, another in Flushing, Queens, and yet another in Brooklyn's Sunset Park. Chinese food is a staple of the New Yorker's diet, and this is the best the city has to offer (p. 131).

12. Grand Central Terminal. New York's magnificent train station, and one of Midtown's anchors. Great for eating (downstairs on the Dining Concourse), travelling (to Westchester and points north), and just staring onto the crowds of New Yorkers. Don't leave without looking up at the ceiling (p. 74).

11. St. Patrick's Cathedral. The most recognizable church in New York gracefully sits on Fifth Avenue among myriad chic store. For a Gothic church, it lacks the requisite flying buttresses, but don't let that keep you down (p. 73).

10. Brooklyn Bridge. It's a cliche, but even locals make it a practice to walk/jog/skate/bike across this suspended masterpiece (p. 90).

9. Washington Square Park. The epicenter of **Greenwich Village,** filled with New York's cool kids, in one of the hippest areas in the city (p. 59).

8. Museum of Modern Art. New York's tribute to modern art. Van Gogh and Matisse adorn the walls of one of New York's greatest museums. The Museum is leaving its digs in Midtown in summer 2002 for renovations. Look out for them in Long Island City (p. 111).

7. Empire State Building. The most visible and recognizable component of the New York skyline (p. 69).

6. Times Square. This is in-your-face New York. Huge advertisements and packed sidewalks mark the area. A great place to fend off pickpockets and catch a Broadway show (p. 76).

5. The Statue of Liberty and Ellis Island. A tourist trap perhaps, but the more you think about it, the cooler it is: a 305-foot high statue off the coast of Manhattan. Don't miss Ellis Island, an excellent museum documenting the history of immigration into America (p. 47).

4. United Nations. Whether you think this institution is the world's savior or if you think it's perfectly useless, you shouldn't leave New York without seeing the UN complex. Technically, this isn't NYC; it's independent from city jurisdiction. All the more reason to go and mail yourself an internationally stamped letter (p. 75).

3. Rockefeller Center. The greatest complex of buildings in the city. Where else can you see Prometheus bring the mortals fire, Conan bring the masses laughter, and the Rockettes bring crowds long legs? (p. 72).

2. Central Park. A huge green paradise in the middle of New York? You'll have to see it to believe it. The park abounds with space to sun yourself, to play ball, or to frolic in the grass (p. 78).

1. The Metropolitan Museum of Art. In our opinion, the greatest museum in the US. You can't *do* the Met. There's just too much to see, too much to do. Visit ancient Egypt or ancient Greece, or just revel in the splendor of their European collection. This one might require a number of visits (p. 110).

SUGGESTED ITINERARIES

THREE-DAY NEW YORK JAUNT

DAY 1. Start your tour of NYC in **Greenwich Village** (p. 58), a neighborhood that has always been synonymous with the rebellious Bohemian lifestyle. Although rising property values keep out starving artists today, the Village has not lost its edge. Explore its meandering streets: make like an **NYU** film student, and challenge one of the chess players in **Washington Square Park** or watch inspiring pick-up basketball at **the Cage.** For lunch, amble to the Italian section of the **Village** around Bleecker St. If you tire of the trendy, visit the Village's cooler sibling in **Chelsea** (p. 68). Home to the avant-garde, you can catch a few of its **galleries** (p. 124) for free before night falls and its **clubs and lounges** (p. 167) pull you away to follow less intellectual pursuits.

DAY 2. Now it's time to get to business—the skyscrapers beckon you uptown. Walk around **Midtown** (p. 71) to see the NY you've always heard about. Look down on the city from the **Empire State Building** (p. 69), and ramble up Fifth Avenue to see the **New York Public Library** (p. 71). After gazing at the reading room, exit the library and head east on 42nd St. to **Grand Central Terminal** (p. 74). At this point, you may continue east on 42nd St. to the **United Nations** (p. 75) or you can head back uptown, making sure you pass by **Rockefeller Center** (p. 72) and **St. Patrick's Cathedral** (p. 73). But enough of this ambling. Slow down and linger in the nearby **Museum of Modern Art** (p. 111, though it may have temporarily relocated to Long Island City if you're in New York after June 2002). After the long day of sightseeing, grab a bite to eat and head to the bars of the **Upper West Side** to unwind in their unpretentious company.

DAY 3. To make up for last night, wake up early and make the trek to the **Cloisters** (p. 113) in Washington Heights, lunch in the beautiful gardens. Instead of running right back to charted lands, stroll around neighboring **Harlem** (p. 86), one-time home of Langston Hughes and Martin Luther King, Jr. View the neighborhood's historic **brownstones.** When that gets boring, walking along **125th Street** should give you all the bustle you crave. Stop in at one of the million sports clothing stores or get some collard green at **Sylvia's** (p. 149). At nightfall, take in some music in one of Harlem's jazz clubs.

FIVE DAYS IN THE CITY THAT NEVER SLEEPS

DAY 4. After three days in the city, it's time to get over your Manhattan-centrism and make a foray into the Big Bad Boroughs. If it's **Brooklyn** (p. 90) you desire, take our Walking Tour (see the end of this chapter) for a taste of its unique flavor. But if its **Queens** you've wanted to visit since you saw *Coming to America*, join us on the **International Express** (more commonly known as the 7 train). Get off right at the entrance to the borough, near Queensboro, and pick a large street to follow for the day. **Astoria Boulevard** will bring you through Greece (Astoria, p. 96), India (Jackson Heights), then, on Northern Blvd., to Korea (Flushing, p. 99). If you choose the less commercial but still very active **Queens Boulevard,** you can visit Ireland (Woodside), sample a United Nations summit (Elmhurst, p. 97), get lost in a Tudor wonderland (Forest Hills, p. 97), and end up in the steamy West Indies (St. Albans). If you liked your World Tour that much, stay in Queens for the nightlife it offers in **Bayside** (p. 167).

DAY 5. Start at the **Metropolitan Museum of Art** (p. 110) and lose yourself in its magical galleries. If the weather is manageable, stroll through **Central Park** (p. 78) with the other New Yorkers—or rest on the beautiful **carousel** with their children—and rush to the **American Museum of Natural History** (p. 112). By the time you're out of there you'll be just in time to walk down to **Times Square** (p. 76) to see the lights of Broadway. Take the splurge and see a **Broadway show** (p. 172) or eat a good dinner among the actors at **Sardi's** (p. 143).

SEVEN-DAY SLICE OF THE APPLE

DAY 6. The **Lower East Side** (p. 56) is the perfect follow-up to Manhattan's touristy side. Start off with an early lunch (that'll stay in your stomach all day) at one of the neighborhood's **delis** (p. 135). Walk off that pastrami and see old, gritty NYC as it butts heads with that tireless force, gentrification. You'll get addicted to the no-name **boutiques** and **antique stores,** so keep shopping just next-door in the hip-and-happening **East Village** (p. 206). While you're there, see the remains of the old, turbulent East Village in the **murals** documenting the neighborhood's **drug wars** and in **Tompkins Square Park** (p. 62). Head up to **Curry Row** (p. 138) and enjoy cheap Indian fare before taking in the East Village and Lower East Side nightlife scene (p. 160).

DAY 7. If you're staying this long you'll have to see the **Statue of Liberty** (p. 47)—no buts about it. Get yourself to the **Staten Island Ferry** Terminal (don't start screaming yet, we're not going to send you there) to get the cheapest, if not closest, view of Lady Liberty. (Make sure you stay on the ferry until it's back safely onto Manhattan shores.) From your southern-most vantage point of the island, you can either take the relaxing path through **Battery Park** (p. 49) to get to the **Stock Exchange** (p. 50), or detour through active **South Street Seaport** (p. 54). Walk through the **Civic Center,** keeping an eye out for **City Hall** (p. 53) and the **Woolworth Building** (p. 52). For dinner and lichee ice cream, move on to **Chinatown** (p. 131). "New York, New York, it's a hell of a town!"

HOLIDAYS AND FESTIVALS IN 2002

DATE	FESTIVAL	INFORMATION
November 22, 2001	Thanksgiving Day	Find a family; eat their turkey. Or attend Macy's Thanksgiving Day Parade, a 75-year tradition that begins at E. 77th St., runs along Central Park West, and goes south on Broadway to 34th St. Ogle the huge balloon floats assembled the night before at 79th St. and Central Park West, and see yourself on television!
Late-November to January	*Nutcracker* Season	The New York City Ballet performs its timeless classic. See p. 183 for ticket information.
November 28	Tree Lighting	At Rockefeller Center. ☎332-6868.
December 25	Christmas	Businesses closed.
December 31	New Year's Eve Celebrations	Millions gather around 42nd St. to glimpse the famous dropping of the Times Square ball–you'll get a better view on TV, without the drunkards and tourists.

DATE	FESTIVAL	INFORMATION
January 1, 2002	New Year's Day	Massive hangovers, massive confetti clean-up. Businesses closed.
January 21	Martin Luther King, Jr.'s Birthday	City offices closed.
February 14	Valentine's Day	Snuggle up to that sweetie in your hostel or eat a candlelit dinner by the Hudson River.
February 18	President's Day	Businesses closed.
March 17	St. Patrick's Day Parade	Along Fifth Avenue, everything's green—even the bagels.
March 29-April 7	International Auto Show	At the Jacob Javits Convention Center.
April 15	Easter Sunday	Businesses closed.
May 5	Bike New York	A 2-decade springtime tradition—bike all 5 boroughs on traffic-free roads with 28,000 other cyclists. ☎932-2453.
May 28	Memorial Day	Concerts and fireworks at the South Street Seaport. Businesses closed.
June	Music in the Anchorage	Rock concert series at the base of the Brooklyn Bridge. ☎206-6674, ext. 252.
Mid-June	Welcome Back to Brooklyn Homecoming Festival	Festival celebrating the borough. Brooklyn natives who've made it big return home to the fanfare of bands, writers' readings, and family activities. Starts at Grand Army Plaza. Free. ☎718-855-7882, ext. 54; www.brooklynX.org/welcome.
June to August	World Financial Center Festival	A full entertainment schedule throughout the summer. Mostly outdoors, mostly free. ☎945-0505.
June to August	Summerstage	Performances in Central Park. Great acts, free. ☎360-2777; www.summerstage.org.
Mid-June to Mid-August	Celebrate Brooklyn	Outdoor performing arts festival at the Park Slope Bandshell. Free.
Late June to Late July	Midsummer Night Swing	Dance under the stars at Lincoln Center to live music. See p. 184 for more information.
Late June to August	Shakespeare in the Park	Quality Shakespeare in Central Park's Delacorte Theater. Free. See p. 175 for more information.
mid-June	Museum Mile Festival	Fifth Avenue closes from 82nd to 104th Sts. from 6-9pm; museums along the strip give free entertainment.
June	JVC Jazz Festival	Prestigious jazz festival with venues across the city. ☎496-9000 for annual dates and schedule.
June 25	Puerto Rican Independence Day	Parade along Fifth Ave. and festivities in El Barrio (Spanish Harlem).
June 26	Mermaid Parade	At Coney Island. A festival of fabulous fishies. See p. 95.
Late June	New York Restaurant Week	New York City's top restaurants allow you to partake of their fine eats for the mere price of the year (i.e., $20.02 in the year 2002). See p. 134.
July 4	Independence Day	Macy's fireworks display around Lower Manhattan and some over the river at the Battery Park esplanade.
Late August	Tap-A-Mania	Sponsored by Macy's, thousands of tap dancers congregate on 34th St. and Broadway. ☎695-4400.
Last week in August, first week in September	US Open	Tennis championship held in the USTA's center in Flushing Meadows, Queens. ☎718-760-6200.
September 2	Labor Day/Labor Day Caribbean Festival	Labor Day honors US workers. Caribbean festival, Children's Carnival at St. John's Place in Brooklyn, and a Labor Day Parade starting at Eastern Parkway in Brooklyn. Free. ☎718-625-15115 or 773-4052.
October 14	Columbus Day	Businesses closed.
Mid-October	Ice Skating begins	Rockefeller Center. ☎332-6868. See p. 191.
October 31	Halloween Parade	Oooh...inventive costumes and debauched fun. Sixth Ave. from Spring St. to 23rd St.
November 3	New York City Marathon	See skinny people sweat. NY Roadrunner's Club ☎423-2233. See p. 188.
November 11	Veterans' Day	Businesses closed.

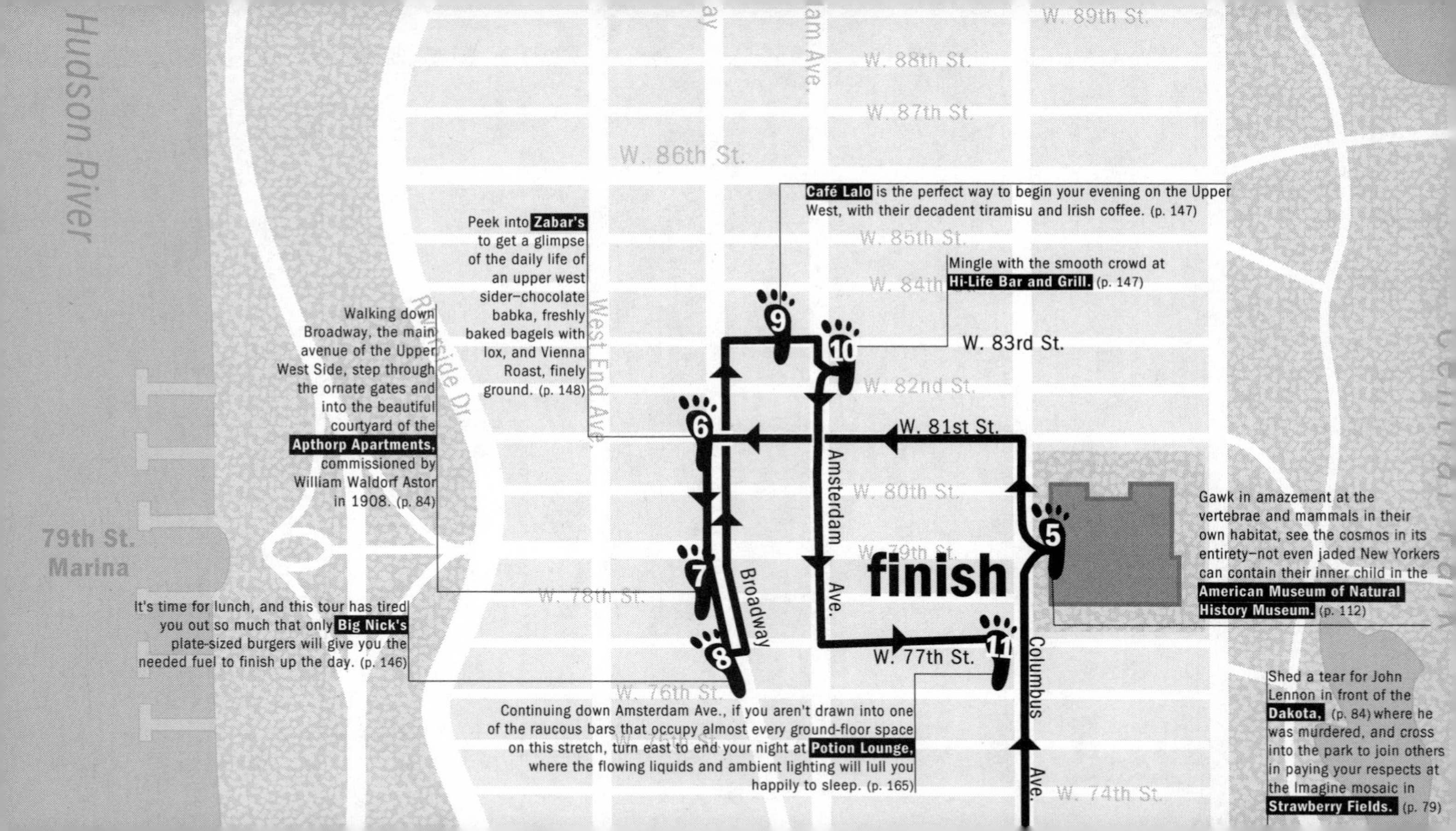
Hudson River
79th St. Marina
W. 89th St.
W. 88th St.
W. 87th St.
W. 86th St.
W. 85th St.
W. 84th St.
W. 83rd St.
W. 82nd St.
W. 81st St.
W. 80th St.
W. 79th St.
W. 78th St.
W. 77th St.
W. 76th St.
W. 74th St.
Riverside Dr.
West End Ave.
Broadway
Amsterdam Ave.
Columbus Ave.
finish
Café Lalo is the perfect way to begin your evening on the Upper West, with their decadent tiramisu and Irish coffee. (p. 147)
Mingle with the smooth crowd at Hi-Life Bar and Grill. (p. 147)
Peek into Zabar's to get a glimpse of the daily life of an upper west sider–chocolate babka, freshly baked bagels with lox, and Vienna Roast, finely ground. (p. 148)
Walking down Broadway, the main avenue of the Upper West Side, step through the ornate gates and into the beautiful courtyard of the Apthorp Apartments, commissioned by William Waldorf Astor in 1908. (p. 84)
It's time for lunch, and this tour has tired you out so much that only Big Nick's plate-sized burgers will give you the needed fuel to finish up the day. (p. 146)
Continuing down Amsterdam Ave., if you aren't drawn into one of the raucous bars that occupy almost every ground-floor space on this stretch, turn east to end your night at Potion Lounge, where the flowing liquids and ambient lighting will lull you happily to sleep. (p. 165)
Gawk in amazement at the vertebrae and mammals in their own habitat, see the cosmos in its entirety–not even jaded New Yorkers can contain their inner child in the American Museum of Natural History Museum. (p. 112)
Shed a tear for John Lennon in front of the Dakota, (p. 84) where he was murdered, and cross into the park to join others in paying your respects at the Imagine mosaic in Strawberry Fields. (p. 79)

UPPER WEST SIDE

Walkintour1

For couples, poets, Beatles fans, Martini-sippers, and big eaters.

EST. CALORIC INTAKE 70,000
EST. FAT CALORIES 40,000

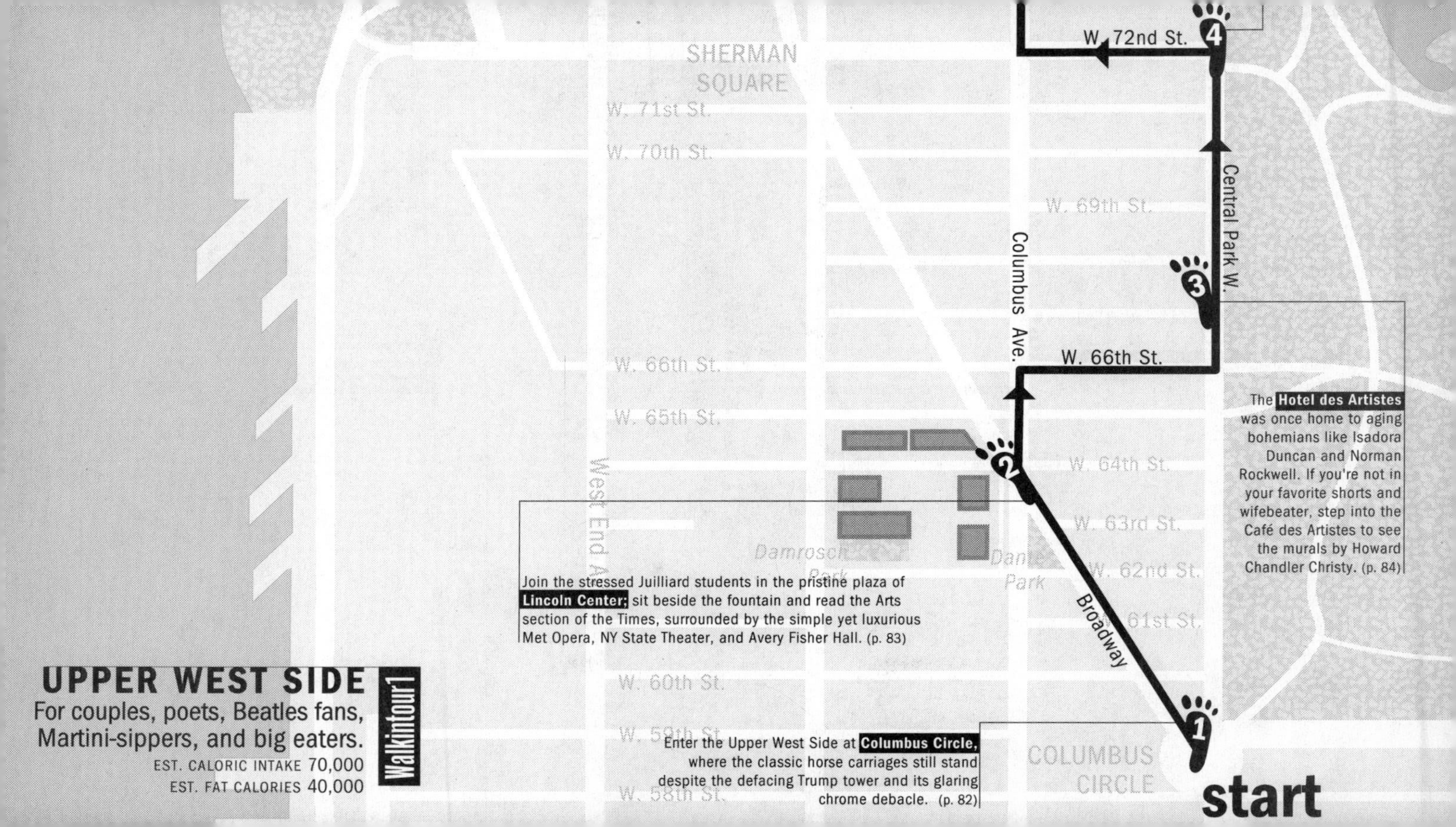

Enter the Upper West Side at **Columbus Circle,** where the classic horse carriages still stand despite the defacing Trump tower and its glaring chrome debacle. (p. 82)

Join the stressed Juilliard students in the pristine plaza of **Lincoln Center;** sit beside the fountain and read the Arts section of the Times, surrounded by the simple yet luxurious Met Opera, NY State Theater, and Avery Fisher Hall. (p. 83)

The **Hotel des Artistes** was once home to aging bohemians like Isadora Duncan and Norman Rockwell. If you're not in your favorite shorts and wifebeater, step into the Café des Artistes to see the murals by Howard Chandler Christy. (p. 84)

finish
If it's late, stop at Galapagos for a drink with the artsy crowd–you could catch anything from an Indie film or an art exhibit to a live band or DJ. (p. 167)
Stop by the Williamsburg Art and Historical Center to see the works of avant-garde artists who can't afford to live in the village. (p. 126)
start
Start off your tour of Brooklyn properly with a walk across the Brooklyn Bridge, one of the most beautiful public monuments in the city–see what Frank Stella and Georgia O'Keefe were so enthralled by. (p. 90)
Walk along the Brooklyn Heights Promenade to get more stunning views of Lower Manhattan; you'll probably bump into a few postcard photographers in your path. (p. 92)
MANHATTAN
WILLIAMSBURG
Hudson River
East River
Williamsburg Bridge
Brooklyn Bridge
Promenade
Kent Ave.
Bedford Ave.
Grand St.
Nassau Ave.
Greenpoint Ave.
Flushing Ave.
278
1
2
3
9
10
M

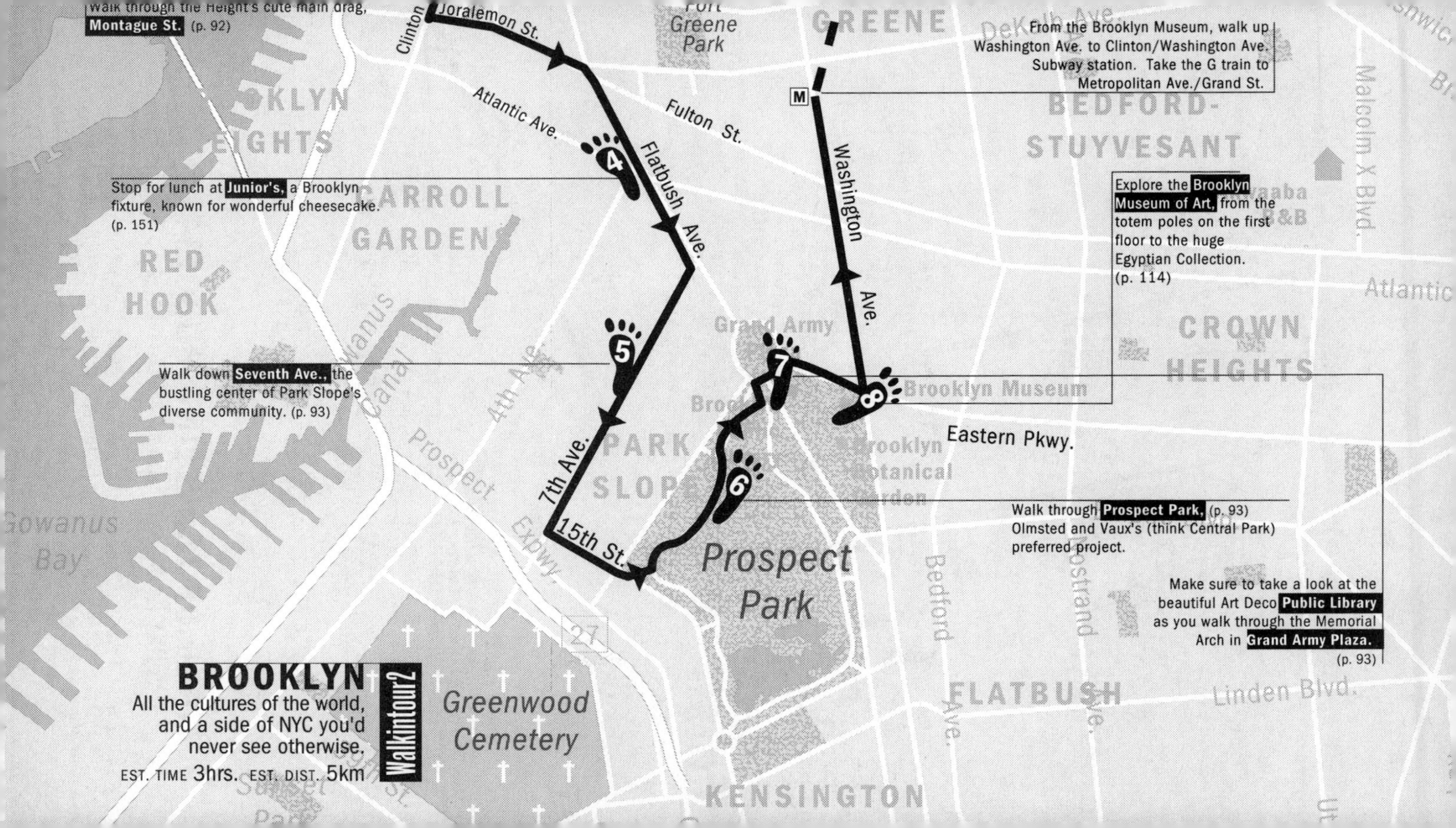

BROOKLYN
Walkintour2
All the cultures of the world, and a side of NYC you'd never see otherwise.
EST. TIME 3hrs. EST. DIST. 5km
Walk through the Height's cute main drag, Montague St. (p. 92)
Stop for lunch at Junior's, a Brooklyn fixture, known for wonderful cheesecake. (p. 151)
Walk down Seventh Ave., the bustling center of Park Slope's diverse community. (p. 93)
Walk through Prospect Park, (p. 93) Olmsted and Vaux's (think Central Park) preferred project.
Make sure to take a look at the beautiful Art Deco Public Library as you walk through the Memorial Arch in Grand Army Plaza. (p. 93)
Explore the Brooklyn Museum of Art, from the totem poles on the first floor to the huge Egyptian Collection. (p. 114)
From the Brooklyn Museum, walk up Washington Ave. to Clinton/Washington Ave. Subway station. Take the G train to Metropolitan Ave./Grand St.
Clinton
Joralemon St.
Atlantic Ave.
Fulton St.
Flatbush Ave.
Washington Ave.
7th Ave.
15th St.
Eastern Pkwy.
Brooklyn Museum
Grand Army
Prospect Expwy.
4th Ave.
Gowanus Canal
Gowanus Bay
Bedford Ave.
Nostrand Ave.
Linden Blvd.
Malcolm X Blvd.
DeKalb Ave.
Atlantic
Fort Greene Park
GREENE
BEDFORD-STUYVESANT
CROWN HEIGHTS
CARROLL GARDENS
RED HOOK
PARK SLOPE
FLATBUSH
KENSINGTON
Prospect Park
Brooklyn Botanical Garden
Greenwood Cemetery
27
M
4
5
6
7
8

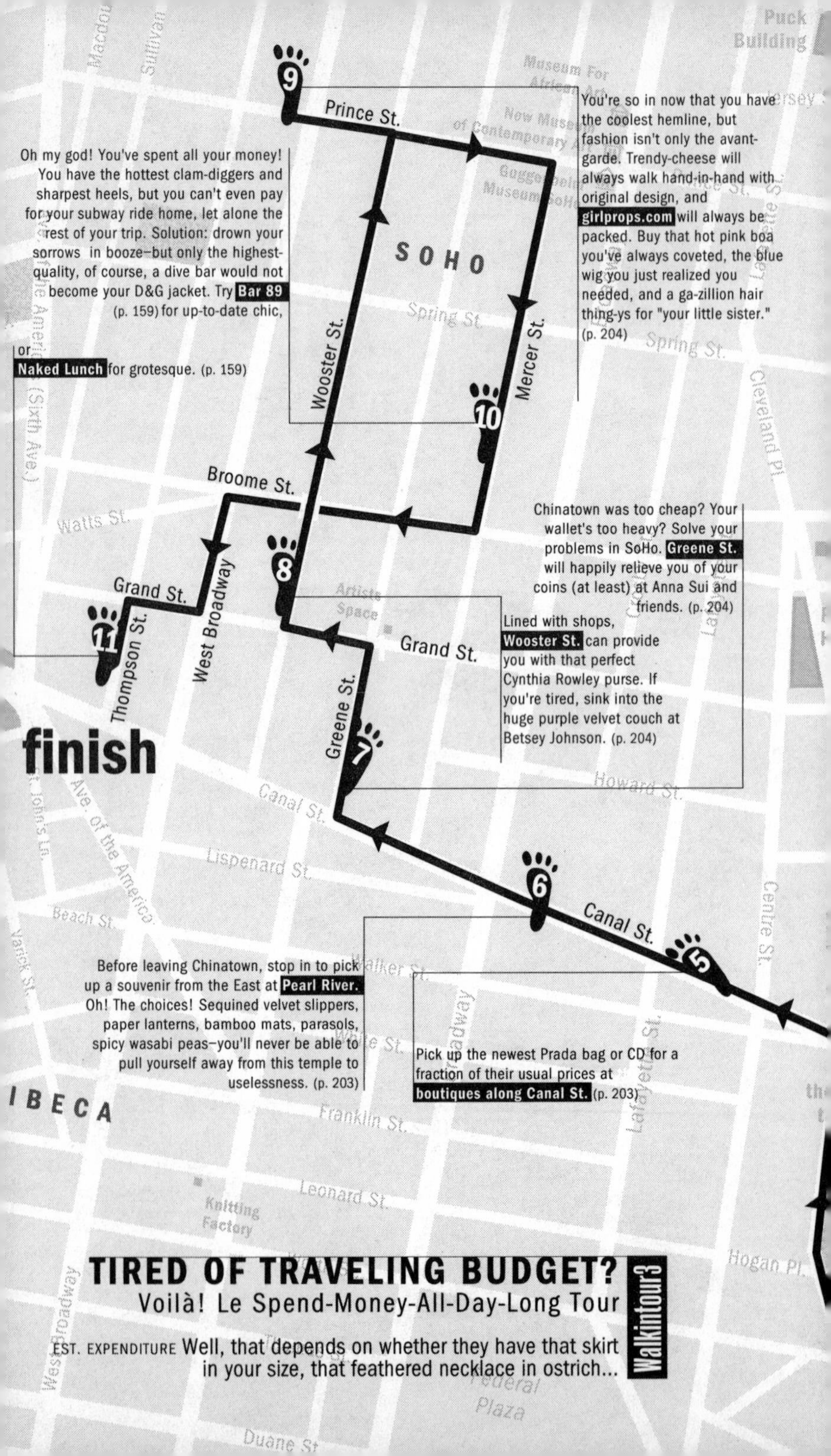

Oh my god! You've spent all your money! You have the hottest clam-diggers and sharpest heels, but you can't even pay for your subway ride home, let alone the rest of your trip. Solution: drown your sorrows in booze–but only the highest-quality, of course, a dive bar would not become your D&G jacket. Try **Bar 89** (p. 159) for up-to-date chic, or **Naked Lunch** for grotesque. (p. 159)

You're so in now that you have the coolest hemline, but fashion isn't only the avant-garde. Trendy-cheese will always walk hand-in-hand with original design, and **girlprops.com** will always be packed. Buy that hot pink boa you've always coveted, the blue wig you just realized you needed, and a ga-zillion hair thing-ys for "your little sister." (p. 204)

Chinatown was too cheap? Your wallet's too heavy? Solve your problems in SoHo. **Greene St.** will happily relieve you of your coins (at least) at Anna Sui and friends. (p. 204)

Lined with shops, **Wooster St.** can provide you with that perfect Cynthia Rowley purse. If you're tired, sink into the huge purple velvet couch at Betsey Johnson. (p. 204)

Before leaving Chinatown, stop in to pick up a souvenir from the East at **Pearl River.** Oh! The choices! Sequined velvet slippers, paper lanterns, bamboo mats, parasols, spicy wasabi peas–you'll never be able to pull yourself away from this temple to uselessness. (p. 203)

Pick up the newest Prada bag or CD for a fraction of their usual prices at **boutiques along Canal St.** (p. 203)

TIRED OF TRAVELING BUDGET?

Voilà! Le Spend-Money-All-Day-Long Tour

EST. EXPENDITURE Well, that depends on whether they have that skirt in your size, that feathered necklace in ostrich...

Walkintour3

E. Houston St.
Start the day off right at the expensive boutiques on the Lower East Side. You too can be hip, prowling the streets for the newest accessory to complement the newest neckline. Need a lead? Lucky Wang (100 Stanton St.) and TG-170 (170 Ludlow St.) are on the cutting edge, but they could be way out by the time you read this. (p.204)
start
Stanton St.
1
St. Patrick's Old Cathedral
Mulberry St.
Chrystie
Forsyth
Rivington St.
2
DeSalvio Playground
Whew! Spending money is so tiring. Pick up candy for the rest of the day at Economy Candy, 108 Rivington St., before setting off to Chinatown. (p. 135)
Sara Delano Roosevelt Park
Eldridge
Allen
Orchard St.
Ludlow St.
Essex St.
LITTLE ITALY
Delancey St.
Elizabeth St.
Pioneer Hotel
Find out right away what Chinatown does best–food. Kick back at H.S.F. Restaurant, as waiters wheel out cart after cart of dim sum. (p. 131)
Broome St.
Grand St.
Bowery Savings Bank
Engine Co. 55
LOWER EAST SIDE
Hester St.
Bowery
Mahayana Buddhist Temple
Canal St.
Oriental Enterprises Co.
CHINATOWN
Bayard St.
3
CONFUCIUS PLAZA
Mott St.
Buddhist Temple
Pell St.
Doyers St.
Division St.
Forsyth St.
Pike
E. Broadway
St.
Market St.
Henry St.
4
Church of the Transfiguration
Relish the city's best mini-cakes as they come off Cecilia Tam's pan at Hong Kong Egg Cake Co. (p. 132)
Mosco St.
Chinatown Fair
Library
Catherine St.
Manhattan Bridge
Worth St.
First Chinese Presbyterian Church

INSIDE

Once in NYC

THE FIVE BOROUGHS

Contrary to popular belief, NYC comprises **five boroughs:** the Bronx, Brooklyn, Manhattan, Queens, and Staten Island. Pervading Manhattan-centrism has deep historical roots. The island's original inhabitants, the Algonquin, called it Manahatta or Heavenly Land. The British were the first to call the island "New York," after James, Duke of York, the brother of Charles II. Only in 1898 did the other four boroughs join the city's government. Flanked on the east by the "East River" (actually a strait) and on the west by the Hudson River, **Manhattan** is a sliver of an island, measuring only 13 mi. long and 2½ mi. wide. Sizeable **Queens** and **Brooklyn** are on the other side of the East River, and **Staten Island** is to the south. North of Manhattan sits the **Bronx,** the only borough connected by land to the rest of the US.

MANHATTAN

The city of right angles and tough, damaged people.
—Pete Hamill

see maps pp. 303-335

Above 14th St. Manhattan is an organized grid of avenues running north-south and streets east-west, the result of an expansion scheme adopted in 1811. Streets run consecutively, and their numbers grow as one travels north. Avenues are slightly less predictable: some are numbered while others are named. The numbers of the avenues increase as one goes west. **Broadway,** which follows an old Algonquin trail, cavalierly defies the rectangular pattern and cuts diagonally across the island, veering east of Fifth Ave. at 23rd St. Central Park and Fifth Ave. (south of 59th St. and north of 110th St.) separate the city into the East Side and West Side.

Grand Central Terminal

Who Loves NY?

View from the Empire State Building

Below 14th St. the city dissolves into a charming but confusing tangle of old, narrow streets, which becomes especially complicated south of Houston St., where streets are not numbered. The **Financial District/Wall St. area,** set over the original Dutch layout, is full of narrow, winding, one-way streets. **Greenwich Village,** only slightly less confusing, is especially complicated west of Sixth Ave. The **East Village and Alphabet City** are grid-like, with alphabetized avenues from Ave. A to Ave. D east of First Ave.

When setting off to find something, make sure you have not only its address (i.e.: 180 East End Ave.), but also its cross-street (in this case, 88th and 89th Sts.).

FINANCIAL DISTRICT

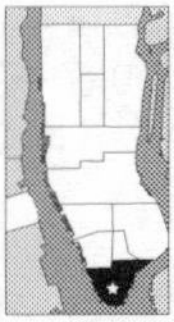

see map pp. 310-311

Subway: 1, 9 to South Ferry, Rector St., Cortlandt St.; 4, 5 to Bowling Green, Wall St.; N,R to Whitehall St., Rector St., Cortlandt St.; 2, 3 to Wall St.; 22, 3, 4, 5, J, M, Z to Fulton St.; A, C to Broadway-Nassau.; J, M, Z to Broad St. ***Sights:*** *p. 49.* ***Food:*** *p. 131.* ***Shopping:*** *p. 203.*

The southern tip of Manhattan is the financial hub of the city and, quite possibly, the entire world. The Financial District is bounded roughly between Battery Park on the south and Fulton St. on the north and extends from the Hudson River and the East River. Broadway runs uptown-downtown and slices through the Financial District's center. The neighborhood's main thoroughfare is Wall St., which runs east-west. Highlights of the Financial District are **Trinity Church, the New York Stock Exchange,** and the site of **the World Trade Center.**

THE CIVIC CENTER

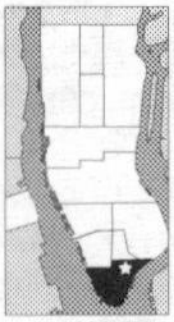

see map pp. 310-311

Subway: N, R to City Hall; 4, 5, 6 to Brooklyn Bridge-City Hall; J, M, Z to Chambers St. ***Sights:*** *p. 52.* ***Food:*** *p. 131.* ***Shopping:*** *p. 203.*

Nearly all of the buildings here house some branch of city, state, or federal government, and most of them sit atop a huge flight of limestone steps. Just north of the Financial District, the neighborhood centers around City Hall. Most government buildings cluster around Broadway, Park Row, and Centre St. Worth St. is the neighborhood's boundary with Chinatown. Be sure to check out City Hall and the **Woolworth Building.**

SOUTH STREET SEAPORT

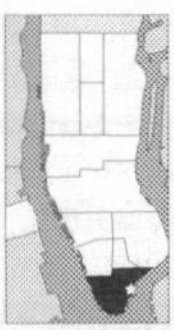

see map pp. 310-311

Subway: 2, 3, 4, 5, J, M, Z to Fulton St.; A, C to Broadway-Nassau. ***Sights:*** *p. 54.*

Bounded by Fulton St. on the south, Dover St. on the north, Pearl St. on the west, and East River on the east, the South Street Seaport is one of New York's most heavily touristed locales. Don't miss the **Fulton Fish Market.**

CHINATOWN

Subway: 6, J, M, N, R, Z to Canal St.; walk east on Canal St. to get to Mott St., follow the curved street to get to the Bowery, Confucius Plaza, and E. Broadway. ***Sights:*** *p. 55.* ***Food:*** *p. 131.* ***Shopping:*** *p. 203.*

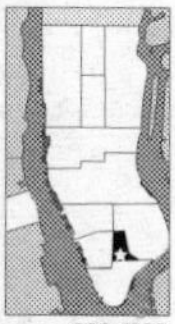

see map pp. 312-313

Chinatown is loosely bounded by Worth St. to the south and Canal St. to the north, Broadway to the west and the Bowery to the east. A vibrant community that maintains seven Chinese newspapers, over 300 garment factories, and innumerable food shops, New York's Chinatown contains the largest Asian community in the US outside San Francisco (over 300,000 estimated residents). Cruise down **Mott St.,** the **Bowery,** and **Canal St.** in search of great Chinese food.

LITTLE ITALY

Subway: 6 to Spring St. 4, 5, 6, N, R, J, M, Z to Canal St., B, D, F, Q to Broadway-Lafayette. ***Sights:*** *p. 55.* ***Food:*** *p. 133.* ***Shopping:*** *p. 203.* ***Accommodations:*** *p. 253.*

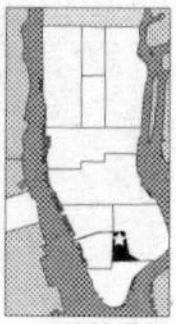

see map pp. 312-313

There's not much of Little Italy left in New York. Immigration giveth, and immigration taketh away. What remains of the neighborhood is mostly located on Mulberry St., east of SoHo, west of the Lower East Side. Perhaps worth walking through for a sense of the old atmosphere, but the food here is not budget by any means.

LOWER EAST SIDE

Subway: F to Second Ave., East Broadway; E, F, J, M, Z to Essex/Delancey St.; ***Sights:*** *p. 56.* ***Food:*** *p. 135.* ***Nightlife:*** *p. 158.* ***Shopping:*** *p. 204.*

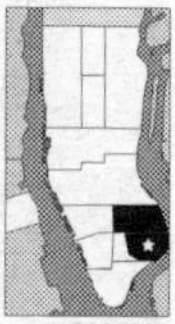

see map pp. 320-321

Down below East Houston and east of the Bowery lurks the trendily seedy Lower East Side, where old-timers rub shoulders with heroin dealers, and twenty-somethings emulate *la vie bohème.* A traditional destination for immigrants, the neighborhood retains its multicultural flavor but is slowly shedding its working-class clothes for what is young, hip, and chic. Highlights include the **Lower East Side Tenement Museum** and **Katz's Delicatessen.** This is a neighborhood worth exploring.

TRIBECA

Subway: 1, 9, A, C, E to Canal St.; 1, 9 to Franklin St.; 1, 2, 3, 9, A, C, E to Chambers St. ***Sights:*** *p. 58.* ***Food:*** *p. 136.* ***Nightlife:*** *p. 159.*

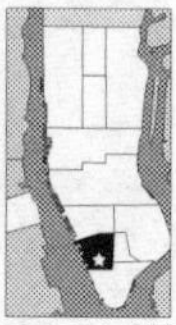

see map p. 315

Bounded by Canal St. on the north, the Hudson River on the west, Vesey St. on the South and East Broadway on the east, **Tri**angle **Be**low **Ca**nal St. is primarily residential neighborhood. There's not much in the way of sights here, but bars and expensive restaurants lurk in Tribeca's nooks.

SOHO

Subway: C, E to Spring St.; N, R to Prince St.; 1, 9 to Houston St. B, D, F, Q to Broadway-Lafayette. ***Sights:*** *p. 57.* ***Galleries:*** *p. 123.* ***Food:*** *p. 136.* ***Nightlife:*** *p. 159.* ***Shopping:*** *p. 204.*

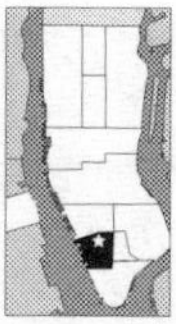

see map p. 315

SoHo, the district **So**uth of **Ho**uston St. (say "HOW-ston"), holds court between Tribeca and Greenwich Village and is bounded by Crosby St. on the east, W. Broadway on the west, and Canal St. on the south. New Yorkers come to the neighborhood for its art galleries and shopping.

GREENWICH VILLAGE

Subway: A, B, C, D, E, F, Q to W. 4th St.; A, C, E, to 14th St.; 1, 9 to Houston St., 1, 2, 3, 9 to Christopher St.; N, R to 8th St.-NYU; L to Sixth Ave., Eighth Ave.; 6 to Bleecker St. ***Sights:*** *p. 58.* ***Food:*** *p. 137.* ***Nightlife:*** *p. 160.* ***Gay Nightlife:*** *p. 196.* ***Shopping:*** *p. 205.* ***Accommodations:*** *p. 253.*

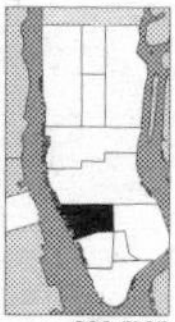

see map pp. 316-317

The Village is located west of Broadway, between Houston and 14th Sts. Between Broadway and Sixth Ave., the streets are organized in grid-like fashion, but west of Sixth Ave., they dissolve into a confusing, tangled web. Use this book's handy map to navigate the neighborhood. While rent is no longer low in the Village, the area is still a center for the rebellious and the intellectual. Highlights include **Washington Square Park** and the neighborhood's **jazz clubs.**

The Subway

see map pp. 320-321

EAST VILLAGE AND ALPHABET CITY

Subway: 6 to Astor Pl., Bleecker St.; L to First Ave., Third Ave.; F to Second Ave. ***Sights:*** *p. 62.* ***Food:*** *p. 138.* ***Nightlife:*** *p. 160.* ***Gay Nightlife:*** *p. 198.* ***Shopping:*** *p. 206.* ***Accommodations:*** *p. 253.*

The East Village, east of Broadway, north of East Houston, and south of 14th St., was carved out of the Bowery and the Lower East Side in the early 1960s, as artists and writers moved here to escape high rents in the West Village. St. Mark's Pl. is the center of the East Village scene. Alphabet City lies to the east of First Ave., south of 14th St., and north of Houston St., where Manhattan gained some weight and never lost it back. Here, the avenues give up on numbers and adopt letters. The area is generally safe during the day, but use caution east of Ave. B after dark. The **nightlife** in the East Village is among the city's best.

On the Cell

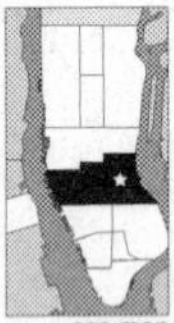
see map pp. 322-323

GRAMERCY PARK, UNION SQUARE, AND MURRAY HILL

Subway: 4, 5, 6, L, N, R to Union Square, 6, N, R to 23rd St., 6 to 28th St., 33rd St. ***Sights:*** *p. 65.* ***Food:*** *p. 142.* ***Nightlife:*** *p. 163.* ***Accommodations:*** *p. 253.*

At 14th St. between Broadway and Park Ave. South, you'll find Union Square. Gramercy Park is located to the northeast, at the southern end of Lexington Ave., between 20th and 21st St. The surrounding neighborhood is called Gramercy, after the park. Murrary Hill, home to the **Pierpont Morgan Museum,** is in the thirties on the East Side.

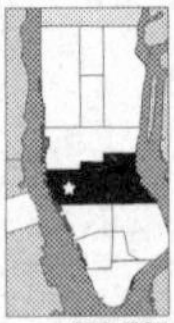
see map pp. 322-323

CHELSEA

Subway: 1, 2, 3, 9, A, C, E to 14th St.; L to Eighth Ave.; 1, 9, C, E to 23rd St.; 1, 9 to 28th St. ***Sights:*** *p. 68.* ***Galleries:*** *p. 124.* ***Food:*** *p. 141.* ***Nightlife:*** *p. 163.* ***Gay Nightlife:*** *p. 197.* ***Shopping:*** *p. 209.* ***Accommodations:*** *p. 255.*

Extending west from Sixth Ave. to the Hudson River between 14th and 28th Sts., Chelsea is home to some of the city's best galleries and clubs. A thriving gay community lives in Chelsea, and fashionable men dine on Eighth Ave. between 20th and 23rd Sts.

Silver Scooter

see map pp. 322-323

HERALD SQUARE AND THE GARMENT DISTRICT

Subway: B, D, F, N, Q, R, W to Herald Sq. ***Sights:*** *p. 69.* ***Food:*** *p. 141.* ***Shopping:*** *p. 210.* ***Accommodations:*** *p. 257.*

Herald Square is located between 34th and 35th Sts. between Broadway and Sixth Ave. The area is a center for shopping. One block to the east is the **Empire State Building**.

HELL'S KITCHEN

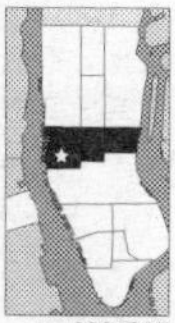

see map pp. 326-327

Subway: 1, 2, 3, 9 to Penn Station; A, C, E to 34th/Eighth Ave.; N, R to 34th St.; or B, D, F, Q to 33rd St. for Herald Sq. and Garment DIstrict. 1, 2, 3, 9, A, C, E, 7, S to Times Sq. for Times Sq. and Theater District. ***Sights:*** *p. 71.* ***Food:*** *p. 143.*

Between Eighth Ave. and the Hudson River, 34th and 59th Sts., is **Hell's Kitchen,** until very recently a violent area inhabited by immigrant gangs with misleading names such as "Battle Row Annie's Ladies' Social and Athletic Club."

MIDTOWN

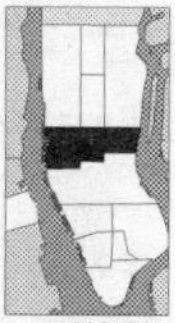

see map pp. 326-327

Subway: 4, 5, 6, 7, S to 42nd St.-Grand Central Terminal; 6 to 51st St.; 4, 5, 6, N, R to 59th St.-Lexington Ave.; B, D, F, 7 to 42nd St.-Bryant Park; B, D, F to 47th-50th Sts.-Rockefeller Center; 1, 2, 3, 7, 9, A, C, E, N, Q, R, S, W to 42nd St.-Times Square; E,F to Fifth Ave.; N,R to 50th St. ***Sights:*** *p. 71.* ***Sights:*** *p. 71.* ***Galleries:*** *p. 125.* ***Food:*** *p. 144.* ***Shopping:*** *p. 211.* ***Accommodations:*** *p. 257.*

East of Eighth Ave., from about 42nd St. to 59th St., lies Midtown. Mammoth office buildings and posh hotels dominate the skies, and the streets are lined with high-brow stores. On the east side of Midtown, you'll find luxurious Fifth Ave., more solemn Park Ave., and the United Nations. On the West Side are Times Square, the Theater District, and Central Park South.

UPPER EAST SIDE

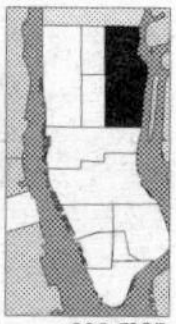

see map pp. 328-329

Subway: 4, 5, 6, N, R to 59th St.-Lexington Ave.; 6 to 68th St., 77th St., 96th St.; 4, 5, 6 to 86th St. ***Sights:*** *p. 80.* ***Galleries:*** *p. 125.* ***Food:*** *p. 145.* ***Nightlife:*** *p. 164.* ***Shopping:*** *p. 212.* ***Accommodations:*** *p. 260.*

The Upper East Side (from 59th St. to 96th St. and East End Ave. to Fifth Ave.) is definitely the Horn of Plenty. The city's best museums are here, such as the **Metropolitan Museum of Art, the Frick,** and the **Guggenheim.**

UPPER WEST SIDE

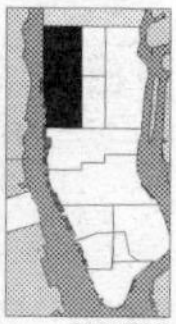

see map pp. 332-333

Subway: 1, 9, A, B, C, D to 59th St.-Columbus Circle; 1, 9 to 66th St.; 1, 2, 3, 9, B, C to 72nd St.; 1, 9 to 79th St.; B, C to 81st St.; 1, 9, B, C to 86th St.; 1, 2, 3, 9, B, C to 96th St. ***Sights:*** *p. 82.* ***Food:*** *p. 146.* ***Bars:*** *p. 165.* ***Shopping:*** *p. 214.* ***Accommodations:*** *p. 260.*

Located between 59th and 110th Sts. west of Central Park, the Upper West Side is home to exciting dining, shopping, and cultural activity. Because of the continuous bustle, Broadway above 96th St. feels safe even late at night, although *Let's Go* can't say the same of the side streets that intersect it or of Amsterdam and Columbus Aves. above 98th St. **Lincoln Center** and **American Museum of Natural History** are the neighborhood's biggest attractions.

MORNINGSIDE HEIGHTS

see map pp. 334-335

Subway: 1, 9 to 110th St., 116th St., 125th St. ***Sights:*** *p. 84.* ***Food:*** *p. 148.*

Above 110th St. and below 125th St., between Amsterdam Ave. and the Hudson River, this area, caught between the chaos of Harlem and the color of the Upper West Side, is dominated by students from Barnard College and Columbia University. Unassuming restaurants dot the active collegiate neighborhood.

HARLEM

see map pp. 334-335

Subway: 6 to 103rd St., 110th St., 116th St.; 4, 5, 6 to 125th St.; 2, 3 to 110th St., 116th St., 125th St., 135th St.; 3 to 145th St., 148th St.; B, C to 110th St., 116th St., 135th St.; B, C, D to 125th St.; A, B, C, D to 145th St.; 1, 9 to 137th St., 145th St. ***Sights:*** *p. 86.* ***Food:*** *p. 149.* ***Shopping:*** *p. 214.* ***Accommodations:*** *p. 265.*

Harlem, the largest neighborhood in all of Manhattan, extends from 110th St. to the 150s, between the Hudson and East Rivers. The dangerous and poor Harlem of urban legend exists largely in the area south of 125th St. in the Manhattan Valley, particularly along Frederick Douglass Boulevard and Adam Clayton Powell Boulevard; avoid this area after dark. Central Harlem's main thoroughfare is 125th St. Many of this neighborhood's streets have been renamed for past black leaders: Sixth/Lenox Ave. is also referred to as Malcolm X. Boulevard, and 125th St. is also Martin Luther King Boulevard.

Spanish Harlem, or El Barrio, sits between 96th to 125th Sts. on the East Side. The neighborhood's main artery, East 116th St., rocks to a salsa beat and overflows with fruit stands, Puerto Rican eateries, and men vending flavored crushed ice on scorching summer days.

WASHINGTON HEIGHTS

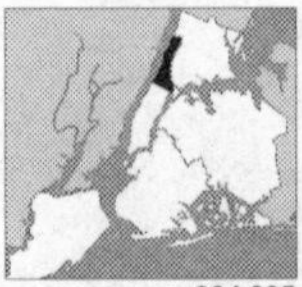

see map pp. 334-335

Subway: C to 155th St., 163rd St.; 1, 9, A, C to 168th St.-Washington Heights; A to 175th St., 181st St., 190th St.; 1, 9 to 181st St., 191st St. **Sights:** *p. 88.*

North of 155th St., Manhattan Island's curves eluded the leveling eye of the postmodern architect and the demolishing hand of the corporate contractor that rendered downtown neighborhoods so many clusters of flattened blocks. You may want to bargain-shop along trinket-filled St. Nicholas Ave. or Broadway, where vendors sell swimwear, household items, and electronics for half the original price.

BROOKLYN

see map pp. 336-337

***Sights:** p. 90. **Galleries:** p. 127. **Food:** p. 150. **Nightlife:** p. 166. **Shopping:** p. 215. **Accommodations:** p. 266.*

Brooklyn's main avenues dissect the borough. The **Brooklyn-Queens Expressway (BQE)** pours into the **Belt Parkway** and circumscribes Brooklyn. Ocean Parkway, Ocean Ave., Coney Island Ave., and diagonal Flatbush Ave. run from the beaches of southern Brooklyn to Prospect Park in the heart of the borough. The streets of western Brooklyn (including those in Sunset Park, Bensonhurst, Borough Park, and Park Slope) are aligned with the western shore and thus collide at a 45-degree angle with central Brooklyn's main arteries. In northern Brooklyn, several avenues—Atlantic Ave., Eastern Parkway, and Flushing Ave.—travel from downtown east into Queens.

NEIGHBORHOODS

Our story begins, as all great stories do, in Brooklyn.
—Jon Kalish

In the borough's northeastern corner is **Greenpoint,** a predominantly Polish neighborhood whose main drag is Manhattan Ave. To the south is artist-haven **Williamsburg.** Centered around Bedford Ave., the neighborhood is among Brooklyn's most trendy. Another art-oriented community is **DUMBO** (Down Under Manhattan Bridge Overpass), which sits southwest of Williamsburg. Its western neighbor, **Fulton Ferry,** is where you'll find the Brooklyn Bridge. **Brooklyn Heights,** a uniformly preserved 19th-century residential area, sprang up with the development of steamboat transportation between Brooklyn and Manhattan in 1814. Rows of posh Greek Revival and Italianate houses in this area essentially created New York's first suburb. **Downtown Brooklyn** is the borough's civic center. To the east, vibrant **Fort Greene,** along DeKalb Ave., is the hub of black artistic and cultural activity. To the south, **Park Slope** centers around Fifth and Seventh Aves.

Just south of Atlantic Ave., west of Park Slope, lies the quiet Italian neighborhood of **Cobble Hill,** whose gorgeous brownstone-lined sidestreets segue into **Carroll Gardens.** The ground floors of Smith and Court Sts. buildings are crowded with thrift stores, antique vendors, artist cooperatives, and craft shops where restaurants leave space. On the other side of the Brooklyn-Queens Expressway (BQE) is the industrial waterfront area of **Red Hook.** Cobblestone streets and Atlantic Ave. lead to warehouses and docks, where there are wonderful views of the Statue of Liberty. Farther south is **Sunset Park,** home to Greenwood Cemetery, the largest in Brooklyn. The nearby Shore Road of **Bay Ridge** is lined with mansions overlooking the Verrazano-Narrows Bridge and New York Harbor. **Bensonhurst,** to the southeast, is centered around Stillwell and Park Aves. Neighboring **Borough Park** is the largest Hassidic Jewish neighborhood in Brooklyn. Just southeast of Prospect Park and east of Borough Park is the **Flatbush,** where Manhattan's turn-of-the-century aristocracy maintained summer homes; you can wander around Argyle St. and Ditmas Ave. to see some of their old mansions.

In southern Brooklyn, you'll find the seaside communities of **Brighton Beach,** or "Little Odessa by the Sea," which is populated heavily by Eastern European immigrants. To the west **Coney Island** will take you back to a Brooklyn of years past.

QUEENS

Sights: *p. 96.* ***Galleries:*** *p. 127.* ***Food:*** *p. 153.* ***Nightlife:*** *p. 167.* ***Accommodations:*** *p. 267.*

see map pp. 340-341

The streets of Queens are neither like the orderly grid of Upper Manhattan nor the haphazard angles of Greenwich Village; instead, a mixed bag of urban planning techniques has resulted in a logical—but extremely complicated—system. Streets generally run north-south and are numbered from west to east, from 1st St. in Astoria to 271st St. in Glen Oaks. Avenues run perpendicular to streets and are numbered from north to south, from Second Ave. to 165th Ave. The address of an establishment or residence often tells you the closest cross-street (for example, 45-07 32nd Ave. is near the intersection with 45th St.). The challenging parts of Queens's geography are its numbered drives, roads, and places set randomly amid the streets and avenues. Use a map; pick up the very useful Queens Bus Map (free) available on most Queens buses.

NEIGHBORHOODS

Unlike Brooklyn, in which the parts make up a cohesive whole, Queens is full of relatively self-contained neighborhoods. You don't mail a letter to Queens, NY, but rather Long Island City, NY or Jackson Heights, NY.

In the borough's western edge are **Astoria** and **Long Island City.** As you move to the east, you'll find **Jackson Heights, Elmhurst,** and **Corona.** To the south of Corona are **Forest Hills** and **Forest Park. Flushing-Corona Park** sits, not surprisingly, between **Flushing** and Corona. **Jamaica** is south of Flushing, and **The Rockaways** are on the borough's southwestern edge.

THE BRONX

Sights: *p. 101.* ***Food:*** *p. 154.* ***Nightlife:*** *p. 167.*

see map pp. 342-343

Major highways cut up Bronx into many pieces. The Major Deegan Expressway (I-87) runs up the western border of the borough, next to the Harlem River. The Cross-Bronx Expressway (I-95) runs across the borough before turning north on its eastern-most edge. Up the center of the borough runs the Bronx River Parkway. Several avenues run north-south including the Grand Concourse and Jerome Ave. on the western side of the borough and White Plains Road and Boston Road on the eastern side of the borough. Streets running east-west include Tremont Ave. and Fordham Road and the Bronx and Pelham Parkway.

NEIGHBORHOODS

High on a hill, **Riverdale** is in the northwestern corner of the Bronx, surveying **Van Cortlandt Park** to the east. Farther to the east, you'll find **Woodlawn Cemetery,** and in the Bronx's northeastern corner is **Pelham Bay Park.** To the southeast of the park is **City Island.** Back in the borough center is **Bronx Park,** home to the Zoo and the Botanical Garden. West of the park are the neighborhoods of **Fordham** and **Belmont.** Farther south, you'll find the **South Bronx,** one of the city's most destitute areas.

STATEN ISLAND

Sights: *p. 106.* ***Food:*** *p. 155.*

see map p. 344

Unlike the rest of the city, Staten Island is quite spread out. Pick up much needed maps of Staten Island's bus routes as well as other pamphlets at the Staten Island **Chamber of Commerce,** 130 Bay St., bear left from the ferry station onto Bay St. (☎718-727-1900. Open M-F 9am-5pm.)

SIGHTSEEING TOURS

WALKING TOURS

Adventure on a Shoestring, (☎265-2663). See the city with veteran guide and budget connoisseur Howard Goldberg. Detailed 1½hr. tours incorporate chats with members of the various communities. Excursions reveal some of New York's better-kept secrets; Mr. Goldberg is a walking treasure trove of information on budget eats and accommodations. Themed tours run on holidays and weekends, like the Valentine's Day Big Apple Lovers' Tour, and fascinating tours like the Greenwich Village Ghosts Galore tour run year-round. Most tours cost $5; the price has never increased during the organization's 39 years of existence.

Big Onion Walking Tours (☎439-1090; www.bigonion.com). Graduate students in American history from Columbia or NYU lead tours of historic districts and ethnic neighborhoods. Themed excursions include "Brooklyn Bridge and Brooklyn Heights at Twilight," "Immigrant New York," "Historic Harlem," and the "Multi-Ethnic Eating Tour," which explores the gastronomical delights of places such as Chinatown and Little Italy. Tours average 2-2½hr. Adults $12-15, students and seniors $10-13. "Show-up" tours are Th-Su. Group tours and bus tours also available.

Joyce Gold's Tours (☎242-5762; www.nyctours.com). Ms. Gold has read over 900 books on Manhattan, the subject she teaches at NYU and at the New School. On 45 days each year she and a company of adventurers give tours focusing on architecture, history, and ethnic groups within the city. Tours last approximately 2-2½hr., depending on the subject, and cost $12.

Lower East Side Tenement Museum Walking Tours, 90 Orchard St. (☎431-0233; www.tenement.org). Neighborhood heritage tour strolls through the Lower East Side Apr.-Dec. and examines how different immigrant groups shaped and continue to shape the area. 1hr. Sa and Su at 1:30pm and 2:30pm. $9 adults, $7 students and seniors; combination tickets available for walking tour and tenement tours. (See **Museums,** p. 119.)

Municipal Art Society (☎439-1049; www.mas.org). Guided walking tours ($10-15); destinations change with the seasons but include most major districts of Manhattan, such as SoHo and Times Square. Free tour of Grand Central Station W 12:30pm, at the info booth on the main concourse. Call in advance.

Museum of the City of New York, 1220 Fifth Ave., and 103rd St. (☎534-1672; www.mcny.org). The museum sponsors popular walking tours Apr.-Oct. on Sa afternoons, lasting a leisurely 1-2hr. ($12). Areas covered include Chelsea, the Lower East Side, and East Harlem, with a focus on the history and architecture of the particular district.

Radical Walking Tours (☎718-492-0069). Historian/activist Bruce Kayton leads tours that cover the alternative history of NYC. For example, tours of Greenwich Village highlight radicals and revolutionaries like John Reed and Emma Goldman, as well as artistic and theatrical movements that flourished around them. Other tours include trips to Wall Street, the Lower East Side, and Central Park. Even lifelong locals will learn fascinating details about the city's history. No reservations required. Call for schedule and departure sites. All tours $10. 2-3hr.

92nd Street Y, 1395 Lexington Ave. (☎415-5628). The Y leads an astounding variety of walking tours covering all boroughs and many aspects of New York life, from the Garment District, SoHo artists, and the brownstones of Brooklyn to literary tours, museum visits, and even an all-night candlelight tour. Tours vary in length and cost $15-30. Call for the latest tours.

BOAT TOURS

Circle Line Tours, W. 42nd St., at the Hudson River, Pier 83 (☎563-3200; www.circleline.com). The Circle Line takes you on a boat around Manhattan. 3hr. full-circle tour that circumnavigates the island $24, children $12, seniors $20. 2hr. semi-circle tour $20, children $10, seniors $17. Call for times. No reservations necessary; arrive 30-45min. early.

BUS TOURS

Brooklyn Attitude, 224 W. 35th St., between Seventh and Eighth Aves. (☎718-398-0939). Bus tour with several walking excursions through ethnic and historic neighborhoods in Brooklyn. Departure points in both mid-Manhattan and Brooklyn. $21-31.

Gray Line Sight-Seeing, 42nd St. and Eighth Ave., at the Port Authority Terminal (☎397-2600; www.gray linenewyork.com). Huge bus-tour company offering many trips, including jaunts through Manhattan and gambling junkets to Atlantic City. Conducted in French, Italian,

Spanish among other languages. The Downtown tour (every 10min., 8:30am-5pm; $30, children 5-11 $20) and Uptown tour (every 20min., 8:30am-5pm; $30, children $20) allow you to get on and off the bus at points to explore on your own. The 6hr. Night on the Town tour ($75, children $55; 6:30pm daily) covers many sights. Reservations aren't required for in-city tours, but arrive at the terminal 30min. early.

Harlem Spirituals, 690 Eighth Ave., between 43rd and 44th Sts. (☎391-0900; www.harlemspiritualtours.com). Offers tours of Manhattan, Brooklyn, and the Bronx. Tours of upper Manhattan, such as the "Spirituals and Gospel" tour, includes trips to historic homes and participation in a Baptist service (4hr.; Su 9:30am, W 9am; $39). The "Soul Food and Jazz" tour (M, Th, Sa 7pm-midnight; $95) features a tour of Harlem, a filling meal at a Harlem restaurant (usually Sylvia's), and an evening at a jazz club. Reserve in advance.

Heart of Brooklyn Trolley, ☎718-282-7789. A trolley system that runs on weekends around major sights around Prospect Park, including stops at the Brooklyn Museum of Art, the Botanic Garden, and the 9th St. Bandshell. Wheelchair accessible. Sa-Su noon-6pm.

GETTING INTO NEW YORK

TO AND FROM THE AIRPORTS

Travel between the airports and Manhattan is a choice between inconvenience and money. **Public transportation** is cheap, but you will almost definitely have to transfer from bus to subway, subway to bus, or subway to subway at least twice (with all your luggage). **Private bus companies** (shuttles) charge slightly more, but will take you directly from the airport to any one of many Manhattan destinations: Grand Central Station (42nd St. and Park Ave.), the Port Authority Bus Terminal (41st St. and Eighth Ave.), the World Trade Center (1 West St.), or to several prominent hotels. Most private services peter out or vanish entirely between midnight and 6am. A **taxi** is the most comfortable way of getting to the city, if you're willing to pay. Heavy traffic makes the trip slightly more expensive; traveling during rush hour (7:30-10am and 4-7:30pm) can be hard on your wallet. Passengers are responsible for paying bridge and tunnel tolls.

The best resource for ground transportation to the airports is the Port Authority of NJ & NY's website, **http://www.panynj.gov.** If you make lodging reservations ahead of time, be sure to ask about **limousine services**—some hostels offer transportation from the airports for reasonable fares.

JFK AIRPORT

*30-60min. from Manhattan. **Taxi** around $30 (plus tolls and tip).*

BY SUBWAY. Catch a free yellow-white-blue JFK Long-Term Parking bus from any airport terminal (every 15min., 24hr.) to the **Howard Beach-JFK Airport subway station.** You can take the **A train** from there to several points in the city ($1.50, exact change only; 1hr.). Heading from Manhattan to JFK, take the Far Rockaway A train.

BY BUS. Local **bus** Q10 ($1.50, exact change only) stops at the airport and connects to the A, E, J, L, F, and R subway lines, which in turn go to Manhattan; tell the driver what subway line you want, and ask him to tell you where to get off. Although these routes are safe during the day, nighttime travelers should check with the information desk to find the safest way into the city.

BY SHUTTLE. The **New York Airport Service Express Bus** (☎718-875-8200), is a private line that runs between JFK and Grand Central Terminal, Penn Station, and Port Authority ($13-15; every 15-30min., 6am-midnight). The **Gray Line Air Shuttle** (☎800-451-0455) will drop you off anywhere in Manhattan between 21st and 103rd. Sts. ($14-19; 6am-11:30pm). The **SuperShuttle** (☎212-258-3826) will drop you anywhere in Manhattan between Battery Park and 227th St. ($13.50-14.50; 24hr.). Inquire about all three at the Ground Transportation Center in JFK. All services take 40-70min.

LAGUARDIA AIRPORT

*15-30min. away from Manhattan. **Taxi** $16-20 (plus tolls and tip).*

BY BUS AND SUBWAY. The **M60 bus** (daily 4:50am-1am; $1.50) connects to the following subways in Manhattan: 1, 9 at 116th St. and Broadway; 2, 3 at 125th St. and

THE BIG APPLE'S SEED

Every time a New York Met hits a home run in Flushing's Shea Stadium, an oversized plastic apple rises from behind the outfield wall in celebration, a physical manifestation of the city's nickname: the Big Apple.

According to scholars Barry Popik and Gerald Cohen, the nickname got its start in the 1920s, when John G. FitzGerald named his horse-racing column "Around the Big Apple." FitzGerald apparently heard New York so dubbed by African-American stablehands in New Orleans who looked upon Gotham as the big time or the big reward for years on the minor tracks.

A less plausible, but more sexy explanation of the nickname comes from Peter Salwen, who claims that the Big Apple is synonymous with Gotham's long history of prostitution. Salwen writes that Evelyn de Saint-Evremond ran a first-class bordello in the early 19th century. When Evelyn was shortened to Eve, the "young men-about-town soon got into the habit of referring to their amorous adventures as 'having a taste of Eve's Apples.'" Hence the Big Apple.

Popik disagrees with Salwen and seems to have the evidence on his side. He told *Let's Go:* "Big Apple doesn't come from whores."

In either case, Big Apple did not become prevalent until Charles Gillett, former president of the New York Convention and Visitors Bureau, popularized the name with his Big Apple Campaign in 1971. His P.R. ploy hit onto something inexplicably catchy.

Lenox Ave.; 4, 5, 6 at 125th St. and Lexington Ave. In Queens, catch the N at Astoria Blvd. and 31st St. Or, take the MTA **Q33 bus** (from the Marine Air Terminal) or the **Q47 bus** (everywhere else; both $1.50). Transfer to the 7, E, F, G, R ($1.50) at the 74th St./Broadway-Roosevelt Ave./Jackson Hts. **subway** stop in Queens. Takes at least 1½hr. Be especially careful traveling these routes at night.

BY SHUTTLE. The **New York Airport Service Express Bus** (☎718-875-8200) runs from LaGuardia to Grand Central Terminal, Penn Station, and Port Authority ($8-10; every 15-30min. 6:40am-11:40pm). The **Gray Line Air Shuttle** (☎800-451-0455) runs from LaGuardia to anywhere between 23rd and 96th Sts. ($13; on demand 7am-11pm). **SuperShuttle** (☎258-3826) will drop you anywhere in Manhattan between Battery Park and 227th St. ($13.50-16.50; 24hr.). All services take 30-60min.

NEWARK AIRPORT

30-60min. from Manhattan. ***Taxi*** *$34-51, including tolls.*

BY BUS. New Jersey Transit Authority, NJTA (☎973-762-5100), runs **Air Link bus #302** from the airport and Newark's Penn Station (not Manhattan's; $4). From there **bus #108** ($3.25, exact change) goes to Port Authority. Takes at least 1½hr.

BY TRAIN. PATH trains (☎800-234-PATH) also run from Newark Penn Station to Manhattan, stopping at Christopher St., Sixth Ave., 9th St., 14th St., 23rd St., and 33rd St. ($1). **NJT** (☎800-772-2222) runs from Newark Penn Station to Manhattan's Penn Station ($2.50). **Amtrak** (☎800-USA-RAIL) also travels from Penn to Penn ($7). Takes at least 1½hr.

BY SHUTTLE. Olympia Airport Express (☎964-6233) run from the airport to Port Authority, Grand Central Terminal, and Penn Station ($11; every 20-30min. 6am-midnight). **Gray Line Air Shuttle** (☎800-451-0455) runs from the airport to anywhere between 23rd and 63rd Sts. ($14; on demand 7am-11pm; takes 30-60min). **SuperShuttle** (☎258-3826) runs from Newark to anywhere between Battery Park and 227th St. ($17.50-22.50; on demand 24hr.; takes 30-60min.).

GETTING AROUND NYC

BY SUBWAY

The 233-mile New York subway system operates 24 hours a day, 365 days a year. It moves 4.5 million people daily through 468 stations. The fare for subways is $1.50, and groups of three and four may find a cab ride to be cheaper and more expedient for short distances. Long distances are best traveled by subway, since once inside a passenger may transfer onto any of the other trains without restrictions. Free, extremely useful subway maps are available at any subway station booth, and additional copies are posted directly downstairs in any station and in every subway car.

The biggest **subway hubs** are 42nd St.-Grand Central on the east side and 42nd St.-Times Square on the west side. From these two, most trains can be connected to, and the two are connected by the 7 and S trains. **The subways are much more useful for traveling north-south** than east-west, as there are only two crosstown shuttle trains (42nd and 14th St.). **Express trains** stop only at certain major stations; **locals** stop everywhere. Be sure to **check the letter or number and the destination of each train,** since trains with different destinations often use the same track. When in doubt, ask a friendly passenger or the conductor, who usually sits near the middle of the train.

You'll see lit glass globes outside most subway entrances. Green means that the entrance is staffed 24hr. a day. Red indicates that the entrance is closed or restricted in some way, usually during off (night) hours; read the sign posted above the stairs.

FARES: METROCARD. The **MetroCard** now serves as the dominant form of currency for transit in New York. The card, containing a magnetic strip, can be used at all subway stations and on all public buses and some private buses. Subway and bus fare is $1.50 per ride with the MetroCard, but purchasing a $15 card gets you one free ride ($30 gets you 2 free rides, etc.). Even more importantly, MetroCards can be used for subway-bus, bus-subway, and bus-bus transfers. When you swipe the card on the initial ride, a free transfer is electronically stored on your MetroCard and is good for up to 2hrs. **Without the MetroCard, bus-subway or subway-bus transfers are not free.** There are certain restrictions on bus-bus transfers (i.e. passengers on a north-south bus can generally only transfer to a bus going east-west).

UNLIMITED METROCARDS. "Unlimited Rides" MetroCards (as opposed to "Pay-Per-Ride" cards) are sold in 1-day ($4), 7-day ($17) and 30-day ($63) denominations and are good for unlimited use of the subway and bus systems during the specified period. **The Unlimited Rides Card is highly recommended for tourists who plan on visiting many sights.** Those with disabilities or over 65 qualify for a Reduced Fare card. For Reduced Fare card information or application, call 718-243-4999 (TTY for hearing impaired, call 718-596-8273). The MetroCard can be purchased in all subway stations and at any newsstand, pharmacy, or grocery store bearing a MetroCard sticker in the storefront window. MetroCard vending machines at many subway stations accept cash, credit, and debit cards.

SAFETY. The subway isn't the cleanest form of transportation, and there are homeless people living in stations and even subway cars themselves, but since everyone uses it all the time, it is generally safe, at least around central Manhattan. Nighttime is not necessarily a dangerous time to travel as long as you are taking a popular subway line and are not going to one of the outer boroughs. Try to be in the same subway car as other people you think are safe and stay near the middle to be close to the conductor (you'll see his face from the platform). During rush hour and in crowded stations (like 42nd St.), try to keep your bag in front of you to avoid falling prey to quick-fingered pickpockets. A real concern for women specifically is sexual molestation—there are quite a few crazies who ride the subways to brush up or grope others. If this happens, be *loud* in your indignation.

BY BUS

Because buses are often mired in traffic, they can take twice as long as subways, but they are almost always safer, cleaner, and quieter. They'll also get you closer to your destination, since they stop every two blocks or so and run crosstown (east-west), as well as uptown and downtown (north-south). For long-distance travel (over 40 north-south blocks), buses can be a nightmare (except late at night, when traffic is manageable), but for shorter—and especially crosstown—trips, buses are often as quick as, and more convenient than, trains. The MTA transfer system provides north-south travelers with a paper slip, valid for a free ride east-west, or vice-versa, but you must ask the driver for a transfer when you board and pay your fare. Make sure you ring when you want to get off.

Bus stops are indicated by a blue sign post announcing the bus number or a glass-walled shelter displaying a map of the bus's route and a schedule of arrival times (they are surprisingly on-point). A flat fare of $1.50 is charged at all times when you board; either a MetroCard (see above for more information), exact change, or a subway token is required—dollar bills are not accepted. If you use a MetroCard, within two hours you can transfer without charge from the bus to the subway or from a bus to another bus. Ask for outer borough bus maps at any outer borough subway station; different restrictions apply to them as many are operated by private companies.

BY TAXI

Even if your stomach survives a harrowing NYC cab ride, your budget may not. The meter starts at $2 and clicks 30¢ for about every four street blocks or one long avenue block; 30¢ is also tacked on for every 75 seconds spent in slow or stopped traffic, a 50¢ surcharge is levied from 8pm to 6am, and passengers pay for all tolls. Don't forget to tip 10-15%; cabbies expect the dough. Before you leave the cab, ask for a receipt, which will have the taxi's identification number (either its meter number or its medallion). This number is necessary to trace lost articles or to make a complaint to the **Taxi Commission** (☎221-8294; open M-F 9am-5pm). Some drivers may illegally try to show the naive visitor the "scenic route"; quickly glance at a street map before embarking so you'll have some clue if you're being taken to your destination, or just being taken for a ride. Use only yellow cabs—they're licensed by the state of New York. Cabs of other colors are unlicensed "gypsy" cabs and are illegal in NYC. When hailing a cab: if the center light on the cab's roof is lit, then the cabbie is picking up fares; if it is dark, the cab is already taken. If you can't find anything on the street, commandeer a radio-dispatched cab (see **Service Directory**, p. 283, for phone numbers). Keep in mind that you can't cram more than four people into a cab.

BY CAR

What do New Yorkers know about driving? Don't do it in the city. When behind the wheel in New York, you are locked in combat with aggressive taxis, careless pedestrians, and lunatic bicycle couriers. If you do choose to drive in Manhattan, note that most avenues and streets run one-way. Streets usually run east if they're even-numbered and west if they're odd-numbered. Wide transverse streets (135th, 125th, 116th, 106th, 96th, 86th, 79th, 72nd, 57th, 42nd, 34th, 23rd and 14th Sts.) are two-way. When traveling uptown or downtown, you are generally better served by taking an avenue on which traffic travels one-way. On these avenues, traffic lights are synchronized such that lights turn from red to green in succession.

But the hassle of parking truly makes having a car nothing but a nuisance. Don't be surprised if you have to park many blocks from your destination. Read the signs carefully; a space is usually legal only on certain days of the week. The city has never been squeamish about towing, and recovering a towed car will cost $100 or more. Some streets have parking meters that cost 25¢ per 15min., with a limit of one or two hours. **Parking lots** are the easiest but the most expensive option. In Midtown lots, expect to pay at least $25 per day and up to $15 for two hours. The cheapest parking lots are downtown—try the far west end of Houston St.

Break-ins and car theft happen often, particularly if you have a radio. The wailing of a car alarm is such a familiar tune to New Yorkers that you may hear them sing along. Never leave anything visible inside your car.

INTERNATIONAL DRIVING PERMIT

For information on how to obtain the **International Driving Permit (IDP),** contact the one of the following organizations in your home country:

Australia: Contact your local Royal Automobile Club (RAC) or the National Royal Motorist Association (NRMA) if in NSW or the ACT (☎08 9421 4298; www.rac.com.au/travel). Permits AUS$15.

Canada: Contact any Canadian Automobile Association (CAA) branch office in Canada, or write to CAA, 1145 Hunt Club Rd., Suite 200, K1V 0Y3 Canada. (☎613-247-0117; fax 247-0118; www.caa.ca/CAAInternet/travelservices/internationaldocumentation/idptravel.htm).Permits CDN$10.

Ireland: Contact the nearest Automobile Association (AA) office or write: The Automobile Association, International Documents, Fanum House, Erskine, Renfrewshire PA8 6BW (☎990 500 600). Permits IR£4.

New Zealand: Contact your local Automobile Association (AA) or their main office at Auckland Central, 99 Albert St. (☎9 377 4660; fax 302 2037; www.nzaa.co.nz.). Permits NZ$8.

South Africa: Contact your local Automobile Association of South Africa office or the head office at P.O. Box 596, 2000 Johannesburg (☎11 799 1000; fax 799 1010). Permits SAR28.50.

U.K.: Visit your local Automobile Association (AA) Shop. To find the location nearest you that issues the IDP, call ☎0990 50 06 00. More information available at www.theaa.co.uk/motoring/idp.asp). Permits UK£4.

CAR RENTAL

All agencies maintain varying minimum-age requirements and require proof of age as well as a security deposit. Agencies in Queens and Yonkers are often less expensive than their Manhattan counterparts, especially for one-day rentals. Most auto insurance policies will cover rented cars, and some credit cards like American Express and Chase Visa take care of your rental insurance costs if you've charged the vehicle to their card (but be sure to ask about all the particulars from the companies themselves; as always, "restrictions apply"). For car rental agencies, refer to the **Service Directory,** p. 279.

BY FOOT

Walking is the cheapest, arguably the most entertaining, and often the fastest way to get around town. During rush hour the sidewalks are packed with suited and sneakered commuters. In between rush hours, sidewalks are still full of street life. Twenty street blocks (north-south) are the equivalent of one mile; one east-west block from one avenue to the next is about triple the distance of a north-south, street-to-street block.

WHEN IN NEW YORK

BLENDING IN

Acting like a tried-and-true New Yorker is your best defense. The New Yorker walks briskly. Be discreet with street maps and cameras; address requests for directions to police officers or store-owners. Consider covering your flagrant *Let's Go* guide with plain paper. Stay out of public bathrooms if you can; they tend to be filthy and unsafe. Instead, try department stores, hotels, or restaurants (Barnes & Noble bookstores are a great place for bathroom stops). If you suspect you're being followed, duck into a nearby store or restaurant.

NEWSPAPERS AND MAGAZINES

New York supports over 100 different newspapers, reflecting the diversity of its urban landscape. Weekly ethnic papers cater to the black, Hispanic, Irish, Japanese, Chinese, Indian, Korean, and Greek communities, among others. The city's best paper, however, is ***The New York Times,*** which soberly claims to publish "all the news that's fit to print." Its editorial page—which has a liberal slant—is a nationally respected forum for political debates. Praise from its Book Review section can revitalize living authors and immortalize dead ones, and its Sunday crossword puzzles enliven brunches from Fresno to Tallahassee. Although it is circulated nationally, the paper remains staunchly centered on New York; theater directors, nervous politicians, and other fervent readers often make late-night Saturday newsstand runs to buy the hefty, definitive Sunday *Times.*

The city's two major tabloids, the ***New York Post*** and ***The Daily News,*** infamously flaunt less-than-demure sensibilities. Both papers have editorial opinions more conservative than their headlines, as well as comics, advice pages, gossip columns, and horoscopes. Both have great sports sections, though *Let's Go* prefers the *Post's.*

The Village Voice, the largest weekly newspaper in the country, captures a spirit of the city each Wednesday that you won't find in the dailies. The left-leaning *Voice* prefers to stage lively political debates and print quirky reflections on New York life. It also sponsors some excellent investigative city reporting—and the city's most intriguing set of personal ads. The real estate and nightlife listings are legendary and indispensable to visitors and natives alike. Best of all, it is free to Manhattanites and can be picked up at any street corner midweek.

New York is undoubtedly the magazine publishing capital of the country; most national periodicals have their headquarters somewhere in the city. Of those that focus on New York, the ***New Yorker*** is the most respected. Led by David Remnick, the magazine publishes articles on anything from science and politics to fiction and poetry. Star writer Adam Gopnik pens a column on city life, and Roz Chast draws witty back-page cartoons. ***Time Out: New York*** also contains helpful entertainment listings and colorful, well-written articles.

RADIO

In New York City, the radio spectrum serves up everything from soulless elevator instrumentals (WLTW 106.7 FM) to pirate radio broadcasts of underground sounds and community activism. The lower on the dial, the less-commercial (and more innovative) the sounds will be. *Let's Go's* favorites include WKCR 89.9, Columbia's radio station which features some great jazz programs; WFUV 90.7, Fordham University's radio station, and WQHT 97.1 (Hot 97), which every evening brings in DJs cut, scratch, and mix on the last major label wax. On WABC 770AM, Michael Kay and John Sterling expertly broadcast New York Yankees games.

The following stations are FM unless otherwise noted:

TYPE	DIAL POSITION
Classical	WNYC 93.9, WQXR 96.3
Jazz	WBGO 88.3, WQCD 101.9
College/Indie/Alternative/Popular	WCWP 88.1, WPSC 88.7, WNYU 89.1, WKCR 89.9, WSOU 89.5, WFMU 91.1, WDRE 92.7, WXRK 92.3
Classic Rock	WQXR 104.3, WNEW 102.7
Top 40	WRKS 98.7, WPLJ 95.5, WHTZ 100.3, WRCN 103.9, WMXV 105.1
Hip-Hop/R&B/Soul	WQHT 97.1, WBLS 107.5, WWRL 1600AM
Oldies	WCBS 101.1
Foreign-Language Programming	WADO 1280AM, WWRV 1330AM, WKDM 1380AM, WZRC 1480AM, WSKQ 97.9, WNWK 105.9, WRTN 93.5
News	WABC 770AM, WCBS 880AM, WINS 1010AM, WBBR 1130AM
Public Radio	WNYC 93.9, WNYC 820AM, WBAI 99.5
Sports	WFAN 660AM, WABC 770AM
Pirate	88.7 Steal This Radio (Lower East Side)

TAXES AND TIPPING

The prices quoted throughout *Let's Go* do not include New York sales tax, which is 8.25%. Hotel tax is also 8.25%. Remember that service is never included on a New York bill, unless you're in a large party at a restaurant (six or more people), and then it is noted. Tip cab drivers and waiters 15%, bellhops around $1 per bag, and bartenders between 50¢ and $1 per drink, depending what type of environment you're in.

KEEPING IN TOUCH

MAIL

SENDING MAIL

Stamps for a normal letter envelope costs 34¢ for domestic mail, 50¢ for international. Most US post offices offer an **International Express Mail** service, which is the fastest way to send an item overseas. (A package under 8oz. can be sent to most foreign destinations in 40-72 hr. for around $13.) If you have questions concerning services, post office branch locations, or hours, dial ☎800-725-2161 for the 24hr. info line which provides information on branch hours and locations, postal rates, and zip codes and addresses. For post office branches in NY, see **Service Directory**, p. 282.

RECEIVING MAIL

Mail can be sent **General Delivery** to New York's **central post office branch,** 421 Eighth Ave. (☎330-2902; open 24hr.), occupying the block between Eighth and Ninth Ave. and 33rd and 32nd St. General Delivery mail should be sent to 390 Ninth Ave.; you must collect your General Delivery mail at the Ninth Ave. entrance. General Delivery letters to you should be labeled like this:

Firstname LASTNAME (capitalize & underline last name for accurate filing)
c/o General Delivery
Main Post Office
James A. Farley Building
390 Ninth Ave.
New York City, NY 10001
USA (if from another country)
HOLD FOR 30 DAYS

When you claim your mail, you'll have to present ID; if you don't claim a letter within two to four weeks, it will be returned to its sender.

Throughout the US, **American Express** acts as a mail service for cardholders if you contact them in advance. Under this free **Client Letter Service,** they will hold mail for 30 days, forward upon request, and accept telegrams. Address the envelope the same as you would for General Delivery. Some offices offer these services to non-cardholders but you must call ahead to make sure (☎800-528-4800).

TELEPHONES

Most of the information you will need about telephones—including area codes for the US, foreign country codes, and rates—is in the front of the local **white pages** telephone directory. The **yellow pages** lists businesses by category. Federal, state, and local government listings are provided in the blue pages at the back of the directory. To obtain local phone numbers or area codes of other cities, call **directory assistance** at 411. **All phone numbers listed without an area code are Manhattan numbers with the area code (212).**

AREA CODES

TELEPHONE CODES			
Manhattan	212, 917, 646	Staten Island	718, 347
Brooklyn	718, 347	Hoboken/NJ	201, 973
The Bronx	718, 347	Long Island	516 (Nassau)
Queens	718, 347		631 (Suffolk)

CALLING HOME FROM NYC

To place international calls from NYC, dial the universal international access code (011) followed by the country code, the city/area code, and the local number. Drop the first zeros of country codes and city codes if they are listed (i.e.: 033 is 011-33).

COUNTRY CODES			
Australia	61	Ireland	353
Austria	43	New Zealand	64
Italy	39	South Africa	13

A calling card is probably your best and cheapest bet. Calls are billed either collect or to your account. MCI WorldPhone also provides access to MCI's Traveler's Assist, which gives legal and medical advice, exchange rate information, and translation services. Other phone companies provide similar services to travelers. To **obtain a calling card** from your national telecommunications service before you leave home, contact the appropriate company below.

US: AT&T (☎888-288-4685; www.att.com/traveler); **Sprint/Global One** (☎800-877-4646; www.globalone.net/calling.html); **MCI/Worldphone** (☎800-444-4141; from abroad dial the country's MCI access number; www.mci.com/worldphone/english/accessnoalpha/shtml).

Canada: Bell Canada **Canada Direct** (☎800-565-4708; www.stentor.ca/canada_direct/eng/travel/cardform.htm).

UK: British Telecom **BT Direct** (☎800 34 51 44; www.chargecard.bt.com/html/access.htm).

Ireland: Telecom Éireann (becomes Eircom in September 1999) **Ireland Direct** (☎800 250 250; www.telecom.ie/eircom).

Australia: Telstar **Australia Direct** (☎13 22 00).

New Zealand: Telecom New Zealand (☎800 000 000; www.telecom.xtra.co.nz/cgi).

South Africa: Telkom South Africa (☎09 03; www.telkom.co.za/international/sadirect/access.htm).

To **call home** with a **calling card,** contact the North American operator for your service provider by dialing:

BT Direct: ☎800-445-5667 AT&T, ☎800-444-2162 MCI, ☎800-800-0008 Sprint.

Australia Direct: ☎800-682-2878 AT&T, ☎800-937-6822 MCI, ☎800-676-0061 Sprint.

Telkom South Africa Direct: ☎800-949-7027.

Wherever possible, use a calling card for international phone calls, as the long-distance rates for national phone services are often exorbitant. Where available, prepaid phone cards and, occasionally, major credit cards can be used for direct international calls, but they are still less cost-efficient. Although incredibly convenient, in-room hotel calls invariably include an arbitrary and sky-high surcharge (as much as $10).

CALLING WITHIN THE US

Telephone numbers in the US consist of a three-digit area code followed by seven digits, written as 123-456-7890. Only the last seven digits are used in a **local call. Calls outside the area code** from which you are dialing require a "1" and the area code and number. In NYC, a call to another borough will be local in terms of price, but you'll still need to dial a "1" and the area code and number. For example, to call the Brooklyn Museum from Manhattan, you would dial 1-718-638-5000, but it would only cost $0.25. Generally, discount rates apply after 5pm on weekdays and Sunday and economy rates every day between 11pm and 8am; on Saturday and on Sunday until 5pm, economy rates are also in effect. Numbers beginning with area code 800 or 888 are **toll-free calls** requiring no coin deposit. Numbers beginning with 900 are **toll calls** and charge you (often exorbitantly) for whatever "service" they provide.

Pay phones (25¢) are plentiful, most often stationed on street corners and in public areas. Be wary of private, more expensive pay phones—the rate they charge per call should be printed on the phone.

SAFETY AND SECURITY

PERSONAL SAFETY

WOMEN TRAVELERS

Women exploring NYC on their own inevitably face additional safety concerns. In general, NYC by day is safe, but from evening to morning some neighborhoods are definitely dangerous—always trust your instincts: if you'd feel better somewhere else, move on. Always carry extra money for a phone call, bus, or taxi. Stick to centrally located accommodations and avoid late-night treks or subway rides.

Look as if you know where you're going (even when you don't) and consider approaching women or couples for directions if you're lost or feel uncomfortable. Your best answer to verbal harassment is no answer at all. Don't hesitate to seek out a police officer or a passerby if you are being harassed. The look on your face is the key to avoiding unwanted attention; have a New Yorker's attitude. These warnings should not discourage women from traveling alone—NYC women manage just fine.

For general information and for information on rape crisis centers and counseling services, contact the **National Organization for Women (NOW),** 105 W. 28th St., #304, **New York,** NY 10010 (☎212-627-9895; fax 627-9891; www.nownyc.org).

EXPLORING BY DAY AND BY NIGHT

Pay attention to the neighborhood that surrounds you. A district can change character dramatically in the course of a single block (e.g., 96th St. and Park Ave.). Many notoriously dangerous districts have safe sections; look for children playing, women walking in the open, and other signs of an active community.

Terrible freak accidents can happen in the securest of neighborhoods, and you can get safely home in the worst of neighborhoods every day. Some quick guidelines: stay out of Central Park when it's dark; by the same token stay away from all large public parks and less-traversed, secluded areas like the Brooklyn Heights Promenade at night. *Let's Go* mentions neighborhoods that are slightly shadier during the night; be careful, but don't let it take over your vacation.

A good self-defense course will give you more concrete ways to react to different types of aggression. **Impact, Prepare, and Model Mugging** can refer you to local self-defense courses in the United States (☎800-345-5425). Workshops (2-3hr.) start at $50 and full courses run $350-500. Both women and men are welcome.

FINANCIAL SECURITY

Rip-off artists seek the wealthy as well as the unwary, so hide your riches, especially in neighborhoods where you feel uncomfortable. Carrying a shoulder bag is better than having a backpack. In the midst of a crowd, it is easy for pickpockets to unzip backpack pockets and remove items. Tourists make especially juicy prey because they tend to carry large quantities of cash—hence *Let's Go*'s advocacy of traveler's checks. Don't count your money in public or use large bills. Tuck your wallet into a less-accessible pocket and keep an extra ten bucks or so in a more obvious one (this is "Mugging Money," a NYC tradition—it appeases the criminals and you aren't left destitute).

Con artists run rampant on New York's streets. Beware of hustlers working in groups. If someone spills ketchup on you, someone else may be picking your pocket. Be distrustful of sob stories that require a donation from you. Remember that no one ever wins at three-card monte. If you take a car into the city, do not leave *anything* visible inside the car—put it all in the trunk, and if your tape deck/radio is removable, remove it and put it in the trunk also. You should never sleep in your car, no matter how low on cash you are.

DRUGS AND ALCOHOL

You must be 21 years old to purchase alcoholic beverages legally in New York State. The more popular drinking spots, as well as more upscale liquor stores, are likely to card. Smaller convenience stores and liquor stores in poorer neighborhoods will usually accept any type of ID, but few stores will let you get away with no proof of age whatsoever.

Possession of marijuana, cocaine, crack, heroin, methamphetamine, MDMA ("ecstasy"), hallucinogens, and most opiate derivatives (among many other chemicals) is punishable by stiff fines and imprisonment. But that doesn't stop New York's thriving **drug trade,** whose marketplaces are street corners, club bathrooms, and parks throughout the city, most conspicuously the Village's Washington Square Park. Whiffs of marijuana smoke are commonplace throughout the city, for this drug is low on the NYPD's list of problems. Trying to acquire drugs brings increasing levels of personal danger (both from the police and sketchy dealers). Attempting to purchase illegal drugs of any sort is a **very bad idea.** Out-of-towners seeking (or on) a high are walking targets—not just for cops, but for thieves, as well.

If you carry **prescription drugs** when you travel, it is vital to have a copy of the prescriptions themselves readily accessible at US Customs. Check with the US Customs Service before your trip for more information.

INSIDE

Life & Times

MONEY AND POLITICS

TRADERS AND TRAITORS: 1624-1811

The **Dutch West Indies Company** founded the colony of **New Amsterdam** on the southernmost tip of Manhattan in 1624 as a trading post, but England soon asserted rival claims to the land. While the mother countries squabbled, the colonists went about their burgeoning business, trading beaver skins, colorful *wampum* (beads made of white or violet seashells), and silver with the neighboring Native Americans. In 1626 New York's tradition of great bargains began when Peter Minuit bought the island from natives for 60 guilders ($24) worth of trade goods.

The rich and fertile land made light work for European settlers. "Children and pigs multiply here rapidly," gloated one colonist. Calvinist **Peter Stuyvesant,** the Dutch governor at the middle of the 17th century, enforced strict rules on the happy-go-lucky settlement. He shot hogs, closed taverns, and whipped Quakers, sparking protest and anger among the citizenry. Inexplicably, the draconian Stuyvesant has since become a local folk hero. New York schools, businesses, and even several neighborhoods (see Bedford-Stuyvesant in Brooklyn, **Sights,** p. 94) bear his name.

Unhappy with Dutch rule, early colonists refused to back Stuyvesant in resisting the English, and the Brits took over the settlement in 1664. The new British governors were slightly less offensive, if only because they were less effective: between 1664 and 1776, New York experienced 22 suspensions of governance.

Left to its own devices, the city continued to mature. The city's first newspaper, the **Gazette,** appeared in 1725. Ten years later, **John Peter Zenger,** editor of the *New York Weekly Journal,* was charged with libel for satirizing public officials. The governor of

SUBTERRANEAN IRT BLUES

On October 27, 1904, the first subway in New York City departed from City Hall Park. Until that point, there had been elevated trains, but the Interborough Rapid Transit Subway (IRT) represented a major advance in New York transportation, both for aesthetic and economic reasons. According to *The New York Times*, the first train made it up to 145th St. in 26 minutes, not bad timing, even by present-day standards.

The *Times* recorded that crowds were furious the first day, and over 150,000 people rode the IRT between 7pm and midnight, some using the subway to commute, others just in it for the ride.

Perhaps most interesting is the *Times'* commentary on the difference between the riders from Manhattan and those from outside of the city: "The up-bound Brooklynites and Jerseyites and Richmondites had boarded the trains with the stolid air of an African chief suddenly admitted into civilization and unwilling to admit that anything surprised him. The Manhattanites boarded the trains with the sneaking air of men who were ashamed to admit that they were doing something new, and attempting to cover up the disgraceful fact."

New York threw Zenger into jail and publicly burned copies of his paper. Zenger's acquittal set a precedent for a great US tradition—freedom of the press. In 1754, higher education arrived in New York in the form of **King's College** (later renamed **Columbia University,** p. 84). By the late 1770s, the city had become a major port with a population of 20,000. Early success made New Yorkers preoccupied with prosperity and uninterested in the first whiffs of revolution. After all, British rule was good for business.

Understandably, the new American army made no great efforts to protect the ungrateful city. New York was held by the British throughout the war, and the **Revolutionary War** was a rough time for the metropolis. Fire destroyed a quarter of the city in 1776, and a large portion was pillaged and deserted. When the defeated British left in 1783, most New Yorkers were relieved.

With its buildings in heaps of rubble and one-third of its population off roaming Canada, New York made a valiant effort to rebuild. "The progress of the city is, as usual, beyond all calculations," wrote one enraptured citizen. New York's post-Revolution comeback entailed briefly serving as the nation's capital and establishing the **first stock exchange,** which met under a buttonwood tree on Wall Street (p. 50). Meanwhile, **the 1811 Commissioner's Plan** established Manhattan's rectilinear street grid with characteristic New York ambition—at the time, the island consisted primarily of marshes and open fields, and boasted fewer than 100,000 residents. Merchants built mansions for themselves on the new streets and tenements for the increasing numbers of immigrants from western and northern Europe.

THE BIG APPLE AND THE WORM: 1812-1898

Political administration and services could not keep pace with irrepressible growth. By the early 19th century, New York was the largest US city, but pigs, dogs, and chickens continued to run freely, fires and riots made street life precarious, while the foul water supply precipitated a cholera epidemic. The notorious corruption of the political machine **Tammany Hall** (whose offices were housed in the original ConEd building in Battery Park City, p. 52), reached its peak in the 1850s under **"Boss" William Tweed**, who bribed voters—often immigrants—with money and jobs. An embezzler *par excellence*, Boss Tweed robbed the city of somewhere between 100 and 200 million dollars. When citizens complained, Tweed asked defiantly, "Well, what are you going to do about it?" Though Tweed was busted in 1875, the Tammany machine exerted its control over New York City politics well into the 20th century.

Amidst internal strife and national crisis, New Yorkers remained loyal to the city. Many citizens initially opposed the **Civil War;** their desire to protect trade with the South outweighed abolitionist and constitutional principles. The attack on South Carolina's Fort Sumter rallied New York to the Northern side, but a class-biased conscription act in July 1863 led to the infamous **New York City Draft Riots,** which erupted throughout Manhattan at the cost of over a thousand lives.

After the war, the city entered a half-century of prosperity, during which New York developed into its recognizable modern self. The **Metropolitan Museum of Art** (p. 110) was founded in 1870, and department store **Bloomingdale's** (p. 213) opened its now-venerable doors in 1872. In 1883, the **Brooklyn Bridge** (p. 90), an engineering marvel, was completed; many still consider it the world's most beautiful bridge. The new transportation gateway allowed the incorporation of the **outer boroughs**—the Bronx (p. 101), Brooklyn (p. 90), Queens (p. 96), and Staten Island (p. 106)—into the City of New York in 1898. During this period of rapid change, **Teddy Roosevelt** headed the police department, reforming New York in time for the turn of the century. He sallied forth at night dressed in a cape, searching for policemen who were sleeping on the job or consorting with prostitutes. At the tail end of the century, **Frederick Law Olmsted** and **Calvin Vaux** created **Central Park** (p. 78) on 843 rolling acres. With 2000 farms still in New York, the city began to spread out, both horizontally and vertically. "It'll be a great place if they ever finish it," O. Henry quipped.

THE "NEW METROPOLIS" 1899-1929

Despite entrepreneurial optimism among the powers-that-were, 70 percent of New York's population dwelled in substandard tenement housing in 1900. The turn-of-the-century war on slums was swept into a new stage of renewal. **Colonel George E. Waring's** army of "White Wings" put "a man instead of a voter behind every broom," thus creating the double benefit of jobs and cleaner streets. New York's most famed photographer of the era, **Jacob Riis** elegized, "It was Colonel Waring's broom that first let light into the slum." The first thirty years of the century witnessed the building of the **Williamsburg Bridge** (p. 90)—then the longest suspension bridge in the world—and a brand new infrastructure. Perhaps the city's greatest development during this era was the opening of its world-renowned **subway** (p. 34) system.

New York's innovations reached such glamorous proportions that the city began to feature prominently in the young art form of cinema. Early films, with such apt titles as *The Cheat* (1915), portrayed the city as the "new" or "great" metropolis, emphasizing a booming business world and foreshadowing the **Roaring Twenties.**

UPS AND DOWNS: 1930-1990

Mayor Fiorello LaGuardia's leadership engendered fierce civic pride that saw New Yorkers through the **The Great Depression**. Post-World War II prosperity brought more immigrants and businesses to the city. In this era, urban planner **Robert Moses** became New York's most powerful official. As chief of staff of the New York State Reconstruction Commission, Moses steamrolled dissenting politicians and councils to mold the physical landscape of New York that we know today. He created 36 parks and a network of roads (parkways) to make them accessible to the public, added 12 bridges and tunnels, and built Lincoln Center (p. 83), Shea Stadum (p. 186), and numerous housing projects (see **Go Down Moses,** p. 220). But even as the world celebrated New York as the capital of the 20th century, cracks in the city's foundations became apparent. By the 1960s, crises in public transportation, education, and housing exacerbated racial tensions and fostered heightened criminal activity.

In 1965, a hopeful **John V. Lindsay** ran for mayor under the slogan, "He is fresh and everyone else is tired." But with a barrage of crime, racial problems, labor unrest, and drought, Lindsay's novelty wore off quickly. City officials raised taxes to provide more services, but higher taxes drove middle-class residents and corporations out of the city. As a series of recessions and budget crises swamped the government, critics deplored **Mayor Robert Wagner**'s "dedicated inactivity." By 1975, in the middle of **Abe Beame's** term as mayor, the city was pleading with President Gerald Ford and the federal government to rescue it from impending bankruptcy, only to be rebuffed. *The* headline the next day read "Ford to New York: Drop Dead."

THE BUMS VERSUS U.S. STEEL

New York once had three baseball teams: the Yankees, the Dodgers, and the Giants. The Yankees were the juggernaut of the Major League, a well-oiled machine meant to plow through the competition. The business-like Yankees had such an edge that it was said that pulling for the club was like "rooting for U.S Steel."

The Dodgers, who played in Brooklyn (see **Sights,** p. 94), were the city's lovable losers. Nicknamed "Dem Bums" by loyal followers, the team always seemed to come up short against the Yankees in the playoffs.

That is, until 1955. Sparked by Jackie Robinson's steal of home plate in the Series' first game, the Dodgers pulled off a huge upset, winning the championship in seven games. After telling his teammates that he would need only one run to win, 23-year old Johnny Podres pitched a shutout in the final game to stop the Yanks for good.

Goliath was slain. David was victorious.

Well, at least for a year. In 1956, things returned to normal. The Yankees won the World Series, beating the Dodgers in seven games. The Dodgers would leave Brooklyn two years later to head to sunnier pastures in California.

However, resilient NYC rebounded with an attitude of streetwise hope. The state's massive (if goofy) **"I Love New York" campaign** spread cheer via bumper stickers. Large manufacturing, which had gone south and west of New York, was supplanted by fresh money from high finance and infotech. In the 1980s, **Wall Street** (p. 49) was hip again (or at least grotesquely profitable), and the upper middle class face of the city recovered some of its lost vitality. In poorer areas, meanwhile, discontent pervaded, manifesting itself in waves of crime and vandalism that scared off potential tourists. With a New Yorker's armor of curmudgeonly humor, **Ed Koch** defended his city's declining reputation and became America's most visible mayor. Koch appeared on Saturday Night Live, providing an endless stream of quotables, most notably his catchphrase, "How'm I doing?"

BROKEN WINDOWS AND LOW BLOWS: 1990-2001

The financial flurry of the 1980s faded into the gray recession of the early 1990s, aggravating class tensions. Racial conflict reached an all-time high in the late 80s and early 90s, when bigoted beatings erupted in the boroughs. A nationally publicized riot in **Crown Heights, Brooklyn** was sparked by a hit-and-run incident, in which an Orthodox Jewish man killed a young West Indian boy. **David Dinkins,** the city's first black mayor, elected in 1989 on a platform that glorified New York's "Gorgeous Mosaic," fought hard to encourage unity between the city's ethnic groups and dismantle bureaucratic corruption. Dinkins's term saw the abolition of the **Board of Estimate** system of municipal government, under which each borough's president had one vote. (This system was blatantly unfair, as borough populations differ vastly.) An expanded 35-member City Council replaced the old system.

Mounting fiscal crises and a persistent crime rate, however, led to Dinkins's defeat at the hands of **Rudy Giuliani** in the 1993 mayoral election. The election was strongly divided along racial lines. Many moderate whites who had supported Dinkins in 1989 defected to the side of the liberal Republican Giuliani, who aimed to deter major crime by cracking down on vandalism, a policy was known as the Broken Windows Theory. Some New Yorkers adore Mayor Giuliani for reducing crime and cleaning up formerly murky areas, such as Times Square (p. 76). Critics believe the Mayor cares only about beautifying and "gentrifying" tourist-heavy Manhattan, at the expense of the outer boroughs. Some say his budget cuts have damaged **The New York City Board of Education,** which seems to have a new leader every year. Still others assert that

Giuliani's war on crime has translated into an overzealous police force. Accusations of police brutality reached a fever pitch in 1997-98, when New York policemen led by Officer Justin Volpe used a toilet plunger to sexually assault **Abner Louima,** an innocent Haitian man. Federal prosecutors concluded a 20-month investigation of the New York City Police Department when Volpe plead guilty in June 1999. But the February 1999 murder of **Amadou Diallo** sparked renewed public outcry. Four officers fired 41 times on Diallo—who allegedly fit the description of a serial rapist—while he stood unarmed in his apartment building's vestibule. The policemen were indicted two months later for second-degree murder, but New Yorkers continued to aim their anger at Giuliani for his immoderate police strategies and his "no-apologies" stance. In November 2001 New Yorkers will elect a new mayor, Giuliani having served the two-term maximum.

ETHNIC NEW YORK

ACROSS THE ATLANTIC

The city's diversity dates back to colonial days. In old New Amsterdam, artisans, sailors, trappers, and slaves all mingled together, speaking no fewer than 18 languages. It was in the 19th century, however, that emigration from western and northern Europe rose dramatically. Germans and Irish came over in droves between 1840 and 1860; in 1855, European-born immigrants constituted nearly half of New York's population. The second wave of immigration—from 1890 to 1930—brought thousands to New York from Central and Southern Europe. Italians, Lithuanians, Russians, Poles, and Greeks left the Old World *en masse,* fleeing famine, religious persecution, and political unrest in their native lands for the promise of America.

But the US didn't always live up to expectations. Immigrants often worked long hours in detestable and unsafe conditions for meager wages; only the **Triangle Shirtwaist Fire** of 1911, which killed 145 female factory workers, brought about enough public protest to force stricter regulations on working conditions. Meanwhile, Tammany Hall-based "ward bosses" took the confused new arrivals under their wing, helping them find jobs and housing and providing them with funds in case of illness or accident—in exchange for votes. Nonetheless, upward mobility was a common thread in the tales of many immigrants, who rose from being employees to employers and moved from downtown (particularly the **Lower East Side,** see p. 56) to parts north.

FROM THE SOUTH TO HARLEM

In the early 20th century, real estate mavericks built hundreds of Harlem tenements with the hope of renting to whites once the subway arrived. The plan backfired, however, as whites bypassed Harlem and moved farther uptown. Working at a failing real estate office, **Philip Payton** convinced renters to open their buildings to the many southern blacks who had rushed north to New York. Payton's business venture paid off, and within the span of a few years, Harlem was transformed from a predominantly Jewish neighborhood to a bustling black city within a city. 80,000 blacks lived in Harlem in 1920; the cultural vitality of the dense population sparked the **Harlem Renaissance** of the 1920s. By 1930, some 100,000 more blacks had settled in Harlem.

Even so, there was not always strength in numbers. People of color were charged more than their white counterparts for the unhealthy tenement rooms, and the **Cotton Club,** Harlem's famous jazz club, didn't allow blacks inside unless they were performing (see **Sights,** p. 86).

THE MODERN MELTING POT

Today the melting pot simmers with over eight million people speaking more than 80 languages. New York boasts more Italians than Rome, more Irish than Dublin, and more Jews than Jerusalem. New Yorkers are proud of the fact that the city is awash with foreigners. While immigration policies were criticized nationwide, Mayor Giuliani staunchly defended immigrants, calling them the lifeblood of New York.

But this saturation of cultures has not always led to racial harmony. Ethnic divisions cause much of the city's strife, dating as far back as the 17th century. In the last few decades, ethnic conflict has led to, and been the result of, extreme segregation and distrust across communities. The 1960s saw riots in Harlem, Bedford-Stuyvesant, and the South Bronx, as angry African-Americans railed against governmental and police injustices. In the late 1980s, racially related deaths in Bensonhurst and Crown Heights in Brooklyn, and Howard Beach in Queens, demonstrated the lethal potential of ethnic tensions.

Even so, ethnic communities thrive throughout the five boroughs. Dominicans are the most heavily represented immigrant group; Washington Heights (see p. 88), the Lower East Side (see p. 56), and Bushwick in Brooklyn are Dominican strongholds. Immigrants from the former Soviet Union have settled in Brooklyn's Brighton Beach (see p. 95) and in Central Queens. The neighborhoods of Sunset Park (p. 95) and Bensonhurst (p. 95) are becoming increasingly Chinese, while Flatbush (p. 94) and the northern Bronx are Jamaican enclaves. Flushing's Main St. (p. 99) is reminiscent of Korea; **Israeli** eateries pepper Queens Blvd. in Forest Hills (p. 97); and Jackson Heights bustles with large **Indian** and **South American** populations. In Brooklyn, an **Arab** community centers around Atlantic Ave. in Brooklyn Heights.

Thanks to immigration, a neighborhood's personality can change quickly. Astoria, Queens (p. 96) hosts a large **Greek** community that is now making room for Egyptians and Croatians. In the Bronx, Belmont's Italian community is now also a home for Albanians. And Mexicans may currently outnumber Puerto Ricans in Spanish Harlem. The city is a revolving door. As people leave Ghana and Nigeria for New York City, Italians move out of Little Italy. The only constant is flux.

ARCHITECTURE

> A hundred times have I thought "New York is a catastrophe" and fifty times: "It is a beautiful catastrophe."
>
> —Le Corbusier, architect

Capricious New York has always warmed to the latest trends in architecture, hastily demolishing old buildings to make way for their stylistic successors. In the 19th century, the surging rhythm of endless destruction and renewal seemed to attest to the city's vigor and enthusiasm. Walt Whitman praised New York's "pull-down-and-build-over-again spirit," and *The Daily Mirror* was an isolated voice when, in 1831, it criticized the city's "irreverence for antiquity."

EARLY YEARS AND EUROPEAN INFLUENCE

Traces of Colonial New York are hard to find. The **original Dutch settlement** consisted mostly of traditional homes with gables and stoops. One example from 1699, the restored **Vechte-Cortelyou House,** stands near Fifth Avenue and 3rd St. in Brooklyn. The British, however, built over most of these Dutch structures with imposing, Greek-influenced, **Federal-style** buildings such as **St. Paul's Church** (p. 52) on Broadway.

Even after the British had been forced out, their architectural tastes lingered, influencing the townhouses built by their prosperous colonists. Through the early 19th century, American architects continued to incorporate such Federal details as dormer windows, stoops, doors with columns and fan lights. Federal houses still line Charlton St., Vandam St., and the South St. Seaport area (p. 54). The old **City Hall,** built by D.C. mastermind Pierre L'Enfant in 1802, is one example of a building that employs Federal detailing (p. 53).

The **Greek Revival** of the 1820s and 30s added porticoes and iron laurel wreaths to New York's streets. Greek Revival prevails on Washington Square North (p. 59), Lafayette St. (p. 64), and W. 20th St. (p. 68). Gray granite **St. Peter's,** built in 1838 with high, vaulted ceilings pointing to the heavens, was the first **Gothic Revival** church in America (p. 68).

While borrowing from the old country and classical tradition, Americans did manage to introduce some architectural innovations. Beginning in the 1850s, thousands of brownstones made from cheap stone quarried in New Jersey sprang up all over New York. Next to skyscrapers, the **brownstone townhouse** may be New York's most characteristic structure. Although beyond most people's means today, the houses were once middle-class residences—the rich lived in block-long mansions on Fifth Avenue, while apartments were for the poor. Brownstones incorporate an essential element of a New Yorker's lifestyle—the raised **stoop.** An innovation brought over by the Dutch in the 17th century to elevate the best rooms in the house, the stoop today has its own urban culture of "stoop ball," checker-playing, and intense neighbor-watching.

In 1884, New York's architectural hierarchy was disrupted by the building of luxurious apartment houses like the **Dakota** (p. 84) and the **Ansonia** (p. 84), both on the Upper West Side.

In the 1890s, American architects studying abroad brought the **Beaux-Arts** style from France and captivated the nation. Beaux-Arts, a blend of Classical detail and lavish decoration, stamped itself on structures built through the 1930s. Memorable examples are the **US Custom House** (p. 50) and the **New York Public Library** (p. 71).

The Flatiron Building

The Algonquin Hotel

THE SKYSCRAPER: AN AMERICAN AESTHETIC

Made possible by combining new technologies—the elevator and the steel frame—skyscrapers allowed the city to explode upward and assuaged the growing pains engendered by New York's spectacular commercial and human growth. The first skyscraper, the **Flatiron Building,** sprouted up on 23rd Street in 1902 (p. 66).

In 1913, Cass Gilbert gilded the 55-story **Woolworth Building** with Gothic flourishes, piling on antique "W"s and dubbing it "Cathedral of Commerce" (p. 52). The Art Deco **Empire State Building** (p. 69) and the **Chrysler Building** (p. 76) were fashioned from stone and steel.

Just 14 years after the first skyscraper came the nation's first zoning resolution, which restricted the height and bulk of the dizzying buildings. Knowledge of the changes in the zoning codes throughout the decades is the key to understanding and dating the city's architectural quirks. Does the building have a stepped, pyramidal roof? Look like a wedding cake? Zoning restrictions of the late 1940s stipulated that tall buildings had to be set back at the summit. New York's first curtain of pure glass was the 1950 **United Nations Secretariat Building,** a nightmare to air-condition (p. 75). Then, in 1958, Ludwig Mies Van der Rohe and Philip Johnson created the **Seagram Building** (p. 75), a glass tower set behind a plaza on Park Avenue. Crowds soon gathered to mingle, sunbathe, and picnic, much to the surprise of planners and builders. A delighted planning commission began offering financial incentives to every builder who offset a high-rise with public open space. Over the next decade,

Woolworth Building

many architects stuck empty plazas next to their towering office complexes. Some of them looked a little too empty to the picky commission, which changed the rules in 1975 to stipulate that every plaza should provide public seating. By the late 70s, plazas moved indoors, and high-tech atriums with gurgling fountains and pricey cafes began to flourish.

The leaner skyscrapers date from the early 1980s, when shrewd developers realized they could get office space, bypass zoning regulations, *and* receive a bonus from the commission if they hoisted up "sliver" buildings. Composed largely of elevators and stairs, the disturbingly anorexic newcomers provoked city-wide grumbles. Those tired of living in the shadow of shafts altered zoning policy in 1983 so that structural planning would encourage more room for air and sun.

Builders have finally recognized the overcrowding problem in Midtown and expanded their horizons somewhat. New residential complexes have risen on the Upper East Side above 95th St., while Donald Trump, the city's most notorious real-estate guru, recently erected the second of his muscular and gaudy towers in Columbus Circle near the Upper West Side; some developers have even ventured into the outer boroughs. The planning commission that oversees the beautiful catastrophe now takes overcrowding and environmental issues into account when making decisions.

Throughout this continual modernization, concern has arisen that New York's history might be quickly disappearing. Mounting public concern climaxed when developers destroyed gracious **Penn Station** in 1965; in response, the city created the **Landmarks Preservation Commission**. Since then, the LPC has successfully claimed and protected 21,000 individual sites as "landmarks." However, developers continue to seek loopholes and air-rights to expand the skyline.

NEW YORK IN MUSIC

I lay puzzle as I backtrack to earlier times
Nothing's equivalent, to the New York state of mind
—Nas, "N.Y. State of Mind"

Between the extremes of Nas's rap lyrics and Frank Sinatra's crooning plea that "It's Up to You New York," lies a world of quick cadence, lyrical meandering, and pleasing dissonance all of which owe their inspiration to New York City. **Leonard Bernstein** captured the bleeding heart of the city in his musical *West Side Story*, while **George Gershwin** used the rhythms of his train rolling into New York for the musical skeleton of his *Rhapsody in Blue*.

From sweet vibrations to killer beats, New York is *the* place to catch new music. Nearly every performer who comes to the States plays

HIP-HOP (R)EVOLUTION

In 1973, Bronx DJ Kool Herc began prolonging songs' funky drum "break" sections by using two turntables and two copies of the same record, switching to the start of the second copy when the first one ended and then doubling back. Dancers took up the rhythm's challenge, by 1975 evolving break-dancing in response to similar turntable manipulations by Afrika Bambaataa, Grandmaster Flash, Kool, and other denizens of the 174th St. area by the Bronx River. Thus, the Bronx birthed the art of DJing, an acrobatic dance style, and a musical genre known as hip-hop/rap that would shape the sound of the new millennium. For more information, hit Davey D's exhaustive web page at www.daveyd.com

here, and thousands of local bands and DJs compete to make a statement and win an audience. Venues range from stadiums to concert halls to back-alley sound-systems. Every day of the year, clubs, bars, and smaller venues serve up sounds from open-mic folk singers to "electronic" DJ recombination. Annual festivals abound, such as summertime's **Next Wave Festival** that takes over the Brooklyn Academy of Music with spectacular, offbeat happenings, crackpot fusions of classical music, theater, and performance art. Whatever your inclination, New York's expansive musical scene should be able to satisfy it. (See **Entertainment,** p. 177)

JAZZ

From the beginning, jazz has expressed the cadence and rhythm of New York. The Big Band sound thrived here in the 1920s and 30s, when Duke Ellington set the trend in clubs around town. **Minton's Playhouse** in Harlem was home to Thelonious Monk and was one of the birthplaces of bebop, a highly sophisticated jazz variant. Miles Davis, Charlie Parker, Dizzy Gillespie, Max Roach, Tommy Potter, Bud Powell, and many others contributed to the New York sound of the late 1940s and 1950s, when beatniks, hepcats, and poor old souls filled 52nd St. clubs. Free-jazz pioneer Cecil Taylor and spaceman Sun Ra set up shop in NYC during the 1960s and 70s. Today, skilled experimentalists like John Zorn and James Blood Ulmer destroy musical conventions at clubs like the **Knitting Factory** (p. 176). At Fez, one can tap into the legacy of the revolutionary era of the 40s and 50s with the **Mingus Big Band** (p. 178), which is dedicated to playing the works of virtuoso bassist and band-leader Charles Mingus.

PUNK AND POST-PUNK

True to the grit of city living, the New York rock sound has always had a harder edge than its West Coast or Southern counterparts. The **Velvet Underground,** Andy Warhol's favorite band and a seminal 1960s rock group, combined jangling guitars with disconcerting lyrics on sex, drugs, and violence that deeply influenced the next generation of bands. In 1976, ambitious avant-garde poets and sometime musicians took over the campy glam-rock scene in downtown barroom clubs like **CBGB's** and Max's Kansas City. Bands and performers like the Ramones, Patti Smith, Blondie, and the Talking Heads brought venom, wit, and a calculated stupidity to the emerging **punk** scene. Ever since, New York has convulsed with musical shocks. In the 1980s, angry kids imported **straight-edge** from Washington, D.C. A bevy of fast-rocking, non-drinking, non-smoking bands packed Sunday all-ages shows at CBGB's. In the 1980s and early 1990s the **post-punk** scene crystallized around bands such as Sonic Youth and Pavement. Obscure vinyl can be found in the city's many used record stores; prices can be absurd, but the selection surpasses that of any other North American city (see **Shopping,** p. 201). As the millennium approaches, **post-rock** proliferates. Locals Bowery Electric and Ui incorporate drum machines and dub techniques in efforts to keep rock radical, while native Brooklynites and indie-rockers extraordinaire, Lady Bug Transistor, make effete rock sexy with flutes, organs, and trumpets.

STREET POETS

Rap and **hip-hop** also began on New York's streets, and the list of NYC artists reads like a History of Urban Music, including such heavyweight emcees as KRS-1, Chuck D, LL Cool J, Run-DMC, EPMD, and Queen Latifah (who leapt across the river from Jersey). Bronx DJs **Grandmaster Flash** and **Afrika Bambaataa** laid the foundations in the late 70s and early 80s with records rooted deeply in electronic processing, scratching, and sampling. In 1979, the **Sugarhill Gang** released *Rapper's Delight*, widely considered the first true rap record.

Predominant in the East Coast hip-hop hierarchy are the **Native Tongues,** a loose collection of New York (OK—some are Long Islanders) acts which includes A Tribe Called Quest, De La Soul, and Black Sheep. Straight out of Staten Island came the Wu-Tang Clan, whose dense, brooding beats have made names for several of its coterie, including **Method Man** and the **GZA.** The Beastie Boys and Luscious Jackson transcended racial lines to broaden the national appeal of the hip-hop genre, incorporating jazz loops, hard-core thrash, and funk samples into their stylistic repertoire.

Other recent NYC area acts to climb the charts include Nas, Mobb Deep, and the Fugees (including Wyclef Jean and 1999 Grammy winner, **Lauryn Hill,** who also have powerful solo personas). And, although highly commercial, Puff Daddy's protege, Mase, put Harlem back on the map with his 1998 release, "Harlem World," before retiring to devote himself to his new-found commitment to Christianity.

For a clearer glimpse of the hip-hop scene in New York (and across the country) pick up a copy of New York-based *The Source*, the genre's premier publication, or check out Davey D's Hip Hop Corner on the web (www.daveyd.com). In Brooklyn, the **Crooklyn Dub Consortium** eschews commercial success to create otherworldly dubhop, where crooked beats fuse with third world instrumentation and Jamaican dub styles.

THE ELECTRONIC WAVE

Although the Big Apple may have pioneered the hip-hop sound, it lags a bit behind Europe on the **techno** frontier. Nevertheless, New York City serves as ground zero for the east coast stage of the **rave** revolution that took hold of European and L.A. club culture. Deeelite and Moby first got the city grooving where **disco** left off with their toe-tapping amalgamation of ambient and techno-funk, and now home-grown superstar DJs like Junior Vasquez, Frankie Bones, and DB keep the crowds dancing to the newest **house, trance, jungle,** and **trip-hop.** Downtown's kitsch-hungry partygoers now groove to "loungecore," a sexy, shmaltzy revival of 1970s soft porn soundtracks and exotica records that goes great with polyester.

LITERARY NEW YORK

Since **William Bradford** was appointed America's first public printer in 1698 and went on to found the country's first newspaper, the *New York Gazette*, New York City has been the literary capital of the Americas. The epicenter of the city's literary vanguard changed with each successive movement, but the Big Apple has never lacked prolific pens.

The city has inspired innumerable authors' greatest achievements. **Herman Melville** and **Washington Irving** were both born in Lower Manhattan at 6 Pearl St. and 131 William St., respectively. Irving, in fact, gave New York its ever-enduring pen- (and movie-) name, **Gotham. Walt Whitman,** born in South Huntington, Long Island, edited the controversial **Brooklyn Eagle** newspaper. **Edgar Allen Poe,** living uptown in the rural Bronx (see p. 104), was so brutally poor that he sent his aging mother-in-law out to scour the area for edible roots. Starving artists filled **Greenwich Village** in the early 20th century—**Willa Cather, John Reed,** and **Theodore Dreiser** parented the American novel in its streets. Over time, the Village came to prevail as the city's literary center; **e.e. cummings** and **Djuna Barnes** both lived off 10th St. at **Patchin' Place** (see p. 61). **Edna St. Vincent Millay** lived in the same neighborhood, at Bedford St., where she founded the **Cherry Lane Theater.**Midtown contains the legendary **Algonquin Hotel,** 59 W. 44th St. (see p. 71). In 1919 the wits of the **Round Table**—writers such as Robert Benchley, Dorothy Parker, Alexander Wollcott, and Edna Ferber—adopted this hotel for their famous weekly lunch meetings and Harold Ross dreamed up the magazine *The New Yorker* here.

The area surrounding Columbia University witnessed one of the most vibrant and important moments in American literary history, the 1920s **Harlem Renaissance**. Novels like George Schuyler's *Black No More* and Claude McKay's *Home to Harlem* are tales of the exoticized underworld of speakeasies and nightclubs. **Zora Neale Hurston,** then a Columbia anthropology student, helped create buzz in Harlem with her novel, *Their Eyes Were Watching God.* Poet **Langston Hughes** and his circle founded radical journals that proposed the idea of a "New Negro." The next generation of black talent, including **Ralph Ellison** and **James Baldwin,** expanded the scope of African-American literature, dealing with issues of whiteness and the idea of America. Ellison's *Invisible Man* offers an epic excursion into the complexities of black and white life in Manhattan, while Baldwin's work, such as *Go Tell It On The Mountain*, wields a grittier edge.

Columbia University continued to be the intellectual magnet of the Upper West Side. The roving Beat crowd swamped the area in the late 1940s when **Allen Ginsberg** and **Jack Kerouac** studied at the college. During the controversial late 60s, Brooklyn resident Paul Auster also honed his writing chops there. **Public School #6,** also on the Upper West Side, boasts such prestigious alums as *Catcher in the Rye* author, **J.D. Salinger.** Later in the 20th century, the **East Village** became the city's literary headquarters when the nomadic Kerouac and Ginsberg moved in next to neighbors Amiri Baraka **(Le Roi Jones)** and **W.H. Auden** (who spent many years at 77 St. Mark's Place, basement entrance).

Today, the city continues to be a literary haven. All of New York's waiters, waitresses, and bar-keeps seem to have half of the Great American novel sitting in their underwear drawer.

Some **must-reads** involving the city of dreams:

The Age of Innocence and **The House of Mirth,** Edith Wharton. Two tales of turn-of-the-century romance and woe among the New York gentry.

Another Country, James Baldwin. Interracial lovers and same-sex couples uncover beauty and tremendous pain trying to relate to one another in 60s Manhattan.

A Tree Grows In Brooklyn, Betty Smith. An Irish woman's coming-of-age in early 20th-century Brooklyn. Also a 1945 film by Elia Kazan.

The Bonfire of the Vanities, Tom Wolfe. A Wall Street financier takes a wrong turn off the Tri-Boro Bridge. Hijinks ensue. For your own sake, miss the movie.

Bright Lights, Big City, Jay MacInerney. 1980s New York. A columnist for the *New Yorker* divides his time between clubs and cocaine. Michael J. Fox starred in the film. Also see *Story of My Life,* another tale of Manhattan self-indulgence.

The Catcher in the Rye, J.D. Salinger. A now-classic fable of alienated youth. Prep-schooler Holden Caulfield visits the city and falls from innocence.

Eloise, Kay Thompson. A classic children's book. Young Eloise lives in the Plaza Hotel, wreaking havoc on every elegant floor and combing her hair with a fork.

The Great Gatsby, F. Scott Fitzgerald. An incisive commentary on the American Dream, vis-à-vis the rise and fall of would-be New Yorker Jay Gatsby.

Jazz, Toni Morrison. This Nobel prize-winning novel is written in jazz form: sensual, cerebral, and experimental. It examines love, murder, and the magical potency of the city in 1920s Harlem.

New York Trilogy, Paul Auster. Three playfully literary short stories set in Brooklyn Heights and Manhattan, riff on the conventions of detective fiction.

Washington Square, Henry James. An oppressed heiress comes to terms with this elegant, stratified neighborhood in the nineteenth century.

Winter's Tale, Mark Helprin. A fantastic voyage into the turn-of the century New York. Intensely lyrical.

NON-FICTION

AIA Guide to New York City, Elliot Willensky, ed. The *definitive* guidebook for those who want to know about every building in the city. Written by architects.

Encyclopedia of the City of New York, Kenneth Jackson. A wonderful reference book of all things Gotham.

Gotham: A History of New York City to 1898, Edwin G. Burrows and Mike Wallace. To date, the definitive history on the city's first 274 years.

Low Life, Luc Sante. A tale of growing up in the city.

The Power Broker, Robert Caro. A biography of the influential city planner Robert Moses.

THE SILVER SCREEN

Always a ham, the Big Apple has never been shy on camera. It's not unusual, on a mid-morning stroll down Fifth Avenue, to encounter production assistants and camera crews in mirrored sunglasses waving their hands and shouting in California-ese. The city encourages film production by granting free permits to those filmmakers who want to shoot on location; there is even a special police task force—the New York Police Movie and Television Unit—to assist with traffic re-routing and scenes involving guns or uniformed police officers. As a testament to how seriously this city takes its film industry, Mayor Giuliani proclaimed May 18, 1998 "Godzilla Day" in honor of the opening of the gargantuan flick that was shot in New York. "The industry," in turn, has rewarded Gotham well. Anywhere between 60 to 90 productions are on location in the city on a given day.

Here is a smattering of quintessential New York films:

Annie Hall (1977). Woody Allen and Diane Keaton play tennis, flirt, and squabble in this funny, romantic ode to the city, crystallizing Allen's image as a neurotic Upper West Side intellectual.

Basquiat (1996). Chronicles the tragic rise to fame of Gotham street artist Jean-Michele Basquiat, protege of an aging Andy Warhol (played with great nuance by David Bowie).

Breakfast at Tiffany's (1961). Audrey Hepburn frolics through Upper East Side society.

Brighton Beach Memoirs (1986). Neil Simon's–imagine it–semi-autobiographical comedy about growing up Jewish in Brooklyn with baseball and sex on the brain.

A Bronx Tale (1993). Robert DeNiro's directing debut: a tale of a boy torn between his Pop and the temptations of mob life. Shot in Brooklyn and Queens.

Coming to America (1988). Eddie Murphy emerges from his utopian jungle community in search of independence in Queens.

Desperately Seeking Susan (1985). A bored housewife finds excitement when she assumes the identity of that hippest of East Village hipsters, Madonna.

Do the Right Thing (1989). Spike Lee's explosive look at one very hot day in the life of Brooklyn's Bed-Stuy. Colorful, stylized cinematography. Racial tensions at the boiling point.

The Fisher King (1991). Shock-jock Jeff Bridges and homeless dude Robin Williams seek redemption in the fantastical dimension of New York.

The French Connection (1971). An all-time great chase scene: Gene Hackman vs. the B train.

Ghostbusters (1984). Bill Murray and Dan Ackroyd try to rid the city (and Sigourney Weaver) of ghosts. Note the New York Public Library and 55 Central Park West, among other landmarks.

The Godfather I, II, and III (1972-1990). Coppola's searing study of one immigrant family and the price of the American Dream. Based on a bestseller by Mario Puzo.

Goodfellas (1990). Scorsese's look at true-life gangster Henry Hill. Great location shots in the city, especially the Bamboo Lounge in Canarsie.

Hair (1979). The love-child musical brought to the screen, complete with hippies tripping in Sheep Meadow in Central Park. Nell Carter sings a solo.

Kids (1995). Larry Clark's study of some baaaaaad NY kids. Not for the queasy.

King Kong (1933). Single giant ape seeks female atop symbol of phallic power.

Little Odessa (1995). Tim Roth in a thriller about the emerging Russian-American mafia in Brooklyn's Brighton Beach. From the book by Joseph Koenig.

Manhattan (1979). Woody Allen's hysterically funny love note to New York. Glimmering skyline, to the tune of Gershwin's *Rhapsody in Blue*.

Mean Streets (1973). Harvey Keitel and Robert DeNiro cruise around Little Italy looking for trouble. This film put Scorsese on the map.

Metropolitan (1990). Whit Stillman chronicles the dying Park Avenue debutante scene: a tale of east (side) meets west (side), conversation, and cocktails.

Midnight Cowboy (1969). Jon Voight as a would-be hustler, and Dustin Hoffman as street rodent Ratso Rizzo, star in this devastating look at the seedy side of NY.

New York Stories (1989). Martin Scorsese, Francis Ford Coppola, and Woody Allen grind their cinematic axes on the Big Apple, to varying success.

On the Town (1949). Start spreading the news–Gene Kelly and Frank Sinatra are sailors with time and money to burn in New York City.

Saturday Night Fever (1977). John Travolta shakes his polyester-clad booty.

Serpico (1973). Al Pacino fights the power in this true tale of NYPD corruption.

The Seven-Year Itch (1955). Marilyn Monroe and subway grates–perfect together.

Taxi Driver (1976). DeNiro is Travis Bickle, a taxi driver with issues. Don't look him in the eye...and tip him well.

West Side Story (1961). Romeo and Juliet retold à la fire escape.

When Harry Met Sally (1989). Meg Ryan and Billy Crystal continually emote about their foibles against a New York backdrop. The ultimate date movie.

Sheep Tickets.
Visit StudentUniverse.com for real deals on student travel anywhere.
StudentUniverse.com
Real Travel Deals
800.272.9676

INSIDE

Sights

You could go on a tour, maybe on a boat, a double-decker bus, or even on foot (See **Tours,** p. 22). But look here—you could also walk around yourself, without those other embarrassing tourists decked out in their Hawaiian-print shirts, camcorders, and oh-so-last-decade haircuts. Just follow our sights write-ups, listed by neighborhood, perfect for a relaxed but informed stroll through the Big City. Shed your insecurities, get into your walking shoes and get to know everything, from the packed and famous to the quiet hidden treasures.

MANHATTAN

THE STATUE OF LIBERTY

...Give me your tired, your poor,
Your huddled masses yearning to breathe free,
The wretched refuse of your teeming shore;
Send these, the homeless, tempest-tost to me,
I lift my lamp beside the golden door!
—Emma Lazarus, 1883

Statue of Liberty information: ☎363-3200. Stands on Liberty Island in New York Harbor, about 1 mi. southwest of Manhattan. Subway: 1,9 to South Ferry; 4,5 to Bowling Green; N,R to Whitehall St. Ferries leave for Liberty Island from the piers at Battery Park, daily every 30min. (9:30am-3:00pm). Ferry hours may be extended slightly during the summer and on certain holidays. Ferry Information: ☎269-5755. Tickets for ferry, access to the Statue of Liberty and Ellis Island: $8, seniors $6, ages 3-17 $3, under 3 free. Buy tickets in Castle Clinton's central courtyard, just to the right of the ferry dock as one faces the harbor. The wait to climb Liberty ranges between 1 and 3 hours. Gift shop with novelty kitsch such as $2 foam Liberty crowns.

on the cheap

Sail-by Shooting

Completely free, the Staten Island ferry may very well offer the world's premier sightseeing bargain. Wave Manhattan goodbye as you pass **Ellis Island,** the **Statue of Liberty,** and Governor's Island in route to Staten Island. The ferry began shuttling commuters in 1810 thanks to the entrepreneurial Cornelius Vanderbilt and his mother's money. It turned public in 1905, but the city charged up to 25¢ for the scenic view until 1997. Postcard photographers flock here for some of the most marketable shots of the city. The ride is particularly exhilarating at sunset or night. (See orientation under Staten Island in **Once in NYC,** p. 21).

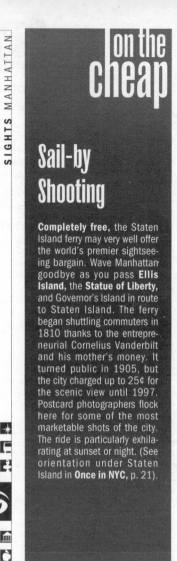

Located in New York Harbor, about a mile away from the southern tip of Manhattan, the Statue of Liberty has welcomed many immigrants to the New World. Because of its symbolic cachet, Lady Liberty has become a world-renowned tourist draw with lines as long as the green lady is tall.

Like most immigrants who arrived by sea, the statue has roots in the Old World. In 1865 French leftist intellectual Edouard-René de Laboulaye dreamt up Liberty as a way of celebrating Franco-American relations, which had been jump-started almost 100 years before when France aided the US in its revolution against the British. Laboulaye selected the sculptor Frederic-Auguste Bartholdi for the job. Bartholdi did reconnaissance in New York, but constructed the actual statue in Paris — with the aid of Gustave Eiffel (yes, that Eiffel) — finishing in 1884 and presenting the statue to the American ambassador on July 4. The good Lady was then disassembled and sent across the Atlantic in 220 crates.

If it were not for Joseph Pulitzer, the tycoon publisher of the New York *World*, Liberty might have remained in pieces. Funding was slow, and only after Pulitzer took charge of the finances of the pedestal construction did Liberty literally get off the ground. Once structurally complete in 1886, the pedestal received its finishing touch: the now-famous words of welcome by poet Emma Lazarus.

Visitors to the monument are encouraged to board an early ferry, ideally the first one out of Battery Park, to avoid the despair-inducing lines that build up over the course of the day. Ferries run in a Battery Park-Liberty Island-Ellis Island loop. The ticket costs the same no matter how long you stay and regardless of whether you want to see only the statue or the immigration station, so you might as well do both. The ferry ride is one long, tourist-pleasing photo-op, with jaw-dropping views of the Lower Manhattan skyline, the Brooklyn Bridge, and, of course, Miss Liberty.

Once you're on the island, head quickly for the statue's back entrance at Fort Wood (dating from the War of 1812), where you will choose one of two lines. The significantly faster line on the right leads to the elevator carting folks to the observation decks atop **Richard Morris Hunt's pedestal.** The line on the left offers the only route to the crown. It's all stairs: 22 narrow, spiraling stories' worth, the last leg a precipitous staircase with lines that move at a snail's pace. There are only two reasons to go to the crown: (1) like Mt. Everest, because it's there; or (2) to glimpse Eiffel's internal support system. Beware—the view boasts little splendor; tiny, airplane-type windows look out not on Manhattan but on the Brooklyn dockyards. Senior citizens, young children, and anyone impatient should avoid the climb. The pedestal's observation decks, on the other hand, offer enchanting views of New York, Ellis Island, and the towering statue above you.

Some of the artifacts on display over the second entrance doors include an actual-size cast of Liberty's face, various artists' renderings of the sculpture, and evidence of Miss Liberty's lasting influence, such as the cover of Supertramp's *Breakfast in America* LP. A third-floor immigration exhibit should whet your appetite for the much more fascinating Ellis Island. Tours are sporadic and depend on staff availability.

If you plan to make a day of it, bring a bag lunch: otherwise, you will be at the culinary mercy of the Liberty Island cafeteria.

ELLIS ISLAND

For instructions on how to get to Ellis Island, see The Statue of Liberty, above. Video documentary: "Island of Hope, Island of Tears." 30min. Shown in two theaters, one with a preceding 15min. talk by a ranger. Play: "Ellis Island Stories," based on oral histories of those who passed through Ellis Island; performed in spring, summer, and fall. The film is free (call for play prices), but you must get tickets at the info desk near the entrance in advance of the showing. Audio Tour: 1¼hr. $4, seniors $3.50, students and under 17 $2.50.

While the Statue of Liberty embodies the American Dream, Ellis Island chronicles the harsh realities of starting over in the New World. Twelve million immigrants were processed here, many winding up with new Americanized names. During the height of immigration (1892-1920), Ellis Island ushered 5000 people per day into the US. The island's exhibits commemorate the site and its history as well as the immigrant experience in America.

Ellis Island opened as a museum in 1990 after multi-million dollar renovations. The museum is housed in a grand red brick and stone building, restored as it stood early in the 20th century. The building's stones are heavily rusticated, and four copper-domed towers give the former immigration depot the air of a military fortress. Two bald eagles, symbols of the US, perch over the building's central arch and entrance.

Since 2001, visitors have had access to a thorough, user-friendly database of computerized records that lists immigrants who passed through Ellis Island. This exhibit, which opened with great fanfare and critical success, gives would-be genealogists 35 minutes of computer time ($5) to track ship records and arrival papers until 1920. The rest of the records are still being computerized.

Other highlights include the overwhelming Registry Room (where most of the processing took place); an exhibit on the "Peopling of America;" and "Treasures from Home," which displays a collection of artifacts and clothing that immigrants brought from the Old World; and the film "Island of Hope, Island of Tears."

FINANCIAL DISTRICT

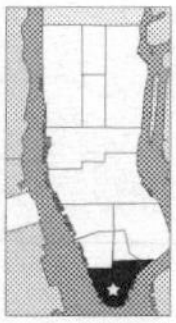
see map pp. 310-311

Money, money, everywhere, and it shows. Once a dock where men shucked their daily oyster catch, Pearl St. is now one of the richest streets in the whole world. Wall St. is the cornerstone of both the district and the entire financial universe. Once the northern border to the New Amsterdam settlement, the street takes its name from the wall built in 1653 to shield the Dutch from the invasion-happy British.

To ensure that sights are open and to get a true sense of the area's bustling atmosphere, explore lower Manhattan during the week. Sights are listed from **south to north.**

BATTERY PARK

Located on the southern tip of Manhattan. Subway: 1, 9 to South Ferry; 4, 5 to Bowling Green; N, R to Whitehall St. ***Castle Clinton:*** *Open daily 8:30am-5pm. 20min. walking tours daily every hr. 10:05am-4:05pm. Free.* ***New York Unearthed:*** *19 State St. ☎ 748-8628. Open M-F noon-6pm. Free.*

At the very bottom of Manhattan rests Battery Park, thanks to landfills that replaced New York Harbor between State St. and the offshore **Castle Clinton.** Today, Castle Clinton acts as the ticket booth for the ferry to the Statue of Liberty and Ellis Island. Along its promenade, the park features beautiful views of Brooklyn and the Statue of Liberty. On the northern border of the park is **New York Unearthed,** an urban archaeology museum that owns about two million excavated shards, trinkets, and gewgaws

City Hall

The World Trade Center

Esplanade Sculpture in Battery Park City

that it keeps in storage. Downstairs, archaeologists try to make sense of it all. The public exhibits are limited but instructive.

BOWLING GREEN

The confluence of Battery Pl., Broadway, and Whitehall St. Subway: 4, 5 to Bowling Green.

The Museum of the American Indian overlooks the site of the city's first mugging—Peter Minuit's purchase of Manhattan for the equivalent of $24 in trade goods. This spot eventually became the city's first park, used for the playing of bowls, an ancestor of American bowling. In 1776 revolutionary New Yorkers tore down a statue of King George here and melted it down for munitions to fight the British. While some historians have suggested that the statue be recreated because of its cultural importance, others pshaw the idea of paying tribute to the very king the Revolution was held against. At present, the governing statue in the park is that of a large charging bull, a shrine to the god of strong stock markets.

US CUSTOM HOUSE

1 Bowling Green. Subway: 4, 5 to Bowling Green.

Completed in 1907, when the city still derived most of its revenue from customs, the Custom House has been transformed into the Smithsonian's **National Museum of the American Indian** (see **Museums and Galleries,** p. 121). The magnificent Beaux-Arts building, designed by Cass Gilbert, is flanked by exquisite sculptures of four women, representing America, Europe, Africa, and Asia. The face of Mercury, the Roman god of commerce, crowns each of the building's 44 columns.

NEW YORK STOCK EXCHANGE

20 Broad St. between Wall St. and Exchange Pl. Subway: 2, 3, 4, 5 to Wall St.; 1, 9 to Rector St.; J, M, Z to Broad St. ☎656-5165 or 656-5168. Open M-F 9am-4:30pm. Tickets handed out on a first come, first served basis beginning at 8:45am.

Designed in the Classical Revival style popular in turn-of-the-century New York, the Stock Exchange is a temple of capitalism. Once inside, you can check your portfolio, ask questions at any of a number of interactive computer stations, or watch a film on the functions and high-tech features of the exchange. The climax of the tour is the opportunity to peek down from the observation gallery at the paper-strewn trading floor, enclosed in glass ever since the 1960s, when activist Abbie Hoffman and his merry band of Yippies threw dollar bills on the floor. The traders stopped their work to chase frantically after the money, just as the protestors had anticipated. Today the only trace of Red Communism you'll find here are the free tickets to get inside.

TRINITY CHURCH

Broadway at Wall St. Subway: 4, 5 to Wall St.; N, R to Rector St. Open M-F 7am-6pm, Sa-Su 8am-4pm. Welcome center open daily 10-11:45am and 1-3pm.

Around the corner from the New York Stock Exchange, this Gothic Revival Episcopal church has the last laugh over its towering, billion-dollar neighbors: Trinity Church owns much of the land on which these temples of commerce sit. Outside, the church seems an anomaly. Its steeple and cemetery—which houses the grave of Alexander Hamilton—are delicately crafted amid the canyons of the Financial District. Once inside, check out the modest museum behind the altar and the welcome center and gift shop to the left of the entrance. When the church was first built in 1846, its Gothic spire served as a beacon for approaching ships.

Wall Street

FEDERAL HALL NATIONAL MEMORIAL

26 Wall St. Disabled entrance: 15 Pine St. Subway: 1, 9, N, R to Rector St.; 2, 3, 4, 5 to Wall St.; J, M, Z to Broad St. ☎ 825-6888. Open M-F 9am-5pm; in summer daily 9am-5pm. Free tours on request.

A tight-pantsed George Washington stands guard in front of this Parthenon look-alike, which housed the original City Hall from 1703. In 1789, the year of Washington's inauguration, the renovated City Hall was renamed "Federal Hall," and it served as the fledgling nation's first seat of government; James Madison first presented the Bill of Rights to Congress here. The original structure was demolished in 1812 and later rebuilt to house numerous federal agencies including the Custom House, the Sub-Treasury, and the FBI.

Trinity Church

THE FEDERAL RESERVE BANK OF NEW YORK

33 Liberty St. ☎ 720-6130. Free 1hr. tours M-F 9:30, 10:30, 11:30am, 1:30, and 2:30pm, but at least 7 days advance notice required. Must be 16+. 30 people per group max. limit.

This mammoth neo-Renaissance building occupies an entire city block. Built in 1924 and modeled after the Palazzo Strozzi, the home of a 15th-century Florentine banking family, the grave facade is designed to keep you away from ¼ of the world's gold bullion. Most of the gold belongs to foreign countries, who store their precious metals in a vault five stories below ground, with 121 triple-locked compartments.

Peking Ship

WORLD TRADE CENTER

On September 11, 2001, two hijacked commercial jets crashed into the Twin Towers. Approximately an hour after the crash, both 110-story buildings collapsed in a cloud of rubble and debris. Thousands were killed in the worst ter-

rorist act ever to have hit the United States. At the time this book went to press, rescue efforts were just underway.

Built in 1972 by Minoru Yamasaki in order to spur business in the Big Apple, the 110-story Twin Towers (One WTC and Two WTC) were the centerpiece of this seven-building complex. The tallest buildings in New York and the second tallest in the US to the Sears Tower, the Twin Towers were actually fraternal. One WTC (the one with the antenna on top) stood 1372ft. tall, four feet taller than its sibling, and would never let him forget it. Both Twin Towers had massive amounts of office space, but Two WTC was where to go for the view. To get to its 107th floor observatory, you could skip the exhibits on commerce and history and get in line for tickets on the mezzanine. When weather permitted, the rooftop observation deck offered an even better view. One could gaze at One WTC and imagine crossing the gap on a tight-rope, as Phillippe Petit did in 1974. Telescopes (25¢) on the roof allowed you to see if any naked people had left their curtains open.

Outside, the main plaza on Church and Dey Sts. provided ample seating space for checking out the comings and goings of Wall St. types. During the summer, the plaza played host to daily lunchtime entertainment, such as public theater, dance, and music.

BATTERY PARK CITY

Subway: 1, 9, N, R to Cortlandt St.; A, C, E to Chambers St.-World Trade Center; 2, 3 to Park Pl.; 4, 5 to Fulton St.

When the World Trade Center was being constructed in the 1970s, the millions of tons of soil dug up were deposited west of West St. The **Battery Park City Apartments,** some of New York's newest and glitziest digs, and the **World Financial Center,** West St. between the World Trade Center and Hudson River (☎945-0505), were built upon the landfill. The four granite-and-glass 40-story towers are covered by distinctive copper roofs. The main public space, the glass-enclosed **Winter Garden,** is a stunning galleria replete with a sprawling marble staircase and sixteen 40-foot-tall palm trees. The garden, which faces the river esplanade, hosts year-round festivals and performances open to the public. Most well known is the spectacular New York International Orchid Show, held in mid-spring each year.

THE CIVIC CENTER

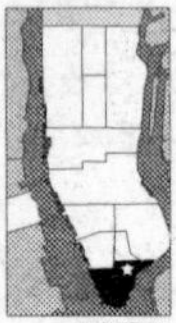

see map pp. 310-311

Subway: 2, 3 to Park Pl; 4, 5, 6 to Brooklyn Bridge; A, C, E to Chambers St.-World Trade Ctr.; J, M, Z to Chambers St.; N, R, to City Hall.

Fittingly, the city's center of government is located immediately north of its financial district, as the city tries to keep shady dealings to a minimum. City Hall is the neighborhood's center, and around it revolve myriad courthouses, civic buildings, and federal buildings. Sights are listed roughly from **south to north**.

ST. PAUL'S CHAPEL

Broadway, between Fulton and Vesey Sts. ☎602-0773. Chapel open M-F 9am-3pm, Su 7am-3pm.

Inspired by the design of London's St. Martin-in-the-Fields, this chapel was built in 1766, with the clock tower and spire added in 1794. Since then, St. Paul's has required precious little renovation. It is Manhattan's oldest church, and George Washington prayed here in his personal pew on Inauguration Day. The inside feels more like a meeting house than a church.

WOOLWORTH BUILDING

233 Broadway, between Barclay St. and Park Pl.

F.W. Woolworth purportedly paid $15.5 million to house the headquarters of his five-and-dime store empire in this sumptuous 1913 skyscraper, once known as the "Cathedral of Commerce." Construction moved at a fast pace—an average of 1½ stories per week—and by the time it was finished, the skyscraper measured at 792 feet, at the time, the tallest in the world. Its lobby is spectacular: replete with Gothic arches and flourishes, glittering mosaics, gold painted mailboxes, imported marble designs and carved caricatures. Note the depictions of Woolworth himself counting change and architect Cass Gilbert holding a model of the building.

CITY HALL

Broadway at Murray St., off Park Row. ☎ 788-6879. Group tours M-F, but call at least 2 weeks in advance. Groups from 10-35 people. Mayor Rudy Giuliani closed City Hall to tourists but when he leaves office in January 2002, it is possible that the new mayor will reopen City Hall to tourists.

The mayor of New York City keeps his offices in this elegant Neoclassical building. Press conferences are often held on its steps, and demonstrations (with permission, of course) may be coordinated to disrupt the mayoral train of thought. In 1865 thousands of mourners paid their respects to the body of Abraham Lincoln under the hall's vaulted rotunda. Winding stairs lead to the Governor's Room, in which portraits of American political heroes adorn the walls. City Hall sits in City Hall Park, once home to a jail, a public execution ground, and a barracks for British soldiers. The area along Park Row, now inhabited by a statue of journalist Horace Greeley, was formerly known as "Newspaper Row," because most of New York's papers were published near the one place they were guaranteed to find scandal.

TWEED COURTHOUSE

Chambers St., between Center St. and Broadway, north of City Hall.

Named after the infamous Boss Tweed of the Tammany Hall scandals, this courthouse took 10 years and $14 million—or the equivalent of $166 million today—to build. Rumor has it that $10 million went to Tweed himself, setting off a public outcry that marked the beginning of the end for Boss Tweed and his embezzling ways. Today you can admire this building's Victorian reinterpretation without paying off any crooked public officials.

SURROGATE'S COURT

31 Chambers St., near Center St. ☎ 374-8244.

Two sculpture groups—*New York in Its Infancy* and *New York in Revolutionary Times*—grace the Beaux-Arts exterior of this overwhelming former Hall of Records. In front of the building's Mansard roof stand eight statues of notable New Yorkers—visitors may want to go across the street for a better view. Inside, Egyptian mosaics and the 12 signs of the Zodiac cover the foyer ceiling.

FEDERAL OFFICE BUILDING

290 Broadway, off Reade St., a block north of City Hall.

The lobby holds powerful public art installations including Clyde Lynd's sculpture "America Song" and Roger Brown's mosaic depicting legions of AIDS-stricken faces descending into a sea of skulls. On the floor of the central rotunda, a work entitled "The New Ring Shout" commemorates the African burial ground on which the building stands. The title of this 40-foot-wide work of terrazzo and polished brass derives from a historical dance of celebration.

AFRICAN BURIAL GROUND

Corner of Duane and Elk Sts.

In 1991 archaeologists found the remains of over 20,000 slaves buried only 20 feet underground, making the site the largest known excavated African cemetery in the world. Congress declared it a national landmark in response to protests against a new Federal Court building slated to be built over the burial ground. The space now stands undisturbed with plans in the works for an elaborate memorial.

BROOKLYN BRIDGE

Off Park Row, east of City Hall Park.

See p. 90 for information.

THE CAGED BIRDS SING

Early-rising ornithologists will want to take a sunrise stroll to **Sara Delano Roosevelt Park,** west of the Bowery, at the corner of Chrystie and Delancey Sts. There, between about 7am and 9am, a group of older Chinese men gather each morning from spring to fall to give sun to the songbirds.

The men arrive at the small garden at the park's northern edge with beautiful wooden bird cages covered in cloth so that their occupants don't wake too early. After positioning the cages, the men gingerly remove the coverings and bid their songbirds good morning. The men do some stretching exercises as they wait for their birds to awake and warm to the sun. Once sufficiently bathed in light, the birds give fanfare to the day. The songs are amazingly loud and melodic, and are easily heard over the roar of early morning traffic. This is an old Chinese tradition intended as a distraction from vice, but as one of the men remarked, it's more "like walking your dog."

Yoga groups practice to the morning song of the birds, including members of Falun Xiulian Dafa, a semi-religious yoga group that is growing rapidly in China and is currently the victim of political oppression from the Chinese government, who sees the group as a potential threat. For more information, visit falun-ny.net

SOUTH STREET SEAPORT MUSEUM

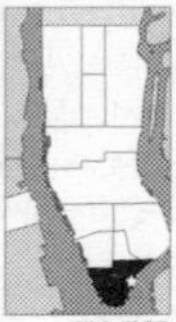

see map pp. 310-311

Subway: 2, 3, 4, 5, J, M, Z to Fulton St.; A, C to Broadway-Nassau.

The shipping industry thrived here for most of the 19th century, when New York was the most important port city in the US. During the 20th century, bars, brothels, and crime flourished in the South St. Seaport. In the mid-1980s, the Seaport Museum teamed up with the Rouse Corporation, which built Boston's Quincy Market, the St. Louis Union Station, and Baltimore's Harborplace, to design the 12-block "museum without walls."

SEAPORT MUSEUM VISITORS CENTER

209 Water St. ☎748-8600. Adults $6, students $4, seniors $5, ages 4-12 $3. Separate ship ticket $3.

Your first stop at the Seaport Museum, the pleasant Visitors Center provides information on and sells passes to any of the galleries, ships, or shops under the museum's auspices.

FULTON FISH MARKET

End of Fulton St. at South St. Seaport. ☎748-8786. Museum tours May-Oct. 1hr; daily 6am, $12. Reservations required 1 week in advance.

The largest fresh fish market in the country, the Fulton Market has repeatedly clashed with the city, but continues to open at 4am as it has for over 160 years. After a suspicious fire, Mayor Giuliani went to town on the organized crime influences that allegedly controlled the market. Nevertheless, New York's store and restaurant owners continue to buy their fresh fish here, as they have done since the Dutch colonial period in the 1600s. Between midnight and 8am you can see buyers surveying the still-gasping catch of the day.

PEKING

On the East River off Fulton St. and next to Pier 16. For a sample of this ship's rich history, catch the 15min. 1929 film of the ship's passage around Cape Horn, shown daily 10am-6pm.

In 1911, a Hamburg-based company built the *Peking*, the second-largest sailing ship ever launched. It spent most of its career on the "nitrate run" to Chile, a route that passes around Cape Horn, one of the most dangerous stretches of water in the world. Help the current crew raise one of the ship's 32 sails or simply take a 30min. tour.

OTHER SEAPORT MUSEUM SIGHTS

In addition to the Peking, there are five other skiffs open to the public. Some ships are stationary, such as the 325-foot *Wavertree*, an iron-hulled, full-rigged ship built in 1885, which is currently undergoing a major restoration, and the *Ambrose*, a floating lighthouse built in 1907 to mark an entrance to New York Harbor. Others take to the open seas: the *Pioneer* (1885) offers wonderful two- and three-hour tours on which you can help keep the ship afloat. Back on land, the museum occupies a number of the area's early 19th-century buildings. **Bowne & Co.,** 211 Water St., a re-creation of a 19th-century printing shop, offers demonstrations of letterpress printing. On Fulton St., between South and Front Sts., is a group of buildings called **Schermerhorn Row.** Constructed between 1811 and 1812, these Georgian-Federal buildings once housed shops that served the throngs exiting the Fulton Ferry.

Lower East Side Tenement Museum

CHINATOWN AND LITTLE ITALY

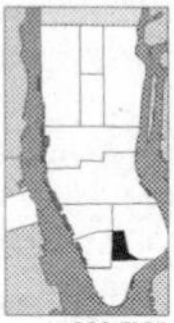
see map pp. 312-313

Subway: 4, 6, J, M, N, R, Z to Canal St.

Mott and Pell Sts., the unofficial centers of Chinatown, boil over with Chinese restaurants and commercial activity. Every inch of the old red and green awnings lining the storefronts are decorated with Chinese-style baby jackets, bamboo hats, stuffed Hello Kittys, and miniature Buddhas. If it's labels you're into, Canal is the street for you; every inch of the sidewalk is used for commercial space. Don't let the low-priced merchandise snooker you, though—creative labeling abounds in several stores and those are *not* Rolexes. During the Chinese New Year, the area's frenetic pace accelerates to a fever pitch.

Immigration has propelled Chinatown into what was once Italian territory. Since the 1960s, Little Italy's borders have receded in the face of an aggressively expanding Chinatown, and much of the neighborhood's authenticity has disappeared due to the temptation of tourism. Mulberry Street remains the heart of the neighborhood. The gift shop on the corner of Grand and Mulberry Streets, however, bears looking into even if you don't want to take home a souvenir. Instead of a tourist bureau, in here you can find Mr. Rossi, the store's proprietor, who may honor you with an exposition of the neighborhood's history.

Sights are listed from **south to north.**

Mahayana Buddhist Temple

FIRST SHEARITH ISRAEL GRAVEYARD

South side of Chatham Sq., at St. James Pl., between James and Oliver Sts.

This historical site attests to Chinatown's previous guise as part of the Jewish Lower East Side. The cemetery served NYC's first Jewish

Chinese Lanterns

Apples for Sale

Little Italy

Wetlands

congregation, the Spanish-Portuguese Shearith Israel Synagogue. Gravestones date from as early as 1683.

MAHAYANA BUDDHIST TEMPLE

133 Canal St., near the Manhattan Bridge.

This modern space, with its large television, spotlights, and state-of-the-art sound system, might be jarring for those who think of Buddhism as a religion practiced in musty old monasteries in ancient Tibet. Here, the path to *satori* is strewn with *tchotchkes.*

MANHATTAN BRIDGE

Between Canal St. and the Bowery.

Walking northeast toward where the Bowery and East Broadway meet will bring you past the grand arch and flanking colonnades that mark the entrance to the Manhattan Bridge. These were designed by Carrère and Hastings, the same firm that designed the New York Public Library (p. 71) and the Frick Mansion (p. 113).

POLICE HEADQUARTERS

240 Centre St., off Broome St.

Well, former police headquarters: in the 1970s this domed Beaux-Arts giant became a luxury co-op apartment building. Gazing at the elegantly refurbished lobby, complete with marble columns and massive chandelier, makes it hard to imagine a more pleasant place to get booked.

LOWER EAST SIDE

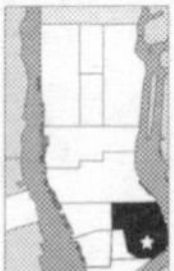

see map pp. 320-321

Everybody ought to have a Lower East Side in their life.
—Irving Berlin

The Lower East Side was once the most densely settled area in New York; 240,000 immigrants lived within one square mile. Initially populated by Irish immigrants in the mid-1800s, the area saw a large influx of Eastern Europeans in the 50 years preceding WWI. Post-WWII migrants to the area were mostly African-Americans and Puerto Ricans, and in the 1980s and 90s Latin Americans and Asians have moved into the area. Main thoroughfares such as East Broadway continue to reflect the multicultural aspect of the neighborhood. Traces of the Jewish ghetto also persist on Orchard St., an historic shopping area that fills up on Sundays with salesmen hawking discount goods in vacuum-sealed bags. If you need guidance, visit the **Lower East Side Visitors Center,** 261 Broome St. between Orchard and Allen Sts. (☎888-825-8374. Open Su-F 10am-4pm.)

Sights are listed from **south to north.**

SUNG TAK BUDDHIST ASSOCIATION

15 Pike St., between East Broadway and Henry St. Subway F to East Broadway. ☎587-5936. Open daily 9:30am-6pm. Free.

Formerly the Congregation Sons of Israel Kalvarie, this building stood abandoned for years, dilapidated and graffiti-covered, until the Buddhist Association moved in. This newly renovated house of worship now serves a different faith but retains its multicultural past in its mixture of Middle Eastern and Asian architectural styles.

ELDRIDGE ST. SYNAGOGUE

12 Eldridge St., near Canal St. Subway: 4, 6, J, M, N, R, Z to Canal St. ☎219-0903. Open Su, Tu-Th noon-4pm. Tours Tu, Th 11:30am and 2:30pm. Tours $4; children, students, and seniors $2.

This Moorish-style synagogue, built in 1886 as the first synagogue for Eastern Europeans in New York, majestically looms over a crowded, noisy block. The synagogue has recently finished the first leg of its multi-million dollar renovation project and is now a national historic sight open to the public.

CONGREGATION ANSHE CHESED

172-176 Norfolk St., at Stanton St. Subway: F to Delancey St. ☎780-0175.

New York's oldest reform synagogue, the red-painted Gothic Revival structure was built in 1849 to seat 1500. While the impressive building is worth a slight detour while strolling around the neighborhood, the synagogue is now a private space owned by the Angel Orensanz Association and is only open for services twice a month on the first and third Friday of the month.

SOHO

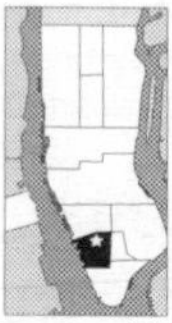

see map p. 315

Bounded in the north by Houston St., south by Canal St., west by West Broadway, and east by Crosby St. Subway: B, D, F, Q to Broadway-Lafayette; 6 to Spring St.

Over the past 10 years, SoHo has solidified into a saucy dish of artsy, commercial-chic. The story of SoHo's evolution is similar to that of many New York neighborhoods. In the earlier part of the century, SoHo was a dark industrial zone: factories and warehouses operated between its alleyways. In the mid-1940s, however, charmed by low rents and airy lofts, artists moved in; the trickle roared to a full-scale waterfall of migration by the 1960s. Until the mid-1980s, SoHo's scene, led by Jean-Michel Basquiat, Keith Haring, and Kenny Scharf, blossomed as the hotbed of NYC artistic innovation, but as the 90s brought Victoria's Secret and J.

Naked Lunch Bar

Double Happiness Bar

Sonnabend Gallery

Crew, the cutting-edge dulled. SoHo may no longer cradle the truly avant-garde, but it still boasts pockets of off-beat culture, high fashion, and meticulous design.

Designated an historic district in 1973 by the Landmarks Preservation Commission, SoHo is filled with cast-iron buildings, the result of a construction boom in the latter half of the 19th century, when the neighborhood was home to warehouses and factories. The cast-iron facades are complemented by a dense collage of windows, thanks to the strength of the cast iron. Especially notable is the **Haughwout Building,** 488 Broadway, with its delicate, yet crowded facade of arched windows set between Corinthian columns. Built in 1857, the five-story Haughwout was the first building to be outfitted with a passenger elevator. Though currently in need of preservation, the building is still definitely worth a stroll-by.

When meandering through SoHo, however, don't concentrate on just one building, but be sure to take in all of the rich architecture that borders each narrow street. Pop in to the galleries (p. 123) and shops (p. 204) that inhabit many of the cast-iron buildings.

TRIBECA

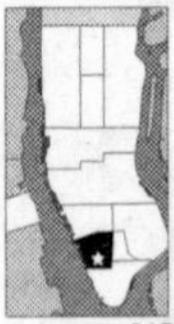

see map p. 315

Subway: 1, 9 to Canal St., Franklin St., or Chambers St.; A, C, E to Canal St., Chambers St.

Once an industrial wasteland, TriBeCa (Triangle Below Canal St.) has steadily evolved into a hip, mostly residential neighborhood full of confusing streets. One of the neighborhood's highlights is **Washington Market Park,** located in the triangle bounded by Greenwich, Chambers, and West Sts. This surprisingly large park hosts Thursday evening concerts each week from late June to early August in its charming blue-and-white gazebo. TriBeCa is also the illustrious home of the firehouse from which Bill Murray, Dan Ackroyd, and fellow **Ghostbusters** helped rid New York of unwanted paranormal activity in two classic 1980s films. To make a pilgrimage, head to 114 Moore St., near White St. If you prefer mafia movies to sci-fi flicks, then pass by the **TriBeCa Grill,** 375 Greenwich St., owned by Robert DeNiro. The restaurant is on the ground floor of the **TriBeCa Films** building, in which Miramax and several other production companies work their cinematic magic. The actor/entrepreneur has also opened the **TriBeCa Bakery** in the middle of the block, and the chic, expensive, and surprisingly friendly **Nobu** on the corner of Franklin St. and Hudson St.

GREENWICH VILLAGE

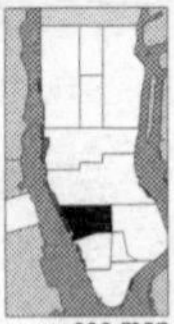

see map pp. 316-317

Greenwich Village has undergone a relentless process of cultural ferment that layered grime, activism, and artistry atop a tangle of quaint, meandering streets. The area, once covered in farms and hills, developed in the mid-19th century into a staid high-society playground that fostered literary creativity. Henry James captured the debonair spirit of the Village in his 1880 novel *Washington Square.*

Real-estate values plummeted at the turn of the century as German, Irish, and Italian immigrants found work in the industries along the Hudson River and in pockets of the Village. Some fifty years later, the Beat movement crystallized in the Village, and the 60s saw the growth of a homosexual community around Christopher St. The Village's nonconformist ethos conflicted with the aims of the city government in the late 60s. Violent clashes between police and homosexuals resulted in the Stonewall Riots of 1969, a powerful moment of awakening in the gay rights movement. In the 70s the punk scene exploded and added mohawked and be-spiked rockers to the Village's diverse cast of characters. The 80s saw the beginnings of a gentrification process that continued through the 90s and has made the Village a fashionable and comfortable settlement for those wealthier New Yorkers with a bit more spunk than their uptown counterparts.

The Village comes out in all of its (non)traditional glory for the wild Village **Halloween Parade.** This is your chance to see people dressed as toilets or condoms. Slap on your own wig, strap on your appendage of choice, and join the crowd—no one will blink a rhinestoned eyelash.

WASHINGTON SQUARE PARK AREA

I know not whether it is owing to the tenderness of early associations, but this portion of New York appears to many persons the most delectable.
—Henry James, *Washington Square*

Washington Square Park: between 4th St. and Washington Sq. Park North, Macdougal St. and Greene St. Subway: A, B, C, D, E, F, Q to W. 4th St.

Washington Square Park has stood at the center of Village life for most of this century. Native Americans once inhabited the marshland here, and by the mid-17th century it had become home to black slaves freed by the Dutch. The latter half of the 18th century saw the area converted into a potter's field for the burial of the poor and unknown (around 15,000 bodies lie buried here) and then as a hanging-grounds during the Revolutionary War. In the 1820s the area metamorphosed into a park and parade ground. Soon, high-toned residences made the area the center of New York's social scene. On the north side of the park is **The Row.** Built largely in the 1830s, this stretch of stately Federal-style brick residences soon became an urban center populated by 19th-century professionals, dandies, and novelists.

In the late 1970s and early 80s, Washington Square Park became a base for low-level drug dealers. The mid-80s saw a noisy clean-up campaign that has made the park fairly safe, though its drug traffic has not altogether vanished. After $900,000 worth of renovations were completed in 1995, the park today hosts musicians, misunderstood teenagers, muttering homeless people, and romping children.

At the north end of the Park stands the **Washington Memorial Arch,** built in 1889 to commemorate the centennial of George Washington's inauguration. Until 1964, Fifth Ave. actually ran through the arch; residents, however, complained of the noisy traffic and the city truncated the most esteemed of avenues.

NEW YORK UNIVERSITY

Campus scattered throughout the Village. NYU Information: 50 W. 4th St. ☎998-4636. Free maps.

The country's largest private university, NYU is most notable for its stellar communications and film departments and some of the least appealing contemporary architecture in the Village. Many desperately functional-looking buildings around Washington Square proudly display the purple NYU flag.

On the southeast side of the park, where Washington Sq. South meets LaGuardia Pl., you'll find NYU's **Loeb Student Center,** garnished with pieces of scrap metal that purportedly represent birds in flight. Mere steps away sits **Gould Plaza** in front of NYU's Stern School of Business and the Courant Institute of Mathematical Sciences. The plaza is home to a shiny aluminum Dadaist sculpture by Jean Arp.

At Green Street and Waverly Place lies NYU's **Brown Building,** the former site of the **Triangle Shirtwaist Company** where a 1911 fire killed most of the primarily female staff—the doors had been chained shut to prevent the workers from taking too many breaks. The ensuing uproar led to new workplace regulations and a rejuvenated worker safety movement. Across the street looms another rust-colored bulk, the **Elmer Holmes Bobst Library,** designed by architects with the idea of unifying the severely disjointed campus through red-sandstone facades. Unfortunately the money ran out before the project was complete, so NYU opted for the purple flags instead.

PICASSO

On Bleecker St., between LaGuardia Pl. and Mercer St., in the courtyard of the building complex on the south side of the street. Subway: A, B, C, D, E, F, Q to W. 4th St.

Proclaimed by the *New York Times* to be the ugliest piece of public art in the city, this masterpiece stands almost unnoticed in all the hubbub of the area.

THE NEW SCHOOL

66 W. 12th St. Subway: F, L to 14th St.-Sixth Ave.

Formerly the New School for Social Research, past faculty of this school include John Dewey and W.E.B. DuBois. During World War II, the New School made itself famous by offering positions to European intellectuals fleeing the Nazis; today, it

SoHo Shopping

Washington Square Park

New School

continues its tradition of progressive-minded thinking. Former politician Bob Kerrey is the university's president.

GRACE CHURCH

800 Broadway, between 10th and 11th Sts. Subway: N, R to 8th St.-NYU.

This church was constructed in 1845 using white marble mined by prisoners of the notorious New York State prison Sing Sing. Despite its creepy Gothic exterior, the church used to be *the* place for weddings and still holds a lovely Passion of St. Matthew at Easter. The interior of the church is extremely dark, but beautifully ornate.

WEST OF SIXTH AVENUE (WEST VILLAGE)

The West Village is the city's literary center and one of its nerve centers for gay and lesbian life. Sights are listed roughly **from south to north.**

75½ BEDFORD STREET

Near the corner of Commerce St. Subway: 1, 9 to Christopher St.

75½ Bedford St. is the narrowest building in the Village, measuring 9½ft. across. The writer Edna St. Vincent Millay lived here in 1923 and 1924, during which she founded the **Cherry Lane Theater,** 38 Commerce St. (See **Entertainment,** p. 174.), which has showcased Off-Broadway theater ever since. Actors Lionel Barrymore and Cary Grant also liked cramped quarters; each lived at 75½ Bedford after her departure.

CHUMLEY'S

86 Bedford St. between Grove and Barrow Sts. Subway: 1, 9 to Christopher St. ☎675-4449. Open Su-Th 4pm-midnight, F-Sa 4pm-2am.

Once the center of the Greenwich Village Literary movement, this bar and restaurant became a speakeasy in Prohibition days. Hundreds of authors, including the literary Johns (Dos Passos and Steinbeck), Ernest Hemingway, William Faulkner, and J.D. Salinger have raised a glass here—and now jackets from their books adorn the walls. The fascinating building—complete with its original trap doors, secret elevators, and hidden escape routes—survived four fires and is open to explore even if you're not drinking here. Partly in homage to its clandestine history, no sign indicates that this cream-colored building with a brown door might be a bar.

CHURCH OF ST. LUKE'S IN THE FIELDS

479-485 Hudson St. between Barrow and Grove Sts. Subway: 1, 9 to Christopher St.

At the western end of Grove St. is the Church of St. Luke's in the Fields. The third-oldest church in Manhattan, this severe brick building was named for the once-remote location at which it was built in 1821. The church is not open to the public.

SHERIDAN SQUARE

Intersection of Seventh Ave., Christopher St., and W. 4th St. Subway: 1, 9 to Christopher St.

Rioters against the Civil War draft gathered here in 1863 for some of the darkest days in NYC's history; protesters brutally murdered hundreds of free blacks. Since then, the area has become much more tolerant, as evident in the diversity of Christopher St. The area of the street near Sheridan Sq. has been renamed Stonewall Pl., alluding to the Stonewall Inn, site of the 60s police raid that sparked the gay rights movement. (See **Gay New York,** p. 193.) Within Sheridan Sq., two sculptures of same-sex couples stand locked in embraces, a tribute to the neighborhood's history. An unhitched and stoic General Sheridan stands nearby, love's looker-on.

JEFFERSON MARKET LIBRARY

425 Sixth Ave. at the intersection of W. 10th St. and Greenwich Ave. Subway: 1, 9 to Christopher St. ☎ 243-4334. Open M and Th 10am-6pm, Tu and F noon-6pm, W noon-8pm, Sa 10am-5pm.

Built as a courthouse in 1876, this beautiful building served as a female detention center until the 1960s. The remarkable structure faced and beat a demolition plot in the early 60s, and was once voted the fifth most beautiful building in the country. Carefully restored in 1967, the building is now a public library whose Victorian Gothic Structure looks like a cross between a castle and a church with its detailed brickwork, stained-glass windows, and a turreted clock tower. It occupies the triangle formed by the intersection of W. 10th St., Sixth Ave., and Greenwich Ave. Just behind the courthouse is a small but beautifully lush garden.

PATCHIN PLACE

10th St. and Sixth Ave. Subway: 1, 9 to Christopher St.

Across from Jefferson Market Library, you'll see an iron gate and a street sign that reads "Patchin Place." The modest, 145-year-old buildings that line the unassuming path housed writers e.e. cummings, Theodore Dreiser, and Djuna Barnes during their Village sojourns.

MEAT-PACKING DISTRICT

Around W. 12th and Gansevoort Sts. Subway: A, C, E, L to 14th St.-Eighth Ave.

Walking up Hudson St. will lead you to the meat-packing district, a super trendy area for those who love the grit of the city. In the past few years, lofts have sprung up in old factories, cafes in old garages, and clubs in old stockyards. This urban renewal, however, has had little effect on the shady weekend late-night scene.

Bleeker and McDougal Streets

Herald Sqaure

Washington Square Park

COLOR ME GREEN

In 1973, Liz Christy and the "Green Guerrillas" began planting neighborhood window boxes and tree pits and throwing water balloons filled with seeds into the East Village and Alphabet City's abandoned lots. By 1986 they had transformed the northeast corner of Bowery and Houston into a flowering oasis they named the **Liz Christy Bowery-Houston Garden.** (110 E. Houston St. Open Sa noon-4pm; May-Sept. also open Tu 6pm-dusk.) To find out more about the Green Guerrillas, call ☎674-8124 or check out www.greenguerilla.org. Other spectacular community gardens in the area include:

Sixth Street and Avenue B Garden. The mother of all community gardens; a fantasy jungle. Edward Boros' towering sculpture never fails to turn heads. Open in summer daily 8am-8pm; other times Sa-Su 1-6pm.

Miracle Garden, E. 3rd St., at Ave. B. (entrance on E. 2nd St.) Small but tall and lush.

Campos Garden, E. 12th St., between Aves. B and C. A plethora of fruits and veggies. Open Mar.-Oct. Su 3-5pm and intermittently during the week.

El Sol Brillante, E. 12th St., between Aves. A and B.

Community Garden, Ave. C (Loisaida Ave.), between E. 8th and 9th Sts.

De Colores Garden, St. Mark's Pl., between Aves. B and C. A spacious garden, with a flea market every Sa at 10am.

THE EAST VILLAGE AND ALPHABET CITY

see map pp. 320-321

The East Village—north of Houston St., east of Broadway, and south of 14th St.—was carved out of the Bowery and the Lower East Side in the early 1960s, when artists and writers moved here to escape high rents in Greenwich Village. Today, East Village residents span a wide spectrum, with punks, hippies, ravers, rastas, guppies, goths, and beatniks all coexisting. Diversity, however, does not always breed harmony; many poorer residents of the East Village feel that wealthier newcomers have pushed them out by raising rents. These tensions have forged the East Village into one of the most overtly politicized regions of New York City.

Heterogeneity and rising rents are not the only hallmarks of this area. Not only is it the basis for the hit musical, *Rent*, the East Village also keeps alive a vigorous tradition of creativity in the everyday. Billie Holiday sang here, and, more recently, the East Village provided early audiences for Sonic Youth, the Talking Heads, Blondie, and Frank Zappa.

East of First Avenue, south of 14th Street, and north of Houston St., the avenues give up on numbers and adopt letters. In its 60s heyday, Jimi Hendrix and the Fugs would play open-air shows to bright-eyed love children. You'll still find East Village "deadbeatniks" and hard-core anarchists, as well as artists and students, hanging out in local cafes and shops. However, the area has also found itself squarely in the growing path of New York's wave of gentrification, manifest in the increasing numbers of boutiques and chic eateries. The area is generally safe during the day. Addictive nightlife on Avenues A and B ensure some protection, but use caution east of Avenue B after dark. For information on current issues and events in Alphabet City, check for free local papers at St. Mark's Bookshop and other stores in the area. Neighborhood posters can also let you in on current happenings. Sights are listed **from west to east.**

ST. MARK'S PLACE

Where E. 8th St. would be, between Cooper Sq. E. and Ave. A. Subway: 6 to Astor Pl.

Full of pot-smoking flower children and musicians in the 1960s, this street gave Haight-Ashbury a run for its hashish. In the late 1970s, it taught London's Kings Road how to do punk, as mohawked youths hassled passersby from the brownstone steps off Astor Pl. Nowadays, those 60s and 70s youths still line the street—in their old-tattooed-geezer incarnations. The present-day St. Mark's Pl. is a drag full of tiny ethnic eateries, street level shops, sidewalk vendors selling trinkets of all kinds—from plastic bug-eye sunglasses to PVC fetish wear—music shops, and, of course, tattoo shops. In a way, St. Mark's resembles a small-town Main Street—a small town with a bad-ass history. Unlike most other areas of the city, people here know one another; sometimes they even talk to and look after one another. Although many more-obscure-than-thou types now shun the commercialized (there's even a Gap) and crowded areas of the street, St. Mark's remains the hub of East Village life and *the* place to start your tour of the neighborhood.

ASTOR PLACE

At the junction of Lafayette Ave., Fourth Ave., and E. 8th St. Subway: 6 to Astor Pl.

Simultaneously a small road and a large cultural intersection, this western border of the East Village simmers with street life. Check out the ever-popular **Beaver Murals** at the Astor Place subway stop—they pay homage to John Jacob Astor's prolific fur trade. Upstairs from the murals, the subway kiosk, a cast-iron Beaux-Arts beauty, was built in 1985 as part of a reconstruction of the station. A **large black cube** balanced on its corner distinguishes Astor Place's position. If you and your friends push hard enough, the cube will rotate, but you may disturb Astor Pl.'s various denizens sitting (or sleeping) underneath it. "The Cube," (officially, "the Alamo," by Bernard Rosenthal) provides a meeting point for countless rallies, marches, and demonstrations, as well as a space for impromptu performances and asphalt for hordes of prepubescent skaters.

THE COOPER UNION FOUNDATION BUILDING

7 E. 7th St., at Cooper Sq. off Astor Pl. Subway: 6 to Astor Pl. ☎353-4199. Gallery open M-Th 11am-7pm.

Peter Cooper, a self-educated industrialist, founded the Cooper Union for the Advancement of Science and Art in 1859 as a tuition-free technical and design school. Both the American Red Cross and the NAACP got their starts here. Cooper Union also stands as the oldest building in the US to incorporate steel beams (made of old railroad rails). The second floor **Houghton Gallery** hosts changing exhibits on design and American history as well as displays by the talented and stylish student body (but not during the summer). Find Cooper's statue in Cooper Sq. in front of the building.

ST. MARK'S CHURCH IN-THE-BOWERY

131 E. 10th St. Subway: 6 to Astor Pl. ☎674-6377. West Yard open Su 11:30am-1pm, Tu 3-5pm, W 3-6pm, Sa 10:30am-12:30pm.

The Cage

Nuyorican Poets Cafe

Empire State Building

Erected in 1799, St. Mark's Church stands on the site of Peter Stuyvesant's estate chapel, and the Dutch governor lies buried in its small cobblestone graveyard. St. Mark's has a long history of political activism and involvement in the arts. It hosts several community companies, including the **Ontological Theater,** which continues to produce some of the better off-Broadway plays, as well as the **Danspace Project** and the **Poetry Project** (see **Entertainment,** p. 176)

COLONNADE ROW

428-434 Lafayette Ave. and 4th Sts. Subway: 6 to Bleecker St.

New York's most famous 19th-century millionaires—John Jacob Astor, Cornelius "Commodore" Vanderbilt, and the Franklin Delano Roosevelt family—dwelled in three of these four-columned houses, built in 1833. There used to be nine of these houses; the four remaining are unfortunately the worse for wear.

MERCHANT'S HOUSE MUSEUM

29 E. 4th St., between Lafayette Ave. and Bowery. Subway: 6 to Bleecker St. ☎ 777-1089; www.merchantshouse.com. Open Th-M 1-5pm. Admission $5, students and seniors $3.

Contained in the preserved townhouse of Seabury Tredwell, a well-off 19th-century merchant, and containing furniture, clothing, and other belongings of the Tredwell family, the Merchant's House Museum spreads over three floors. Admission is somewhat pricey, but architectural buffs will get a kick out of the incongruousness of a beautiful townhouse in the middle of ultra-hip NoHo.

THE 2ND AVE. DELI

156 Second Ave., at E. 10th St. Subway: 6 to Astor Pl. *See **Food,** p. 139.*

This famous Jewish landmark, founded by Abe Lebewohl, is all that remains of the "Yiddish Rialto," the stretch of Second Ave. between Houston and 14th Sts. that contained the Yiddish theater district in the early part of the 20th century. Stars of David in the sidewalk out front contain the names of actors and actresses who spent their lives entertaining Jewish immigrants. While this community no longer remains the Jewish enclave it once was, the historic deli stands as a loyal mainstay; it still serves up the meanest pastrami sandwich in town. Across the street is **Abe Lebewohl Park,** built to commemorate the founder of the deli, who was murdered in 1996.

NEW YORK MARBLE CEMETERIES

Second Ave. between E. 2nd and 3rd Sts. and 52-74 E. 2nd St., between First and Second Aves. Subway: F to Second Ave. Open F 1-5pm and Sa 10am-2pm

The New York Marble Cemeteries (so named because burials were in one of the underground vaults, made of white marble) were the city's first two non-sectarian graveyards. Both cemeteries can be viewed through the iron fences around them.

ST. GEORGE UKRAINIAN CATHOLIC CHURCH

On Taras Sevchenko Pl., near Cooper Sq. East. Subway: 6 to Astor Pl.

Ukrainian-American life centers on E. 7th St., with cafes and several churches. The most remarkable is St. George Ukrainian Catholic Church. The artwork inside, viewable only if you stop by Sunday after mass, eclipses even the haunting icons that ornament the outer doors.

TOMPKINS SQUARE PARK

Between Aves. A and B and E. 7th and 10th Sts. Subway: L to First Ave. Open daily 6am-midnight.

Tompkins Square Park's history is one of clashes, protests, and marches, although you'd be hard-pressed to tell that today. In 1988 police officers precipitated a riot when they attempted to forcibly evict a band of the homeless and their supporters from the park. An aspiring video artist recorded scenes of police brutality, sparking a public outcry and further police-inspired violence. "East Side Anarchists"—who hoofed down to Tompkins Sq. after tearing through St. Mark's Pl.—incited one of many riots that erupted in New York City following the Rodney King verdict in 1992. The **dog run** in the park, a designated area for letting man's best friend romp about, affords marvelous opportunities for canine-watching. In the summer, you're bound to stumble upon **impromptu concerts** here.

LOWER MIDTOWN

Between 14th and 42nd Sts. stretching all the way across Manhattan.

UNION SQUARE AND GRAMERCY

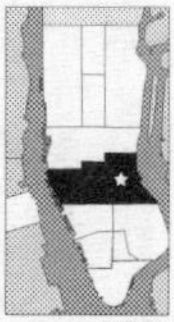

see map pp. 322-323

Anchored by four parks—Union Square, Stuyvesant Park, Madison Square Park, and Gramercy Park—this portion of midtown is more residential, and, therefore, less crazed, than the bordering neighborhood to the north. Sights are listed from **south to north.**

UNION SQUARE

Between Broadway and Park Ave. South, 14th and 17th Sts. Subway: 4, 5, 6, L, N, R to Union Sq. Greenmarket open M, W, F-Sa 7am-6pm. Info on events taking place in the square: ☎ 460-1208; www.unionsquarenyc.org. Walking tours Sa 2pm, by the Lincoln Statue.

So named because it was a "union" of two main roads (the Bowery and Bloomingdale Rd., now Fourth Ave. and Broadway), Union Square and the surrounding area sizzled with high-society aristocrats before the Civil War. Early in the 20th century, the square's name became doubly significant when the neighborhood served as a center of New York's Socialist movement, which held its popular May Day celebrations in the park. As the century sped onward, Union Square Park was abandoned to drug dealers and derelicts until 1989 when the city stepped in and cleaned up. Today, the park is pleasant and generally safe, although not pristine. The scent of herbs and fresh bread wafts through the air, courtesy of the **Union Square Greenmarket.** Farmers, fisherman, and bakers from all over the region come to sell fresh produce, jellies, and baked goods.

UNION SQUARE THEATRE

100 E. 17th St. Subway: 4, 5, 6, L, N, R to Union Sq.

The Union Square Theatre building (see **Entertainment,** p. 174) was once the headquarters of Tammany Hall, a feared political machine that almost always got its candidates elected into office. Now musicals show on the site—how the mighty have fallen. The "Society of Tammany or Columbian Order" inscription on top of the door is about the only reminder of the building's past.

UNION SQUARE SAVINGS BANK

20 Union Sq. East. For tickets ☎ 239-6200. Subway: 4, 5, 6, L, N, R to Union Sq.

Although designed by Henry Bacon, architect of the Lincoln Memorial in Washington, D.C., this old neoclassical building was never declared an historic landmark. The bank is now the site of the **Daryl Roth Theatre,** currently home of the much talked-about De La Guarda (see **Entertainment,** p. 183).

STUYVESANT SQUARE

Second Ave., between 15th and 17th Sts. Subway: L to Third Ave. or First Ave.

A park divided by Second Ave., Stuyvesant Sq. is named after Governor Peter Stuyvesant (see **Life and Times,** p. 33) who owned farm property here in the 17th century. The statue of the Governor in the square was created by Gertrude Vanderbilt Whitney, later the founder of the Whitney Museum (see **Museums and Galleries,** p. 115). On Rutherford Pl. is **St. George's Episcopal Church,** created in 1856 in the style of Romanesque Revival, as well as a Quaker **Friends Meeting House,** built in Greek Revival style in 1860.

GRAMERCY PARK

At the south end of Lexington Ave., between 20th and 21st Sts. Subway: 6 to 23rd St. Closed to the public.

In 1831 Samuel Ruggles, a developer fond of greenery, drained a marsh to create Gramercy Park and laid out 66 building lots around its perimeter. Buyers of Ruggles' lots received keys to enter the park; for many years, the keys were made of solid gold. Over 150 years later, little has changed. Gramercy, with its wide gravel paths, remains the only private park in New York, immaculately kept by its owners. The surrounding real estate is some of the choicest in the city. A charming mix of Greek Revival and Victorian Gothic-style townhouses surround the park.

SANTA CLAUS WAS A CABBIE

Late Christmas Eve in 1822, or so the story goes, Clement Clarke Moore was taking a sleigh ride through Greenwich Village. Moore, a noted scholar and Chelsea landowner par excellence, was returning from a local butcher with a turkey in hand for Christmas dinner. A portly white-bearded Dutchman drove the sleigh through the wintry night. He would prove to be one of the greatest inspirations in 19th century American verse.

The next day Moore presented his poem "A Visit from St. Nicholas" with its famous opening lines "Twas the night before Christmas and all through the house / Not a creature was stirring, not even a mouse" and its legendary depiction of St. Nick, or Santa Claus himself, "His droll little mouth was drawn up like a bow, / and the beard on his chin was as white as the snow."

Moore's poem, which was published anonymously in *The Sentinel* and for which Moore did not take credit for ten years, cemented the image of St. Nicholas in the minds of New Yorkers and Americans. Moreover, it inextricably tied Santa Claus to Christmas Eve, sparking today's modern-day mythology.

The curious traveler may check up on Moore at Trinity Church (see p. 51), where he is now buried.

NATIONAL ARTS CLUB

15 Gramercy Park South. Subway: 6 to 23rd St. ☎475-3424. Gallery open M-F 10am-5pm, Sa-Su noon-5pm. Free.

Founded in 1898, the National Arts Club boasts members such as Martin Scorcese, Robert Redford, and Uma Thurman. The club occupies the former mansion of Samuel Tilden (another would-be American President who won the popular vote and lost the Electoral College). Some of the rooms are used as gallery space for temporary exhibitions.

PLAYERS CLUB

16 Gramercy Park South. Subway: 6 to 23rd St. ☎228-7611. Tours for groups of 10 or more. Suggested contribution $5, students and seniors $3.

Actor Edwin Booth (brother of Lincoln's assassin) established the Players Club in 1888 as an exclusive social club where actors could congregate. Members have included Mark Twain, Sir Laurence Olivier, Frank Sinatra, Walter Cronkite, and Richard Gere. The building, built in 1845, is one of the oldest brownstones in New York.

THE THEODORE ROOSEVELT BIRTHPLACE

28 E. 20th St. between Broadway and Park Ave. South. Subway: N, R to 23rd St. ☎260-1616; www.nps.gov/thrb. Open W-Su 9am-5pm. Guided tours 10am-4pm; 30min; $2, under 18 free.

This brownstone is a reproduction of the house Teddy Roosevelt lived in until he was 14. The museum now consists of five elegant period rooms, decorated as they would have appeared in Teddy's childhood. The free exhibit downstairs highlights events in the 26th president's life.

MADISON SQUARE PARK

Southern end of Madison Ave., between 23rd and 26th Sts. Subway: N, R to 23rd St.; 6 to 23rd St.

More peaceful than Central Park, Madison Square Park allows for wonderful views of the surrounding skyscrapers, including the Flatiron Building and the New York Life Insurance Building. Before the park's opening, it was in this public space that a game formerly known as "New York ball" was played by a group called the Knickerbockers. This game evolved to become America's favorite pastime—baseball. Around the park today stand statues of famous 19th-century generals.

FLATIRON BUILDING

175 Fifth Ave., off the southwest corner of Madison Square Park. Subway: N, R to 23rd St.; 6 to 23rd St.

Eminently photogenic, this building acquired its name because of its resemblance to the clothes-pressing device. The intersection of Broadway, Fifth Ave., and 23rd St. forced the construction of its dramatic wedge shape (only

6-feet wide at its point). In 1902, the Fuller Building, as it was originally named, was the city's first skyscraper over 20 stories high; it was one of the first buildings in which exterior walls were hung on a steel frame. Today, a publishing company rests within the narrow confines.

METROPOLITAN LIFE INSURANCE TOWER

1 Madison Ave., on the corner of Madison Ave. and 23rd St. Subway: N, R to 23rd St.; 6 to 23rd St.

Surveying Madison Square Park from 700 ft. above ground, the rather unaesthetic-looking tower, a 1909 addition to the 1893 building, once made this building a member of New York's tallest-building-in-the-world club. The minute hands of the clocks (one on each of the building's four faces) weigh 1,000 pounds each. The annex on 24th St., connected by a walkway, features an eye-catching neo-Gothic facade.

69TH REGIMENT ARMORY

68 Lexington Ave., at 26th St. Subway: 6 to 28th St. Open M, W-Su 11am-7pm.

A large structure in the Beaux Arts style, the armory is notable for having hosted the infamous International Exhibition of Modern Art in 1913 that brought Picasso, Matisse, and Duchamp—whom Teddy Roosevelt called "a bunch of lunatics"—to the shores of America. Perhaps in homage to its history of exhibiting art, temporary installations can sometimes still be found in its old basketball courts.

NEW YORK LIFE INSURANCE BUILDING

51 Madison Ave. between 26th and 27th Sts. Subway: N, R to 28th St.; 6 to 28th St.

Built by Cass Gilbert (of **Woolworth Building** fame, see p. 52) in 1928, this multi-tiered structure is topped by a golden pyramid-shaped roof. The building is located on the former site of circusmeister P.T. Barnum's "Hippodrome," which was rebuilt by Stanford White and served as the original Madison Square Garden from 1890 to 1925. It soon became the premier spot for New York's trademark entertainment spectacles. Star architect and man-about-town White was fatally shot here in 1906 by the unstable husband of a former mistress; the story was later fictionalized in E.L. Doctorow's *Ragtime.*

CHURCH OF THE TRANSFIGURATION

29th St. between Fifth and Madison Aves. ☎684-6770; www.littlechurch.org. Open daily 8am-6pm.Subway: N, R to 28th St.; 6 to 28th St.

Better known as "The Little Church Around the Corner," this church has been the home parish of New York's theater world ever since a pastor agreed to bury Shakespearean actor George Holland here in 1870, when actors were considered low-lives. The charming neo-Gothic cottage features the beautiful Lich Gate, peculiar green roofs, and a manicured garden with a bubbling fountain. Check out the stained-glass windows: they may look like a scene from the Bible, but look again—the vignette is from *Hamlet.*

MURRAY HILL

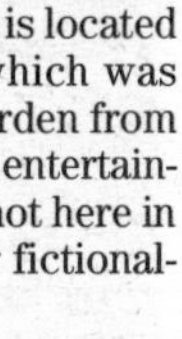
see map pp. 322-323

Subway: 6 to 33rd St.

So named because Robert Murray, a rich man in revolutionary times, made his country home close to the present-day intersection of 37th St. and Park Avenue. The upper crust of the late 19th and early 20th century dwelled in this sedate residential area, lined with streets of warm brownstones and apartments.

On the neighborhood's southern border is the **American Academy of Dramatic Arts,** 120 Madison Ave., between 30th and 31st Sts., one of America's premier schools for actors. A peek at the class photos hanging in the lobby reveals the fresh faces of Kirk Douglas, Class of 1941; Grace Kelly, Class of 1948-49; and Robert Redford, Class of 1958-59. Would-be thespians in town for a longer period can check out the six-week summer program. The highlight of Murray Hill, however, is the **Pierpont Morgan Library,** 29 E. 36th St. at Madison Ave. The original library building was completed in 1906 and designed by Charles McKim. In the style of a Renaissance *palazzo*, the library is both understated and elegant; it is definitely worth a visit both for architectural beauty and for its collection devoted to the printed word (see **Museums,** p. 114).

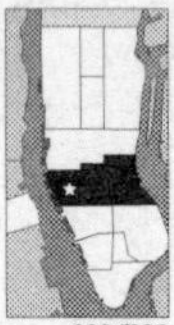

see map pp. 322-323

CHELSEA

Chelsea is probably best known today for its visible and vocal gay community, which is most apparent during **Pride Weekend** (usually the last weekend in June). The neighborhood is also synonymous with art, and the waterfront factories and warehouses from a bygone industrial era now contain artistic spaces and underground hangouts. Though Chelsea retains some of its former grit, the superb galleries around **Tenth** and **Eleventh Avenues** and **22nd Street** house some of the most cutting-edge art in the city. Sights are listed from **east to west**.

HOTEL CHELSEA

222 W. 23rd St. between Seventh and Eighth Aves. Subway: 1, 9 to 23rd St.; C, E to 23rd St. ☎243-3700.

This is hallowed ground for literati. In this cavernous 400-room complex some 150 books have been penned, including works by Arthur Miller, Mark Twain, Vladimir Nabokov, and Dylan Thomas. The Chelsea also has numerous rock and roll associations: Joni Mitchell wrote the song "Chelsea Morning" here. Yet, despite the hype, the hotel is discreet and maintains a charming seediness. Ethan Hawke is rumored to live here periodically, but the doorpeople aren't telling secrets. For pricing info, see **Accommodations,** p. 255.

ST. PETER'S CHURCH

346 W. 20th St. between Eighth and Ninth Aves. Subway: C, E to 23rd St. ☎929-2390.

A Greek Revival rectory and a Gothic Review main church building provide an interesting architectural mix. St. Peter's shares space with the non-denominational Chelsea Community Church. Episcopal services on Sunday at 10am.

GENERAL THEOLOGICAL SEMINARY

175 Ninth Ave., between 20th and 21st Sts. Subway: C, E to 23rd St. ☎243-5150. Open M-F noon-3pm, Sa 11am-3pm.

The oldest Episcopal seminary in America (founded in 1817), the complex stands on Chelsea Square on land donated by Clement Clarke Moore (see **Santa Claus was a Cabbie,** (p. 66), who taught here. The calming grounds are open to the public: go through the regrettable 1960 exterior to find a serene, peaceful oasis punctuated by a 161-foot bell tower. If you're lucky, you may catch some aspiring priests playing tennis.

CHELSEA MARKET

75 Ninth Ave., between W. 15th St. and W. 16th St. Subway: A, C, E, L to 14th St.-Eighth Ave. Open M-F 8am-7pm, Sa-Su 10am-6pm.

A cavernous Nabisco factory complex, converted with industrial-themed decor (an indoor waterfall that comes out of a pipe, exposed brick). The sprawling building contains a bakery, florist, wine store, soup stand, and more high-quality wholesalers, but it's worth walking around even if you don't need any produce.

CUSHMAN ROW

406-418 W. 20th St. between Ninth and Tenth Aves. Subway: C, E to 23rd St.

Named for Don Alonzo Cushman, a 19th-century dry-goods mogul, this terrace of brownstones (complete with wrought-iron railings) is one of the city's finest examples of the Greek Revival architectural style.

CHELSEA PIERS

On the Hudson River, at the far west end of 23rd St. Subway: C, E to 23rd St. ☎336-6666.

This massive space eschews urban grit in favor of ludicrously bright colors and scrubbed-clean surfaces. Ocean liners once docked here—the *Carpathia* landed in Chelsea Piers after rescuing survivors from the *Titanic*—but after years of disuse, the Piers were reincarnated in the 90s as a sports-entertainment complex. Various diversions populate the complex, including ice-skating rinks (see **Sky Rink,** p. 191), bowling alleys, and even a golf driving range.

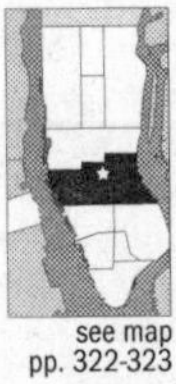

see map pp. 322-323

HERALD SQUARE AREA AND THE GARMENT DISTRICT

The *New York Herald* used to publish its daily newspaper in a building at the intersection of Broadway and 6th Ave. between 34th and 35th Sts. The newspaper is long gone, but the (triangular) square survives. Sights are arranged from **east to west.**

THE EMPIRE STATE BUILDING

350 Fifth Ave and 34th St. Subway: B, D, F, N, Q, R to 34th St./Herald Sq. Observatory: ☎736-3100. Open daily 9:30am-midnight (last elevator up at 11:30pm); tickets sold until 11:30pm. $9; seniors $7; children under 12 $4. Skyride: ☎279-9777. Open daily 10am-10pm. $11.50; ages 4-12 and seniors $8.50. Combination Pass $17; seniors $13; children $10.

Ever since King Kong first climbed the Empire State Building with his main squeeze in 1933, the skyscraper has attracted scores of tourists. The observatories welcome nearly four million visitors each year. Even alien "tourists" chose the landmark as the epicenter of their destruction in *Independence Day.*

Built on the site of the original Waldorf-Astoria hotel and completed in 1931, the limestone, granite, and stainless-steel-sheathed structure pioneered Art Deco design. The Empire State was among the first of the truly spectacular skyscrapers, stretching 1454 feet into the sky and containing 2 miles of shafts for its 73 elevators.

The lobby stands as a gleaming shrine to Art Deco interior decorating, right down to its mail drops and elevator doors. It contains 8 vaulted panels on The Seven Wonders of the Ancient World and the Eighth Wonder of the Modern World, the building itself (hmm...). Follow the arrows to find the escalator to the concourse level, where you can purchase observatory tickets. Note the sign indicating visibility level—a day with perfect visibility offers views for 80 miles in any direction. Although the elevator shoots you up to the observation deck in less than one minute, prepare to wait up to an hour during peak visiting times in the summer. For those wary of heights, stay indoors once at the main observatory.

If the view isn't exciting enough, the Empire State offers the New York Skyride, a simulation of a spaceship journey through the city.

MACY'S

151 W. 34th St. between Broadway and Seventh Ave. Subway: B, D, F, N, Q, R to 34th St./Herald Sq.; 1, 2, 3, 9, A, C, E to 34th St. ☎695-4400. Open M-Sa 10am-8:30pm, Su 11am-7pm.

Stretching 10 floors up and housing two million square feet of merchandise (ranging from designer clothes to housewares), Macy's has come a long way from its beginnings in 1858, when on its first day of business it grossed

Union Square

Chelsea Piers

Max Protech Gallery

$11.06. No longer in top form as seen in the movie *Miracle on 34th St.*, the store retains some antique touches: check out the wooden escalators on the upper floors. The store sponsors the **Macy's Thanksgiving Day Parade,** a New York tradition buoyed by helium-filled, 10-story Snoopys and Bullwinkles, as well as marching bands, floats, and general hoopla. Other annual Macy-sponsored events include the **4th of July fireworks** extravaganza on the East River, and "Tapamania," when hundreds of tap-dancers cut loose on the sidewalks of 34th St. in late August.

PENNSYLVANIA STATION

Between 31st and 34th Sts., Seventh and Eighth Aves. Subway: 1, 2, 3, 9, A, C, E to 34th St.

The original Penn Station was built in 1910. Modeled on the Roman baths of Caracalla, it featured a grand waiting room with a 150-foot-high glass ceiling. In an act Lewis Mumford deemed "irresponsible public vandalism," that building was demolished in the 1960s in favor of a more practical space 50 feet below. This boring underground station is what now greets visitors coming into New York from Jersey, Long Island, and points further afield.

MADISON SQUARE GARDEN

Between 31st and 34th Sts., Seventh and Eighth Aves. Subway: 1, 2, 3, 9, A, C, E to 34th St. ☎465-5800; www.thegarden.com. Tours every hour on the hour M-Sa 10am-3pm, Su and holidays 11am-3pm; 1hr.; $14, children under 12 $12.

Upstairs from Penn Station, the Garden is home to basketball's New York Knicks and hockey's New York Rangers. Other sporting highlights include boxing and the annual Westminster Dog Show. MSG doubles as New York's premier entertainment complex, host to a wide array of top acts. A visit behind the scenes includes glimpses of the locker rooms, the arena and concert stage, backstage areas, and luxury boxes.

THE JAMES A. FARLEY BUILDING

421 Eighth Ave., between 31st and 33rd St. Subway: 1, 2, 3, 9, A, C, E to 34th St. Open M-Sa 7:30am-6pm.

New York's immense main post office confronts Madison Square Garden with 53-foot high Corinthian columns. The broad portico of this neoclassical building (completed in 1913 and later named for a Postmaster-General of the U.S.) bears a quotation from Herodotus, now the adopted motto of the US Postal Service: "Neither snow nor rain nor heat nor gloom of night stays these couriers from the swift completion of their appointed rounds." Don't count on it.

GARMENT DISTRICT

West 30s between Broadway and Eighth Ave. Subway: 1, 2, 3, 9, A, C, E to 34th St.

The Garment District was once a redlight district known as the Tenderloin. By the 1930s, it had the largest concentration of apparel manufacturers in the world. Today, a small statue named *The Garment Worker*, depicting an aged man huddled over a sewing machine, sits near the corner of 39th St. and Seventh Ave. to commemorate the neighborhood's formative era. Walk along Broadway from the upper 20s and lower 30s for the accoutrements of the latest fashion trends, including wholesale and retail fabric, jewelry, clothing, perfume, accessories, and leather stores. If you want to create your own clothes, the **Fashion Institute of Technology** is on the corner of Seventh Ave. and 27th St. One block uptown blooms the **Flower District,** 28th St. between Sixth and Seventh Aves. No garments here. Wholesale distributors and buyers of flora congregate each morning to stock the city's florists and garden centers.

HELL'S KITCHEN (OR CLINTON)

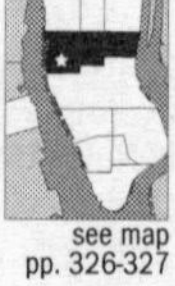

see map pp. 326-327

Located from 34th St. to 59th St. west of Eighth Avenue, Hell's Kitchen purportedly got its name from a policemen fed-up with his beat. Once a badland for ruffians and a breeding-ground for violence, this is the neighborhood that bore the "Westies"—the gangs that inspired Leonard Bernstein's 1957 *West Side Story* and Marvel Comics crime-fighter Daredevil. Slowly swept by a wave of gentrification, this neighborhood paints urban renewal over a gritty core. Though Hell's Kitchen is mostly residential and lacks actual "sights," the neighborhood, on the cusp of a complete metamorphosis, is an interesting one to explore.

JACOB K. JAVITS CONVENTION CENTER

Along Twelfth Ave. between 34th and 38th Sts. Subway: A, C, E to 34th St. ☎216-2000; www.javitscenter.com.

This black behemoth covers five blocks and hosts some of the grandest-scale events in the world, including international boat, car, and motorcycle shows. The April Auto Show brings in the biggest crowds, but the expos are not limited to transportation—a toy fair, stationary expo and fashion boutique are just some of the center's other offerings.

JOHN JAY COLLEGE OF CRIMINAL JUSTICE

899 Tenth Ave. at 58th St. Subway: A, B, C, D, 1, 9 to 59th St.-Columbus Circle.

Though the school got its start as the College of Police Science in 1965, John Jay trains civil servants of all kinds (not just the gun-totin' ones). Renovations have given the 1903 neo-Victorian central building, formerly DeWitt Clinton High School (attended by Calvin Klein), a postmodern atrium and extension.

MIDTOWN

From 42nd St. to 59th St. stretching all the way across Manhattan.

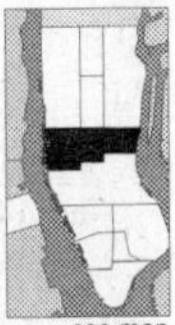

see map pp. 326-327

ON AND OFF FIFTH AVENUE

This is New York's glamour avenue and, along with Times Square, possibly the most heavily touristed area of the city. Expensive stores line the avenue, in addition to a slew of office buildings. Sights are listed from **south to north**.

NEW YORK PUBLIC LIBRARY

42nd St. and Fifth Ave. Subway: B, D, F, 7 to 42nd St.-Bryant Park. ☎869-8089. Open M and Th-Sa 10am-6pm, Tu-W 11am-7:30pm. Free ***tours*** *Tu-Sa at 11am and 2pm, leaving from the Friends Desk in Astor Hall.*

A monumental research library in the style of a classical temple, the main branch of the New York Public Library is a breath of fresh air from the skyscrapers lining Fifth Avenue. With stairs leading to the entrance and the pediment pushed back behind the frieze, the library seems to invite you inside, so long as you remain humble. The Beaux-Arts Fifth Avenue facade is loosely modeled after that of the Louvre. Featured in the hit 80s film *Ghostbusters*, two marble lions, Patience and Fortitude, dutifully guard the library against ghosts, Rick Moranis, and illiteracy. Inside, the main reading room is located on the third floor. It's not the most comfortable place to read, but the room is built on a grand scale and is worth a peek. The stacks at the library are not open, but books are readily available with a library card.

BRYANT PARK

Sixth Ave., between 40th and 42nd Sts., behind the library. Subway: B, D, F, 7 to 42nd St.-Bryant Park. Open daily 7am-9pm. The New York Convention and Visitors Bureau, ☎484-1222 or 517-5700, provides a schedule of events. Film festival M during the summer.

A century and a half after hosting the 1853 World's Fair, Bryant Park remains a busy park filled with interesting characters. The stage at the head of the park's open field plays host to a variety of free cultural events throughout the summer, including jazz concerts, classic film screenings, and amateur comedy.

THE ALGONQUIN HOTEL

44th St., between Fifth and Sixth Aves. Subway: B, D, F, 7 to 42nd St.-Bryant Park.

Alexander Woollcott's "Round Table," a regular gathering of the 1920s' brightest theatrical and literary luminaries, made this hotel famous. The Algonquin's proximity to the offices of *The New Yorker* attracted the "vicious circle" of Robert Benchley, Dorothy Parker, and Harold Ross, among other barbed tongues. The Oak Room still serves tea every afternoon, and folks say that—for better or for worse—the restaurant's menu and decor have not changed in 50 years.

MIDTOWN MURALS

Midtown is at once the theatrical nexus, business pulse, and shopping center of New York. But as the best things in life are free, Midtown's public art is also some of its most interesting.

Cloud Scenes in the NY Public Library Reading Room.The Main Reading Room has recently undergone a $15 million dollar restoration project that has returned it to its original brilliance. The intricate woodwork and restored ceiling mural have transformed the enormous room into a magnificent space.

Mural with Blue Brush Stroke, in the Atrium of the Equitable Building (787 7th Ave. between 51st and 52st). Roy Lichtenstein's 68-foot master-piece dominates the atrium of this office building. One of Manhattan's largest paintings, the work incorporates over a dozen colors and Lichtenstein signature style into the famous work.

America Today, in the Equitable Building. Painted by Thomas Hart Benton, the prominent artist made famous of his portraits of pre-Depression life, this 1932 mural has been completely restored.

ROCKEFELLER CENTER

Between 48th and 51st Sts. and Fifth and Sixth Aves. Subway: B, D, F, Q to 47th-50th St./Sixth Ave. ***NBC Tour:*** *from the GE Building. Admission $17.50, children and seniors $15; ☎664-3700.* ***Radio City Music Hall Tour:*** *Tours given M-Sa 10am-5pm, Su 9am-5pm. Admission $16, kids under 12 $10.*

Rockefeller Center got its start in the Roaring 1920s when tycoon John D. Rockefeller Jr. wanted to move the Metropolitan Opera to midtown. Depression struck in 1929, and the scheme to move the opera was nixed. Still desiring to use the space for good, Rockefeller scrapped his plan to bring culture to midtown and instead invited in the media. The Center, which was built during the 30s, became home to such radio companies as RKO, RCA, and NBC. Rockefeller's dream is now considered to be one of the most impressive architectural feats in New York City.

The main entrance to Rockefeller Center is on Fifth Ave. between 49th and 50th Sts. **The Channel Gardens,** so named because they sit between the **Maison Francaise** on the left and the **British Empire Building** on the right, usher the pedestrian toward **Tower Plaza**. This sunken space, topped by the gold-leafed statue of **Prometheus**, is surrounded by the flags of over 100 countries. During spring and summer an **ice-skating rink** lies dormant beneath an overpriced cafe. The rink, which is better for people-watching than skating, reopens in winter in time for the **annual Christmas tree lighting,** one of New York's greatest traditions.

Behind Tower Plaza is **The General Electric Building,** 30 Rockefeller Plaza. This 70-story tower, once home to RCA, is the jewel of the complex. The GE Building is notable not only for its scale but also for its extensive artwork. Outside the building's main entrance is Lee Lawrie's limestone and glass frieze of Wisdom. On the inside, Jose Maria Sert's "American Progress" adorns the lobby's walls. NBC, which makes its home here, offers an hour-long tour that traces the history of the network, from their first radio broadcast in 1926 through the heyday of TV programming in the 1950s and 60s to today's sitcoms. The tour visits six studios including the infamous 8H studio, home of Saturday Night Live.

A block north, on the corner of Sixth Ave. and 51st St. is **Radio City Music Hall**. Narrowly escaping demolition in 1979, this Art Deco landmark received a complete interior restoration shortly thereafter. Built in 1932, the 5874-seat theater remains the largest in the world. It functioned as a movie theater between 1933 and 1975, premiering films like *King Kong* and *Breakfast at Tiffany's*. Now it is being used mostly for its original purpose: live performance. Radio City's main attraction is the Rockettes, a high-stepping long-legged troupe of dancers. Tours of the Music Hall take the visitor through The Great Stage and various rehearsal halls.

Back on Fifth Avenue, in front of the **International Building** between 50th and 51st Sts., stands a bronze sculpture of a well-built **Atlas** holding up the weight of the world. Originally, the statue was not welcomed because of its purported resemblance to Italian dictator Benito Mussolini.

If you prefer American consumerism to Fascist rule, try Rockefeller Center's underground concourse, full of shops and restaurants.

ST. PATRICK'S CATHEDRAL

Southeast corner of Fifth Ave. and 51st St. Subway: E, F to 53rd St.-Fifth Ave. ☎ 753-2261.

New York's most famous church and America's largest Catholic cathedral opened in 1879, 21 years after work on it had begun. The construction was not a continuous project, however; the American Civil War put it on hold in the 1860s, and even after its functional opening, the cathedral's famed steeples had yet to be erected. These twin spires, which flank the Fifth Ave. facade and have been captured in countless photos and postcards, reach a height of 330 feet. The Gothic exterior of the cathedral recalls similar European structures, but the interior's majestic nave is close kin to those of Westminster, Exeter, and other English cathedrals. Once inside, it is hard to miss the Great Organ (especially when it is being played). It commands attention with its nearly eight thousand pipes, some of which are as many as thirty-two feet long; it even has a mechanism to simulate the sound of a sixty-four-foot pipe by joining two of these. On the titular window in the South Transept, on the 50th St. side, you'll find a stained-glass portrayal of the life of Saint Patrick.

UNIVERSITY CLUB

NW corner of Fifth Ave. and 54th St. Subway: E, F to 53rd St.-Fifth Ave.

This turn-of-the-century granite palace accommodates aging, rich white guys, and since 1987, aging rich white women. As indicated by its name, this organization was among the first men's clubs to require its members to hold college degrees. Twenty prestigious university crests adorn its facade, which is as close as you'll get to the interior; entrance to the club is for members and guests only.

SONY PLAZA

550 Madison Ave. between 55th and 56th Sts. Subway: N, R to Fifth Ave.–59th St. ☎ 833-8830. Lab open Tu-Sa 10am-6pm, Su noon-6pm. Free.

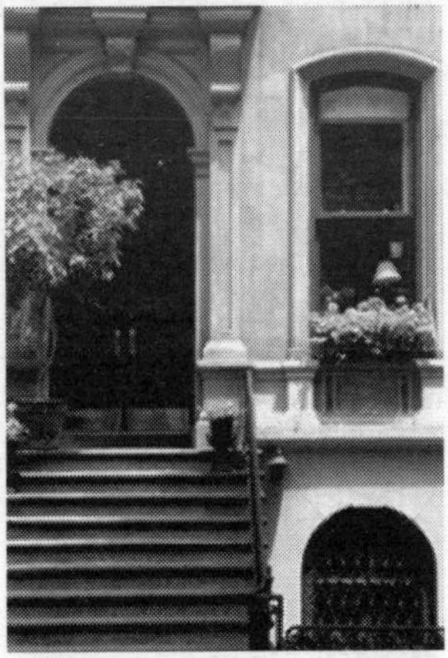

Murray Hill

NY Public Library

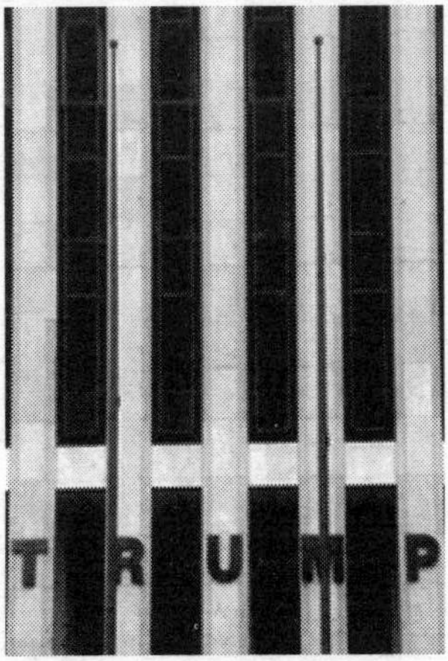

Trump Tower

The Sony Corporation recently bought Philip Johnson's postmodern masterpiece, the erstwhile AT&T Building, and renamed it. It now features two massive superstores offering interaction with state-of-the-art products and free movie screenings of releases by Sony-owned Columbia Pictures. The new Sony Wonder technology lab is an introduction to communications technology. Stop by and play free video games.

CROWN BUILDING

730 Fifth Ave., between 56th and 57th Sts. Subway: N, R to Fifth Ave.-59th St.

Completed in 1919, the Crown Building was originally topped by a 6-foot copper goddess, who was later melted down for the World War II effort. In 1978 (when the building was owned by Ferdinand and Imelda Marcos) the upper tier was overlaid with 24½-carat gold leaf and embedded with colored glass. As the sun sets, the reflected light creates a magnificent crown. The building houses, among others, Playboy Enterprises.

TRUMP TOWER

725 Fifth Ave., at 56th St. Subway: N, R to Fifth Ave.-59th St.

The skyscraper shines as a beacon to excess. Inside, a ludicrous 80-foot waterfall washes into an atrium of orange, pink, and brown marble. The result is tacky with a capital T.

PARK AVENUE

A luxurious boulevard with greenery running down its center, Park Avenue from 45th St. to 59th St. is lined with office buildings and hotels. The avenue fades into apartment buildings as one travels uptown. Sights are listed from **south to north.**

GRAND CENTRAL TERMINAL

E. 42nd St. between Madison and Lexington Aves, where Park Ave. should be. Subway: 4, 5, 6, 7, S to Grand Central-42nd St. Free tours: W 12:30pm from information booth, run by Municipal Arts Society (☎935-3960); F 12:30pm from Philip Morris/Whitney Museum, on 42nd St. across the street from Grand Central, run by the Grand Central Partnership (☎697-1245).

Completed in 1913, Grand Central is a train station of monumental proportions. The richly classical main facade is on 42nd St.; on top of the facade stands a beautiful sculpture of Mercury, Roman god of transportation. Inside, the Main Concourse is the terminal's central space. After a four-year renovation, it has been restored to mint condition, with zodiac constellations lining the newly cleaned ceiling. In the middle of the Concourse sits an information booth, which may be the most popular meeting place in New York. For a sense of the fast pace in the Terminal, follow commuters onto the Main Concourse during rush hour and try doing a few turns around the info booth. Whereas in the past, the whirring masses departed from Grand Central to take voyages across the continent, today trains from the station only travel to Westchester and points north. Some trains leave from the station's lower level, which also contains the **Dining Concourse,** a sleek gallery of 18 restaurants and cafes of various cuisine.

MET LIFE BUILDING

200 Park Ave. Subway: 4, 5, 6, 7, S to Grand Central-42nd St.

An oversized knife stabbing Grand Central Terminal in the back, this building punctuates Park Avenue. Visible from anywhere on the avenue, the building accommodates 2.4 million sq. ft. of corporate cubicles and all the pink marble you can handle.

THE WALDORF-ASTORIA HOTEL

301 Park Ave., between 49th and 50th Sts. Subway: 6 to 51st St.; E, F to 53rd St. ☎355-3000.

Ritzier than the Ritz, the Waldorf-Astoria is the crème de la crème of Park Avenue hotels. The hotel was originally on the site of the Empire State Building, but relocated farther uptown in 1931. Cole Porter's piano sits in the front lounge, and a huge chandelier dominates the lobby. Every US President since Hoover has spent a night or two here while away from the White House. Bask in the luxury that you've been missing in your hostel. $205-$495 for guest rooms, $265-670 for suites.

ST. BARTHOLOMEW'S CHURCH

109 E. 50th St., at Park Ave. Subway: 6 to 51st St; E, F to 53rd St. ☎378-0200.

This Byzantine church draws heavily upon medieval European religious architecture for its inspiration. Completed in 1919, the church features a large mosaic of the Resurrection and a life-sized marble angel in the devotional area left of the altar. St. Bart's hosts a summer festival of classical music on Sundays at 11am as part of its weekly service. Outside of the church is Cafe St. Bart's—a lovely but sinfully expensive—outdoor cafe.

SEAGRAM BUILDING

375 Park Ave., at 53rd St. Subway: 6 to 51st St.; E, F to 53rd St.

This bronze skyscraper, built in 1958, is the only building in the city designed by the architect Ludwig Mies van der Rohe. The plaza in front helps create a sense of grandeur that is out of place along the understated Park Avenue.

CITIGROUP CENTER

The corner of 53rd St. and Lexington Ave. Subway: 6 to 51st St.; E, F to 53rd St.

Built on 10-story stilts to accommodate a Lutheran church, the Citigroup Center is one of the more distinctive buildings in midtown. The 45-degree angled roof was intended to be a solar collector; today, the roof supports a high-tech gadget, the TMD (Tuned Mass Damper), which senses and records the tremors of the earth and warns of earthquakes.

TURTLE BAY AND UNITED NATIONS

Named after an 18th-century farm and located in the east 40s, this neighborhood now plays host to the United Nations, and the diplomats who work there. Sights are listed from **east to west**.

THE UNITED NATIONS BUILDING

First Ave. between 42nd and 48th Sts. Subway: 4, 5, 6, 7, S to Grand Central-42nd St. ☎963-4475; General Assembly ☎963-7713. Tours, in 20 languages, depart from the UN visitor's entrance at First Ave. and 46th St. $7.50, students $5, children 4-14 $4, over 62 $6; disabled 20% discount. Children under 5 not admitted on tour. 1hr; every 15min.; daily 9:15am-4:45pm.

Founded in 1945 in the aftermath of World War II to serve as "a center for harmonizing the actions of nations," the United Nations fittingly makes its home in the world's most diverse city. Though located along what would be First Ave., the UN is international territory and not under the jurisdiction of the US, let alone New York—as evinced by the member nations' 189 flags flying outside at equal height, in flagrant violation of American custom. The complex consists of the Secretariat Building (the skyscraper), the General Assembly Building, the Hammarskjöld Library, and the Conference Building. The only way to view the expansive General Assembly and the council rooms is by guided tour. Outside, a rose garden and statuary park provide a lovely view of the multi-hued East River and the industrial wastelands of western Queens. Also note the statue depicting a muscle-bound man beating a sword into a plowshare; the buff Socialist was a gift to the UN by the former USSR in 1959.

DAILY NEWS BUILDING

220 E. 42nd St., at 2nd Ave. Subway: 4, 5, 6, 7, S to Grand Central-42nd St.

When the building was undertaken in 1930, the *Daily News* had the largest circulation of all the newspapers in New York. Today, the paper, along with the *New York Post*, is one of the two major tabloids in the city. Check out the lobby, a popular tourist attraction when the building opened.

THE CHRYSLER BUILDING

405 Lexington Ave., at 42nd St. Subway: 4, 5, 6, 7, S to Grand Central-42nd St.

A spire influenced by radiator grille design tops this Art Deco palace of industry—one of many details meant to evoke the romance of the automobile in the Chrysler's "Golden Age." Other monuments to motoring include stylized lightning-bolt designs symbolizing the energy of the new machine and flared gargoyles styled after 1929 hood ornaments and hubcaps. During construction in 1929, the Chrysler Building engaged in a race with the Bank of Manhattan building for the title of the world's tallest structure. When the building appeared to be finished, the Bank of Manhattan's building was taller. But with capitalist ingenuity, devious Chrysler machinists then brought out and added the spire that had been secretly assembled inside. While many consider it to be the most aesthetically pleasing building in New York, it ruined architect William Van Alen's career: Walter Chrysler, unsatisfied with the final product, accused Van Alen of embezzlement and refused to pay him. Today, Chrysler no longer has offices in the building.

TIMES SQUARE AND THE THEATER DISTRICT

At 42nd St., Seventh Ave., and Broadway, the city offers up one of the largest electronic extravaganzas in the world. Times Square may have given New York its reputation as a dark metropolis covered with strip clubs, neon, and filth, but today the smut is at least partially cleaned up. Madame Tussaud's and AMC united to rebuild the Liberty, Empire, and Harris theaters into a wax museum and 29-screen movie megaplex. The historic Victory Theater, where Abbot met Costello and Houdini made an elephant disappear, is now the eerily Orwellian "New Victory" Theater. Even though Times Square has become more white bread, one-and-a-half million people still pass through every day. Theater-goers, tourists, and wanderers crowd the streets well into the night.

ONE TIMES SQUARE

At 42nd St., Seventh Ave., and Broadway. Subway: 1, 2, 3, 9, A, C, E, N, Q, R, S.

In 1904, publisher of the *New York Times* Adolph Ochs moved the paper's offices here. Today, however, the *Times'* tackles "all the news that's fit to print" at 229 W. 43rd St., and One Times Square is no more than a giant billboard. On New Year's Eve, millions gravitate to the building to see the ball drop. If you want to get within a half-mile, arrive before 8pm.

THEATER DISTRICT

From 41st to 57th Sts, Broadway to Eighth Ave. Subway: 1, 2, 3, 9, A, C, E, N, Q, R, S. For information on specific theaters, see ***Entertainment**, p. 172.*

While some theaters have been converted into movie houses or simply left to rot as the cost of live productions has skyrocketed, approximately 40 theaters remain active (most of them grouped around 45th St.), 22 of which have been declared historical landmarks. One highlight of the Theater District is **Shubert Alley,** a half-block west of Broadway between 44th and 45th Sts. Originally built as a fire exit between the Booth and Shubert Theaters, the alley now serves as a private street for pedestrians. After shows, fans often hover at stage doors to get their playbills signed.

CENTRAL PARK SOUTH, 57TH ST., AND VICINITY

Luxury hotels, such as the **Essex House,** the **St. Moritz,** and the **Plaza,** overlook Central Park from their perch on Central Park South, between Fifth and Eighth Aves., where 59th St. should be. Two blocks south is 57th St., filled with galleries, stores, and New York's musical mecca, **Carnegie Hall**. Sights are located from **west to east**.

CARNEGIE HALL

881 Seventh Avenue at 57th St. Subway: N, R, W to 57th St.; B, D, E to 53rd St.-Seventh Ave. ☎903-9791 for tours. 1-hr tours M-Tu and Th-F at 11:30am, 2pm, and 3pm. $6, students and seniors $5, under 12 $3. Small museum displaying artifacts and memorabilia, open M-Tu and Th-F 11am-4:30p; free. Museum and tours closed July-Aug. *See Entertainment, p. 182 for concert information.*

Throughout its illustrious and eclectic career, which was inaugurated by the American debut of Tchaikovsky, Carnegie Hall has hosted such artists as Caruso, Toscanini, and Bernstein; jazz greats like Dizzy Gillepsie, Ella Fitzgerald, and Billie Holiday; and rock-and-rollers the Beatles and the Rolling Stones. In the late 1950s, the threat of Carnegie's replacement by an enormous red skyscraper generated a city-wide campaign, led by violinist Isaac Stern, to save the building. In 1960, the campaign convinced the City of New York to purchase the building for $5 million. Decades of patchwork maintenance and periodic face-lifts left the building in various stages of disrepair until 1985 when a $60 million restoration and repair program returned the building to its earlier splendor. Legend has it that prior to the renovation, a hole in the ceiling gave the hall perfect acoustics.

Rockefeller Center

CITY CENTER THEATER

130 W. 55th St. between Sixth and Seventh Ave. Subway: N, R, W to 57th St.; B, D, E to 53rd St.-Seventh Ave.

City Center Theater replaced a mosque in 1943 to become the city's first performing art center. Sickles and crescents still adorn each doorway, four tiny windows face Mecca (or at least the East Side) from the limestone upper stories, and a Moorish dome caps the roof. Venture inside the lobby to see the elaborate tile mosaics surrounding the elevators.

F.A.O. Schwarz

PLAZA HOTEL

Fifth Ave. and 59th St. at Central Park South. Subway: N, R to Fifth Ave.–59th St.

This Henry J. Hardenberg French Renaissance style luxury hotel and historic landmark opened in 1907. Splendid in its carved marble fireplaces and crystal chandeliers, The Plaza consists of Specialty Suites (with names such as Louis XVI and the Vanderbilt), costing up to $15,000 per night, and houses four world-renowned restaurants, including the Oak Room and the Oak Bar. Past guests have included Frank Lloyd Wright, the Beatles, Mark Twain, F. Scott Fitzgerald, and Kay Thompson's fictional character, Eloise.

Times Square at Night

GRAND ARMY PLAZA

59th St. and Fifth Ave. Subway: N, R to Fifth Ave.-59th St.

Inspired by Parisian style, Grand Army Plaza sits in front of the Plaza Hotel and doubles as an entrance to Central Park. The Pulitzer Fountain, with Karl Bitter's bronze statue of Pomona, the goddess of abundance, is set to one side, while directly across from it sits Saint-Gaudens' gilt equestrian statue of Union General William Tecumseh Sherman.

kids IN THE CITY

Wee Ones' Wonderland

Kids love Central Park; these are some of the tots' favorites.

The Friedsam Memorial **Carousel,** brought from Coney Island and restored in 1893, stands at 65th St., west of Center Dr., with its 58 hand-carved horses. (Open M-Sa 10am-6pm, Su 10am-6:30pm, weather permitting; Thanksgiving to mid-Mar. Sa-Su 10am-4:30pm. $1.)

Alice in Wonderland and her friends live at 74th St. off Fifth Ave. A statue of **Hans Christian Andersen,** a gift from Copenhagen in 1956, depicts him with the Ugly Duckling. Children scramble over the statues, sitting in Andersen's lap or clinging precariously to the Mad Hatter's oversized *chapeau.* The NY Public Library sponsors summer storytelling at the Andersen statue, usually Sa 11am; call ☎340-0849 for info.

Formerly a Swedish 19th-century schoolhouse placed in the park in 1876, the **Swedish Cottage Marionette Theater,** at 81st St. mid-park, puts on regular puppet shows. (☎988-9093. Reservations required. Shows usually Tu-F 10:30am and noon, Sa 1pm. Adults $5, children $4.)

With a $20 deposit and valid ID, older children can rent equipment at the Dairy and square off at the nearby **Chess and Checkers House.**

CENTRAL PARK

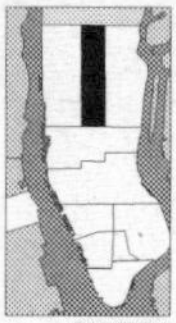

see map p. 336

There is no greenery; it is enough to make a stone sad.
—Nikita Khrushchev, on New York, 1960

Between 59th St. and 110th St., Fifth Avenue and Central Park West. ***General Information:*** *☎360-3444; for parks and recreation info: ☎360-8111 (M-F 9am-5pm). The Central Park Conservancy, which runs the park and offers public programs, has four visitors centers that offer brochures, calendars of events, and* ***free park maps,*** *at* ***Belvedere Castle*** *(☎772-0210), located mid-park at 79th St.; the* ***Charles A. Dana Discovery Center*** *(☎860-1370), at 110th St. near 5th Ave.; the* ***North Meadow Recreation Center*** *(☎348-4867), mid-park at 97th St.; and the* ***Dairy,*** *mid-park near 65th St. The Dairy also showcases exhibits, books, and other collectibles reflecting the history of the park; open Apr.-Oct. Tu-Su 10am-5pm, Nov.-Mar. Tu-Su 10am-4pm.* ***Tours:*** *Trolley tours: from Grand Army Plaza. ☎397-3809. May 1-Nov. M-F 10:30am, 1, and 3pm. Carriage tours: from Central Park South. ☎246-0520. $34 for first 20min., $10 each additional 15min. Central Park Bicycle Tour: from 2 Columbus Circle. ☎541-8759. 10am, 1, and 4pm from 2 Columbus Circle. $30 for 2hr., under 16 $20. New York Skateout: from 72nd St. and Central Park West. ☎486-1919. Tours daily 9am and 5pm. $25 for 1½hr.*

Until the mid-1800s the 843 acres that are now Central Park were considered a social and geographical wasteland. The area was home to over 1600 of the city's poorest residents, including Irish pig farmers, German gardeners, and the black Seneca Village population, all squatters, who occupied shantytowns, huts, and caves on the site. Around 1850 some of New York's wealthiest citizens began to advocate for the creation of a park, claiming that the public space would ameliorate social ills. In truth, the upper class had long envied the public grounds of London and Paris and now sought a playground of their own. Their voices were heard, and in 1857 Frederick Law Olmstead collaborated with Calvert Vaux to win the rights to design the park. Their Greensward Plan, inspired by the English romantic tradition, took 15 years to implement, employing over 20,000 workers.

Olmstead and Vaux's masterpiece is a delicate balance of the natural and the man-made and a must-see for visitors. Sights are listed **from south to north.**

THE CHILDREN'S DISTRICT

Between 59th and 65th Sts. ***The Dairy:*** *65th St., mid-park.* ***Wollman Memorial Rink:*** *between 62nd and 63rd Sts., mid-park. For skating info, see p. 191.* ***Central Park Wildlife Center:*** *between 63rd and 65th Sts., off Fifth Ave. ☎439-6500. Open: Apr.-Oct. M-F 10am-5pm, Sa-Su 10:30am-5:30pm; Nov.-Mar. daily 10am-4:30pm. Last entry 30min. before closing.* ***Tisch Children's Zoo:*** *between 65th and 66th Sts. Combined* *admission to both zoos: $3.50, seniors $1.25, ages 3-12 50¢, under 2 free.*

Vaux and Olmsted designated this area as a place for the young to frolic and receive affordable nourishment. At that time, **The Dairy** distributed food and purity-tested milk to poor families susceptible to food poisoning. Today it is one of the park's information centers. To the south is **Wollman Memorial Rink,** where New Yorkers ice-skate in the winter. To the east is the **Central Park Wildlife Center,** a.k.a. The Zoo, which features polar bears and other mammals that enjoy splashing in the water. North of the zoo is the **Tisch Children's Zoo,** a petting zoo.

SHEEP MEADOW AND THE MALL

Sheep Meadow: From about 66th to 69th St. on the western side of Central Park, directly north of the Hecksher Ballfields. ***Tavern on the Green:*** *West of Sheep Meadow, between 66th and 67th Sts. ☎873-3200. On average, lunch $11-26, dinner $15-37 . Open M-F noon-3:30pm and 5:30-11:30pm, Sa-Su 10am-3:30pm and 5-11:30pm.* ***The Mall:*** *runs roughly on a north-south line between 66th St to 71st St.* ***Bethesda Terrace and Fountain:*** *at the end of the mall, about 72nd St., mid-park.*

Named for the sheep who grazed there until lawnmowers put the flock out of work in 1934, the **Sheep Meadow** was a popular spot for love-ins and drug fests in the 60s and 70s. On summer days, so many tanning bodies cover the Sheep Meadow that some locals have morbidly dubbed it Gettysburg. The restaurant **Tavern on the Green** is located just to the west of the Sheep Meadow. Built in 1870, this rural Victorian Gothic structure originally was home to the sheep who grazed in Sheep Meadow and was only launched as a restaurant in 1934. Even if you can't afford a meal, drop by to stare at the chandeliers, antique prints, paintings, and stained glass.

The Mall, to the east of the Sheep Meadow, is lined with statues of famous artists, especially towards its southern end. Towards the northern part of the walk is **Naumberg Bandshell** and **Rumsey Playfield,** home to Summerstage. At the end of the Mall is **Bethesda Terrace and Fountain,** where crazy skaters pull stunts and hopefully don't land on your head.

THE LAKE AND STRAWBERRY FIELDS

The Lake: *On the west side of the park from approximately 72nd to 77th Sts.* ***Strawberry Fields:*** *West of the Lake at 72nd St. and West Dr.* ***Conservatory Water:*** *At 74th St., off Fifth Ave. ☎673-1102. Boat rental $10 per hr.* ***The Ramble:*** *74th to 79th Sts., mid-park.*

Would-be romantics awkwardly maneuver rowboats around the **Lake.** You can woo your loved one as well, by renting a boat at the **Loeb Boathouse,** mid-park at 75th St. (see **Entertainment,** p. 191.) To the west is **Strawberry Fields,** a memorial to John Lennon, which stands directly across

Strawberry Fields

Merry-Go-Round

Harmony Atrium

from the Dakota Apartments where he was assassinated. Yoko Ono battled for this space against city-council members who had planned a Bing Crosby memorial on the same spot. On John Lennon's birthday, October 9th, thousands gather around the **"Imagine" mosaic** to remember the legend.

To the east of the Terrace and the Lake, competitive model-yachters gather to race at the **Conservatory Water.** Less serious yachters can rent remote-control sailboats. North of the Lake is the **Ramble,** full of narrow trails that will make you forget you're in New York.

THE GREAT LAWN AND TURTLE POND

Great Lawn: *80th to 85th Sts., mid-park.* ***Turtle Pond:*** *Between 79th and 80th Sts., mid-park.* ***Belvedere Castle:*** *Just off the 79th St. Transverse. Observatory open Tu–Su 11am-5pm.* ***Delacorte Theater:*** *80th St., mid-park.*

The Great Lawn dominates the park in the lower 80s. The New York Philharmonic and the Metropolitan Opera Company hold summer performances here (see **Entertainment,** p. 177). Overlooking the lawn and neighboring **Turtle Pond** is **Belvedere Castle,** a whimsical fancy designed by Vaux in 1869. The castle rises from Vista Rock. For many years a weather station, Belvedere Castle has been reincarnated as an education and information center.

The **Delacorte Theater,** home to Shakespeare in the Park, sits adjacent to Turtle Pond. The **Shakespeare Garden,** containing every plant, flower, and herb mentioned in the Bard's works, sits near the Cottage.

THE RESERVOIR AND POINTS NORTH

Reservoir: *from 86th to 95th Sts.* ***Conservatory Garden:*** *105th St., near Fifth Ave. ☎860-1382. Free tours of the Garden summer Sa at 11am. Gates open spring-fall daily 8am-dusk.* ***Harlem Meer:*** *110th St. near Fifth Ave., at the northeast corner of the park. ☎860-1370. Open Tu-Su Apr.-Oct. 10am-5pm; Nov.-Mar. 10am-4pm.*

New Yorkers who jog around the **Reservoir** are treated to wonderful views of the Central Park West skyline. To the north is **Conservatory Garden.** Inspired by the European tradition of formal landscaping, this romantic haven is full of ordered paths and colorful flowers. The Burnett Fountain, located in the center of the south (English) section, depicts Mary and Dickon, from Frances Hodgson Burnett's classic novel *The Secret Garden.* Sundays from late May to early September, this 11-acre lake holds the **Harlem Meer Performance Festival.** The **Charles A. Dana Discovery Center** features exhibitions and activities presenting Central Park as an environmental space to be explored by amateur and professional biologists alike. The Center also leads tours and loans out free fishing rods and bait for use in the Meer; carp, largemouth bass, and chain pickerel abound, but there is a catch-and-release policy in effect.

UPPER EAST SIDE

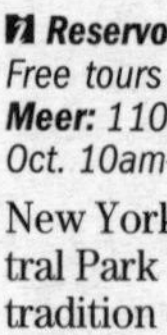

see map pp. 328-329

Since the late 19th and early 20th centuries, when some of New York's wealthiest citizens built elaborate mansions along **Fifth Avenue,** the Upper East Side has been home to the city's richest residents. Today, some of these parkside mansions have been turned into museums, such as the Frick Collection and the Cooper-Hewitt Museum. They are just two of the world-famous museums—including the Metropolitan, the Guggenheim, the Museum of the City of New York—that line **Museum Mile,** from 82nd to 104th Sts. on Fifth Ave.

Madison Avenue, where you might not even be able to afford to window shop, is a fashion mecca. High-end designer boutiques, including Ralph Lauren, Vera Wang, Gucci, Dolce and Gabbana, Max Azria, and Versace, line this expensive walkway (see **Shopping,** p. 212). **Park Avenue** from 59th to 96th Sts. is lined with dignified apartment buildings. North of 96th St., where a train emerges from underground, the avenue takes a sudden change for the worse.

To generalize about the rest of the Upper East Side, **Lexington** and **Third Aves.** are intensely commercial, but as you go east, the neighborhood becomes more and more residential. The area east of Third Ave. between 75th and 96th Sts. was a German neighborhood in the late 19th and early-to-mid 20th century, but today, the only sign of its heritage is the **Schaller and Weber** on 86th St. and Third Ave. Sights are listed **from south to north.**

OLD BOYS CLUBS

i ***Metropolitan Club:** 1 E. 60th St.,* ***Union Club:** 101 E. 69th St.,* ***Knickerbocker Club:** 2 E. 62nd St. Subway: 4, 5, 6, N, R to 59th St.-Lexington Ave.; 6 to 68th St.*

Designed by Stanford White and built by David H. King Jr. to perfectly resemble a 16th-century Italian palazzo, **The Metropolitan Club,** 1 E. 60th St. (first president: J.P. Morgan), was founded in 1891 by a group of distinguished gentlemen who were disgruntled with the rejection of some of their friends from the very exclusive **Union Club,** 101 E. 69th St. Inversely, **The Knickerbocker Club** was founded in 1871 by Union men who believed that the club's admissions policies had become *too* lax and liberal. Member names you might recognize: Hamilton, Eisenhower, Roosevelt, Rockefeller, dare we continue?

ARTS CLUBS

i ***Grolier Club:** 47 E. 60th St., between Madison and Park Aves. ☎838-6690.* ***Lotos Club:** E. 66th St. between Madison and Fifth Aves. Subway: 4, 5, 6, N, R to 59th St.-Lexington Ave.; 6 to 68th St.*

The **Grolier Club,** an organization of book collectors, was founded in 1884 and named in honor of Jean Grolier, prominent bibliophile during the Renaissance. Completed in 1917, this Georgian structure houses a collection of fine bookbindings, quarterly exhibitions, and a specialized research library open by appointment. The French Renaissance style, Richard Hunt-designed **Lotos Club,** an organization of actors, musicians, and journalists, was founded in 1870.

TEMPLE EMANU-EL

i 1 E. 65th St. at Fifth Ave. Subway: 6 to 68th St. ☎744-1400.

The largest Reform Jewish house of worship in the world, Temple Emanu-El was built in 1929 for a primarily German-American congregation. The Romanesque facade of the building is imposing, but the inside is home to some remarkable stained-glass windows.

CHURCH OF ST. JEAN BAPTISTE

i Corner of Lexington Ave. and 76th St. Subway: 6 to 77th St. ☎472-2853.

The multi-domed Catholic **Church of St. Jean Baptiste** seems seriously out of place on busy Lexington Ave. To get a good look at its splendid paired towers and Corinthian porticoes, cross over to the other side of Lexington Ave. The inside of the building is rich, and the lively acoustics make it a wonderful place to hear music.

Bryant Park

Sotheby's

Lincoln Center

CARL SCHURZ PARK

Between 84th and 90th St. along East End Ave. Subway: 4, 5, 6 to 86th St. Closes at 1am. ***Gracie Mansion:*** *☎570-4751. 50min. tours by reservation only; Open Mar. to mid-Nov. W at 10 and 11am, and 1 and 2pm. Suggested donation $4; seniors $3.*

Named for the German immigrant who served as a a Missouri senator and editor of the *New York Tribune*, the park overlooks the turbulent waters of Hell's Gate. **John Finley Walk,** which begins at E. 82nd St., forms a border on the eastern side of the park. Perfect for a romantic stroll, this strip also provides a spectacular view of the East River. **Gracie Mansion,** at the northern end of the park (E. 88th St.), has been the official home of the mayor of New York City since 1942.

HENDERSON PLACE HISTORIC DISTRICT

East End Ave., between 86th and 87th Sts. Subway: 4, 5, 6, to 86th St.

The remaining 24 of the original 32 connected, Queen Anne-style inspired houses of the Henderson Place Historic District. Completed in 1882 and intended for "persons of moderate means" (no longer), they flaunt beautiful gables, dormers, mansards, and, some say, ghosts.

CHURCH OF THE HOLY TRINITY

316 E. 88th St. between First and Second Aves. Subway: 4, 5, 6 to 86th St.

This French Gothic-influenced church was originally built to minister Episcopalian services to the poorer residents of Yorkville. Though there are no longer poor residents, the church, set back from the street, nicely complements the surroundings and graces the neighborhood with a small garden in front.

ST. NICHOLAS RUSSIAN ORTHODOX CATHEDRAL

15 E. 97th St. Subway: 6 to 96th St.

Five onion domes exuberantly top this cathedral designed in Russian Baroque style. The church was built in 1901 with money from Tsar Nicholas II and today continues to attract Russian immigrants in New York.

UPPER WEST SIDE

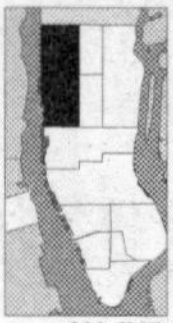

see map pp. 332-333

While **Central Park West** and **Riverside Drive** flank the Upper West Side with residential quietude, **Columbus Avenue, Amsterdam Avenue,** and **Broadway** are abuzz with action. The gods of organic fruit and progressive politics will reward you for wandering their domain. Sights are listed from **south to north.**

COLUMBUS CIRCLE

Intersection of Broadway, Eighth Ave., and Central Park South. Subway: A, B, C, D, 1, 9 to 59th St./Columbus Circle.

This bustling nexus of pedestrian and automobile traffic is where Midtown ends and the Upper West Side begins. The circle takes its name from the memorial to Columbus that stands in the middle of the traffic circle. On the west side of the circle you'll see the **New York Coliseum,** built in 1954 by the TriBoro Bridge and Tunnel Authority to serve as the city's convention center. Nearby, a monument on the entrance to Central Park commemorates those who died on the *USS Maine*, while at 1 Central Park West stands the black glass facade of Donald Trump's gargantuan monstrosity, the **Trump International Hotel and Towers.** A shiny, silver globe adorns the Towers' facade—a sign of Trump's next real estate acquisition, perhaps?

THE GALLERY AT THE AMERICAN BIBLE SOCIETY

1865 Broadway, at 61st St. Subway: A, B, C, D, 1, 9 to 59th St.-Columbus Circle. ☎408-1500; www.americanbible.org. Wheelchair access. Gallery open M-W and F 10am-6pm, Th 10am-7pm, Sa 10am-5pm. Library open M-F 10am-5pm. Free.

The American Bible Society distributes the Good Book in nearly every tongue. Its gallery showcases rotating exhibitions of Judeo-Christian art, as well as rare and unorthodox Bibles, a smattering of Guttenberg pages, and an online Bible. In 2002, exhibitions will include *In Search of Mary Magdalene* (April 5-June 29) and *Icons or Portraits? Images of Jesus and Mary Across Ten Centuries* (July 26-November 15).

LINCOLN CENTER

Columbus Ave., between 62nd and 66th Sts. Subway: 1, 9 to 66th St. ☎546-2656, 875-5350; www.lincolncenter.org. ***Info booth*** *near the Avery Hall entrance.* ***Tours*** *of theaters and galleries start daily at the concourse, under the Met Opera House; 1hr.; 10:30am, 12:30pm, 2:30pm, 4:30pm; $9.50; students and seniors $8; children $4.75. Backstage Met Opera House tours M-F 3:45pm, Sa 10am; ☎769-7020 to reserve.*

The seven facilities that constitute New York's center for established art cover 16 acres and at full capacity accommodate over 13,000 spectators. Power broker Robert Moses masterminded Lincoln Center when Carnegie Hall (see p. 76) seemed fated for destruction in 1955. The ensuing construction forced the eviction of thousands and erased a major part of the Hell's Kitchen area (see p. 70). The complex was designed as a modern version of the public plazas of Rome and Venice, and despite the opinions of critics (the *Times* called it "a hulking disgrace"), the spacious, uncluttered architecture—as well as the performances that take place here—have made it one of New York's most admired locales.

The buildings of Lincoln Center are set around the **Josie Robertson Plaza,** where the cast of *Fame* danced at the beginning of each show. Straight ahead is the Mondrian-inspired glass facade of Lincoln Center's 1966 centerpiece, the **Metropolitan Opera House,** designed by Wallace K. Harrison. Chagall murals grace the plaza and lobby, where a grand, multi-tiered staircase await the humble opera buff. (See **Entertainment,** p. 182.)

To the left side of the plaza as you face the Opera House is the **New York State Theater,** home of the New York City Ballet and the New York City Opera (see **Entertainment,** p. 182). **Damrosch Park,** behind the theater, hosts frequent outdoor concerts and the perennially popular Big Apple Circus in the Guggenheim Bandshell.

On the right side of the plaza is **Avery Fisher Hall,** designed in 1966 by Max Abramovitz and home to the New York Philharmonic (see **Entertainment,** p. 181). To the right of the opera house are the **Vivian Beaumont Theater** and **Mitzi E. Newhouse Theater,** both housed in an Eero Saarinen-designed glass box.

A footbridge across 66th St. leads to the prestigious **Juilliard School.** Here Itzhak Perlman and Pinchas Zukerman fine-tuned their skills, and Robin Williams tried out his first comedy routines. Within the Juilliard building complex you'll find the intimate **Alice Tully Hall,** home to the Chamber Music Society of Lincoln Center (see **Entertainment,** p. 181). Behind Juilliard stands the **Walter E. Reade Theater,** which features foreign films and special festivals (see **Entertainment,** p. 184).

Zabar's

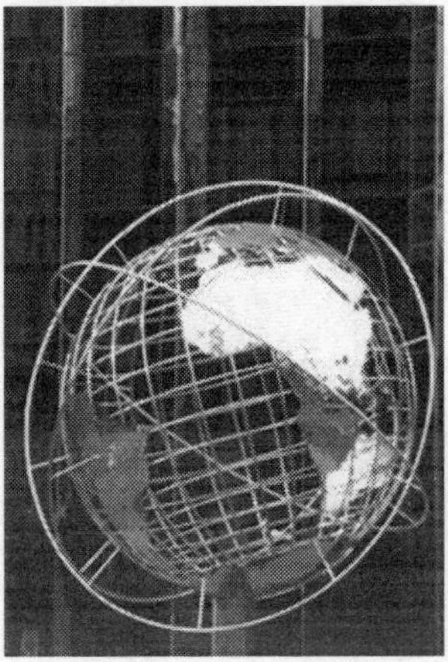
Columbus Circle

Malcolm X Church

HOTEL DES ARTISTES

1 W. 67th St. between Central Park W. and Columbus Ave. Subway: 1, 9 to 66th St.; B, C to 72nd St.

Built by George Mort Pollard in 1913, this stately mass of luxury co-ops was originally designed to house bohemians who had moved beyond their romantic garret stage. Here you will also find the famously romantic—but prohibitively expensive—**Café des Artistes.** The pastoral murals of reclining nudes, painted in 1934 by Howard Chandler Christy, deserve a peek.

DAKOTA APARTMENTS

1 W. 72nd St., at the corner of Central Park West. Subway: B, C to 72nd St.

Perhaps Manhattan's most famous apartment building, the Dakota counts Lauren Bacall, Leonard Bernstein, Roberta Flack, and Boris Karloff as its former residents. When constructed in 1884, the complex was surrounded by open land and shanties, and so far removed from the city that someone remarked, "It might as well be in the Dakota Territory." The name stuck, and architect Henry Hardenbergh (later architect of the Plaza Hotel) even gave the elegant building a frontier flare—look for the bas-relief Native American head and the stone garnish of corn and arrowheads that adorn the "territory." Beyond its history, the Dakota's claims to fame are rather macabre: *Rosemary's Baby* was filmed here, and resident John Lennon was assassinated outside on December 8, 1980.

ANSONIA HOTEL

2109 Broadway, between 73rd and 74th Sts. Subway: 1, 2, 3, 9 to 72nd St.

The *grande dame* of *beaux* apartments bristles with ornaments, curved Veronese balconies, and towers. Constructed in the Beaux-Arts style in 1904, the Ansonia has 2,500 apartments as well as various cafes, tea rooms, writing rooms, and a dining room seating 550. Its soundproof walls and thick floors enticed illustrious musically-inclined tenants like Enrico Caruso, Arturo Toscanini, and Igor Stravinsky. William Stokes, the developer of the Ansonia, used the building for an entirely different purpose—he raised chickens, ducks, and a pet bear on its roof. Worth strolling by, but you can't venture inside.

APTHORP APARTMENTS

2211 Broadway, at 79th St. Subway: 1, 9 to 79th St.

The Apthorp's ornate iron gates, vaulted carriageways, and spacious interior courtyard have starred in a number of New York-based films such as *The Cotton Club* and *Network*. Its simple marble facade features bas-relief vestal virgins. The apartments were built in 1908 on commission from William Waldorf Astor, who named them after the man who owned the site in 1763. Ask the guard to let you check out the courtyard.

EL DORADO APARTMENTS

300 Central Park West, between 90th and 91st Sts. Subway: B, C to 86th St., 96th St.

This appropriately named residence showcases flashy Art Deco detailing in a full array of golds. The El Dorado lobby is a national landmark, and well worth a stop if you can convince the numerous security guards that you won't sneak a visit to the stars who reside there.

RIVERSIDE PARK

West of Riverside Dr., from 72nd St. to the George Washington Bridge/175th St.

Along the Hudson River lies Riverside Park, where Upper West Siders walk their pooches. The park is desolate at night, but provides wonderful views of the river and the Palisades in New Jersey.

see map pp. 334-335

MORNINGSIDE HEIGHTS

Above 110th Street and below 125th, this area, caught between the chaos of Harlem and the color of the Upper West Side, is dominated by Barnard College and Columbia University.

Sights are listed from **south to north**.

CATHEDRAL OF ST. JOHN THE DIVINE

Amsterdam Ave. between 110th and 113th Sts. Subway: 1, 9 to 110th St. ☎316-7540; tours ☎932-7347. Open M-Sa 7am-6pm, Su 7am-8pm. Suggested donation $2, students and seniors $1. Vertical tours (you go up 124ft.) noon and 2pm on 1st and 3rd Sa of month; $10; reservations necessary. Regular horizontal tours Tu-Sa 11am, Su 1pm; $3.

A cathedral where creation is not only for the divine, unfinished St. John's has been under construction since 1892. St. John's is the largest cathedral in the world and one of the most worldly, featuring altars and bays dedicated not only to the sufferings of Christ, but also to the experiences of immigrants and victims of genocide and AIDS. The central nave contains a 100-million-year-old nautilus fossil; the world's second largest organ stop, which consists of some 8035 pipes; and a "Poet's Corner" honoring writers such as Nathaniel Hawthorne and Edith Wharton. Stained-glass windows depict everything from religious scenes to a 1925 prototype television. With a poet and two dance companies in residence, the Cathedral's extensive secular schedule complements Episcopal services with concerts, art exhibitions, poetry readings, lectures, theater, and dance events. The complex also contains a Greek amphitheater (still under construction), a peace fountain, a children's sculpture garden, and a Biblical Garden.

COLUMBIA UNIVERSITY

Morningside Dr. and Broadway, from 114th to 120th Sts. Subway: 1 or 9 to 116th St. Group tours for prospective students late fall through spring, but no regularly scheduled public tours.

Chartered in 1754 as King's College, the university lost its original name in the American Revolution. In 1897 President Seth Low, seeking a healthy academic environment for students and professors, moved the school to its current location. The campus, designed by prominent New York architects McKim, Mead & White, is urban (don't come looking for grass), yet removed from surrounding Morningside Heights. Its centerpiece, the majestic Roman Classical **Low Library,** looms over **College Walk,** the school's central promenade bustling with academics, students, and quacks. The statue of **Alma Mater** in front of the building was a rallying point during the riots of 1968. Resilient and proud, Alma survived a bomb during student protests in 1970. Just to the east of Low Library stands **St. Paul's Chapel,** a small but beautiful space with magnificent acoustics.

RIVERSIDE CHURCH

120th St. and Riverside Dr. Subway: 1, 9 to 116th St. ☎870-6792. Bell tower open Tu-Sa 10:30am-5pm, Su 9:45-10:45am and noon-4pm. Admission to observation deck Tu-Sa $2, students and seniors $1. Free tours Su 12:30pm.

Apollo Theater

Fort Tyron Park

125th Street

This steel-framed imitation of the Cathedral in Chartres was constructed in only two years, thanks to John D. Rockefeller Jr.'s philanthropy. Officially opened in 1930, this church is interdenominational. The tower observation deck looms 362 feet above Riverside Dr. and commands an amazing view both of the bells within and the expanse of the Hudson River and Riverside Park below. Best heard from the parks around the church, concerts on the world's largest carillon—74 bells built in memory of Rockefeller's mother—resonate on Su at 10:30am, 12:30pm, and 3pm.

GRANT'S TOMB

Near the intersection of Riverside Dr. and 122nd St. Subway: 1, 9 to 125th St. ☎666-1640. Open daily 9am-5pm. Free. Informal ranger-guided tours on request.

This massive granite mausoleum—the largest of its kind in America—rests atop a hill overlooking the Hudson River. Once covered with graffiti, the monument to Civil War general and 18th US President Ulysses S. Grant is now pristine. Bronze casts of other Union generals surround the tomb where Grant and his wife Julia lie. Vibrant and surrealist mosaic tile benches sit around the monument, inspired by Antonio Gaudí and added in the mid-1970s.

HARLEM

see map pp. 334-335

Harlem is a place where I like to eat, sleep, drink, and be in love.
-Langston Hughes

Over the years Harlem has entered the popular psyche as the archetype of America's frayed edges, but you won't believe the hype once you've actually visited the place.

The largest neighborhood in all of Manhattan, Harlem extends from 110th Street to the 150s, between the Hudson and East Rivers. Between 1910 and 1920, during a collapse in the real-estate market, Harlem began its transformation into a black neighborhood. The 1920s brought prosperity to Harlem and an artistic and literary movement known as the Harlem Renaissance was launched (see **Life & Times,** p. 42).

In the 1960s, riding the tidal wave of the Civil Rights movement, the radical Black Power movement thrived here. LeRoi Jones's Revolutionary Theater performed one-act plays in the streets, and Malcolm X, Stokely Carmichael, and H. Rap Brown spoke against racism and injustice. But in spite of the activism, Harlem's economic welfare was declining rapidly. In the 1970s and 80s, members of the community recognized the need for economic revitalization as a route to empowerment. Today, thanks to the economic boom of the 1990s, pockets of Harlem are thriving again.

NATURAL NEW YORK

Due to its size and residential nature, Harlem has many parks perfect for a relaxing picnic or stroll after the bustle of Midtown. Visit one of the following if NYC is getting too stifling for your suburban sensibilities.

Morningside Park. You too can discuss your sexual fantasies in this strolling park, just like Meg Ryan in *When Harry Met Sally. (Along the Hudson River, between 110th and 123rd Sts.)*

Sakura Park. Japanese for "cherry blossoms," the sakura were a gift to the city in 1912. Features a statue of General Daniel Butterfield, best known for composing "Taps." *(Across the street from Grant's Tomb.)*

Riverbank State Park. The state resolved to put a sewage plant here in 1993, an act many considered racist, so Gov. Cuomo built a state-run park over it. Ice and roller rinks, pool, tennis, tracks, baseball diamonds, and picnic fields make up for the sewage. The officials have vanquished the odor problem ("really, it's tidewater")—the park is surprisingly clean. *(Off the West Side Highway, enter at 135th St. ☎693-3654.)*

Jackie Robinson Park. Originally Colonial Park, these 12.8 acres were renamed in 1978; the hero himself stands in bronze at its center. *(145th-152nd St. between Edgecombe and Bradhurst Aves.)*

Marcus Garvey Park. Named after the "Back-to-Africa" movement advocate, this park features huge canopy trees and sloping rocks. *(120th-124th Sts. between Fifth and Madison Aves.)*

Spanish Harlem or El Barrio sits between 96th and 125th Sts. on the East Side. A large Mexican and Puerto Rican population resides here. The neighborhood's main artery is E. 116th St. On your way up Park Avenue on the east side, you will be confronted by stark examples of social and cultural stratification: north of 96th Street, bedraggled men sleeping in doorways take the place of uniformed doormen. There are still pockets of brilliance within this poverty, however, such as the **Graffitti Wall of Fame** at 106th Street and Park Avenue. El Barrio is at its best on **Puerto Rican Independence Day,** June 20, when streets close off for serious festivity. Sights are listed from **south to north.**

TERESA HOTEL

Southwest corner of 125th St. and Powell Ave. Subway: 2, 3 to 125th St.

After its segregation policy was dropped in 1940, the Teresa reigned for some years as the "Waldorf of Harlem." Despite the hotel's significance in the community as a center for civil rights advocacy, the historic building has been reduced to a corporate space and can now only be appreciated from the outside.

CITY COLLEGE

Convent Ave. from 135th to 41st St., enter at 138th St. Subway: 1, 9 to 137th St.

The sloping campus shelters Collegiate Gothic style buildings and sprawling green lawns. Founded in 1847 by Townsend Harris to provide immigrants and the poor a chance to receive a higher education, City College is the nation's first public college and the alma mater of Woody Allen and Colin Powell.

THE SCHOMBURG CENTER FOR RESEARCH IN BLACK CULTURE

135th St. and Lenox Ave. Subway: 2, 3 to 135th St. ☎491-2265 or 491-2200. Open M-Sa 10am-6pm, Su 1-5pm. Free.

This research branch of the public library houses the city's archives on black history and culture. The center's namesake, avid black history scholar Arturo Schomburg, collected photographs, oral histories, and artwork, all of which are incorporated into the center's collection (a five-million object bounty). The center also houses the **American Negro Theater,** famous during the 1940s, and **The Langston Hughes Auditorium,** a venue for a wide range of entertainment including concerts and plays featuring both local talent and celebrities. The center also features impressive exhibits of photographs and other artwork, in addition to providing a wealth of information for minority travelers (see **Living in NYC,** p. 277). The

Cathedral of St. John the Divine

The Dakota Apartments

Columbia University

SUGAR DADDY

Perhaps Harlem's most prized possessions are its historic buildings, especially its beautiful brownstones. Below are the neighborhood's most famous.

SUGAR HILL. In the 1920s and 30s, African-Americans with "sugar" (a.k.a. money) moved here. In addition to leaders W.E.B. DuBois and Thurgood Marshall—both of whom lived at 409 Edgecombe—and musical legends Duke Ellington and W.C. Handy, some of the city's most notable gangsters operated here. (Wesley Snipes starred as one in the film *Sugar Hill.*) The area is also the birthplace of Sugarhill Records, the rap label that created the Sugarhill Gang, whose 1979 "Rapper's Delight" became the first hip-hop song to reach the Top 40. *(143rd to 155th St. between St. Nicholas and Edgecombe Aves.)*

STRIVER'S ROW. A group of impressive 1891 brownstones presents a combination of architectures, from neo-Colonial to Italian Renaissance. Originally envisioned as a "model housing project" for middle-class whites, legend says Striver's Row acquired its nickname from lower class Harlemites who felt their neighbors were striving to attain uppity middle-class status. Now part of the St. Nicholas Historic District, the neighborhood appears in Spike Lee's *Jungle Fever. (138th and 139th Sts. between Powell and Fredrick Douglass Blvds.)*

research library is large and impressive with a year-round exhibit featuring brief biographies of 100 notable black New Yorkers.

THE ABYSSINIAN BAPTIST CHURCH

132 W. 138th St. between Malcolm X and Powell Blvds. Subway: 2, 3 to 135th St. ☎862-7474. Su services 9am and 11am.

Postured nobly on a dilapidated block, this church has seen its share of famous pastors. Adam Clayton Powell Jr. presided over the pulpit until 1930 before becoming NYC's first black congressman. Powell's father, Adam Clayton Powell Sr., a legendary figure credited with catalyzing the black migration to Harlem, preceded his son at this church. Today, the eloquent Calvin Butts, also a well-known local political leader, preaches to the over 5000-member congregation and draws an enormous crowd each Sunday.

HAMILTON HEIGHTS

Between Convent and Edgecombe Aves., 145th and 149th Sts. Subway 1 or 9 to 145th St. station. ***Hamilton Grange*** *open F-Su 9am-5pm.*

Between Convent and St. Nicholas Aves. rests a residential neighborhood full of intricately designed brownstones. The two-story Colonial-style **Hamilton Grange,** 287 Convent Ave., was built by founding father and co-author of the *Federalist Papers*, Alexander Hamilton. In the next few years, the National Parks Service will restore the house, making it a national landmark and moving it to a more spacious lot in St. Nicholas Park.

WASHINGTON HEIGHTS

see map pp. 334-335

The hilly Washington Heights out-slopes Park Slope (p. 93), and its several parks make it one of the greenest neighborhoods in the five boroughs. Buildings perched atop high ridges peer down hundreds of feet onto their next-door neighbors. Once predominantly Irish, Washington Heights now joins large Latino, black, Greek, Armenian, and Jewish communities, and has had to deal with its share of cultural clashes.

Sights are listed from **south to north.**

MORRIS-JUMEL MANSION

65 Jumel Terrace between 160th and 162nd Sts. Subway: C to 163rd St. ☎923-8008. Open W-Su 10am-4pm. $3; seniors and students $2. Accompanied children under 12 free. Guided tours by appointment; add 50¢ to admission, $1.50 for children under 12.

Built in 1765, the Georgian Morris-Jumel Mansion is Manhattan's oldest free-standing house.

George Washington lived here while devising his battle plan for the successful (but little-known) Battle of Harlem Heights in 1776. In 1810 Stephen and Eliza Jumel purchased the house, and after Stephen died in 1832, Eliza married Aaron Burr in the front room in 1833. In addition to both Washington and Burr's bed chambers, the house boasts elaborate carved and gilded furniture and an interesting two-floor octagonal wing. The gardens are exceptional, with a great view of the Harlem River. Don't be afraid to knock if the house seems closed. Across the street on **Sylvan Terrace,** French colonial houses vie for attention.

AUDUBON BALLROOM

165th St. between Broadway and St. Nicholas Ave. Subway: C to 163rd St.

On February 21, 1965, during a rally, black leader Malcolm X was assassinated on the grounds of this building by three of his former supporters. The Audubon was rededicated by Mayor Rudy Giuliani in 1997, partly as a memorial to Malcolm X and primarily as a medical research center. While most of the ballroom has been swallowed by commercial space (a bank and a restaurant) a memorial to Malcolm X will be opening in the next few years.

GEORGE WASHINGTON BRIDGE

Best view from the corner of 181st St. and Riverside Dr. Subway: A to 181st St. Great views of Manhattan from the walking path on the bridge itself. Toll: $6 from NJ to NY, free from NY to NJ.

The construction of this 14-lane, 3500-foot suspension bridge coincided with the beginning of the Great Depression, and the ensuing purse-tightening left the bridge's two towers without the granite sheathing designer Othmar Amman had intended. The naked steelwork creates the precociously postmodern, erector-set look that so excited Le Corbusier: he proclaimed it "the most beautiful bridge in the world."

LITTLE RED LIGHTHOUSE

Subway: A to 181st. St. From the intersection of Riverside Dr. and 181st St., go west across the suspended walkway. From there, follow the path to the edge of the water. ☎304-2365. Tours available, if you call ahead.

Originally constructed in 1921 to steer barges away from Jeffrey's Hook, the lighthouse is perhaps best known from Hildegarde Hoyt Swift's book **The Little Red Lighthouse and the Great Grey Bridge**. The trail to the Lighthouse is spooky—don't travel it alone or at night.

YESHIVA UNIVERSITY

Amsterdam Ave. from 182nd to 186th Sts. Subway: 1, 9 to 181st St.

An island of pallid university buildings, Yeshiva sits in the middle of a bustling Hispanic neighborhood. The recently renamed David H. Zysman Hall is the centerpiece of the campus. The Gothic building features Romanesque windows and colorful minarets that contrast with the drab, institutional architecture of the rest of the campus.

FORT TRYON PARK

Bounded by Broadway on the east, the Hudson River on the west, Riverside Dr. on the north, and Overlook Terrace to the south. Subway: 1, 9 to 190th St.; A to 190th St. Conservancy instructors take people to climb about twice a month. ☎342-4865.

Central Park's Frederick Law Olmstead lovingly landscaped this park, which was donated to the city by John D. Rockefeller in 1935 in exchange for permission to construct Rockefeller University. You can still see the crumbling remains of Fort Tryon, a Revolutionary War bulwark captured by the British in 1776. The park also contains a path that offering views of the Palisades and **The Cloisters,** the Met's palatial sanctuary for medieval art (see **Museums,** p. 113). If you're an experienced climber you can register to climb up and rappel down the 50-ft. face of the cliff on the eastern side of the park.

BROOKLYN

see map pp. 336-337

The Dutch named this area Breuckelen, or "Broken Land." Displaying typical resilience, the city of Brooklyn refused when asked to join New York City in 1833, claiming that the two cities shared no interests except common waterways. Not until 1898 did the citizenry decide in a close vote to join New York City's boroughs. In the early 20th century, European immigrants flowed into the borough in great numbers, and after the Great Depression black Southerners also sought haven in Brooklyn. Today, Brooklyn is New York City's most populous borough.

In the coverage below, **neighborhoods are arranged from north to south.**

WILLIAMSBURG AND GREENPOINT

Having become home to a growing number of artists in the last decade, **Williamsburg** has the galleries to match its artsy population (see **Museums and Galleries,** p. 123). The neighborhood's flare for the funky centers around Bedford Avenue and Berry Streets. In the south side of town, along Broadway, Heyward Street, Wythe Street, and Bedford Avenue, thrives a Hassidic Jewish community, where men wear long black coats and hats that recall the garb of the Polish nobility of Eastern Europe. North of Broadway is predominantly Latino. **Greenpoint,** bounded by Java St. to the north, Meserole St. to the south, and Franklin St. to the west, is Brooklyn's northernmost border with Queens and home to a large Polish population. The birthplace of Mae West, Brooklynese, and the Union's Civil War ironclad **Monitor,** Greenpoint is also home to charming Italianate and Grecian houses built during the shipbuilding boom of the 1850s.

RUSSIAN ORTHODOX CATHEDRAL OF THE TRANSFIGURATION

228 N. 12th St. Subway: L to Bedford Ave.; G to Nassau Ave.

Five striking, copper-covered, onion-shaped domes carry you off to Mother Russia. Built between 1916 and 1921, the cathedral's gorgeous stained-glass windows and triple-slashed crosses are just a hint of the beauty within.

BROOKLYN BREWERY

79 N. 11th St. Subway: L to Bedford Ave.; G to Nassau Ave. ☎718-486-7422. Tap room open F 6-10pm, Sa noon-5pm; tours and tastings Sa noon-4:30pm.

In the days when beer was an alternative to an unsanitary water supply, thirsty immigrants with brewing know-how began a century-long Brooklyn legacy. Although poor business in the 1960s brought the beer boom to an end, the spirit continues in the Brooklyn Brewery, established in 1987. Making Brooklyn Lager and Brooklyn Brown Ale, beer that you'll find in the borough's bars, the brewery is a busy factory during the week and a lively spot on the weekend for the curious and for those who just want to knock one back.

FULTON LANDING AND DUMBO

Fulton Landing hearkens back to days when the ferry—not the subway or the car— was the primary means of transportation between Brooklyn and Manhattan. The Fulton Ferry traveled between the Fulton St. in Brooklyn and the Fulton St. in Manhattan. DUMBO, which stands for Down Under Manhattan Bridge Overpass (ugh), is home to a thriving arts scene.

BROOKLYN BRIDGE

From Brooklyn: entrance from the end of Adams St. Subway: A, C to High St.-Brooklyn Bridge. From Manhattan: entrance from Park Row. Subway: 4, 5, 6 to Brooklyn Bridge-City Hall.

A walk across the Brooklyn Bridge at sunrise or sunset is one of the most exhilarating strolls New York City has to offer—especially when you're dodging the cyclists on the pedestrian path. The bridge gracefully spans the gap between Lower Manhattan's dense cluster of skyscrapers and Brooklyn's less intimidating shore. Georgia O'Keefe and Joseph Stella have memorialized this technological and aesthetic triumph on canvas, while Hart Crane and Walt Whitman expressed their admiration in verse.

Completed in 1883, the bridge is the product of elegant calculation, careful design, and human exertion. After chief architect John Augustus Roebling crushed his foot in a surveying accident and died of gangrene, his son Washington took over. When Washington himself succumbed to the bends, Washington's wife Emily Warren inherited the project. Plaques at either end of the walkway commemorate the Roeblings and the 20 workers who died in the bridge's underwater chambers during construction. A gallery and performance space is housed within the bridge's cavernous suspension cable storage chambers. See **Museums and Galleries,** p. 123.

Brooklyn Heights Promenade

FULTON FERRY

At the East River end of Old Fulton St. Subway: A, C to High St.-Brooklyn Bridge

From 1642 until 1924, a ferry ran services from here to Manhattan, and in the 19th century this was one of Brooklyn's major centers of trade. The bustle is gone now, but there are still beautiful views of Lower Manhattan and the Brooklyn Bridge to be had from the pier.

Brooklyn Bridge

THE EAGLE WAREHOUSE AND STORAGE CO.

28 Old Fulton St., at Front St. Subway: A, C to High St.-Brooklyn Bridge.

The *Brooklyn Eagle* newspaper was once printed in a building on this site. Its editor, Brooklyn poet-laureate Walt Whitman, was fired due either to laziness or to his bold anti-slavery views, depending upon the slant of your source. The current structure is an impressive 1894 warehouse that has been converted into apartments.

DOWN UNDER MANHATTAN BRIDGE OVERPASS (DUMBO)

The area between the Brooklyn Bridge and the Manhattan Bridge. Subway: F to York St., A, C to High St.-Brooklyn Bridge.

The area surrounding the Manhattan Bridge has long been an artistic haven. Some old warehouse spaces in this growing artistic area have been made into galleries by Brooklyn's volunteer artist militia: the numerous tacked-on buzzers on the door of **135 Plymouth St.,** at Anchorage Pl., indicate the building's several makeshift galleries (see **Museums and Galleries,** p. 123).

Brooklyn Brownstones

BROOKLYN HEIGHTS AND DOWNTOWN

Subway: M, N, R, 2, 3, 4, 5 to Court St./Borough Hall.

Brooklyn Heights, a well-preserved 19th-century residential area, sprang up with the development of steamboat transportation between Brooklyn and Manhattan in 1814. Rows of posh Greek Revival and Italianate houses in this area essentially created New York's first suburb. **Montague Street,** the neighborhood's main drag, has the stores, cafes, and mid-priced restaurants of a cute college town. Arthur Miller and W.H. Auden called this area home in the 1940s and 50s. Young, upwardly mobile types make this area home, while **Atlantic Ave.** has a thriving Middle Eastern community. **Downtown** is the location of Brooklyn's Civic Center, and strolling through you'll find several grand municipal buildings. Sights are listed **from north to south.**

PROMENADE

By the East River between Remsen and Orange Sts. Subway: 2, 3 to Clark St.

The view of the lower Manhattan skyline and the Brooklyn Bridge from this waterfront walkway is one of *the* New York sights to see—even if it doubles as the roof of the toxic Brooklyn-Queens Expressway (BQE). To the left, Lady Liberty peeps from behind Staten Island, and in fair weather, Ellis Island appears in full view.

PLYMOUTH CHURCH OF PILGRIMS

75 Hicks St., off Henry St. ☎ 718-624-4743. Subway: 2, 3 to Clark St.

Before the Civil War, this simple red-brick church was part of the underground railroad and the center of New York abolitionist sentiments. Created in 1849, its courageous first minister and head abolitionist was Henry Ward Beecher, brother of *Uncle Tom's Cabin* author Harriet Beecher Stowe. A section of Plymouth Rock is used in the adjoining arcade. Beecher's statue sits in the beautifully-cultivated courtyard alongside a bas-relief of Abraham Lincoln, who twice visited the church.

WILLOW STREET

Willow St. between Clark and Pierrepont Sts. Subway: 2, 3 to Clark St.

To see the Heights' potpourri of 19th-century styles, which range from Italianate to Classical Revival, explore the Federal-style Willow Street. Numbers 155-159 were the earliest houses here (c. 1825), and boast dormer windows punctuating the sloping roofs.

BROOKLYN HISTORICAL SOCIETY

128 Pierrepont St., off Clinton St. Subway: M, N, R to Court St.; 2, 3, 4, 5 to Borough Hall. ☎ 718-624-0890; www.brooklynhistory.org. Open M and Th-Sa noon-5pm.

This striking building, lined with gargoyle-busts of Shakespeare, Beethoven, and others, houses both the very informative historical society and a museum. The research library is closed indefinitely for renovations.

ST. ANN'S AND THE HOLY TRINITY EPISCOPAL CHURCH

Montague St., on the corner of Clinton St. Subway: M, N, R to Court St.; 2, 3, 4, 5 to Borough Hall. ☎ 718-834-8794. Arts at St. Ann's: ☎ 718-858-2424.

One of the more impressive landmarks on Montague St., St. Ann's contains over 4000 square feet of stained glass. An alternative and illustrious **private school** operates on the church grounds, as does the **Arts at St. Ann's,** an acoustically superb cultural center that has attracted performers like Lou Reed and Marianne Faithfull. The church hosts weekly free organ concerts (W; 1:10pm).

BOROUGH HALL

209 Joralemon St., at the southern end of Fulton St. Mall. Subway: 2, 3, 4, 5, to Borough Hall; M, N, R to Court St. Free tours Tu 1pm.

Completed in 1851, this beautiful Greek temple-inspired edifice topped by a cupola once housed the city hall of an independent Brooklyn. It now houses the Borough President's office.

PROSPECT PARK AND PARK SLOPE

Park Slope is a residential neighborhood with charming brownstones. Restaurants and stores line the north-south avenues; **Seventh Avenue** has long been the neighborhood's main drag, but Fifth Avenue's budding thrift stores, gay bars, and even an art gallery or two, give it a hipper edge. The neighboring **Propect Park** is the borough's answer to Manhattan's Central Park (see p. 78).

PROSPECT PARK

Bounded by Prospect Park West, Flatbush Ave., Ocean Ave., Parkside Ave., and Prospect Park Southwest. Subway: 2, 3 to Grand Army Plaza; F to 15 St./Prospect Park; D, Q, S to Prospect Park. ☎ 718-965-8951; events hotline ☎ 718-965-8999; www.prospectpark.org. Free. ***Paddle Boat and horse rental:*** *☎ 718-282-7789. Th-F 11am-4pm, Sa-Su noon-6pm. Paddle boat $10 per hr., $10 deposit; horses $25-30 per hr.* ***Memorial Arch:*** *Open to climbers Sa-Su 1-5pm. Free.* ***Leffert's Homestead:*** *At Flatbush Ave. and Empire Blvd. ☎ 718-965-6505. Open Th-F 1-4pm, Sa-Su and holidays 1pm-5pm; July-Aug. also open W 1-4pm. Free.* ***Zoo:*** *Flatbush Ave., at Empire Blvd. ☎ 718-399-7339. Open M-F 10am-5pm, Sa-Su 10am-5:30pm. Admission $2.50, seniors $1.25, children $0.50.*

Frederick Law Olmsted and Calvert Vaux designed the park in the mid-1800s and supposedly liked it better than their Manhattan project, Central Park. Today, sunbathers and ball players alike congregate on **Long Meadow. Prospect Lake,** south of the meadow, and **Lookout Hill** both offer peaceful views of glacial pools. In the middle of Grand Army Plaza, the 80-foot-high **Memorial Arch,** built in the 1890s to commemorate the North's Civil War victory, marks one of the entrances into Prospect Park. Those who climb to its top are rewarded with stunning views of the park. The charioteer atop the arch is an emblem of the maiden Columbia, the symbol of the victorious Union.

In summer, concerts are held at the **Bandshell** in the northwestern corner of the park—enter at Prospect Park W. and 9th St. Paddle boats and horses are available for rent at **Wollman Rink.**

Prospect Park also contains a children's museum and a zoo. **Leffert's Homestead,** a preserved Dutch-style farmhouse built between 1777 and 1783 and moved from its original location on Flatbush Ave. and Maple St. in 1918, houses the Children's Historic House Museum and gives children the chance to play with toys from various cultures (Dutch, African-American, Native American). Prospect Park Zoo's exotic fauna in the zoo include a pair of capybaras, a red panda, and a cotton-topped tamarin. The sea lions get fed at 11:30am, 2pm, and 4pm.

THE BROOKLYN BOTANIC GARDEN

1000 Washington Ave.; other entrances on Eastern Parkway and on Flatbush Ave. ☎ 718-623-7000; www.bbg.org. Open Apr.-Sept. Tu-F 8am-6pm, Sa-Su 10am-6pm; Oct.-Mar. Tu-F 8am-4:30pm, Sa-Su 10am-4:30pm. Admission $3; students and seniors $1.50; under 16 free; free Tu all day and Sa 10am-noon; seniors free every F.

This 52-acre fairyland was founded in 1910 by the Brooklyn Institute of Art and Sciences on a reclaimed waste dump. If you've gotten over that traumatic bee stinging in grade school, the **Fragrance Garden for the Blind** is an olfactory carnival—with mint, lemon, violet, and other appetizing aromas. The more formal **Cranford Rose Garden** crams in over 100 blooming varieties of roses. Every spring, visitors can take part in the **Sakura Matsuri** (Japanese cherry blossom festival) at the Cherry Walk and Cherry Esplanade. The woodsy **Japanese Garden** contains weeping willows and a viewing pavilion over a pond. The artificial scenery's authenticity fools the many water birds that flock to the site. The **Shakespeare Garden** displays 80 plants mentioned in Will's works. The various pavilions of the **Steinhardt Conservatory** are climate-controlled to show desert, tropical, and other flora. You should not miss the 100 varieties of tropical water-lilies and the sacred lotus that radiate in the summer in the **Lily Pool Terrace,** as well as the rainbow assortment of flowering annuals in the **Annual Border**—both just outside of the conservatory.

THE BROOKLYN PUBLIC LIBRARY

Corner of Eastern Pkwy. and Flatbush Ave. ☎ 718-780-7700; www.brooklynpubliclibrary.org. Open M-Th 9am-8pm, F-Sa 9am-6pm, Su 1-5pm; closed Su mid-June to mid-Sept.

kids IN THE CITY

Coney Island

This is Brooklyn the way it was during its Golden Era. The amusement park is not quite as exciting in our highly-technological age as it must have been in the past. Still, this is a good place for kids if they're bored of brownstones.

Take a 100-second-long, rickety, screaming whirl on the legendary **Cyclone,** built in 1927. It's a historic place according to the National Register, and couples have been married on it. (834 Surf Ave, and W. 10th St. Open daily mid-June to Sept. noon-midnight; Easter weekend to mid-June F-Su noon-midnight. $5.)

The **Wonder Wheel,** at 150feet, was the world's tallest when it was built. (In Deno's, on Surf Ave. $3.50)

The Ghost Hall is as scary as the *Munsters,* but it's pure Coney Island camp. (12th St., off Bowery. $3.50.)

For the extra small, **Deno's,** right next to Astroland, has rides kiddie-sized, like the Sea Serpent roller coaster. ($2 per ride, $15 for 10.)

The real spirit of Coney Island, however, is at the **Coney Island Circus Sideshow,** which has sword swallowers, snake charmers, jugglers, and "freaks." (1208 Surf Ave., at 12th St. Open F 2-10pm, Sa-Su 1pm-midnight. $3, children $2.)

The striking Art Deco main branch of the Brooklyn Public Library system stands majestically on Grand Army Plaza. The library has spawned 53 branches and contains 1,600,000 volumes. There are changing exhibitions on the second floor.

BEDFORD-STUYVESANT

Bounded by Classon Ave. on the west, Atlantic Ave. on the south, Broadway on the east, and Flushing Ave. on the north. Subway: A, C to Franklin Ave., Nostrand Ave., Kingston-Throop Aves.

A predominantly African-American community, Bed-Stuy is not a heavily-touristed part of town, in part because it is *not a very safe* neighborhood. If you walk its streets during the day, however, you will be treated to some of the city's finest brownstones, especially in the southernmost part of the neighborhood, on Macon, MacDonough, Decatur, Bainbridge, and Chauncey Sts.

COBBLE HILL, CARROLL GARDENS, AND RED HOOK

Together bounded by the water, on the south and west, Hoyt St. on the east, and Atlantic Ave. on the north. Subway: F, G to Bergen St., Carroll Gardens, Smith St., 9th St.

Just south of Atlantic Avenue lies the quiet Italian neighborhood of **Cobble Hill,** whose gorgeous brownstone-lined sidestreets segue into **Carroll Gardens.** The large Italian population is evidenced by the many pasta and pastry shops and the old *padrones* sitting in lawn chairs talking with their hands. The ground floors of **Smith** and **Court** Streets' buildings are crowded with thrift stores, antique vendors, artist cooperatives, and craft shops.

FLATBUSH

Bounded by Coney Island Ave. on the west, Ave. H on the south, Nostrand Ave. on the east, and Parkside Ave. on the north. Subway: D, Q, M to Church Ave., Newkirk Ave.; 2, 5 to Flatbush Ave./Brooklyn College.

Transformed by the introduction of the trolley in the late 19th century, Flatbush grew from a small town into a stomping ground for the well-to-do. You can wander around Argyle Street and Ditmas Avenue to see some of their old mansions. In the first half of the 20th century, the neighborhood was home to the beloved Brooklyn Dodgers, who played in **Ebbets Field.** The stadium was demolished when owner Walter O'Malley moved the club to Los Angeles. A housing complex now stands in its stead. Home plate was located close to the corner of Sullivan Place and Franklin Avenue. The neighborhood's extant highlight is **Erasmus Hall Acad-**

emy, 911 Flatbush Ave. at Church Ave., the second-oldest high school in North America. Constructed in 1787 with the participation of Aaron Burr, John Jay, and Alexander Hamilton, no brick can be moved from the school's central building or, according to an antiquated charter, a neighboring Dutch Reform Church will repossess it. Once a predominantly Jewish immigrant neighborhood, Flatbush is now home to significant Jamaican and West Indian populations. Reggae music and exotic fruit stands fill major thoroughfares like Nostrand Avenue on summer days.

SUNSET PARK AND GREENWOOD CEMETERY

Bounded by the water on the west, 65th St. to the south, 8th Ave. and Greenwood Cemetery to the east, and the Prospect Expressway to the north. Subway: R to 25th St., 36th St., 45th St., 53rd St., 59th St.; N to 36th St., 59th St.

Home to a melange of ethnic groups, most notably Latinos and Chinese, Sunset Park is the embodiment of the melting pot. Avid consumers flock to the area's Fifth Avenue, which is lined with discount stores and hybrid restaurants. Just to the northeast of the neighborhood is **Greenwood Cemetery,** Fifth Ave. and 25th St. Laid out over various hills (some of which offer views all the way to Manhattan and beyond), and with lakes and a chapel, Greenwood is as peaceful as the name suggests. On a clear day, Lady Liberty is visible from the elaborate Gothic Revival entrance on 25th St. This vast (478-acre), hilly kingdom of ornate mausoleums and tombstones makes for a pleasant, if morbid, walk. Samuel Morse, Horace Greeley, and William "Boss" Tweed slumber at this Victorian Necropolis, as do Leonard Bernstein and Mae West: come up and see her sometime. (Open daily 8am-4pm. Tours: 2hr.; Su 1pm; $6.)

BENSONHURST AND BOROUGH PARK

Bensonhurst bounded by 26th St. on the southeast, 61st St. on the northeast, Fourteenth Ave. on the northwest, and Gravesend Bay on the southwest. Subway: N to 18th Ave. Borough Park is north of Bensonhurst.

Bensonhurst, centered around Stillwell and Park Avenues, is a primarily Italian neighborhood in southern Brooklyn that has seen an increasing number of Russians move from Brighton Beach. This is the authentic Italian neighborhood that you couldn't find in Manhattan's Little Italy. Walk down to 18th Avenue to see the neighborhood at its most bustling. **Borough Park** is the largest Hassidic Jewish neighborhood in Brooklyn. In contrast to the more visible Crown Heights Lubavitchers, the Bobovers of Borough Park prefer to maintain an insular community. As in the other Hassidic neighborhoods of Brooklyn, visitors will feel more welcome if they are dressed conservatively.

BAY RIDGE

Bounded by Belt Parkway on the west, 101st St. on the south, Fort Hamilton Pkwy on the east, 65th St. on the north. Subway: R to Bay Ridge Ave., 77th St., 86th St., Bay Ridge-95th St.

The nearby Shore Road of **Bay Ridge** is lined with mansions overlooking New York Harbor. Bay Ridge was the scene of John Travolta's strutting in the classic *Saturday Night Fever.* Although the 2001 Odyssey disco is no longer operational, the predominantly Italian neighborhood centers around 86th Street, and is chock full of Italian bakeries, pizza joints, rowdy youths, and discount stores, especially around 17th Avenue. The **Verrazano-Narrows Bridge** is Staten Island's only connection by automobile to the other boroughs, a majestic suspension bridge stretching a smashing 4,260 ft. (1,298 m). When it opened in 1964, it was the world's longest, and people still marvel at is engineering though several have since toppled its record.

CONEY ISLAND AND BRIGHTON BEACH

Coney Island is Brooklyn straight out of the 1940s and 50s. Outdated amusement parks reign in Coney Island, and rides such as the Parachute Jump, the Wonder Wheel, and the Cyclone are legendary in these parts (see p. 94). Beyond Ocean

Parkway, east of Coney Island, lies **Brighton Beach,** or "Little Odessa by the Sea," an area populated heavily by Eastern European immigrants and written about in Neil Simon's Brighton Beach Memoirs. By day it is home to Eastern-European delis, grocery stores, and shops; at night, Russian music, from disco to folk, livens up the neighborhood.

NEW YORK AQUARIUM

At Surf and W. 8th Sts. ☎ 718-265-3474. Summer tickets sold M-F 10am-5:15pm, Sa-Su 10am-6:15pm. $9.75; children 2-12 and seniors $6.

Home to the first beluga whale born in captivity, the aquarium has all the expected marine inhabitants here, from penguins and piranhas to sharks and jellyfish, as well as a few surprises. They even have some coneys, the fish that gave Coney Island its name. An outdoor theater serves up wonderful performances by a sea lion and two bottle-nosed dolphins.

KEYSPAN PARK

On the south side of Surf Ave. between W. 17th and W. 19th Sts. ☎ 718-449-TIXS for game tickets $6-$10

After 43 years, baseball is back in Brooklyn. The newly erected stadium for the minor league Brooklyn Cyclones (the Class A affiliate of the Mets), Keyspan Park interacts with other relics of yesteryear: ruins of Coney Island rides recall the days when the carnival-grounds extended farther west. One may still see some rusted cars from the deceased **Thunderbolt** coaster, half-sunk, and the tall, worn skeleton of the **Parachute Jump**.

QUEENS

see map pp. 340-341

Less a borough of famous sights or museums, Queens is notable primarily for its ethnic communities. Unlike Brooklyn—which contains many distinctive neighborhoods—but remains united as a whole, Queens is a more of a collection of independent towns. Those exploring Queens in detail should pick up the large foldout Queens **bus map,** available at any subway station or on any bus within the borough. **Neighborhoods are listed from west to east.**

ASTORIA AND LONG ISLAND CITY

Astoria is located in the northwestern corner of Queens across the river from Manhattan. Long Island City is located southwest of Astoria. Subway: All N stops between 36 Ave. and Astoria Ditmars Blvd. G, R to 36 St. or Steinway St.

Just under half of Astoria's population is ethnically Greek, and the average block is likely to have a Greek bakery, as well as an Italian grocery. **30th Ave.** is the major thoroughfare, while the blocks surrounding the **Ditmars Blvd.** subway stop are known as "Little Athens." Avid shoppers head east on **Broadway** to **Steinway St.**

Long Island City, almost parallel to Roosevelt Island, is mostly industrial in nature, but has experienced a resurgence as Queens's artistic center, a revival anchored by **PS1** (see **Museums and Galleries,** p. 127) and the temporary coming of **MoMA** (see **Museums and Galleries,** p. 111). Stretches on Vernon Blvd. have pleasant boardwalk sections along the water that end near the Socrates Sculpture Park.

THE STEINWAY PIANO FACTORY

19th Rd. and 77th St. Subway: N to Ditmars Blvd. ☎ 718-721-2600. Tours run every other Th; call for information.

The world-famous Steinway pianos have been manufactured in the same spot, in the same way, since the 1870s. The 12,000 parts of a typical Steinway include a 340lb. plate of cast iron and tiny bits of Brazilian deer skin. Over 95% of piano performances in the US are played on Steinway grands.

THE SOCRATES SCULPTURE PARK

At the end of Broadway, across the Vernon Blvd. intersection. Subway: N to Broadway. ☎ 718-956-1819. Open daily 10am-dusk. Free.

Sculptor Mark di Suvero created this curiosity. Thirty-five stunning, if unnerving, dayglo and rusted metal abstractions cluster on the site of what was once an illegal dump.

KAUFMAN-ASTORIA STUDIOS

Corner of 35th St. and 35th Ave. Subway: N to 36th Ave.

The US's largest studio outside of Los Angeles sits on a 13-acre plot with eight sound stages. Paramount Pictures used these facilities to make such films as *Scent of a Woman* and *The Secret of My Success*. Television's *The Cosby Show* and *Sesame Street* were taped here as well. To get to Sesame Street, exit the 36th Ave. N station, walk one block to 35th Ave. and down to 35th St. The studios are closed to the public, but next door is the **American Museum of the Moving Image** (see **Museums,** p. 116).

CITICORP BUILDING

Court Sq., at Jackson Ave. Subway: E, F to 23 St.-Ely Ave.; G to 21 St.

At 48 stories, this structure of blue glass is the tallest New York building outside of Manhattan. Bankers and other office workers mill around the plaza at lunchtime, creating a scene seemingly incongruous with the otherwise industrial/artsy surroundings.

ELMHURST AND CORONA

Elmhurst: Subway: R to Elmhurst Ave. or Grand Ave.-Newtown. Corona: Subway: 7 to 103rd St.-Corona Plaza, 111th St.

Elmhurst is arguably the most ethnically diverse part of the most ethnically diverse of boroughs, with immigrants from more than 100 countries. The corner of Broadway and Whitney Ave. holds a plethora of great ethnic restaurants (see **Food,** p. 153). Now a largely Hispanic part of town, Corona was the site of Archie Bunker's house in "All in the Family." Besides nearby Flushing Meadow-Corona Park, the main attraction of the area is the **Lemon Ice King of Corona** (see **Food,** p. 153). Jazz fans can visit **Louis Armstrong's House,** 34-56 107th St. (☎997-3670). Malcolm X lived in **23-11 97th St.,** in nearby East Elmhurst, from 1954 until his death in 1965.

FOREST HILLS AND FOREST PARK

Subway: E, F, G, R to Forest Hills-71st Ave. ***Forest Park:*** *☎ 718-235-4100; events info ☎ 718-520-5941; golf ☎ 718-296-0999. Subway: J, Z to Woodhaven Blvd. Open daily 6am-9pm.*

Forest Hills is an upscale, residential part of town, with many private streets and houses more suited to suburbia than New York City (two-car garages!). It's pleasant to walk around, although there aren't too many particular attractions. To the south stands **Forest Park,** a densely wooded area with miles of park trails, a bandshell, a golf course, a carousel ($1), baseball diamonds, tennis courts, and horseback riding (see **Sports,** p. 188).

FLUSHING MEADOWS-CORONA PARK

Subway: 7 to 111th St. or Willets Point-Shea Stadium.

From the Van Wyck Expressway, motorists gaze upon the ruins of a more glamorous past. Rusting towers and half-eaten buildings punctuate the serene trees of Flushing Meadows-Corona Park, home to the 1939 and 1964 World's Fairs. The 1255-acre swamp, nestled between Corona and Flushing, became a huge rubbish dump until city planners decided to turn the area into fairgrounds. The remnants from the first fair are long gone, and the monuments from the second are fast deteriorating. Yet, behind the trees hide several excellent attractions, sculptured gardens, and one or two well-kept monuments. The grounds are worth a visit, not only for these hidden gems, but for the old steel and concrete dinosaurs themselves.

PHUN PHACTORY

A yellow brick road spray-painted on the sidewalk leads up to the entrance of the superintendent's office of this Queens factory. Inside sits Pat Delillo, doling out permission to young street artists to "write" their colorful drawings on the outer walls, rooftop, and inner sanctuary of this factory warehouse. In 1993 he initiated the first not-for-profit organization for graffiti writers, encouraging them move off the streets and focus their talents in legal locations. In general, the colorful murals (visible from the 7 train) turn over every few months, except for the ones dedicated to writers killed in street violence. Pat encourages visitors, as he wants to spread the word for his cause. *(45-14 Davis St., off Jackson Ave. Subway: 7 to 45 Rd.-Court House Sq. or E, F, G, R to 23 St.-Ely Ave. ☎718-482-7486; www.phunphactory.org. Open daily 9am-6pm.*

NEW YORK HALL OF SCIENCE

47-01 111th St., at 48th Ave. ☎718-699-0005; www.nyhallsci.org. Open July-Aug. M 9:30am-2pm, Tu-Su 9:30am-5pm; Sept.-Jun. Tu-W 9:30am-2pm, Th-Su 9:30am-5pm. Admission $7.50, seniors and under 17 $5; under 4 free. Free Sept.-June Th-F 2-5pm.

Futuristic when it was constructed in 1964, the concrete hall now stands flanked by rusty rockets. Its vision of the future may not have aged well on the outside, but a recent renovation and expansion have made the exhibitions inside current and engaging. Although largely oriented toward children, this museum will keep visitors of all ages occupied with over 150 hands-on displays.

THE UNISPHERE

In front of the Arthur Ashe Stadium.

A 380-ton steel globe tilting in retro-futuristic glory over a fountain. Constructed by the steel industry for the 1964 World's Fair, the Unisphere dramatically symbolizes "man's aspirations toward peace and his achievements in an expanding universe." Rings encircling the globe represent the three man-made satellites then in orbit. On sweltering summer afternoons you may be tempted to romp around the fountain with everyone else despite the "No Wading" signs.

NEW YORK STATE PAVILION

In Flushing Meadows Park.

A true eyesore. The two towers of the New York State Pavilion were the original center of the 1964 World's Fair. The architect Philip Johnson probably never envisioned the towers as hideouts for alien spacecraft—their role in *Men In Black.* Part of the pavilion is now the **Queens Theater in the Park** (see **Entertainment,** p. 175). South of the Pavilion, across the expressway overpass and behind the Planet of the Apes Fountain, is a restored **Coney Island carousel** that pipes out silly chipmunk tunes.

OTHER SIGHTS

While in the park, you can try your hand at a full course of **pitch 'n' putt golf**. (☎718-271-8182. Open daily 8am-7pm. Greens fee Sa-Su $7.25, M-F $8.25. Club rental $1 each.) In the southern part of the park, **Meadow Lake** offers paddle- and row-boating, while **Willow Lake Nature Area** hosts an occasional free tour. **Shea Stadium** (☎718-507-8499), to the north of the park, was built for the 1964 Fair; it is now home to the Mets (see **Entertainment,** p. 186). Nearby, the **USTA National Tennis Center** and **Arthur Ashe Stadium** (☎718-760-6200) host the US Open.

The Queens Wildlife Center/Zoo, 53-51 111th St., near 53rd Ave., features North American animals as well as more exotic species, including bison and sea lions. Sheep, goats, cows, and other cuddly creatures frolic in the petting zoo. (☎718-271-1500. Open Apr.-Oct. M-F 10am-5pm, Sa-Su 10am-5:30pm; Nov.-Mar. daily 10am-4:30pm. Admission $2.50, seniors $1.25, under 12 50¢). **The Queens Museum of Art's** "Panorama of the City of New York," is the world's largest scale model of an urban area at 9335 sq. ft.; one inch corresponds to 100 ft. of New York. (In the north wing of the New York City Building, next to the Unisphere. ☎718-592-9700; Open W-F 10am-5pm, Sa-Su noon-5pm. Suggested donation $4, seniors and children $2.)

FLUSHING

Subway: 7 to Flushing-Main St.

Flushing started life as a village in 1654 (its name is a corruption of Vlissingen, the Dutch name for the village). **Main St.** and **Roosevelt Ave.** form the commercial hub of the neighborhood. Today, many signs around those streets are penned in Korean or Chinese characters, and ducks and dumplings adorn shop windows.

THE KINGSLAND HOMESTEAD

143-35 37th Ave. ☎718-939-0647; www.preserve.org/queens. Open Tu and Sa-Su 2:30-4:30pm. Historical Society open by appointment M-F 9:30am-5pm.

Built in 1775 (and moved to its current location in 1968), the Homestead was a typical home of the time, but few similar structures remain today. It holds a permanent collection of antique china and memorabilia that belonged to early trader Captain Joseph King. There is also a collection of antique dolls and a fully-furnished "Victorian Room," depicting the typical furnishings of a middle-class citizen of the time. As home of the **Queens Historical Society,** the Homestead also displays three or four temporary exhibits each year depicting aspects of the borough's history.

QUEENS BOTANICAL GARDEN

43-15 Main St. ☎718-886-3800. Walk from the Flushing-Main St. 7 station or take the Q44 bus toward Jamaica. Open Apr.-Oct. Tu-F 8am-6pm, Sa-Su 8am-7pm; Nov.-Mar. 8am-4:30pm. Admission free.

An exhibition for the 1939 World's Fair in nearby Flushing Meadows-Corona Park (see p. 97), the garden had to move when the park was redesigned for the 1964 World's Fair. At its present site it boasts a 5000-bush rose garden, a 23-acre arboretum, more than nine acres of "theme gardens," and a new home compost demonstration site. On weekends, the Garden plays host to a cavalcade of wedding parties, each competing for gazebos, fountains, and the home compost demonstration site as a backdrop for commemorative photos.

FLUSHING TOWN HALL

137-35 Northern Blvd. ☎718-463-7700; www.flushing townhall.org. Concerts $20, students and seniors $15. Admission free.

Or rather, former town hall: the building, built in 1862, now functions as a gallery and a performing space, as well as home to the **Flushing Council of Culture and the Arts.** Local art and historical exhibitions await inside. A small permanent exhibit on jazz in Queens includes original postcards and letters written by Louis Armstrong; pick up the free *Queens Jazz Trail* map for details of how to get to the former homes of Dizzy Gillespie, Ella Fitzgerald, and ol' Satchmo himself. Live jazz and classical concerts on occasional F nights and Su afternoons; call for schedule.

BOWNE HOUSE

37-01 Bowne St. ☎718-359-0528. Open Tu and Sa-Su 2:30-4:30pm. Admission $2, seniors and under 14 $1.

This low, unassuming house, built in 1661, is the oldest remaining residence in New York City and is filled with interesting antiques. Here, John Bowne defied Dutch governor Peter Stuyvesant's 1657 ban on Quaker meetings and was exiled for his efforts. The house is currently undergoing major renovations, so call ahead if you want to go inside.

JAMAICA

Subway: E, J, Z to Jamaica Center.

Jamaica's main strip is the section of Jamaica Ave. stretching from 150th to 168th St. Restaurants selling succulent Jamaican beef patties, stores peddling African clothing and braids, and mobs of local shoppers rushing to get a deal crowd the brick-lined **pedestrian mall** on 165th St. Saint Albans can best be explored by a walk down Linden Blvd. The West Indian culture is concentrated on both sides of Hillside Ave. eastward.

On Jamaica Ave. and 153rd St. sits the **King Manor Museum.** This colonial residence belonged (between 1805 and 1827) to Rufus King, an early abolitionist, framer and signer of the Constitution, senator for New York, Presidential candidate, and ambassador to Great Britain. The house, set in 11-acre **King Park,** dates back to the 1750s and combines Georgian and Federal architecture. The period rooms downstairs give you an idea of how they lived back in the day. (☎718-206-0545. Open Mar.-Dec. Sa-Su noon-4pm; second and last Tu of the month noon-4pm. Admission with guided tours only; $2, students and seniors $1, families $5).

The graveyard of **Grace Church,** 155-03 Jamaica Ave., contains the grave of Rufus King. The church itself is a Gothic Revival structure, one of the oldest churches in Queens (open daily 11am-1pm). The elaborate Moorish facade of the **Tabernacle of Prayer,** 165-11 Jamaica Ave., is a remnant of the building's past as a movie theater, the Loews Valencia.

THE ROCKAWAYS

Take the A train to the end of the line and land at the beach in the far-eastern reaches of Queens.

THE JAMAICA BAY WILDLIFE REFUGE

On Broad Channel, Jamaica Bay. Subway: A to Broad Channel. Walk west along Noel Rd., which is just in front of the station, to Cross Bay Blvd., then turn right and walk to the center. ☎718-318-4340. Park open daily dawn to dusk. Visitor/Nature Center open daily 8:30am-5pm. Free, but pick up map and permit at visitors center.

Roughly the size of Manhattan and 10 times larger than Flushing Meadows-Corona Park, this park is one of the most important urban wildlife refuges in the US, harboring more than 325 species of birds and small animals. Environmental slide shows and tours are held on weekends.

ROCKAWAY BEACH

From Beach 3rd St. in Far Rockaway to Beach 149th St. in the west. Subway: A (marked "Far Rockaway") to all stops between Beach 36th St. and Beach 67th St. or A (marked "Rockaways") or S to all stops between Beach 90 St. and Rockaway Park-Beach 116 St. ☎718-318-4000. Lifeguards Memorial Day-Labor Day.

Immortalized by the Ramones in one of their pop-punk tributes, the 10-mile-long public beach is lined by a **boardwalk.** It's often pleasantly free of crowds, and always free of tacky souvenir stalls. Supplies can be found at Beach 116th and Beach 129th Sts., including at the Sand Bar (see **Entertainment,** p. 188).

FIRST PRESBYTERIAN CHURCH

1324 Beach 12th St., at Central Ave. Subway: A to Far Rockaway-Mott Ave. ☎718-327-2440.

Railroad tycoon Russell Sage donated the money to build this church, noted for its enormous, magnificent Louis Tiffany stained glass window. The landscape of the window appears different depending on the time of day outside.

JACOB RIIS PARK

Just west of Rockaway Beach, separated from it by a huge chain-link fence. Subway: A (marked Rockaways) or S; stop at Rockaway Pk., then transfer to Q22 westward. ☎718-318-4300. Open 6am-midnight.

Part of the 26,000-acre Gateway National Recreation Area that extends into Brooklyn, Staten Island, and New Jersey, the park was named for Jacob Riis, a photojournalist and activist in the early 1900s who persuaded the city to turn this overgrown beach into a public park. Today, the area is lined with its own gorgeous beach and boardwalk, as well as basketball and handball courts and a golf course. To the west of the entrance, nature trails run through the remnants of Fort Tilden, a former U.S. Army base. A former nude beach is at the eastern end; in the 1980s the beach decided to "clean up its act" and now only allows you to go topless.

ROOSEVELT ISLAND

Subway: Q to Roosevelt Island; 4, 5, 6, N, R to 59th St. (at Lexington Ave.), then walk to 59th St. and Second Ave. and hop the tram. ☎832-4555. Every 15min. Su-Th 6am-2am, F-Sa 6am-3:30am; twice as frequently at rush hour. One-way $1.50; no metro cards accepted. 6min. each way.

The only reason to travel to Roosevelt Island is the bright red tram that shuttles residents and tourists across the East River. The ride allows a grand view of the East Side as you rise to 250 ft. above the United Nations complex. One of the few publicly operated commuter cable cars in the world, it operates at an annual loss of $1 million, and its future has become uncertain since the subway opened to the island about 10 years ago. Once on the island, walk north or take the mini-bus (25¢) up **Main St.** and roam around a bit. A **walking/skating path** encircles the island, and gardens and playgrounds abound on the northern half. The southern tip of the island is currently off-limits while the city restores the ruins of the asylum and hospital. **Lighthouse Park,** at the northernmost tip of the island, is a pleasant retreat offering views of the swirling East River.

THE BRONX

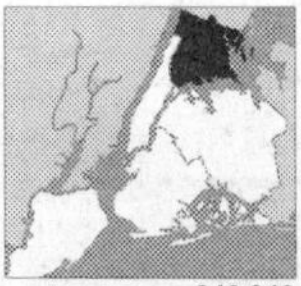

see map pp. 342-343

The borough takes its name from Jonas Bronck, the European who settled in the area with his family in 1639. Until the turn of the 19th century, the area consisted largely of cottages, farmlands, and wild marshes. In the 1840s, the tide of immigration swelled and brought scores of Italian and Irish settlers to the borough. Since then, the flow of immigrants (now mostly Hispanic and Russian) has never stopped. This relentless stream has created vibrant ethnic neighborhoods (including a Little Italy to shame its Manhattan counterpart). The Bronx will give any visitor insight into the dynamics of burgeoning urban life, not to mention a peek at numerous attractions. In the coverage below, **neighborhoods are arranged from south to north.**

SOUTH BRONX

Thirty fires a night raged in the South Bronx during the 1970s. Landlords torched buildings to collect insurance, and tenants burned down their own houses to collect welfare. When Ronald Reagan visited, he compared the South Bronx to a bombed-out London after the Battle of Britain. Thanks to a huge inflow of government funds and a stronger economy, the South Bronx and the borough as a whole have taken steps away from poverty and violence. Still, for the most part, the South Bronx is not a traditional tourist destination and is not a safe place to walk around, especially at night.

YANKEE STADIUM

E. 161st St., at River Ave. Subway: 4, B, D to 161st St. ☎718-293-6000. Tours: Daily at noon. Admission $10; 14 and under and seniors $5.

In 1923, Babe Ruth's success as a hitter inspired the construction of the Yankees' own ballpark, and to this day "The House That Ruth Built" remains one of the Bronx's main attractions. The aging stadium's frequent face-lifts have kept it on par with younger structures. The Yankees played the first night game here in 1946, and the first message scoreboard tallied runs here in 1954. Inside the 11.6-acre park (the field measures only 3.5 acres), monuments honor Yankee greats like Lou Gehrig, Joe

DiMaggio, and Babe Ruth. Despite the parade of baseball legends that have graced the Yankee lineup, no major leaguer has ever hit a home run ball out of the stadium, although legend has it Josh Gibson did once in a Negro League game. The Yankees offer tours of the Stadium, but do yourself a favor and go to a ballgame.

THE BRONX MUSEUM OF THE ARTS

1040 Grand Concourse, at 165th St. ☎718-681-6000. Open W 3-9pm, Th-F 10am-5pm, Sa-Su noon-6pm. Suggested donation $3, students and seniors $2; W free.

Set in the rotunda of the Bronx Courthouse, the museum's two small galleries exhibit works by contemporary artists as well as local talent, with a focus on Latino, African-American, and women artists. The museum encourages the community to create textual and visual responses to the permanent collection and mounts the (often nutty) viewer feedback alongside the original work.

ART AND ANTIQUE MARKET

Subway: 6 to Third Ave.; walk south a few blocks to Bruckner Blvd.

Antique Road Show buffs looking for a good deal might consider taking a look in northeastern Bronx on Bruckner Blvd., between Alexander and Willis Sts.

BRONX PARK

Perhaps the highlight of the Bronx is this park, which features both the Bronx Zoo and New York Botanical Garden, both the best of their kind in the city.

BRONX ZOO

Entrances on Bronx Park S., Southern Blvd., E. Fordham Rd., and the Bronx River Parkway. Subway: 2, 5 to West Farms Sq./E. Tremont Ave. Follow Boston Rd. for three blocks until the Bronx Park S. gate. Bus: Bx9, Bx19, Bx22, and Q44 pass various entrances to the zoo. Liberty Lines bus leaves from Madison Ave. in Midtown for the Bronxdale entrance to the zoo ($3 each way); ☎718-652-8400 for Liberty Lines info. Zoo: ☎718-367-1010 or 718-220-5100. Open daily M-F 10am-5pm, Sa-Su 10am-5:30pm. Parts of the zoo closed Nov.-Apr. Admission: $9, seniors and children 2-12 $5; W free (but they suggest a donation). Congo Gorilla Forest $3. Disabled-access info: ☎718-220-5188.

The Bronx Zoo/Wildlife Conservation Park, also known as the New York Zoological Society, is perhaps the borough's biggest attraction. The largest urban zoo in the United States, it provides a home for over 4000 animals. While the odd building dots the zoo, this newly environmentally conscious park prefers to showcase its stars within the 265-acre expanse of natural habitats created for each species' dwelling pleasure. The timber rattlesnake and Samantha the python (the largest snake in the US) serve life in the **Reptile House,** but more benign beasts wander free in the Park's "protected sanctuary," occasionally allowing for startlingly close interaction between inhabitant and visitor. Indian elephants frolic unfettered in a **Wild Asia** while white-cheeked gibbons tree-hop in the **JungleWorld.** More apes can be seen at the **Congo Gorilla Forest,** which also features okapi, but that requires a separate entrance.Other noteworthy habitats include the **Himalayan Highlands, South America,** and the **World of Darkness.** Kids imitate animals at the hands-on **Children's Zoo,** where they can climb a spider's web or try on a turtle shell. If you tire of the kids, the crocodiles are fed Mondays and Thursdays at 2pm, sea lions daily at 3pm.

NEW YORK BOTANICAL GARDEN

*Kazimiroff Blvd., Subway: 4 to Bedford Park Blvd./Lehman College; B, D to Bedford Park Blvd. Walk 8 blocks east or take the Bx26 bus. **Bus:** Bx19 or Bx26. Train: Metro-North Harlem line goes from Grand Central Terminal to Botanical Garden station, which is right outside the main gate. ☎212-532-4900 for info.☎718-817-8700. **Open** Apr.-Oct. Tu-Su 10am-6pm; July-Aug. Th and Sa grounds open until 8pm; Nov.-Mar. Tu-Su 10am-4pm. **Admission** $3; students and seniors $2; children 2-12 $1; W all day and Sa 10am-noon free. Certain exhibits throughout the garden incur an additional charge; "passports" ($10; students and seniors $7.50; children $4) allow you to see all exhibits. Various **tours** (both paid and free) depart daily; inquire at the Visitor's Information Center.*

North across East Fordham Rd. from the zoo sprawls the beautiful, labyrinthine New York Botanical Garden. Here, urban captives cavort amid such oddities as trees, flowers, and the open sky. Snatches of forest and water attempt to recreate the area's original landscape. The 250-acre garden, an outstanding horticultural preserve, serves as both a research laboratory and a plant and tree museum. One can scope out the 40-acre **hemlock forest,** (the last of the forests that once covered the city) kept in its natural state, the **Peggy Rockefeller Rose Garden, the T.H. Everett Rock Garden** and waterfall, and a hands-on children's adventure garden. Although it costs an extra few dollars to enter, the **Conservatory** deserves a visit; the gorgeous domed greenhouse contains a few different ecosystems of exquisite plant life. If you go exploring by yourself, get a garden map; it's a jungle out there. The crowded 30-minute **tram ride** ($1) skirts most of the major sights.

Flushing Meadows

FORDHAM AND BELMONT

Fordham is the Bronx's largest college, and its peaceful grounds offer refuge from the fast-paced surroundings. Belmont, well-positioned for a visit after a day at the Bronx Zoo or the New York Botanical Garden, is the Bronx's Little Italy.

Little Asia

FORDHAM UNIVERSITY

Webster Ave. between E. Fordham Rd. and Dr. Theodore Kazimiroff Blvd. Subway: ☎ 718-817-1000.

Opened in 1841 by John Hughes as St. John's College, 80-acre Fordham has matured into one of the nation's foremost Jesuit schools. Robert S. Riley built the campus in classic collegiate Gothic style in 1936—so Gothic, in fact, that *The Exorcist* was filmed here. The Fordham Rams basketball and baseball teams turn heads at Rose Hill Gymnasium and Coffey Field.

EAST FORDHAM ROAD

E. Fordham Rd. from Webster Ave. to University Ave. Subway: 4, B, D to Fordham Rd.

Perhaps the busiest shopping district in New York City, the strip is one long marketplace. Music blaring from storefront speakers attracts customers. Street vendors vie with department and specialty stores, while wizened women dish out *helado* alongside bargain beepers and gold figurines of the Madonna.

Bronx Zoo

BELMONT

Centering on Arther Ave. and E. 187th St., near the Southern Blvd. entrance to the Bronx Zoo. Subway: 4, B, D to Fordham Rd.; then walk 10 blocks east (or take Bx12) to Arthur Ave. and head south.

This uptown "Little Italy," with its two-story rowhouses and narrow alleyways, cooks up some of the best Italian food west of Naples. **Arthur Ave.** is home to some wonderful homestyle southern Italian cooking. At **Dominick's,** between 186th and 187th Sts., boisterous crowds blindly put away pasta (see **Food,** p. 101). To get a concentrated sense of the area, stop into **Arthur Avenue Retail Market,** 2334 Arthur Ave. between 186th and Crescent Sts. This indoor market is indeed a Little Italy unto itself, with *caffè*, a butcher, grocer, cheese shop, deli, and other stalls selling Italian necessities. The **Church of Our Lady of Mt. Carmel,** 627 187th St., at Belmont Ave., holds high mass in Italian daily at 10:15am, 12:45, and 7:30pm. The church lights up the street and the neighborhood every July 15th with its **festival** of the Lady of Mt. Carmel. Across and up the street is the **Belmont Italian-American Playhouse,** 2385 Arthur Ave., between 186th and 187th Sts. (☎718-364-4700). The theater also puts on Italian language productions, ranging from Eduardo de Filippo's *Filumena* to the satires of wacky Nobel Prize-winner Dario Fo. The theater is usually closed during the summer. Signs of a recent Kosovar influx permeate the area; the Kosovar flag with its red background and spidery bird is hung in the window fronts of many stores and eateries.

EDGAR ALLAN POE COTTAGE

E. Kingsbridge Rd. and Grand Concourse, five blocks west of Fordham University. Subway: 4, D to Kingsbridge Rd. ☎718-881-8900. Open Sa 10am-4pm, Su 1-5pm. Admission $2.

The morbid writer and his tubercular cousin/wife Virginia (whom Poe married when he was 26 and she 13) lived spartanly in the cottage from 1846 until 1848. Here Poe wrote *Annabel Lee*, *Eureka*, and *The Bells*, a tale of the neighboring Fordham bells. The museum displays a slew of Poe's manuscripts and macabrabilia.

KINGSBRIDGE AND BEDFORD PARK

Subway: 4 to Bedford Park Blvd./Lehman College.

This neighborhood is located north of Fordham and contains two schools worth noting. Founded in 1931 as Hunter College, **Herbert H. Lehman College,** 250 Bedford Park Blvd. West, bounded by W. 198th St. and Jerome Ave., is a fiefdom in the CUNY empire. The UN Security Council met in the gymnasium building in 1946. In 1980, the Lehmans endowed the first cultural center in the Bronx, the **Lehman Center for the Performing Arts,** on the Bedford Park Blvd. side of campus (☎718-960-8000). Close by is the **Bronx High School of Science,** 75 W. 205th St., an established center of academic excellence, as evidenced by the five Nobel Prize winners who matriculated here, the most of any high school in the world (☎718-817-7700).

RIVERDALE AND VAN CORTLANDT PARK

In direct contrast to much of the poverty-stricken borough, Riverdale features some extremely wealthy residences and a triumvirate of esteemed private schools—**Fieldston School,** on Fieldston St. at Manhattan College Parkway (featured in Francis Ford Coppola's short film in *New York Stories*), **Horace Mann,** 231 W. 246th St., and **Riverdale,** 5250 Fieldston Road. Sycamore Ave. between W. 252nd and W. 254th St. is the **Riverdale Historic District.**

VAN CORTLANDT PARK

Sprawling east of Broadway and north of Van Cortlandt Park South, all the way to the Westchester border. Subway: 1, 9 to 242nd St. ☎718-430-1890. The park's ***special events office*** *(☎718-430-1848) offers info about the many concerts and sports activities that take place during the warmer months. Park closes at 10pm.*

Van Cortlandt Park spreads across 1146 acres of ridges and valleys in the northwest Bronx. The slightly grungy park has two golf courses, tennis courts, baseball diamonds, soccer, football, and cricket fields, kiddie recreation areas, a large swimming pool, and barbecue facilities. Hikers have plenty of clambering options: the **Cass Gallagher Nature Trail** in the park's northwestern section leads to rock outcroppings from the last ice age and to what is arguably the most untamed wilderness in the city. The **Old Putnam Railroad Track,** once the city's first rail link to Boston, now leads past the quarry that supplied marble for Grand Central Terminal. Ballplayers have a choice between the baseball and softball diamonds of the **Indian Field recreation area** (laid atop the burial grounds of pro-rebel Stockbridge Indians who were ambushed and massacred by British troops during the Revolutionary War) or the **Parade Grounds**.

VAN CORTLANDT MANSION

Broadway, at W. 246th St. Subway: 1, 9 to 242nd St. ☎ 718-543-3344. Open Tu-F 10am-3pm, Sa-Su 11am-4pm. Admission $2, seniors and students $1.50, children under 12 free.

This national landmark, built in 1748 by the prominent political clan of the same name, is the oldest building in the Bronx. George Washington held his 1781 meeting with Rochambeau to determine his strategy in the last days of the Revolutionary War here. He also began his triumphal march into NYC from here in 1783. These days, the stone house contains various rooms decorated in period styles. Besides featuring the oldest doll house in the US, the house also sports a colonial-era garden and sundial.

MANHATTAN COLLEGE

From corner of Broadway and 242nd St., take 242nd St. uphill all the way. Subway: 1, 9 to 242nd St. ☎ 718-862-8000; www.manhattan.edu.

As you walk up 242nd St., you'll see the red-brick buildings and chapel of this 139-year-old private liberal arts institution that began as a high school. The campus sprawls over stairs, squares, and plateaus like a life-sized game of Chutes and Ladders. Hardy souls who ascend the campus's peaks can take in a cinemascopic view of the Bronx. The college takes its name from its original location, 131st St. and Broadway in Manhattan. The college's teams are called the Jaspers, after the first baseball coach, Brother Jasper of Mary, who may have invented the 7th-inning stretch.

WAVE HILL

Independence Ave., at W. 249th St. ☎ 718-549-3200; www.wavehill.org. Subway: 1, 9 to 231st St., then bus Bx7 or Bx10 to 252nd St. Walk across the Henry Hudson Pkwy. and turn left; walk to 249th St., turn right and walk to Wave Hill Gate. Open June-July Tu-Th and Sa-Su 9am-5:30pm, W 9:30am-dusk; mid-April to May and Aug. to mid-Oct. Tu-Su 9am-5:30pm; mid-Oct. to mid-April 9am-4:30pm. Wheelchair access. Admission $4, students and seniors $2; Tu free, Sa free until noon; mid-Nov. to mid-Mar. free.

This pastoral estate in Riverdale commands a broad, amazing view of the Hudson and the Palisades. Samuel Langhorne Clemens (a.k.a. Mark Twain), conductor Arturo Toscanini, and Teddy Roosevelt all resided in Wave Hill House. Horticultural enthusiasts will enjoy the greenhouses and spectacular formal gardens. Also on the grounds is Glyndor House, which shows exhibitions of contemporary art.

WOODLAWN AND WOODLAWN CEMETERY

East of Van Cortlandt Park. Subway: 4 to Woodlawn. Open daily 9am-4:30pm.

Music lovers pay tribute at the resting place of jazz legends Miles Davis, Duke Ellington, and Lionel Hampton. Other famous individuals, such as Herman Melville, are buried here, some of them in impressive mausoleums. To the north is Woodlawn, a neighborhood filled with Irish ex-patriates.

PELHAM BAY PARK

In the northeast corner of the Bronx. Subway: 6 to Pelham Bay Park. Rangers: ☎ 718-430-1890. Open dawn to dusk. Stables: Shore Rd. at City Island Dr.; take Bx29 from the Pelham Bay Park station. ☎ 718-885-0551. Open daily 9am-dusk. $25 per hr. ***Bartow-Pell Mansion:*** *895 Shore Rd., opposite the golf courses. ☎ 718-885-1461. Open W and Sa-Su noon-4pm. Closed in Aug. Admission $2.50; students and seniors $1.25, under 12 free.*

New York City's largest park, **Pelham Bay Park** boasts over 2700 acres of green saturated with playing fields, tennis courts, golf courses, wildlife sanctuaries, Orchard Beach (see **Entertainment,** p. 188), and even training grounds for the city's mounted police force. The deeply knowledgeable **park rangers** lead a variety of history- and nature-oriented walks. From the **Pelham Bay stables,** you can take a guided ride around the park on horseback. The Empire/Greek Revival **Bartow-Pell Mansion Museum** sits among a prize-winning formal herb garden landscaped in 1915. The house's wonders include a free-standing spiral staircase and an herb garden arranged around a pond, complete with goldfish and spouting cherub.

CITY ISLAND

Subway: 6 to Pelham Bay Park; board bus Bx29 outside the station and get off at the first stop on City Island.

For a whiff of New England in New York, visit **City Island,** a community of century-old houses, sailboats, and a shipyard. Would-be sea salts can visit the **North Wind Undersea Institute,** 610 City Island Ave. at Bridge St., a maritime museum. Aquatic life can be sampled in the many seafood restaurants lining City Island Ave., the main artery; a careful search will yield the elusive $10 lobster. The food chain stops dead in its tracks at the nearby **Pelham Cemetery** on the west end of Reville Rd. Emblazoned on the gate is: "Lives are commemorated...deaths are recorded...love is undisguised...this is a cemetery." Hmmm. Thoughts to ponder as you wait for the Bx29 bus, which leaves every 30 minutes.

STATEN ISLAND

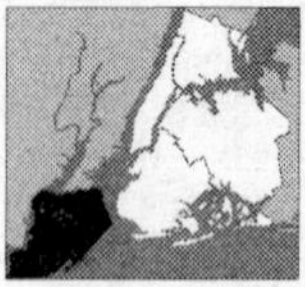
see map p. 344

Unless a specific site from the following list particularly piques a personal interest, Staten Island is, on the whole, not worth the trek. But perhaps, to some, the few fine attractions may seem better for their mystique. Because of the hills and the distances (and some dangerous neighborhoods in between), it's a bad idea to *walk* from one site to the next. **Make sure to plan your excursion with the bus schedule in mind.** You can pick one up from the VISIT booth on the Manhattan side of the ferry, or from the Staten Island chamber of commerce, who also sell street maps ($2).

SNUG HARBOR CULTURAL CENTER

Cultural Center: *1000 Richmond Terrace. Bus S40. ☎ 718-448-2500; www.statenisland-arts.org. Free tours of the grounds offered Sa-Su 2pm, starting at the Visitors Center.* ***Botanical Garden:*** *☎ 718-273-8200; www.sibg.org. Open daily dawn-dusk.* ***Scholar's Garden:*** *Open Tu-Su 10am-5pm. $5. Tours W, Sa, Su on the hour noon-4pm.* ***Newhouse Center:*** *☎ 718-448-2500 ext. 260. Open W-Su noon-5pm. Suggested donation $2.* ***Noble collection:*** *☎ 718-447-6490. Call for hours.* ***Children's Museum:*** *☎ 718-273-2060. Open Tu-Su 11am-5pm. $4; under 2 free.*

Founded in 1801, Sailors' Snug Harbor originally served as a home for retired sailors (the iron fence that barricades it originally kept old mariners from quenching their thirst at nearby bars). Purchased by the city and opened in 1976 as a cultural center, it now includes 28 historic buildings scattered over wonderfully placid, unpopulated parkland—83 sprawling, green, and amazingly well-kept acres of national historic landmark. Gardens of various styles are cultivated throughout the grounds of the Center as part of the **Staten Island Botanical Garden:** the **Connie Gretz Secret Garden, the New York Chinese Scholar's Garden,** and the **White Garden** (which offers tea every other Su) are a few. The Center provides various spaces as resources for the arts. The **Newhouse Center for Contemporary Art** shows revolving exhibits of contemporary art; the **Noble Maritime collection** houses Noble's artwork that focuses on NY's working waterfront. The **Children's Museum** features interactive exhibits. Plays, recitals, and concerts occur often. Snug Harbor also offers free summer concerts Su on the North Lawn.

HISTORIC RICHMOND TOWN

441 Clarke Ave. Bus S74 to Richmond Rd. and St. Patrick's Pl.; 30min. ☎ 718-351-1611. Open July-Aug. W-F 10am-5pm, Sa-Su 1-5pm; Sept.-Dec. W-Su 1-5pm. $4; students, seniors, and 6-18 $2.50.

A huge, recreated village complex documenting three centuries of Staten Island's culture and history, Historic Richmond Town features reconstructed 17th- to 19th-century dwellings exhibiting artifacts from the collection of the SI Historical Society as well as authentic "inhabitants" (costumed master craftspeople and their apprentices), who also give well-informed tours of the grounds. Head for the **Voorlezer's House,** the oldest surviving elementary school in the US (built in 1695). The museum rotates the buildings it opens to the public, so call in advance to find out what you can see and to get info about the summertime "living history" events.

MORAVIAN CEMETERY

On Richmond Rd., at Todt Hill Rd., in Dongan Hills. Bus S74 to Todt Hill Rd. Open daily 8am-6pm.

Here, Commodore Cornelius Vanderbilt (the creator of the ferry) and his monied clan lie in an ornate crypt, designed in 1886 by Richard Morris Hunt. The grounds around the Vanderbilt mausoleum were landscaped by Frederick Law Olmsted, designer of Central Park.

INSIDE

Museums & Galleries

New York may never sleep, but it is always collecting. While the past may be shown little respect on New York's streets, temples to history, art, and science dominate the city's landscape. The Museum of the City of New York houses Gotham's own relics, while wonderful collections of paintings, sculpture, and fossils are strewn throughout the city. The options are endless: swoon under a life-sized replica of a great blue whale at the American Museum of Natural History. Peer into the cockpit of a Blackbird spy plane at the Intrepid Sea-Air-Space Museum. Slip into the world of the 2000-year-old Egyptian Temple of Dendur at the Metropolitan Museum of Art. Relax alongside Monet's *Water Lilies* at the Museum of Modern Art. New York has accumulated more artwork in more museums than any other city in the New World, and it shows no signs of letting up.

During the annual **Museum Mile Festival** in mid-June, Fifth Ave. museums keep their doors open until late at night, stage engaging exhibits, involve city kids in mural painting, and fill the streets with music. Many museums also sponsor film series and live concerts throughout the year (see **Entertainment,** p. 181). Be aware that many major museums, including the Met, the Cloisters, The Frick, and the Whitney, are not open on Monday. The MoMA is closed Wednesday.

MUSEUMS BY NEIGHBORHOOD

FINANCIAL DISTRICT		SOHO	
Museum of Jewish Heritage	(120)	Museum for African Art	(120)
National Museum of the American Indian	(121)	New Museum of Contemporary Art	(121)
New York City Police Museum	(122)	New York City Fire Museum	(118)

MUSEUMS BY NEIGHBORHOOD, CONTINUED

MUSEUM DIRECTORY

METROPOLITAN MUSEUM OF ART

1000 Fifth Ave., at 82nd St. Subway: 4, 5, 6 to 86th St. Recorded info 535-7710, upcoming concerts and lectures 570-3949; www.metmuseum.org Open Su and Tu-Th 9:30am-5:15pm, F-Sa 9:30am-8:45pm. Suggested donation: $10, students and seniors $5, members and children under 12 (with an adult) free. Foreign Visitors Desk: Maps, brochures, and assistance in a number of languages; call 650-2987. Gallery Tours: Free. Daily. Inquire at the main info desk for schedules, topics, and meeting places, or call 570-3930. Key to the Met Audio Guides: $5, $4.50 for members, discounts for groups. Disabled Access: ☎535-7710. Wheelchairs at the coat-check areas; enter through the 81st St. entrance. TTY: ☎396-5057.

Founded in 1870 by a group of distinguished art collectors, philanthropists, civic leaders, and artists, the Met, whose collection includes more than two million works of art spanning over 5,000 years, is one of the largest and finest museums in the world. Don't rush the Metropolitan experience; you could camp out here for a month—in fact, two youngsters did exactly that in the children's book *From the Mixed-up Files of Mrs. Basil E. Frankweiler*. For those desiring more direction, tour and audio guide information is listed above.

If you decide to brave the Met without such guidance, here is one suggested strategy: focus on examining a limited number of collections in depth. The **European paintings** collection, a whopping 2,500 works, is the greatest collection of its kind in the world, and is so prodigious that it could easily be the first and only stop for visitors to the Met. The entrance to these labyrinthine galleries of old and more-modern masters is centrally located at the top of the main staircase on the second floor. Jacques-Louis David's larger-than-life portrait of the French chemist Lavoisier and his wife hangs on the western wall of this first chamber. Pressing onwards, you'll see familiar masterpieces by van Gogh, Cézanne, Vermeer, and Monet, not to mention such seminal works as van Eyck's *The Crucifixion* and *The Last Judgement*, El Greco's luminous *View of Toledo*, Botticelli's *The Last Communion of Saint Jerome*, and Brueghel's starkly realistic *The Harvesters*.

If oils don't set your interest aflame, you may want to try scarabs (which are often more popular with younger children), to the right of the main entrance in the **Egyptian Art** collection. The finest assembly of ancient Egyptian artifacts outside of the Egyptian Museum in Cairo, the Metropolitan Museum has added to the department through a sustained program of acquisitions and excavations between 1874 and the present with the permission of the Egyptian government. The 36,000 pieces in this department, most of which are on permanent public display, date from the Prehistoric Period (from 30,000 BC) to the Byzantine Period (ending in AD 641) and include beautiful and compelling vestiges of ancient Egyptian culture: jewelry, mummies in their wrappings, potsherds, and the fully intact **Temple of Dendur,** a monument reassembled with precision after its trip from the shore of the Nile to the Museum Mile.

Nearby, a line of ghostly European knights stand guard in the **Arms and Armor** hall. In addition to the stereotypical medieval European suits, swords, and firearms from the 5th to the 19th centuries, the collection also displays a striking set of Japanese armaments. Most of the antiques presented here are spectacular examples of craftsmanship, never intended for use in actual battle. One of the treasures of the collection is a tremendously ornate suit of armor created in the mid-16th century for the French king Henry II.

Directly above the Northern wing and the Egyptian galleries, you'll find the largest and most comprehensive collection of **Asian Art** in the West, from monumental Chinese Buddhist sculptures and ancient statuettes to Japanese prints, not to mention an exquisite and preeminently serene re-creation of a Ming scholar's garden. In a more bellicose vein and a different part of Asia, though on the same level of the building, one can hardly miss the huge winged guardian icons flanking a passageway in the **Ancient Near Eastern Art** gallery. They originally kept an imposing lookout at the palace of Ashurnasirpal at Nimrud in the 9th century BC. Unique bas-reliefs of the Assyrian kings and their entourages of bird-men and eunuchs adorn the walls.

Another exhibit that should not be overlooked is the world-renowned **Costume Institute,** at the north end of the museum's Ground Floor. This collection houses over 75,000 costumes and accessories from five continents from the 17th century to the present and offers interesting rotating exhibits such as the 1998 memorial to Gianni Versace.

The list of stupendously well-appointed galleries continues from there. The **American Art** exhibition possesses such classics as Sargent's *Madame X* as well as works by Gilbert Stuart (the renowned painter of George Washington), Mary Cassatt, James McNeill Whistler, and others. Also worth a gander is one of the most famous canvases in all of American art: the 1851 painting *Washington Crossing the Delaware*, by Emanuel Gottlieb Leutze.

The department of **Greek and Roman Art** has assembled a strong and meticulously attentive display of classical forms: the traditional museum complement of ancient marble torsos and heads pose for the public, along with wall paintings from Roman villas, Greek painted urns on which the Romantic intellectual movement rhapsodized, and superb glass- and silver-wares.

Many of the pieces in the department of **Musical Instruments** are playable and can be heard in recordings as well as at live concerts and lectures. One historic American pipe organ is used in a recital on the first Wednesday of each month, from October to May. Another seasonal display, not to be missed: the annual **Christmas tree** that goes up at the end of November on the first floor, covered with the Met's stunning collection of papier-mache angels and accompanied by their Neapolitan crêche (nativity).

MUSEUM OF MODERN ART (MOMA)

***Until Spring 2002**: 11 W. 53rd St. between 5th and 6th Aves. Subway: E, F to Fifth Ave.-53rd St.; or B, D, F to 47th-50th St.-Rockefeller Center. ☎ 708-9400; info and film schedules 708-9480; www.moma.org. Admission: $10, students and seniors $6.50, under 16 free. Pay what you wish F 4:30-8:30pm. Extra fee for some special exhibitions; audio guide rental $4. Open Sa-Tu and Th*

REST YER BONES

If you aim to see the **Met** in its entirety, you'll need a place to rest. Many charming courts and gardens offer a romantic setting for foot relief. Try the **Charles Engelhardt Court** in the American Wing, or the **European Sculpture Garden** between the Wrightsman Galleries and the Kravis Wing. Do a little meditating in the **Astor Court,** a Chinese scholar's garden complete with goldfish in the Asian art wing. **The Temple of Dendur** also offers an area upon which you can sit like a Nubian bird on a wire, while enormous windows grant a splendid view of Central Park and a ponderous stone offers a bed of sorts beside mummies of yore. On cool summer days, the **Gerald and Iris B. Cantor Roof Garden** (6th floor) allows you sunbathe alongside sculpture, while a view of the skyline proves that most gardens in the world lack a little altitude.

10:30am-5:45pm, F 10:30am-8:15pm. Free brochures and film tickets at information desk. ***Summer 2002-Late 2004, Location Change to MoMA Queens:*** *45-20 33rd St. in Long Island City. Subway: 7 to 33rd St.*

The MoMA commands one of the world's most impressive collections of post-Impressionist, late 19th- and 20th-century art. Founded in 1929 by scholar Alfred Barr in response to the Met's refusal to display cutting-edge work, the museum's first exhibit, held in a Fifth Ave. office building, displayed then unknowns Cézanne, Gaugin, Seurat, and van Gogh. But as the groundbreaking works of 1900 to 1950 moved from cult to masterpiece status, MoMA, in turn, shifted from revolution to institution. In 2000, the museum reclaimed its innovative edge by commissioning Japanese architect Yoshio Taniguchi to expand and renovate the museum—a $650-million project lasting until 2005. This enormous undertaking will double the museum's size. Temporary exhibits partly make up for the interim closing of parts of the permanent collection.

Construction reaches its peak in the middle of 2002, and from summer 2002 until late 2004, the Museum will be temporarily relocated to **MoMA Queens. MoMA Queens** will be housed in a converted Swingline factory. Planned shows include an exhibition of contemporary drawings in fall 2002 and a display of Picasso and Matisse works in spring 2003.

Until Summer 2002, the MoMA in Manhattan will continue to display cutting-edge art. The third floor of the museum tracks American and European painting from the end of World War II to the late 1960s. Some of the collection's most renowned works are Rodin's *John the Baptist;* van Gogh's *The Starry Night;* Duchamp's dadaist *To Be Looked at (from the Other Side of the Glass) with One Eye, Close To, for Almost an Hour; White on White* by the Russian Constructivist Malevich; Henri Matisse's *Dance (First Version);* Mark Rothko's *Red, Brown, and Black*, and Andy Warhol's signature pieces, the gold *Marilyn Monroe* and the *Campbell Soup Cans.* However, MoMA owns much more 20th-century art than it will ever have space to display. An ever-changing assortment of works lurks behind the third-floor stairwell, in a chamber full of the museum's recent acquisitions. The museum's fourth floor summit houses the architecture and design collections, with scale models by notables such as Frank Lloyd Wright and Buckminster Fuller.

AMERICAN MUSEUM OF NATURAL HISTORY

Central Park West, between 77th and 81st Sts. Subway: B, C to 81st St. Entrances at 77th St., Columbus Ave., Central Park W., and 81st St. ☎ 769-5100; www.amnh.org. Open Su-Th 10am-5:45pm, F-Sa 10am-

8:45pm. Suggested donation $10; students and seniors $7.50; children $6. Highlight Tours: 6 per day from 10:15am-3pm, usually leaving 15min. past the hr.; free. Imax: ☎ 769-5034. Combo-ticket (Museum and Imax) $15, students and seniors $11, children 2-12 $9. Double Feature: F-Sa at 9pm $21, students and seniors $15.50, children $12.50. Rose Center Hayden Planetarium (Museum and Space Show): $19, students and seniors $14, children $11.50. Wheelchair access.

You're never too old for the Natural History Museum, one of the world's largest museums devoted to science. The main draw is the fourth-floor **dinosaur halls,** which display real fossils in 85 percent of the exhibits (most museums use fossil casts). The bones of T. Rex, Triceratops, and the rest of the gang are overwhelmingly impressive, although chances are you'll have to fight off overly enthusiastic kids to get close to them.

If you're not into the Jurassic or the Cretaceous, chart the development of world cultures as displayed in life-sized dioramas on the second floor or dodge the 90-foot blue whale suspended from the ceiling of the first-floor. The **Alexander White Natural Science Center,** the museum's only room holding *live* animals, explains the ecology of New York City to children, while the **Discovery Room** gives them artifacts they can touch. The museum also houses an **Imax** cinematic extravaganza on one of New York's largest movie screens—four stories high and 66 feet wide.

But perhaps the most impressive part of the museum is the sparkling **Hayden Plantarium** within the **Rose Center for Earth and Space.** The sheer size of the 87 ft. (26.5m) sphere that holds the planetarium is awe-inspiring enough to make one appreciate the wonders of space discovery. And the view of the Planetarium from the outside at night, in which the sphere looks like it's floating within a glass and steel box, is nothing short of spectacular.

THE CLOISTERS

Fort Tryon Park in Washington Heights. Subway: A to 190th St.; then follow Margaret Corbin Dr. 5 blocks north. ☎ 923-3700. Open Mar.-Oct. Tu-Su 9:30am-5:15pm; Nov.-Feb. Tu-Su 9:30am-4:45pm. Museum tours Mar.-Oct. Tu-F 3pm, Su noon. Suggested donation: $10; students and seniors $5. Includes same day admission to the Met's main building in Central Park.

Crowning a hilltop at the northern tip of Manhattan, this tranquil branch of the Metropolitan Museum of Art incorporates pieces of 12th- and 13th-century French monasteries into its own medieval design. The Cuxa Cloister, taken from a 12th century Benedictine monastery, is an especially beautiful portion of the mueseum. John D. Rockefeller donated the site (now Ft. Tryon Park) and many of the works that make up the Cloisters' rich collection of medieval art, including frescoes, panel paintings, and stained glass. Highlights of the collection include the sublimely detailed Unicorn Tapestries, which tell the tale of a hunt for a magic unicorn; the Treasury, where the museum's most fragile offerings are found; and the Robert Campin's altarpiece, one of the first known oil paintings. When the museum tires you out, make like a monk and sit in the two small gardens planned according to the aesthetic sensibilities of medieval horticulture.

FRICK COLLECTION

1 E. 70th St., at Fifth Avenue. Subway: 6 to 68th St. ☎ 288-0700; www.frick.org. Open: Tu-Sa 10am-6pm, Su 1-6pm. Admission: $10, students and seniors $5. No children under 10 admitted; children under 16 must be accompanied by an adult. Group visits by appointment only. Free audio guides. Wheelchair accessible.

Designed by Thomas Hastings in the style of an 18th-century mansion, the former residence of Henry Clay Frick, the Pittsburgh coke and steel industrialist, is now home to a magnificent ensemble of fine art. This extraordinary collection of works, two-thirds of which belonged to Frick himself, consists of impressive Western masterpieces of the early Renaissance through the late 19th century. Paintings by the world's greatest Old Masters are displayed here, in addition to vases, 18th-century French sculptures, Renaissance bronzes, and porcelains.

The distinguished list of artists on view at the Frick include Renoir, van Eyck, Goya, Whistler, El Greco, Holbein, Corot, and Titian. A stately self-portrait of Rembrandt, in the West Gallery, is one of the artist's most keenly perceptive works. Vermeer, too, is particularly well represented in the collection; the Frick owns three of the roughly 40 works to which he has lent his brush. Also be sure to note the gold desk-watch in the Garden Court, which conforms to the odd 10-hour-day standard mandated by the French revolution. Free audio guides or nicely detailed guide books ($1) will help you navigate the exhibits. A slide show on the history of the collection and the grounds runs every hour on the half-hour. Frick's favorite organ music sometimes plays in the relaxing Garden Court (see **Entertainment,** p. 182). The Frick Collection also operates an art reference library at 10 E. 71st St., which is one of the leading institutions for research in the history of art.

PIERPONT MORGAN LIBRARY

29 E. 36th St., at Madison Ave. Subway: 6 to 33rd St. ☎685-0610; www.morganlibrary.org. Open Tu-F 10:30am-5pm, Sa 10:30am-6pm, Su noon-6pm. Admission: $8, students and seniors $6; under 12 free.

The Pierpont Morgan Library contains a stunning collection of rare books, manuscripts, and Near Eastern seals gathered by banker J.P. Morgan and his son. Completed in 1907, the library remained private until 1924, when J.P. Morgan, Jr. opened it to the public. In 1991, the museum doubled its size with the acquisition of Morgan's former townhouse. Its permanent collection includes drawings and prints by Blake and Dürer, illuminated Renaissance manuscripts, Thoreau's journals, a manuscript copy of Dickens's *A Christmas Carol*, and sheet music handwritten by Beethoven and Mozart. The **West Room,** Morgan Sr.'s sumptuous former office, has a carved ceiling made during the Italian Renaissance and stained glass from 15th- and 17th-century Switzerland.

But the heart of the library is the **East Room,** which features stacks of mahogany-toned, hand-bound volumes encircled by two balconies. Among the more notable items in the room are one of three existing likenesses of John Milton and a copy of the Gutenberg Bible, the first printed book (only 11 survive in the world). The Morgan also displays the Stavelot Triptych, a jewel-encrusted 12th-century triptych believed to contain fragments from the Holy Cross.

The Morgan's temporary exhibitions for 2002 include *Pierre Matisse and His Artists*, a display of major artworks by artists represented by the dealer (Feb. 14-May 19).

GUGGENHEIM MUSEUM

1071 Fifth Ave., at 89th St. Subway: 4, 5, 6 to 86th St. ☎423-3500; www.guggenheim.org. Open Su-W 9am-6pm, F-Sa 9am-8pm. Admission: $12, students and seniors $8, under 12 free; F 6-8pm "pay-what-you-wish." Another Branch: Guggenheim Museum SoHo (see p. 118). Wheelchair accessible: ☎423-3539.

The Guggenheim's most famous exhibit? The building itself, surely. The inverted white quasi-ziggurat, designed by Frank Lloyd Wright, is a modern architectural masterpiece. In his attempt to embrace nature and emphasize its plasticity, Wright produced a spiral design reminiscent of a nautilus shell, with interdependent spaces, dividing the galleries similar to the membranes of a citrus fruit.

The Guggenheim contains a large collection of non-objective paintings, including significant works in the fields of cubism, surrealism, American minimalism, and abstract expressionism. Each spin of the museum's spiral holds one sequence or exhibit, while a portion of the **Tower Galleries** exhibits the **Thannhauser Collection.** Donated by Justin K. Thannhauser in 1976, the group of 19th- and 20th-century works includes several by Picasso and Matisse, and a beautiful collection of Impressionist-era paintings by van Gogh, Gaugin, Manet, and Cézanne. The rest of the permanent collection features geometric art, including that of Mondrian and his Dutch De Stijl school, the Bauhaus experiments of German Josef Albers, and the Russian modernists. The collection also holds several Degas sculptures and works by such artists as Kandinsky and Klee, and German Expressionists such as Kirchner.

BROOKLYN MUSEUM OF ART

200 Eastern Pkwy., at Washington Ave. Subway: 2, 3 to Eastern Parkway/Brooklyn Museum. ☎718-638-5000; www.brooklynart.org. Open W-F 10am-5pm, Sa-Su 11am-6pm. Open first Sa of the month 11am-11pm. Suggested donation $6 students and seniors $3 under 12 free. Free on first Sa of each month after 5pm.

The Brooklyn Museum is home to a fine collection of art from all over the world. Its enormous Oceanic and New World art collection takes up the central two-story space on the first floor—the towering totem poles covered with human/animal hybrids could fit nowhere else—and the impressive African art collection was the first of its kind in an American museum when it opened in 1923.

You'll find outstanding Ancient Greek, Roman, Middle Eastern, and Egyptian galleries on the third floor; only London's British Museum and Cairo's Egyptian Museum have larger Egyptian collections. Crafts, textiles, and period rooms on the fourth floor tell the story of American upper class interiors from the 17th to the 19th centuries, including the Moorish Room, a lush bit of exotica from John D. Rockefeller's Manhattan townhouse. John Singer Sargent and the Hudson River School grace the American Collection on the fifth floor. Nearby, the contemporary gallery contains noteworthy work by Alfredo Jaar and Francis Bacon. European art from the early Renaissance to Post-Impressionism, including works by Renoir and Monet also appear on the floor. Galleries downstairs host temporary exhibits and weekend talks.

WHITNEY MUSEUM OF AMERICAN ART

945 Madison Ave., at 75th St. Subway: 6 to 77th St. ☎570-3676; www.whitney.org. Open Tu-Th 11am-6pm, F 1pm-9pm, Sa-Su 11am-6pm. Admission $10, students and seniors $8, children under 12 free; F 6-9pm pay-what-you-wish. ***Another branch*** *is located in the Philip Morris building (120 Park Ave., at 42nd St.; ☎917-663-2453), where a sculpture court features a changing array of installation pieces. Admission and frequent gallery talks (M, W, F at 1pm) free. Wheelchair accessible.*

When the Metropolitan Museum declined a donation of over 500 works from Gertrude Vanderbilt Whitney in 1929, the wealthy patron and sculptor formed her own museum, which in 1966 settled within its present-day walls: a futuristic fortress-style building designed by Marcel Breuer.

This museum, the only one with a historical mandate to champion the works of living American artists, has assembled the largest collection, consisting of 12,000 objects, of 20th- and 21st-century American art in the world. Even the modern-art skeptic will be impressed by Jasper John's *Three Flags*, Frank Stella's *Brooklyn Bridge*, Ad Reinhardt's *Abstract Painting, Number 33*, Willem De Kooning's *Woman on Bicycle*, and Georgia O'Keefe's Flower Collection. The mezzanine-level galleries, accessible from the top floor, hosts a collection of Alexander Calder's called *Circus*; he approaches modernism with a sure feel for the joy and vibrancy of color and the clean smoothness of form and motion. The result: mobiles that appeal to the child within everyone.

OTHER MAJOR COLLECTIONS

ALICE AUSTEN HOUSE MUSEUM AND GARDEN

2 Hylan Blvd., in Staten Island. Bus S51 to Hylan Blvd. Walk 1 block toward the water. ☎718-816-4506. Open Mar.-Dec. Th-Su noon-5pm; grounds open daily until dusk. Admission: $2, children free.

This 18th-century cottage was home of photographer Alice Austen, who took more than 8000 photographs of her upper-middle-class life. After the 1929 stock market crash, Austen languished in the poorhouse until the Staten Island Historical Society discovered her work and published it in *Life* months before her death. This quiet museum displays Austen's photos and has a garden with great views of the Verrazano-Narrows Bridge.

AMERICAN CRAFT MUSEUM

40 W. 53rd St. Subway: B, D, F, Q to 47th-50th St.-Rockefeller Center. ☎956-3535. Open Tu-W, Th 10am-8pm, F-Su 10am-6pm. Admission: $7.50, students and seniors $4, under 12 free; Th pay as you wish.

No wooden *chachkas* here. Three floors of phenomenal ceramic, glass, metal, wood, fiber, and origami displays by contemporary artists. The changing exhibits range from elegant paper architecture to light screens. In the works for 2002 is an exhibit of turned and sculpted wood and a presentation of modern Native American art.

The Cloisters

Guggenhein Museum

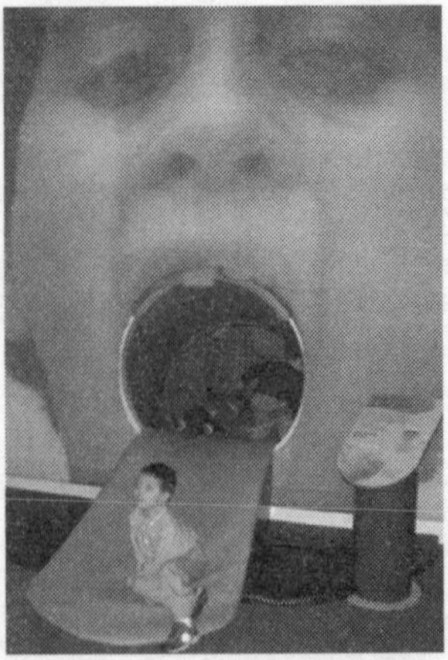
The Children's Museum

AMERICAN MUSEUM OF THE MOVING IMAGE

35th Ave., at 36th St., in Astoria, Queens. Subway: G, R to Steinway St. Walk one block down and turn right onto 35th Ave. ☎718-784-0077; www.ammi.org. Open Tu-F noon-5pm, Sa-Su 11am-6pm. $8.50; students and seniors $5.50; children $4.50; under 4 free. Screening tickets free with admission.

A museum dedicated to the art of film and television production, with displays of cameras, projectors, and movie-related memorabilia. The Monk's Cafe set from "Seinfeld" is here, as are handwritten scripts by Larry David. On the third floor, you can create your own digitally animated film sequence, dub your voice into scenes from *Taxi Driver*, or alter sound effects from movies like *Terminator 2*. Demonstrations of film- and TV-related processes add depth to the displays. Nonetheless, the admission fee would be steep if it did not cover the price of screenings of classic movies on weekends.

THE ASIA SOCIETY

Midtown: *502 Park Ave., at 59th St. Subway: 4, 5, 6, N, R to 59th St.-Lexington Ave.* ***Uptown:*** *725 Park Ave., at 70th St. Subway: 6 to 68th St. ☎517-ASIA or 288-6400. Open M-Sa 10am-6pm. Admission: $4, students and seniors $2, free noon-2pm daily. Tours Sa 12:30pm.*

The Asia Society shows exhibitions of Asian art, from Iran and Japan to Yemen and Mongolia, in addition to works by Asian-American artists. After an 18-month renovation, the headquarters in Midtown will reopen in October 2001. Planned exhibits include *Monks and Merchants: Silk Road Treasures from Northwest China, Gansu and Ningxia, 4th to 7th Century* and *Conversations with Traditions*.

AUDUBON TERRACE MUSEUM GROUP

613 W. 155th St. between Broadway and Riverside Dr. Subway: 1, 9 to 157th St. ***Hispanic Society:*** *☎926-2234. Open Tu-Sa 10am-4:30pm, Su 1-4pm. Free.* ***Numismatic Society:*** *☎234-3130. Open Tu-F 9am-4:30pm, Su 1-4pm. Free.* ***Academy of Arts and Letters:*** *☎368-5900. Open mid-May- mid-June Th-Su 1-4 but call ahead for more info.*

Once part of John James Audubon's estate and game preserve, the regal terrace now contains an unlikely collection of museums. The **Hispanic Society of America,** devoted to Spanish and Portuguese arts and culture, includes mosaics, ceramics, and paintings by El Greco, Velázquez, and Goya. In addition to the vast collection of Spanish tiles and the ornate details of the building itself, students of Hispanic culture will enjoy the 100,000-volume research library. The much less trammeled **American Numismatic Society** presents...the fascinating history of the penny! (Who knew?) An extraordinary collection of coinage and paper money from prehistoric times to the present is on display in the exhibition room. The **American Academy of Arts and Letters** honors American artists, writers, and composers. Only open to the public for one month per year (mid-May to mid-June, call ahead for exact dates), the Academy exhibits manuscripts, paintings, sculptures, and first editions.

BROOKLYN CHILDREN'S MUSEUM

145 Brooklyn Ave., at St. Mark's Ave. Subway: 3 to Kingston Ave.; C to Kingston-Throop Aves. ☎718-735-4400; www.brooklynkids.org. Suggested admission $4; July-Aug. free F after 5pm. Open July-Aug. M and W-Th noon-5pm, F noon-7pm, Sa-Su 10am-5pm; Sept.-June W-F 2-5pm, Sa-Su 10am-5pm.

Founded in 1899, the Brooklyn Children's Museum is the oldest museum of its kind in America. The many exciting interactive exhibits tackle myriad subjects: from cultural artifacts to the natural sciences. The "Together in the City" exhibit discusses the communal life of New Yorkers.

COOPER-HEWITT NATIONAL DESIGN MUSEUM

2 E. 91st St., at Fifth Ave. Subway: 4, 5, 6 to 86th St.; 6 to 96th St. ☎849-8400. Open: Tu 10am-9pm, W-Sa 10am-5pm, Su noon-5pm. Admission: $8, students and seniors $5, under 12 free; Tu 5-9pm free. Library: ☎849-8330. Open by appointment until 5:30pm daily. Wheelchair accessible.

Founded in 1897 by the Hewitt sisters, the National Design Museum was the first—and remains the only—museum in the US devoted exclusively to historical and contemporary design. Occupying the splendid Carnegie Mansion since 1967, the Cooper-Hewitt holds a collection of over 250,000 objects—one of the largest collections of design in the world. However, the vast majority of this permanent collection is never on display to the public; design students with something particular in mind and tourists instilled with a preternatural fascination for 19th-century pottery are advised to make an appointment to privately explore these extensive archives. The public exhibitions, while only representing a small selection of works, are engaging and unusual.

FORBES MAGAZINE GALLERIES

62 Fifth Ave., at 12th St. Subway: R to 8th St.-NYU; L, N, R, 4, 5, 6 to Union Sq. ☎206-5548. Open Tu-Sa 10am-4pm; hours subject to change. Free. Children under 16 must be accompanied by an adult. Th reserved for group tours; call in advance.

Just one more multi-millionaire financier who turned over his personal collection to the public. The late Malcolm Forbes's irrepressible penchant for the offbeat permeates this collection of eclectic exhibits. Some of the more interesting include the world's largest private collection of Fabergé *objets d'art* and an exhibit tracing the evolution of the game Monopoly.

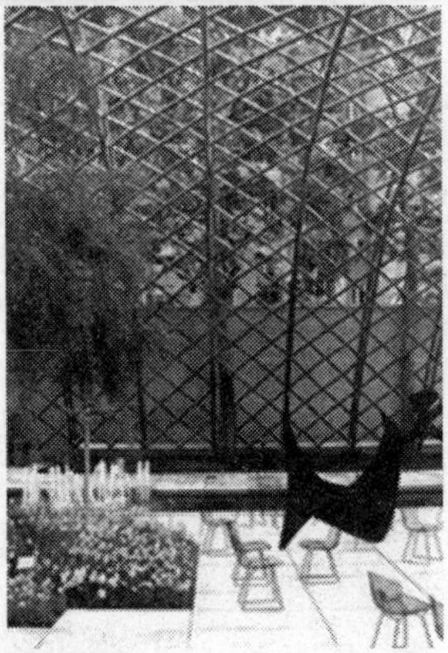
Inside MOMA

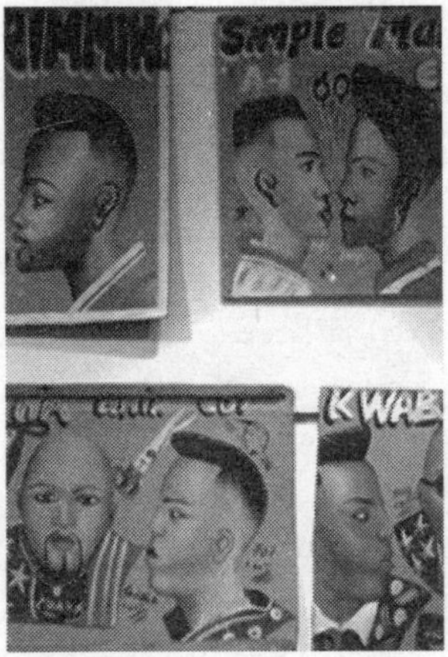

Museum for African Art

American Museum of Natural History

kids
IN THE CITY

Child's Play

Founded in 1973 by Harlem and Upper West Side artists and educators in response to the elimination of music and cultural programs in public schools, the **Children's Museum of Manhattan** is full of interactive exhibits fun for kids. Check out the "Body Odyssey" exhibit that allows you and your child to crawl through, climb on, and pedal through the gears of creaky machines. *(212 W. 83rd St., off Amsterdam Ave. ☎721-1223. Subway: 1, 9 to 79th St., 86th St. Open W-Su 10am-5pm. Adults and children $6, seniors $3, under 1 free. Wheelchair accessible.)*

Housed in a renovated 1904 firehouse, the **New York City Fire Museum** is perfect both for those kids who want to be firemen when they grow up and for those who keep trying to light the cat on fire. Impressive relics of fire-fighting past are on display, such as a hand-pulled truck from when George Washington was a volunteer NYC fire-fighter. Big moments in NYC history are honored, like the P.T. Barnum Museum fire, in which several firemen were injured rescuing the 400lb. fat lady. *(278 Spring St. between Varick and Hudson Sts. ☎691-1303. Subway: 1, 9 to Houston St. Open Tu-Su 10am-4pm. Suggested donation $4, students and seniors $2, under 12 $1.)*

GUGGENHEIM MUSEUM SOHO

575 Broadway, at Prince St. ☎423-3500. Subway: N, R to Prince St.; 6 to Spring St. Open Th-M 11am-6pm. Free. Wheelchair accessible.

This downtown branch of the Guggenheim fills two floors of a historic 19th-century building with selections from the museum's mammoth permanent collection. The gallery store peddles artsy trinkets perfect for browsing.

HALL OF FAME FOR GREAT AMERICANS

181st St. and Martin Luther King Jr. Blvd. on the campus of Bronx Community College. ☎718-289-5161. Subway: 4 to Burnside Ave. Walk 6 blocks west on Burnside Ave. as it becomes 179th St., then 1 block north. Open daily 10am-5pm. Free.

This poignant hall features over 100 bronze busts of America's immortals solemnly whiling away the years, among them Alexander Graham Bell, Abraham Lincoln, Booker T. Washington, and the Wright brothers.

INTERNATIONAL CENTER OF PHOTOGRAPHY

1133 Ave. of the Americas, at 43rd St. Subway: B, D, F, Q to 42nd St. ☎860-1777. Open Tu-Th 10am-5pm, F 10am-8pm, Sa-Su 10am-6pm. Admission: $8, students and seniors $6, under 12 $1.

Housed in a chic Midtown skyscraper, ICP is the city's only photography museum. The center showcases historical and contemporary works, from fine art to photo-journalism. The two floors rotate exhibits every three months and draw in famous international photographers such as Sebastio Salgado.

INTREPID SEA-AIR-SPACE MUSEUM

Pier 86 at 46th St. and 12th Ave. Subway: A, C, E to 42nd St. ☎245-0072.Open May 1-Sept. 30 M-F 10am-5pm, Sa-Su 10am-6pm; Oct. 1-Apr. 30 W-Su 10am-5pm. Last admission 1hr. before closing. Admission: $12; seniors, students, ages 12-17, and veterans $9; ages 6-11 $6, ages 2-5 $2; active duty servicemen, and children under 2 free, wheelchair patrons half price.

A dream come true for kids of all ages (even the adult ones), the museum features the veteran World War II and Vietnam War aircraft carrier *Intrepid*, the Vietnam War destroyer *Edson*, and the only publicly displayed guided-missile submarine *Growler*. Pioneer's Hall displays models, antiques, and film shorts of flying devices from the turn of the century to the 1930s. You can also climb aboard the *Intrepid's* 900 ft. flight deck to view old and new warplanes—including a declassified CIA A-12 Blackbird, the world's fastest spy plane. The excitement doesn't stop there: check out the Iraqi tanks parked near the gift shop (captured in the Gulf War) or the piece of the Berlin wall outside.

ISAMU NOGUCHI GARDEN MUSEUM

32-37 Vernon Blvd., at 10th St. and 33rd Rd., in Long Island City, Queens. Subway: N to Broadway. Walk along Broadway toward Manhattan until the end, then turn left on Vernon Blvd. ☎718-204-7088; www.noguchi.org. On weekends, a ***shuttle bus*** *leaves from the Asia Society, 70th St. and Park Ave. in Manhattan, every 30min. 11:30am-3:30pm; $5; return trips every hr. noon-5pm. Open Apr.-Oct. W-F 10am-5pm, Sa-Su 11am-6pm. Suggested donation $4, students and seniors $2. Lengthy free tour at 2pm.*

The late Isamu Nogughi designed this museum full of his own works in 1985. Located next to the world-renowned sculptor's studio, the museum contains 13 galleries and an outdoor sculpture garden. Noguchi's breathtaking work covers a wide range: from the sculptures that stand around the shimmering water of *The Well*, to his *akari* lamps, to Italian playground slides. Not on exhibit at the museum but perhaps indicative of the artist's vision is Noguchi's *Sculpture to Be Seen From Mars*, a 2 mi. long face carved in the dirt next to Newark International Airport.

JACQUES MARCHAIS MUSEUM OF TIBETAN ART

338 Lighthouse Ave., in Staten Island. Bus S74 to Richmond Rd. & Lighthouse Ave.; turn right and walk up the fairly steep hill. ☎718-987-3500. Open Apr.-Nov. W-Su 1-5pm; Dec.-Mar. W-F 1-5pm. Admission: $5, seniors and students $3, under 12 $2.

One of the largest private collections of Tibetan art in the West. Bronzes, paintings, and sculpture from Tibet and other Buddhist cultures are found in this serene hilltop museum. Its terraced sculpture gardens look down on the distant Lower Bay. Programs on Asian culture (fees vary) cover topics ranging from mask-making to meditation.

JAPAN SOCIETY

333 E. 47th St. and First Ave. Subway: 6 to 51st St. ☎832-1155. Open Tu-F 11am-6pm, Sa-Su 11am-5pm. Admission: $5, students and seniors $3.

By juxtaposing a plain, Western facade with an entirely Asian interior, Junzo Yoshimura sought to embody the attempt to bring together the people of Japan and the US. In the spirit of a traditional Japanese home, there is an interior pool garden on the first floor, complete with stones and bamboo trees. The gallery on the second floor exhibits traditional and contemporary Japanese art. The Society also sponsors Japanese language courses, lectures, meetings with notable leaders, a film series, and performances.

THE JEWISH MUSEUM

1109 Fifth Ave., at 92nd St. Subway: 6 to 96th St. ☎423-3200; www.thejewishmuseum.org. Open Su-M and W-Th 11am-5:45pm, Tu 11am-8pm. Admission: $8, students and seniors $5.50; Tu 5-8pm pay-what-you-wish. Wheelchair access info: ☎423-3225.

The gallery's permanent collection *Culture and Continuity: The Jewish Journey*, details the Jewish experience throughout history, ranging from ancient Biblical artifacts and ceremonial objects to contemporary masterpieces by Marc Chagall, Frank Stella, and George Segal, and culminating in hypermodernity with a deconstructivist mezuzah, and an interactive Talmud exhibit. Popular rotating exhibits usually emphasize the interpretation of art through the lens of social history. Summer Nights movie and sitcom programs run through July and August.

LOWER EAST SIDE TENEMENT MUSEUM

90 Orchard St., at Broome St. Subway: F to Delancey St.; J, M, Z to Essex St. ☎431-0233; www.tenement.org. Visitor Center and Gift Shop open daily 11am-5pm. 1hr. tours of the tenement leave from the Visitor's Center Tu-F every 30 min. 1-4pm; Th 4:30, 5, and 6pm; Sa-Su every 20 min. 11am-4:30pm. Walking tours Sa-Su 1 and 2:30 pm. Admission: $9, students and seniors $7.

Tours lead through three meticulously restored apartments that recreate the experiences of immigrant families who once inhabited the tenement: the Gumpertzes in 1870, the Rogarshevskys in 1918, and the Baldizzis in 1939. One-hour walking tours of the neighborhood, which also start at the Visitors Center, detail immigrant experiences in the Lower East Side (past and present) and highlight historical buildings.

MOUNT VERNON HOTEL MUSEUM AND GARDEN

421 E. 61st St. between York and First Aves. Subway: 4, 5, 6, N, R to 59th St.-Lexington Ave. ☎838-6878. Open Sept.-July W–Su 11am-4pm, Tu 11am-9pm. Admission: $4, students and seniors $3, under 12 free.

Formerly the Abigail Adams Smith Museum, this museum reconstructs the rooms of the Mount Vernon Hotel (1826-1833). In addition, a variety of programs, including tours, lectures, and concerts, helps to illuminate early 19th-century hotel life. For children the Summer Garden evenings offer games and music from the 19th century.

EL MUSEO DEL BARRIO

1230 Fifth Ave., at 104th St. Subway: 6 to 103rd St. ☎831-7272. Open W-Su 11am-5pm. Suggested contribution $4, students and seniors $2.

Founded in 1969 by Puerto Rican artists and activists, this museum has evolved into an expansive Latino cultural institution, representing art and culture from throughout the Caribbean and Latin America. The permanent collection, which has grown immensely in the past decade, includes works by Santos de Palo, hand-crafted wooden saint figures from Latin America, and a vast exhibit on pre-Columbian and Taino art and ceramics that date back to AD 1200. The artistic treasures culled from the permanent collection (such as the colorful Chicano prints and Haitian Vodun flags) complement the contemporary exhibits and celebrate Latin American culture past and present.

THE MUSEUM FOR AFRICAN ART

593 Broadway between Houston and Prince Sts. Subway: N, R to Prince St.; 6 to Spring St. ☎966-1313. Open Tu-F 10:30am-5:30pm, Sa-Su noon-6pm. Admission $5, students and seniors $2.50. Su free.

Features two major exhibits a year, along with several smaller exhibitions of stunning African and African-American art on such themes as storytelling, magic, religion, and mask-making. Objects on display span centuries, from ancient to contemporary, and come from all over Africa. Many hands-on family-oriented workshops on African culture are offered, providing instruction in traditional activities such as weaving and drumming.

MUSEUM OF AMERICAN ILLUSTRATION

128 E. 63rd St. between Lexington and Park Aves. Subway: 4, 5, 6, to 59th St.; N, R to Lexington Ave. ☎838-2560. Open Tu 9am-8pm, W-F 9am-5pm, Sa noon-4pm. Free.

Established in 1981 by the Society of Illustrators, this treasure of a museum owns over 1,500 works by such legendary artists as Rockwell, Pyle, and Wyeth. At any one time, a small exhibit in the main gallery focuses on the interplay between past, present, and future in the field of illustration.

MUSEUM OF THE CITY OF NEW YORK

1220 Fifth Ave., at 103rd St. Subway: 6 to 103rd St. ☎534-1672. Open W-Sa 10am-5pm, Su noon-5pm. Suggested contribution: $7; seniors, students, and children $4. Also sells tickets to theaters, other museums, and various city attractions.

This fascinating museum details the history of the Big Apple, from the construction of the Empire State Building to the history of Broadway theater. Cultural history of all varieties is on parade: from model ships and NYC paintings to hot pants and Yankees World Series trophies. The vast collection also includes an extensive photography exhibit documenting the evolution of New York in the first half of the 20th century, an exhibit on the consolidation of the boroughs in 1898, a toy gallery, and a variety of non-permanent exhibits.

MUSEUM OF JEWISH HERITAGE

18 First Pl. Subway: 4, 5 to Bowling Green; 1, 9 to South Ferry; N, R to Whitehall St. ☎968-1800. Open Su-W 9am-5pm, Th 9am-8pm, F 9am-2pm, closed on Jewish holidays. Admission: $7; students and seniors $5, under 5 free.

A painful yet uplifting tribute to the Jewish people in a sleek six-sided building recalling the Star of David. The collection of poignant personal artifacts complements hours of personal narratives to present a larger picture of Jewish life. While the exhibits on the Holocaust are inherently upsetting, they are tempered by the hopeful final displays.

MUSEUM OF TELEVISION AND RADIO

25 W. 52nd St. between Fifth and Sixth Aves. Subway: B, D, F to Rockefeller Center; or E, F to 53rd St.-Fifth Ave. ☎621-6600, daily activity schedule 621-6800. Open Tu-W and F-Su noon-6pm, Th noon-8pm. Hours extended until 9pm on F for theaters only. Admission: $6, students and seniors $4, under 13 $3, ISIC and AAA members free.

More archive than museum, this shrine to modern media contains over 100,000 TV and radio programs that are easily accessible through a computerized cataloguing system. In addition, the museum hosts a number of film screenings that focus on topics of social, historical, popular, or artistic interest (read: *Monty Python* marathons); daily schedule at the front counter.

NATIONAL ACADEMY MUSEUM

1083 Fifth Ave. between 89th and 90th Sts. Subway: 4, 5, 6, to 86th St. ☎369-4880. Open W-Th noon-5pm, F 10am-6pm, Sa-Tu 10am-5pm. Admission: $8; seniors, students, and children under 16 $4.50.

Founded in 1825 to "promote the fine arts through exhibition and instruction," the academy hosts exhibits and trains young artists. Such notables as Winslow Homer, Frederic Edwin Church, John Singer Sargent, and Thomas Eakins represent the 19th century in the permanent collection. The Academy also annually features America's oldest, continuously held juried art competition, scheduled to appear on exhibition in April 2002.

NATIONAL MUSEUM AND ARCHIVE OF LESBIAN AND GAY HISTORY

208 W. 13th St. between Seventh and Eighth Aves. Subway: 1, 2, 3, 9 to 14th St.; A, C, E, L to 14th St.-Eighth Ave. ☎620-7310; www.gaycenter.org. Open daily 6-9pm.

This museum, devoted to artwork that explores gay, lesbian, bisexual, and transgendered life, is housed in the Lesbian and Gay Community Services Center (p. 194). The museum includes a wide variety of exhibits that range from works by lesbian artists to photos of transgendered lives. Not to be missed is the Keith Haring bathroom (which is actually a conference room), every inch of which was transformed by Haring's brush.

NATIONAL MUSEUM OF THE AMERICAN INDIAN

1 Bowling Green. Subway: 4, 5 to Bowling Green. ☎668-6624. Open daily 10am-5pm, Th closes at 8pm. Free.

Housed in the stunning Custom House, this excellent museum exhibits the best of the Smithsonian's vast collection of Native American artifacts. The museum's exhibitions are entirely conceived and designed by Native American artists and craftsmen. Until July 2002, the museum will display *Spirit Capture: Native Americans and the Photographic Image*, an exhibit documenting Native American history in the last two centuries.

NEW MUSEUM OF CONTEMPORARY ART

583 Broadway between Prince and Houston Sts. ☎219-1222. Subway: 6 to Spring St.; N, R to Prince St.; B, D, F, Q to Broadway-Lafayette. Open W and Su noon-6pm, Th-Sa noon-8pm. Admission: $6, students and seniors $3, under 18 free. Th 6-8pm free.

Founded in 1977, the New Museum supports the newest and, usually, the most controversial in contemporary art, making it one of the premier museums of modern art in the world. Three galleries feature innovative art in many media. The museum sponsors free lectures, symposia, panel discussions, and film screenings that attempt to find connections between the art world and contemporary social issues. Most major exhibitions are complemented by "gallery talks" in which the artist holds court at the museum to discuss the work and answer questions.

NEW YORK CITY POLICE MUSEUM

25 Broadway, 2nd fl. Subway: 4, 5 to Bowling Green. ☎301-4440. Open Tu-Sa 10am-6pm. Suggested donation $2-5.

For devotees of criminal history, the police museum houses an extensive collection of memorabilia, most of which has never before been on public display. An impressive array of badges, guns, and criminal profiles appeals to the public's desire for luridness. Children may be fascinated by the "Interactive Crime Scene" exhibit, an exercise in deduction; adults can arrange a turn on the Firearms and Tactics Simulator used to train members of the police force (call in advance for reservations).

NEW YORK HISTORICAL SOCIETY

2 W. 77th St., at Central Park West. Subway: B, C to 72nd St., 81st St. ☎873-3400; www.nyhistory.org. Museum open Tu-Su 11am-5pm. Library open Tu-Su 11am-5pm, summer Tu-Sa 11am-5pm. Wheelchair access. Suggested donation $5, students and seniors $3, children free.

Founded in 1804, this is New York's oldest continuously operated museum. The block-long Neoclassical building houses both a library and museum for history buffs. The Society's extensive, six-million-object collection includes 132 Tiffany lamps and 435 Audubon watercolors. The **Henry Luce III Center,** on the fourth floor, houses the museum's collection. Children should visit the permanent "Kid City" installation, a delightful chronicle of the history of New York.

NEW YORK TRANSIT MUSEUM

Corner of Schermerhorn St. and Boerum Pl. Subway: 2, 3, 4, 5, M, N, R to Court St./Borough Hall. ☎718-243-3060. Open Tu-F 10am-4pm, Sa-Su noon-5pm. Admission $3, children and senior citizens $1.50, seniors free W noon-4pm.

Housed in the now-defunct Court St. subway station, this museum describes the birth and evolution of every aspect of New York's mass transit system, from subways to buses to commuter rails. The walk-through exhibit includes various subway maps from over the years, turnstiles, and even the trains themselves.

PARSONS EXHIBITION CENTER

2 W. 13th St., at Parsons School of Design on Fifth Ave. ☎229-8987. Subway: 4, 5, 6, L, N, R to 14th St. Open M-F 9am-6pm. Free.

A variety of exhibitions, many of student and faculty work, including photography, computer art, painting, and sculpture.

P.S.1 CONTEMPORARY ART CENTER

22-25 Jackson Ave., Long Island City, Queens. Subway: 7 to 45 Rd.-Courthouse Sq.; E, F to 23rd St.-Ely Ave.; G to 21st St. ☎718-784-2084; www.ps1.org. Wheelchair access. Open W-Su noon-6pm. Suggested donation $5, students and seniors $2.

Proving it is hip indeed to stay in school, P.S.1 presents cutting-edge exhibitions within a converted public school, the first in then-independent Long Island City. Rotating exhibits—even the staircase landings are used as display spaces—continue to keep up the museum's reputation for being on the pulse of contemporary art (artists featured in 2001 include Miri Segal and Kim Sooja). A partnership with MoMA has allowed P.S.1 access to that museum's resources, while giving the larger institution street credibility. Getting to the fourth floor might involve a climb up a precarious staircase (there's an elevator), but it leads to a spectacular view of the surroundings and Manhattan, not to mention the occasional work by 80s *enfant terrible* Julian Schnabel.

STUDIO MUSEUM

144 W. 125th St. between Adam Clayton Powell Jr. Blvd. and Lenox Ave. ☎864-4500. Subway: 2, 3 to 125th St. Open W-Th noon-6pm, F noon-8pm, Sa-Su 10am-6pm. Public Gallery Talks and Tour Sa at 1pm. Suggested donation $5, students and seniors $3, under 12 $1.

Born in 1967 at the height of the Civil Rights movement, the Studio Museum is dedicated to the collection and exhibition of works by contemporary black artists. Currently undergoing a major growth spurt that will add gallery space, an auditorium and a cafe, this museum features two vibrant exhibitions a year which include multimedia works, installations, paintings, sculptures, and photographs.

WATERFRONT MUSEUM

290 Conover St., at Barge #79, Pier 45, in Red Hook, Brooklyn. Subway: A, C, F, 2, 3, 4, 5 to Jay St.-Borough Hall; M, N, R to Court St.; then bus #B61 to Beard St.; walk a block in the opposite direction from bus; left onto Conover St. and it's 2 blocks to the waterfront. Free shuttle bus from surrounding Brooklyn neighborhoods (see website for details). ☎718-624-4719; www.waterfrontmuseum.org.
This is not your typical museum. First, it's located on a barge floating in the New York Harbor (the Lehigh Valley Railroad Barge #79, to be specific). Second, the focus of the museum is the barge, the pier, and the stunning view, in addition to the exhibits themselves. The proprietor of the museum pulled the barge out of a muddy bank himself and took years to restore it to its present state; currently, it is the only functional wooden barge left in New York Harbor. The museum hosts a great **Sunset Concert Series** (July-August Sa 8-11pm; doors open 7:30pm; suggested donation $5) and **Circus Sundays** in June when jugglers and acrobats come to entertain Red Hook's kids ($5, shows at 2pm and 4pm).

GALLERIES

New York's galleries are where contemporary art *goes down.* What's even better, gallery proprietors don't expect the sassy traveler (read: you with *Let's Go: NYC)* to buy anything (read: be able to afford anything on display). And they don't even charge for entrance—yes, sometimes the best of culture can be free.

To get started, ask for a free copy of *The Gallery Guide* (www.galleryguideonline.com) at any major museum or gallery. Published every two-to-three months, it lists the addresses, phone numbers, and hours of virtually every showplace in the city. Extensive gallery info can also be found in the "Choices" listings of the free *Village Voice*, the Art section of *Time Out* and *New York* magazines, the complimentary *The New York Art World* (www.thenewyorkartworld.com) available in select galleries, and in *The New Yorker*'s "Goings On About Town."

Most galleries are open Tuesday to Saturday, from 10 or 11am to 5 or 6pm. Galleries are usually only open on weekdays in the summer, and many are closed from late July to early September, as gallery types head to the Hamptons in droves for their late summer vacation. The **Art Shuttle** transports gallery-goers between SoHo, Chelsea, and beyond on Saturdays (☎769-8100; www.artshuttle.org; Sa 11am-6pm).

SOHO

Subway: B, D, F, Q to Broadway-Lafayette; N, R to Prince St.

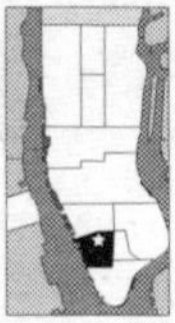

see map p. 315

SoHo galleries open and close with amazing rapidity, and many of them unfortunately have had to cut their losses and sell what they call "bread and butter" commercial art—a landscape that goes well with a sofa or a sunset dangerously verging on airbrush. Still, the avant-garde does make a stand here. The most cutting edge offerings have trouble making it to the ground-level, commercial galleries that line West Broadway and Broadway, so if you want to see SoHo's more experimental art, explore the second or third floors of gallery-packed buildings. The addresses 560-594 Broadway are known as the **Broadway Gallery Buildings,** with many small galleries packed inside. The following is only a sampling of this packed neighborhood.

Drawing Center, 35 Wooster St. between Grand and Broome Sts. (☎219-2166). Specializing exclusively in original works on paper, this non-profit space sets up reliably high-quality exhibits. Both historical and contemporary works are on show–everything from Picasso to Kara Walker. Open Tu-F 10am-6pm, Sa 11am-6pm; closed Aug.

Artists Space, 38 Greene St., 3rd fl., at Grand St. (☎226-3970). Non-profit gallery open since 1972. Its space is usually divided into several small exhibits by lesser-known artists. Slide file of unaffiliated artists gives those without backing a chance to shine. Open Tu-Sa 11am-6pm. Slide file open by appointment, usually F-Sa.

Pop International Galleries, Inc., 473 W. Broadway, between Prince and W. Houston Sts. One of the more commercial galleries, this space offers works by pop art icons such as Warhol, Lichtenstein, and Haring. Open M-Sa 10am-7pm, Su 11am-6pm.

Shakespeare's Fvlcrum, 500 Canal St. (☎966-6848). This is a gallery like no other; the owner wears transparent vixen clothing and displays Actual Art: art that requires the forces of nature for completion. Open Tu-Sa 11am-6pm, Su-M 1-6pm.

Exit Art/The First World, 548 Broadway, between Prince and Spring Sts., 2nd fl. (☎966-7745). A fun and happening "transcultural" and "transmedia" non-profit space, featuring experiments in the presentation of visual art, theater, film, and video. About as friendly and young as it gets in the NYC art scene. Suggested contribution $2. Open Tu-F 10am-6pm, Sa 11am-6pm; closed Aug.

Thread Waxing Space, 476 Broadway between Broome and Grand Sts., 2nd fl. (☎966-9520). An eclectic space that shows in various media. Open Tu-Sa 10am-6pm.

Tony Shafrazi, 119 Wooster St. between Prince and Spring Sts. (☎274-9300). A commercial highbrow gallery that boasts being one of the first to display art by 1980s greats such as Haring and Basquiat. Open M-F 10am-6pm.

Illustration House, 96 Spring St. between Mercer and Broadway., 7th fl. (☎966-9444). Devoted to exhibiting American illustration history. Works by Rockwell and Nyeth can be found here. Open Tu-Sa 10am-6pm.

Dia Center for the Arts, 141 Wooster St. between Houston and Prince Sts., 2nd fl. (☎473-8072). An extension of the Chelsea gallery (see below), it has been showing Walter De Maria's The New York Earth Room since 1980. W-Sa noon-6pm. Closed summers.

David Zwirner, 43 Greene St. between Grand and Broome Sts. (☎966-9074). Both established and up-and-coming artists. Open Tu-Sa 10am-6pm; summer M-F 10am-6pm.

The Painting Center, 52 Greene St. 2nd fl., at Broome Sts. (☎343-1060). Paintings of all shapes and sizes. Open Tu-Sa 11am-6pm.

Deitch Projects, 76 Grand St. between Greene and Wooster Sts. (☎343-7300). Often has group shows of up-and-coming artists. Open Tu-Sa noon-6pm.

Staley-Wise, 560 Broadway, 3rd fl., at Prince St. (☎966-6223). The focus here is on fashion photography–Louise Dahl-Wolfe, Helmut Newton, Man Ray, etc. Open Tu-Sa 11am-5pm.

The Work Space, 96 Spring St., 8th fl., between Broadway and Mercer St. (☎219-2790). Open M-F 10am-5pm, Sa 1-5pm.

CHELSEA

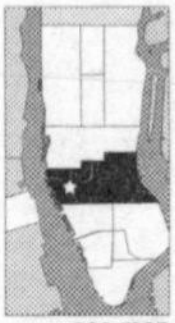

see map pp. 322-323

Subway: A, C, E, L to 14th St.; C, E to 23rd St.

Many of the galleries originally in SoHo have been lured by cheaper rents to Chelsea's warehouses; the area west of Ninth Ave., between 17th and 26th Sts., is full of display spaces. Be sure to check out the building at **529 W. 20th St.** between Tenth and Eleventh Aves.; with 11 floors, it is a treasure trove of contemporary art. I-20 (see below) is on the top floor of this building. The area between Fifth and Sixth Ave. and 17th and 21st Sts. is known as the **Photography District,** with its professional developing labs. Cutting-edge outposts of contemporary art have recently emerged in **Chelsea** in reclaimed industrial spaces centered around W. 14th St. between Ninth and Tenth Aves. and W. 22nd St. between Tenth and Eleventh Aves.

Dia Center for the Arts, 548 W. 22nd St. between Tenth and Eleventh Aves. (☎989-5566). A space with a definite sensibility for catching the pulse of current art. Four floors of changing exhibits covering a balanced range of media and styles. The roof holds Dan Graham's installation piece *Rooftop Urban Park Project*, as well as a cafe and a decent view of Chelsea. Open W-Su noon-6pm; closed mid-June to mid-Sept. Admission $6, students and seniors $3.

Sonnabend, 536 W. 22nd St. between Tenth and Eleventh Aves. (☎627-1018). Originally located in SoHo, this famous gallery has shown works by well-known American and European contemporary artists for 40 years. Open Tu-Sa 10am-6pm; closed Aug.

Matthew Marks Gallery, 523 W. 24th St. and 525 W. 22nd St., both between Tenth and Eleventh Aves. (☎243-0200). One of the doyennes of the Chelsea gallery scene, with exhibits by major modern and contemporary artists (Willem de Kooning, Ellsworth Kelly, Nan Goldin) in the 2 large spaces. Open Tu-Sa 10am-6pm; summer M-F 11am-6pm.

The Museum at Fashion Institute of Technology, Seventh Ave. and 27th St. (☎217-5800). A heavenly place for fashionistas. Several changing exhibits related to anything and everything fashionable–from photography to mannequin displays. Open Tu-F noon-8pm, Sa 10am-5pm.

I-20, 529 W. 20th St., 11th fl. (☎645-1100). A gallery exhibiting high-quality contemporary art displayed in a beautiful 11th-floor space. Also commands a stirring view of the river and piers below. Open Tu-Sa 10:30am-6pm.

Gavin Brown's Enterprise Corp., 436 W. 15th St. between Ninth and Tenth Aves. (☎627-5258). An interactive space that is both a gallery and a social area. The bar, Passerby, has DJs Tu and Th. Open Tu-Sa 10am-6pm.

Max Protetch, 511 W. 22nd St. between Tenth and Eleventh Aves. (☎633-6999). Having started as an exhibition space for architectural drawings, Protetch now hosts impressive and intelligent contemporary shows of painting, sculpture, and all things in between. Open Tu-Sa 10am-6pm; summer M-F 10am-6pm; closed Aug.

D'Amelio Terras, 525 W. 22nd St. between Tenth and Eleventh Aves. (☎352-9460). Shows works in sculpture and photography. Open Tu-Sa 10am-6pm; summer M-F 10am-5pm.

535 W. 22nd St., 535 W. 22nd St. between Tenth and Eleventh Aves. Home to an assortment of galleries, including the **Frederick Taylor Gallery** and the **CRG Gallery.**

DCA Gallery, 525 W. 22nd St. between Tenth and Eleventh Aves. ☎255-5511. Open Tu-F 10am-6pm, Sa noon-6pm; closed Aug.

MIDTOWN AND THE UPPER EAST SIDE

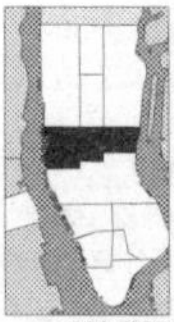

see map pp. 326-327

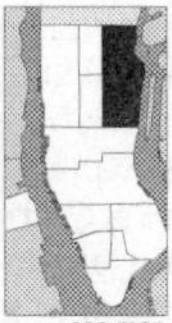

see map pp. 328-329

Madison Avenue between E. 63rd and E. 81st Sts. has a generous sampling of ritzy showplaces, and another group of galleries sits on **57th St.** between Madison and Park Aves.

Fuller Building, 41 E. 57th St. between Park and Madison Aves. Subway: N, R to 59th St.-Fifth Ave.; 4, 5, 6 to 59th St. This stylish Art Deco building harbors 12 floors of galleries with frequent turnover, featuring contemporary notables, ancient works like Frederick Schultz, and several modern works galleries. Most open M-Sa 10am-5:30pm, but call ahead to make sure; Oct.-May most closed M.

Pace Gallery, 32 E. 57th St. between Park and Madison Aves. (Pace Prints and Primitive ☎421-3237, Pace-MacGill 759-7999, and Pace Wildenstein 421-3292). Subway: N, R to 59th St.-Fifth Ave.; 4, 5, 6 to 59th St. Four floors dedicated to the promotion of widely disparate forms of art. Open June-Sept. M-Th 9:30am-6pm, F 9:30am-4pm; Oct.-May Tu-Sa 9:30am-6pm.

Sotheby's, 1334 York Ave., at 72nd St. (☎606-7000, ticket office 606-7171). Subway: 6 to 68th St. One of the most respected auction houses in the city, offering everything from Degas to Disney. Auctions open to anyone, but a few of the more popular require a ticket (first come, first served). They also have several galleries for works soon to be auctioned off. Open M-Sa 10am-5pm, Su 1-5pm; closed Sa-Su in summer.

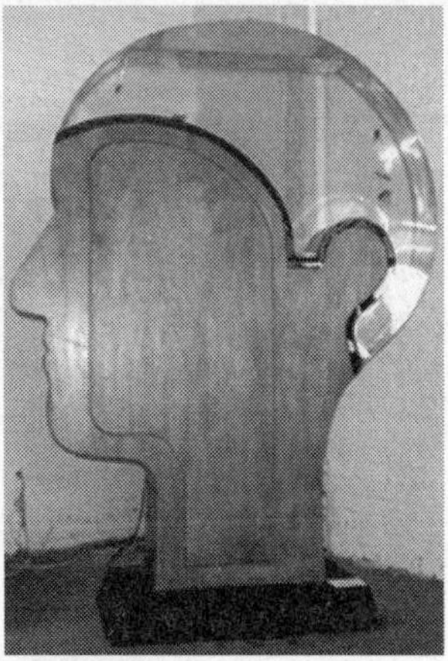

Stuart Parr

P.S.1

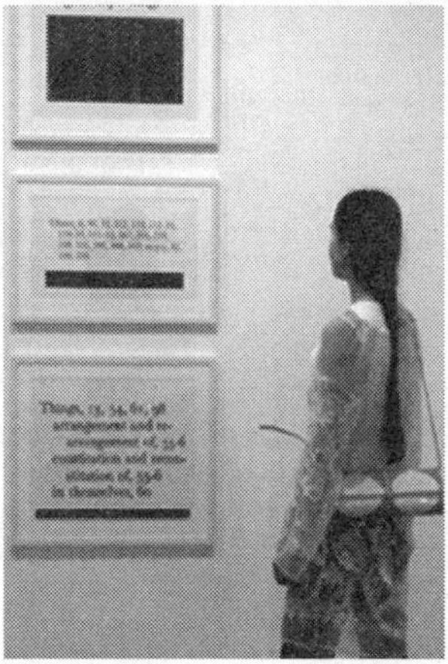

D'Amelio Terras

Christie's, 20 Rockefeller Plaza at 49th St. (☎636-2000). Subway: B, D, F, Q to 47th-50th St.-Rockefeller Center. This famous international auction house flaunts an impressive collection of valuable wares that range from a Giovanni painting to a dress worn by Marilyn Monroe. The 6 galleries and auctions are open to the public. During the height of the season, there are 2-3 sales per week, while the summer months are much slower. Call ahead for a schedule. Open M-Sa 10am-5pm, Su 1-5pm.

Leo Castelli, 59 E. 79th St., between Park and Madison Aves. (☎249-4470). Subway: 6 to 77th St. Showing a selection of contemporary artists such as Jasper Johns and Ed Ruscha. Open Tu-Sa 10am-6pm; summer Tu-F 10am-5pm.

Gagosian, 980 Madison Ave., at 77th St. (☎744-2313). Subway: 6 to 77th St. Represents an impressive group of artists such as Warhol and Richard Serra. Open M-Sa 10am-6pm.

M. Knoedler & Co., Inc., 19 E. 70th St. between Madison and Fifth Aves. (☎794-0550). Subway: 6 to 68th St. One of the oldest and most respected galleries in the city. Mounts exhibits such as "The Collector as Patron in the 20th Century." Open Tu-Sa 9:30am-6pm; summer Tu-F 9:30am-5pm.

Hirschl and Adler Galleries, 21 E. 70th St. between Madison and Fifth Aves. (☎535-8810). Subway: 6 to 68th St. Two floors of selected art: on the 1st floor is a wide variety of 18th- and 19th-century European art; upstairs, at Hirschl and Adler Modern, more contemporary works are displayed. Open Tu-F 9:30am-5:15pm, Sa 9:30am-4:45pm; summer M-F 9:30am-4:45pm.

Acquavella, 18 E. 79th St. between Madison and Fifth Aves. (☎734-6300). Subway: 6 to 77th St. This majestic building houses exhibitions specializing in post-Impressionist paintings, drawings, and sculpture. Big names such as Picasso, Degas, Cézanne, and Giacometti. Open M-F 10am-5pm; open Sa-Su for larger shows.

BROOKLYN

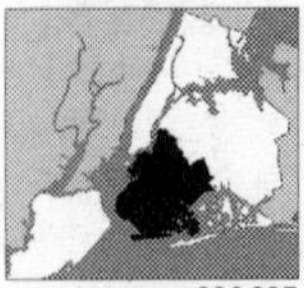
see map pp. 336-337

The few Bohemian pilgrims that moved into Williamsburg in the 80s have witnessed the neighborhood transform into a full-scale artistic mecca. The neighborhood boasts over 30 galleries--with new ones constantly springing up--that provide a forum for cutting-edge artists who have yet to break into the commercialized world of downtown Manhattan. As a result, the art here is current and fresh. While many of the galleries cluster around Bedford Ave. and Grand St., smaller gems are tucked deeper into Williamsburg such as the tiny (but who says size matters?) and ultra-modern **Rome** (103 Havermayer St.; ☎718-388-2009; open Sa-Su noon-6pm), **Arena @ Feed** (173A North 3rd St.; ☎646-389-3213, open Sa-Su noon-6pm), and many others.

Pierogi, 177 N. 9th St., between Bedford and Driggs Aves. (☎718-599-2144). Subway: L to Bedford Ave. Hosts 2 big-name solo shows a month, but still displays hundreds of affordable works by emerging artists in front files. If you happen to be lucky enough to visit one of the openings, expect free pierogis. Open F-M noon-6pm.

The Williamsburg Art and Historical Center, 135 Broadway between Bedford and Driggs Aves. (☎718-486-7372). Subway: J, M, Z to Marcy Ave.; L to Bedford Ave. The epicenter of the Williamsburg arts scene, this historic building harbors space for theater, and music as well as a beautiful 2nd floor gallery exhibiting the work of local and international artists. A monthly musical performance and biannual international show keep this Center bustling with artists from all backgrounds. Open Sa-Su noon-6pm.

Lunar Base, 197 Grand St. (☎718-599-2905). Subway: L to Bedford Ave. Amidst a gaggle of other galleries on Grand St., this new gallery boasts bold abstract and contemporary works from international artists. Open Th-Su 1-7pm.

Brooklyn Bridge Anchorage, Cadman Plaza West, on the corner of Hicks and Old Front Sts. (☎718-802-1215). Subway: A, C to High St. A gallery/performance space is housed within the bridge's cavernous suspension cable storage chambers; it features cutting-edge, multimedia installations that make good use of the vaulted, 80-ft. ceilings. Creative Time runs the under-bridge space, and uses it to put on hip music performances. Open mid-May to mid-Oct. Th-Tu noon-8pm, W noon-7pm. Creative Time open Th-F 3-8pm, Sa-Su 1-6pm.

QUEENS

see map pp. 340-341

Long Island City is the center of the Queens arts scene. In addition to these spaces, don't miss P.S. 1, (see Other Major Collections above). **Queens Artlink** runs on weekends from the Museum of Modern Art in Manhattan to connecting major Queens sites. The route takes in P.S.1, the Isamu Noguchi Museum, Socrates Sculpture Park, and the Museum of the Moving Image. (☎718-708-9750; www.queensartlink.com; runs Sa-Su 11:30am-5:30pm.)

New York Center for Media Arts, 45-12 Davis St., off Jackson Ave. under the 7 line. (☎718-472-9414; www.nycmediaarts.org). Subway: E, F to 23 St.-Ely Ave.; G to 21 St.; 7 to 45 Rd.-Courthouse Sq. A spacious converted warehouse, featuring rotating installations of multimedia art work. Exhibits rotate every few months—when *Let's Go* visited, pieces included Candice Beitz's "Karaoke 2000," a circle of TVs playing videos of people singing "Killing Me Softly With His Song." Open Th-Su noon-6pm.

Holocenter (Center for the Holographic arts), 45-10 Court Sq. (☎718-784-5065; www.holocenter.com). Subway: E, F to 23 St.-Ely Ave.; G to 21 St.; 7 to 45 Rd.-Courthouse Sq. An exhibition space dedicated to artwork involving holograms. Open by appointment.

Jamaica Center for Arts, 161-04 Jamaica Ave., at 161st St. (☎718-658-7400; www.jcal.org). Subway: E, J, Z to Jamaica Center. The small gallery offers workshops and art exhibits by local and international artists. The JCA also organizes talks and classes. Open M-Tu and F-Sa 9am-6pm, W-Th 9am-8pm. Free.

THE BRONX

see map pp. 342-343

The community-oriented galleries here often showcase local talent and address issues of neighborhood and ethnic identity.

Lehman Art Gallery, 250 Bedford Park Blvd. between West and Goulden Aves. On the campus of Herbert Lehman College, in the Fine Arts Building. (☎718-960-8731). Subway: 4, B, D to Bedford Park. Housed in a building designed by Marcel Breuer, the gallery's past exhibitions have included artifacts from Papua New Guinea and a series of paintings commemorating Puerto Rican victims of domestic violence. Every June, Lehman holds a children's show displaying art made by local youngsters in the museum's education program. Open June M-F 10am-4pm; July M-Th 10am-4pm; Aug. by appointment only.; Sept.-May Tu-Sa 10am-4pm.

INSIDE

Food & Drink

"What can I get for ten dollars?" "Anything you want." Yes, it's true. New York is home to every kind of food imaginable, and with our attitude good quality is a must.

Besides the ethnic enclaves that dot the city, certain types of food pervade every area. **Chinese food, pizza,** and **bagels** are the best examples—MSG reaches every borough through so many plates of beef and broccoli, neon orange tomato sauce fills the arteries of every self-respecting New Yorker, and no native could be *phklemped* after starting the day with cream cheese and lox on a bagel.

Take advantage of all that the city has to offer, from cheap bar stool grub to the luxurious Tavern on the Green, but do not miss NYC's **street food:** sweet roasted peanuts in the winter, mustard and sauerkraut-slathered hot dogs or pretzels throughout the year, and a summer favorite: flavored ice in any color of the fluorescent rainbow.

ORGANIZATION

We have prefaced the neighborhood food listings with a chart of our favorite restaurants categorized **by cuisine.** These restaurants are "*Let's Go* Picks" and feature extraordinary combinations of low prices and high quality. We base our appraisals on price, quality, and atmosphere. For more complete listings, turn to the **By Neighborhood** section, in which we list many more good values.

PRICE SYMBOLS

$	$5-10 entree	$$	$10-15 entree	$$$	$15-20 entree

LET'S GO PICKS BY CUISINE

AMERICAN, STANDARD
Barking Dog Luncheonette (145) UES
Big Nick's Burger Joint (146) UWS
Corner Bistro (137) GV
Space Untitled (136) SoHo

AMERICAN, NEW
Brooklyn Moon (151) BC
Henry's (146) UWS
Rice (134) NoL

BAKERIES
Galaxy Pastry Shop (154) QUE
Hong Kong Egg Cake Co. (132) CHI
Le Pain Quotidien (145) UES
Little Pie Co. (142) CHE

CAFES
Cafe Lalo (147) UWS
drip (147) UWS
Rivington 99 Cafe (135) LES

CARIBBEAN
National Cafe (139) EV

CENTRAL AND EASTERN EUROPEAN
Primorksi Restaurant (152) BS

CHINESE
Flushing Noodle (153) QUE
Hop Kee (131) CHI
H.S.F. Restaurant (131) CHI
Joe's Shanghai (132) CHI, QUE
New Silver Palace (131) CHI

DELICATESSENS
Katz's Delicatessen (135) LES
Second Ave. Deli (139) EV

FRENCH
Bouley Bakery (136) TBC
Le Gamin Cafe (136) SoHo

GREEK
Elias Corner (153) QUE

ICE CREAM AND CANDY
Chinatown Ice Cream Factory (132) CHI
Ciao Bella (134) NoL
Economy Candy (135) LES
The Lemon Ice King of Corona (154) QUE

INDIAN, PAKISTANI, AND AFGHAN
Curry in a Hurry (142) MID
Jackson Diner (153) QUE

ITALIAN
Dominick's (154) BX
Emilia's (154) BX
Frank (139) EV
Max (138) EV

JAPANESE AND KOREAN
Yakitori Taisho (138) EV

MALAYSIAN
Penang (136) SoHo, QUE

MARKETS
Fairway (149) MH
Zabar's (148) UWS

MEXICAN
El Sombrero (135) LES
Kitchen (141) CHE

MIDDLE EASTERN
Alfanoose (131) LOW
Amir's Falafel (148) MH
Oznot's Dish (150) WIL

PIZZA
Grimaldi's (151) BC
John's Pizzeria (137) GV
Lombardi's (133) LIT
Nick's Pizza (153) QUE
Totonno Pizzeria (152) BS

PUBS AND TAVERNS
Hourglass Tavern (144) THE

SOUL
Copeland's (149) HAR
Manna's Too (149) HAR
Sugar Shack (149) HAR
Sylvia's (149) HAR

THAI
Jai-Ya (153) QUE
Planet Thailand (150) WIL
Thailand Restaurant (131) CHI

VEGETARIAN
Bliss (150) WIL

VIETNAMESE
Saigon Grill (145) UES
Vietnam (132) CHI

BX	Bronx	**HAR**	Harlem	**QUE**	Queens
BC	Central Brooklyn	**LIT**	Little Italy	**SoHo**	SoHo
BS	South Brooklyn	**LES**	Lower East Side	**TBC**	TriBeCa
CHE	Chelsea	**LM**	Lower Manhattan	**THE**	Theater District
CHI	Chinatown	**MH**	Morningside Heights	**UES**	Upper East Side
EV	East Village	**MID**	Midtown	**UWS**	Upper West Side
GV	Greenwich Village	**NoL**	NoLita	**WIL**	Williamsburg

BY NEIGHBORHOOD

Neighborhoods are listed in geographical order (from south to north in Manhattan and from north to south in Brooklyn), and restaurants within each area are in order of preference. Restaurants take major credit cards unless otherwise noted.

FINANCIAL DISTRICT AND CIVIC CENTER

Lower Manhattan eateries tailor their schedules to the lunch breaks of Wall St. brokers. Fast food joints abound on Broadway near Dey and John Sts. In the summer, food pushcarts offer tempting deals on falafel, burritos, and gyros, but be wary of what you eat on the street.

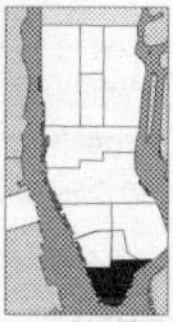
see map pp. 310-311

Alfanoose, 150 Fulton St., at Broadway (☎349-3622). Subway: 2, 3, 4, 5, A, C, J, M, Z to Fulton St. Don't waste time with pushcart vendors; the falafel here is the real thing. Each sandwich is carefully crafted so that all the flavors explode in every bite. Word of the shop's gustatory wizardry has spread throughout the business district, and the line is known to go out the door during lunch hours. If you can skirt the rush, their falafels are well worth the price ($3.25). Open M-F 10am-9:30pm, Sa-Su 11am-9:30pm. **$**

Zigolini's, 66 Pearl St., at Coenties Alley (☎425-7171). Subway: N, R to Whitehall St. Serving tasty sandwiches ($5-7) and great pasta ($7), Zigolini's also has a deli-style counter in the back. Open M-F 7am-7pm. **$-SS**

Caruso's, 204 Broadway between Fulton and John Sts. (☎349-3622). Subway: 2, 3, 4, 5, A, C, J, M, Z to Fulton St. A local alternative to Italian fast-food chains. Fresh pizza (slices $1.75) and pasta ($5-6). Open M-F 9am-9pm, Sa 10am-8pm, Su 11am-7pm. **$**

CHINATOWN

Subway: 4, 6, J, M, N, R, Z to Canal St.

Fresh food abounds in Chinatown. Open-air markets selling live turtles, eels, and crabs spill onto the sidewalk. For food you don't have to kill yourself, head to **Mott St.,** around Canal St., which has some of the best seafood and produce in the city. The neighborhood's 300-plus restaurants won't burn a hole in your wallet and cook up fantastic Chinese, Thai, and Vietnamese cuisine. Be prepared, however, for waiters with a poor grasp of English and restaurants with little ambiance. Many restaurants are **cash only** (unless where noted) and don't serve alcohol. After dinner you can take a stroll through technicolor streets, as you delight in Chinese ice cream or Vietnamese desserts.

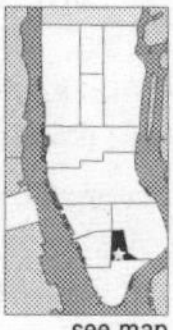
see map pp. 312-313

Hop Kee, 21 Mott St., down the stairs at the corner of Mosco St. (☎964-8365). Bare bones in the ambiance department, but this is *real* Chinese food. Their specialties include salted pork chop with hot peppers ($8.25) and seafood in a basket ($16.95); the latter's basket is edible, made from taro root. Open daily 11am-4am. Cash only. **$-$$**

New Silver Palace, 52 Bowery, at Canal St. (☎964-1204). An enormous mecca for dim-sum lovers ($3-5; served until 4pm) and a popular spot for Chinatown wedding banquets. Open daily 9am-10:30pm. **$-$$**

H.S.F. Restaurant, 46 Bowery between Bayard and Canal Sts. (☎374-1319). Wonderful dim sum ($3-5; served 11am-5pm), but to be adventurous, order the buffet special and cook up vegetables, dumplings, etc. in a pot of boiling broth at your table ($19.95 per person; served after 5). Open Su-Th 8am-midnight, F-Sa 8am-2am. **$-$$**

Thailand Restaurant, 106 Bayard St. between Baxter and Mulberry Sts. (☎349-3132). Chinatown's first Thai restaurant has dealt well with the mushrooming competition. Simple and quiet, but head and shoulders above the other joints. Taste the killer *pad thai* ($5.50) and roasted duck in curry with coconut milk, bamboo shoots, onions, and bell peppers ($9.50). Known for homemade Thai desserts like sweet rice with egg custard and coconut milk ($1.50). Open daily 11:30am-11pm. **$**

Vietnam, 11-13 Doyers St. between Bowery and Pell St. (☎693-0725). All of the standards—brittle spring rolls, shrimp on sugar cane, noodle soups—and then some. Try the tasty, filling Vietnamese crepes ($6) for a distinct, assertive flavor. Ask about the more innovative items on the menu like the stir-fried salmon with black bean sauce ($7). Beer. Open daily 11am-9:30pm. **$**

Joe's Shanghai, 9 Pell St. between Bowery and Mott St. (☎233-8888). From fried turnip cakes ($3.25) to crispy fried whole yellowfish ($13), this branch of the Queens legend serves up all sorts of tasty Shanghai specialties. The true source of Joe's acclaim is his *xiao long bao* ($7), crab meat and pork dumplings in a savory soup. Be prepared for communal tables and long lines of *bao* addicts on weekends. Beer. Open daily 11am-11:15pm. Cash only. **$-$$**

Excellent Dumpling House, 111 Lafayette St., just south of Canal St. (☎219-0212). Small, unassuming, and perennially crowded with folks enjoying splendid food and fast service. Terrific veggie and meat dumplings fried, steamed, or boiled ($4 for 8). Huge bowls of noodle soups $3.50-4. Beer. Open daily 11am-9pm. Cash only. **$**

Shanghai Cuisine, 89-91 Bayard St., at Mulberry St. (☎732-8988). The house specialty, braised soy duck with 8 treasures ($34), must be ordered a day in advance and is the richest dish you will ever taste—attack it only in large groups. Less intense dishes also, such as spicy pepper salt prawns ($13), and mixed vegetables ($7). Beer and wine. Open daily 11am-11pm. Cash only. **$$**

Bo-Ky, 80 Bayard St. between Mott and Mulberry Sts. (☎406-2292). Tourists rarely grace this Vietnamese joint specializing in soups (most under $5). The curry chicken noodle ($4.50) will clear that nasty head cold instantly. *Pho,* the beef broth king of Vietnamese soups, will fill you up without emptying your wallet ($3-5). Open daily 8am-9:30pm. Cash only. **$**

Sweet-n-Tart Cafe, 76 Mott St., at Canal St. (☎334-8088). In addition to inexpensive standard Chinese fare, this small crowded cafe offers *tong shui,* sweet Chinese "tonics" (soups), each believed to have medicinal value for a specific part of the body: dry bean curd with gingko for healthy skin ($2.35), lotus seeds in herbal tea with egg for the liver and kidneys ($3). Open daily 9am-11:30pm. Cash only. **$**

Vegetarian Dim Sum House, 24 Pell St. between Canal and Bayard Sts. (☎226-6572). All animals are ersatz on the huge menu of this small and appropriately green eatery; soy and wheat by-products, taro root, and mushroom disguise themselves as beef, chicken, and fish. Fantastic dumplings (3 for $2) should please both vegetarians and carnivores alike. Most entrees $6-10. Ice-cold lotus-seed or lychee drink $2. Open daily 11am-11pm. Cash only. **$**

Nyonya, 194 Grand St. between Mulberry and Mott Sts. (☎334-3669). Popular, excellent Malaysian dishes in a cool, wood-lined interior. The delectably spicy *nasi lemak* ($4) puts chili anchovies and curry chicken in a bed of coconut rice. For an unusual dessert, ask for the "ABC"—a sort of shaved-ice sundae with red bean, corn, palm seeds, and jelly rose syrup. Beer and wine. Open daily 11am-11:30pm. Cash only. **$-$$**

SHOPS

Hong Kong Egg Cake Co., on the corner of Mott and Mosco Sts. Located in a small red shack—just follow the line wrapped around the corner. Cecelia Tam will make you a dozen bite-size, sweet egg cakes ($1) fresh from the skillet that she's been working 20 years. Open W-Th and Sa-Su 10:30am-5pm.

Chinatown Ice Cream Factory, 65 Bayard St. at Elizabeth St. (☎608-4170). Satisfy your sweet-tooth with homemade lychee, taro, ginger, red bean, or green tea ice cream. One scoop $2.20, two $3.95, three $4.80. Open summer M-Th 11:30am-11:30 pm, F-Su 11:30am-midnight; rest of the year daily noon-11pm.

Ten Ren Tea and Ginseng Company, 75 Mott St. between Canal and Bayard Sts. (☎349-2286). Comfortable and classy, Ten Ren boasts a huge selection of rare, delectable teas ranging in price from the very cheap to hundreds of dollars for a pound. To beat the heat in the summer, get the Green Tea Powder ($4-7), and add a packet's worth to a cold bottle of water. Drop in some apple juice for sweetener, and you've got a very refreshing, very *green* caffeine drink. Open daily 10am-8pm.

Dynasty Supermarket Corp., 69 Elizabeth St., at Hester St. (☎966-4943). One of the most extensive markets in the area and an air-conditioned refuge from the tumult of the street. Find ginseng, sea cucumber, live mudskipper, chicken feet, exotic flavored gummy candies, and Hostess cupcakes all in one stop. Open daily 9:30am-8:30pm.

Green Tea Cafe, 45 Mott St., between Bayard and Pell Sts. (☎693-2888). Teas are the first order of business at this trendy new hangout, and the "in" drink at the moment is the unusual "bubble tea," usually taken cold and sipped through an extra-wide straw to accommodate the chewy tapioca pearls at the bottom. Open daily 10am-midnight.

LITTLE ITALY

Subway: 6 to Spring St.

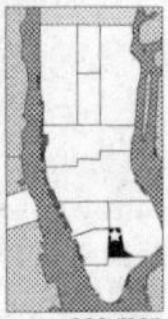

see map pp. 312-313

The three blocks of Mulberry St. between Grand and Canal Sts. are packed tight with the tables of myriad trattorie and caffe. At 7pm, the street comes to life; arrive a bit earlier for one of the better tables. On weekends, reservations are a must. Three tips for choosing a restaurant or caffe: first, just because someone famous ate there doesn't mean it's good; second, just because it's really old doesn't mean it's good; and third, just because the waiters all have heavy Italian accents...well, you know. Most restaurants really milk their old world "charm." A full meal can run $60-70, particularly when you bring a bottle of wine into the equation. Save money with sizable appetizers (antipasti) or a snack at one of the many shops and groceries.

Lombardi's Coal Oven Pizza, 32 Spring St. between Mott and Mulberry Sts. (☎941-7994). Perhaps the oldest pizzeria in the United States (opened 1905), credited with creating the famous New York-style thin-crust, coal-oven pizza (they don't take credit for the grease). A large pie feeds 2 ($13.50). Toppings are pricey ($3 for one, $5 for two, $6 for three) but they're worth it. Reservations for groups of 6 or more. Open M-Th 11:30am-11pm, F-Sa 11:30am-midnight, Su 11:30am-10pm. Cash only. **$-$$**

Da Nico, 164 Mulberry St. between Broome and Grand Sts. (☎343-1212). Tasty food in a lovely environment: the tree-shaded garden in back is frequented by Al Pacino and Johnny Depp. Chicken marsala ($12.50) is one of their specialties. Lunch: pasta $6-10, entrees $6.50-12.50. Dinner: pasta $11-19, entrees $12-29. Open Su-Th 11am-11pm, F-Sa 11am-midnight. **$$**

La Mela, 167 Mulberry St. between Broome and Grand Sts. (☎431-9493). Plastered with photos and postcards, La Mela is the place to come for a raucous time. The chummy, boisterous waitstaff serve up generous portions family style. The house wine is inexpensive and plentiful ($20 for 1.5L). Pasta $6-8, entrees $11-15. Open daily noon-11pm. **$$**

Rocky's Italian Restaurant, 45 Spring St., at Mulberry St. (☎274-9756). A true neighborhood joint, Rocky's buzzes with strains of the Old Country. For lunch, try a pizza hero ($4.50) or sandwich ($4.50-9), served until 5pm. Pasta $7-13, entrees $10-19. The chicken with garlic sauce ($14) is a treat. Wine is cheap (carafe $14). Open Tu-Su 11am-11pm; kitchen closes at 10:30pm. **$$**

CAFFÈS

Caffè Palermo, 148 Mulberry St. between Hester and Grand Sts. (☎431-4205). The best of the *caffè* offerings along Mulberry. During summer, Palermo opens onto the street with an espresso bar up front. Most pastries $3-5. The staff takes much pride in its tasty *tiramisù* ($5); the cannoli ($2.75) and cappuccino ($3.25) are also quite good. Open Su-Th 10am-midnight, F-Sa 10am-2am.

La Bella Ferrara, 110 Mulberry St. between Canal and Hester Sts. (☎966-1488). The name is cribbed from the larger, factory-like Caffè Ferrara on Grand St. and basically means "better Ferrara." The local choice for after-dinner dessert. Pastries $2-2.50, cakes $4-5, cappuccino $3. Cash only. Open daily 9am-2am.

SHOPS

Di Palo's, 206 Grand St., at Mott St. (☎226-1033). Even the toughest budget traveler cannot live on bread alone; enter Di Palo's. The shop offers a selection of breads, meats, and pastas, but specializes in cheeses. The homemade soft, fleshy mozzarella ($4.89 per lb.) is their mainstay, but the goat cheese and the *ricotta fresca* are also delicious. The proprietor cultivates knows all his regular customers by name, and he'll offer tasty tidbits or chat about cheese varieties with relish. Open M-Sa 9am-6:30pm, Su 9am-3:30pm.

the BIG $plurge

Not Quite a Free Lunch

Most budget travelers spend their sojourn in New York City without ever stepping foot into one of the city's swankier restaurants, but there are ways to treat yourself to an *extremely* fine meal without completely busting your wallet. Every summer, many restaurants participate in **NY Restaurant Week,** during which the price of lunch corresponds to the current year. For example, the 2002 price will be $20.02. While this still might seem like a lot, at ritzy places like Lutece, Gramercy Tavern, Peter Luger, and Le Cirque, it's quite a bargain. The program has begun expanding to include the entire summer, and reservations tend to go quickly. For a list of participating restaurants, send a stamped envelope to: NYC Restaurants, New York Convention and Visitors Bureau, 2 Columbus Circle, New York, NY 100

NOLITA

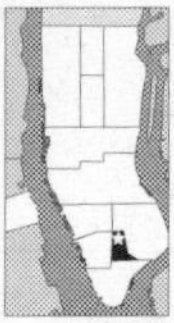

see map pp. 312-313

Subway: 6 to Spring St.

NoLIta (northern Little Italy) is a budding pocket of culinary action. Since you'll pay the price for ambiance around Elizabeth, Mott, and Mulberry Sts., you might want to go early for drinks and an appetizer or late for drinks and dessert.

Rice, 227 Mott St. between Prince and Spring Sts. (☎226-5775). Fantastic food on rice. The basics—basmati, brown, sticky, Japanese—are options, in addition to the more exotic Thai black or Bhutanese red ($1-4). The sauces range from mango chutney to Aleppo yogurt ($1). You can also add ratatouille or chicken satay, among other enticing toppings ($3.50-8). Open daily noon-midnight. Cash only. **$**

Cafe Gitane, 242 Mott St., at Prince St. (☎334-9552). A focal point of NoLIta life, this cafe is a prime spot to see and be seen. A rack of glossy fashion mags invites the fashionable to linger. Salads $5-7, glass of wine $5-7, tasty dishes like the grilled eggplant with goat cheese and pesto on rice pilaf $8, and tiramisu $4. Open daily 9am-midnight. Cash only. **$**

Cafe Colonial Restaurant, 276 Elizabeth St., at the corner of Houston St. (☎274-0044). Great entree options like the veggie burger ($7.50) and soft-shell crab sandwich ($13). Beers $4.50. Open Su-Th 8am-11pm, F-Sa 8am-midnight. **$$**

M&R Bar, 264 Elizabeth St. between Houston and Prince Sts. (☎226-0559). Comfortable neighborhood bar with just a bit of attitude. Weekend brunch 11:30am-4pm, $8-10. Sandwiches $10-12; appetizers $6. Late-night menu until 1am during the week, 2am on weekends. Beer $4-5. Open M-Th 5pm-midnight, F 5pm-4am, Sa 11:30am-4pm and 5:30pm-midnight, Su 11:30am-4pm and 5pm-midnight. **$-$$**

Mottsu, 285 Mott St. between Prince and Houston Sts. (☎343-8017). One of the only sushi restaurants in the neighborhood, Mottsu serves up fresh sushi and sashimi at downtown prices. Try the excellent tuna rolls ($2.50). Open for lunch M-F noon-3pm; dinner Su-Th 5-11pm, F-Sa 5-11:30pm; Su brunch 3-5pm. **$$**

Cafe Habana, 229 Elizabeth St. between Prince and Houston Sts. (☎625-2002). Inexpensive but stylish. The chicken diablo (blackened chicken, mesclun, and black beans, $6.25) will leave you singing Satan's praises. Other entrees range from rice and beans ($4) to grilled steak ($10.50). Open daily noon-10pm. **$**

SHOPS

Ciao Bella, 285 Mott St. between Prince and E. Houston Sts. (☎431-3591). Possibly the best ice cream in the city: dense, smooth and rich. Their downtown location is little more than a storefront, but benches outside invite devotees to linger. Small $3.50, large $4.50. Open M-Sa 11am-11pm, Su 11am-10pm.

LOWER EAST SIDE

The neighborhood's multiethnic character and rich history are reflected in the endless and diverse dining options. The delis along Essex St. are reminiscent of the area's Yiddish past. Many of the stores close in observance of the Jewish Sabbath, sundown Friday to sundown Saturday, so make sure you stock up on your deli delectables during the week.

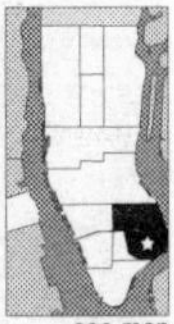

see map pp. 320-321

El Sombrero, 108 Stanton St., at Ludlow St. (☎254-4188). Subway: F, J, M, Z to Delancey St.-Essex St. If the gods ate at a Mexican restaurant, lived on a budget, and didn't mind a little kitsch, they'd dine here. Vegetable enchiladas ($8) make a satisfying meal, but you'll marvel at the Fajitas Mexicana ($10). Quench your thirst with margaritas (small $3) and beer. Hours vary, but opens daily around 10am and closes at approximately midnight during the week and 3am on the weekends. Cash only. **$$**

Katz's Delicatessen, 205 E. Houston St. between Orchard and Ludlow Sts. (☎254-2246). Subway: F to Second Ave. A Lower East Side institution since 1888. Every president in the last three decades has proudly received a Katz salami, and you can sit at the same table where Bill Clinton shoveled in his lunch (2 hotdogs, a pastrami sandwich, fries and a *diet* ginger ale). The food is orgasmic (as Meg Ryan confirmed in *When Harry Met Sally*), but you pay extra for the atmosphere. Heroes $5.10, knishes $2.25, franks $2.15, sandwiches around $9. Open Su-Tu 8am-10pm, W-Th 8am-11pm, F-Sa 8am-3am. **$-$$**

Grilled Cheese, 168 Ludlow St. between Stanton and Houston Sts. (☎982-6600). Subway: F, J, M, Z to Delancey St.-Essex St. This tiny sliver of a joint serves up freshly made sandwiches, salads ($5-6), and homemade ice cream sandwiches ($4), as well as delectable drinks (espresso milkshakes $4). The varieties of grilled cheese sandwiches ($3.50-5) are savory. Pop in and enjoy the simple things in life. Open daily noon-midnight. **$**

Casa Mexicana, 133 Ludlow St., at Rivington St. (☎473-4100). Subway: F, J, M, Z to Delancey St.-Essex St. Serving authentic Mexican food in a tasteful setting, Casa Mexicana excels in service and style. Try the *molcajete ranchero* (chicken $9, sirloin $11), a meat dish served with charred cactus and salsa. Dine late and check out the bar and lounge downstairs where a DJ spins house every night. Open Su-Th 11am-5pm and 6pm-midnight, F-Sa 11am-5pm and 6pm-1am. Lounge open 10pm-4am, no cover. **$-$$**

Tiengarden, 170 Allen St. between Rivington and Stanton Sts. (☎388-1364). Subway: F to Second Ave. A Vegan restaurant that makes health food a spiritual experience by not including any of the five impurities that could damage your *Chi*. The spicy organic tofu ($6.50) still has plenty of flavor. No alcohol. Open Su-F noon-4pm and 5-10pm. Cash only. **$**

Sentosa, 3 Allen St. between Canal and Division Sts. (☎925-8018). Subway: F to East Broadway. Down on a banal section of the Lower East Side, Sentosa delivers really cheap Malaysian food with a Singaporean (read: slightly more Chinese-influenced) twist. Hainanese chicken rice $6.95, rice dishes $3.95. Open 9am-midnight.

CAFES

Rivington 99 Cafe, 99 Rivington St., at Ludlow St. (☎358-1191). Subway: F, J, M, Z to Delancey St.-Essex St. This signless coffee haven is a local hangout. The perfect place to read the paper cover-to-cover while sipping on a cup of joe. Open M-Sa 9am-7pm, Su 10am-6pm.

SHOPS

Economy Candy, 108 Rivington St. between Ludlow and Essex Sts. (☎254-1531). Subway: F, J, M, Z to Delancey St.-Essex St. This candy warehouse sells imported chocolates, jams, and countless confections, all at rock-bottom prices. Treat yourself to a huge bag of dried cantaloupe ($5) or a 10 lb bag of assorted candy ($12). Open Su-F 8:30am-6pm, Sa 10am-5pm.

Guss' Lower East Side Pickle Corp., 35 Essex St., at Hester St. Subway: F, J, M, Z to Delancey St.-Essex St. (☎254-4477 or 800-252-4877). Glorious gherkins are sold straight out of vats, from super-sour to sweet (individual 50¢-$2; quart $5,25). Guss' also offers cole slaw, pickled tomatoes, carrots, and t-shirts ($10). Open Su-Th 9am-6pm, F 9am-4pm.

Yonah Schimmel Knishery, 137 E. Houston St. (☎477-2858). Subway: F to Second Ave. The knish is an artform at Rabbi Schimmel's Lower East Side institution. A dozen varieties of these Eastern European potato-filled pastries are available for $1.75. Open daily 8:30am-6pm except during the Jewish Sabbath.

TRIBECA

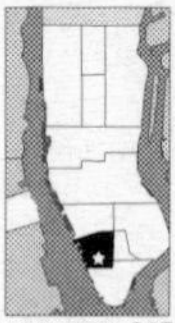
see map p. 315

Restaurants here cater to middle-aged adults with money to burn. For really cheap fare head to the borders of TriBeCa, especially around **Chambers and Church Sts.** (which have a handful of **halal** eateries).

Bouley Bakery, 120 W. Broadway between Duane and Reade Sts. (☎964-8362). Subway: 1, 2, 3, 9, A, C to Chambers St. This world-class restaurant also has an adjoining cafe, which serves breakfast, brunch, and light meals. Peckish travelers can take away sandwiches such as the satisfying roast beef on mountain bread ($7.25), or the "torpedo", a baguette roll with prosciutto and mozzarella ($2.50). The restaurant's desserts (tarts $5) are also available at the cafe–you'll find yourself returning to sample them all. Cafe open daily 8am-6pm. **$**

Bubby's, 120 Hudson St., at N. Moore St. (☎219-0666). Subway: 1, 9 to Franklin St. Rough brick walls, un-upholstered window seats, and two walls of windows add to this cafe's stylish simplicity. The great weekend brunch and the pies keep this joint packed with locals. Entrees $9-15. Open M-Th 8am-11pm, F 8am-midnight, Sa 9am-midnight, Su 9am-10pm. **$$-$$$**

El Teddy's, 219 W. Broadway between Franklin and White Sts. (☎941-7070). Subway: 1, 9 to Franklin St. You'll definitely have no trouble finding it–the oddly-shaped nacre awning hangs over windows of light-up whirligigs. Creative Mexican cuisine with a strong dose of California health food. Soups and salads $7-9; quesadillas around $8. By night, El Teddy's brims with carousing bar patrons. Open M-W noon-3pm 6-11:30pm, Th-Sa 6pm-1am, Su 6-11pm. **$-$$**

Yaffa's Tea Room, 19 Harrison St., at Greenwich St. (☎274-9403). Subway: 1, 9 to Franklin St. Amidst an eclectic arrangement of used furniture, Yaffa's serves high tea, from M-Sa 2-6pm; the meal includes cucumber, salmon, or watercress finger sandwiches, fresh-baked scones, a dessert sampler, and a pot of tea ($20, reservations required). Sandwiches $8.50-11; salads $6-11; entrees $9-15. Open 8:30am-midnight. **$$-$$$**

Pakistan Tea House, 176 Church St. between Duane and Reade Sts. (☎240-9800). Subway: 1, 2, 3, 9, A, C to Chambers St. Perennially busy hole-in-the-wall eatery simmers with Tandoori dishes and other traditional Pakistani favorites. Their combo plates ($4) are an amazing deal. All meat is halal. Open daily 11am-4:30am. **$**

SOHO

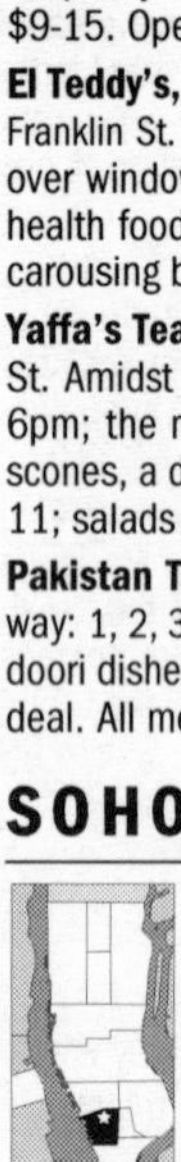
see map p. 315

Food is all about image in SoHo. It comes in a variety of exquisite and pricey forms, precious little of it fried or served over a counter. Often the best deal in SoHo is brunch, when the neighborhood shows its cozy, good-natured front. **W. Houston** between Macdougal and Thompson St. offers some delicious finds. Strolling along any one of the side streets, such as **Sullivan St.,** is a good bet for people-watching and latte-sipping.

Penang, 109 Spring St. between Mercer and Greene Sts. (☎274-8883). Subway: N, R to Prince St. Excellent Malaysian cuisine served in a beautiful and exotic setting. Admire the waterfall in the back while you savor the *roti canai* $4.25 or the hearty *poh-piah*, steamed spring rolls $6. Vegetarians: try the delectable *kari sayur campur* ($12.50). Cocktails $9. Expect a wait on the weekends. Open M-Th noon-midnight, F-Sa noon-1am. **$$-$$$**

Le Gamin Cafe, 50 MacDougal St. between Prince and Houston Sts. (☎254-4678). Subway: C, E to Spring St. Always brimming with locals, this cafe offers simple but elegant French fare. The *salade de chevre chaud aux noix* (goat cheese croutons, tomato, mesclun, and walnuts, $9) is a favorite. Cafe au lait $3. Crepes $3.25-9.50. Open daily 8am-midnight. **$$**

Space Untitled, 133 Greene St. between Prince and Houston Sts. (☎260-8962). Subway: N, R to Prince St. Huge, warehouse-like cafe with plenty of bar stools and chairs to make yourself comfortable. Sandwiches $3-6; sumptuous desserts $1.75-4.50. Coffee $1.50-4; wine and beer $4.50. Open M-Th 7am-10pm, F 7am-11pm, Sa 8am-11pm, Su 8am-9pm. **$**

Lucky's Juice Joint, 75 W. Houston St. between Wooster St. and W. Broadway (☎388-0300). Subway: B, D, F, Q to Broadway-Lafayette. Delightful stop specializes in fresh juice combos. Exotic smoothies ($4-5) made with a whole banana and a choice of everything from soy milk to peaches; anything from ginseng to bee pollen can be included for a dollar more. Fresh and healthy food for the weary gallery-goer available in the outdoor cafe. Open M-Sa 9am-8pm, Su 10am-8pm. **$**

Brisas del Caribe, 489 Broadway, at Broome St. Subway: 6 Spring St. Caribbean food in a decidedly un-SoHo setting. During lunchtime this dark dive is populated by men on break from crew-work here for the very cheap food (french fries $2; hot sandwiches $2.35-6.50) and roast pork that is rumored to be the best in town ($4.50). Open daily 7am-6pm. **$**

Jerry's, 101 Prince St. between Mercer and Greene Sts. (☎966-9464). Subway: N, R to Prince St. The calamari salad ($11) will definitely add some spice to your life. Great selection of sandwiches. Try the country ham and brie on sourdough ($8.50). Open M-W 9am-11pm, Th-F 9am-11:30pm, Sa 10:30am-11:30pm, Su 10:30am-5pm. **$$-$$$**

Kelley and Ping Asian Grocery and Noodle Shop, 127 Greene St. between Houston and Prince Sts. (☎228-1212). Subway: N, R to Prince St. In a hollowed-out SoHo warehouse space now decorated with sleek Asian food products, Kelley and Ping serves up filling noodle dishes for $8-9. Wraps $4; soups $6-10. Also has a tea counter for all things not Lipton. Open daily 11:30am-11pm. **$**

Lupe's East L.A. Kitchen, 110 Sixth Ave., at Watts St. (☎966-1326). Subway: C, E to Spring St. A small, down-scale cantina with extremely filling burritos and enchiladas ($8-10). The Super Vegetarian Burrito ($7.50) and the Taquito Platter ($7.50) are worthy of the City of Angels, as are the *huevos cubanos*—eggs with black beans and sweet plantain ($6-7). Four types of hot-pepper sauce available for those who play with fire. Brunch ($4-8) served Sa-Su 11:30am-4pm; open Su-Tu 11:30am-11pm, W-Sa 11:30am-midnight. **$**

SHOPS

Dean and Deluca, 560 Broadway, at Prince St. (☎226-6800). Subway: N, R to Prince St. This gourmet shop is more gallery than grocery with food too pretty to eat. You might be able to afford a lollipop. Open M-Sa 9am-8pm, Su 9am-7pm.

GREENWICH VILLAGE

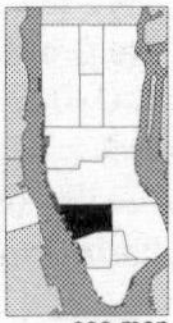
see map pp. 316-317

The West Village's artistic spirit spawns many creative eateries and makes stumbling around looking for food as much fun as dining. Around the intersection of Bleecker and Carmine Sts. are a cluster of Italian restaurants. On Hudson St. you'll find a number of gourmet shops which serve great sandwiches.

Corner Bistro, 331 W. 4th St., on the corner of Jane St. at Eighth Ave. (☎242-9502). Subway: A, C, E, L to 14th St.-Eighth Ave. Known for transcendent hamburgers ($4.50-5.50) and cold beer ($2-3). Arrive early—or late—if you want to get a seat. Open M-Sa 11:30am-4am, Su noon-4am. Cash only.

John's Pizzeria, 278 Bleecker St. between Seventh Ave. S. and Morton St. (☎243-1680). Subway: 1, 9 to Christopher St. Widely regarded as Manhattan's best pizzeria and a great place to sit down and enjoy a pie. Two sizes, small and large, $10-20. No slices. Open M-Th 11:30am-11:30pm, F-Sa 11:30am-12:30pm, Su noon-11:30pm. Cash only. **$-$$**

Chez Brigitte, 77 Greenwich Ave. between Seventh Ave. and Bank St. (☎929-6736). Subway: 1, 2, 3, 9 to 14th St. This hole-in-the-wall French diner-cum-bistro has no pretensions with its $4.50-9 French entrees. Just as its menu boasts, it "serves 250 people, 11 people at a time" with diner-style counter service. Open daily 11am-10pm. Cash only. **$**

Tartine, 253 W. 11th St., at W. 4th St. (☎229-2611). Subway: 1, 2, 3, 9 to 14th St.; 1, 9 to Christopher St. Bring your own wine to complement a fine Continental lunch, brunch or dinner in the serene sidewalk seating of this secluded West Village bistro. Entrees are delicately prepared and reasonably priced (chicken sauteed in lemon and sage $13). Prix-fixe Su brunch $9.75. Open Tu-Sa 9am-10:30pm, Su 9am-10pm. Cash only. **$$**

Moustache, 90 Bedford St. between Barrow and Grove Sts. (☎229-2220). Subway: 1, 9 to Christopher St. Sumptuous Middle-Eastern fare served on copper table-tops. Lentil soup $3.50, salads $4-9.50, *tabouleh* $3.50. Falafel sandwich $5.50. Open daily noon-11pm. **$**

Arturo's Pizza, 106 W. Houston St., at Thompson St. (☎677-3820). Subway: 1, 9 to Houston St. Arturo's has served up great, cheap pizza and divey class for decades now. The big, cheesy pies ($10-17) are divine. Entrees range from $11-28. Live jazz M-Th 8pm-1am, F-Sa 9pm-2am, Su 7pm-midnight. Open M-Th 4pm-1am, F-Sa 4pm-2am, Su 3pm-midnight. **$**

Olive Tree Cafe, 117 MacDougal St. between Bleecker St. and Minetta Lane (☎254-3480). Standard Middle Eastern food offset by endless stimulation. If you get bored by the old movies on the wide screen, you can rent chess and backgammon sets ($1 per person per hour), doodle with chalk on the slate tables, or sit on the patio and survey the Village nightlife. Falafel sandwich $2.75; chicken kebab platter with salad, rice pilaf, and vegetable $8.75; delicious egg creams $2. Open daily 11am-4am. **$**

Peanut Butter & Co., 240 Sullivan St., at 3rd St. (☎677-3995). Subway: A, B, C, D, E, F, Q to W. 4th St. All sandwiches include fresh peanut butter (ground daily) at this restaurant perfect for the kids. Sandwiches $4-7. Open Su-Th 11am-9pm, F-Sa 11am-10pm.

Ray's Pizza, 465 Sixth Ave. at 11th St. (243-2253). Subway: 1, 2, 3, 9 to 14th St.; L to Sixth Ave. Half the uptown joints claim the title of "Original Ray's," but here's the real McCoy. Tourists from Europe wait in line with students from neighboring P.S. 41 for cheese-heavy pies. Plain slice $1.90, "Famous Slice," $3.75. Scant seating near large mirrors; get pizza to go. Open Su-Th 11am-2am, F-Sa 11am-3am. **$**

Spain, 113 W. 13th St. between Sixth and Seventh Aves. (☎929-9580). Subway: 1, 2, 3, 9 to 14th St. L to Sixth Ave. Enormous tureens of traditional Spanish food for $9-19 in a charming Spanish dining room. The entrees can easily satisfy 2 or even 3 people (sharing incurs an extra $2 charge). Try the *paellas* or anything with garlic. Tantalizing and *free* appetizers such as *chorizo.* Open daily noon-1am. Cash only. **$$**

Day-O, 103 Greenwich Ave. (☎924-3168) between Jane and W. 12th St. Spicy concoctions of Caribbean and Southern cuisine with the most soul–and possibly the most funk–in the West Village. Firebird Jerk Chicken Wings $8. BBQ Ribs $17. Open Su-W noon-10:30pm, Th-Sa noon-1am. **$$**

Eva's, 11 W. 8th St. between MacDougal St. and Fifth Ave. (☎677-3496). Subway: A, B, C, D, E, F, Q to W. 4th St. Refreshing fast-service health food. Massive veggie plate with falafel, grape leaves, and eggplant salad $6. Vitamin store in back adds to the anti-ambience. Open M-Sa 11am-11pm, Su 11am-10pm. **$**

CAFES

The Grey Dog, 33 Carmine St. between Bleecker and Bedford Sts. (☎462-0041). Subway: A, B, C, D, E, F, Q to W. 4th St. Hip *can* be cheap, as this cafe's happy young patrons are well aware. A caffeine-lover's best friend, coffee is just $.80. Salads and sandwiches are also reasonable ($5.50-$8). Open M-F 6:30am-11:30pm, Sa-Su 7am-12:30am.

Caffe Dante, 79-81 MacDougal St. between Houston and Bleecker Sts. (☎982-5275). Subway: A, B, C, D, E, F, Q to W. 4th St. A Village staple, with black-and-white photos of Italy and atmospheric lighting. *Frutta di bosco* (cream pastry with fruit) $5.50, coffee-based drinks $2-6, nice gelati $6. A great place to take Beatrice. Open Su-Th 10am-2am, F-Sa 10am-3am.

Caffe Mona Lisa, 282 Bleecker St. between Jones and Barrow Sts. (☎929-1262). Subway: 1, 9 to Christopher St. Like the coffee here, *La Gioconda*'s recurring image is strong but not overpowering. Well-brewed beverages ($1.25-4.50) and other cafe fare (sandwiches and crepes $7-11). Mona Lisa's oversized mirrors, old stuffed chairs, and eccentric furniture pieces might make you smile enigmatically. Open daily 11am-2am.

EAST VILLAGE

see map pp. 320-321

St. Mark's Pl. hosts a slew of inexpensive and popular village institutions. At night, **Avenue A** throbs with bars and sidewalk cafes. Among the East Village's famous centers of ethnic cuisine are the row of Indian restaurants that line **E. 6th St.** between First and Second Aves., the Japanese eating spots on **E. 9th St.** and **Stuyvesant St.** between Second and Third Aves., and the Eastern European restaurants along **Second Ave.**

Yakitori Taisho, 5 St. Mark's Pl. between Second and Third Aves. (☎228-5086). Subway: 6 to Astor Pl. Look for the huge red paper lantern out front. This tiny eating space serves good Japanese fare at wonderful prices. 10 *yakitori* (skewers of exquisitely tender pieces of chicken and vegetables) $12, cold ramen $4, chicken teriyaki $7. Open daily 11am-11pm. **$**

Max, 51 Ave. B between E. 3rd and 4th Sts. (☎539-0111). Subway: F to Second Ave. Eating in the back garden of Max is like having dinner in an old Italian-American neighborhood: clothes hang off faux washing lines. And the food (pasta $8.95-10.95, entrees $10.95-14.95) tastes lovingly hand-made. Open daily noon-midnight. Cash only. **$$**

National Cafe, 210 First Ave., at E. 13th St. (☎473-9354). Subway: L to First Ave. The decor may not be much to talk about, but this is great home cooking, Cuban style. It's hard to find a better Cuban lunch special in the city; from 10:30am-3pm the National serves an entree of the day, rice and beans or salad, plantain, a cup of soup, and bread for $4.60. Everything on the garlic-heavy menu is well under $10. Open M-Sa 10:30am-10pm. **$**

Frank, 88 Second Ave. between E. 5th and E. 6th Sts. (☎420-0202). Subway: 6 to Astor Pl. An adorable sliver of a place with a friendly bistro feel. The lunch menu centers around healthy sandwiches ($6-8) and pasta ($9-10). Dinner fare is more expensive (pasta $8.95-12.95; entrees $11.95-13.95). M-F 5:30-7pm is Aperitivo Hour—free antipasti until 6:30pm. Expect to wait on the sidewalk for seats; no reservations unless you're a party of 8 or more. Open M-Th 10:30am-4pm and 5pm-1am, F-Sa 10:30am-4pm and 5pm-2am, Su 10:30am-4pm and 5pm-midnight. **$-$$**

Second Ave. Delicatessen, 156 Second Ave., at 10th St. (☎677-0606). Subway: 6 to Astor Pl. *The* definitive New York deli. The Lebewohl family has proudly maintained this strictly kosher joint since 1954. Meals served with an array of pickles. Try the chopped liver ($6.50), *babka* ($3.25), *kasha varnishkes* ($4), or mushroom barley ($4), all reputed to be among the best in the city, or go for the classic pastrami or corned beef sandwiches ($7.95-10.95). Open M-Sa 10am-8:30pm, Su 11am-7pm (See **Sights,** p. 64.) **$$**

Bulgin' Waffles Cafe, 49.5 First Ave., at E. 3rd St. (☎477-6555). With its plush, colorful chairs, this cute cafe is a good spot for taking a *siesta* in between meal hours. Serves waffles ($4) and wafflettes (hazelnut $2). Open M-Th 8am-10pm, F 8am-2am, Su 9am-2am, Su 9am-10pm. **$**

Cucina di Pesce, 87 E. 4th St. between Second and Third Aves. (☎260-6800). Subway: 6 to Astor Pl. A classic little Italian place with oil paintings, rosily-lit nooks, and sidewalk seating. Dishes are relatively inexpensive and portions are large. Spinach penne (with asparagus, sun-dried tomatoes, and fontina cheese) $7.95; salmon with sauteed mushrooms and pasta $10.95. Free mussels at the bar. The daily special is a steal: full dinner with soup, entree, and glass of wine $9.95 (M-F 4-6:30pm, Sa-Su 4-6pm). Open daily 2:30pm-midnight. **$-$$**

Dojo Restaurant, 26 St. Mark's Pl. between Second and Third Aves. (☎674-9821). Subway: 6 to Astor Pl. One of the most popular restaurants and hangouts in the East Village serving an incredible variety of (largely) vegetarian and Japanese foods with St. Mark's Pl. ambiance. Soyburgers with brown rice and salad $3.50. Dojo salad with carrot dressing $5. Yakisoba $5-7. Open Su-Th 11am-1am, F-Sa 11am-2am. Cash only. **$**

Elvie's Turo-Turo, 214 First Ave. between E. 12th and 13th Sts. (☎473-7785). Subway: L to First Ave. Filipino food served cafeteria-style—just point to what you want. Dishes include *pancit* (a stir-fried rice noodle dish), an excellent chicken adobo, and barbecued pork and chicken. One dish (plus rice) $4, two for $5.75. Open M-Sa 11am-9pm, Su 11am-8pm. **$**

Flor's Kitchen, 149 First Ave., at E. 9th St. (☎387-8949). Subway: 6 to Astor Pl., L to First Ave. A tiny, brightly-colored Venezuelan restaurant serving up all sorts of *arepas* (filled corn cakes, $3-4) and *empanadas* ($2.75). The beet soup is quite good (bowl $4.50). Entrees $8-13. Open M-Th 11am-11pm, F-Sa 11am-midnight, Su 10am-10pm. **$**

Kate's Joint, 58 Ave. B, between E. 4th and 5th Sts. (☎777-7059). Subway: F to Second Ave. A good vegan restaurant serving hearty food. This colorful, couch-lined, chill eatery delivers veggie fare like tofu teriyaki ($10), Southern-fried unchicken cutlets ($9.95), and unturkey club ($7). Lunch special daily 9am-4pm for $5 (selections like vegan pancakes and cheese omelette). Open daily 9am-1am. **$$**

La Focacceria, 128 First Ave., between St. Mark's Pl. and E. 7th St. (☎254-4946). Subway: 6 to Astor Pl. Serving delectable Sicilian eats for 85 years. The *vesteddi* (fried ricotta and kashkaval cheese, $2) and Sicilian-style eggplant sandwiches ($5) are exceptional. Open M-Th 11am-10pm, F-Sa 1-11pm. **$**

Mama's Food Shop, 200 E. 3rd St. between Aves. A and B (☎777-4425). Subway: F to Second Ave. See laid-back East Villagers obeying Mama's order to "shut up and eat." Fried chicken or salmon (each $7) with sides like honey-glazed sweet potatoes and broccoli or couscous ($1 each). Vegetarian dinner includes any 3 sides ($7). Bread pudding and cobbler come by the ½ pint ($3), if you have room left for dessert. Open M-Sa 11am-11pm. Mama has recently created a doppelganger with **Step Mama's,** across the street at 199 E. 3rd St. (☎228-2663), which sells sandwiches, soups, and sides. The nourishment continues next door at **Mama's Milk,** a new, creative smoothie shop. **$**

Mare Chiaro's

Tom's Restaurant

Tavern on the Green

Pommes Frites, 123 Second Ave. between E. 7th St. and St. Mark's Pl. (☎674-1234). Subway: 6 to Astor Pl. A hole in the wall vending lovely Belgian fries, topped with your choice of one of a large variety of sauces. Regular fries $3, large $5.

St. Dymphna's, 118 St. Mark's Pl. between First Ave. and Ave. A (☎254-6636). Subway: L to First Ave. Irish pub grub cooked well, a full bar, and a lush garden out back. The beef and Guinness casserole ($10) shames average pies. Open for lunch M-F 10am-4pm; dinner daily 5pm-midnight; brunch Sa-Su 10am-5pm. Bar open daily until 4am. **$-$$**

Two Boots Restaurant, 37 Ave. A, at E. 3rd St. (☎505-2276). Subway: F to Second Ave. Which two boots? Italy and Louisiana. A swinging combination of Cajun and Italian, the restaurant draws locals in with its hybrid pizzas (individual $6.50-9.95) and po'boys ($5-6). **Two Boots To Go,** the nearby takeout pizzeria (at 42-44 Ave. A; ☎254-1919) has an attached, amazingly well-stocked video store. **Den of Cin** (below the video store) is a screening room/performance space (☎254-0800). Open daily noon-midnight. **$**

Veselka, 144 Second Ave., at E. 9th St. (☎228-9682). Subway: 6 to Astor Pl. Big, beautiful murals adorn this Ukrainian restaurant. The enormous menu includes 7 varieties of soups, as well as salads ($3.50-7.75), blintzes ($7.25), Ukrainian meatballs ($8.25), and other Eastern European fare. Combination special gets you soup, salad, stuffed cabbage, and four melt-in-your-mouth *pierogi* ($8.25). Open 24hr. **$**

Whole Earth Bakery and Kitchen, 130 St. Mark's Pl. between First Ave. and Ave. A (☎677-7597). Subway: 6 to Astor Pl. Inspired by the owner's 87-year-old mother, Whole Earth gives home cooking a strictly vegan tweak. The baked goods (all without egg, naturally) are shockingly tasty. Ask for flavorful tofu/garlic spread on other items. Cookies 50¢-$2; fruit cobbler $1.50; oil/sugar-free muffins $1.50. Open M-F 8am-midnight, Sa-Su 10:30am-midnight. **$**

Yaffa Cafe, 97 St. Mark's Pl. between First Ave. and Ave. A (☎674-9302 or 677-9001). Subway: 6 to Astor Pl. Cocktail garden party meets Middle Eastern disco lounge. Yaffa Cafe features all sorts of sandwiches ($4.50-6.95), salads (around $6), and a multitude of entrees (veggie entrees $6.95, chicken $8.95). Beer $3.50. The beautiful outdoor garden is open all summer. Open 24hr. **$**

CAFES

Alt.Coffee, 139 Ave. A, at E. 9th St. (☎529-2233). Subway: 6 to Astor Pl. This cafe is a haven for artists, anarchists, and alterna-types galore. Offering all sorts of (non-alcoholic) drinks ($1.50-3.75), sandwiches, and vegan cookies ($2.25), as well as internet access ($10/hour). Local art adorns the walls. And yes, you can smoke here. Open M-Th 8:30am-1:30am, F 8:30am-3am, Sa 10am-3am, Su 10am-1:30am.

SHOPS

Moishe's Bake Shop, 115 Second Ave. between E. 6th and 7th Sts. (☎505-8555). Subway: 6 to Astor Pl. For 30 years this bake shop has served up strictly kosher, *geshmak* (that's Yiddish for tasty) breads and cookies. Challah $2.75. Open Su 7am-8pm, M-Th 7:30am-8:30pm, F 7am until 1hr. before sunset.

Veniero's, 342 E. 11th St., between First and Second Aves. (☎674-7070). Subway: L to First Ave. Established in 1894, this Italian pastry shop has clogged the arteries of many sweets-lovers. Spacious, if not particularly atmospheric, cafe seating. But with cheesecake this light and tasty, who's worrying about decor? Cannolis $2.25; cheesecakes $3.50-4. Open Su-Th 8am-11:30pm, F-Sa 8am-12:30pm.

Something Sweet, 177 First Ave., at 11th St. (☎533-9986). Subway: L to First Ave. Delectable and inventive sweets that give Veniero's a run for its money. Indulge in a tropical fruit tart ($2.25), a mousse tart ($2), or *crème brulée* ($2.25). Open M-Sa 8am-8pm, Su 9:30am-5:30pm.

CHELSEA AND HERALD SQUARE

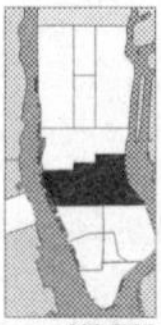

see map pp. 322-323

Chelsea's restaurants are a mix of Central American and Chinese cuisine, as well as varieties of Cajun and Creole specialties. A variety of fashionable watering holes and diners cater to the neighborhood's visible and enthusiastic gay contingent. The heart of Chelsea dining is **Eighth Ave.,** between 14th and 23rd Sts., a center of great cafes and stylish restaurants. (See also **Gay New York,** p. 196.)

Kitchen, 218 Eighth Ave., at 21st St. (☎243-4433). Subway: C, E to 23rd St. Bear with the narrow confines of Kitchen—the Mexican dishes (takeout only) are well worth the squeeze. The store also hawks books, Mexican paraphernalia, and a staggering array of international hot sauces Burrito stuffed with a filling of your choice, pinto beans, rice, and green salsa $6.75. Open M-Sa 9am-10:30pm, Su 11am-10:30pm. **$**

Minar, 5 W. 31st St. between Fifth Ave. and Broadway (☎684-2199). Subway: B, D, F, N, Q, R, W to Herald Sq. Long and narrow, this Indian restaurant still manages to pack in many neighborhood South Asians for lunch and dinner. Spicy vegetable curries ($4.25) and regular curries ($5.25-5.50) are served at the counter with a small salad and choice of bread or rice. Open M-F 10am-7:30pm, Sa 10am-5:30. **$**

Bendix Diner, 219 Eighth Ave., at 21st St. (☎366-0560). Subway: C, E to 23rd St. A successful new hybrid—the Thai greasy spoon—Bendix encourages its patrons to "Get Fat!". Entrees at this prime people-

Gray's Papaya

Milady's Bar

Outdoor Seating

watching spot range from Pork Chops to Pad Nur and will set you back around $7-8. Sandwiches $4-8, "Thai breakfast" $3-3.50. Breakfast available all day. Open M-W 8am-midnight, Th-Sa 8am-1am, Su 8am-11pm. **$**

Negril, 362 W. 23rd St. between Eighth and Ninth Aves. (☎807-6411). Subway: C, E to 23rd St. Colorful decor, excellent Jamaican food, and a lively bar with 12 kinds of martinis–what more could you ask for? Dinner options are mid-priced, but lunch is affordable (entrees $8.50-13.50). The jerk chicken ($8.50) is tender and just spicy enough. Open M 5pm-midnight, Tu-Th noon-midnight, F-Sa noon-1am (bar open till 2am), Su 2-11pm.

Wild Lily Tea Room, 511-A W. 22nd St. between Tenth and Eleventh Aves. (☎691-2258). Subway: C, E to 23rd St. Sparse menu is full of Asian ingredients like shiitake mushrooms and mesclun greens. Sip a jasmine or green mattcha iced tea ($5 for a tall glass) while you wax philosophical within the minimalist Tea Room, featuring a circular pond full of koi fish and floating flowers. Open Tu-Su 11am-10pm.

Blue Moon Mexican Cafe, 150 Eighth Ave., between 17th and 18th Sts. (☎463-0560). Subway: A, C, E, L to 14th St.-Eighth Ave. A funky hangout, popular both for the food and the margaritas. Giant burritos $8.95; entrees $10.95-12.95. Weekend brunch includes one alcoholic beverage (omelettes or french toast, $7.95; pancakes $6.95). Open Su-Th noon-11pm, F-Sa 11:30am-midnight. **$-$$**

Mary Ann's, 116 Eighth Ave., at 16th St. (☎633-0877). Subway: A, C, E, L to 14th St.-Eighth Ave. Waiters serve up huge portions of inventive Mexican food in this white-walled restaurant slung with lights. Entrees $8-12. $1 Corona with entree on Th. Open M-Tu noon-10:30pm, W-Th 11:30am-11pm, F-Sa 11:30am-11:30pm, Su noon-10pm. Cash only. **$-$$**

Spring Joy, 172 Eighth Ave. between 18th and 19th Sts. (☎243-1688). Subway: A, C, E, L to 14th St.-Eighth Ave.; C, E to 23rd St. Although Chinese food is not as trendy as Chelsea, Spring Joy serves up good food at decent prices. Numerous lunch options under $5; dinner $6.25-8.95. Design your own dish $6.95; diet options $6.25-8.95. *And* free white wine with your dinner. Open M-F 11:30am-midnight, Sa-Su noon-midnight. **$**

Food Bar, 149 Eighth Ave. (☎243-2020). See **Gay Hangouts and Restaurants**, p. 196.

SHOPS

Little Pie Co., 407 W. 14th St. between Ninth and Tenth Aves. (☎414-2324). Subway: A, C, E, L to 14th St.-Eighth Ave. Small but perfect. Grab a 5" old-fashioned apple pie ($5 of fresh apples and great crust) to go, or snack on it on the red diner-style bar counter. Open M-F 10am-8pm, Sa-Su noon-7pm.

F & B, 269 W. 23rd St. between Seventh and Eighth Aves. (☎646-486-4441). Subway: 1, 9, C, E to 23rd St. Street food, European-style–the name stands for 'frites and beignets,' and the brushed-metal look completes the look. Hot dogs ($2.35-5.50, most $3.50) come with a lot more toppings than your street-corner Sabrett's. The juicy *frites* ($2.25-3.25) are amazing with one of the 12 kinds of dips ($0.60). Veggie dogs available. Open M-Th 11am-11pm, F 11am-midnight, Sa 9am-midnight, Su 9am-11pm.

UNION SQUARE, GRAMERCY, & MURRAY HILL

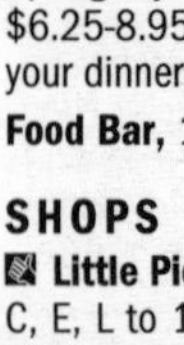

see map pp. 322-323

A small cluster of Pakistani and Indian restaurants and other ethnic cuisine restaurants battle for customers on Lexington and Third Aves., in the upper 20s and lower 30s (an area jocularly known as Curry Hill). Trendy, upscale restaurants (**Union Square Cafe** and **Bluewater Grill** are among New York's finest eating spots, although hardly the sort of place one would call 'budget') and yuppie watering holes cluster around Union Square and Park Ave. South.

Curry in a Hurry, 119 Lexington Ave., at 28th St. (☎683-0900). Subway: 6 to 28th St. Lots of tasty food at good prices make this one of our favorite Curry Hill locales. Chicken or lamb curries $4.50; vegetarian dishes $3.50-3.75; platters (main dishes, basmati rice, naan, and salad) $6.50-8.50. Open daily noon-midnight. **$**

Pete's Tavern, 129 E. 18th St., at Irving Pl. (☎473-7676). Subway: 4, 5, 6, L, N, Q, R, W to Union Sq. "NY's oldest original bar," having served alcohol since 1864. Photos on the wall show Pete's during its speakeasy days during Prohibition. Legend has it that O. Henry wrote *The Gift of the Magi* in the first booth as you enter. Sandwiches $7-7.50; entrees $8-14.50. Kitchen open daily 11am-1am. **$-$$**

71 Irving Place, 71 Irving Pl. between 18th and 19th Sts. (☎995-5252). Subway: 4, 5, 6, L, N, Q, R, W to Union Sq. In its original incarnation at 52 Irving Pl., this cafe was a Gramercy favorite. The new setting looks like the inside of a Gramercy brownstone, and it's still a great place to read one of the magazines on the rack amidst neighborhood residents. Soft fresh-made waffles ($4.95-6.95) and fresh coffee from their upstate farm ($1.15). Open M-W 7am-11pm, Th-F 7am-midnight, Sa 8am-midnight, Su 8am-11pm. **$**

Chat 'n' Chew, 10 E. 16th St. between Union Sq. and Fifth Ave. (☎243-1616). Subway: 4, 5, 6, L, N, Q, R, W to Union Sq. The menus proclaim "real American homestyle," and indeed Chat 'n' Chew's down-home food is just like your Mom used to make—if your Mom was a '50s sitcom housewife. Heaping plates of macaroni and cheese ($7.95), classic grilled cheese with tomato ($6), and "Not your Mother's Meatloaf" ($10.95). Open M-Th 11:30am-11:30pm, F-Sa 10:30am-11:30pm, Su 10:30am-11pm. **$-$$**

Molly's, 287 Third Ave., between 22nd and 23rd Sts. (☎889-3361). Subway: 6 to 23rd St. Wooden beams and dim lighting give Molly's the feel of a pub in the Irish countryside; the sawdust that covers the floor just adds to the feel of being in Killarney. Good burgers ($7.95-9.95). Open daily 11am-4am; kitchen closes at midnight. **$-$$**

Republic, 37 Union Square W. (☎627-7168). Subway: 4, 5, 6, L, N, Q, R, W to Union Sq. Its storefront may look small but this very popular Japanese noodle bar is surprisingly capacious on the inside. High ceilings and wooden tables. Still, be prepared to share your table on crowded days. Soup noodles $6-8; pad thai $8; a few vegetarian options. Open Su-Th 11am-11:30am, F-Sa 11am-midnight. **$$**

Tibetan Kitchen, 444 Third Ave. between 30th and 31st Sts. (☎679-6286). Subway: 6 to 28th St. This tiny place serves food true to its Tibetan roots—meatier than Chinese, with a dollop of Indian. *Momo* (beef dumplings, $7.50) and *bocha* (buttered, salted tea, $3.25) are both delicious. Veggie dishes are plentiful ($6.75-8). Open M-F noon-3pm and 5-11pm, Sa 5-11pm. **$**

Zen Palate, 34 Union Sq. East, (☎614-9291). Subway: 4, 5, 6, L, N, Q, R, W to Union Sq. Asian-inspired vegetarian/vegan cuisine, including soothing, healthy, and fresh treats like "Shredded Heaven" (assorted veggies and spring rolls with brown rice, $8.45), stir-fried rice fettuccini with mushrooms ($7.65), or other concoctions on brown rice/seaweed/kale. Fresh-squeezed juices or rice milkshakes $1.50-3.50 Open M-Th and Su 11am-10:45pm, F-Sa 11am-11:45pm. **$-$$**

CAFES AND SHOPS

Sunburst Espresso Bar, 206 Third Ave., at 18th St. (☎674-1702). Locals stroll in for this cafe's impressive selection of sandwiches ($4.25-5.95), H&H bagels ($1.25), and low-fat muffins ($1.75) to go with their espressos ($0.85). The shakes and smoothies ($3.25-4.95) are dreamy Open M-Th 7am-11pm, F-Sa 7am-midnight, Su 8am-11pm. **$**

Coffee Shop Bar, 29 Union Sq. West (☎243-7969). Ugly building, but beautiful people. The restaurant features classic American diner fare with a Brazilian twist (eggs Ipanema $8.95). Waifs abound, but the Kate Moss-like figures aren't a likely result of such delicious food as the *media noche* sandwich ($9). Beers $4-6. Open M 7am-2am, Tu 7am-4am, W-F 7am-5:30am, Sa 8am-5:30am, Su 8am-2am. They card (21+) in the wee hours. **$$**

THE THEATER DISTRICT AND HELL'S KITCHEN

Subway: 1, 2, 3, 7, 9, A, C, E, N, R, S to 42nd St.-Times Square or Port Authority

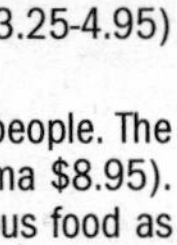

see map pp. 326-327

Your best budget bets generally lie along Eighth Ave. between 34th and 59th St. Those willing to spend more should try a meal on posh **Restaurant Row** on 46th St. between Eighth and Ninth Ave. The block caters to a pre-theater crowd, so arriving after 8pm will make it easier to get a table. Celebrities occasionally drift over to **Sardi's,** 234 W. 44th St. (☎221-8440), and take a seat on the plush red leather, surrounded by caricatures of themselves and their best friends. Traditionally, on the opening night of a major Broadway play, the main star makes an entrance at Sardi's following the show—to hearty cheers for a superb performance or polite applause for a bomb. Don't rule out the top restaurants in this area; several of the city's finest have excellent prix fixe lunch deals. **Le Beaujolais,** 364 W. 46th St. (☎974-7464), is a charming French bistro with a $14.25 lunch special.

Hourglass Tavern, 373 W. 46th St. between Eighth and Ninth Aves. (☎265-2060). A dark, crowded, two-floor triangular joint on Restaurant Row that is not for the slow-moving. Servers flip an hour-glass at your table when you sit down and the 59-min. time limit is strictly enforced when crowds are waiting. The changing prix-fixe entrees ($12-14)–which regularly feature fresh fish and filet mignon–make it worth the rush. Open M-W 5-11:15pm, Th-F 5-11:30pm. **$$**

Manganaro's, 488 Ninth Ave. between 37th and 38th Sts. (☎563-5331). If you don't mind a little chaos, this Italian deli and restaurant promises a lively and delicious lunch break with the authentic flavor of pre-gentrified Hell's Kitchen. Home of the six-foot sub, the restaurant prides itself on its gargantuan portions. Sandwiches $3-12. Open M-F 8am-7pm, Sa 9am-7pm; Dec.-May also Su 11am-5pm. **$-$$**

Becco, 355 W. 46th St. between Eighth and Ninth Aves. (☎397-7597). Gourmet cuisine that makes you forget your budget. Their 70 wines priced at $18 a bottle allows the luxury of selectivity minus the guilt of dropping a c-note before a Broadway show. For a $17 prix fixe lunch (dinner $22) you can have a gourmet antipasto platter or caesar salad, plus unlimited servings of the 3 pastas of the day. $16 dollar food minimum/person for dinner, $14 for lunch. Open daily noon-3pm and 5pm-midnight. **$$$**

Original Fresco Tortillas, 536 Ninth Ave. between 39th and 40th Sts. (☎465-8898). This tiny 9-seater serves up excellent homemade food at fast-food prices: fajitas and tacos $1-2, quesadillas $2-4, giant burritos $4-5. No artificial or chemical spices, no MSG, no preservatives, no kidding. Open M-F 11am-11pm, Sa-Su noon-10pm. **$**

MIDTOWN

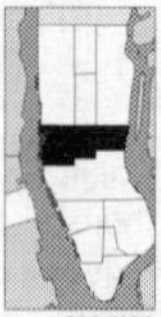

see map pp. 326-327

Keep in mind that in Midtown, cash is king. Here, CEOs run their corporate empires by wining and dining their clients, while socialite shoppers drop as much money on a late lunch as on a Fendi tote. Budget travelers don't despair—underpaid underlings all scour for cheap lunches here. From noon to 2pm, harried junior executives trying to eat and run swamp delis and cafes. If you do want to splurge, many top restaurants offer relatively reasonable *prix fixe* lunch menus that include an appetizer, entree, and dessert. Try **Aureole,** 34 E. 61st St. between Madison and Park Aves., one of the best restaurants in the city. (☎319-1660; Reservations required. M-F 2-2:30pm, three-course *prix fixe* $20.) Also, don't miss the city's best food court at **Grand Central Terminal Dining Concourse,** between 42nd and 45th St., Lexington and Vanderbilt Aves.

Sapporo, 152 W. 49th St. between Sixth and Seventh Aves. (☎869-8972). Subway: B, D, F, Q to 47th-50th Sts.-Rockefeller Center. A simple Japanese diner, with entrees listed on the wall in Japanese (the menu explains in English). A favorite spot for Broadway cast members and corporate types. Filling portions and astounding flavors. Sapporo ramen special $7.30. Open M-Sa 11am-11:30pm, Su 11am-10:30pm. **$-$$**

Dishes, 47 E. 44th St. between Vanderbilt and Madison Aves. (☎687-5511). Subway: 4, 5, 6, 7, S to 42nd St.-Grand Central. Relatively new and sleekly designed gourmet cafeteria. A score of sandwiches is available for the busy traveler's delectation, in addition to a number of combination juices and smoothies for the natural-food conscious. Open M-F 7am-5pm. **$-$$**

Mangia, 16 E. 48th St. between Madison and Fifth Aves. (☎754-7600). Subway: 6 to 51st St. An upscale prepared-food market. Its tidy and attractive cakes, pies, candy tid-bits, and tartlets are so artfully presented that it almost seems a shame to eat them. Open M-F 7am-6pm; restaurant open M-F 11:30am-4pm. **$-$$**

Fresco by Scotto, on the go, 40 E. 52nd St. between Park and Madison Aves. (☎754-2700). Subway: 6 to 51st St.; E, F to 53rd St.-Fifth Ave. Italian-inspired fare, mainly grilled pizzas and sandwiches. Huge salads $5-10. Open M-F 6:30am-6pm. **$-$$**

SHOPS

Teuscher Chocolatier, 620 Fifth Ave., on the promenade at Rockefeller Center (☎246-4416). Subway: B, D, F, Q to 47th-50th Sts.-Rockefeller Center. No Snickers or Kit-Kats here. A chocoholic's paradise, Teuscher offers the freshest chocolates flown in from Zurich weekly, and unfortunately have the prices to prove it. But don't let a little transatlantic overhead keep you from this experience–you can still savor a single piece for under $2. Open M-W 10am-6pm, Th 10am-7:30pm, F-Sa 10am-6pm, Su noon-5pm.

UPPER EAST SIDE

Meals on the Upper East Side descend in price as you move east away from Fifth Avenue's glitzy, mildly exorbitant museum cafes toward Lexington, Third, and Second Aves. Second and Third Aves., especially from the mid-70s to the mid-80s, boast approximately six restaurants per block.

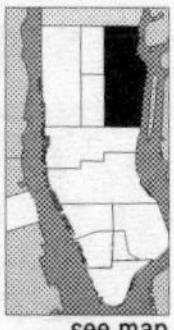

see map pp. 328-329

Saigon Grill, 1700 Second Ave., at 88th St. (☎996-4600). Subway: 4, 5, 6 to 86th St. Some of the best Vietnamese in the city and a rare bargain on the Upper East Side. Dishes come chock full with vegetables. Open daily 11:30am-11:30pm. Also at 2381 Broadway (☎875-9072). **$**

Barking Dog Luncheonette, 1678 Third Ave., at 94th St. (☎831-1800). Subway: 6 to 96th St. Enjoy big, tasty portions like "'Mom's Lovin' Meatloaf" ($11) in this restaurant full of dog paraphernalia, from the doghouse-shaped entrance to the pictures of celebrities and their hounds. Salads $5-9; sandwiches $6-8. Specials (M-F 5-7pm) come with soup or salad and dessert. Open daily 8am-11pm. **$-$$**

El Pollo, 1746 First Ave. between 90th and 91st Sts. (☎996-7810). Subway: 4, 5, 6 to 86th St. Excellent Peruvian fare. While known for its roasted, marinated, 7-flavored chicken, this restaurant also serves up delicacies like fried sweet plantains ($3) and papas con aji ($5). Half-chicken $6. Open M-F 11am-11pm, Sa-Su 12:30pm-10:45pm. **$-$$**

EJ's Luncheonette, 1271 Third Ave., at 73rd St. (☎472-0600). Subway: 6 to 68th, 77th Sts. The Scrumptious fare, like the buttermilk pancakes ($6), has won the devotion of Upper East-siders. After all, what could be better than breakfast served all day? Open M-Sa 8am-11pm, Su 8am-10:30pm. **Other locations:** 447 Amsterdam Ave. between 81st and 82nd Sts. (☎873-3444); 432 Sixth Ave. between 9th and 10th Sts. (☎473-5555). **$**

Jackson Hole, 232 E. 64th St. between Second and Third Aves. (☎371-7187). Subway: 6 to 68th St. Home of the famed 7oz. burger and offering over 25 different kinds of burgers and chicken sandwiches, Jackson Hole is synonymous with grease, which is synonymous with TASTE! Burgers, chicken sandwiches, and platters $6-11. Open M-Sa 10am-1am, Su 10am-midnight. **Some other locations:** 91st St. and Madison Ave. (☎427-2820); 85th St. and Columbus Ave. (☎362-5177); and 70th St. and Astoria Blvd. (☎718-204-7070). **$-$$**

Candle Cafe, 1307 Third Ave., at 75th St. (☎472-0970). Subway: 6 to 77th St. A vegan's delight, this restaurant adds a twist to organic ingredients. Try the excellent Classic Caesar ($6) or Herbed Tofu Roller with grilled portabello mushrooms. Open M-Sa 11:30am-10:30pm, Su 11:30am-9:30pm. **$-$$**

Papaya King, 179 E. 86th St., at Third Ave. (☎369-0648). Subway: 4, 5, 6 to 86th St. Since 1972 New Yorkers have tolerated no seating and tacky tropical decor at this dive for the "tastier than filet mignon" hot dogs ($1.45). It's hard to just have one, though, so you might opt for the special: 2 hot dogs and a 16-oz. taste of their famous tropical drinks for $4, a rare deal for the Upper East Side. Open Su-W 8am-midnight, Th-Sa 8am-1am. **$**

Viand, 673 Madison Ave., at 61st St. (☎751-6622). Subway: N, R to 59th St.-Fifth Ave. Locals sing the praises of this coffee shop's turkey sandwich ($7.35), which is rumored to be among the best in the city. Open M-Sa 6am-10pm, Su 7am-9pm. **$-$$**

Dallas BBQ, 1265 Third Ave., at 73rd St. (☎772-9393). Subway 6 to 68th St., 77th St. Big portions, tasty rib and shrimp dishes, and piña coladas ($7) and daiquiris ($7) bigger than Texas. Open Su-Th 11:30am-midnight, F-Sa 11:30am-1am. **$-$$**

Tony's di Napoli, 1606 Second Ave., between 83rd and 84th Sts. (☎861-8686). Subway: 4, 5, 6 to 86th St. Family-style southern Italian food served in a festive atmosphere. All dishes serve 2-3. The veal parmigiana ($20) is a perennial favorite. Open M-F 5-11pm, Sa-Su 2pm-11pm.

SHOPS

Le Pain Quotidien, 1131 Madison Ave., between 84th and 85th Sts. (☎327-4900). Subway: 4, 5, 6 to 86th St. Purveyors of some of the best, and freshest, breads in the city. Stop in and pick up a *baguette à l'ancienne* ($2.50). Hungry travelers may sit for a meal at their trademark communal wooden tables. Open M-F 7:30am-7pm, Sa-Su 8am-7pm. **$-$$**

Grace's Marketplace, 1237 Third Ave., at 71st St. (☎737-0600). Subway: 6 to 68th St. Your tongue will be plastered to the counter's window once you see the cornucopia of fresh goodies this gourmet shop has to offer. Even if you can't afford a thing at this market, Grace's is a education in Upper East Side life. Open M-F, Sa 7am-8:30pm, Su 8am-7pm.

on the cheap

The Best Bagels in New York

New York City's bagels are legendary. Crisp on the outside and chewy on the inside, a bagel is a New York breakfast tradition and a great midday snack. Here are three of the best places to buy a bagel in the city.

H&H Bagels, 2239 Broadway, at 80th St. (☎692-2435). H&H has fed Upper West Siders for years with bagels (95¢) that hold a reputation for being the best in Manhattan. Send a dozen ($11.40) home to mom—H&H ships anywhere in the world. Open 24hr.

Ess-a-Bagel, 831 Third Ave. between 52nd and 53rd Sts. (☎980-1010). A real New-York-style delicatessen, with the usual array of spreads, fillings and garnishes, but the centerpiece of the whole procedure is the bagel that the sandwich is made from (70¢, $8.40 for a baker's dozen). Open M-F 6am-9pm, Sa-Su 8am-5pm.

Tal Bagel, 333 E. 86th St. between First and Second Aves. (☎427-6811). Large, chewy bagels at a good price (65¢). An Upper East Side mainstay. Open M-Sa 5:30am-10pm; Su 5:30-7pm.

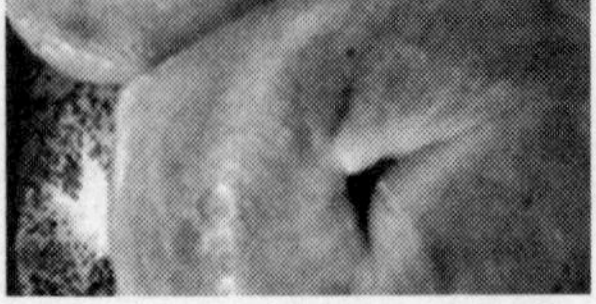

UPPER WEST SIDE

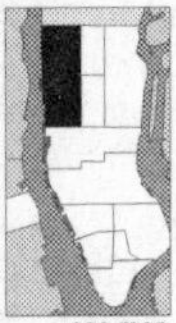

see map pp. 332-333

The Upper West Side offers a variety of ethnic cuisine. If you're not in the mood to dine fancy, check out the countless pizza shops and diners. Browse around Columbus Ave., Amsterdam Ave., and Broadway to find cute sidewalk cafes in the summer.

Big Nick's Burger Joint and Pizza Joint, 2175 Broadway, at 77th St. (☎362-9238). Subway: 1, 9 to 79th St. Two times a joint, Big Nick's will satisfy your munchies and then some. Nick's has been dishing tried-and-true pizza, plate-sized burgers ($4.95-6.75, or go for the 1-lb. sumo burger, $7.50), and breakfast dishes from their vast menu. Free delivery. Open 24hr., "sometimes 25." Also at 70 W. 71st St. at Columbus Ave. (☎799-4444). **$**

Henry's, 2745 Broadway, at 105th St. (☎866-0600). Subway: 1, 9 to 103rd St. A pleasant neighborhood restaurant with compulsively fresh and attentively prepared dishes. Of particular interest are the duck confit spring roll ($8) and the crab cakes with fennel-orange salad ($18). The dessert menu boasts such showstoppers as the Grand Marnier cheesecake with grapefruit and orange ($6). Open M noon-11pm, Tu-Th noon-midnight, F noon-1am, Sa 11am-1am, Su 11am-11pm. **$$-$$$**

Good Enough to Eat, 483 Amsterdam Ave. between 83rd and 84th Sts. (☎496-0163). Subway: 1, 9 to 86th St. The farmhouse motif makes for glorious breakfast eating. Breads and desserts made on premises. Vermont cheddar and apple omelette with buttermilk biscuits $7.25; strawberry almond waffles $8.50. Healthy salads (about $10) and vegetarian options abound. Open M-Th 8am-4pm and 5:30-10:30pm, F 8am-4pm and 5:30-11pm, Sa 9am-4pm and 5:30-11pm, Su 9am-4pm and 5:30-10:30pm. **$-$$**

Gray's Papaya, 2090 Broadway, at 72nd St. (☎799-0243). Subway: 1, 9 to 72nd St. Satiate your hunger with amazing deals on hot dogs at this takeout. Gray's never-ending "recession special" sells 2 franks and 1 fruit drink (banana daiquiri, pineapple, piña colada, papaya) for a mere $2.45. Open 24hr. **$**

Mama Mexico, 2672 Broadway, at 102nd St. (☎864-2323). Subway: 1, 9 to 103rd St. Wonderful Mexican food in a festive atmosphere. With colored lanterns, a *loud* mariachi band, and a vivacious crowd, Mama promises a lively dinner. Amazing margaritas in 14 tropical flavors $6. Entrees $12-23. Reservations strongly recommended. Open Su-Th noon-midnight, F-Sa noon-2am. **$$-$$$**

Ollie's, 1991 Broadway, between 67th and 68th Sts. (☎595-8181). Subway: 1, 9 to 66th St. One of NY's most well-known noodle shops, with decor more in line with its neighbors than the typical Chinese restaurant. Just looking at the extensive menu of noodle soups ($6.25-7.50), fried rice (around $7), seafood

($10-14), and meat dishes ($8.50-10.25) will make you full. Great vegetarian options, too ($7.75-8.50). Lunch special M-F 11:30am-3pm $6 (entree, soup, and rice). Open Su-Th 11:30am-midnight, F-Sa 11:30am-1am. **$$**

La Caridad 78 Restaurant, 2197-2199 Broadway, at 78th St. (☎874-2780). Subway: 1, 9 to 79th St. A packed Chinese-Cuban hybrid. Ebullient waiters charm in 3 languages. The delicious cooking makes up for the rather mediocre decor. Prices around (and often well below) $10. Lunch special M-F 11:30am-4pm $5. Open M-Sa 11:30am-midnight Su 11:30am-10:30pm. Cash only. **$**

The Lemongrass Grill, 2534 Broadway, at 95th St. (☎666-0888). Subway: 1, 2, 3, 9 to 96th St. A culinary mainstay of the Upper West Side. Thai noodles and vegetables ($6.95-8.50) sate locals. Chicken entrees $8.95. Great appetizers (spring rolls $3.50) and salads (*yum pla muk*, Thai calamari salad, $6.95). Open Su 1pm-11:30pm, M-Th noon-11:30pm, F-Sa noon-12:30am. Also at: 138 E. 34th St., between Park Ave. S. and Lexington Ave. (☎ 213-3317); 80 Univ. Pl. **$**

Hi-Life Bar and Grill, 477 Amsterdam Ave., at 83rd St. (☎787-7199). Subway: 1, 9 to 79th St., 86th St. Step into the 1950s at this sleek hangout with a friendly waitstaff and late-night menu. Burgers $6.95-8.50; entrees $8.95-16.95. Sushi ½-price M-Tu, big bowls of pasta $7.95 W and Su, grilled chicken fajitas $8.50 Th and Sa. Other early dinner specials daily 5-7:30pm. DJ Th-Sa. Open M-F 4:30pm-late, Sa-Su 10:30am-4pm for brunch and 4:30pm-late.

Ivy's Cafe, 154 W. 72nd St. between Amsterdam and Columbus Aves. (☎787-3333 or 787-0165). Subway: 1, 2, 3, 9 to 72nd St.; B, C to 72nd St. A Chinese-Japanese restaurant that claims the distinction of having catered to both Jiang Zemin and Li Peng. Standard Chinese menu dishes done well (most entrees $7.95-10.95), as well as a large Japanese menu (teriyaki dishes $9.50-15.50; tempura $8.95-13.75). Sushi $1.50-2.50 per piece. Open M-Th 11:30am-11:30pm, F-Sa 11:30am-midnight, Su noon-11:30pm. **$-$$**

CAFES

Cafe Lalo, 201 W. 83rd St. between Broadway and Amsterdam Ave. (☎496-6031). Subway: 1, 9 to 79th St., 86th St. Jazz flies onto the street out of a wall of French windows. Sample Cafe Lalo's immense selection of near-perfect cakes ($4.95 per slice), pies ($4.75 per slice), and tarts ($5.25 per slice); full bar available. Open M-Th 8am-2am, F 8am-4am, Sa 9am-4am, Su 9am-2am.

drip, 489 Amsterdam Ave. between 83rd and 84th Sts. (☎875-1032) Subway: 1, 9 to 79th St., 86th St. A pastel interior and comfy couches set the backdrop for students on laptops, young ladies reading complimentary magazines, and single Upper West Siders nervously eyeing each other over coffee. Drip's **dating service** ($10 to sign up, $3 to request a date) has no

Street Vendor

Pizza!

Pina Colada

fewer than 24,500 heartsick participants in its database. Coffee $1.25-2; cocktails $6-7. Open M-Th 8:30am-1am, F-Sa 8:30am-3am, Su 9am-midnight.

Cafe Mozart, 154 70th St. between Amsterdam and Columbus Aves. (☎595-9797). Subway: 1, 2, 3, 9 to 72nd St.; B, C to 72nd St. A relaxing, elegant cafe illustrated with pictures of the eponymous child prodigy. Gourmet coffee $0.75-2; cannoli $3.50; tiramisu $6.25. Live music (usually classical or jazz piano) M-Sa 9pm-midnight, Su 1-4pm and 9pm-midnight. Open M-Th 8am-1am, F 8am-3am, Sa 10am-3am, Su 10am-1am.

Cafe La Fortuna, 69 71st St., at Columbus Ave. (☎724-5846). Subway: 1, 2, 3, 9 to 72nd St.; B, C to 72nd St. Italian pastries, coffees, and sandwiches served in an intimate grotto. The oldest cafe in the Upper West Side. Espresso $2.50; pies about $4.50; sandwiches $5.95; and salads $4.75-6.75. In the summer, they sell flavored ices out front ($1.35-4) in 8 delightful flavors. Open Su-Th noon-midnight, F noon-1am, Sa noon-1:30am; Cash only.

SHOPS

Zabar's, 2245 Broadway between 80th and 81st Sts. (☎787-2000). Subway: 1, 9 to 79th St. This Upper West Side institution sells everything you need for a 4-star meal at home. Cheese of every imaginable sort, smoked salmon, beautiful bread, lure droves of shoppers into the gourmet grocery store. On weekend mornings, hordes of hungry New Yorkers stand in line for bagels and coffee. Upstairs kitchen gadgets and coffee pots co-mingle. Open M-F 8am-7:30pm, Sa 8am-8pm, Su 9am-6pm.

MORNINGSIDE HEIGHTS

see map pp. 334-335

Morningside Heights caters mostly to Columbia students, faculty, and their families. This usually means that hours run late and the price range fits that of a starving student. If you walk along Broadway, you'll find everything from old-fashioned coffee shops and new-age diners to romantic Italian restaurants and quick-service Chinese food.

Amir's Falafel, 2911A Broadway between 113th and 114th Sts. (☎749-7500). Subway: 1, 9 to 110th St., 116th St. Small and simple with low-priced Middle Eastern staples like *shawerma, baba ghanoush,* and *musakaa* (cold eggplant salad) for vegetarians and meat-lovers alike. Sandwiches ($3-5) and vegetarian platters ($5) made with care. Open daily 11am-11pm. Cash only. **$**

Koronet Pizza, 2848 Broadway, at 110th St. (☎222-1566). Subway: 1, 9 to 110th St. Slices larger than life for $2.25. Open Su-W 10am-2am, Th-Sa 10am-4am. Cash only. **$**

Massawa, 1239 Amsterdam Ave., at 121st St. (☎663-0505). Subway: 1, 9 to 116th St., 125th St. Wash your hands before heading to this restaurant specializing in Ethiopian and Eritrean cuisine–traditional finger food. Veggie dishes ($5-7) served with spongy *ingera* bread or rice. Massawa offers a great luncheon buffet ($7), not to mention lunch specials like lamb stew and collard green/potato platters ($6-7). Open daily 11:30am-midnight. **$-$$**

Obaa Koryoe, 3143 Broadway between Tiemann and La Salle, near 125th St. (☎316-2950). Excellent West African food in casual but vibrant dining room. Try the bean stew and fried plantains, with *jollof* rice ($9) or chicken, bean stew, *wachey,* and *gari* ($10). Indulge in a bottle of "budget" South African wine ($14-19) or ginger beer ($3). Lunch specials 11:30am-4pm. Open daily 11am-midnight. **$$**

Toast, 3157 Broadway between La Salle and Tiemann, near 125th St. (☎662-1144). Subway: 1, 9 to 125th St. Offering a variety of sandwiches ($4-9), this artsy joint provides the perfect setting for a relaxed and tasty meal. Check weekend brunch specials. Beer on tap $4. Happy Hour daily 5-7pm. Open M-F 11am-midnight, Sa-Su 9am-midnight. **$-$$**

Tom's Restaurant, 2880 Broadway, at 112th St. (☎864-6137). Subway: 1, 9 to 110th St. Immortalized as the storefront featured in *Seinfeld* and in the famous pop song "Tom's Diner," this restaurant is about as average as it gets. Greasy, but tasty, burgers ($3-8). Open Su-Th 6am-1:30am, F-Sa 24hr. Cash only. **$**

SHOPS

The Hungarian Pastry Shop, 1030 Amsterdam Ave., at 111th St. (☎866-4230). Subway: 1, 9 to 110th St. Come get your *phyla* at this friendly neighborhood hot spot. Eclairs, cake slices, and other goodies for around $2. Pleasant outdoor seating. Open daily 8:30am-10:30pm. Cash only. **$**

HARLEM

see map pp. 334-335

The cuisine ranges from East and West African to Caribbean, Creole, and some of the best soul food north of the Mason-Dixon Line. In Spanish Harlem, you'll find Puerto Rican and other Latino food.

Copeland's, 547 W. 145th St. between Broadway and Amsterdam Ave. (☎234-2357). Subway: 1, 9 to 145th St.; A, B, C, D to 145th St. Excellent soul food accompanied by live music in an elegant dining room. Entrees pricey ($11-26), so you may want to check out Copeland's "cafeteria" next door—no atmosphere but same food and more options, entrees $4-11. Gospel brunch Su with live jazz, all-you-can-eat buffet, and complimentary champagne; $17. Except for Su (noon-9pm), only open for dinner; cafeteria M-F 8am-11:30pm, Sa 8am-12:30am, Su 8am-1am. **$$**

Sugar Shack, 2611 Frederick Douglass Blvd/Eighth Ave., at 139th St. (☎491-4422). An artsy crowd frequents this sexy lounge and soul food restaurant (entrees $10-12). Try the phenomenal daiquiris or the chocolate martini ($6-12). M and W poetry night, Th caters to a gay and lesbian crowd, F and Sa a live DJ spins everything from house to reggae. Tu night Ladies night with $5 mixed drinks. Cover only on poetry nights: $6. 2 drink min. Reservations recommended. Open M 7pm-midnight, Tu-W 5:30pm-11pm, Th 5:30pm-1am, F-Sa 5:30pm-2am, Su brunch all you can eat buffet ($14) 11am-5pm. V, MC.

Sylvia's, 328 Lenox Ave., at 126th St. (☎996-0660). Subway: 2, 3, to 125th St. The sumptuous soul food has enticed New Yorkers for close to 40 years; now European tour groups arrive in buses. Sylvia accents her "World-Famous Talked-About BBQ Ribs Special" with sweet spicy sauce and a side of collard greens and macaroni and cheese ($11). Lunch special of salmon croquette, pork chop, fried chicken leg, collard greens, and candied yams ($7). Free live jazz and R&B Sa 11am-2pm. Gospel Brunch Su. Open M-Sa 7:30am-10:30pm, Su 11am-8pm. **$$**

Manna's Too!!, 486 Lenox Ave. between 134th and 135th Sts. (☎234-4488). Subway: 2, 3, to 135th St. This restaurant and deli boasts the best salad bar in Harlem, along with a variety of soul food options and fresh veggies. Homemade cakes $2.50; an enormous and sinful piece of double chocolate cake $2. Open M-Sa 7am-8pm, Su 10am-7pm. Cash only. **$**

La Marmite, 2264 Frederick Douglass Blvd. between 121st and 122nd Sts. (☎666-0653). Subway: B, C to 116th St. or 125th St. Nothing too fancy, this small restaurant serves up authentic French and African cuisine in a cramped but colorful setting. Beware the bite of some of the spices. Popular dishes on the lunch menu (noon-4pm) include *thiebou djeun*, a famous West African dish of fried rice served with fish and vegetables. Patrons rave about the dinner menu's *dibi* and *poisson grille* (served 4pm-6am). Open M-Sa 12:30pm-6am. **$-$$**

Londel's, 2620 Eighth Ave./Frederick Douglass Blvd. between 139th and 140th Sts. (☎234-6114). Subway: B, C to 135th St.; A, B, C, D to 145th St. With its sleek black tables and oak-wood floors, this sophisticated supper club brings loads of class and nouveau Southern cuisine to Sugar Hill. Traditional and Southern entrees $12-20. Drinks $7. F and Sa nights feature live jazz and blues from 8-11pm. Cover $5; $10 food/drink min. Open Tu-Sa 11:30am-midnight, Su brunch noon-5pm. **$$-$$$**

Gary's Jamaican Hot Pot, 2260 Adam Clayton Powell Blvd./Seventh Ave. between 134th and 135th Sts. (☎491-5270). Subway: B, C to 135th St.; 2, 3 to 135th St. The ultimate in Caribbean cuisine in a relaxed atmosphere, this restaurant cooks up a mean oxtail stew ($10) and hot, spicy jerk chicken ($10) that keeps locals begging for more. Open Su-Th 11am-1am, F-Sa 11am-2am. **$-$$**

La Fonda Boricua, 169 E. 106th St. between Lexington and Third Aves. (☎410-7292). Subway: 6 to 103rd St. Community art adorns the brick walls of this friendly and recently renovated Puerto Rican restaurant. Lots of seafood, like the popular seafood shrimp salad (small $7, combo $10). Dinner entrees $7-10. Daily lunch specials $5-8. Open M-Sa 10am-8pm. **$**

SHOPS

Fairway, 2328 12th Ave., at W. 132nd St., on the Hudson River. (☎234-3883). This super supermarket offers a ridiculous selection of food at wholesale prices. From the fresh bakery and gourmet cheeses to the huge variety of fruits and deli options, Fairway is brimming with bargains. Open daily 8am-11pm.

BROOKLYN

see map pp. 336-337

WILLIAMSBURG AND GREENPOINT

Trendy Williamsburg is rife with trendy food in trendy spaces, especially along **Bedford Ave**. If you're not into cool and you want to shell out wads of cash, **Peter Luger,** 78 Broadway, might serve the best steak in the city (☎718-387-7400). North of Williamsburg, Greenpoint features authentic Polish fare. **All establishments accept credit cards unless otherwise noted.**

Bliss, 191 Bedford Ave. between 6th and 7th Sts. (☎718-599-2547). Subway: L to Bedford Ave. Don't be surprised when your chili con pan comes meat-free in this almost-vegan (they use eggs and cheese) hot spot. Specialties include the marinated-tofu sandwich with horseradish sauce ($7) or the Bliss Bowl ($8). BYOB. Open M-F 8am-11pm, Sa-Su 10am-11pm. Cash only. **$**

Oznot's Dish, 79 Berry St., at N. 9th St. (☎718-599-6596). Subway: L to Bedford Ave. An artistic work in progress: Oznot's exterior resembles a modern painting, and the interior is exquisite. The Mediterranean food is good, especially the lunch *meze* platter of pita, hummus and olives ($7), but it is the tiled mosaic bar and glass dining area that make the restaurant truly unique. Open daily 11am-4:30pm and 6pm-midnight. **$-$$**

Planet Thailand, 115 Berry St. between N. 7th and 8th Sts. (☎718-599-5758). Subway: L to Bedford Ave. Recently reopened, the restaurant has been reincarnated in a sassy, high-ceilinged space that's too trendy for a sign. The menu is expansive, with Thai entrees reasonably priced ($8) and a new Japanese menu which is a bit pricier (sushi dinner $11). DJ every night at 9pm. Open Su-W 11:30am-1am, Th-Sa 11:30am-2am. Cash only. **$$**

L Cafe, 189 Bedford Ave. between N. 6th and 7th Sts. (☎718-388-6792). Subway: L to Bedford Ave. A colorful joint that embodies Williamsburg cool. Check out the flyers up front and the nice garden out back. Beers $3.25; veggie burger $6. Sandwiches named after artsy revolutionary types like Joni Mitchell and Leonard Cohen ($4.50-8). Open M-F 9am-midnight, Sa-Su 10am-midnight. Cash only. **$**

Miyako, 143 Berry St., at N. 6th St. (☎718-486-0837). Subway: L to Bedford Ave. Affordable sushi in a classy restaurant; most entrees under $11. Williamsburg Roll ($7). Open M-F 11:30am-11pm, Sa 3:30-11:30pm. **$-$$**

Stylowa Restaurant, 694 Manhattan Ave. between Norman and Nassau Aves. (☎718-383-8993). Subway: G to Nassau Ave. In the heart of predominantly Polish Greenpoint, Stylowa cooks up cheap, filling Polish cuisine; sample *kielbasa* (Polish sausage) with fried onions, sauerkraut, and bread ($4.50). Excellent potato pancakes $3. All other entrees ($2.75-7.25) served with a glass of *compote* (pink, apple-flavored fruit drink). Open M-Th noon-9pm, F noon-10pm, Sa 11am-10pm, Su 11am-9pm. Cash only. **$**

Vera Cruz, 195 Bedford Ave. between 6th and 7th Sts. (☎718-599-7914). Subway: L to Bedford Ave. Mexican food in a cozy indoor dining room and lively outdoor garden. Try the Mexican-styled corn, corn on the cob covered in Mexican cheese and sprinkled with lime and chili powder ($2.50). Happy Hour M-F 4-7pm. Open M 4-11pm, Tu-Th 4-11:30pm, F-Sa 4pm-midnight, Su 11am-midnight. **$-$$**

CAFES

The Read Cafe and Bookshop, 158 Bedford Ave. (☎718-599-3032). Subway: L to Bedford Ave. A quiet and cozy sanctuary, this cafe lines its pale green walls with bookshelves and magazines. Garden seating out back. Don't leave without trying one of their homemade scones ($1.50). Open M-F 8am-11pm, Sa-Su 9am-11pm.

Phoebe's, 323 Graham Ave. (☎718-599-3215). Subway: L to Graham Ave. For those venturing slightly east from Bedford Ave: this cafe boasts cheap eats, good coffee, and a young hip crowd. The menu doesn't provide many choices, but no one seems to mind. Cash only. Open M-F 8am-10pm, Sa-Su 10am-10pm.

BROOKLYN HEIGHTS, DOWNTOWN, FORT GREENE

Old-school Brooklyn (pizzerias and diners) rubs up against Middle Eastern newcomers on **Atlantic Ave. Fulton St.** around the **Fort Greene** area has a variety of cafes and ethnic food joints. **Establishments take credit cards unless otherwise noted.**

Grimaldi's, 19 Old Fulton St. between Front and Water Sts. (☎718-858-4300). Subway: A, C to High St. Delicious thin crust brick-oven pizza with wonderfully fresh mozzarella, sold only by the pie. Come admire the all-Sinatra decor (it was one of his favorite joints) and hear Ol' Blue Eyes on the jukebox. Small pies $12, large $14; toppings $2 each. Open M-Th 11:30am-11pm, F-Sa noon-midnight, Su noon-11pm. Cash only. **$-$$**

Caravan, 193 Atlantic Ave. between Court and Clinton Sts. (☎718-488-7111). Subway: 2, 3, 4, 5, M, N, R to Court St./Borough Hall. Caravan prides itself on its couscous and tandoori oven-baked bread. Prix fixe lunch ($7.95) includes an entree, hummus and *baba ghanoush,* soup or salad, dessert, and Moroccan coffee. Belly-dancing and live band Sa at 8pm. Open M-F 11am-10pm, Sa-Su noon-midnight. **$$**

Brooklyn Moon, 745 Fulton St., at S. Elliott Pl., in Fort Greene (☎718-243-0424). Subway: G to Fulton St.; C to Lafayette Ave. Comfy couches and amiably mismatched furniture. Salmon burger (with tasty spicy fries on the side) $6.50; apple salad $4.25. The Moon holds open mic night on F at 10:30pm, when aspiring bards from all over NYC come forth. Occasional performances and readings by authors like Jamaica Kincaid and Amiri Baraka. The preferred method of applause (at least by the upstairs neighbors) is to snap your fingers. Open M-Th noon-10pm, F-Sa 11:30am-midnight; Su 11:30am-10pm. **$$**

Fountain Cafe, 183 Atlantic Ave. (☎718-624-6764). Subway: 2, 3, 4, 5, M, N, R to Court St./Borough Hall. Named for the rumbling little fountain in its center, this eatery serves inexpensive and filling Middle Eastern food. *Shawerma* or shish kebab sandwich $4.65, falafel sandwich $3.30. Open M-Th 11am-10:30pm, F-Sa 11am-11pm. **$**

Keur N'Deye, 737 Fulton St. at S. Elliott Pl., in Fort Greene (☎718-875-4937). Subway: G to Fulton St.; C to Lafayette Ave. Even in New York's culinary melting pot, there aren't many Senegalese restaurants. *Tiebou dieun* (bluefish with vegetables stewed in a tomato sauce) is Senegal's most popular dish ($9). Meat entrees $8-9; vegetarian entrees $7.50. Open Tu-Su noon-10:30pm. **$**

Junior's, 386 Flatbush Ave. Extension, at De Kalb Ave. (☎718-852-5257). Subway: D, M, N, Q, R to DeKalb Ave. A 1970 *New York* magazine article touted Junior's diner as the home of "the world's finest cheescake," and this Brooklyn institution continues to dish out thousands of slices ($4.40) a week. Come bask in the glow of orange diner light to eat roast beef and brisket to your heart's delight. 10oz. steakburgers start at $6.50. Open Su-Th 6am-12:30am, F-Sa 6am-2am. **$-$$**

Petite Crevette, 127 Atlantic Ave. between Henry and Clinton Sts. (☎718-858-6660). Subway: 2, 3, 4, 5, M, N, R to Court St./Borough Hall. A small restaurant serving the ocean's fruits with expertise. Lunch special (whiting fillet or chicken salad sandwich with soup) $7. Sandwiches $5.75-8.25; entrees $7-13. Open M-Th 11:45am-10:30pm, F 11:45am-11pm, Sa noon-11pm. Cash only. **$-$$**

SHOPS

Sahadi Importing Company, 187-189 Atlantic Ave., between Court and Clinton Sts. (☎718-624-4550). Subway: 2, 3, 4, 5, M, N, R to Court St./Borough Hall. A popular Middle Eastern emporium that stocks spices and seasonings, dried fruits, and an array of spreads and dips like hummus and *baba ghanoush.* Open M-F 9am-7pm, Sa 8:30am-7pm.

Damascus Bakery, 195 Atlantic Ave., between Court and Clinton Sts. (☎718-625-7070). Subway: 2, 3, 4, 5, M, N, R to Court St./Borough Hall. Friendly bakery serving up all kinds of goods, Middle Eastern and otherwise. Package of fresh pita bread 50¢; baklava $1.50; spinach and feta pies $1.35; pistachio turkish delights $8/lb. Open daily 7am-7pm.

PARK SLOPE AND CARROLL GARDENS

For the most trendy in Brooklyn restaurants, head to **Smith St.** in **Carroll Gardens.** Upscale **Park Slope** brims with good eats, especially off **Fifth Ave.**

Patois, 225 Smith St. between DeGraw and Douglass Sts., in Carroll Gardens (☎718-855-1535). Subway: F, G to Bergen St. A quaint French bistro. Entrees are a bit pricey ($12-17), but traditional starters like garlic snails, puff pastry, and spinach and chives (around $8) are delicious too. Open Tu-Th 6-10:30pm, F-Sa 6-11:30pm, Su 11am-3pm and 5-10pm. **$$**

12th Street Bar and Grill, 1123 Eighth Ave. (☎718-965-9526). Subway: F to Seventh Ave.-Park Slope. An American restaurant specializing in steak and fish. Hanger steak $17; shell steak $21. The menu is seasonal and changes about every 2½ months. Prix fixe menu on M and Tu: $20 for appetizer, main course, and dessert. Open M-Th 5-11pm, F 5pm-midnight, Sa 11am-3pm 5pm-midnight, Su 11am-3pm 5-11pm.

CocoRoco, 392 Fifth Ave. (☎718-965-3376). Subway: F, M, N, R to Fourth Ave.-9th St. Peruvian fare pulled off with expertise. Lunch specials $5. The restaurant's specialty is the ceviche, which can be ordered as appetizers or as a main course. Mixed seafood ceviche $11, Papaya ceviche $13. Open M-Th noon-10:30pm, F 11:30am-11:30pm.

Sotto Voce, 225 Seventh Ave. (☎718-369-9322). Subway: F to Seventh Ave.-Park Slope. A pleasant Italian restaurant with popular pasta dishes such as the homemade fettuccini with shrimp ($11) and the fuscilli with 4 cheeses ($9). Perfect for the early-afternoon lush: brunch ($11) includes unlimited champagne among other drinks. Open: M-Th noon-11pm, F noon-midnight, Sa 10am-midnight, Su 10am-11pm.

SUNSET PARK AND FLATBUSH

Flatbush, especially on **Church Ave.,** is the spot for West Indian eateries. Brooklyn's Chinatown is located in **Sunset Park. Eighth Ave.** is the neighborhood's center.

Gia Lam, 5402 Eighth Ave., at 54th St., in Sunset Park. (☎718-854-8818). Subway: N to Eighth Ave. This popular Vietnamese restaurant in Brooklyn's Chinatown serves large portions at low prices. The squid with lemongrass on rice ($3.75) is an excellent lunch choice. Lunches $3-5, dinner entrees $7-10. Open daily 10:30am-10:30pm. Cash only. **$-$$**

Roy's Jerk Chicken, 3125 Church Ave., in Flatbush (☎718-826-0987), between 31st and 32nd Sts. Subway: 2, 5 to Church Ave. Excellent jerk chicken. Other enticing entrees $6-7. Open M-Th 9am-2am, F-Su 24hr. Cash only. **$**

Hammond's Finger Lickin' Bakery, 5014 Church Ave., at Utica Ave. in Flatbush (☎718-342-5770). Subway: 3, 4 to Utica Ave. West Indian pastries $1-2, including carrot cake ($1.25). Open M-F 8:30am-8pm, Sa-Su 8:30am-9pm. Cash only.

CONEY ISLAND AND BRIGHTON BEACH

Ethnic enclave Brighton Beach is full of Russian and Ukrainian food, while Coney Island is known for its pizza and hot dogs. **Restaurants take credit cards unless otherwise noted.**

Totonno Pizzeria Napolitano, 1524 Neptune Ave. between 15th and 16th Sts. (☎718-372-8606). Subway: B, D, F, N to Coney Island. A Coney Island legend, this joint serves pizza by the pie that vies for the coveted title of finest pizza in New York. Pies $13-14.50. No slices. Open W-Su noon-8:30pm. Cash only. **$**

Primorski Restaurant, 282 Brighton Beach Ave. between Brighton Beach 2nd and 3rd Sts. (☎718-891-3111). Subway: D to Brighton Beach. This restaurant serves Ukrainian *borscht* ($3.50) in an atmosphere that is best described as Sinatra-meets-Russian-wedding-hall. Eminently affordable lunch special (M-F 11am-5pm, Sa-Su 11am-4pm; $4). Russian music and disco M-Th 8pm-midnight, F-Sa 9pm-2am, Su 8pm-1am. Open daily 11am-2am. **$**

Nathan's, 1310 Surf Ave. between Stillwell and 15th Sts., in Coney Island (☎718-946-2202). Subway: B, D, F, N to Coney Island. 74 years ago, Nathan Handwerker became famous for underselling his competitors on the boardwalk: his hot dogs cost a nickel, theirs a dime. His crunchy dogs have since become famous world-over. A classic frank now sells for $1.95; cheese-fries $2.19-2.59. Sauerkraut available in winter, fried onions in summer. Open M-Th 6am-2am, F-Su 6am-4am. **$**

Cafe Glechik, 3159 Coney Island Ave. (☎718-616-0494). Subway: B, D, F, N to Coney Island. A Russian eatery renowned for its traditional cold appetizers, notably herring with potatoes and smoked mackerel (both $4). Open daily 9am-10pm. **$**

SHOPS

Sea Lane of Odessa Bakery, 615 Brighton Beach Ave. between 6th and 7th Sts. (☎718-934-8877). Subway: D to Brighton Beach. The best Jewish bakery in Brighton. Then again, you can't go wrong with 99¢ danishes or strudel with mixed fruit ($4 per lb.). Open daily 6am-9pm.

QUEENS

see map pp. 340-341

As one might expect, Queens offers visitors some of the best and most reasonably priced ethnic cuisine in town, including Greek fish, Indian *daal*, Italian ices, and Jamaican beef. In **Astoria** Greek restaurants proliferate around the elevated station at Broadway and 31st St., where you can catch the N train north to Ditmars Blvd. for still more dining options. In **Flushing** you'll find excellent Chinese and Korean eateries. Restaurants here often make use of rarely seen ingredients like skatefish, squid, and tripe, which more Americanized Asian restaurants tend to avoid. Come to **Jackson Heights** for great Indian food or to buy spices in bulk. Thai, Chinese, and Vietnamese proliferates in **Elmhurst.** Broadway and Elmhurst Ave. are the centers of the feast. West Indian, Central American, and Caribbean cuisine are the norm in **Jamaica.** Linden Boulevard and Jamaica Avenue are the best bets for a tropical fix.

Elias Corner, 24-02 31st St., at 24th Ave., in Astoria (☎718-932-1510). Subway: N, W to Astoria Blvd. With no menus, outdoor dining, and fresh everything, this fantastic seafood restaurant has a distinctly Greek character. Try the delicious *tsatziki,* calamari, or grilled octopus as appetizers ($3-6 depending on plate size). Whole grilled fish $7-14. Often crowded. No reservations. Open daily 4-11pm or midnight. Cash only. **$-$$**

Joe's Shanghai, 136-21 37th Ave., in Flushing (☎718-539-3838). Subway: 7 to Main St.-Flushing. The original Queens outpost for New York's favorite purveyor of Shanghai cuisine, including the inimitable *xiao long bao*, soup-filled dumplings. Open daily 11am-11pm. Cash only. **$-$$**

Flushing Noodle, 135-42 Roosevelt Ave., in Flushing (☎718-353-1166). Subway: 7 to Main St.-Flushing. Duck from the bustle of Flushing's main arteries into this Chinese noodle shop, among the finest in Flushing. Noodles $3.75-4.95. Lunch specials $4.95.

Jackson Diner, 37-47 74th St., in Jackson Heights, at 37th Ave. (☎718-672-1232). Subway: E, F, G, R to Jackson Heights/Roosevelt Ave.; 7 to 74th St./Broadway. Possibly the best Indian food in New York, in a bright, colorful setting that's a departure from other, more traditionally ornate Indian restaurants. Savor the *saag gosht* (lamb with spinach, tomato, ginger, and cumin; $10.95), and don't forget the samosas ($2.50). Lunch specials $6-7.50. Weekend lunch buffet $7.95 (11:30am-4pm). Open M-F 11:30am-10pm, Sa-Su 11:30am-10:30pm. Cash only. **$**

Nick's Pizza, 108-26 Ascan Ave., between Austin and Burns Sts., in Forest Hills (☎718-263-1126). Subway: E, F, G, R to Forest Hills/71st Ave.; then walk 3 blocks on Queens Blvd. (the numbers should be going up) and take a right on Ascan Ave. Some of the best pizza in Queens, served in a classy setting. Flaky crust and delectable sauce and toppings (small pizzas $11, large $13, toppings $2 extra; no individual slices). Open M-Th 11:30am-9:30pm, F 11:30am-11:30pm, Sa 12:30-11:30pm, Su 12:30-9:30pm. **$-$$**

Penang, 82-84 Broadway, at Whitney Ave., in Elmhurst (☎718-672-7380). Subway: R to Elmhurst Ave. Yes, branches of Penang have now proliferated all over Manhattan, but this is one of the best of the venerable Malaysian chain. Rice dishes $4.25-4.95; try the Hainanese chicken rice ($4.25). The crisp *roti canai* (Indian pancakes, $1.95) is a favorite appetizer. Open daily 11am-12 midnight. Cash only. Also at: 240 Columbus Ave., at 71st St. (☎212-769-8889); 1596 Second Ave., at 83rd St. (☎212-585-1968); 109 Spring St. (☎212-941-8868). **$**

Jai-Ya, 81-11 Broadway, in Elmhurst (☎718-651-1330). Subway: R to Elmhurst Ave. Great Thai food, with 3 degrees of spiciness, from mild to "help-me-I'm-on-fire." The soothing interior tangos with budget prices and a decidedly upscale look. Most dishes $7-11.25. Vegetarian options available. Lunch specials ($5.25-8.50) M-F 11:30am-3pm. Open M-F 11am-midnight, Sa 11:30am-midnight, Su 5pm-midnight. **$-$$**

Uncle George's, 33-19 Broadway, at 33rd St., in Astoria (☎718-626-0593). Subway: N to Broadway, then 2 blocks east; or G, R to Steinway St., then 4 blocks west. Crowded, noisy, and friendly, this popular restaurant serves hearty Greek fare around the clock. All entrees under $12. Diehard fans feed on roast leg of lamb with potatoes ($9) or octopus sauteed with vinegar ($7). Open 24hr. **$**

Kum Gang San, 138-28 Northern Blvd., in Flushing (☎718-461-0909). Subway: 7 to Main St.; walk north on Main St. and take a right on Northern Blvd. (about 10min.). Good Korean food in an elegant setting with marble floors and dark wood tables. A complete lunch special can get you chicken teriyaki with salad, noodles, a California roll, and a dumpling all for $6-9. Open 24hr. **$**

Anand Bhavan, 35-66 73rd St., in Jackson Heights (☎718-507-1600). Subway: E, F, G, R to Roosevelt Ave. or 7 to 74th St.-Broadway. Tasty vegetarian South Indian restaurant. Piquant lunch specials (noon-4:30pm) $6-8. The Anand Bhavan special, a 4-course meal ($13), includes *sambar* (spicy lentil soup) and a choice of *iddly* (rice crepe with peppers and onions) or *vada* (stuffed lentil dough). Open daily noon-9:30pm. **$**

Più Bello, 70-09 Austin St., in Forest Hills (☎718-268-4400). Subway: E, F, G, R to Forest Hills/71st Ave.; walk west on Queens Blvd. past 70th Rd. to 70th Ave., then take a left. A slick, family-owned restaurant where the neighborhood's cool kids hang out. Unfortunately, the Tower Mall setting detracts from the romantic Italian cafe feel. The Argentine expatriate owners make their smooth *gelato* and delicious cakes on the premises. Entrees $7-8. Individual pizzas from $4. More than 20 *gelato* flavors ($6). Open M-Th 9am-1am, F-Sa 9am-2am, Su 10am-1am. **$**

Rincon Salvadoreño, 92-15 149th St., at Jamaica Ave., in Jamaica (☎718-526-3220). Subway: E, J, Z to Jamaica Center. Heaping portions of tasty El Salvadorean food such as *pupusas* (tortillas with various fillings) $1.25-2. Meat entrees $8-12. Live music Sa-M, Th at 8pm. **$**

SHOPS

The Lemon Ice King of Corona, 52-02 108th St., at Corona Ave., in Corona (☎718-699-5133). Subway: 7 to 111th St.; a healthy walk back 1 block to 108th and south 10 blocks. Keep walking—it's worth it (it's near Flushing Meadow-Corona Park anyway). One of the most famous sites in Queens, on par with the Unisphere. The Emperor of Cool scrapes up juicy frozen treats outdoors. Every flavor you could want, including bubble gum, blueberry, cantaloupe, cherry, and, of course, lemon ($0.80-2). Open daily 10am-12:30am. **$**

Galaxy Pastry Shop, 37-11 30th Ave., in Astoria (☎718-545-3181). Subway: N to 30th Ave.; make a right on 30th Ave. and walk east to 37th St. A hangout for young locals, the Galaxy offers great pastries to ruin your diet. The baklava ($1.20) tastes like the answer to a Dionysian prayer. Relax in outdoor cafe seating during summer. Open daily 6:30am-3am. **$**

Eddie's Sweet Shop, 105-29 Metropolitan Ave., at 72nd Rd., in Forest Hills (☎718-520-8514). Subway: E, F, G, R to Forest Hills/71st Ave.; then take the Q23 to Metropolitan Ave. or a 15min. walk through the suburbs. The decor evokes parlors of the 1950s: get your ice cream ($2) from a metal cup on a marble countertop. Open Tu-F 1pm-11:30pm, Sa-Su noon-11:30pm. **$**

THE BRONX

see map pp. 342-343

Arthur Ave. in Belmont is the culinary heart of the Bronx. Subway: C, D to Fordham Rd. and walk 5 blocks east; or 2 to Pelham Pkwy., then bus Bx12 2 stops west.

The cuisine of the Bronx reflects its diverse make-up, but the local Italian fare is the culinary magnet of the borough. The Italian immigrants settling in the Bronx brought with them their recipes and a tradition of hearty communal dining. The neighborhood of **Belmont** (see **Sights,** p. 103) brims with raw bars (try **Cosenza's,** 2354 Arthur Ave.; ☎718-364-8510), pastry shops, pizzerias, restaurants, and mom-and-pop emporiums, without the touristy frills of Manhattan's Mulberry St. For a 50¢ treat, try a dixie cup of Italian ice from street vendors.

Dominick's, 2335 Arthur Ave., near E. 186th St., in Belmont. (☎718-733-2807). No menu here and no set prices—regulars are happy to give advice. At this small family-style Italian eatery, waiters seat you at a long table and simply ask what you want. Linguine with mussels and marinara ($7), marinated artichoke ($7), and veal *francese* ($12) are all house specials. Arrive before 6pm or after 9pm, or expect a 20min. wait. Open M, W, Th, Sa noon-10pm; F noon-11pm; Su 1-9pm. **$-$$**

Emilia's, 2331 Arthur Ave., near E. 186th St., in Belmont. (☎718-367-5915). Delicious food in large portions. The *calamari fra diavolo* ($15) is especially good. Appetizers $5-10; pasta $10; entrees $13-18. Lunch special $10. Open M-F and Su noon-10pm, Sa noon-11pm. **$$**

Pasquale's Rigoletto, 2311 Arthur Ave., in Belmont. (☎718-365-6644). Pasquale's will soothe you with luscious arias; if you have a favorite in mind, ask to have it played—or sing it yourself on amateur night (Sa). Favorite customer Joe Pesci's pictures adorn the front door. Pasta $13; meat dishes $15 and up; poultry $15; seafood $17. Open Su-F noon-9:30, Sa noon-10:30. **$$**

Giovanni's, 2343 Arthur Ave., between E. 186th St. and Crescent Ave. (☎718-933-4141). Hanging plants match the green of the tablecloths and the waiters' outfits in this restaurant. Arguably one of the best places to get a brick-oven pizza (individual-sized $6-9, regular-sized $11-14) in Belmont, and that's saying something. Open M-Sa 11am-midnight, Su noon-midnight. **$-$$**

Reef Restaurant (a.k.a. Johnny's Reef), 2 City Island Ave. (☎718-885-2086). Subway: 6 to Pelham Bay Park, then Bx29 to City Island. Surrounded by squawking seagulls and grease, Johnny's serves up cheap, fresh seafood, steamed or fried. Fish and chips $9. Open daily 11am-midnight. **$**

SHOPS

De Lillo Pastry Shop, 606 E. 187th St., between Hughes and Arthur Aves. (☎718-367-8198). Crowded, but it's worth your while to sample the excellent baked goods ($1-2) along with a cappuccino ($2.25) or espresso ($2). Open daily 8am-7pm; closed M July-Aug.

Egidio Pastry Shop, 622 E. 187th St., at Hughes Ave. (☎718-295-6077). A neighborhood tradition. Since 1912, Egidio has baked up mountains of Italian pastries and cakes. The ever-popular cannoli ($1.25) tastes divine with a steaming cappuccino ($2.75). Homemade ices 75¢-$2.50. Open daily 8am-8pm.

STATEN ISLAND

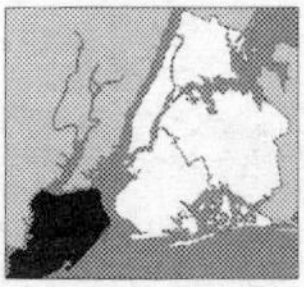
see map p. 344

Cargo Cafe, 120 Bay St. (☎718-876-0539) near the SI Chamber of Commerce, away from the Ferry Terminal. A large exterior mural and open windows with iron fencing cut at different heights give this bar/restaurant a funky feel. Art on walls and bar games add to the chill atmosphere. Lunch special (daily special and beer) $5.25, dinner entrees $15-20. Open mic M 9:30pm-midnight, big band W 8-10pm. Open daily noon-4am.

The Elbow Beach Restaurant (at The Old Bermuda Inn), 2512 Arthur Kill Road (☎718-948-7600), difficult to reach by public transportation. Anticipate a lovely meal. The fare is well-balanced, showcasing seafood entrees but presenting pork, steak, and chicken with the same craft. Early bird special $12.50 per person, W-F 4pm-6pm. Su brunch $18.50 per person. Open W-Th 4-9pm, F-Sa 4-10pm, Su 11am-6pm. **$$-$$$**

INSIDE

Nightlife

A city like this one makes me dream tall and feel in on things.
—Toni Morrison, *Jazz*

When the sun sets over the Hudson, the insomniac empress Gotham loosens her corset and takes down her hair. The city is awash with nightlife options: see performance art; hear live hip-hop; sip a highball; work it at a drag show; learn to salsa. Do as you wish, so long as you keep up with your hungry hostess, the city herself. In New York's night kitchen, you could easily cook up a different feast for the senses every evening of your life. Whether you prefer Times Square's blinding lights or a Harlem jazz club, a smoky Brooklyn bar or a Lower East Side be-seen-ery, allow yourself to succumb to the city's dark side. At the end of it all, a 4:30am cab ride home through empty streets with the windows down will inevitably make your spirits soar. A number of publications print daily, weekly, and monthly nightlife calendars; try *Time Out: New York*, the *Village Voice*, *New York* magazine, *The New York Press*, and *The New York Times* (particularly the Sunday edition). The monthly *Free Time* calendar ($1.25) lists free cultural events throughout Manhattan. For gay and lesbian nightlife options see **Gay New York,** p. 196.

BARS AND HANGOUTS

No one bar scene defines NYC in the way that pubs define Ireland or cruisy Hollywood bars define Los Angeles. NYC doesn't merely have every type of bar, but does them all well. Bars listed by neighborhood are loosely ranked, but personal preference depends on your own social or alcoholic slant.

FLYERS! GET YOUR FRESH FLYERS!

Too good for our recommendations? Keep your eyes peeled as you travel the city by day to find nighttime options. Although NYC doesn't have the flyer culture that other big cities do, there are plenty of places to pick up party, club, or concert ads. Here are a few good stores to look into if you're around the East Village. And if it's a special type of music you're into, ask around at record stores—smaller, specialized stores generally have in-the-know staff.

Etherea, 66 Ave. A. Flyers for house/loungecore/techno events.

8th St. Lab, 69 E. 8th St. Huge selection of club flyers and the coveted *Flyer* monthly mag.

Dance Tracks, corner of First Ave. and E. 3rd St. Flyers for house music and techno events.

Throb, 211 E. 14th St. Techno event flyers.

Metropolis, 43 Third Ave. Club flyers.

A-1 Record Shop, 439 E. 6th St. Various flyers for hip-hop as well as techno club flyers.

House of Trance, 122 St. Mark's Pl. Trance/ambient event flyers.

Store, 325 E. 9th St. Mostly techno club flyers.

LOWER EAST SIDE

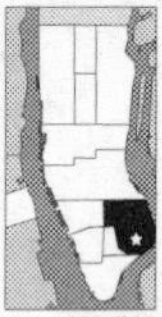

see map pp. 320-321

bOb Bar, 235 Eldridge St. between Houston and Stanton Sts. (☎777-0588). Subway: F to Second Ave. Small and laid-back, with a hip-hop-inclined crowd and graffiti-esque paintings covering the walls. Happy Hour F 7-10pm $3 beers. While Tu alternates between Latin, reggae, and hip-hop (free), Th is strictly hip-hop ($5 cover after 10pm; $3 for women). Open daily 7pm-4am.

Idlewild, 145 E. Houston St. between First and Second Aves. (☎477-5005). Subway: F to Second Ave. This eclectic bar appropriated JFK's former name to lift the theme bar to new heights. Idlewild is shaped like an airplane, replete with a fuselage-shaped interior, reclining seats with tray tables, and a boarding ramp. Beer $4-5. Drinks $7-10. Open Tu-W 8pm-3am, Th-Sa 8pm-4am.

Orchard Bar, 200 Orchard St. between Houston and Stanton Sts. (☎673-5350). Subway: F to Second Ave. A long, narrow haunt frequented by hip Lower East Side scene-sters. The bar is too cool for a sign—keep your eyes wide. DJ after 10pm on some weekend nights. F is house with one of NY's best DJs, Rob Salmon (free). Beer $4-5. Other drinks $5-6. Open W-Su 6pm-4am.

Fun, 130 Madison St., at Pike St. (☎964-0303). Subway: F to East Broadway. In-the-know hipsters chill at this "never a cover, never a guest list" hangout. Its whimsical decor (complete with hydraulic lifts for the bartenders and wall video projections) merit the self-titled "integrated sound and video environment." VJs and DJs rotate nightly. Tu playstation nights. Drinks start at $9 but are worth the fun. Open M-Sa 8pm-4am.

Motor City Bar, 127 Ludlow St. between Rivington and Delancey Sts. (☎358-1595). Subway: F to Delancey St. Locals and musicians kick back on the Dodge Dakota car seats and vinyl bar stools at this rock-and-roll bar. Pin ball and video games for the less conversation savvy. DJ spins rock and roll, punk, and new wave nightly. No cover. Happy hour daily 4-7pm. Beer $3-4. Open daily 4pm-4am.

The Rivertown Lounge, 187 Orchard St. between Houston and Stanton Sts. (☎388-1288). Subway: F to Second Ave. This dark lounge has been a staple of the LES bar scene for six years. A pool table, couches, a jukebox, and a "No Dancing" sign set the scene. Beer $4-5. Open daily 1pm-4am.

Max Fish, 178 Ludlow St., at Houston St. (☎529-3959). Subway: F to Second Ave. This self-consciously hip bar draws big crowds of cool people F-Sa, and small crowds of cool people on other days. Perhaps the best jukebox in town, playing everything from the Fugees to the Stooges. Keeps all the great things about a bar: pinball, pool tables, and relatively inexpensive drinks. Beer $3-4.50. Bingo games the first Su of the month at 9. Open daily 5:30pm-4am.

SOHO AND TRIBECA

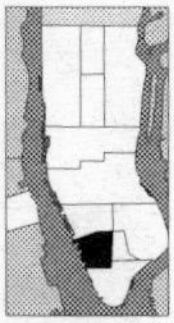

see map p. 315

Naked Lunch Bar and Lounge, 17 Thompson St., at Grand St. (☎343-0828). Subway: 1, 9, A, C, E to Canal St. Adorned with the roach-and-typewriter theme found in the William Boroughs book of the same name. The after-work crowd has no qualms about dancing in the aisle alongside the bar. Unbeatable martinis like the Tanqueray tea $8. Free barbecues monthly in summer. All beers $6. Sometimes a $7 cover F and Sa after 10pm. $2 off all drinks during Happy hour Tu-F 5-9pm. Open Tu-F 5pm-4am, Sa 9pm-4am.

Milady's, 160 Prince St., at Thompson St. (☎226-9069). Subway: C, E to Spring St. A rough in the overbearing diamond mine that is SoHo. Down-to-earth neighborhood haunt that claims the only pool table in SoHo (a bit of a stretch) and a cast of affable regulars. Everything (even martinis) under $6. Good, inexpensive food served M-Th 11am-midnight, F-Sa 11am-1am, Su 11am-11pm. Open daily 11am-4am.

Cafe Noir, 32 Grand St., at Thompson St. (☎431-7910). Subway: 1, 9, A, C, E to Canal St. Cool in so many ways. The patrons, the bartenders, and the street-front windows all provide this bar/lounge/restaurant with a classy but unaffected feel. Draft beers $5-6. Entrees $12-22. Open daily noon-4am.

Lucky Strike, 59 Grand St., at W. Broadway (☎941-0772). Subway: 1, 9, A, C, E to Canal St. The people here are beautiful, but don't let that stop you. They're too secure to be pretentious, and all are welcome. Lovely food and divine drinks ($5 and up). The vanilla shanti ($8.50) tastes like a carnival in a martini glass. Open Su-Th noon-3am, F-Sa noon-4am.

MercBar, 151 Mercer St. between Prince and Houston Sts. (☎966-2727). Subway: N, R to Prince St. Trendy bar with a good-looking crowd. Cozy couches and dim lighting set a relaxing mood. Looking for Love? Maybe the drink will suffice ($11). All beers $6; mixed drinks start at $6. Open M-Tu 5pm-1:30am, W 5pm-2am, Th 5pm-2:30, F-Sa 5pm-3:30am, Su 6pm-1:30am.

Circa Tabac, 32 Watts St. between Sixth Ave. and Thompson St. (☎941-1781). Subway: C, E to Spring St. Claims to be the first, and perhaps only, cigarette lounge in the world. As the war against smoking has become entrenched even in downtown NYC, Circa Tabac remains a haven for cigarette-lovers. Enhancing its atmosphere of taboo, Tabac's trendy decor recalls a Prohibition-era speakeasy, with protective curtains and Art Deco pieces. A jazz soundtrack replete with old standards completes the spell. State-of-the-art air purifiers and odor killers keep the air clear and sweet-smelling. 180 different kinds of cigarettes ($5-25) are available. Open Su-W 5pm-2am, Th-Sa 5pm-4am; in summer, closed Su.

X-R Bar, 128 Houston St., at Sullivan St. (☎674-4080). Subway: 1, 9 to Houston St. Comfortable but lively bar caters to a young crowd. M-Tu live music, often New Orleans bluegrass, jazz, or folk; Th-Sa DJ. Beers $4-5; drinks $6-8. Happy Hour daily 3-7pm; all drinks $1 off. Open M-Sa 3pm-4am, Su 4pm-4am.

Fanelli's, 94 Prince St., at Mercer St. (☎226-9412). Subway: N, R to Prince St. A casual neighborhood hangout, where it always feels like it's late. Offers a full menu with great burgers ($7.50). Standard bar fare, cheap brew ($4 for domestic drafts, $4.50 for imports and microbrews), and slightly older crowd than neighboring bars. Open M-Th 10am-1:30am, F-Sa 10am-2:30am, Su 11am-1:30am.

Denizen, 73 Thompson St. between Broome and Spring Sts. (☎966-7299 or 226-9858). Subway: C, E to Spring St. This elegant and sexy bar/restaurant features some of the best cosmopolitans the city has to offer ($9). Check out the rock wall bathrooms. Restaurant open M-F 5pm-2am, Sa-Su noon-2am; bar stays open until 4am.

Bar 89, 89 Mercer St. between Spring and Broome Sts. (☎274-0989). Subway: N, R to Prince St. Upscale bar/restaurant serving American fare to a stylish crowd. Salads $7-11; sandwiches $7.50-$11. The main attraction, however, is the unisex bathroom, which features glass doors that only become opaque when latched precisely. Open Su-Th noon-1:15am, F-Sa noon-2:15am.

Scharmann's, 386 West Broadway between Broome and Spring Sts. (☎219-2561). Subway: C, E to Spring St. Mismatched sofas and a high ceiling make this a nice alternative to a traditional bar. Classy and loungy. Beer $4. Open Su-W 10am-1am, Th-Sa 10am-3am.

GREENWICH VILLAGE

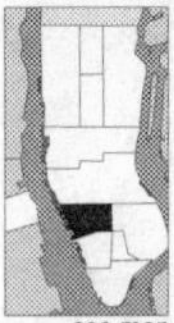

see map pp. 316-317

The Whitehorse Tavern, 567 Hudson St., at W. 11th St. (☎243-9260). Subway: 1, 9 to Christopher St. Dylan Thomas drank himself to death here, pouring 18 straight whiskies through an already tattered liver. Boisterous students and locals squeeze into one of New York's oldest bars to pay the poet homage by tattering their own livers. Great jukebox. Outdoor patio. Beer $3.50-5. Open Su-Th 11am-2am, F-Sa 11am-4am.

The Village Idiot, 355 W. 14th St. between Eighth and Ninth Aves. (☎989-7334). Subway: A, C, E, L to 14th St.-Eighth Ave. No Myshkins here, just honky-tonk, New York style. The beer is still cheap ($1.25 mugs of MGD), the music still loud (and still country), and the ambiance still as close to a roadhouse as this city gets. As if the customers' drunken antics or the bras hanging from the bar weren't enough, the (female) staff occasionally dances on the bar. Open daily noon-4am.

Automatic Slims, 733 Washington St., at Bank St. (☎645-8660). Subway: 1, 9 to Christopher St. Stop by this 60s diner-esque bar for a dose of nostalgia or a glass of beer. 20-somethings sit on red and white bar stools and tables with classic vinyls under glass. Weekends pack a more diverse crowd. American cooking served 6pm-midnight. Entrees $7.50-14. Open Tu-Sa 6pm-4am.

Absolutely 4th, 228 W. 4th St., at Seventh Ave. S. (☎414-4345). Subway: 1, 9 to Christopher St. A sexy splash in the ocean of West Village nightlife. The plush, high-backed, fan-shaped booths are constantly rearranged for the upscale crowd, giving the bar a new feel every night. Karaoke W, DJ on weekends. Drinks $5-10. Open daily 4pm-4am.

Bar 6, 502 Sixth Ave. between 12th and 13th Sts. (☎691-1363). Subway: 1, 2, 3, 9 to 14th St.; L to Sixth Ave. French-Moroccan bistro by day, sizzling bar by night. Live DJ spins (primarily house) F-Su nights for an upscale crowd. Beers on tap ($4-5 per pint) usually from local Brooklyn Brewery. Kitchen open Su-Th noon-2am, F-Sa noon-3am.

Kava Lounge, 605 Hudson St. between Bethune and W. 12th Sts. (☎989-7504). Subway: A, C, E, L to 14th St.-Eighth Ave. Kava is a few blocks removed from the colorful center of the West Village and attracts a tame and relaxed crowd. The bar prides itself on its Polynesian theme and boasts a vast selection of Aussie and New Zealander wines. 2-for-1 Happy Hour M-F 5-7pm. Open Su-Th 5pm-1am, F-Su 5pm-3am.

Hell, 59 Gansevoort St. between Greenwich and Washington Sts. (☎727-1666). Subway: A, C, E, L to 14th St.-Eighth Ave. A sultry lounge decorated with red velvet curtains, this bar took its theme just a little too far with photos of famous people graffitied with red horns and mustaches. Hard-to-find, but worth the trip. Both gay and straight crowd. Open Sa-Th 7pm-4am, F 5pm-4am.

Panache Brasserie, 470 Sixth Ave. between 11th and 12th Sts. (☎243-2222). Subway: F to 14th St.; L to Sixth Ave. This subdued bar and cafe invites the posturing of failed poets and philosophers, cigarette and chalice in hand. 60s avant-garde music, and delicious crepes ($3.25-5). Open Su-M 11am-2am, Tu-F 11am-4am.

The Slaughtered Lamb Pub, 182 W. 4th St., at Jones St. (☎627-5262). Subway: A, B, C, D, E, F, Q to W. 4th St. Transylvanian kitsch. A labyrinthine English pub with a dungeon downstairs and wax museum rejects in the back room. Patronized by locals, tourists, and an NYU crowd. More than 150 types of beer ($5-25 per bottle) and ale. $3 special on rotating beers. Open Su-Th noon-2am, F-Sa noon-4am.

Bowlmor, 110 University Pl. See **Entertainment,** p. 190, for info. An after-hours, lights-out bowling alley with glowing pins where DJs spin jungle, trip-hop, and house.

EAST VILLAGE

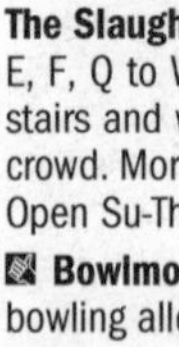

see map pp. 320-321

Tribe, 132 First Ave., at St. Mark's Pl. (☎979-8965). Subway: 6 to Astor Pl. Behind the frosted glass windows lies a chic, friendly bar with colorful but subtle back lighting, complete with comfortable lounging areas. DJ nightly: M live music and DJ, Tu Salsa/Latin. Beer $5; cocktails $5-10. Open daily 5pm-4am.

Izzy Bar, 166 First Ave., at E. 10th St. (☎228-0444). Subway: L to First Ave. Izzy Bar is a wooden-decor-laden, votive-glowing hangout; it's also one of the East Village's best music spots, whether it be for the DJs spinning house or hip-hop, or for the live jazz (Su). Corona $5. Cover up to $10. Open daily 7pm-4am.

d.b.a., 41 First Ave. between E. 2nd and 3rd Sts. (☎475-5097). Subway: F to Second Ave. A bar for the serious beer drinker. With 19 premium beers on tap (around $5), well over 100 bottled imports and microbrews, classy bourbons and whiskeys ($6), and 45 different tequilas, this extremely friendly space lives up to its motto—"drink good stuff." Mellow jazz and a sassy crowd. The popular outdoor beer garden is open until 10pm. Open daily 1pm-4am.

Beauty Bar, 231 E. 14th St., between Second and Third Aves. (☎539-1389). Subway: L to Third Ave. Unless you knew this was a bar, it would be easy enough to walk by "Thomas Hair Salon." Both the exterior and interior retain the look of an old beauty parlor, although the bar's customers are well primped in slightly punk East Village-style. Crowded all week, with patrons drawn by the cheap cocktails (Amaretto sour $4). Beer $3-4.50. During Happy hour (M-F 5-8pm) all drinks $1 off. Open Su-Th 5pm-4am, F-Sa 7pm-4am.

Bbar (Bowery Bar), 40 E. 4th St., at the Bowery (☎475-2220). Subway: F to Second Ave. Bbar has long held court on Bowery as a flagship of cooler-than-thou-ness. While newer spots may challenge its cachet, this white and blue building—with garden patio—and its frequenters still have attitude to burn. Beer $5. Tu night is "Beige," Erich Conrad's wonderfully flamboyant gay party. Open Su-Th 11:30am-3am, F-Sa 11:30am-4am.

Coup, 509 E. 6th St., between Aves. A and B (☎979-2815; www.coupnyc.com). Subway: 6 to Astor Pl. Wood floors, silver beams, and capsule-esque lights create a restaurant-bar that's a modernist's dream, all angles and sharp lines. The sleekness is toned down by the back garden. Beer $5; wine $7. DJs on F-Sa; no cover. Open Su-Th 6pm-midnight, F-Sa 6pm-4am.

The Anyway Cafe, 34 E. 2nd St., at Second Ave. (☎533-3412). Subway: F to Second Ave. Sample Russian-American culture at this dark, relaxed, leopard-spotted hangout. Numerous literary readings during the week, as well as jazz F and Sa nights, and Russian folk on Su. Music every night from 9pm. Friendly and free of pretension. A great place to kick back with homemade sangria and sample gourmet Russian specialties ($8-12). Open M-Th 5pm-2am, F-Sa 5pm-4am, Su noon-1am.

Korova Milk Bar, 200 Ave. A, between E. 12th and 13th Sts. (☎254-8838). Subway: L to First Ave. A tribute to Stanley Kubrick's twisted vision, this is a mock-up of little Alex's "moloko plus" bar in *A Clockwork Orange,* replete with sultry naked female mannequins, lusciously shaped couches, Kubrick's movie playing on various screens, and an anarchist atmosphere. Perhaps too self-consciously hip, but they do make a mean martini. Open daily 5pm-4am.

McSorley's Old Ale House, 15 E. 7th St., at Third Ave. (☎473-9148). Subway: 6 to Astor Pl. Their motto is, "We were here before you were born," and unless you're 148 years old, they're right. McSorley's

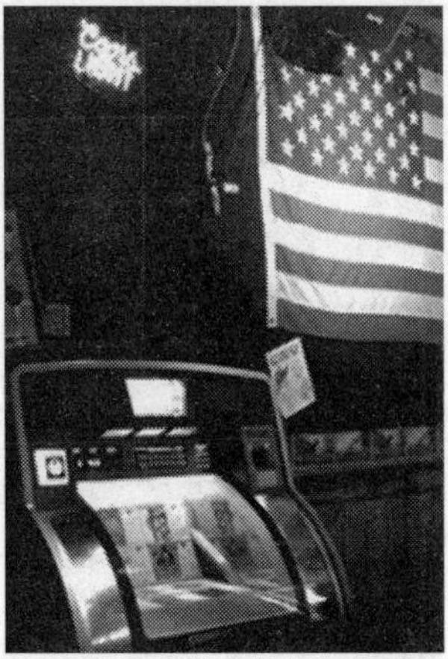

Yogi's Bar

Naked Lunch Bar

Knitting Factory

WELCOME TO THE JUNGLE

Early in the 90s, black Londoners spawned jungle, a frantic urban music style that has adapted well to New York City. NYC is the original urban jungle, although here the crowd is comprised mostly of white post-ravers. Jungle incorporates the slow, dubby basslines of reggae with sped-up hip-hop breakbeats and recombinant sampling strategies, stewed thick and fast with inflections of techno. The result is edgy, experimental, and futuristic. New York now offers a few jungle club nights a week. **Konkrete Jungle** (☎604-4224) is the most established, while **Jungle Nation** (☎802-7495) throbs with a more serious crowd. The legendary, though mainstream, Limelight hosts a Global Bass party once a summer; call for date and details. (660 6th Ave., at 20th St. ☎807-7780. $20 advance tickets, $25 at the door.) For slightly more drum 'n' bass-oriented clubbing, try Thursday nights at **Aria,** 539 W. 21st St., presented by DJ Cassien and friends. ($8 before midnight, $10 after; 21+ only.) DJs to look for include Dara, Delmar, Soulslinger, DB, Cassien, and Peshay. Smaller music stores probably offer the best resource for finding jungle nights, with flyers and knowledgeable staff.

has played host to such luminaries as Abe Lincoln, the Roosevelts (Teddy and Franklin), and John Kennedy; women were not allowed in until 1970. It can get frat-boyish at times, but then that might just be your thing. Only 2 beers: light and dark. Two-fisters take note: mugs come 2 at a time ($3 for 2). Open M-Sa 11am-1am, Su 1pm-1am.

Sake Bar Decibel, 240 E. 9th St. between Stuyvesant St. and Second Ave. (☎979-2733). Subway: 6 to Astor Pl. All things Japanese are seriously fashionable in the East Village, and sake is no exception. This quasi-hidden bar (the entrance is down a flight of stairs) draws in a mix of Japanese patrons and random hipsters. Over 60 kinds of *sake* $4-6 per glass. Minimum order $8 per person during busy weekend hours. Open M-Sa 8pm-3am, Su 8pm-1am.

La Linea, 15 First Ave. between E. 1st and 2nd Sts. (☎777-1571). Subway: F to Second Ave. A long, narrow bar with three rooms: a friendly, lantern-laden bar room, a comfortable lounge area in the middle, and a grotto-like back room. Despite the quality music coming from the speakers, La Linea manages to be a good spot for chatting. Beer $4; happy hour (daily 3-9pm) $1 off. Open daily 3pm-4am.

Lucky Cheng's, 24 First Ave. between E. 1st and 2nd Sts. (☎473-0516; www.luckychengs.citysearch.com). Subway: F to Second Ave. One of New York's better-known drag clubs. Both the upstairs restaurant and downstairs bar are decorated in over-the-top Asian kitsch, serviced by gorgeous "girls." 3-4 Drag shows nightly. Martinis $7.50; plum wine $5. Bar open Su-Th 5pm-2am, F-Sa 5pm-4am.

Tenth Street Lounge, 212 E. 10th St. between First and Second Aves. (☎473-5252). Subway: L to First Ave. A chic East Village hangout with a matching clientele. The high ceiling, spacious bar, and large couches make this a gorgeous place for an early-evening drink. Beers $4-5; cocktails $6-10. Open M-Sa 5pm-3am, Su 3pm-2am.

Joe's Pub, 425 Lafayette St., at Astor Pl. (☎539-8777). Subway: 6 to Astor Pl. Despite its name, this Public Theater spot is really more a bar/lounge than a pub. Still, high ceilings and couches make Joe's a great place to soak in the great, eclectic selection of live performers. (Or sit on the tables outside and watch theatergoers walk into the Public Theater.) Performances start around 7-9pm. Cover for performances $10-30. Occasional two-drink minimum. Open daily 6pm-4am.

Open Air, 121 St. Mark's Pl., between First Ave. and Ave. A. (☎979-1459). Subway: 6 to Astor Pl. Not much gives this bar away from the outside: all you see is black frosted glass and the Chinese character for "wine." But Open Air is a sleek, intimate space, with good DJs. Occasional cover ($5) on Sa. Open Tu-Th 6pm-2 or 3am, F-Sa 7pm-4am.

Nuyorican Poets Cafe, 236 E. 3rd St., between Aves. B and C. Subway: F to Second Ave. (☎505-8183; www.nuyorican.org). New York's leading joint for poetry slams (check out the Friday night slam at 10pm) and spoken-word performances; several regulars have been featured on MTV. A mixed bag of doggerel and occasional gems. If you don't like the poets, don't worry—there's likely to be a heckler in the house. Cover $5-12.

Barmacy, 538 E. 14th St. between Aves. A and B (☎228-2240). Subway: L to First Ave. Essentially a preserved old-style pharmacy (think neighborhood apothecary, not Duane Reade) with a bar thrown in. Barmacy is filled with East Village hipsters, who come as much for the music coming from the DJ booth as for the cheap drinks (Amaretto sour $4; $1 off all drinks before 8pm). Open 5:30pm-4am, Sa-Su 7pm-4am.

Coyote Ugly, 153 First Ave. between E. 9th and 10th Sts. (☎477-4431). Subway: L to First Ave. If you've seen the movie based on this bar, you know what Coyote Ugly's like: a honky-tonk bar with good-looking bartenders and people whoopin' it up atop the bar, with occasional bra liberations. For those who like country music on the jukebox and a cheap beer in the hand. Open noon-4am.

KGB, 85 E. 4th St., at Second Ave. (☎505-3360). Subway: F to Second Ave. Formerly a meeting place for the Ukrainian Communist Party, this hangout for literati and Slavophiles retains its original furnishings, including the Lenin propaganda banner and candle-illuminated photos of factories. The 2nd-story, tiny space hosts frequent readings by major and minor authors. Over 20 different kinds of Stoli ($3 per shot). Open daily 7:30pm-4am.

Joe's Bar, 520 E. 6th St. between Aves. A and B (☎473-9093). Subway: F to Second Ave. An eclectic, typically East Village neighborhood crowd makes up most of the regulars at Joe's, a bar about as laid-back as its name suggests. Pilsner, Bass, and Fosters on tap. Beers $2-3 a mug. Serious pool on M nights. Open daily noon-4am.

The Bar, 510 E. 11th St. between Aves. A and B. (☎982-3929). Subway: L to First Ave. Call it whatever you want, this nameless drinking spot, with its solid oak bar and tables, is still a great bar for conversation or just for watching the TV and munching on bar snacks. Open daily 4pm-4am.

Patio, 31 Second Ave. between E. 1st and 2nd Sts. (☎460-9171). Subway: F to Second Ave. Sadly, sitting by Second Ave. is a poor substitute for being at the beach. But Patio does its best with what it has. With the bamboo bar and the open storefront, it's like getting drinks from someone's outdoor bar. Open daily 5pm-2am.

CHELSEA AND UNION SQUARE

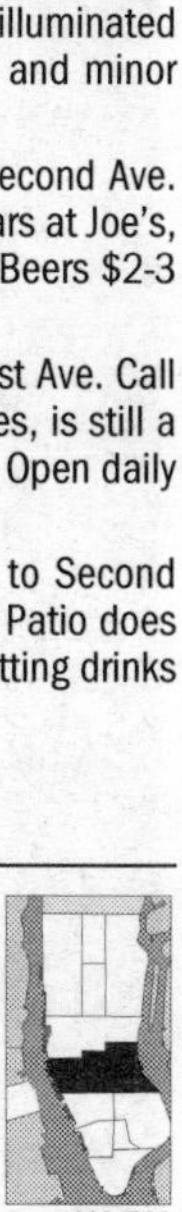
see map pp. 322-323

Billiard Club, 220 W. 19th St. between Seventh and Eighth Aves. (☎206-7665). Subway: 1, 9 to 23rd St. Red-felted tables of this pool hall await both the hustlin' type and those who just enjoy a game of eight-ball. $8 per hr. before 6pm, Su-W $13 per hr. after 6pm, Th-Sa $14 per hr. after 6pm. You must be over 21 to play after 6pm. Open M-Th 1pm-1am, F-Sa 1pm-3am, Su 2pm-1am.

Lemon, 230 Park Ave. South, between 18th and 19th Sts. (☎614-1200). Subway: 4, 5, 6, L, N, R to Union Sq. A two-story restaurant-bar, and perhaps the best (or at least the most popular) of the Park Ave. South yuppie hangouts. Large variety of martinis (around $8). Open M-W and Su 11:30am-midnight, Th-Sa 11:30am-3am.

Old Town Bar and Grill, 45 E. 18th St. between Park Ave. South and Broadway (☎529-6732). Subway: 4, 5, 6, L, N, R to Union Sq. A dark, 104-year-old hideaway, with the wood and brass furniture you'd expect from a traditional bar. Seen on the old "Late Night with David Letterman" opening montage. Popular with a late-20s/early-30s crowd: beware of perpetual after-work and weekend mobs. Beer on tap $4, Heineken $3.75. Open M-Sa 11:30am-1am, Su 3pm-midnight.

Passerby, 436 W. 15th St. between Ninth and Tenth Aves. (☎266-7321). Subway: A, C, E. L to 14th St.-Eighth Ave. Adjacent to owner Gavin Brown's gallery (see **Museums and Galleries,** p. 125), Passerby's mirror and neon floor panels create a dizzying space-age-meets-70s-disco optical illusion on the outskirts of the meat-packing district. Most drinks $8. Open Su-M 6pm-1am, Tu-W 6pm-2am, Th-Sa 6pm-4am.

Heartland Brewery, 35 Union Sq. West. between 16th and 17th Sts. (☎645-3400). Subway: 4, 5, 6, L, N, R to Union Sq. A packed, loud, and friendly brew pub with a "down home" American menu ($10-16) and an after-work corporate crowd. The family feel of the brewery during the day gives way to a singles' scene at night. Draught beers $5-6. Open M-Th noon-1am, F-Sa noon-2am, Su noon-midnight; restaurant closes 2hr. earlier. Also at: 1285 Ave. of the Americas, at 51st St. (☎582-8244).

THE RETURN OF VAUDEVILLE

Vaudeville once represented a ticket out of poverty for immigrants living on the Lower East Side. From 1870 to 1930, variety acts that featured everything from magic to dancing were all the rage. But with the coming of the motion picture in 1930, vaudeville faded off the stage and into the history books.

That is, until recently. An attitude of "Vaudeville is dead. Long live Vaudeville" has come to rule in parts of New York, as performers self-consciously imitate their counterparts of yore.

To take a step back in time, head to **The Slipper Room**, 167 Orchard St. A new addition to the Orchard St. scene, this converted sneaker store serves up a mixed bag of vaudeville entertainment: from sketch comedy to sword-swallowers. An artsy crowds swarms during the weekend, especially for the Saturday night feature. Beer $4-5. (☎253-7276. Open daily 8pm-4am. No cover.)

Peter McManus, 152 Seventh Ave., at 19th St. (☎929-6196). Subway: 1, 9 to 23rd St. Made famous by a *New York Times* article on the timeless appeal of ordinary bars, of which this is the epitome. Ordinary drinks, ordinary clientele (with some tourists thrown in), slightly-higher-than-ordinary prices. The carved mahogany bar and leaded glass windows add to the pub's charm. A smattering of video games and a jukebox. Dinner specials $6-8 until midnight. Draught beers $2-4.50. Open daily 10:30am-3am.

B.M.W. Bar, 199 Seventh Ave. between 21st and 22nd Sts. (☎229-1807). Subway: 1, 9 to 23rd St. A funky dive with local art and unique objects adorning the walls. Beer, Music, Wine ($4-6), and Coffee, an option that didn't make it into its name. Happy hour M-F 4-8pm: house wine and beer $3. Open mic Tu from 10pm-late. Live music. Open daily 4pm-4am.

Lola, 30 W. 22nd St., between Fifth and Sixth Aves. (☎675-6700). Although entrees are expensive (lunch $11.50-14, dinner $26-32) in this sleek restaurant, the lounge (2-drink minimum) hosts an elegant after-work crowd. Beers $5. "Lola is soul" they claim, and they have live music every day: M varies, Tu jazz music, W-Sa R&B, funk, and soul. Open M 6pm-1am, Tu-F noon-3pm and 6pm-1am, Sa-Su 6pm-1am.

Coffee Shop Bar, see **Food,** p. 143.

UPPER EAST SIDE

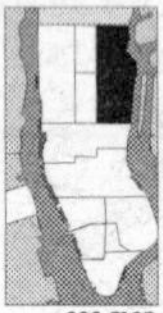

see map pp. 328-329

Ozone, 1720 Second Ave. between 89th and 90th Sts. (☎860-8950). Subway: 4, 5, 6 to 86th St. Dimly-lit and elegant, Ozone's front room holds a classy bar, while the back has a mellow and comfortable lounge. Wear black and walk in with an attitude—you'll fit right in. Large selection of imported ($4) and domestic ($3) beers. Happy hour daily 4-7pm; live DJ spinning the latest in funk, jazz, and hip-hop F-Sa. Open Su-Th 4pm-2am, F-Sa 6pm-4am.

Match, Uptown, 33 E. 60th St. between Park and Madison Aves. (☎906-9177). Subway: 4, 5, 6, N, R to 59th St.-Lexington Ave. Sleek and elegant bar in a nouveau-Asian restaurant. Dim lighting and a sophisticated crowd dressed-to-impress make this an Upper East Side hotspot. Beer $5, cocktails $7-8, dim sum rack $9.50. Open daily 11:30am-midnight. **Downtown:** 160 Mercer St. between Houston and Prince Sts. (☎343-0020).

Mo's Caribbean Bar and Grille, 1454 Second Ave., at 76th St. (☎650-0561). Subway: 6 to 77th St. Lively, friendly bar with the island touch. Big screen TV keeps the crowd's attention on sporting events. Sign onto website for 2 free drinks. Beer, imported and Caribbean, $4.50; domestic $4. Try the mixed drinks, like the famous Mo' Betta Colada ($6). Happy hour 4-7pm. Open M-F 4pm-4am, Sa 11am-4am, Su 11am-2am.

Auction House, 300 E. 89th St. between First and Second Aves. (☎427-4458). Subway: 4, 5, 6 to 86th

St. Don't be intimidated by the name of the bar or its seemingly calculated "antique" appearance. Inside this classy establishment are rooms of ornately-carved, comfortable wood chairs, gilt oil paintings of naked women, and crimson velvet curtains. Sit back and watch the young elite mingle and drink. Beers $5. Open Su-Th 7:30pm-2am, F-Sa 7:30pm-4am.

Brother Jimmy's Carolina Kitchen BBQ, 1461 First Ave., at 76th St. (☎545-7427). Subway: 6 to 77th St. The sign advertises "BBQ and booze," and this greasy-chops Carolina kitchen serves up plenty of both. Ribs are a bit pricey ($17), but the bar is where the action is—light weights, watch out. Lots of original drinks; "Swampwater" comes with a toy alligator. Happy hour M-F 5-7pm. Open M-F 5pm-midnight, Sa-Su noon-midnight. Bar stays open until M-Sa 4am, Su until 1am.

Spancill Hill, 1715 First Ave., at 89th St. (☎410-6301). Subway: 4, 5, 6 to 86th St. Named after a little horseracing town in Ireland, Spancill Hill is friendly and relaxing with colorful murals and red candle-lighting. Imported beer $4.50, domestic $4, draft $4.50-5. Open daily 11pm-4am.

American Trash, 1471 First Ave. between 76th and 77th Sts. (☎988-9008). Subway: 6 to 77th St. Cavernous barroom hung with "trash" (read: twisted metal bits) from NASCAR go-carts to Molly Hatchet posters. Live music Su (JJ and the All-American-Trash band), live DJ M. Known for their wide variety of beers (domestic $4, imported $4.50). Happy Hour M-F noon-7pm, Sa-Su 5-7pm. Open daily noon-4am.

UPPER WEST SIDE

The Evelyn Lounge, 380 Columbus Ave., at 78th St. (☎724-2363). Subway: B, C to 81st St. A somewhat upscale bar for the after-work set, with fireplaces and settees creating a homey setting. Great live music downstairs Tu-Th 9:30pm-1:30am. Drinks ($9 martinis) are a bit pricey but cover the cost of comfy couches colonized by cultured cliques. Enticing bar menu $7-14. Open daily 6pm-4am.

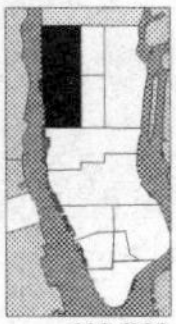

see map pp. 332-333

Potion Lounge, 370 Columbus Ave. between 77th and 78th Sts. (☎721-4386). Subway: B, C to 81st St. A silvery-blue lounge complete with local art on the walls, bubbles rising through pipes in the windows, and velvety sofas. The lounge takes its name from the colorful layered drinks ("potions" $10) it serves. DJs on weekends. Draught beers $5-6; martinis $9. Open M-Th 6pm-midnight, F-Sa 6pm-4am.

Yogi's, 2156 Broadway, at 76th St. (☎873-9852). Subway: 1, 9 to 79th St. Midriff-baring bartenders pour seriously cheap beer and alcohol (mugs $1.25-2.25; pitchers $5; shots from $1.50), as a constant stream of country music twangs out of the jukebox. The bar's namesake bear greets outside. Open daily 11:30am-4am.

SOB's

Ozone Bar

bOb Bar

THOU SHALT NOT DANCE

As you bar-hop across town, you may notice deliberately placed signs that read "NO DANCING." These signs are not atmospheric attempts at machismo. They are for real.

In 1926, New York City passed a law that prohibited dancing in a bar without a cabaret license. The law fadded into obscurity over time, and liquored-up bar patrons giddily fell back into a clumsy two-step.

That is, until Mayor Rudy Giuliani cut in. Beginning in 1997, as part of his effort to clean up New York, Giuliani enforced the law anew, wreaking havoc for bars where feet moved a little too ryhthmically and dispatched the "Dance Police" to regulate the city that never sleeps.

Needless to say, reaction to the law's enforcement has been overwhelmingly negative and has earned Giuliani comparisons to Mussolini and Hitler. To stay on the former mayor's good side, save your dancing for law-abiding cabarets.

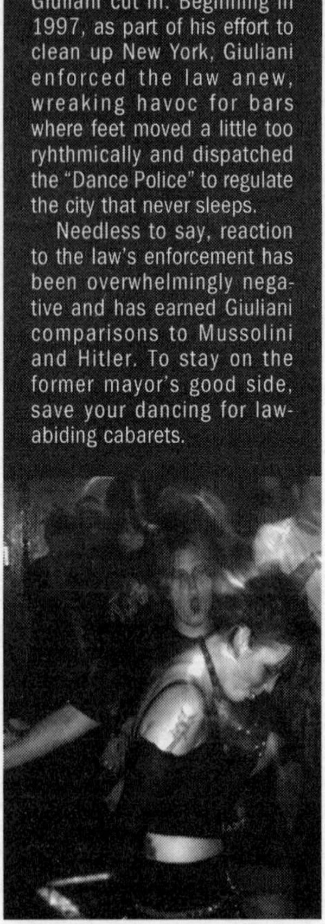

Merchants, 521 Columbus Ave. between 85th and 86th Sts. (☎721-3689). Subway: B, C to 86th St. Intimate tables by the fireplace in winter and a happening sidewalk scene in the summer makes Merchants popular. Upscale singles scene. Draughts $5; cocktails $5-9. Open daily 11:30am-4am.

BROOKLYN

see map pp. 336-337

Montero's Bar & Grill, 73 Atlantic Ave., at Hicks St.-(☎718-624-9799). Subway: 2, 3, 4, 5, M, N, R to Court St./Borough Hall. Heavily bedecked with nautical paraphernalia, this friendly dive still looks like the longshoremen's bar it once was. Beer $3. Open M-Sa 10am-4am, Su noon-4pm.

Waterfront Ale House, 155 Atlantic Ave. between Henry and Clinton Sts. (☎718-522-3794). Subway: 2, 3, 4, 5, M, N, R to Court St./Borough Hall. A friendly neighborhood joint, and a great spot to go for beer and burgers. The 15 beers on tap change seasonally; try to get a pint of Brooklyn Brown. Specials like mussels in a *weiss* beer broth broaden the definition of pub grub. Mugs $3.50, pints $4.50. Happy hour (pints $3) M-F 4-7pm. Live jazz Sa 11pm-2am. Open daily noon-11pm; bar open until 3 or 4am.

Brooklyn Ale House, 103 Berry St., at N. 8th St. (☎718-302-9811). Subway: L to Bedford Ave. Less self-consciously hip than the Williamsburg "scene," this lively neighborhood joint welcomes all with cheap beer ($4). The rustic wooden tables and benches are more structurally sound than they look. Open daily 3pm-4am.

Yabby's, 265 Bedford Ave., at N. 1st St. (☎718-384-1664). Subway: L to Bedford Ave. A mellow crowd packs into this converted auto-repair shop to lounge on the mismatched vintage furniture and hangout on the large outdoor patio. The vast outdoor space makes this a hot spot during the summer. Live music F, Su; DJ on Th, Sa. Open Tu-Th 3pm-2am, F 3pm-4am, Sa noon-4am, and Su noon-2am.

Teddy's, 96 Berry St., at N. 8th St., in Greenpoint (☎718-384-9787). Subway: L to Bedford Ave. An eclectic mix of artists and wizened Brooklynites visits Teddy's for its great jukebox and friendly atmosphere. A wide variety of specialty martinis and low-priced Brooklyn beers ($2-4). Th is honky tonk and the first W of the month is a spirited tap-jazz jam. Happy hour M-F 4-7pm. Open Su-Th 10am-2:30am, F-Sa 11am-4am.

Pete's Candy Store, 709 Lorimer St. between Frost and Richardson Sts. (☎718-302-3770). Subway: L to Lorimer St. A labor of the owner's love, this hand-painted bar includes a small performance room in the back and a "makeout" hallway. The lively local crowd flocks to the soda-shop-turned-bar for the free live music every night. Bingo on Tu and the Quiz-Off on W (both 7-9pm) are both extremely popular, but it's the

Bucket of Joy (Stoli, Red Bull, 7-up and straws) that makes this place more than worth the walk ($6). Open Su-Tu 5pm-2am, W-Sa 5pm-4am.

Halcyon, 227 Smith St., between Butler and Douglass Sts. (☎718-260-9299; www.halcyon-line.com). Subway: F, G to Bergen St. The hippest Brooklyn hangout south of Flatbush Ave., Halcyon combines record store, cafe, and lounge (and even furniture store). The laid back atmosphere allows you to soak in the sounds of the DJ while playing one of their old, forgotten board games like Twixt, or smoking in the back garden. BYOB. No cover. Open Su and Tu-Th 8pm-midnight, F-Sa 9pm-2am.

Galapagos, 70 N. 6th St., between Kent and Wythe Sts. (☎718-782-5188; www.galapagosartspace.com). Subway: L to Bedford Ave. A bit deserted at night; go with a friend. Once a mayonnaise factory, this space is now one of the hipper cultural spots in the city. Great bar in an interesting futuro-sleek decor, complete with an enormous reflecting pool, makes for an interesting hangout. Puts up parties, vaudeville performances on M, as well as Ocularis, their weekly film series (Su 7 and 9:30pm, M 8:30pm; $5 cover). DJ's every Tu-Sa. Events sometimes charge $5 cover. Happy Hour M-Sa 6pm-8pm. Open Su-Th 6pm-2am, F-Sa 6pm-4am.

Montague Street Saloon, 122 Montague St., at Henry St. (☎718-522-6770). Subway: 2, 3 to Clark St. The yuppie crowd congregates here to eat, drink, and be merry on this fashionable street in Brooklyn Heights. Open Su-W 11:30am-2am, Th-Sa 11:30am-4am.

THE BRONX AND QUEENS

see map pp. 340-341

see map pp. 342-343

Located on City Island in the Bronx, **The Boat Livery, Inc.,** 663 City Island Ave., at Bridge St., is the place to come if you want cheap beer, bloodworms, and fishing tackle. Bud $1. (☎718-885-1843. Subway: 6 to Pelham Bay Park, then bus Bx29 to City Island Ave. and Kilroe St. Boat rental open 5am-4:30pm; bait shop open 5am-8pm; bar open 5am-10pm.)

Bell Blvd., out east near the Nassau County border in Bayside, is the center of Queens nightlife for the borough's young and semi-affluent, with blocks of restaurants, bars, and clubs lining the boulevard. **Bourbon Street,** 40-12 Bell Blvd. (☎718-224-2200), has a noisy pub-like atmosphere and plays frequent live jazz. **Victorian Lounge,** 47-39 Bell Blvd. (☎718-229-0167), is another good option. In the Rockaways, you'll find **Sand Bar,** on the Rockaway Beach boardwalk at Beach 116th St. It's far from fancy (count 'em—two beers on tap), but there's something about drinking a Bud from a plastic cup ($1.50), while sitting on the tables looking out onto the boardwalk and Rockaway Beach. (Open Memorial Day-Labor Day 10am-midnight.)

DANCE CLUBS

A wilderness of human flesh
Crazed with avarice, lust and rum
New York, thy name's Delirium.
—Byron R. Newton, "Ode to New York"

Carefree crowds, hype music, unlimited fun, massive pocket book damage—these foundations of the New York club scene make it an unparalleled institution of boogie. Some of the best parties stay underground, advertised only by word of mouth, or by flyer. Many parties move from space to space each week. The rules to clubbing in New York are simple. Door people, the clubs' fashion police, forbid anything drab or conventional. That means don't wear khaki shorts and a purse across your chest. Above all, just look confident—attitude is at least half the battle. Come after 11pm unless you crave solitude, but the real party starts around 1 or 2am. A few after-hours clubs keep at it until 5-6am, or even later.

Centrofly, 45 W. 21st St. between Fifth and Sixth Aves. (☎627-7770; www.centrofly.com). Where the beautiful people and music aficionados come to dance to the latest house and techno, often by big-name DJs. Although the patrons rave about the martinis ($11), it's the psychedelic lights and retro-chic decor that put the "fly" in Centrofly. Manhattan's clubbing elite tend to show up here on Th. Cover $20. Mixed drinks $8-10. Open M-Sa 10pm-5am.

Cheetah, 12 W. 21st St. between Fifth and Sixth Aves. (☎206-7770). Subway: F, N, R to 23rd St. Cheetah-print sofas and greenery create the setting for this club. A self-consciously trendy crowd struts it. Beers $6. Cover charge usually $20-25. Th is Clique, a female DJ rotation with open bar 10-11pm. F is Great British House with open bar 10-11pm. Sa is Cherchez La Femme, hip hop and R&B with open bar 10-11pm. Open 10pm-4am.

Hush, 17 W. 19th St. between Fifth and Sixth Aves. (☎989-4874; www.hushnyc.net or www.atnight.com/hush). Subway: F, N, R to 23rd St. This medium-sized club, run in part by the former head of security at Studio 54, spreads house, trance, and hip-hop over two rooms. Dress nicely. Open F-Sa 11pm-4am.

Kilimanjaro, 95 Leonard St., at Broadway. (☎343-2824). Subway: 1, 9 to Franklin St. Features the latest in hip-hop, reggae, African music, and R&B. Cover: women $10; men $15. Drinks $7. Open Sa 11pm-4:30am.

Metronome, 915 Broadway, at W. 21st St. (☎505-7400; www.metronomenyc.com). Subway: F, N, R to 23rd St. This high-ceilinged restaurant/lounge becomes a club late nights. There's only one dance floor and a catch-all music policy, which means you'll be hearing a mix of (fairly standard) hip-hop, house, and reggae most nights. Cover $25. Open (as a club) F-Sa until 4am.

Nell's, 246 W. 14th St. between Seventh and Eighth Ave. (☎675-1567; www.nells.com). Subway: 1, 2, 3, 9, A, C, E to 14th St.; L to Eighth Ave. This declining hotspot has recently become less exclusive and now packs in a diverse crowd. Upstairs is a mellow space for mingling; downstairs is for dancing. The DJ spins hip-hop and house, and the bar/club boasts various theme nights from Israeli and Middle Eastern house on M to Comedy on F. No sneakers, jeans, or work boots. Cover M-W $10, Th-Su $15. Open M 8pm-2am, Tu and Th-Su 10pm-4am, W 9pm-3am.

NV/289 Lounge, 289 Spring St., near Varick St. (☎929-6868). Subway: C, E to Spring St. Gothic playground meets post-industrialism and results in a web of ceiling pipes over curtain-laden, sconce-enhanced chambers. Two bars and dance floors. As long as the club remains up and coming, you can enter the iron gates without too much bouncer inspection. Mixed drinks are club priced ($8-10) and the cover ($10-20) could be much more substantial for a night of pure fun. W and Su nights feature great R&B, hip-hop, and reggae vibes. Happy Hour W-Th 6-10pm. Open W-Su 10pm-4am.

Ohm, 16 W. 22nd St., between Fifth and Sixth Aves. (☎229-2000; guest list 774-7749; www.ohmnyc.com). Subway: F, N, R to 23rd St. A flashy, stylish club, with a towering ceiling, three bars, and a quality restaurant. House (of the high-BPM Euro variety) dominates the playlist on Sa, and gets mixed up with Latin (salsa, merengue, freestyle) on F. Downstairs, hip-hop beats reign. Open Th-Sa 10pm-4am. Cover $20.

Shine, 285 West Broadway, at Canal St. (☎941-0900; www.shinelive.com). Subway: A, C, E to Canal St. "Touch" on F nights showcases house and trance, while "Reminisce Reggae" on Su is for all those nostalgic for old school, Jamaican style. But it's "The Show" on Sa that lives up to its name, with not just great hip-hop and house but also dancers and the occasional Elvis impersonator. Cover Th $10, F-Sa $20, Su $5. Open Th-Sa 10pm-4am, Su 6pm.

Spa, 76 E. 13th St. between Broadway and Fourth Ave. (☎388-1062). Subway: 4, 5, 6, L, N, Q, R, W to Union Sq. Don't be intimidated by the elegance of the crowd or the Herculean-sized bouncers. Just wear black and walk in with attitude. "Rock and Roll W;" other nights have hip-hop, house, and R&B to get you in the dancing groove. Th is a very popular gay night. Open Tu-Sa 10pm-4am. Cover F-Sa $20-25.

Tunnel, 220 Twelfth Ave. at 27th St. (☎695-7292; www.limelight-tunnel.com). Subway: C, E to 23rd St. The premier club in the late 80s and early 90s, this warehouse of a space has seen better days, but with five rooms, lounges, glass-walled live shows, and cages for dancing, this party still attracts a diverse crowd including celebrities, drag queens, and hip-hop heads alike. With massive crowds of about 3000 to control, it's no wonder security is so tight. F and Sa are regular party nights featuring techno, trance, house, R&B, hip-hop, and other genres. Dress clean and casual. Cover $25. Open F-Su 10pm-7am.

2i's, 248 W. 14th St. between Seventh and Eighth Aves. (☎807-1775). Subway: 1, 2, 3, 9, A, C, E to 14th St.; L to Eighth Ave. Two metallic floors—one at street level, one below—throbbing to hip-hop. While bare midriffs are the norm, they are not necessary to get through the velvet rope–just no sneaks or sportswear. Reggae M-Su; Hip Hop W-Sa. Th is G-Spot (lesbian night). Women free before midnight F-Sa. Cover $5-15. Drinks $6-12. Open W-M 11pm-4am.

Webster Hall, 125 E. 11th St., between Third and Fourth Aves. (☎353-1600; www.websterhall.com). Subway: 4, 5, 6, L, N, Q, R, W to Union Sq. This popular (if somewhat mainstream) club offers 4 floors dedicated to R&B/hip hop, 70s and 80s/Top 40, house/techno/trance, and Latin. Sports bar and coffee bar to boot. One of the only 19+ clubs in the city. Cover Th $20 for men, free for women before midnight, $10 after; F-Sa $25, Su $20; the website has guest passes that get you $5 off. Open Th-Su 10pm-4am.

COMEDY CLUBS

Comic Strip Live, 1568 Second Ave. between 81st and 82nd Sts. (☎861-9386). Subway: 4, 5, 6 to 86th St. Sunday comics' characters Dagwood and Dick Tracy line the 4-color walls of this well-established pub-style club. Former regulars include just about everyone in the post-SNL pantheon. Usually a 2-drink min. Su and Tu-Th $10 cover; F-Sa $14 cover. Make reservations, especially for weekends. Shows Su-Th around 8pm, additional shows on weekends.

Dangerfield's, 1118 First Ave. between 61st and 62nd Sts. (☎593-1650). Subway: 4, 5, 6, N, R to 59th St.-Lexington Ave. Rodney's respectable comic-launching pad. HBO specials featuring Roseanne Barr and Jerry Seinfeld have been taped at the club. Be prepared for a surprise—the line-up is only available the day of the show, and unannounced guest comedians appear occasionally. Cover Su-Th $12.50, F-Sa $15, Sa 10:30pm show $20. Su-Th shows at 8:45pm; F shows at 9pm and 11:15pm; Sa shows at 8pm, 10:30pm, and 12:30am; doors open 1hr. before 1st show.

Gotham Comedy Club, 34 W. 22nd St. between Fifth and Sixth Aves. (☎367-9000; www.gothamcomedyclub.com). Subway: F, N, R to 23rd St. One of New York's more upscale comedy clubs. Usually a 2-drink min. Cover Su-Th $10, F-Sa $15. Shows Su-Th 8:30pm, F-Sa 8:30 and 10:30pm. Amateur night F 7pm, Sa 6:30pm.

Stand Up New York, 236 W. 78th St. between Amsterdam Ave. and Broadway (☎595-0850). Subway: 1, 9 to 79th St. A stand-up club with good lineup. Neighborhood man Jerry Seinfeld has performed here. Shows Su-W 7, 9pm; Th 7, 9, 11:30pm; F-Sa 8, 10pm. Cover $5-12; two-drink min.

Upright Citizens Brigade Theater, 161 W. 22nd St. between Sixth and Seventh Aves. (☎366-9176; www.uprightcitizens.org or www.ucbtheatre.com). Subway: 1, 9, F to 23rd St. Funny, offbeat sketch and improv comedy, as seen on their Comedy Central show. 2-3 shows per night, usually 8 and 9:30pm. The original gang show up for Su performances. Tickets M-Th $5, F-Su $7, Su 9:30pm show free.

INSIDE

Entertainment

In Manhattan, every flat surface is a potential stage and every inattentive waiter an unemployed, possibly unemployable, actor.
—Quentin Crisp

New York is the country's center for both established and up-and-coming artists. The talent is overwhelming. You could go to a rock show Monday, a NY Philharmonic concert Tuesday, a jazz club and cabaret on Wednesday, a poetry reading Thursday, a baseball game Friday, a musical on Saturday, and the ballet on Sunday. *Let's Go* lists New York's most essential venues and hot spots, but be sure to check local sources to get the scoop on current offerings. After all, it's the shows that are good, not the venue. Look through publications for the most up-to-date run-down on entertainment in the city: try *Time Out: New York*, the *Village Voice*, *New York* magazine, and *The New York Times* (particularly the Sunday edition). The monthly *Free Time* calendar ($1.25) lists free cultural events throughout Manhattan. Try the NYC Parks Department's **entertainment hotline** (☎360-3456; 24hr.) for the lowdown on special events in parks throughout the city. Call the **NYC/ON STAGE hotline** (☎768-1818) for a comprehensive listing of theater, dance, and music events taking place each week.

THEATER

Broadway war-horses like *The Phantom of the Opera* and *Les Misérables* have ushered armies of tourists, senior citizens, and suburbanites through the theater doors for interminable runs. The recent resurrection of Broadway has triggered an equally vibrant theater scene throughout the city—off-Broadway, off-off-Broadway, in dance and studio spaces, museums, cafes, parks, and even parking lots.

on the cheap

CheapSeats

The Great White Way's major theatrical draws may seem locked away in gilded Broadway cages, but you *can* find cheap tickets. Should **Ticketmaster** (☎307-7171) not work, try the standby ticket distributor, **TKTS,** or any of the following options.

Rush Tickets: Some theaters distribute them on the morning of the performance; others make student rush tickets available 30 minutes before showtime. Lines can be extremely long, so get there *early*.

Cancellation Line: No rush luck? Some theaters redistribute returned or unclaimed tickets a few hours before curtain. However, this might mean sacrificing your afternoon.

Sold-out Shows: Even if a show is sold out to the general public, theaters reserve prime house seats for VIPs. When no one important shows up, the theatre will sell them to the masses.

Standing-room Only: Sold on the day of the show, tend to be around $15 or $20. Call first, as some theaters can't accommodate standing room.

Hit Show Club: 630 Ninth Ave. (☎581-4211), between 44th and 45th St. This free service distributes coupons redeemable at the box office for over 1/3 off regular ticket prices. Call for coupons via mail or pick them up at the club office.

Though Broadway tickets usually run upwards of $50, many money-saving schemes exist. **TKTS** sells tickets at a 25-50% discount on the day of the performance of many Broadway and some larger off-Broadway shows. The lines begin to form an hour or so before the booths open, but move fairly quickly. More tickets become available as showtime approaches, so you may find fewer possibilities if you go too early. (☎768-1818. Duffy Square, at 47th St. and Broadway. Tickets sold M-Sa 3-8pm for evening performances; W and Sa 10am-2pm for matinees; and Su 11am-7pm for matinees and evening performances. Less competitive lines form downtown, where TKTS has a branch in the mezzanine of 2 World Trade Center. Open M-F 11am-5:30pm, Sa 11am-3:30pm; Su matinee tickets sold on Sa.)

Theatre Development Fund (TDF) offers discount vouchers for off- and off-off-Broadway productions and other events sponsored by small, independent production companies. Those eligible—students, teachers, performing-arts professionals, retirees, union and armed forces members, and clergy—have to first join the TDF mailing list by sending in an application and enclosing $20. Once you are a member, which may take six-to-eight weeks after you turn in the application, you can purchase four vouchers for $28, which are redeemable at the box office of any participating production (☎221-0885; www.tdf.org).

You may reserve full-price tickets over the phone and pay by credit card through: **Tele-Charge** (☎239-6200 or outside NYC 800-432-7250; 24hr.; www.telecharge.com) for Broadway shows; **Ticket Central** (☎279-4200; www.ticketcentral.org) for off-Broadway shows; and **Ticketmaster** (☎307-4100 or outside NYC 800-755-4000; www.ticketmaster.com; 24hr.) for all types of shows. All three services assess a per-ticket service charge; ask before purchasing. You can avoid these fees if you buy tickets directly from the box office.

BROADWAY

Most Broadway theaters are north of Times Square and are not actually on Broadway itself, but between Eighth Ave. and Broadway. Here's a list of some current blockbusters. For more information, go to www.nytheatre.com.

Annie Get Your Gun, Marquis Theatre, 1535 Broadway between 45th and 46th Sts. (www.anniegetyourgun.com). This Grammy-winning musical stars Crystal Bernardas. Tickets $35-75. Students get 50% off $60 seats.

Beauty and the Beast, Lunt-Fontanne Theatre, 205 W. 46th St., at Broadway. (www.disneyonbroadway.com). Sarah Litzsinger as Belle, Steve Blanchard as Beast. Tickets $30-85.

Cabaret, Studio 54, 254 W. 54th St. between Broadway and Eighth Ave. (www.cabaret-54.com). Was the hottest ticket on Broadway in the summer of 1998. Now starring Brooke Shields and Matt McGrath. Tickets $45-90.

Chicago, Shubert Theater, 225 W. 44th St. between Broadway and Eighth Ave. (www.chicagothemusical.com). An excellent revival with stunning choreography by Anne Reinking. Winner of six 1997 Tony Awards. $20 tickets available at box office 10am day of performance, subject to availability (two per person, line forms early). Tickets $42.50-90.

Les Miserables, Imperial Theater, 249 W. 45th St., between Broadway and Eighth Ave. (www.lesmis.com). Rapidly approaching its 15th year on Broadway. Tickets $20-85.

The Lion King, New Amsterdam Theater, 216 W. 42nd St., at Broadway (www.disneyonbroadway.com). The intricate costumes and actors' graceful body movements make this elaborate show an aesthetic masterpiece. $20 rush tickets available 10am day of performance. Tickets $25-90.

The Music Man, Neil Simon Theater, 250 W. 52nd St., between Broadway and Eighth Ave. (www.themusicmanbroadway.com). The feel-good story of a con artist/salesman, a boys band, and a librarian. Tickets $40-90.

Phantom of the Opera, Majestic Theater, 247 W. 44th St., between Broadway and Eighth Ave. (www.thephantomoftheopera.com). Classic Broadway production. Tickets $20-85.

The Producers, St. James Theater, 246 W. 44th St. between Broadway and Eighth Ave. (www.producersonbroadway.com). This new Mel Brooks musical won 12 Tony Awards in 2001. Based on a 1967 movie, the extremely popular show stars Nathan Lane and Matthew Broderick. Tickets $35-99.

Rent, Nederlander Theater, 208 W. 41st St., at Seventh Ave. (www.siteforrent.com). A modern version of *La Bohème* set in NYC. $20 tickets available after 5:30pm line-up for 6pm lottery at the box office for evening shows Tu-F; 2 tickets per person, cash only. Tickets $35-80.

A Thousand Clowns, Longacre Theater, 220 W. 48th St. between Broadway and Eighth Ave. (www.athousandclowns.net). This revival comedy stars Tom Selleck. Tickets $40-77.50.

OFF-BROADWAY

Off-Broadway theaters, by definition, feature less mainstream presentations for crowds of 499 or fewer. Runs are generally short; however, shows occasionally jump to Broadway houses (as in the case of *Rent*). Many of the best off-Broadway houses huddle in the Sheridan Square area of the West Village, while others are located to the west of Times Square. Off-Broadway tickets cost $15-45. You may see shows for free by arranging to

MoreCheapSeats

High 5 Tickets to the Arts (☎445-8587; www.high5tix.com): Through this program any junior high or high school student between the ages of 13 and 18 can attend theater shows, concerts, and museum exhibitions for only $5. Tickets are sold at all New York Ticketmaster locations; proof of age is required, and tickets must be purchased at least one day prior to the performance.

Kids' Night on Broadway (☎563-2929): This annual program, sponsored by TDF and the League of American Theatres, gives children ages 6 to 18 free admission (with the purchase of one regularly priced ticket) on four specified nights. Kids' Night debuted in NY last year and was so successful that it has expanded to 20 cities. Tickets start selling in October; performances are Jan.-Feb.

CareTix (☎840-0770, ext. 230): Sponsored by Broadway Cares/Equity Fights AIDS, CareTix sells house seats for sold-out Broadway and off-Broadway shows, and for some non-theatrical events. Tickets are twice the regular box office price, but it's for a good cause.

Audience Extras (☎989-9550): A little-known program with a lot of leftover tickets (many for prime house seats) to theater shows, concerts, and dance performances. You must pay a one-time membership fee of $130 and an annual fee of $85; after that, however, each ticket will only cost you $3. Most tickets sold on a day-of-show basis.

usher; this usually entails dressing neatly and showing up at the theater around 45 minutes ahead of curtain, helping to seat ticket-holders, and then staying after the performance to help clean up. Speak with the house manager far in advance.

Listings and reviews appear the first Wednesday of every month in **Simon Says,** a *Village Voice* guide tailored to unconventional theater happenings around the city. Other publications with theater listings include *New York* magazine, the *New York Press*, the *New Yorker*, *Time Out: New York*.

Actors Playhouse, 100 Seventh Ave. South between Christopher and Bleecker Sts. (☎463-0060). Tickets $35-45. Box office open 3-8pm on show days and Sa-Su noon-8pm.

Astor Place Theater, 436 Lafayette St. between E. 4th St. and Astor Pl. (☎800-BLUEMAN). Home to the infectious *Blue Man Group*. Tickets $45-55. Box office open daily noon-8pm or until 15min. before last show. Shows Tu-Th 8pm, F-Sa 7pm and 10pm, Su 4pm and 7pm.

Cherry Lane, 38 Commerce St., at Grove St. (☎989-2020). This converted box-factory has hosted a slew of magnificent plays by famous playwrights such as Beckett, Albee, O'Neill, and others. Tickets $35-55. An alternative theater in the same building has more experimental productions. Tickets $12. Box office open Tu-F 2-8pm, Sa 2-9pm, Su noon-7pm.

The Joseph Papp Public Theater, 425 Lafayette St. between E. 4th St. and Astor Pl. (☎539-8750). The Public's six venues present a wide variety of productions and have hosted a decade-long marathon of Shakespeare's every last work, right down to *Timon of Athens*. Shakespeare in the Park tickets are handed out here. Box office Su-M 1pm-6pm, Tu-Sa 1pm-7:30pm.

Lamb's, 130 W. 44th St. (☎997-1780 or 575-0300). A 349-seat theater and a 29-seater host family-oriented plays and musicals. Tickets $25-35.

Manhattan Theater Club, 131 W. 55th St. between Sixth and Seventh Ave. (☎399-3000 or 581-1212). A popular venue for new plays. Tickets $40-55.

New York Theatre Workshop, 79 E. 4th St., between the Bowery and Second Ave. (☎460-5475; www.nytw.org). A small (150-seat) theater. Wheelchair access. Line for cheap tickets ($10, two per person, cash only) 2 hrs. before curtain. Student tickets $15; seniors $28. Box office open Tu-Sa 1-6pm.

Orpheum, 126 Second Ave. between E. 7th St. and St. Mark's Pl., in the East Village (☎477-2477; www.stomponline.com). Now playing the infectious, rhythmic *Stomp*: a percussive feast that makes instruments out of garbage cans. Tickets $30-50. Box office open M 1-6pm, Tu-F 1-7pm, Sa 1-9pm, Su noon-6pm.

Primary Stages, 354 W. 45th St. between Eighth and Ninth Ave. (☎333-4052). This theater, opening its 17th season, features new American plays. Box office open M-Sa noon-6pm.

Samuel Beckett Theater, 410 W. 42nd St. between Ninth and Tenth Aves. (☎574-2826). Mostly productions of contemporary drama, sometimes including post-performance discussions with members of the cast. Tickets $45, students and seniors $35. Box office open Tu, Th-F noon-8pm, W noon-3:30, 5-8pm, Sa noon-3pm, 5:30-8pm, Su noon-3pm.

SoHo Repertory Theatre, 46 Walker St. between Broadway and Church St. (☎941-8632; reservations 946-5469). Tickets $8-25.

SoHo Think Tank Ohio Theater, 66 Wooster St. between Grand and Broome Sts. (☎966-4844). A theater that puts on provocative intellectual pieces combining theater, performance art, dancing, and sketch comedy. "Cafe Ohio" opens before shows at 6pm for "drinks and conversation." Shows usually W-Sa at 7pm. $15.

Sullivan Street Playhouse, 181 Sullivan St. between W. Houston and Bleecker Sts. (☎674-3838). Home to *The Fantasticks*, the longest running show in US history. The city has renamed this section of road "The Fantasticks Way." All seats Tu-Th and Su $37.50, F-Sa $40. Shows Tu-F 8pm, Sa 3 and 7pm, Su 3 and 7:30pm. Box office open Tu-Su noon-showtime.

Theater for the New City, 155 First Ave. between E. 9th and 10th Sts. (☎254-1109; www.theaterforthenewcity.com). New avant-garde productions. Productions Th-Su 8pm. Tickets around $10. Dispatches a roving theater troupe throughout the city that performs in parks and streets (late July-Sept.; free; call for locations). Box office open M-F 10am-6pm.

Union Square Theatre, 100 E. 17th St., at Union Sq. East (☎505-0700). A respectable off-Broadway theatre, housed in what was once Tammany Hall. Box office open Tu-Sa 1-7pm, Su 1pm-6:30pm. Tickets $55.

Vineyard Theater Company's Dimson Theatre, 108 E. 15th St., between Union Sq. East and Irving Pl. (☎353-3366).

OUTDOOR THEATERS

Queens Theater in the Park, in Flushing Meadows-Corona Park (☎718-760-0064; www.queenstheatre.org). Film and performing arts center that hosts an annual Latino arts festival (late-July to mid-Aug.), among other events. Call for dance and theater listings.

Shakespeare in the Park, (☎539-8750), near the West 81st St. entrance of Central Park, just north of the 79th St. Transverse. This renowned series is a New York summer tradition. Two Shakespeare plays, one late June to mid-July and the second early August to September, bring outstanding actors and directors to the outdoor Delacorte amphitheater in Central Park. Tickets available 1pm the day of performance at the Delacorte and 1-3pm at the Public Theatre at 425 Lafayette St.; try to get there by 10:30am. Stand-by line forms at 6pm. Limit 2 tickets per person. Doors open Tu-Su at 7:30pm; shows start at 8pm.

GENERAL ENTERTAINMENT VENUES

ABC No Rio, 156 Rivington St. between Clinton and Suffolk Sts. (☎254-3694). A non-profit, community-run art space with a vibrant mural marking its entrance. The center is open to the public and hosts a myriad of community events from art exhibitions of local teenagers to hard-core and punk shows. No alcohol or beverages served. All ages. Cover $2-5.

Beacon Theater, 2130 Broadway, at 74th St. (☎307-7171). Subway: 1, 2, 3, 9 to 72nd St. Attached to the Beacon Hotel, this mid-sized venue hosts a wide variety of music acts, as well as other performances and plays. Call for schedule. Tickets usually $25-50. Box office open M-F 11am-6pm, Su noon-5pm.

Brooklyn Academy of Music, 30 Lafayette Ave. between St. Felix St. and Ashland Pl. (☎718-636-4100; www.bam.org). Subway: 2, 3, 4, 5, D, Q to Atlantic Ave.; B, M, N, R to Pacific St. The oldest performing arts center in the country, the Brooklyn Academy of Music (BAM) has compiled a colorful history of magnificent performances: here Pavlova danced, Caruso sang, and Sarah Bernhardt played Camille. Now, it focuses on new, non-traditional, multicultural programs—with the occasional early classical music performance. Jazz, blues, performance art, opera, and dance also take the stage. Late spring brings Dance Africa. BAM's annual **Next Wave Festival,** Oct.-Dec., features contemporary music, dance, theater, and performance art. Call about student rush. The **Brooklyn Philharmonic Orchestra** performs here Oct.-Mar. and hosts a brief opera season Feb.-Jun. Orchestra and opera tickets $30-50. Manhattan Express Bus ("BAM bus") departs round-trip from 120 Park Ave. at 42nd St. for each performance ($5, round-trip $10).

Brooklyn Center for Performing Arts, 2900 Campus Road and Hillel Place, one block west of the junction of Flatbush and Nostrand Aves. on the campus of Brooklyn College. (☎718-951-4500 or 718-951-4522; www.brooklyncenter.com). Performers scheduled to appear on one of the two stages in 2002 include tap dancer Gregory Hines (Apr. 13), Isaac Hayes (Feb. 9), and the Grigorovich Ballet (Mar. 31). Season Oct.-May. Tickets $20-40.

Cathedral of St. John the Divine, 1047 Amsterdam Ave., at 112th St. (☎662-2133). This beautiful church offers an impressive array of classical concerts, art exhibitions, lectures, plays, movies, and dance events. The NY Philharmonic performs on occasion, and soprano saxophonist Paul Winter gives annual Winter Solstice concert. Prices vary.

Colden Center for the Performing Arts, 65-30 Kissena Blvd., at Queens College in Flushing, Queens (☎718-793-8080). Subway: 7 to Flushing-Main St.; then buses Q17, Q25, or Q34 to the corner of Kissena Blvd. and the Long Island Expressway. Beautiful, 2143-seat theater hosts an excellent program of jazz, classical, and dance concerts Sept.-May. Summer box office hours M-W noon-4pm.

Collective Unconscious, 145 Ludlow St. between Rivington and Stanton Sts. (☎254-5277). Subway: F to Delancey St. A popular performance space run by 21 local artists, this venue and studio space debuts performances from the downtown artistic community. Rev. Jen's Anti-Slam Comedy Act (W) brings in a big crowd, and other nights run the gamut from a reading series to a "Famous Drunks In History" Party. No alcohol served, but BYOB welcome. Cover $3-5.

Cultural Institutes. These centers for expats are valuable for their libraries, small but interesting exhibits, classes, and lectures. Some of these services are only open to members, but all the institutes have highly useful lists of cultural events throughout the city.

Alliance Française, 22 E. 60th St. between Madison and Fifth Aves. (☎355-6100), the cultural arm of the French Embassy, offers Gallic lectures, classes, programs, and films. (Open M-Th 9am-8pm, F 9am-6pm, Sa 9am-2pm; box office at 55 E. 59th St., ☎355-6160.)

Americas Society, the **Spanish Institute,** and the **Italian Cultural Institute** occupy three historically landmarked buildings on Park Ave. between 68th and 69th St. (680 Park Ave., ☎249-8950; 684 Park Ave., ☎628-0420; and 686 Park Ave., ☎879-4242; respectively.)

Asia Society, see **Museums,** p. 116, also has films from or about Asia. (Box office open: M-F 10am-5pm; adults $7, students and seniors $5.)

China Institute, 125 E. 65th St. between Park and Lexington Aves. (☎744-8181), aims to promote the understanding of Chinese culture and history through classes, lectures, performances, and film series; its gallery showcases a broad spectrum of Chinese art and architecture from the Neolithic period to the present. (Gallery hours: M-W, F-Sa 10am-5pm, Tu-Th 10am-8pm, Su 10am-5pm; $3, students and seniors $2, under 12 free, Tu and Th 6-8pm free.)

Goethe Institute, 1014 Fifth Ave. between 82nd and 83rd Sts. (☎439-8700), imports Germanic culture also through the medium of films, concerts, classes, and lectures. (Open Tu and Th 9am-7pm, M, W, F 9am-5pm.)

The Kitchen, 512 W. 19th St. between Tenth and Eleventh Aves. (☎255-5793; www.thekitchen.org). Subway: C, E to 23rd St. World-renowned showcase for arts events in an unassuming location. Features experimental and avant-garde film and video, as well as concerts, dance performances, and poetry readings. Ticket prices vary by event.

Knitting Factory, 74 Leonard St. between Broadway and Church St. (☎219-3055). Features several shows nightly, ranging from avant-garde and indy rock to jazz and hip-hop. The multi-level performance space also hosts a summertime jazz festival. Cover $5-20. Box office open M-F 10am-11pm, Sa-Su 2-11pm. Bar open M-F 4:30pm-2am, Sa-Su 6pm-2am.

Merkin Concert Hall, 129 W. 67th St. between Broadway and Amsterdam Ave. (☎501-3330; www.ekcc.org/merkin.html). Subway: 1, 9 to 66th St. An intimate theater, sometimes known as "the little hall with the big sound." This division of the Elaine Kaufman Cultural Center offers musically-diverse programs. Season Sept.-June. Tickets $8-50, with occasional free concerts. Box office open M-F noon-4pm.

92nd Street Y, 1395 Lexington Ave., at 92nd St. (☎996-1100). The Upper East Side's cultural mecca. The Y's Kaufmann Concert Hall seats only 916 people and offers an intimate setting unmatched by New York's larger halls, with flawless acoustics and the oaken ambience of a Viennese salon. Notable series include Jazz in July, Chamber Music at the Y, Lyrics and Lyricists, and Young Concert Artists. Also hosts an ongoing series of literary readings at the Poetry Center and some of the most engaging lectures in New York. $15-35 for tickets to all events. Closed in summer.

The Point, 940 Garrison Ave., in the Bronx, at the corner of Manida St. in Hunts Point. (☎718-542-4139; www.thepoint.org). Subway: 6 to Hunts Point. On the fringe of one of NY's poorest neighborhoods, The Point houses a growing artistic community and is home to dancer/choreographer Arthur Aviles. Monthly Latin jazz and hip-hop performances are offered, as well as studio facilities, a theater, and classes in art. Community-based efforts like the South Bronx Film and Video Festival enable Hunts Point to call itself "the artistic capital of the Bronx." Call for schedule of events. Open M-F 8am-7pm, Sa 10am-5pm.

Radio City Music Hall, 1260 Sixth Ave., at 50th St. (☎247-4777; see **Sights,** p. 72) boasts a bill of great performers that reads like an invitation list to the Music Hall of Fame; Ella Fitzgerald, Frank Sinatra, Ringo Starr, Linda Ronstadt, and Sting, among others, have all performed at the legendary venue. Tickets for events generally start at $30. Box office 50th St. and Sixth Ave. Open regularly M-Sa 10am-8pm, Su 11am-8pm. In summer, M-F 10am-8pm, Sa-Su noon-5pm.

St. Mark's Church in the Bowery, 131 E. 10th St., at Second Ave. Home to the **Ontological Theater** (☎533-4650), **Danspace Project** (☎674-8194), and **Poetry Project** (☎674-0910). While the Ontological Theater pioneered the wackiness of playwright Richard Foreman, Danspace has provided a venue for emerging dancers and experimental styles of movement since the 1920s (Isadora Duncan danced in this space). The Poetry Project stages evening readings (M, W, F). Call for info on upcoming events, or check the board outside; you'll need to make reservations for theater tickets and arrive 15min. early for the show. Tickets for Danspace $10-15, Poetry Project $4-7.

Soundlab (☎726-1724). Locations vary. Expect a smart, funky, racially-mixed crowd absorbing smart, funky, radically mixed sound. Call to find where the next Lab goes down; past locales include the base of the Brooklyn Bridge, the 15th floor of a Financial District skyscraper, and a Chinatown park.

Symphony Space, 2537 Broadway, at 95th St. (☎864-5400; www.symphonyspace.org). Subway: 1, 2, 3, 9 to 96th St. Under renovation until March 2002. Open Tu-Sa 1-7pm. Tickets by phone Th-Sa noon-6pm. Most movies $8, other events up to $45.

World Financial Center, in Battery Park City (☎945-0505 or 528-2733; www.worldfinancialcenter.com). A variety of festivals are held here year-round, but are more common during the summer. Diversity is the only constant: there may be swing dancing one day and a Far East cultural exposition the next. Other dance and music concerts appear at the nearby World Trade Center. Admission free.

FESTIVALS

Central Park Summerstage, at the Rumsey Playfield, at 72nd St, near Fifth Ave., in Central Park (☎360-2777; www.SummerStage.org). Mid-June to late Aug., Summerstage hosts free cultural events, like concerts, dance, and spoken word. Past performers have included everyone from the Fugees and the Rocksteady Crew to the Gypsy Kings and They Might Be Giants. Big names from all genres, but also an outstanding selection of up-and-coming performers.

Lincoln Center Out-of-Doors (☎875-5108; www.lincolncenter.org), For three weeks in Aug., Lincoln Center sponsors a completely free performance arts festival. Performances run the gamut from dance to Chinese opera.

Lincoln Center Festival, box office at Avery Fisher Hall, Lincoln Center (☎875-5928; www.lincolncenter.org). Cutting-edge events spanning dance, theater, opera, and music throughout the Lincoln Center complex in July. Tickets $20-75. Ask for student discounts at the Avery Fisher Hall box office.

JAZZ

Since its beginnings in the early 20th century, jazz has played a pivotal role in New York's music scene. Uptown at Minton's during the 50s, Charlie Parker, Dizzy Gillespie, and Thelonious Monk were overthrowing traditional swing and planting, arguably, the roots of new genres, such as R&B and Rock N' Roll. Today, New York remains the jazz capital of the world, with a multitude of genres, from Big Band orchestras and traditional stylists to free, fusion, and avant-garde artists, thriving in venues throughout the city. Downtown's crowd is more young, funky, and commercialized whilst Uptown in Harlem, you'll find a more intimate and smooth type of jazz. You can check out one of the many hazy dens that bred lingo like "cat" and "hip" (a "hippie" was originally someone on the fringes of jazz culture who talked the talk but was never really in the know), or more formal shows at Lincoln Center. Summer means open-air (often free) sets in parks and plazas. Check the papers to find listings of jazz venues around the city.

Apollo Theater

Small's

Lenox Lounge

JAZZ CLUBS

You can expect high covers and drink minimums at the legendary jazz spots, but a few bars supply reliable up-and-comers free of charge. And, although some "classier" joints take credit cards, bring cash just in case.

Apollo Theatre, 253 W. 125th St. between Frederick Douglass and Adam Clayton Powell Blvds. (☎749-5838; box office ☎531-5305). Subway: A, B, C, D to 125th St. This Harlem landmark has heard Duke Ellington, Count Basie, Ella Fitzgerald, and Billie Holliday. A young Malcolm X shined shoes here. A big draw is W's legendary Amateur Night ($13-30), in which the audience assumes the starring role of judge, jury, and often, executioner. Order tickets through Ticketmaster (☎307-7171) or at the box office. (Open M, Tu, Th, F 10am-6pm, W 10am-8:30pm, Sa noon-6pm).

Arthur's Tavern, 57 Grove St. between Bleecker and Seventh Ave. S. (☎675-6879). Subway: 1, 9 to Christopher St. A largely local crowd flocks to hear decent live jazz and blues played where Al Bundy jammed and Charlie Parker stomped. The dark and cavernous decor brightens with an animated crowd and swinging tunes. Also features a full American Italian menu. Open Su-M 8pm-3am, Tu-Th 6:30pm-3am, F-Sa 6:30pm-4am. Sets begin at 7pm. No Cover. 1-drink minimum. Drinks $5. Cash only.

Birdland, 315 W. 44th St. between Eighth and Ninth Aves. (☎581-3080). Subway: 1, 2, 3, 7, 9, C, E, N, Q, R, W to 42nd St. Said by Charlie Parker to be the "jazz corner of the world," this dinner club serves up Cajun food and splendid jazz in a classy, neon-accented setting. The gumbo ($16) and the popcorn shrimp ($10) are as famous as the club itself. Music charge, including a complimentary drink, $20-35. An additional $10 minimum food/drink. Open daily 5pm-2am; first set nightly at 9pm, 2nd at 11pm. Reservations recommended. AmEx/D/MC/V.

Blue Note, 131 W. 3rd St., near 6th Ave. (☎475-8592). Subway: A, B, C, D, E, F, Q to W. 4th St. The legendary jazz club is now more of a commercialized concert space. But the Blue Note still brings in many of today's all-stars, such as Take 6. Cover for big-name performers $20-70. $5 food/drink minimum. Students half-off cover Su-Th 11:30pm set only. For a great deal, go to the after hours, when the cover for late night jam sessions drops to $5 (F-Sa, 1am-4am). Open Su-Th 7pm-2am, F-Sa 7pm-4am. AmEx/DC/MC/V.

Cotton Club, 656 W. 125th St., on the corner of Riverside Dr. (☎663-7980). Subway: 1, 9 to 125th St. This jazz hall of the greats is often clogged with tourists. Cover for brunch and Gospel Shows $25; jazz shows $32; no minimum, dinner included. Call ahead (two weeks is standard) for reservations and information. MC/V.

Detour, 349 E. 13th St. between First and Second Aves. (☎533-6212; www.jazzatdetour.com). Subway: L to First Ave. Great nightly jazz and no cover–a perfect mix. One-drink minimum. Happy hour M-F 4-7pm, drinks 2-for-1. Mixed drinks ($6), bottled beer ($4). Open M-Th 3pm-2am, F-Su 3pm-4am. Wheelchair access.

Fez, 380 Lafayette St. between 3rd and 4th Sts., under Time Cafe (☎533-2680). Subway: 6 to Bleecker St. This lushly-appointed, Moroccan-decorated performance club draws an extremely photogenic crowd, especially on Thursday nights when the Mingus Big Band holds court. Sets at 9:30pm and 11:30pm. $18, students pay $10 for second set. Reservations suggested.) Cover $5-30; 2-drink minimum. Open Su-Th 6pm-2am, F-Sa 6pm-4am. Cash only at the door but MC, V for food/drink.

Lenox Lounge, 288 Lenox Ave. between 124th and 125th Sts. (☎427-0253). Subway: 2, 3 to 125th St. The lounge is quintessential Harlem; intimate, offbeat, and bursting with great jazz. The original 1939 decor–smooth red booths and tiled floors–make this one of Harlem's hidden gems. Jazz Th-M $10-15; M night jam session $5. 2-drink minimum. First set 10pm; last set 1am. Open daily noon-4am.

101 Club, 101 Seventh Ave. South, at Grove St. (☎620-4000). Subway: 1, 9 to Christopher St. This jumping spot is hard to walk past. An eclectic crowd listens to live jazz, funk, soul, and rock seven nights a week. Happy Hour 6-9pm, all drinks half-price. Open Su-Th 6pm-3am, F-Sa 6pm-4am. No cover. 1 drink min. Beer $5.50. Mixed drinks $6-8.

St. Nick's Pub, 773 St. Nicholas Ave. between 148th and 149th Sts. (☎283-9728). Subway: A, B, C, D to 145th St. Small and unpretentious with a dedicated crowd, this pub is quintessential Sugar Hill. M nights especially notable: Patience Higgins and the Sugar Hill Jazz Quartet host a laid-back jam session. Cover $3, or 2 people for $5 with 2-drink minimum. Mixed drinks $5-6. Bar opens at 12:30pm, jazz shows M-Sa 9:30pm until 3 or 4am. Cash only.

Showman's Cafe, 375 W. 125th St. between St. Nicholas and Morningside Aves. (☎864-8941). Subway: A, B, C, D to 125th St. A reprise of the original 1942 Showman's, this intimate jazz club attracts a largely local crowd. Showtimes: M-Th 8:30, 10:00pm and 11:30 am, F-Sa 10:30pm, 12:30 am, 2:30 am. No cover. 2 drink minimum. Open M-Sa noon-4am.

Small's, 183 W. 10th St., at Seventh Ave. (☎929-7565). Subway: 1, 9 to Christopher St. The fact that it doesn't serve alcohol allows it to stay open all night, often providing over 10hr. of great music. It's a splendid after-hours spot and a late, late night showcase for musicians who still have chops left over from performances at other clubs. Cover $10. Free show Sa 6:30-9pm. Free non-alcoholic beverages (juice). Call ahead for early bird specials (no cover). Open Su-Th 10pm-8am, F-Sa 6:30pm-8am.

Smoke, 2751 Broadway, between 105th and 106th Sts. (☎864-6662). This sultry cocktail lounge jumps with excellent jazz seven nights a week. Although slightly congested, the intimate space swells with music and an animated atmosphere. Jam sessions M at 10pm and Th at midnight. Also Funk W and Latin Jazz Su. Happy Hour 5-8pm. Su-W no cover; Th-Sa $10-20. $10 drink min. Open daily 5pm-4am.

Swing 46, 349 W. 46th St. between Eighth and Ninth Aves. (☎262-9554). This jazz and supper club has jumped on the big band wagon and delivers all kinds of smooth grooves like Swingtime M, Jump Tu, and Big Band Th. Sunday brings Buster Brown's Crazy Tap Jam and its devoted crowd. Cover includes swing lessons at 9:15pm. Su-W $7, Th-Sa $12 with 2-drink minimum (drinks $10-16). Happy Hour, with half-price drinks, daily 5-8pm. Dinner ($14-24) served daily 5pm-midnight. Sets begin at 10:30pm.

Village Vanguard, 178 Seventh Ave. between W. 11th and Greenwich Sts. (☎255-4037). This windowless, wedge-shaped basement den is 65-years-thick with memories of Lenny Bruce, Leadbelly, Miles Davis, and Sonny Rollins. Every M the Vanguard Orchestra unleashes its torrential Big Band sound on sentimental journeymen at 9:30 and 11:30pm. Cover M-Sa $15, plus $10 minimum. Sets Su-Th 9:30 and 11:30pm, F-Sa 9:30, 11:30pm, and 1am. Doors open at 8:30pm. Reservations recommended. Cash and traveler's checks only.

OTHER JAZZ VENUES

Guggenheim Museum, (☎423-3500; see **Museums,** p. 114). Live jazz, Brazilian, and world beat music in its rotunda F and Sa 5-8pm year-round. Museum admission required, but F 6-8pm is pay-as-you-wish.

Jazz at Lincoln Center, 33 W. 60th St. (www.jazzatlincolncenter.org). A year-round festival celebrating one of America's great music forms, under the direction of Wynton Marsalis as Artistic Director. Plans are afoot for a jazz-specific performance space on Columbus Circle.

Saint Peter's, 619 Lexington Ave., at 52nd St. (☎935-2200). Su jazz vespers at 5pm, usually followed at 7pm by a jazz concert ($5-10 donation for the concert). Informal jazz concerts often held W evenings at 6pm. October 8th, the annual All Night Soul session rocks 5pm-5am. Call ahead for a current schedule of St. Peter's offerings. Dale R. Lind, Pastor to the Jazz Community, oversees all tuneful good deeds.

SUMMER JAZZ AND FESTIVALS

The **JVC Jazz Festival** blows into the city from June to July. All-star performances of past series have included Elvin Jones, Ray Charles, Tito Puente, and Mel Torme. Tickets go on sale in early May, but many events take place outdoors in the parks and are free. Check the newspaper for listings. **Bryant Park,** which has events all summer, also hosts a large number of these concerts, as does **Damrosch Park** at Lincoln Center. Call 501-1390 in the spring for info, or write to: JVC Jazz Festival New York, P.O. Box 1169, New York, NY 10023. Annual festivals sponsored by major corporations bring in local talent and industry giants on the forefront of innovation. The concerts take place throughout the city (some free) but center at TriBeCa's **Knitting Factory** (☎219-3055 in spring).

Central Park Summerstage, at 72nd St. in Central Park (☎360-2777), divides its attention among many performing arts, including jazz. Call or pick up Central Park's calendar of events, available at the Dairy in Central Park (see **Central Park,** p. 78). The free concerts run mid-June to early August.

The **World Financial Center Plaza** (☎945-0505) infrequently hosts free concerts between June and September, featuring jazz styles ranging from Little Jimmy Scott to the Kit McClure Big Band, an all-female jazz orchestra. Two performers are featured

Wednesday to Friday after work and Tuesday to Friday at lunchtime from July until early September. Two performers are featured each week, one performing at noon and the other at 1pm. The **South Street Seaport** (☎732-7678) sponsors a series of outdoor concerts from July to early September at Pier 17, Ambrose Stage, and the Atrium.

ROCK, POP, PUNK, FUNK

Rock & roll and its bastard stepchildren have long been part of New York's scene; the Velvet Underground moaned to Gotham as the city flirted with heroin, languor, and insipid conversation, Patti Smith and Television layered poetry and guitar lines over a beat you couldn't dance to in the dark days of Disco, Sonic Youth drowned out an otherwise disposable decade in a riot of noise and feedback, and Public Enemy fought the power before anybody had ever heard the name Giuliani.

Music festivals are hot tickets and provide the opportunity to see tons of bands at a (relatively) low price. The **CMJ Music Marathon** (☎877-6-FESTIVAL; www.cmj.com) runs for four nights in the fall and includes over 400 bands and workshops on alternative music culture and college radio production. **The Digital Club Festival** (☎677-3530), a newly reconfigured indie-fest, visits New York in late July. The **Macintosh New York Music Festival** presents over 350 bands over a week-long period. For more electronic experimental sounds, check out Creative Time's **Music in the Anchorage,** a June concert series happening in the massive stone chambers in the base of the Brooklyn Bridge. (☎206-6674).

If arena rock is more your style, check out **Madison Square Garden** (☎465-6000), at Seventh Ave. and W. 33rd St., perhaps America's premier entertainment facility. MSG hosts over 600 events and nearly 6,000,000 spectators every year. **New Jersey's Meadowlands** (☎201-935-3900) and the **Nassau Coliseum** (☎516-888-9000) also stage high-priced performances. From June to early September the **Coca-Cola Concert Series** (☎516-221-1000) brings rock, jazz, and reggae concerts to Jones Beach. (Tickets $15-40; See **Long Island,** p. 221, for transportation info.)

Arlene Grocery and Butcher Bar, 95 Stanton St. between Ludlow and Orchard Sts. (☎358-1633). Every night this venue hosts at least three bands back-to-back. Mostly local indie acts, but big names like Sheryl Crow have also played in this intimate space. Bob Dylan once stopped by, but only to use the bathroom. Show starts at 7. Stop by next door at the Butcher Bar–a leg of the "grocery"–where drafts cost $5. Cover on the weekend $5.

The Bitter End, 147 Bleecker St. between Thompson and LaGuardia Sts. (☎673-7030). Small space hosts folk, country, and roots rock acts; they claim artists like Billy Joel, Stevie Wonder, Woody Allen, and Rita Rudner performed here as unknowns. Look for their likenesses in the gaudy mural. Call for show times. Cover $5-12. Open Su-Th 7:30pm-2am, F-Sa 7:30pm-4am.

Bottom Line, 15. W. 4th St., at Mercer St. (228-7880 for info; 228-6300 for box office). A gothic space with a mixed bag of music entertainment–from jazz to kitsch to country to the theater to rock-and-roll by over-the-hill singers. Recent shows run the spectrum from Roger McGuinn to Broadway Diva Betty Berkeley. Crowd and mood varies from show to show in this large, cave-like venue. Double proof of age required, or come with a parent or guardian. Some all-ages performances. Cover $15-25; Shows nightly 7:30 and 10:30 pm.

Bowery Ballroom, 6 Delancey St. between Chrystie St. and The Bowery. (☎533-2111; for tickets call 866-468-7619). Subway: J, M, Z to Bowery. This medium-sized club retains some of the details from its original 1929 Beaux Arts construction. The venue attracts popular bands, and its stage has recently been graced by REM, the Black Crowes, and the Red Hot Chili Peppers. Tickets $10-20.

CBGB/OMFUG (CBGB's), 315 Bowery, at Bleecker St. (☎982-4052). The initials have stood for "country, bluegrass, blues, and other music for uplifting gourmandizers," since CBGB's 1973 opening, but the New York Dolls, Television, the Ramones, Patti Smith, and Talking Heads rendered this venue synonymous with punk. The music remains loud, raw, and hungry. Shows nightly around 8pm. Cover $3-10. Next door, **CB's Gallery,** 313 Bowery (☎677-0455) presents softer live music.

Continental, 25 Third Ave., at Stuyvesant St. (☎529-6924; www.continentalnyc.com). A dark club that hosts the loud set nightly. Come for noise, rock, and local punk. Iggy Pop, Debbie Harry, and Patti Smith have all played here–recently. Check lamp posts and fliers for shows and times. Happy Hour daily half-price drinks. Shot of anything $2 with a beer. Cover free-$7.

The Cooler, 416 W. 14th St., at Greenwich St. (☎229-0785; www.thecooler.com). In the heart of the meat-packing district. The Cooler showcases indie, dub, and electronic music by some of the town's smartest DJs in a huge vault of a room. Randomly hosts good underground hip-hop shows as well. Cover varies. Free Mondays. Doors open Su-Th 8pm, F-Sa 9pm.

Elbow Room, 144 Bleecker St. between Thompson St. and LaGuardia Pl. (☎979-8434). Features three to six live bands a night playing rock, jazz, and blues to a house that fits 400. Call for nightly schedule. Cover usually $7 Tu-Th, $9 F-Sa. Open Tu-Th 7:30pm-2:30am, F-Sa 7pm-4am.

Irving Plaza, 17 Irving Pl., at 15th St. (☎777-6800 or 777-1224 for concert info; www.irvingplaza.com). A mid-sized club decorated in a puzzling chinoiserie style. Rock, comedy, performance art, and other entertainment. Purchase tickets in advance for the bigger shows. Cover varies. Doors generally open at 8pm. "Savoy Sundays" feature live big bands and swing dancing ($13, seniors $5; doors open 7pm; bands play 8pm-midnight). Box office open M-F noon-6:30pm, Sa 1-4pm.

Mercury Lounge, 217 E. Houston St., between Essex and Ludlow Sts. (☎260-4700; www.mercuryloungenyc.com). Once a gravestone parlor, the Mercury has attracted an amazing number of big-name acts, running the gamut from folk to pop to noise, to its fairly small-time room. Past standouts: spoken-word artist Maggie Estep, Morphine, and Mary Lou Lord. A spectacular sound system attracts arbiters of hip to the nightly shows. Cover varies (cash only). Box office open M-Sa noon-7pm.

Roseland Ballroom, 239 W. 52nd St., between Broadway and Eighth Ave. (☎777-6800). Sizzling in the 40s as a swing dance hall, the ballroom is now a decently priced concert club featuring major-label Alt-rock and Hip-Hop. In the past year, Bob Dylan, Dave Mathews, Beck, Jamiroquai and many, many others have rocked this newly renovated space. Tickets $15-30.

Tonic, 107 Norfolk St. between Delancey and Rivington Sts. (☎358-7501; www.tonicnyc.com). This converted wine brewery is home to a small-sized performance space for avant-garde musicians (cover $6-12) and a downstairs lounge (DJ; no cover). In the lounge, wine barrels ten feet in diameter have been carved open and filled with chairs and couches for seating. Lounge open daily 9pm-3am. Evening performance times vary. Sunday brunch with $10 cover and a band.

CLASSICAL MUSIC

Musicians advertise themselves vigorously in New York City, so you should have no trouble finding the notes. Free recitals are common, especially in smaller spaces; just look in *Time Out* and *The Free Time* calendar ($2) for listings of priceless events.

LINCOLN CENTER

Lincoln Center, between Columbus and Amsterdam Aves. and W. 62nd and 66th Sts. (☎LIN-COLN; www.lincolncenter.org; Subway: 1, 9 to 66th St.; see **Sights,** p. 83) remains the great depot of New York's classical music establishment. Regular tickets are pricey, but student and rush rates exist for select performances. You can buy all Lincoln Center tickets through **CenterCharge.** (☎721-6500; open M-Sa 10am-8pm, Su noon-8pm) or online at www.lincolncenter.org. **Alice Tully Hall** box office hours are daily 11am to 6pm (opens Su at noon) and also until 30min. after the start of every performance. **Avery Fisher Hall** box office hours are daily 10am to 6pm (opens Su at noon) and 30min. after the start of every performance.

Chamber Symphony Orchestra, at Alice Tully Hall (☎875-5788; www.ChamberMusicSociety.org). Season Nov.-May. Most tickets $35; some $25 student tickets available.

Great Performers Series, at Alice Tully and Avery Fisher Halls, and some other locations. ☎875-5030 for Avery Fisher Hall events; ☎875-5050 for Alice Tully Hall events). A series that features quality classical music (with ticket prices to match), innovative programming, films, and occasional guests. Performers scheduled for 2002 include such luminaries as Anne Sofie von Otter (March), James Galway (March), and the American Symphony Orchestra (April and May). Tickets start at $28 for a series.

Mostly Mozart, at Alice Tully and Avery Fisher Halls (☎875-5030). A summer festival (end of July to Aug.) featuring a program its name suggests, performed by leading classical music performers–2001's program included Itzhak Perlman and the Emerson String Quartet, for instance. Tickets $15-52. A few free events. 50 tickets for every event are set aside for $10, available on the day of the event, at the box office.

National Chorale, at Avery Fisher Hall (☎333-5333). Choral music to make your soul soar. During the Christmas season, the Chorale puts on Handel's *Messiah;* in 2002, look also for a Bernstein and Sondheim performance on April 12 and Orff's *Carmina Burana* on May 17. Season Nov.-May. Tickets $21-83.

New York Philharmonic, at Avery Fisher Hall (☎875-5656; www.newyorkphilharmonic.org). Perhaps the country's best orchestra. Previous Philharmonic directors include Leonard Bernstein, Arturo Toscanini, and Leopold Stokowski; the current director is Kurt Masur. Season mid-Sept. to May. Tickets $10-60. On the day of select performances students can get $10 tickets. Come early or call ahead. Box office open M-F 10am-5pm.

VENUES ELSEWHERE

Carnegie Hall, Seventh Ave., at 57th St. (CarnegieCharge: ☎247-7800). Subway: N, R to 57th St.; B, D, E to Seventh Ave. The New York Philharmonic's original home is still the favorite coming-out locale of musical debutantes. Top soloists and chamber groups are booked regularly. Box office open M-Sa 11am-6pm, Su noon-6pm. Some shows have $10 rush tickets—call for information. See p. 76 for more information on the hall.

Frick Collection, 1 East 70th St., at Fifth Ave. (☎288-0700). From Sept. through May, the Frick Collection hosts free classical concerts Su 5pm (summer concerts in July and Aug.). Tickets limited to 2 per applicant; written requests must be received by the 3rd M before the concert, or show up 30min. before the show and try to steal seats of no-shows (see **Museums,** p. 113).

Metropolitan Museum of Art, 1000 Fifth Ave., at 82nd St. (☎570-3949). Subway: 4, 5, 6 to 86th St. The Met posts a schedule of performances covering the spectrum from traditional Japanese music and Russian balalaika to all-star classical music recitals Sept.-June. Call for more info. Chamber music in the bar and piano music in the cafeteria F-Sa evenings; free with museum admission (see **Museums,** p. 110).

FESTIVALS

Concerts in the Park, (☎875-5709; www.newyorkphilharmonic.org), in parks throughout the five boroughs and Long Island July-Aug. The Philharmonic plays magnificent outdoor concerts in parks during July. Concerts 8pm, followed by fireworks. Some (great) things in life *are* free.

Cooper-Hewitt Museum, 2 E. 91st St., at Fifth Ave. (☎849-8400; see **Museums,** p. 117). Subway: 4, 5, 6 to 86th St.; 6 to 96th St. Free Cross-Currents concert series brings everything from classical to hip-hop to the museum's garden from late June through July. Tu 6:30-8pm.

Museum of Modern Art, (☎708-9491; for more info see **Museums,** p. 111). "Summergarden," an contemporary classical music series, features Juilliard students performing in **Bryant Park**, behind the New York Public Library. Sponsored by MoMA, this series used to be held in their sculpture garden prior to renovations. July and Aug. F-Sa at 6pm. Free.

MUSIC SCHOOLS

Visiting a music school promises low cost and high quality music—a panacea for a weary budget traveler's soul. Except for opera and ballet productions ($5-12), concerts at the following schools are free and frequent, especially during the school year (Sept.-May): the **Mannes College of Music,** 150 W. 85th St. (☎580-0210), between Columbus and Amsterdam Ave.; the **Manhattan School of Music,** 122 Broadway (☎749-2802); and the **Bloomingdale School of Music,** 323 W. 108th St. (☎663-6021), near Broadway. The **Juilliard School of Music,** at Lincoln Center (☎769-7406; www.juilliard.edu), is New York's most prominent music school, and its **Paul Recital Hall** hosts free student recitals almost daily Sept.-May. Alice Tully Hall holds larger student recitals, also free, most W Sept.-May at 1pm. Orchestral recitals, faculty performances, chamber music, and dance and theater events take place regularly at Juilliard and never cost more than $10.

OPERA

Dicapo Opera Company, at the Dicapo Opera Theater, 184 East 76th St., between Third and Lexington Aves. (☎288-9438). This east side opera company has been earning critical acclaim and standing ovations at every performance—it's easy to understand why tickets go very quickly (usually around $40, senior discounts available). The 2001-2002 season has the company putting on four operas, each for approximately a week and a half.

The Metropolitan Opera Company, at the Lincoln Center's Metropolitan Opera House (☎362-6000; www.metopera.org). North America's premier opera outfit, performing on a stage as big as a football field. Artistic Director James Levine directs the likes of Luciano Pavarotti, Bryn Terfel, and Placido Domingo in new productions and favorite repertory classics. Regular tickets run upwards of $250, so go for the upper balcony at around $50–the cheapest seats have an obstructed view. You can stand in the orchestra ($16) along with the opera buffs who've brought along the score, or all the way back in the Family Circle ($12). Season Sept.-Apr. M-Sa; box office open M-Sa 10am-8pm, Su noon-6pm. In summer, call for info on free park concerts.

The New York City Opera, at the New York State Theater, Lincoln Center (☎870-5630; 496-0600 for tickets). It may not be the juggernaut that the Met Opera is, but this smaller opera company has come into its own under the direction of Christopher Keene, general director since 1989, gaining a reputation for inventive programming. City now has a split season (Sept.-Nov. and Mar.-Apr.), and keeps its ticket prices low year-round ($25-92). Call M to check the availability of $10 rush tickets, then wait in line the next morning. Box office open M 10am-7:30pm, Tu-Sa 10am-8:30pm, Su 11:30am-7:30pm.

DANCE

COMPANIES

American Ballet Theater, at the Metropolitan Opera House, Lincoln Center (☎477-3030; box office ☎362-6000). The company founded by George Balanchine and now run by former premier danseur Peter Martins puts on the opulent classics of ballet such as *Swan Lake* and *Sleeping Beauty.* They also perform some more contemporary works by established modern choreographers like Twyla Tharp. Tickets $17-75; available at the box office.

De La Guarda, at the Daryl Roth Theater, 20 Union Sq. East, at 15th St. (☎239-6200; www.delaguardaonline.com). Think disco in the rain forest with an air show overhead. In a nutshell, that's De la Guarda, an Argentinian performance art troupe whose shows are perpetually sold out. Tickets ($45-50) are standing room only, and a limited number are sold for $20 two hours before each show. Box office open Tu-Th 1pm-8:15pm, F 1pm-10:30pm, Sa 1pm-10pm, Su 1pm-7:15pm.

New York City Ballet, at the New York State Theater, Lincoln Center (☎870-5570; www.nycballet.com). The company's most critically acclaimed works have been the more modern pieces like *Serenade and Apollo,* but they are most famous for that New York Christmas tradition–George Balanchine's staging of **The Nutcracker** (late Nov. to New Year's Eve), replete with a one-ton Christmas tree. Reserve early for this classic. Season Nov.-Feb. and May-June. Tickets $16-88. Tickets can be purchased at the NY State Theater.

Theater District

Waiting For Tickets

Swing 46

VENUES

Dance Theater Workshop, 219 W. 19th St. between Seventh and Eighth Aves. (☎924-0077; www.dtw.org). Subway: 1, 9 to 18th St. Supports emerging dancers. Also hosts innovative dance performances throughout the year. Students get 1/3 off regular ticket prices for most shows. Box office open M-F 10am-6pm.

Joyce Theater, 175 Eighth Ave. between 18th and 19th Sts. (☎242-0800; www.joyce.org). Subway: 1, 9 to 18th St. *The* place to go for modern dance, the Joyce runs energetic, eclectic programming year-round. If you are in the city for a while it may be worth it to buy a series of tickets to get a 40% discount. Such companies as the Parsons, Les Ballet Trockadero, and Pilobolus have all staged stints at the Joyce. Tickets $25-40. Box office open M-F noon-7pm, Sa noon-1pm and 2:30-7pm, Su noon-6pm; hours differ slightly in the winter.

Mark Morris Dance Center, 3 Lafayette Ave. (☎718-624-8400). One of America's leading dance troupes finally has a permanent space to call home, right next to the Brooklyn Academy of Music. Morris is a Brooklyn boy, and this is his return home.

Thalia Spanish Theater, 41-17 Greenpoint Ave., between 41st and 42nd Sts., in Sunnyside, Queens (☎718-729-3880; www.thaliatheatre.org). Subway: 7 to 40th St./Lowery St. Dedicated to the arts of Spanish-speaking cultures. Their dance performances are exquisite, and the theater was showcasing these dance forms long before they became popular. The mid-Nov. to Feb. season brings flamenco. In spring and summer, Thalia heats it up with Tango Tango and theater pieces. Shows usually Th-Su evenings. Plays in English W-Th 8pm, Sa 3pm; in Spanish F-Sa 8pm, Su 4pm. Dance performances Th-F 8pm, Sa 3pm and 8pm, Su 4pm. Tickets $20, students $18.

FESTIVALS AND SEASONAL EVENTS

Dances for Wave Hill, W. 249th St. and Independence Ave., at Wave Hill in the Bronx (☎718-549-3200). Six annual performances in July, inspired by the Wave Hill landscape. Free with admission to Wave Hill. $4, students and seniors $2, under 6 and members free.

PARTICIPATORY EVENTS

Midsummer Night Swing, outdoors in Lincoln Center Plaza, (☎875-5766; www.lincolncenter.org). For the past two decades, some of the best names in jazz, big band, swing, Latin, and even line dancing have been coming to play at this exuberant month-long (late June to July) happening. Come with or without a partner to dance the night away, see couples swishing around you, or merely to take in the ambience. If access to the plaza dance floor is sold out, you can strut your stuff (along with other hapless dancing feet) anywhere on the plaza. Tickets go on sale at the plaza at 5:45pm, but the line often begins at 5pm. Dancing 8-11pm; free lessons 6:30pm. Tickets $12 (cash only); 6-night pass $62.

Dancing on the Plaza, at Dana Discovery Center, Fifth Ave. and 110th St, in Central Park (☎860-1370). Free dancing under the stars to the sounds of salsa, classic disco, swing, and ballroom every Th in Aug. 6-8:30pm. The first 45min. are devoted to lessons for the toe-tied.

Warm Up, at P.S.1, 22-25 Jackson Ave. in Long Island City. (☎718-784-2084; www.ps1.org). Summer Saturdays seem slow? This popular showcase of DJs in P.S.1's outdoor courtyard should slake your thirst for dancing. For those who prefer others to do the dancing, dance performances in the museum begin at 6pm. Runs 3-9pm. Admission $5.

FILM

Typical movie theaters showing big box office hits are easy to find in the city. Just look in any paper. The following listings are for theaters where you may find something special.

American Museum of the Moving Image, 35th Ave., at 36th St., Astoria, Queens (☎718-784-0077; www.ammi.org; see **Museums,** p. 116). Three full theaters showing everything from silent classics to retrospectives of great directors. Free with admission to museum: $8.50, seniors and students $5.50, children under 12 $4.50. Screenings Sa-Su; call for hours.

Angelika Film Center, 18 W. Houston St., at Mercer St. (☎995-2000; box office 995-2570). "K" is for *Kultur:* 6 screens of alternative, independent, and foreign cinema. Show up early on weekends; tickets frequently sell out far in advance. $10, seniors and under 12 $6.

Anthology Film Archives, 32 Second Ave., at E. 2nd St. (☎505-5181; www.anthologyfilmarchives.org). Housed in what used to be the Second Avenue Courthouse, the AFA is a forum for independent films, focusing on the contemporary, offbeat, and avant-garde, chosen from both US and foreign productions. The AFA hosts the annual **New York Underground Film Festival** (Mar.) and **Mix Festival** (Nov.), a les-bi-gay film festival. Tickets $8, students and seniors $5, children under 12 $2.

Cinema Classics, 332 E. 11th St. between First and Second Ave. (☎677-5368; www.cinemaclassics.com). By day it may seem like your standard East Village cafe, but by night the screenings of arthouse films attract cineastes from all over. (Screenings around 8pm and 10pm; $5.50). Coffee $1.75-3.50. If you'd rather watch films in your own home, there's an attached video store (open M-F 11:30am-7:30pm, Sa noon-6pm).

Cinema Village, 22 E. 12th St. between University Pl. and Fifth Ave. (☎924-3363). Features independent documentaries and hard-to-find foreign films. Great seats that lean back. $8.50, students $6.50, children and seniors $5.50.

Film Forum, 209 W. Houston St. between Sixth Ave. and Varick St. (☎727-8110). Three screens with a strong selection in classics, foreign films, documentaries, and independent films. $9, seniors $5 (M-F before 5pm).

Millennium Film Workshop, 66 E. 4th St. between Bowery and Second Ave. (☎673-0090; www.millenniumfilm.org). Subway: F to Second Ave. More than just a theater, this media arts center presents an extensive program of experimental film and video Sept.-June and offers classes and workshops on various aspects of film-making. Also has equipment available for use. Tickets $7. Gallery open M-W and F 7-10:30pm, Sa 1-5pm.

Museum of Modern Art: Roy and Niuta Titus Theaters, 11 W. 53rd St. between Fifth and Sixth Aves (☎708-9480; see **Museums,** p. 111). The MoMA shows a great selection of films daily in its lower-level theater. Film tickets are included in the price of admission and are available upon request. Also ask about screenings in the video gallery on the 3rd floor.

New York Public Libraries: For a real deal, check out a library, any library. All show free films: documentaries, classics, and last year's blockbusters. Screening times may be a bit erratic, but you can't beat the price. (For complete info on New York libraries, see **Service Directory,** p. 282.)

Walter Reade Theater, 165 W. 65th St., at Lincoln Center (☎875-5600; box office 875-5601; www.filmlinc.com). Subway: 1, 9 to 66th St. New York's performing arts octopus flexes yet another cultural tentacle with this theater next to the Juilliard School. Foreign and critically acclaimed independent films dominate. Tickets $9, seniors $4.50 at weekday matinees, 'movies for kids' $3. Box office open daily 30min. before start of first film, closes 15min. after start of last show.

Ziegfeld, 141 W. 54th St. between Sixth and Seventh Aves. (☎765-7600). One of the largest screens left in America, showing first-run films. A must-visit for big-screen aficionados. Consult local newspapers for complete listings. $9.75; $6.25 for seniors and under 11. Not handicap accessible.

FESTIVALS

Bryant Park Film Festival, at Bryant Park, between 40th and 42nd Sts. and Sixth Ave. (☎512-5700). Subway: B, D, F, 7 to 42nd St. Running from late June to August, this free outdoor series features classic revivals such as *Rear Window, Dr. Zhivago,* and *An American in Paris*. Movies begin Mondays at sunset; rain date Tuesday nights.

Living on the Edge, at Socrates Sculpture Park, Vernon Blvd. at Broadway (☎718-956-1819; www.socratessculpturepark.org). A series of films from various cultures, preceded by musical performances and food from neighborhood restaurants. Performances start 7:30pm; movies start at sunset. Runs W evenings; mid-July to mid-Aug.

New York Video Festival, at Walter Reade Theater in Lincoln Center (☎496-3809; www.filmlinc.com). Runs in mid-July. Tickets $9, seniors $4.50 at weekday matinees.

LIVE TELEVISION

Late Show with David Letterman (CBS), at the Ed Sullivan Theater, 1697 Broadway, at 53rd St. (☎975-1003). The cuddly-yet-acerbic host performs his antics in front of a studio audience. If you are lucky enough to get tickets, bring a sweater–the studio is notoriously cold. Order tickets for his *Late Show* well in advance by writing: Late Show Tickets, 1697 Broadway, NY, NY 10019.

Tapings are M-Th 5:30pm and another Th 8pm. For standby tickets on the day of the show, call 247-6497 at 11am on tape days (M-Th). Tickets are no longer given out at the theater.

Late Night with Conan O'Brien (NBC), at the G.E. Building in Rockefeller Center. (☎664-3056). Tapings Tu-F 5:30-6:30pm. To order in advance call or send a postcard to NBC Tickets, 30 Rockefeller Plaza, NY, NY 10012. You may receive up to 4 tickets at a time, but must book a month and a half in advance. Standby tickets also available tape days (Tu-F) at 9am at the 49th St. entrance, but you must show up at 4:15pm to see if there is enough room. Note: A standby ticket does not guarantee admission. Active in summer. Must be 16 or older.

Saturday Night Live (NBC), at the G.E. Building in Rockefeller Center. (☎664-3056). *SNL* goes on hiatus June-Aug. and only accepts ticket requests in Aug. Order tickets by sending a postcard to Rockefeller Plaza (see **Conan,** above). Warning: they don't accept requests for a specific date and only award two tickets per household. Standby: get in line on the mezzanine level of Rockefeller Center (49th St. side) at 9:15 am the morning of the show (for dress rehearsal or live show). One standby ticket per person, with no guaranteed admission. You must be at least 16. Don't hold your breath.

Rosie O'Donnell (NBC), at the G.E. Building in Rockefeller Center. (☎664-3056). Send postcards March-June to NBC Tickets at Rockefeller Plaza (see **Conan,** above). A completely random lottery cares not for your desired dates or number of tickets (they award two per household). Standby tickets, available at 7:30am taping days (M-Th, Sa), are also based on a lottery (read: you don't have to break your neck to get in line by 4am) from 30 Rockefeller Plaza. Ages 6-16 must be accompanied by adult.

The Today Show (NBC), at the corner of 49th St. and Rockefeller Plaza. If you're up between weekdays 7-10am, go look into the windows of this morning news show.

Live with Regis and Kelly (ABC), 67th St. and Columbus Ave. (☎456-3537). Send a postcard with name, address, phone number, approximate date of show you'd like to attend and your request for up to 4 tickets to: Live Tickets, Ansonia Station, P.O. Box 230-777, NY, NY 10023. Expect a year-long wait. For standby tickets, line up at the corner of 67th St. and Columbus Ave. at 7am or earlier on weekdays. Must be 10 or older.

The Daily Show (Comedy Central), 513 W. 54th St. (☎586-2477). Call for tickets. The show tapes from M-Th. Doors open at 5:45pm. Must be 18 or older.

SPORTS

SPECTATOR SPORTS

BASEBALL

Founded in 1903, the vaunted **New York Yankees** (team of Joe DiMaggio, Whitey Ford, Mickey Mantle, Babe Ruth, and Lou Gehrig) are baseball's most storied franchise. Possessing 26 World championships and 36 American League Championships, they have won more championships than any other team in American sports. The Bombers, as they're affectionately known, are led by graceful centerfielder Bernie Williams, matinee idol shortstop Derek Jeter, and intense veteran pitcher Roger Clemens. The team plays ball at **Yankee Stadium** in the South Bronx. (☎718-293-4300. Subway: 4, B, D to Yankee Stadium.) The Yankees have won three straight World Series. As this book goes to press, everyone waits hopefully for a fourth consecutive championship in 2001. (Tickets usually available day of the game; $8 to $30; you can also find them on the web at www.tix.com.)

Created in 1962 to replace the much-mourned Giants and Dodgers (who had moved to California in 1958), the **New York Mets** (short for "Metropolitans") set the still-unbroken major league record for losses in a season during their first year. Seven years later, the "Miracle Mets" captured the World Series. Although the Mets won again in 1986, they quickly wound up deep in the cellar, spawning a David Letterman catchphrase: "We're so close to spring you can almost hear the Mets suck." In 2000, however, the Mets made it to the World Series, where they met their crosstown rivals, the Yanks. The Mets lost. Perhaps feeling the repercussions of defeat, the team has struggled in 2001, despite the efforts of star catcher Mike Piazza. Watch them go to bat at Shea Stadium in Queens. (☎718-507-6387. Subway: 7 to Willets Point/Shea Stadium. Tickets $13-30.)

SUBWAY SERIES. The two teams face off every summer in the popular Subway Series. The Yanks took the 2001 season series 4-2. The actual subways involved in the Subway Series? From the Willets Pt.-Shea Stadium station, take the 7 train to 42nd St.-Grand Central Terminal, and transfer to the uptown 4 train to 161st St.-Yankee Stadium.

BASKETBALL

Although they've been unable to regain the heights of their 1969 Championship Season, the New York Knickerbockers (usually referred to as the **Knicks**) are still a force in the NBA. Led by the tandem of Allan Houston and Latrell Sprewell, the Knicks do their dribbling at **Madison Square Garden** (☎465-5867) from early November to late April. Tickets, which start at $22, are fairly hard to come by unless you order well in advance. On the **collegiate level,** the Garden plays host to Big East Conference contender St. John's Red Storm during the winter and the NIT and Big East tournaments in March. Also playing at the Garden are the **New York Liberty** (☎564-9622) of the Women's National Basketball Association (WNBA). Season June-Aug. Tickets start at $8.

FOOTBALL

Both New York teams play across the Hudson at **Giants Stadium** in East Rutherford, New Jersey. The **Giants** surprised the entire football world when they captured the NFC title in 2000, only to lose in the Super Bowl to the Baltimore Ravens. Over the past 20 years, the Giants's strength has been their linebacking corps and defensive line. What will determine the team's fate in 2001 is their offense, quarterbacked by Kerry Collins. Tickets are nigh impossible to get—season ticket holders have booked them all for the next 40 years, and the waiting list names over 15,000 people. See *Let's Go: New York City 2042* for details. Make friends with a fan, or try any local sports bar for the best view of the action you're likely to get. The **Jets** had a subpar 2000 season, but hope to change their fortunes in 2001, led by quarterback Vinny Testaverde, scrappy wide receiver Wayne Chrebet, and hard-working running back Curtis Martin. (Tickets start at $25; cash only at the Meadowlands box office.) The season begins in early September and runs to early January.

HOCKEY

In a town known for its speed and turbulence, it's not hard to understand why New Yorkers attend hockey games with such fervor. The **New York Rangers** hit the ice at **Madison Square Garden** (MSG ☎465-6741; Rangers ☎308-6977) from October to April. After enduring 54 championship-less years, the Rangers finally captured the

Swing 46

Carnegie Hall

Joyce Theater

Stanley Cup in June 1994. Since that time, the Rangers have been stuck in a rut of mediocrity, but that hasn't hurt attendance. (Ticket on sale Aug. They start at $25; reserve well in advance.) Similarly, after winning four consecutive Stanley Cups in the early 1980s, the so-called "Dynasty Years," the **New York Islanders** are one of the few teams worse than the Rangers. They hang their skates at the **Nassau Coliseum** in Uniondale, Long Island. (☎516-794-9300. Season also runs Oct.-Apr. Tickets $27-70.) For some good hockey, head to **Continental Arena** to see the **New Jersey Devils,** Stanley Cup winners in 2000 and runner-ups in 2001 (☎201-507-8900).

SOCCER

Buoyed by swelling youth interest and the 1994 World Cup in the US, soccer has undergone a meteoric rise in popularity in the past few years, culminating in the start of a new American league, **Major League Soccer.** Since the league's inception in 1996, New Yorkers have been turning out to see the **New York/New Jersey Metrostars** play at **Giants Stadium.** (☎888-4-METROTIX/463-8768. Season late Mar. to early Sept. Tickets $15-30.)

TENNIS

Tennis enthusiasts who get their tickets three months in advance can attend the prestigious **US Open,** one of tennis's four Grand Slam events, held in late August and early September at the United States Tennis Association's (USTA) Tennis Center in Flushing Meadows Park, Queens. (☎718-760-6200. Tickets $33-69. On sale by early June; call 888-673-6849 to buy.) The **Chase Championship,** formerly the Virginia Slims, featuring the world's top women players, comes to Madison Square Garden in mid-November, 2000, for its last year. (☎465-6741. Tickets for opening rounds $20-50, final rounds $35-80.)

HORSERACING

Forsake the rat race for some equine excitement. Fans can watch the stallions at **Belmont Park** (☎718-641-4700) Wednesday to Sunday, May through July and September to mid-October, and may even catch a grand slam event. The **Belmont Stakes,** run the first Saturday in June, is one leg in the Triple Crown. ("Belmont Special" train leaves Penn Station twice per day. $8 round-trip, includes $1 off admission.) The **Aqueduct Racetrack,** near JFK Airport (☎718-641-4700), has races from late October to early May, also Wednesday through Sunday. (Subway: A to Aqueduct.) Grandstand seating at both tracks $2. Racing in New York is suspended during August, when the action goes upstate to Saratoga.

THE NEW YORK CITY MARATHON

On the first Sunday in November, two million spectators line rooftops, sidewalks, and promenades to cheer 22,000 runners in the **New York City Marathon** (16,000 racers actually finish). The race begins on the Verrazano Bridge and ends at Central Park's Tavern on the Green. Call the NY Roadrunner's Club (☎860-4455) for info on signing up.

PARTICIPATORY SPORTS

Whether trying to slim down at the health club or commuting to work via bicycle, endless amateur and recreational athletes twist and flex in New York. Although space in much of the city is at a premium, the **City of New York Parks and Recreation Department** (☎800-201-PARK/7275 for a recording of park events) manages to maintain numerous playgrounds and parks in all boroughs, for everything from baseball and basketball to croquet and shuffleboard.

BEACHES

Manhattan Beach (¼ mi.-long), on the Atlantic Ocean. Ocean Ave. to Mackenzie St. in Brooklyn (☎718-946-1373). Subway: D to Brighton Beach; then bus B1.

Orchard Beach and Promenade (1¼ mi.-long), in Pelham Bay Park, Bronx (☎718-885-2275). Subway: 6 to Pelham Bay Park; then bus Bx5 (summer weekends only) or Bx12 (summer only) to Orchard Beach. A sandy strip facing Long Island Sound, Orchard Beach gets mobbed on hot summer days. Snack stands satiate the sun-seeking throngs. Lifeguards keep watch between Memorial Day to Labor Day (daily 10am-7pm).

Rockaway Beach and Boardwalk (7½ mi.-long), on the Atlantic Ocean (☎718-318-4000). Lifeguards Memorial Day-Labor Day daily 10am-6pm. Subway: A or S between Beach 36th St. and Rockaway Park-Beach 116th St. stations. See **Sights,** p. 100.

Staten Island: South Beach, Midland Beach, and **Franklin D. Roosevelt Boardwalk** (2½ mi.-long), on Lower New York Bay. South Beach is touted one of NYC's "best beaches," and offers spectacular views of the Narrows. Bus S51 from the ferry terminal.

POOLS

Some of the city's nicer public pools include **John Jay Pool** (☎794-6566), east of York Ave. at 77th St., and **Asser Levy Pool** (☎447-2020), at 23rd St. and Asser Levy Pl. (next to the East River). All outdoor pools are open early July through Labor Day, 11am or noon to 7pm, depending on the weather. Both pools listed above are free, although the latter's heated indoor pool is open only to members. Call 800-201-PARK/7275 for other locations.Indoor pools can be somewhat safer than outdoor pools, but most require some sort of annual membership fee ($10 or more).

BASKETBALL

Basketball is one of New York's favorite pastimes. Courts can be found in parks and playgrounds all over the city, and most are frequently occupied. **Pickup basketball** games can also be found in various parts of the city, each with its own rituals, rulers, and degree of intensity. **The Cage,** at W. 4th and Sixth Ave., is home to some of the city's best amateur players: rumor has it that scouts for college and pro teams occasionally drop by incognito to ferret out new talent. Other pickup spots worth checking out (if you're any good) include **Central Park, 96th and Lexington Ave., Tompkins Square Park,** and **76th and Columbus Ave.**

BICYCLING

From spring to fall, daily at dawn and dusk and throughout the weekend, packs of dedicated (and spandex-ed) cyclists navigate the trails and wide roads of **Central Park.** The circular drive is car-free Monday-Thursday 10am-3pm and 7-10pm, Friday 10am-3pm, and Friday 7pm until Monday 6am. On the West Side between 72nd and 110th Sts., along the Hudson bank, **Riverside Park** draws more laid-back riders. Other excellent places to cycle on the weekends include the deserted **Wall Street** area and the unadorned roads of Brooklyn's **Prospect Park.** If you must leave your bike unattended, use a strong "U" lock. Thieves laugh at (then cut through) chain locks. Don't leave quick-release items unattended; you will find them very quickly released.

Loeb Boathouse, mid-park at 75th St., in Central Park (☎861-4137; 717-9048). 3-speeds $8 per hr., 10-speeds $10, tandems $15. Valid ID and $100 cash or credit card deposit required. Open Apr.-Sept. daily 10am-5pm, weather permitting.

Metro Bicycle Stores, Lexington Ave. at 88th St. (☎427-4450). Seven convenient locations throughout the city. Entry-level mountain bikes and hybrids. $7 per hr., $35 per day, $45 overnight. Daily rentals due back 30min. before store closes and overnight rentals next day at 10am. $250 cash or credit card deposit and valid ID required. Helmet rental $2.50 per bike. Open F-Tu 9:30am-6:30pm, W-Th 9:30am-7:30pm.

Pedal Pushers, 1306 Second Ave. between 68th and 69th Sts. (☎288-5592). The best rates in the city. 3-speeds $4 per hr., $10 per day, $12 overnight; 10-speeds $5 per hr., $14 per day, $14 overnight; mountain bikes $6 per hr., $17 per day, $25 overnight. Overnight rentals require $150 deposit on a major credit card, but regular rentals only need major credit card, passport, or a NY state driver's license deposit. Open F-M 10am-6pm, W 10am-7pm, Th 10am-8pm. Rent a helmet for an extra $2 per day.

RUNNING

When running in **Central Park** during no-traffic hours (see **Bicycling,** above), stay in the right-hand runners' lane to avoid being mowed down by reckless pedal-pushers. **Stay in populated areas and stay out of the park after dark.** Recommended courses include the 1.58mi. jaunt around the Reservoir (between 84th and 96th Sts.) and a picturesque 1.72 mi. route along West Dr., starting at Tavern on the Green, heading south to East Dr., and circling back west on 72nd St. Another beautiful place to run is **Riverside Park,** which stretches along the Hudson River bank from 72nd to 116th St.; **don't stray too far north.** For information on running clubs, clinics, and racing events around the city, call the **New York Roadrunner's Club,** 9 E. 89th St. between Madison and Fifth Aves. (☎860-4455). They host races in Central Park on summer weekends.

IN-LINE SKATING

For speed on wheels, there are many in-line skate rental locations throughout the city. For low prices and convenience, **Blades** (☎888-55-Blades) has over eight stores in the Metropolitan area. (Open M-Sa 11am-8pm, Su 11am-6pm. Flat rate $20; includes all protective gear. $200 deposit or credit is required.) In addition, Blades also has various sister stores that feature the same prices and conditions, like **Peck and Goodie Skates,** 917 Eighth Ave. (☎246-6123), between 54th and 55th St., where they'll also hold your shoes while you whiz past your favorite New York sights. They also offer private lessons for a fee of $40/hr. (open M-Sa 10am-8pm, Su 10am-6pm). Good places to skate in the city include **Battery Park, West Street** between Christopher to Horatio Sts., **Chelsea Piers, East River Promenade** between 60th and 81st St., and **Central Park,** which has several roller zones, including the Outer Loop, a slalom course near Tavern on the Green.

BOWLING

For some quality ten-pin, head to **Bowlmor Lanes,** 110 University Pl., near 13th St. where you'll find bowling, music, and alcohol all in one place. Watch your game deteriorate as you knock a couple back. (☎255-8188. Imported beer $6-7, domestic $5. Open Tu-W 10am-1am, Th 10am-2am, F 10am-4am, Sa 11am-4am, Su 11am-1am. Shoe rental $4. M-Th and F before 5pm $6 per person per game, after 5pm F and all day Sa-Su, rates increase $1. After 6pm, becomes 21+).

GOLF

Although New York golf courses don't measure up to those at Pebble Beach, New Yorkers remain avid golfers, jamming all of the 13 well-manicured city courses during the weekends. Most are found in the Bronx or Queens, including **Pelham Bay Park** (☎718-885-1258), **Van Cortlandt Park** (☎718-543-4595), and **Forest Park** (☎718-296-0999). Greens fees are approximately $11-20 for NYC residents and $17-26 for non-NYC residents. Reserve at least one week in advance for summer weekends. Long

Island is home to some of the country's best public courses. **Bethpage** (☎516-249-7000) is home to five top-notch golf courses. The Black course is hosting the 2002 U.S. Open. On the eastern tip of Long Island is **Montauk Downs** (☎631-668-5000), which is among the top 50 public courses in the country.

ICE SKATING

The first gust of cold winter air brings out droves of aspiring Paul Wylies and Tara Lipinskis. While each of the rinks in the city has its own character, nearly all have lockers, skate rentals, and a snack bar.

Rockefeller Center, Fifth Ave. and 50th St. (☎332-7654). Famous and expensive sunken plaza that doubles as the chic American Festival Cafe during the warm months. Always crowded, with throngs of spectators around the outside edges. Call for prices.

Sky Rink, at W. 21st St. and the Hudson River (☎336-6100). Learn to skate or practice on one of the two full-sized indoor Olympic ice-skating rinks. Open M-F 4:30am-midnight, Sa 6am-1am, Su 8am-11:30pm. General skating times are M 12:30-2:20pm and 4-9:20pm, Tu 12:30-2:20pm and 4-5:20pm, W and F 12:30-2:20pm and 4-6pm, Th 4-6:30pm, Sa noon-6:50pm, and Su noon-5:50pm in summer; daily 11:30am-5:30pm in winter. Adults $11.50, children 12 and under and seniors $8. Skate rentals $5.

Wollman Memorial Rink (☎396-1010) is located in a particularly scenic section of Central Park, near 64th St. $15 for 2hr., $25 all day; includes helmet and pads; $100 deposit required.

HORSEBACK RIDING

Central Park horseback riding, for those well-versed in English equitation, operates out of **Claremont Stables,** 175 W. 89th St. (☎724-5100. Open M-F 6:30am-10pm, Sa-Su 6am-5pm. $45 per hr. Make reservations.) **Queens'** Forest Park has guided trail rides by **Dixie Dew Stables,** 88-11 70th Rd. (☎718-263-3500; www.dixie-dew.com. Subway J, Z to Woodhaven Blvd. Open M 8am-7pm; M, W, F last ride 4:30pm. $25 per hr.) **Lynne's Riding School,** 88-03 70th Rd. also offers guided trail rides in Forest Park. (☎718-261-7679. Subway: J, Z to Woodhaven Blvd. Open daily 9am-4pm; call and make an appointment. $25 per hr.)

CLIMBING

You can climb to your heart's content in the center of Manhattan at the **ExtraVertical Climbing Center** in the Harmony Atrium, 61 W. 62nd St.; no experience necessary. (☎586-5382. Day pass $16, students $12, challenge climbs $9 for 2, equipment rental $6; lessons $55-110; monthly passes $75, students $50. Open summer M-F 1-10pm, Sa 10am-10pm, Su noon-8pm; winter M-F 5-10pm, Sa 10am-10pm, Su noon-8pm.) In addition, **North Meadow Recreation Center,** mid-park at 97th St. in **Central Park,** offers 4-week courses for $200 per person. (☎348-4867 for reservations. Every Su 10am.)

ROWBOATS

You can rent them at the **Loeb Boathouse** in Central Park. (☎517-2233; 517-3623. Open daily Apr.-Sept. 10am-6pm, weather permitting. $10 per hr.; refundable $30 deposit.)

INSIDE

Gay New York

New York has been a major center for American gay life since the 19th century, when an open bohemian lifestyle flourished in Greenwich Village. During the 1920s and 30s, the fledgling community found its way uptown to Harlem, where the clubs were more tolerant and the scene vibrant and creative. Gay life throughout the mid-20th century was nonetheless an underground affair, existing in secret societies and private "bottle clubs." Persecution was common: gay establishments were routinely raided and their patrons harassed or arrested. It was during one such police raid of the Stonewall Inn in Greenwich Village, on June 27, 1969, that tensions erupted. In the now-legendary incident, the bar's transsexual, gay, and hustler patrons spontaneously fought the police as they were being led to the paddy-wagon. This singular act of rebellion ignited the community and set off four days of protest, as hundreds of gay men and lesbians took to the streets of NYC to combat injustice. The incident has since become known as the **Stonewall Riot,** and is often credited as the inspiration for the modern gay rights movement.

In the decades since Stonewall, the gay community of New York has grown into a vital and varied community, with a remarkable ability to celebrate itself and respond to adversity. In 1981, in the face of AIDS and the frustration associated with an excess of media hype and lack of helpful action, gay New Yorkers founded the **Gay Men's Health Crisis (GMHC),** the first medical organization dedicated to serving those with AIDS. When the political and medical establishment persisted in its silence about AIDS, activists formed **The AIDS Coalition to Unleash Power (ACT-Up),** a "leaderless" gay militant group whose aggressive actions have spurred the development of effective treatments for the disease and that continues to stage political events throughout the city and nation.

Gay pride is celebrated in late June every year, when hundreds of thousands turn out for the **Pride Parade,** which wends its way down Fifth Avenue and into Greenwich Village. This ecstatic event is jam-packed with juggling drag queens, jubilant confetti-tossers, and cheering throngs toting the banners of gay organizations as varied as the gay volleyball league to **Dykes on Bikes.** The scent of hair spray fills the air on Labor Day weekend during **Wigstock,** the day-long celebration of cross-dressing, during which New York's astounding variety of drag queens cinch, pad, and strut their stuff. (At Pier 54 in the West Village; ☎800-494-TIXS for tickets and information.)

Today, gay and lesbian neighborhoods thrive in New York. An established and well-heeled contingent still clusters around **Christopher Street** in the West Village (see p. 17), while the center of gay life has shifted uptown a few blocks to **Chelsea** (see p. 18). Here, buff men waltz from gym to juice-bar, and rainbow flags fly over dry cleaners and taxi dispatch centers. An edgier, often younger, group rocks out in the **East Village** on First and Second Avenues, south of East 12th Street (see p. 18). A large lesbian community in **Park Slope** has lent the neighborhood the moniker "Dyke Slope" (see p. 178).

RESOURCES AND SHOPS

The **Lesbian and Gay Community Services Center,** 208 W. 13th St. between Seventh and Eighth Aves. (☎620-7310; www.gaycenter.org), is a vast resource center which provides information and referral services and hosts myriad programs, groups, and social activities of interest to the gay community. The second largest lesbian, gay, bisexual and transgender community center in the world, this enormous hub provides space for 300 groups, 27 programs and facilitates over 5,000 visitors each week. (Subway: A, C, E, to 14th St. Open daily 9am-11pm.)

There are numerous **publications** dedicated to the gay and lesbian community of New York. *HomoXtra* (*HX* and *HX for Her*) and *Next* both have listings of nightlife and activities, and are available free at gay hangouts around the city. The free *LGNY* (no, that's not *Let's Go NY*, but *Lesbian-Gay NY*) and the *New York Blade News* are community broadsheets and are distributed throughout the boroughs. The nationally distributed *Advocate* magazine has a New York section; also check out the *Village Voice*, which details events, services, and occasional feature articles of interest to gays and lesbians. In addition, some **websites** will give you info that the printed rags don't reveal. Check out www.gmad.org, a resource for gay men of African descent, and www.pridelinks.com.

The helpful **Gayellow Pages,** P.O. Box 533, Village Station, New York, NY 10014 (☎674-0120; fax 420-1126; gayellowpages.com), has a special New York edition ($16) that lists accommodations, organizations, and services in the city.

HEALTH AND SUPPORT SERVICES

Callen-Lorde Community Health Center, 356 W. 18th St. between Eighth and Ninth Aves. (☎271-7200; www.callen-lorde.org). Subway: A, C, E to 14th St.; L to Eighth Ave. Comprehensive general health services for the queer community, plus counseling and a health resource department. Callen-Lorde offers a sliding-scale fee structure for individuals without insurance coverage, and no one is turned away. Open M 12:30-8pm, W 8:30am-1pm and 3-8pm, Tu and Th-F 9am-4:30pm.

Gay Men's Health Crisis (GMHC), 119 W. 24th St. between Sixth and Seventh Aves. (☎367-1000). Subway: 1, 9, F to 23rd St. Healthcare, support groups, physician referrals, and counseling for men and women with HIV and AIDS. Walk-in counseling M-F 11am-8pm. GMHC's **Geffen Center** provides confidential (not anonymous) HIV testing (☎367-1100). **Hotline:** ☎800-243-7692 or 807-6655 (open M-F 10am-9pm, Sa noon-3pm).

Gay and Lesbian Switchboard (☎989-0999; glnh.@glnh.org). Information, peer counseling, or referrals for the gay or lesbian traveler. Open M-F 6-10pm, Sa noon-5pm. 24hr. recording.

BOOKSTORES

Oscar Wilde Gay and Lesbian Bookshop, 15 Christopher St., at Sixth Ave. (☎255-8097). Subway: 1, 9 to Christopher St. This cozy shop claims to be the world's first gay and lesbian bookstore. In addition to a number of rare and first edition books, the store stocks a multitude of travel guides and magazines. Open M-Sa 11am-8pm, Su noon-7pm.

RELIGIOUS SERVICES

Church of St. Paul and St. Andrew, 86th St., at West End Ave. (☎362-3179). Subway: 1,9 to 86th St. United Methodist Church dating from 1897. Check out the octagonal tower and the angles in the spandrels. Gay-friendly services Su 11am.

Congregation Beth Simchat Torah, 57 Bethune St. (☎929-9498; www.cbst.org). Synagogue catering to the NY lesbian and gay community. Services F at 8pm at the **Church of the Holy Apostle,** at 9th Ave. and 28th St.

Metropolitan Community Church of New York, 446 W. 36th St. between 9th and 10th Sts. (☎629-7440). Subway: A, C, E to 34th St. This Christian Church has been serving the queer community for 26 years. Services Su 10am, 12:30pm (in Spanish), 7pm; and W 7pm.

ACCOMMODATIONS

If you're moving to New York and want help finding a gay, lesbian, bi- or transsexual roommate, it might be worthwhile to pay a visit to **Rainbow Roommates,** 268 W. 22nd St., between Seventh and Eighth Aves. (☎627-8612; www.rainbowroommates.com. Open M-Sa noon-6pm.) Rainbow Roommates provides you with a subscription to personalized listings matching the roommate criteria you have requested. Updates sent daily by e-mail or fax. Subscription $145 for three months, $165 for six months. You may also want to try **DG Neary Realty,** 57 W. 16th St., on the corner of Sixth Ave., which hosts "G.R.I.N."—the Gay Roommate Information Network. (☎627-4242; fax 989-1207. Registration fee $50. Open Su-F 10am-6pm.) Here are some more B, G, L, T accommodation options.

Colonial House Inn, 318 W. 22nd St. between Eighth and Ninth Aves. (☎800-689-3779 or 243-9669; fax 633-1612; houseinn@aol.com; www.colonialhouseinn.com). Subway: C, E to 23rd St. A very comfortable B&B in a classy Chelsea brownstone owned by Mel Cheren, former owner of legendary club Paradise Garage. All rooms have cable TV, A/C, and phone; some have bath and fireplace. Sun deck with a "clothing optional" area. 24hr. desk and concierge. Continental breakfast included, and served in a lounge/art gallery. Check-in 2pm. Check-out noon. Reservations are encouraged and require two nights' deposit within 10 days of reservation. Double bed "economy" room $80-99; queen-size bedroom $99-125, with private bath and fridge $125-140.

Chelsea Pines Inn, 317 W. 14th St. between Eighth and Ninth Aves. (☎929-1023; fax 620-5646; cpiny@aol.com; www.chelseapinesinn.com). Subway: A, C, E to 14th St.; L to Eighth Ave. This fabulous gay-owned and operated inn is a friendly, amenity-laden haven of rooms decorated with vintage film posters. Gorgeous garden and "greenhouse" out back. A/C, cable TV, phone with answering machine, refrigerator, and showers in all rooms. 3-day min. stay on weekends. Continental breakfast included, with fresh homemade bread. Reservations are essential. Rooms with private showers and shared toilet $99-169; with queen-size bed and private bath $129-189, with queen-size bed, private bath, day bed, stereos and breakfast area $139-199. $20 for extra person. AmEx, D, MC, V.

Dancing the Night Away

Cowboy Gear

Disco

Incentra Village House, 32 Eighth Ave. between W. 12th and Jane Sts. (☎206-0007; fax 604-0625). Subway: A, C, E to 14th St. Lovely brick landmark townhouse, built in 1941, with a cozy double Victorian parlor, antique furnishings, and a 1930s baby grand piano. Most rooms have fireplace and kitchenette. Profits are held in a trust benefiting various AIDS service organizations. Check-in 2pm. Check-out noon. Reservations encouraged. Studios: single $99, double $149, triple $179, quad $209; suites: single $129, double $179, triple $209, quad $239.

HANGOUTS AND RESTAURANTS

For general restaurant information, see **Food,** p. 129. For restaurants with a largely gay crowd, one need not look farther than any of the well-adorned restaurants on Eighth Avenue between 14th and 23rd Sts.

Food Bar, 149 Eighth Ave. (☎243-2020). A sharply dressed, almost all-male crowd populates this popular, very chic gay hangout. Features tasty, relatively cheap sandwiches ($6.50-7.50) and large-portioned entrees ($7-12). Chic, minimalist decor. Open M-Th 11am-4pm and 5-11:30pm, F 11am-4pm and 5pm-midnight, Sa 5pm-midnight, Su 5-11:30pm. **$-$$**

Big Cup, 228 Eighth Ave. between 21st and 22nd Sts. (☎206-0059). Bright, campy colors and comfy velvet chairs make this a great place to curl up with a cup of joe ($1.30) and wink at cute Chelsea boys. Sandwiches $6.50. Open M-Th 7am-1am, F-Sa 8am-2am, Su 8am-1am.

Caffe Raffaella, 134 Seventh Ave S., north of Christopher St. (☎929-7247). This unpretentious old-world style cafe serves Italian food to a largely gay, male clientele. This intimate, unpretentious place is famous for their delightful desserts and delicious eye-candy. Sip steamed milk with *orzata* (sweet almond syrup, $3) while reclining in the embrace of an overstuffed chair. Sandwiches $6.50-9; pizza $8-10; crepes ($7-8); cakes and pastries ($4-5). Open daily 10am-2am.

Lips, 2 Bank St., at Greenwich Ave. (☎675-7710). Italian-Continental cuisine with a sassy twist. Impromptu performances from a high-heeled staff in a room festooned with lips. What more could a boy dressed as a girl want? Try the Rupaul for dinner ($14) or the Miss Understood to start ($7.50). Entrees $12-22. Open Su-Th 5:30pm-midnight, F-Sa 5:30pm-2am; Su brunch 11:30am-4pm.

NIGHTLIFE

Following is a list of clubs (some of them dance-oriented, others geared toward conversation and drinking) at the center of gay and lesbian nightlife. Some of these clubs are geared exclusively toward lesbians or gay men, and may frown on letting in hopefuls of the opposite sex. If you and a friend of the opposite sex want to go to any of these clubs together, it might be wise to avoid behaving like a heterosexual couple, especially in front of the bouncer. To find out where the next dance party is being held, lesbians should call the **Sheescape Danceline** (☎686-5665). **Her/She Bar** (☎631-1093 or 631-1102) and **Lovergirl** (☎631-1000) also throw female fetes; call to find out current locations. Also keep in mind **Hot: The NYC Celebration of Queer Culture,** Vineyard 26, 309 E. 26th St., at Dixon Pl. (☎532-1546; www.dixonplace.org.) In addition, there is always a great deal of excellent **gay theater** off-off- and off-Broadway, and the **New York Gay and Lesbian Film Festival** opens its celluloid closet every year in June (keep your eyes peeled in *HX*, *Next*, and the *Village Voice* for listings).

GREENWICH VILLAGE AND BELOW

Bar d'O, 29 Bedford St. (☎627-1580). Subway: 1, 9 to Christopher St. A cozy, sultry-lit lounge. Superb performances by drag divas Joey Arias and Raven O (Tu and Sa-Su nights 10:30pm, $5). Even without the fine chanteuses, this is a damn fine place for a drink. M night is "Pleasure" for women. The bar packs a glam night of drag kings. Go early for the atmosphere, around midnight for the performances, and 2am to people-watch/gender-guess. Don't try to leave in the middle of a show, or you'll be in for a nasty tongue-lashing. Cover $3. Opens at 10pm.

Stonewall, 53 Christopher St. (☎463-0950). Subway: 1, 9 to Christopher St. Legendary bar of the Stonewall Riots (see p. 193). Join the lively and diversified crowd in this recently renovated bar to toast the brave drag queens who fought back. Upstairs, the Club at Stonewall has a dance floor. 2-for-1 Happy Hour M-F 3-9pm. $2 frozen margaritas Sa-Su 2:30-9pm. Open daily 2:30pm-4am.

International Student Identity Card
STUDENT
Stanford University
Gonzalez, Julie
27/09/81
09/2001-12/2002
ISIC

Henrietta Hudson, 438 Hudson St. between Morton and Barrow Sts. (☎243-9079). Subway: 1, 9 to Christopher St. A young, clean-cut lesbian crowd presides at this neighborhood bar. Mellow in the afternoon, jam-packed at night and on the weekends. Also gay male and straight friendly. Try a Double D shot ($6). Happy hour (2-for-1) M-F 5-7pm. DJ's Th-Sa (Cover $3-5). Su is Girl Parts, a cover band highlighting lesbian-friendly music. Open M-F 4pm-4am, Sa-Su 1pm-4am.

The Lure, 409 W. 13th St. between Ninth and Tenth Aves. (☎741-3919). Subway: A, C, E, L to 14th St.-Eighth Ave. In the heart of the meat-packing district, this is one of the world's great leather bars. Complete with cages, homo-erotic porn projections, and a St. Andrew's cross (if you don't know what that is, you probably shouldn't go). Wednesday night is Pork, a more diverse, less uniformly leather evening than other nights, featuring live S/M and fetish performances. Pork opens at 10pm. Weekend dress code is strictly leather, Levis, tees, rubber, and uniforms. No cologne. Open daily 8pm-4am.

Guilty Pleasure and **Living Legends,** at Nowbar, 22 Seventh Ave. S., at Leroy St. (☎802-9502). Subway: 1, 9 to Christopher St. Glorya Wholesome hosts hot parties for "ladies, trannies, gentlemen, gay, straight, lesbian, conservative, liberal, blue collar, white collar, big boned, and anorexics and their admirers!" Expect a more specific crowd of trannies, go-gos, and lap dancers. Legends Sa, Guilty Th; both 10pm-4am. Cover $5 for trannie/drag queens, $10 for ladies, $15 for men.

Body & Soul, at Vinyl, 6 Hubert St., at Hudson St. (☎330-9169). Subway: 1, 9 to Canal St. On Su evening throngs pack Vinyl to wiggle-n-jiggle amid the lights and house music. A New York must. Doors open at 4pm, but things really grind 5pm-midnight. $15 for nonmembers, $10 for members.

The Duplex, 61 Christopher St. (☎255-5438). Subway: 1, 9 to Christopher St. A renowned piano bar always abuzz with performances by the talented waitstaff. The Duplex is filled with merry theatrical throngs who can recite every lyric from *On the Twentieth Century,* and will. The crowd mingles on the colorful outdoor "beach" patio. Cabaret performance room and game room with pool, poker and darts upstairs. Mixed gay and straight crowd. Beer $4. Open daily 5pm-4am.

Chi Chiz, 135 Christopher St., at Hudson St. (☎462-0027). Subway: 1, 9 to Christopher St. *The* Manhattan hot spot for African-American and Latino men. Bar packs a younger, rowdier crowd on weekends, and a mellower neighborhood crowd during the week. Open M-Sa 5pm-4am, Su noon-4am.

The Cubbyhole, 281 W. 12th St., at W. 4th St. (☎243-9041). Subway: A, C, E, L to 14th St.-Eighth Ave. The bar's hanging fish and flowers are reminiscent of something in between a magic underwater garden and a kindergarten class room. Intimate and funky with a predominantly female crowd. Mixed gay and straight crowd. Happy hour M-Sa until 7pm. No cover. Open M-Th 4pm-3am, F 4pm-4am, Sa 2pm-4am, Su 3pm-4am.

Crazy Nanny's, 21 Seventh Ave. S., near LeRoy St. (☎929-8356). Subway: 1, 9 to Houston St. As the door promises, this bar is for "Gay women, biologically or otherwise." Glamour dykes come here to shoot some pool, play video games, eat free popcorn, or just hang out. Dancing nightly in the two-floored, two-bar space. 2-for-1 Happy Hour M-Sa 4-7pm. Karaoke W, Su 8pm; free. F is Sweat, a go-go dance party; doors open 9pm, $10. Sa is Mixer, a party for gay men and women; doors open 9pm, $8. Open daily 4pm-4am.

Rose's Turn, 55 Grove St. between Bleecker St. and Seventh Ave. South (☎366-5438). Subway: 1, 9 to Christopher St. Mixed piano bar with open mic and perhaps the most musically talented bar staff in New York. Basement bar is packed F-Sa; Su provides a small-to-medium crowd for a pleasant balance of liveliness and intimacy. Come F-Su 9pm-4am to hear singer Terri White (who also tends bar)—her voice is one of the city's undiscovered wonders. Cabaret upstairs with varying cover and a two-drink minimum. Beer $5-6. Drinks $5-6. Open daily 4pm-4am.

CHELSEA, HELL'S KITCHEN, AND UPPER WEST SIDE

Splash, 50 W. 17th St. between Fifth and Sixth Aves. (☎691-0073). Subway: 1, 9 to 18th St.; F to 23rd St. One of the most popular gay mega-bars. Enormous complex on two floors. Cool, almost sci-fi decor provides a sleek backdrop for a very crowded scene, with a dance floor that completes the evening. Cover varies, peaking at $7. Drinks $4-7. Open Su-Th 4pm-4am, F-Sa 4pm-5am.

g, 223 W. 19th St. between Seventh and Eighth Aves. (☎929-1085). Subway: 1, 9 to 18th St. Glitzy, popular bar shaped like an oval racetrack–somehow an appropriate architectural metaphor, given the pumped-up Chelsea clientele that speeds around this circuit trying to win glances. Fortunately, the famous frozen Cosmos satisfy the thirst of those logging their miles. No cover. Open daily 4pm-4am.

La Nueva Escuelita, 301 W. 39th St., at Eighth Ave. (☎631-0588). Subway: A, C, E to 42nd St. Drag Latin dance club that throbs with merengue, salsa, soul, hip-hop, and arguably the best drag shows in New York. Largely but not entirely, gay Latin crowd. F, starting at 10pm, is Her/She Bar, with go-go gals, performances, and special events. (Her/She: ☎631-1093; $8 before midnight, $10 after.) Open Th-Sa 10pm-5am, Su 7pm-5am. Cover Th $5; F $10; Sa $15; Su 7-10pm $5, after 10pm $8.

Barracuda, 275 W. 22nd St., at Eighth Ave. (☎645-8613). Subway: C, E to 23rd St. 1950s decor, complete with sofas, a pool table, and a dazzling collection of kitsch furniture, makes for a cozy hangout in the back. Drinks $4-7. 2-for-1 Happy Hour M-F 4-9pm. Open daily 4pm-4am.

The Roxy, 515 W. 18th St., at Tenth Ave. (☎645-5156). Currently *the* place to be on Sa nights. Hundreds of gay men dance and drink in the Roxy's gigantic, luxurious space. Upstairs, lounge/bar provides a different DJ and more intimate setting. Downstairs you'll find high ceilings, a beautiful dance floor, and lounge space. Beer $5. Drinks $6+. Cover $25. Prime hours are 11pm-6am.

The Big Apple Ranch, at Dance Manhattan, 39 W. 19th St. between Fifth and Sixth Aves., 5th fl. (☎358-5752). Subway: F, N, R to 23rd St. A friendly crowd of urban cowboys and girls welcomes all to a romping evening of gay and lesbian two-stepping. $10 cover includes lesson. Sa only 8pm-1am; lessons 8-9pm.

Chase, 255 W. 55th St. between Broadway and Eighth Aves. (☎333-3400). Subway: 1, 9, C, E to 50th St. Trendy and chic, Chase brings a little bit of Chelsea to Hell's Kitchen, drawing in well-groomed men and the neighborhood theatrical community. Happy hour daily 4-7pm. Open daily 3pm-4am.

The Works, 428 Columbus Ave., at 81st St. (☎799-7365). Subway: B, C to 81st St. An Upper West Side hangout for the Banana Republic set. The Works packs them in Th and Su, when aspiring guppies seek genuine bargains in $1 frozen margaritas and cosmos (Th 8pm-2am) and the $5 all-you-can-drink Beer Blast (Su 6pm-1am). Open daily 4pm-4am.

EAST VILLAGE AND ALPHABET CITY

The Cock, 188 Ave. A, at E. 12th St. (☎946-1871). Subway: L to First Ave. A crowded boy bar with a full offering of nightly gay diversions. Foxy Saturday asks the patrons to multiply their "Foxy dollars" through a gamut of risqué challenges. Call for the nightly change of entertainment fare. Open daily 9:30pm-4am.

Boiler Room, 86 E. 4th St. between First and Second Aves. (☎254-7536). Subway: F to Second Ave. A popular locale catering to alluring alternative types, NYU college students, and eager refugees from the sometimes stifling Chelsea clone scene. Terrific jukebox gives the evening a democratic spin. Open daily 4pm-4am.

Wonder Bar, 505 E. 6th St. between Aves. A and B (☎777-9105). Done up in zebra chic and laid back neutrals, the Wonder Bar is frequented by a chill gay bohemian crowd and the occasional curious breeder. Open daily 6pm-4am.

DAYTRIPPING TO FIRE ISLAND

For transportation info, see ***Daytrips****, p. 224.*

Two prominent Fire Island resort hamlets, **Cherry Grove** and **The Pines,** host largely gay communities. Crowded "streets," wooden pathways, border spectacular Atlantic Ocean beaches, and the scene rages late into the night. Weekdays provide an excellent opportunity to enjoy the beauty and charm of the island in a low-key setting, with Thursdays and Sundays offering an ideal balance of sanity and scene—Friday and Saturday see mounting crowds and prices.

Both towns host establishments that advertise themselves as "guest houses." Be aware that some of these may not be legally accredited (due to such things as fire code violations), and that some may not be lesbian-friendly. When planning lodging, be advised that many places require a two-night minimum on the weekends, so call ahead. **The Cherry Grove Beach Hotel** (☎631-597-6600) is a good bet, centrally located on the Main Walk of Cherry Grove and close to the beach. The economy room starts at $90 mid-week during July, but costs $450 for a two-night stay during the weekend. Weekday prices are lower (full price the first night and $30 each additional night). Reservations are required. The hotel is open May to October. Another option is **Holly House** (☎631-597-6911), on Holly Walk, right behind the Ice Palace. The three-bedroom guest house offers rooms with shared baths, $100-$125 weekday, $250 for a two-night stay during the weekend.

NIGHTLIFE

There is a very established schedule to gay nightlife in Fire Island. Both Cherry Grove and The Pines are not very big—it's best to just ask around, either at your hotel or restaurant. In the wooded area between the Pines and the Grove is a loosely-bounded area that those in the know call the **Meat Rack.** There are lots of walkways leading in myriad directions, and this is where things go down—Gay Men's Health Crisis actually puts condoms in the trees to keep everyone safe. Another similar cruising location has recently sprung up on Harbor Walk between Fire Island Blvd and Ocean Walk.

CHERRY GROVE. In this more commercial of the two resort towns, narrow, raised boardwalks line the road-less area and lead to small, uniformly shingled houses that overflow with men, although lesbian couples make up the majority of the town's population. A night in Cherry Grove usually begins at the **Ice Palace** (☎516-597-6600), attached to the Cherry Grove Beach Hotel, where you can disco till dawn. Most go to the Pines for late-night partying; you can catch a water taxi from the docks at Cherry Grove.

THE PINES. A 10-minute walk up the beach from Cherry Grove, the Pines has traditionally looked down its nose at its uninhibited neighbor. Houses here are spacious and often stunningly modern, with an asymmetric aesthetic and huge windows. You may want to bring along a flashlight to navigate the often poorly lit boardwalks here. The Pines' active, upscale nighttime scene, unfortunately, has a bit of a secret club feel to it—you need to be in the know or somehow be able to look like you know the schedule. **Low Tea,** from 5-8pm, is at the bar/club next to the Botel (big hotel). Move on to disco **High Tea** at 8pm at the Pavilion, but make sure you have somewhere to disappear to during "disco nap" time (after 10pm). Around 1:30am you can emerge unabashedly to dance till dawn at the **Island Club and Bistro,** better known as the Sip and Twirl. The Pavilion becomes hot again late-night on weekends, including Sundays during the summer.

INSIDE
shopping by type **201**
shopping by neighborhood **203**

Shopping

There is perhaps no easier place to spend money than New York City. With everything you could ever imagine, from the (former) largest department store in the world to the hottest new boutique to the hardest-to-find underground used-clothing store, how can you, a mere first-time visitor, ever find what you want? Read on, loyal follower: this is your bible to the largest, the cutest, and the hippest. Find a department store; find a designer flagship store; find an out-of-print import CD; find the cheapest, tightest shirt for tonight; find $10 Prada bags and Rolex watches (ok, so maybe they're not always real); even find hard-core mall shopping (although that's banished to Long Island and Westchester).

SHOPPING BY TYPE

BC	Central Brooklyn	**GV**	Greenwich Village	**NoL**	Nolita
CHE	Chelsea	**HAR**	Harlem	**SH**	SoHo
CHI	Chinatown	**LES**	Lower East Side	**UES**	Upper East Side
EV	East Village	**LOW**	Lower Manhattan	**UWS**	Upper West Side
FD	Flatiron District	**MID**	Midtown	**WIL**	Williamsburg

ACCESSORIES		**ACCESSORIES, CONTINUED**	
Adorned (207)	EV	Starfish & Jelli (209)	EV
It's a Mod, Mod World (207)	EV	Ugly Luggage (215)	WIL
Lucky Wang (204)	LES	**ARMY/NAVY SURPLUS**	
Manhattan Portage (208)	EV	Uncle Sam's Army Navy (206)	GV
Pearl River (203)	CHI	Weiss and Mahoney (210)	CHE
Reminiscence (210)	CHE

SHOPPING BY NEIGHBORHOOD

FINANCIAL DISTRICT AND CIVIC CENTER

The southernmost portion of Manhattan is not known for its shopping, but there are a few stores worth noting.

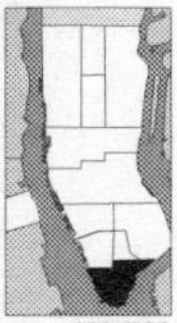

see map pp. 310-311

Century 21, 22 Cortlandt St. between Broadway and Church St. (☎227-9092). Subway: 1, 9, N, R to Cortlandt St. A shopper's dream—a department store with discounted designer wares. Sift through the bargain basement duds to find that Armani suit you could never afford. At the time this book went to press, the store had sustained serious damage during the World Trade Center collapse. Open Su 11am-7pm, M-W and F 7:45am-8pm, Th 7:45am-8:30pm, Sa 10am-7:30pm.

J & R Music World/Computer World, 23 Park Row between Ann and Barclay Sts. (☎732-8600 or 238-9000). Subway: N, R, 4, 5, 6 to City Hall. Will meet most of your electronics needs with competitive prices. Open M-W and F-Sa 9am-7pm, Th 9am-7:30pm, Su 10:30am-6:30pm.

Nassau St. Pedestrian Mall, on Nassau St. located west of City Hall. Subway: N, R, 4, 5, 6 to City Hall. Stores here offer discounted clothing, often for $10 or less. If you know what you're looking for, it's worth the rummage.

Pier 17 Pavilion, near the river on Fulton St. Subway: 2, 3, 4, 5, J, M, Z to Fulton St.; A, C to Broadway-Nassau. If you thought you were getting out of this area without seeing a mall, you couldn't be more wrong. Pier 17 Pavilion is an expansive shopping mall and restaurant arcade.

Strand Book Annex, 95 Fulton St. between William and Gold Sts. (☎732-6070). Subway: N, R, 4, 5, 6 to City Hall. Seek and ye shall find in the remainder books section and the hearty supply of $1 used books. Open M-F 9:30am-9pm, Sa-Su 11am-8pm.

CHINATOWN AND LITTLE ITALY

So long as authenticity doesn't concern you, Chinatown is the perfect place to bargain hunt. You can find Asian imports, $5 burned CDs, and that wicker Kate Spade bag you've been eyeing. And if the stores along Canal St. don't have the nice black vinyl bag with the Prada logo, ask them to stick one on—they're in the back.

Northern Little Italy (or NoLIta) is rife with fashionable boutiques. You might like them, but your wallet won't.

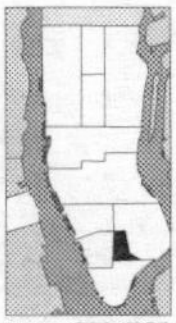

see map pp. 312-313

Find Outlet, 229 Mott St. between Prince and Spring Sts. (☎226-5167). Subway: 6 to Spring St. This outlet store sells wares from costly NoLIta boutiques at a substantial discount. Often 50-80% off the original. **Other location:** 361 W. 17th St. (☎243-3177). Open Th-Su noon-7pm.

Language, 238 Mulberry St. between Prince and Spring Sts. (☎431-5566). Subway: 6 to Spring St. Tremendous—though not affordable—merchandise, stylish and whimsically varied. Where else does one see a silver moped on display next to a gold-trimmed leather jacket and Amazon feather-masks? Open M-W Sa 11am-7pm, Th 11am-8pm, Su noon-7pm.

The Oriental Culture Enterprise, 13-17 Elizabeth St., 2nd fl. between Bayard and Canal Sts. (☎226-8461). Subway: J, M, N, R, Z, 4, 5, 6 to Canal St. Specializing in Chinese literature, the store also sells tapes, CDs, newspapers, calligraphy equipment, and musical instruments. Open daily 10am-7pm.

Pearl River, 277 Canal St., at Broadway (☎431-4770). Subway: N, R, J, M, Z, 4, 5, 6 to Canal St. This Chinese department store sells all the basic necessities, along with a few hard-to-find luxuries: silk slippers, paper lanterns, the miraculous Japanese buckwheat pillow. All cheap, all under one roof. Open daily 10am-7:30pm.

The Pop Shop, 292 Lafayette St., at Jersey St. (☎219-2784). Subway: B, D, F, Q to Broadway-Lafayette. 1980s pop artist Keith Haring's cartoonish, socially conscious work can be found on posters and postcards all over the city, but where else can you find Haring-decorated umbrellas ($40), t-shirts ($20), and everything pop? Opened in 1985, the shop was painted by the late artist in his distinctive style, and all proceeds benefit the Keith Haring Foundation. Open M-Sa noon-7pm, Su noon-6pm.

LOWER EAST SIDE

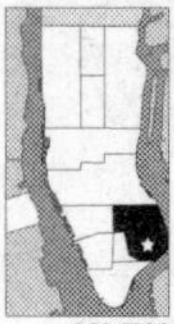
see map pp. 320-321

Shopping in the Lower East Side is slowly becoming an expensive venture. Up-and-coming designers and select shops often display their handmade, cutting-edge wares in stores that look more like museums. Trendy boutiques abound on Orchard, Stanton, and Ludlow Sts.

JBJ Discount Pet Shop, 151 E. Houston St., at Eldridge St. (☎982-5310). Subway: J, M to Bowery. This shop sells bizarre pets at discount rates. Their petite pests have made it big: the Madagascar Hissing roaches appeared in *Men In Black,* and many other species have debuted on David Letterman. The owners have a sense of humor, evidenced by the sign reading "Hug me" in the South American Boa cage. Open M-Sa 10am-6:30pm.

Las Venus Lounge 20th Century Pop Culture, 163 Ludlow St., at Stanton St. (☎982-0608). Subway: F to Delancey St. A wild vintage store, this lounge sells everything from giant lily lamps to 1960s porn magazines. Scenesters stroll in to this romantic hotspot on the weekend, kickback on the pleather couches, and transform what seems like an overcrowded vintage furniture store into a spontaneous party. Open Su-F noon-8pm, Sa noon-midnight.

Lucky Wang, 100 Stanton St. (☎353-2850). Subway: J, M, Z to Essex St. A temple to nylon day-glo fur, the designers here focus on accessories made of "cyberfur," a material reminiscent of tinsel. The store also stocks designer t-shirts ($22), pompom key chains ($1.85), and various types of bags (starting at $10). Open W-F noon-7pm, Sa 1-7pm, Su 1-6pm.

Zao, 175 Orchard St., between Stanton and Houston Sts. (☎505-0500). J, M, Z to Essex St. Flashy and truly chi-chi, this store is worth a browse. If you don't think the racks of Tahari and Zao clothing are worth the price tag, at least peruse the cutting-edge fashion mags (*Inside Out* and other imports) and the home goods in the mezzanine. Open daily 11am-7pm.

SOHO

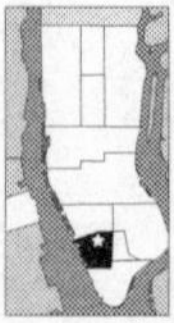
see map p. 315

SoHo is upscale, but you can still find some deals at the district's used clothing stores and streetside stands. Check out the daily "fair" that sets up shop in a lot on **Wooster and Spring Sts.** The bargain hunt continues on Broadway with a wide selection of used clothing stores, like **Alice Underground.** Flea market devotees should check out the outdoor **SoHo Flea Market** at the western end of Canal St., and the **Antiques Fair and Collectibles Market** (☎682-2000; open Sa-Su 9am-5pm), held year-round, hosting some 50-100 vendors on the corner of Broadway and Grand St.

Canal Jean Co., 504 Broadway between Spring and Broome Sts. (☎226-1130). Subway: 6 to Spring St.; N, R to Prince St. This enormous home of surplus bargains brims with 4 floors of neon ties, baggy pants, alterna-tees, and silk smoking jackets. Poke around bargain central in the basement. Open daily 9:30am-9pm.

Girlprops.com, 153 Prince St. between W. Broadway and Thompson Sts. (☎505-7615). Subway: C, E to Spring St.; N, R to Prince St. Heaven for accessory-lovers with every variety of hair clip, lariat, body glitter, rhinestone belt, make-up, or tiara currently in style. Individually inexpensive—but beware, those sparkly bobby pins do add up. Most under $10. Open M-Tu 9am-11pm, W 9am-midnight, Th and Su 10am-midnight, F-Sa 10am-1am.

K. Trimming Co., 519 Broadway between Spring and Broome Sts. (☎431-8829). Subway: 6 to Spring St.; N, R to Prince St. A cavernous warehouse featuring every variety of sewing product you could ever want: doilies, swaths of colored fabrics, embroidered trimmings, pompoms, etc. It's a tempting sartorial jungle where aspiring SoHo designers can come to find their wares. Open Su-Th 9am-7pm, F 9am-2pm.

Sephora, 555 Broadway between Spring and Prince Sts. (☎625-1309). Subway: 6 to Spring St.; N, R to Prince St. An overwhelming array of cosmetic products. The tantalizing rainbow arrangements and the sheer magnitude of perfumes, powders, and exfoliaters at Sephora could convince even Snow White that she needed Shiseido's help. Open M-Sa 11am-8:30pm, Su 11am-7pm.

Universal News and Cafe Corp., 484 Broadway between Broome and Grand Sts. (☎965-9042). Subway: 6 to Spring St. Over 7000 magazine titles (foreign and domestic) covering everything from fashion to fishing to politics. Doubles as a cafe with so-so fare. Open daily 6am-11pm.

Untitled, 159 Prince St. between W. Broadway and Thompson St. (☎982-2088). Subway: C, E to Spring St.; N, R to Prince St. In SoHo since 1970, this fine arts store specializes in design and typography. An amazing library of postcards, catalogued for your convenience (each 85¢). Open daily 10am-8pm.

GREENWICH VILLAGE

For better or for worse, the Village is not trodden ground for the mainstream. If you're shopping here, you're tasting New York.

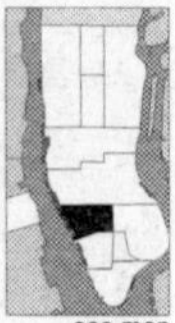

see map pp. 316-317

Andy's Chee-pee's, 691 Broadway between E. 4th St. and Great Jones St. (☎420-5980). Subway: N, R to 8th St.-NYU. Not really cheap at all, but worth a peek, if only for that vintage clothing aroma. Open M-Sa 11am-9pm, Su noon-8pm.

Antique Boutique, 712 Broadway between W. 4th St. and Washington Pl. (☎460-8830). Subway: N, R to 8th St.-NYU. Blares better techno than many clubs, and sells both stunning vintage clothing and interesting new designs (both *very* expensive). Expect a lot of shiny plastics and outrageous attitudes. Open Su-Th noon-8pm, F-Sa 11am-9pm.

Biography Bookstore, 400 Bleecker St., at W. 11th St. (☎807-8655). Subway: 1, 9 to Christopher St. Representing biography-browsing at its best, this small corner shop stocks the myriad life-stories of kings, rock idols, and presidents. Strong gay/lesbian section, as well as best-sellers, travel books, film, and drama. Open M-Th 11am-10pm, F-Sa 11am-11pm, Su 11am-7pm.

Cheap Jack's Vintage Clothing, 841 Broadway between 13th and 14th Sts. (☎777-9564). Subway: L, N, R, 4, 5, 6 to Union Sq. Yet another vintage store using the word "cheap" a bit too loosely. Jack sells racks of worn jeans, leather jackets, and other vintage "gems." Open M-Sa 11am-8pm, Su noon-7pm.

Disc-O-Rama, 186 W. 4th St. between Sixth and Seventh Aves. (☎206-8417). Subway: A, B, C, D, E, F, Q to W. 4th St. All CDs $11 or below. Strong alternative section in addition to more standard Top 40 choices. The CDs aren't always in order and the store is a little packed, so be prepared for a search (only the top 200 are organized). Vinyl downstairs. Open M-Th 10:30am-11pm, F 10:30am-midnight, Sa 10:30am-1am, Su noon-8pm. **Other locations:** Annex at 40 Union Sq. East (☎260-8616) and classical and clearance store at 146 W. 4th St. (☎477-9410).

Forbidden Planet, 840 Broadway, at 13th St. (☎473-1576). Subway: L, N, R, 4, 5, 6 to Union Sq. A repository of all things sci-fi. Comics, posters, models, toys, Play Station games (to buy, sell, and trade), and art books. Unhealthily skinny boys and the death-goth girls who love them congregate here. Open M-Sa 10am-10pm, Su 11am-8pm.

Generation Records, 210 Thompson St. between Bleecker and 3rd Sts. (☎254-1100). Subway: A, B, C, D, E, F, Q to W. 4th St. All kinds of alternative and underground rock on CD and vinyl; the hard-core and industrial/experimental selection is especially impressive. Fairly low prices (CDs $11-13) and the best assortment of hard-to-find imports in the Village. Great deals on used merchandise downstairs (CDs usually $6 or less). Open M-Th 11am-10pm, F-Sa 11am-1am, Su noon-10pm.

La Petite Coquette, 51 University Pl. between 9th and 10th Sts. (☎473-2478). Subway: N, R to 8th St.-NYU. This shop offers all things beaded, embroidered, laced, fringed, and tied. Celebrity photos on the walls testify that La Petite Coquette will elude your budget, but the prices won't drive away the true lingerie enthusiast. Come for their post-Valentine's Day sale when most items are 40% off. Open M-W 11am-7pm, Th 11am-8pm, F-Sa 11am-7pm, Su noon-6pm.

The Leather Man, 111 Christopher St. between Bleecker and Hudson Sts. (☎243-5339). Subway: 1, 9 to Christopher St. A sex shop, not a superhero. The upstairs is dominated by leather apparel but braving the spiral staircase downstairs drops you in a new world of kink. Friendly staff, helpful to all genders and orientations. Open M-Sa noon-10pm, Su noon-8pm.

Patricia Field, 10 E. 8th St., at Fifth Ave. (☎254-1699). Subway: N, R to 8th St.-NYU. Fabulous array of costly, kinky, hip gear with a perpetual "prostitute sale." The fabric of choice is vinyl and the colors are neon. Extensive selection of "pasties" (nipple tassels, $12-22). Open Su-F noon-8pm, Sa noon-9pm.

Second Coming Records, 231 and 235 Sullivan St. between Bleecker and W. 3rd Sts. (☎228-1313). Subway: A, B, C, D, E, F, Q to W. 4th St. Heaven-sent vinyl, and lots of it. The CD stock accommodates a wide range of alternative and popular releases, both new and used. Also good for alternative imports and bootlegs. Open M-Th 11am-7pm; F-Sa 11am-9pm; Su noon-7pm.

FREE-LOVE, VILLAGE-STYLE

Given the Village's radical legacy, it doesn't seem that surprising that the birth control movement flowered here. When Anthony Comstock banned Margaret Sanger's article, "What Every Girl should Know," the Village radicals rose to defend birth control's leading voice. Resolute local presses published her works which sparked an important free-love dialogue about the "New Woman." Today, the sex shop-laden Village does her proud, bringing birth control to new heights. To pay her homage, or just to get some condoms:

Condomania, 351 Bleecker St., at W. 10th St. (☎691-9442). "America's first condom store" stocks over 150 types of condoms as well as various other accoutrements. Pick up some X-rated fortune cookies, a box of "Penis Pasta," or their best-selling pecker sipping straws with your order. Friendly staff answers all questions and gives safe-sex tips. Open Su-Th 11am-11pm, F-Sa 11am-midnight.

Shakespeare and Company, 716 Broadway, at Washington Pl. (☎529-1330). Subway: N, R to 8th St.-NYU. There's more than just words, words, words at this New York institution. Shakespeare & Co. carries high-quality literature, high-brow journals, and a great selection of vintage crime, art, and theater books that won't cost you a pound of flesh. Open Su-Th 10am-11pm, F-Sa 10am-midnight.

Strand Bookstore, 828 Broadway, at 12th St. (☎473-1452). Subway: 4, 5, 6, L, N, R to Union Sq. The world's largest used bookstore. A must-see, with 8 mi. of shelf space that holds nearly 2 million books including rare titles and first editions. 50% off review copies and paperbacks. Vast collection of art books. Check the outdoor carts for extreme bargains. Staffers will search out obscure titles at your bidding. Ask for a catalog, or better yet, get lost in the shelves on your own. Open M-Sa 9:30am-9:20pm, Su 11am-9:20pm.

Tower Records, 692 Broadway, at 4th St. (☎505-1500). Subway: 6 to Bleecker St.; N, R to 8th St-NYU. One-stop music emporium, nearly a block long with 4 full floors of merchandise. Open daily 9am-midnight.

Uncle Sam's Army Navy, 37 W. 8th St. between Fifth and Sixth Aves. (☎674-2222). Subway: N, R to 8th St.-NYU. Eclectic supply of military garb from around the world (we're talkin' *East* German uniform pants). Selection of helmets $14-19 (sometimes on sale for $12). Also houses good selection of less official wear for when you're at ease. Work pants "that will never tear" $15. No tax (Uncle Sam's pays it for you). Open M-W 10am-9pm, Th-Sa 10am-10pm, Su 11am-9pm.

Village Chess Shop, 230 Thompson St. between Bleecker and W. 3rd Sts. (☎475-9580). Subway: A, B, C, D, E, F, Q to W. 4th St. The Village's keenest intellects square off in rigorous strategic combat while sipping coffee ($1) and juice ($1.50). Play is $1 or $1.50 for clocked play per hour per person ($3 per hour to watch). Don't &!$%@ swear or you'll be penalized $1.25. Novices can get their game analyzed for $3. The shop also showcases several breathtaking antique chess sets. Open daily noon-midnight.

Village Comics, 214 Sullivan St. between Bleecker and W. 3rd St. (☎777-2770). Subway: A, B, C, D, E, F, Q to W. 4th St. The requisite comics jostle for space with collectible figurines, sci-fi trinkets, horror-movie doodads, and, in the back, porn movies and magazines. Open M-Tu 10am-7:30pm, W-Sa 10am-8:30pm, Su 11am-7pm.

EAST VILLAGE

see map pp. 320-321

As might be expected from an area populated by self-styled avatars of what's hip, the East Village shopping scene is dominated by small, specialized stores. Those looking for brand names would be better off in SoHo, but those seeking vintage clothing shall find. St. Mark's Pl. shops sell a fantastic assortment of silver jewelry and odd trinkets. **Record Stores** line both sides of St. Mark's Pl., mostly between Third Ave. and Ave. A. You'll be browsing barely organized shelves/racks/drawers for hours, but you'll find the best price for used and new CDs here, as well as a decent variety of records. Especially good: **Sounds,** at 20 St. Mark's Pl. (☎677-3444). Open daily noon-11pm. **CD & Cassette Annex,** at 16 St. Mark's Pl. (☎677-2727). Open daily noon-usually 11pm. Check out any of the boutiques selling handmade, fashionable one-of-a-kinds along 9th St. off Ave. A.

Adorned, 47 Second Ave. between E. 2nd and 3rd Sts. (☎473-0007). Subway: F to Second Ave. Comfortable, safe, and friendly place to add bauble to your body. As they see it, they're here to "make you beautiful, not mutilated." Nose piercing $15; navel $20. Jewelry not included. Skilled, traditional *henna* work (hands and feet) $20 and up. Tattoos $75 and up. Open Su-Th noon-8pm, F-Sa noon-10pm.

Astor Place Hairstylist, 2 Astor Pl., at Broadway (☎475-9854). Subway: 6 to Astor Pl.; N, R to 8th St.-NYU. The largest haircutting establishment in the world is famed for its low-priced production-line approach to style. One observer noted, "It's like Club MTV with clippers." Run DMC, Adam Sandler, and Joan Rivers represent some of the celeb clientele. 85 people work in the 3-story complex. Haircuts $11-25; Su $2 extra. Open M-Sa 8am-8pm, Su 9am-6pm.

Downtown Music Gallery, 211 E. 5th St. between Second and Third Aves. (☎473-0043). Subway: F to Second Ave. Dense and diverse, the selection of CDs and records should please most non-mainstream music enthusiasts. A knowledgable and helpful staff presides over all sorts of music, including jazz, folk, classical, and electronic. When you're alone and life is making you lonely, you can go here Su-Th noon-9pm, F-Sa noon-11pm.

Honeymoon, 105 Ave. B., at E. 7th St. (☎477-8768). Subway: 6 to Astor Place. 40s to 80s vintage clothing; from Pucci dresses ($650) to skirts ($3-5). Open Tu-Sa 1-8pm, Su 1-6pm. Another location **(Second Honeymoon)** at 620 E. 6th St., between Aves. B and C (☎473-4942). Open Tu-Su 2-8pm.

House of Trance, 122 St. Mark's Pl. between First Ave. and Ave A (☎533-6700). Subway: 6 to Astor Pl. Step into the blacklight-lit ambience of this store to chill with Goa-trancers, the modern-day version of psychedelic flower children. Day-glo T-shirts $17-20, camisoles $17. Also the trance records to set the mood. Open daily 11am-midnight.

It's a Mod, Mod World, 85 First Ave. between E. 3rd and 4th Sts. (☎460-8004). Subway: F to Second Ave. A beaded day-glo-painted temple to the unnecessary but wonderful delights in life, including an absolutely fabulous selection of gift items and jewelry. On display are *Barbie* doll installations (available

girlprops.com

Garment District

Music in the Bronx

the BIG $plurge

Soho Spending

When the urge to conspicuously consume begins to tug at your heartstrings, you can browse through SoHo's extensive selection of clothing boutiques, handmade stationers, and home furnishing stores. Broadway is lined with the likes of such high-end stores as **Scoop** (532 Broadway). **Joseph** (115 Greene St.) and neighbor **Anna Sui** (113 Greene St.) are right off Broadway. Along Prince St., you'll find the classic streamlined clothing of **Agnès B.** and Prada's more affordable and street-oriented sibling, **Miu Miu.** (Although, as if in response to the ever-increasing level of gentrification obvious in this neighborhood, **Prada** proper is moving in.) If you're looking for a store where the decor is as off-beat and luxurious as the clothing, **Betsey Johnson,** on Wooster St., might just be your bed of velvet. Wooster St. is also home to quirky but established designers like **Cythnia Rowley** and **Todd Oldham.** Caution to the uninitiated: these are not bargain designer boutiques. Some stores, like **INA** (21 Prince St.), which features top names like Prada and Helmut Lang at up to ½-off the original price, may be the next best thing, but they'll still run you a pretty penny.

for sale), as well as clocks made of cereal and candy boxes ($20). Open M-Th noon-10pm, F-Sa noon-11pm, Su noon-8pm.

Jammyland, 60 E. 3rd St. between First and Second Aves. (☎614-0185; www.jammyland.com). Subway: F to Second Ave. Stocks a wide selection of reggae, dub, dance hall, ska, and other Jamaican innovations, along with a decent world music supply. Open M-Sa noon-midnight, Su noon-10pm.

Kiehl's, 109 Third Ave. between E. 13th and 14th Sts. (☎677-3171). Subway: N, R, 4, 5, 6 to Union Sq.; L to 3rd Ave. A specialty cosmetics store, with prices matching the luxury of their products (toner $15, lip balm $5). So why list this in a budget travel guide? Because their policy of giving out free (and conveniently travel-sized) samples is possibly one of New York's best deals. And might just convince you to actually spend some money in the store. Open M-W and F 10am-6:30pm, Th 10am-7:30pm, Sa 10am-6pm.

Kim's Video and Audio, 6 St. Mark's Pl. between Second and Third Aves. (☎598-9985). Subway: 6 to Astor Place. Three floors of hip entertainment selections. The ground floor has a startlingly strong selection of independent and import CDs, with beats ranging from 1970s Jamaican dub to avant-jazz; the 2nd floor holds new and used vinyl and a tremendous video showcase specializing in independent and foreign films. Open daily 9am-midnight.

Lot 76 NYC, E. Houston St. between First and Second Aves. (☎505-8699). Subway: F to Second Ave. Take home a piece of the subway, legally: Lot 76 NYC sells New York subway signs, as well as old Coke machines and other antiques. True, you're probably not going to fit furniture into your backpack but this outdoor store is still a lot of fun to walk around. Open daily 10am-6pm, weather permitting.

Love Saves the Day, 119 Second Ave., at E. 7th St. (☎228-3802). Subway: 6 to Astor Pl. Since 1966, this store has been selling vintage clothing ($15 shirts) and random collectibles (we spotted ALF memorabilia and old issues of *Life* magazine). Open daily 1-8:30pm.

Manhattan Portage, 333 E. 9th St. between First and Second Aves. (☎995-5490; www.manhattanportage.com). Subway: 6 to Astor Pl. You don't have to be a DJ or a bike messenger to carry these utility bags ($60); you will, however, look like a member of one of those two exalted professions. Urban Outfitters sells these bags all over the country now: here's where they got their start. $35-70. Open Su-Th noon-7pm, F-Sa noon-8pm.

Metropolis, 43 Third Ave. between E. 9th and 10th Sts. (☎358-0795). Subway: 6 to Astor Pl. A selection of new and vintage club wear and shoes, heavy on the funk and slightly cyber-y. Complete with a DJ booth; make sure to pick up flyers at the front of the store on the way out. Open M-Th noon-8pm, F-Sa noon-9pm. Also at 96 Ave. B, between E. 6th and 7th Sts. (☎477-3941).

Miracle on St. Mark's, 100 St. Mark's Pl. between First Ave. and Ave. A (☎614-7262). Subway: 6 to Astor Pl. A tiny but wonderful selection of fashionable wear for women. Open W-Sa noon-8pm, Su 2-6pm.

Other Music, 15 E. 4th St. between Lafayette St. and Broadway (☎477-8150). Subway: 6 to Bleecker St. Specializing in the alternative and avant-garde. Obscure stuff abounds, but you can avoid steep import prices with the sizeable used CD section. Posters and flyers keep the clientele updated on where to see their favorite performers, and the staff is an even better source of information. Open M-Sa noon-9pm, Su noon-7pm.

Rags-A-Go-Go, 75 E. 7th St. between First and Second Aves. (☎254-4771). Subway: 6 to Astor Pl. A well-organized selection of basic vintage gear: T-shirts $6 and the multi-purpose urban hoodie $12. Open M-Sa noon-8pm, Su noon-7pm.

Religious Sex, 7 St. Marks Pl. between Second and Third Aves. (☎477-9037). Subway: 6 to Astor Pl. Supplies vinyl corsets, opulent boas, and sequined tutus to East Village fetishists. Amazing array of kinky outerwear that delights in the outlandish and dabbles in the gothic. 4" PVC stiletto heels $49. Open M-W noon-8pm, Th-Sa noon-9pm, Su 1-8pm.

See Hear, 59 E. 7th St. between First and Second Aves. (☎505-9781). Subway: 6 to Astor Pl. An underground store, both literally and figuratively. See Hear stocks rock music books, 'zines, music mags, and comics. A good place to pick up old copies of *Mojo* magazine. Open daily noon-8pm.

Starfish & Jelli, 96 St. Mark's Pl. between First Ave. and Ave. A (☎388-0007). Subway: 6 to Astor Pl. Handmade jewelry with shiny beads and feathers. Delightfully feminine. Open W-F 2-8pm, Sa noon-10pm, Su noon-8pm.

St. Mark's Bookshop, 31 Third Ave., at E. 9th St. (☎260-7853; www.stmarksbookshop.com). Subway: 6 to Astor Pl. The ultimate East Village bookstore. Excellent selection of books, with an emphasis on current literary theory, fiction, and poetry, and a good selection of mainstream and avant-garde magazines. Helpful staff. Open M-Sa 10am-midnight, Su 11am-midnight.

Throb, 211 E. 14th St. between Second and Third Aves. (☎533-2328). Subway: 4, 5, 6, N, R to Union Sq.; L to 3rd Ave. House, drum 'n' bass, trip-hop, psychedelic trance, and more. Throb caters to folks who are serious about their beats. Wax for the DJs, CDs for the audiophiles, flyers for those looking to party, and a (cute) staff to assist the (gasp) unfamiliar. Open M-Sa noon-9pm, Su 1-9pm.

Tokyo Joe, 334 E. 11th St., between First and Second Aves. (☎532-3605). Subway: 6 to Astor Pl.; L to First Ave. A consignment store with extremely well-priced brand-name clothing, as well as hard-to-find Japanese brands like Pluto Cat on the Earth. Open daily noon-9pm. Also at 240 E. 28th St., between Second and Third Aves. (☎532-3605).

Vintage Stores: Physical Graffiti, 96 St. Mark's Pl. (☎477-7334). Open M-Sa 1pm-midnight, Su 1-10pm. **Tatiana,** 111 St. Mark's Pl., between First Ave. and Ave. A (☎717-7684); open daily noon-8pm. **Shoshana's Place,** 315 E. 9th St. between First and Second Aves. (☎654-6594); open daily 1-9pm. **Fab 288,** 79 E. 7th St. between First and Second Aves.; open W-Su noon-7:45pm. **Tokyo 7 Consignment Store,** 64 E. 7th St. between First and Second Aves. (☎353-8443).

CHELSEA AND THE FLATIRON DISTRICT

Ladies' Mile, in the Flatiron District between Broadway and Sixth Ave., was once a major shopping district: Macy's first store was here, at Sixth Ave. and 14th St. It still remains a shopping hub, and those seeking to avoid the hordes farther uptown will find the chain stores here somewhat less crowded.

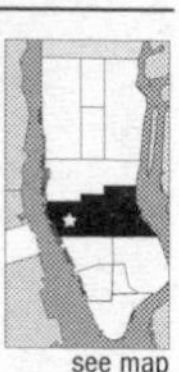
see map pp. 322-323

Books of Wonder, 16 W. 18th St. between Fifth and Sixth Aves. (☎989-3270). Subway: F, Q to 23rd St. A jewel of a children's bookstore, with an amazing antique book section. The store hosts a variety of programs related to children's books; storytime is Su at 11:45am. Open M-Sa 10am-7pm, Su noon-6pm.

Midnight Records, 263 W. 23rd St. between Seventh and Eighth Aves. (☎675-2768). Subway: 1, 9 to 23rd St. A mail-order and retail store specializing in hard-to-find rock records. Posters plaster the walls; every last nook of the store is crammed with records—over 10,000 in stock. Lots of 60s and 70s titles. Most LPs $9-20. Open Tu and Th-Sa noon-6pm.

MOVING ON UP

Mirroring Manhattan's south-to-north development, the main shopping district in the borough progressed northward from 14th St. in the 1870's to 23rd St. in the 1890's. In the early 1900s Macy's move uptown to Herald Square at 34th St., along with the opening of a Saks and Gimbels retail stores in Herald Square, created a new northernmost shopping mecca on Broadway.

But Broadway was about to share the commercial spotlight. In 1906, the B. Altman department store moved from its location on Sixth Ave. and 19th St. to Fifth Ave. at 34th St. To mollify the appalled residents of the mansions along Fifth Ave., Benjamin Altman disguised his store behind a stately French limestone, Florentine-styled exterior, unmarked by his name. Once B. Altman opened, however, there was no stopping the spread of commerce and the shopping area steadily spread northward along Fifth and Madison Aves. By 1924, Saks had relocated from Herald Square to Fifth Ave. and 50th St. into a building whose grand Italian Renaissance facade was in keeping with the expectations of its moneyed clientele and the affluent character of the avenue. This move signaled what was to become the final northward surge of the major retail stores. Saks Fifth Avenue (see p. 212) flourishes today, but B. Altman closed its doors in 1990.

Reminiscence, 50 W. 23rd St. between Fifth and Sixth Aves. (☎243-2292). Subway: R to 23rd St. Happily stuck in a 1970s groove, the store features a wide selection of gifts (inflatable flamingo cups $5; plastic straw bags $3-10), 70s jewelry, and vintage gear (slips $10, jeans $12). Open M-Sa 11am-7:30pm, Su noon-7pm.

Revolution Books, 9 W. 19th St. between Fifth and Sixth Aves. (☎691-3345). Subway: F, Q to 23rd St. America's largest explicitly revolutionary bookstore stocks works on radical struggles from around the world. Large collection of works on Marx, Mao, and Malcolm X. Radical works range from political science to manifestos, posters to children's books. Not-for-profit and mostly staffed by clued-in volunteers. Open M-Sa 10am-7pm, Su noon-5pm.

Second Hand Rose Records, 127 W. 22nd St. (☎675-3735). Subway: 1, 9 to 23rd St. A good selection of second-hand CDs and records of all genres, including old 12" records from Sugarhill Records and Salsoul Records. Open M-F 11am-7:30pm, Sa 10:30am-7pm, Su noon-6pm.

Weiss and Mahoney, 142 Fifth Ave., at 19th St. (☎675-1915). Subway: F, Q to 23rd St. A "peaceful" army/navy store selling surplus gear and camping equipment. The fashion militant can indulge in cargo pants ($25-30) and jungle boots ($20). Buy Carhartt at original (not designer) prices (denim jeans $20). Open M-F 9am-7pm, Sa 10am-6pm, Su 11am-5pm.

HERALD SQUARE

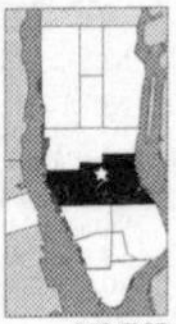

see map pp. 322-323

Dominated by Macy's, once the world' s largest store, Herald Square is full of deparment stores.

The Complete Traveller Bookstore, 199 Madison Ave., at 35th St. (☎685-9007). Subway: 6 to 33rd St. Arnold and Harriet Greenberg stock possibly the widest selection of guidebooks on the Eastern Seaboard. They also carry a well-kept selection of antique travel guides (*Baedekers*, *A&C Blacks*) and travelogues about distant lands. Most importantly, the store carries a full assortment of *Let's Go* guidebooks (priceless). Wheelchair accessible. Open M-F 9am-7pm, Sa 10am-6pm, Su 11am-5pm.

H&M, 1328 Broadway, at 34th St. (☎564-9922). Subway: B, D, F, N, Q, R to Herald Sq. When this Swedish chain opened its first New York branch, lines formed round the block. The crowds may only have eased somewhat, but knock-offs of the latest styles and accessories, both at ridiculously low prices (we spotted an eyelash comb for $1.50), make it worth braving the lines for both the fitting rooms and cashier. Open M-Sa 10am-9pm, Su 11am-8pm. Other branches: 640 Fifth Ave., at 51st St. (☎489-0930; open M-F 10am-8pm, Sa 10am-9pm, Su 11am-7pm), and 558 Broadway, (open M-Sa 10am-9pm, Su 11am-5pm).

Macy's, 151 W. 34th St. between Broadway and Seventh Ave. (☎695-4400; www.macys.com). Subway: B, D, F, N, Q, R to Herald Sq. This New York institution alternately provides thrills and frustration. Just don't get in the way of crazed shoppers on sale days. In its labyrinth-like interior, you can purchase a book, grab a snack or an all-out meal, get a facial or a haircut, have your jewelry appraised, exchange currency, purchase theater tickets, and get lost. Open M-Sa 10am-8:30pm, Su 11am-7pm. (See **Sights,** p. 69.)

Manhattan Mall, Sixth Ave. and 33rd St. (☎465-0500). Subway: B, D, F, N, Q, R to Herald Sq. Eight levels of cheesy Malldom, USA in a neon shell. There's nothing but branches of chain stores, from Express to Victoria's Secret, and the top level is an entire floor of homogenized, multi-cultured fast food. You didn't come to New York to shop the same way as back home, did you? Go outside: you could do so much better. Open M-Sa 10am-8pm, Su 11am-6pm.

Rock and Soul, 462 Seventh Ave. between 35th and 36th Sts. (☎695-3953). Subway: 1, 2, 3, 9 to 34th St. Behind the storefront selling hi-fi electronics, DJ equipment, and gold jewelry is a pathway to full crates of vinyls. Great if you're looking for old-school classics or new releases in soul, R&B, reggae, or hip-hop. Open M-Sa 9:30am-7pm.

The Wiz, 871 Sixth Ave., at 31st St. (☎594-2300), and 17 Union Sq. West, at 15th St. (☎741-9500). Subway: B, D, F, N, Q, R to Herald Sq. In desperate need of a camcorder or camera to make memories of NYC permanent? Check out this chain store's selection of electronics, often at great value prices. If you bring in an advertisement for an item that is priced lower than at the Wiz, they will discount the item 10% for you. Both locations open M-Sa 10am-8:30pm, Su 11am-7pm.

MIDTOWN

High-priced boutiques line Fifth Ave. south of Central Park. Most are not listed, but they are among the most fashionable New York has to offer.

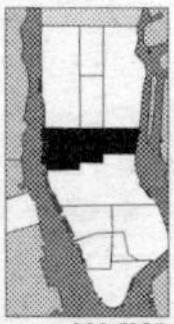

see map pp. 326-327

Bergdorff-Goodman, 754 Fifth Ave. between 57th and 58th Sts. (☎753-7300). Subway: N, R to 59th St.-Fifth Ave. In addition to housing all of the top designers of high fashion, this legendary mansion of clothing (and pomp), splendid in its marble and chandelier surroundings, is every celebrity's one-stop shopping choice when they want to be left alone. Open M-W 10am-7pm, Th 10am-8pm, F-Sa 10am-7pm, Su noon-6pm.

The Counter Spy Shop, 444 Madison Ave. between 49th and 50th St. (☎688-8500). Subway: 6 to 51st St. James Bond fans and clinical paranoids will love this store, devoted to the technology of subterfuge and deception. Bullet-proof vests, hidden cameras, and domestic lie detectors share the racks with false-bottom cans ($20). One useful title: *How To Get Even with Anybody, Anytime.* Open M 9am-6pm, Tu-Th 9am-7pm, F 9am-6pm, Sa 10am-4pm.

The Drama Book Shop, 723 Seventh Ave., 2nd fl., at 48th St. (☎944-0595; www.dramabookshop.com). Subway: 1, 9, to 51st St. If it ever appeared onstage, you'll find it in print here. Find half the aspiring actors in the city and the monologues they seek, all in one compact location. A necessary stop for any theater, film or plain ol' performing arts buff. Open M-F 9:30am-7pm, W 9:30am-8pm, Sa 10:30am-5:30pm, Su noon-5pm.

F.A.O. Schwarz, 767 Fifth Ave., at 58th St. (☎644-9400). Subway: N, R to Fifth Ave.-59th St. A child's ultimate fantasy world: everything that whirs, flies, or begs to be assembled appears in this huge hands-on toy store. But, like Tom Hanks in *Big,* adults, too, can reclaim their inner spoiled brat. With amusement-park-like lines outside and frenzied shoppers inside, the store celebrates the Christmas season with a ritual that resembles the running of the bulls in Pamplona. For the young ones, storytime is held daily at 1, 3, and 5pm. Open M-W 10am-7pm, Th-Sa 10am-8pm, Su 11am-6pm.

Fine Line, 954 Third Ave. between 57th and 58th Sts. (☎527-2603). Subway: 4, 5, 6, N, R to Lexington Ave.-59th St. This clothing company is one of the cheapest boutiques around, offering items from $10-$60. Open M-F 8am-8pm, Sa 10am-8pm, Su 11am-7pm.

Gotham Book Mart, 41 W. 47th St. between Fifth and Sixth Aves. (☎719-4448). The sign outside reads "Wise men fish here." Legendary and venerable, Gotham's renowned selection of new and used volumes of 20th-century writing has long made it a favorite to New York bibliophiles. This little renegade store smuggled censored copies of works by Joyce, Lawrence, and Miller to America. Then-unknowns LeRoi Jones, Tennessee Williams, and Allen Ginsberg all worked here as clerks. Open M-F 9:30am-6:30pm, Sa 9:30am-6pm.

SoHo Shopping

Shoe Heaven (west of 6th Ave.)

Generation Records

Hacker Art Books, 45 W. 57th St. between Fifth and Sixth Ave. (☎688-7600). Subway: B, Q to 57th St. Five flights up from the rumble of the street, this store is hard to find but worth the effort (look for street numbers). The city's oldest remaining art book store, Hacker's volumes comprise one of the best art book selections anywhere. The wide array of books should satisfy art historians, birdhouse builders, and fans of prehistoric stoneware alike. Open Sept.-June M-Sa 9:30am-6pm; July-Aug. M-F 9:30am-6pm.

Hammacher Schlemmer, 147 E. 57th St. between Third and Lexington Aves. (☎421-9000). Subway: 4, 5, 6, N, R to Lexington Ave.-59th St. Known for its unique and innovative products, Hammacher Schlemmer was the first to carry such items as the steam iron, the electric razor, the microwave, and the cordless telephone. The innovation of tomorrow? Silver-plated teak chopsticks ($34.95). Open M-Sa 10am-6pm.

Lord and Taylor, 424-434 Fifth Ave. between 38th and 39th St. (☎391-3344). Subway: B, D, F, Q to 42nd St.; 7 to 5th Ave. During an unusually balmy December in 1905, Lord and Taylor filled its windows with mock blizzards, reviving the Christmas spirit for gloomy city-dwellers and starting a tradition of the display window as stage. Today, the courtly, albeit claustrophobic store features 10 floors of fashion frenzy. Scores of New Yorkers come to be shod at the acclaimed shoe department and treated to caring service and free early morning coffee. Open M-W and Sa 10am-7pm, Th-F 10am-8:30pm, Su 11am-7pm.

Saks Fifth Avenue, 611 Fifth Ave. between 49th and 50th St. (☎753-4000). Subdued and chic. This institution has aged well and continues to combine inflated prices with smooth courtesy. At Saks you truly get what you pay for; in this case, it's expensive clothes. During Christmastime, crowds line up to see the window displays. Open M-W and F-Sa 10am-7pm, Th 10am-8pm, Su noon-6pm.

Tiffany & Co., 727 Fifth Ave., at 57th St. (☎605-4222). Subway: N, R to Fifth Ave.–59th St. Although you (like Holly Golightly) may not be able to afford any of the precious gemstones, there is still much to feast your eyes upon in this world-renowned jewel sanctuary. Open M-F 10am-7pm, Sa 10am-6pm.

UPPER EAST SIDE

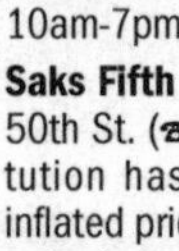
see map pp. 328-329

For the most expensive in New York shopping, stroll down Madison Ave. from the 60s to the 80s.

Argosy Bookstore, 116 E. 59th St. between Lexington and Park Aves. (☎753-4455). Subway: 4, 5, 6, N, R to 59th St. Specializes in old, rare, and out-of-print books, along with autographed editions, Americana, and antique maps and prints. Look for the racks of $1 books. Open M-F 10am-6pm; Oct.-Apr. also Sa 10am-5pm.

Barneys New York, 660 Madison Ave., at 61st St. (☎833-2466). Subway: 4, 5, 6, N, R to 59th St. An exclusive department store whose claim to fame is its discovery and cultivation of relative unknowns into cutting-edge designers. Some lively tropical fish add an extra splash of color to their jewelry displays. Open M-F 10am-8pm, Sa 10am-7pm, Su 11am-6pm.

Bloomingdale's, 1000 Third Ave., at 59th St. (☎705-2000). Founded in 1872 by two brothers, Bloomie's is "not just a store, it's a destination." Not only was Bloomingdale's the first "department" store, it also invented the designer shopping bag in 1961 and made such designers as Ralph Lauren, Donna Karan, and Fendi. If you're lucky enough to survive the mob of perfume assailants, tourists, and casual shoppers, you'll find that it's fun to get lost in this colorful store. Open M-F 10am-8:30pm, Sa 10am-7pm, Su 11am-7pm.

Chick Darrow's Fun Antiques & Collectibles, 1101 First Ave., between 60th and 61st Sts. (☎838-0730). Subway: 4, 5, 6, N, R to 59th St. Established in 1962, Chick Darrow's is the world's first antique toy shop. Possessing a wide variety of items, from 19th-century carpet toys to *Star Trek* memorabilia and *everything* in between, this store will definitely delight seekers of the usual and the unusual. Open Tu-F noon-7pm, Sa noon-5pm.

Corner Bookstore, 1313 Madison Ave., at 93rd St. (☎831-3554). Subway: 6 to 96th St. Careful selection and a friendly staff make this cozy neighborhood bookstore a treasure for Upper East Side book lovers. Note the antique cash register and the zaftig cat named Murphy. Open M-Th 10am-8pm, F 10am-7pm, Sa-Su 11am-6pm.

Encore, 1132 Madison Ave., at 84th St., 2nd fl. (☎879-2850). Second-hand designer clothes. Open M-W and F 10:30am-6:30pm, Th 10:30am-7:30pm, Sa 10:30am-6pm, Su noon-6pm; closed Su July to mid-Aug.

HMV, 1280 Lexington Ave., at 86th St. (☎348-0800). Subway: 4, 5, 6 to 86th St. A music megastore, His Master's Voice also houses a *Ticketmaster* outlet. Open M-Sa 9am-11pm, Su 10am-10pm. **Other locations:** 57 W. 34th St., at 6th Ave.; 234 W. 42nd St. between Seventh and Eighth Aves.; 565 Fifth Ave., at 46th St.; and 308 W. 125th St. between St. Nicholas and Eighth Aves.

Michael's, 1041 Madison Ave., 2nd fl. between 79th and 80th Sts. (☎737-7273). Subway: 6 to 77th St. Peddles "gently-used" designer threads. Open M-W and F-Sa 9:30am-6pm, Th 9:30am-8pm; closed Sa July-Aug.

Rita Ford Music Boxes, 19 E. 65th St. between Madison and Fifth Aves. (☎535-6717). Subway: 6 to 68th St. The first, and only, store in the US to service, repair, and sell both antique and contemporary music boxes, Rita Ford's has been winding up beautiful music since 1947 and has designed exclusive boxes for the White House, the State Department, and overseas royalty. Open M-Sa 9am-5pm.

Book Browsing

St. Mark's Place

Chinatown Street Scene

on the cheap

Harlem Hotspots

Welcome or not, mega-stores have burrowed into Harlem's fertile cultural soil. The main Harlem shopping drag, 125th St., already stomachs the first off-shoots of major corporations. But while Old Navy and the Disney Store might suck the non-conformist spirit out of 125th St., the following depots are more original than their grafted neighbors. Check out these other stores—less money, less mega, and much less mall.

Liberation Bookstore, 421 Lenox Ave., at 131st St. (☎281-4615). This small store houses a great selection of African and African-American history, art, poetry, and fiction. Open Tu-F 3-7pm, Sa noon-4pm. Cash only.

Sugar Hill Thrift Shop, 409 W. 145th St. between St. Nicholas and Convent Aves. (☎281-2396). Ripe with quality vintage clothing and used household merchandise and antiques, this shop is definitely the sweet side of Sugar Hill. Come see what all the buzz is about. Open M-F 10am-6pm, Sa noon-5pm.

Tender Buttons, 143 E. 62nd St. between Third and Lexington Aves. (☎758-7004). Subway: 4, 5, 6, N, R to 59th St. A treasure trove of billions of buttons. If you carelessly lost the button on your favorite Renaissance doublet, you will find a replacement here. Also has cuff links and buckles. Open M-F 10:30am-6pm, Sa 10:30am-5:30pm.

UPPER WEST SIDE

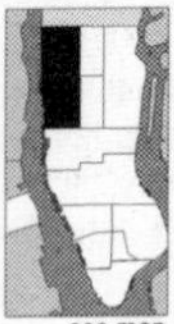

see map pp. 332-333

This is uptown and therefore expensive in general, but, unlike the East Side, the Upper West Side does not have a reputation for being elitist.

Allan and Suzi, 416 Amsterdam Ave., at 80th St. (☎724-7445). Subway: 1, 9 to 79th St.; B, C to 81st St. From new Gaultier Madonna-wear at 70% off to that coveted conservative Prada jacket, this store is *haute couture* discounted (although still expensive). A large assortment of fabulously authentic platform shoes and feather boas all colors of the synthetic, chemically-dyed rainbow surround the melée. Men's clothing includes Armani and Versace suits. Celeb-spotters take note: RuPaul, Courtney Love, and Annie Lennox have been spotted shopping here. Open M-F noon-7:30pm, Sa noon-7pm, Su noon-6pm.

Applause Theater and Cinema Books, 211 W. 71st St. between Broadway and West End Ave. (☎496-7511). Subway: 1, 2, 3, 9 to 72nd St. Great selection of scripts, screenplays, and books on everything about theater and cinema, from John Wayne to tap dancing. Over 4000 titles. Look out for their intermittent $1 sale, 50%-off shelves and the odd celebrity. Knowledgable staff. Open M-Sa 10am-9pm, Su noon-6pm.

Gryphon Bookshops, 2246 Broadway between 80th and 81st Sts. (☎362-0706). Subway: 1, 9 to 79th St. Open for 25 years, this sliver of a bookstore is filled from floor to ceiling with used books and the occasional LP. Sift through fiction, play scripts sorted by author, and cookbooks; you're bound to find something that will catch your eye. Very knowledgable staff. The mezzanine floor holds first editions and art books; you'll have to negotiate the narrow book-filled staircase to get there, though. Frequent sales. Open daily 10am-midnight.

Gryphon Record Shop, 233 W. 72nd St., at Broadway (☎874-1588). Subway: 1, 2, 3, 9 to 72nd St. A relaxed place with wall-to-wall shelves of classical, Broadway, and jazz LPs, many rare or out of print. Great books on music. Proprietor has the knowledge to match. Open M-F 9:30am-7pm, Sa 11am-7pm, Su noon-6pm.

Maxilla & Mandible, 451 Columbus Ave. between 81st and 82nd Sts. (☎724-6173). Subway: B, C to 81st St. Just the store for those who had to be forced out of the nearby Museum of Natural History at closing time. Shelves and boxes of well-displayed shells, fossils, eggs, preserved insects, and bones from every imaginable vertebrate (including *Homo sapiens*). A giant walking-stick insect under glass and an 11 ft. alligator skeleton stand out prominently among the merchandise. "Dinosaur dung" for the little ones ($3); real shark teeth ($5) for the incisive. Open M-Sa 11am-7pm.

Murder Ink, Twilight. He jumped off the 1/9 at 96th St. and walked to 2486 Broadway. He was supposed to meet her at the old haunt. The bookstore. He had been thinking about that dame for some time now. She was swell but always looked out for herself first. Today, she was late and she hadn't phoned (☎362-8905). This place was their hideaway, but it always made him antsy. The whodunits. The black and red walls. It all got him thinking that he had about as much time left as that stool pigeon back at the precinct. And then she walked in. She wore a devilish grin and a skirt that didn't leave much to the imagination. She was trying to get a rise out of him. He knew it, and he wouldn't budge. He picked up a mystery and made like he didn't know the broad. She slipped him a note. Inside was a wad of cash. He looked at his watch. 6:55. Let's scram he said. This place closes in five minutes.

Ordning & Reda, 253 Columbus Ave. between 71st and 72nd Sts. Subway: 1, 2, 3, 9 to 72nd St. (☎799-0828). A minimalist-design addict's dream, in living (primary and secondary) color. Pop into this American outpost of the famed Swedish stationer and drool at the paper, notebooks, and binders all organized by hue. Notebooks a pricey $11-29.50. Open M-Sa 11am-8pm, Su 11am-6pm.

BROOKLYN

A borough with some great deals. Atlantic Ave. is known for its antique shops.

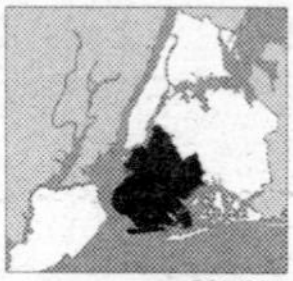

see map pp. 336-337

Beat Street, 494 Fulton St., in Fort Greene. (☎718-624-7465). Subway: 2, 3, 4, 5 to Nevins St.; A, C, G to Hoyt St./Schermerhorn. Hip hop par excellence with great vinyl to boot. Open M-W 10am-7pm, Th-Sa 10am-7:30pm, Su 10am-6pm.

Bird, 430 Seventh Ave., in Park Slope. (☎718-768-4940). Subway: F to Seventh Ave. A fashionable women's clothing store that also sells accessories and bags. Open Tu-F noon-8pm, Sa-Su noon-6pm.

Clovis Press, 229 Bedford Ave., in Williamsburg. (☎718-302-3751). Subway: L to Bedford Ave. The store crams a comfy couch and a great selection of used books, magazines, art, and locally published editions into its cozy confines. Junk furniture and $1 books spill out onto the street in haphazard displays. Open daily noon-8pm.

Domsey's, 431 Kent Ave., in Williamsburg (☎718-384-6000). Subway: J, M, Z to Marcy Ave. Poorly paid Manhattanites and hipsters alike head to Domsey's, located far from the main drag of Williamsburg. Astounding bargains await the diligent shopper in this sprawling warehouse. Check out the tuxedos for $15 and corduroy Levi's in all sorts of colors ($5). The store is huge and the selection vast for those willing to brave the abyss. Next door, a second, even more chaotic store has opened where clothing is sold per pound.Open M-F 8am-5:30pm, Sa 8am-6:30pm, Su 11am-5:30pm.

Girdle Factory, 218 Bedford Ave., in Williamsburg. Subway: L to Bedford Ave. A cavernous collective of small spaces, inhabited by artist's studios, cafes, a beauty salon (Hello, Beautiful), shops, and chairs to just sit and relax. Check out Mini Minimarket (☎718-302-9337) for kitschy, nostalgic, Tokyo-inspired stuff and the store after which the alternative complex was named, The Girdle Factory, for hip vintage clothes. On Su, Lili Fearless sets up on a rug with her wonder-dog Sophie to give absolutely free advice. Open daily noon-9pm.

Ugly Luggage, 214 Bedford Ave. at 5th St., in Williamsburg. (☎718-384-0724). Subway: L to Bedford Ave. Even with a bright orange storefront, this vintage store is surprisingly inconspicuous. Full of retro accessories, such as fake snake skin phones or archaic type-writers. Open M-F 1-8pm, Sa-Su noon-7pm.

INSIDE

Daytripping

DESTINATION	HIGHLIGHTS	TRAVEL TIME
Oyster Bay	The Gold Coast	45 minutes-1 hour
Jones Beach	Waves, sand, sunbathers	1 hour
Fire Island	Beaches, gay scene	1½-2 hours
The Hamptons and Montauk	Beaches, rich people	2-3 hours
Tarrytown and Sleepy Hollow	Estates	45 minutes-1 hour
West Point	Boot camp	1-1½ hours
Woodstock	Hippies in artsy community	2½-3 hours
Bear Mountain State Park	Hiking, bears	1-1½ hours
Hoboken, NJ	Bars, Sinatra	10-20 minutes
Atlantic City, NJ	Casinos	2½-3 hours

LONG ISLAND

TRANSPORTATION

Trains: Long Island Railroad, LIRR (automated info ☎718-217-5477 or 516-822-5477; TDD ☎718-558-3022; daily 7:20am-7:20pm). Trains leave from **Penn Station** in Manhattan (34th St. at Seventh Ave.; subway: 1, 2, 3, 9, A, C, E) and meet in **Jamaica, Queens** (subway: E, J, Z). LIRR also connects in Queens at the 7 subway **Hunters' Point Ave., Woodside, Jamaica,** and **Main St.-Flushing** stations, and in Brooklyn at the **Flatbush Ave.** station (subway: 2, 3, 4, 5, D, Q to Atlantic Ave.; B, M, N, R to Pacific St.) Fares vary daily and by zone. Rush hour peak tickets (Manhattan-bound 5am-9am, outbound 4-8pm) $5 more than off-peak fares. Tickets can be purchased aboard

SCENIC DRIVING

The closest you'll get to a scenic drive in Manhattan is a rush-hour crawl down Park Avenue. There is no peace in city-driving—just ask the cab drivers who brave the streets every day. Too much road rage, too many cars. Life doesn't have to be short: seek calmer pastures and do your driving out of the city. The following make for peaceful and beautiful drives.

The Palisades. Take the George Washington Bridge into New Jersey and find the Palisades Parkway, a picturesque 42-mile ride to Bear Mountain State Park (see **p. 228**).

The North Fork of Long Island. An unspoiled portion of Long Island home to myriad vineyards, the North Fork has character that the South Fork lacks. Take the Long Island Expressway to Exit 73 (this is not scenic) and follow Route 58 to Route 25.

The Merritt Parkway. A narrow two-lane highway (Route 10) that is gorgeous when the leaves turn in autumn. Take I-95 to Milford and follow the steep curves.

Lake George. Located about four hours north the city. Drive up I-87 and take it to Route 9N, which hugs the western portion of the lake and offers some wonderful views.

trains, but you will be surcharged if the station ticket office is open. The LIRR offers 18 expensive but convenient **day tours** May-Nov. ($15-58).

BUSES

MTA Long Island Bus (☎516-766-6722; open M-Sa 7am-5pm). Daytime bus service in eastern Queens, Nassau, and western Suffolk. Runs along major streets, but routes are complex and irregular—confirm your destination with the driver. Some buses run every 15min., others every hr. Fare $1.50; transfers 25¢, free with Metrocard. Disabled travelers and senior citizens pay half fare. Serves Jones Beach daily during summer; every 25 min from the LIRR station in Freeport.

Suffolk Transit (☎631-852-5200; open M-F 8am-4:30pm). Runs from Lindenhurst to the eastern end of Long Island. The 10a, 10b, and 10c lines make frequent stops along the South Fork. No service Su. Fare $1.50; seniors and the disabled 50¢; transfers 25¢; under 5 free. Buses run in summer from the LIRR station in Babylon to Robert Moses State Park on Fire Island, hourly M-F and more frequently on the weekends.

Hampton Jitney (☎800-936-0440 or 631-283-4600; www.hamptonjitney.com). The luxury bus serving the Hamptons. More expensive, but more comfortable and comprehensive than other buses. Departs from various Manhattan locales. One-way $24, round-trip $43. Reservations advisable; call in advance, especially on weekends.

OYSTER BAY

By car: *Take Long Island Expressway to Exit 41N. Take Route 106N and follow signs to Oyster Bay.* ***By train:*** *LIRR to Oyster Bay branch to Oyster Bay.* ***Taxi*** *☎516-921-2141.*

Oyster Bay, a town on the monied North Shore, is Long Island at its most picturesque, with beautiful estates lining the seashore. Depending on your source, the town got its name either for the plentiful oysters located in the offshore waters or for the oyster-like shape of its harbor.

SIGHTS

The town's most illustrious resident was President Theodore Roosevelt, and today his summertime estate **Sagamore Hill,** Sagamore Hill Rd. off Cove Neck Rd., is the most precious jewel in the crown of Oyster Bay. To get there from the LIE, get off at Exit 41N, and take Route 106N for 4 miles to Rte. 25A. Turn right on Rte. 25A east and travel 2½ miles to the third traffic light, at which you will take a left onto Cove Road. After 1½ miles, you'll see a sign for Sagamore Hill. You'll make the next right. In 1905 Roosevelt met in the Queen Anne Style house with envoys from Japan and Russia to set in motion negotiations that would lead to the Treaty of Portsmouth, effectively the end of the Russo-Japanese War. Roosevelt won the Nobel Peace Prize for his part

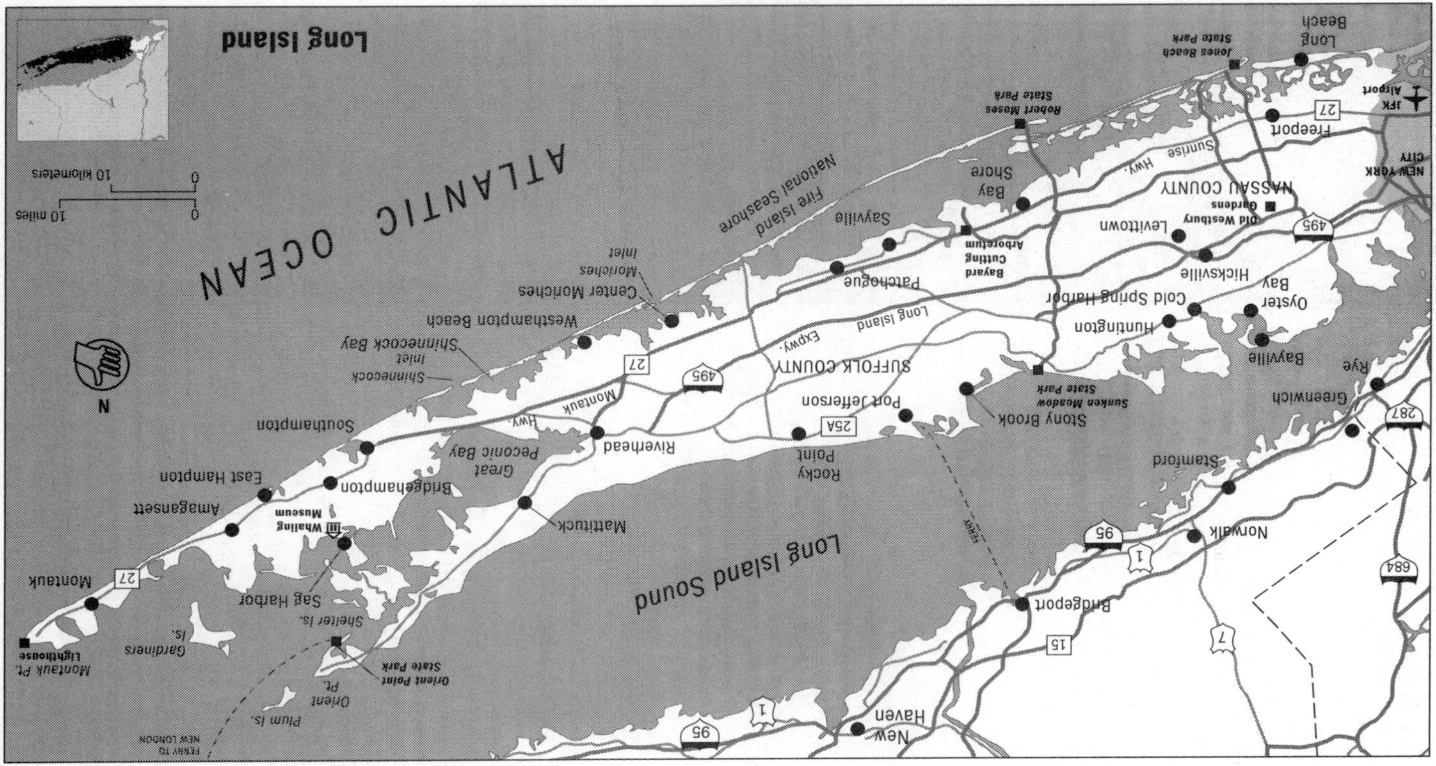
Long Island
Long Island Sound
ATLANTIC OCEAN
N
0 10 miles
0 10 kilometers
Montauk Pt. Lighthouse
Montauk
27
Gardiners Is.
Amagansett
East Hampton
Sag Harbor
Whaling Museum
Shelter Is.
Orient Pt.
Orient Point State Park
Plum Is.
FERRY TO NEW LONDON
Bridgehampton
Southampton
Shinnecock Inlet
Shinnecock Bay
Shinnecock Beach
Westhampton Beach
Great Peconic Bay
Mattituck
Riverhead
Montauk Hwy.
Center Moriches
Moriches Inlet
495
Rocky Point
25A
Port Jefferson
SUFFOLK COUNTY
Long Island Expwy.
Patchogue
Sayville
Fire Island National Seashore
Bayard Cutting Arboretum
Bay Shore
Robert Moses State Park
Stony Brook
Sunken Meadow State Park
Huntington
Cold Spring Harbor
Levittown
Hicksville
Old Westbury Gardens
NASSAU COUNTY
Sunrise Hwy.
Jones Beach State Park
Bayville
Oyster Bay
Freeport
Long Beach
NEW YORK CITY
JFK Airport
Greenwich
Rye
287
684
Stamford
Norwalk
7
1
95
Bridgeport
15
FERRY
New Haven

GO DOWN, MOSES

Robert Moses, New York's most influential builder, executed his first projects on the barren sandbars of Long Island. Moses freed up huge areas of land for public recreation and established the power base from which he would eventually build $27 billion worth of public works. Before Moses took over the Long Island Parks Commission, New Yorkers had nowhere to take their first automobiles—only a few strips of beaches lay open to them, and it took up to four dust-choked hours to get there from downtown Manhattan. Moses finagled $14 million from a graft-ridden state budget, built tree-lined highways (Northern State and Southern State Parkways), and developed Jones Beach, a recreation area with lavish facilities and a Disney-like attention to detail. To wrest right-of-way and parkland from its owners, Moses attacked the rich, who owned most of the island; failing to win their cooperation, he rerouted his plans, obliterating small farmers. To keep his beaches "clean," he had the bridges over the parkways built too low to accommodate city buses, blocked the Long Island Railroad from building a stop, and made it nearly impossible for charter companies carrying African-Americans to get permits for Jones Beach. Those who could not pay parking fees were directed to "poor lots" far from the beach. With Long Island a precedent was set for grand public works projects, accommodation of a large and mobile middle class, and institutional racism and classicism, with which Moses would revolutionize public building.

in the negotiations. The house is packed with memorabilia (such as samurai swords presented by a Japanese emperor) and an impressive collection of "preserved" wildlife. In addition to stuffed deer, buffalo and zebra heads, an old family pet, a rhinoceros foot inkwell, and an elephant's foot trash can adorn his home. (☎516-922-4447 or 516-922-4788. **Visitors Center** open daily 9:30am-4pm; off-season W-Su 9:30am-4pm. $5, under 16 free. **Tours** of the house every 30min. Come early; only 200 tickets available each day. **Grounds** free.)

If the presidential ethos proves overwhelming, try the **Planting Fields Arboretum,** another coastal gem. Purchased by insurance magnate William Robinson Coe and his wife in 1913, the 409-acre estate is filled with flowers in two greenhouses, a rhododendron park, and other quirky highlights such as the "synoptic garden" of plants obsessively alphabetized according to their Latin names. The flowers bloom during the unlikely months of December, January, and February, when most city-dwellers have begun to forget what flora looks like.

The **Fall Flower Show,** held for two weeks in early October, attracts huge crowds every year. The arboretum hosts a summer jazz festival and concert series; past seasons have seen Joan Baez, the Indigo Girls, and Aretha Franklin. Call ahead for a concert schedule. At the center of the historic site sits Coe Hall, the Coe's Tudor revival estate. Constructed in 1921, the mansion has rows upon rows of mind-boggling windows with stained glass that dates to the 12th century. To get to Planting Fields, once in Oyster Bay, turn left at the light onto Lexington Avenue and turn left again at the next light Mill River Road. Follow the signs to Planting Fields Arboretum. (☎516-922-9200. Main greenhouse **open** daily 10am-4:30pm. **Admission** free. **Coe Hall** ☎516-922-0061. Open daily May-Sept. noon-3:30pm. $5; students and seniors $3.50; 7-12 $1. Parking on the grounds 9am-5pm; $5.)

FOOD AND OYSTERS

While its Gold Coast relics and sea-side charm draw a heavy tourist population during the summer, the bay town beckons the masses with an oyster-shucking contest during its October Oysterfest. Oyster-shucking opportunities abound in the summer as well as at the local hotspot for 18 years, **Oyster Bay Fish and Clam Bar.** Oysters run $14/dozen and buckets of clams cost $10. (103 Rte. 106. ☎516-922-5522. Apr.-Oct. M-Th 3 pm-11pm, F-Sa 11am-midnight, Su 11am-11pm.) For more pricey oysters on an outdoor patio, try the brand new **South Street Oyster Bar**. (100 South St. ☎516-922-1545. Su-Th 6pm-midnight, F-Sa 3pm-midnight.) For non-seafood, try **Taby's** famous hamburgers ($4.25-$6.05) (28 Audrey St. ☎516-624-7781).

JONES BEACH

☎516-785-1600. ***By car:*** *From Northern State Parkway East to Wantagh Parkway South to State Park. Parking $7 before 4pm, free after 4pm; open till sundown, Lot 4 until midnight.* ***By train:*** *LIRR to Freeport, shuttle bus to Jones Beach. In the summer, the LIRR runs a package deal for the trip ($11 from Manhattan, June 29-Sept. 7).*

When New York State Parks Commissioner Robert Moses discovered Jones Beach in 1921, it was a barren spit of land off the Atlantic shore of Nassau County. Within 10 years, he had bought up the surrounding land, imported tons of sand, planted beach grass to preserve the new dunes, and completed dozens of buildings for purposes as diverse as diaper-changing and archery. His industrious efforts created six and a half miles of popular public beaches. Although the water is not the bluest nor the sun the strongest, Jones Beach State Park still attracts an army of beach-goers, due to its wealth of attractions and proximity to Manhattan. The parking fields accommodate 23,000 cars, and there are nearly 2500 acres of beachfront with eight different public beaches on the rough Atlantic Ocean and calmer Zachs Bay. Only 40 minutes from the city, barely a patch of sand shows under all the umbrellas and blankets in the summertime. Along the one and a half mile **boardwalk** you can find two Olympic-sized pools, softball fields, roller-skating, mini-golf, a fitness course, basketball, and nightly dancing. The **Marine Theater** inside the park often hosts big-name rockers such as Pearl Jam.

THE HAMPTONS AND MONTAUK

By car: *Long Island Expressway to Exit 70. Make a right onto Rte. 111 (Manorville Rd.). When the road ends, make a left and get on the Montauk Highway. Towns are located either directly off of, or on, the highway.* ***By train:*** *LIRR from Penn Station serves all towns directly except Sag Harbor.*

A prized location for vacation houses, the Hamptons are best visited in the summer. Flowers are in bloom, the upper crust of society mill about on the sidewalks, and beachgoers bravely confront the ocean's waves. Located on the South Fork of Long Island, the Hamptons are a curious amalgam of the serene and the sexy. That is, the promise of serenity has attracted the sexy, who have consequently rid the place of some of its sleepiness. Summering Manhattanites, artists, writers, and displaced West Coast stars make the Hamptons their home come Memorial Day. The Hamptons' sex and star appeal translates into burgeoning development, crowded main streets, and conspicuous consumption.

The Hamptons can be visited for a single day if you set out early in the morning. While most inns and guest houses in the Hamptons run fairly steep, especially in the summer, Montauk might be the most realistic option with its host of motels. Nonetheless, it is imperative to call ahead. For a deal, try coming in the weeks directly following Labor Day, when the water's warm, the place empties out, and prices fall.

SOUTHAMPTON

From the Southampton LIRR station, head right out of the parking lot along Railroad Plaza to North Main St.; turn left onto N. Main and walk to the stop sign; bear left and keep walking as N. Main becomes Main St. and takes you to the center of town (about a ½-mile altogether). ***Taxis:*** *Atlantic Taxi ☎631-283-1900; Southampton ☎631-283-0242; Up Island Connection ☎631-287-7180.*

Founded in 1640 as the first English colony in what would become New York State, Southampton is a beautiful town of sprawling houses that grow as one approaches the ocean. While wandering through Southampton's residential sections, you can peek through hedges at houses designed by Stanford White and other luminaries of the late 19th century. On Dune Rd., by the ocean, enormous gates and rows of Normandy-esque hedges hide the beachfront mansions of some of the town's wealthiest residents. Most **beaches** require resident parking permits, but lots at the end of Beach Rd. D., off Meadow Lane, offer free parking. To get there from town, take Main St. south to Dune Rd. Make a left onto Dune Rd. Follow Dune Rd. to First Neck Lane. Make a left, and find Meadow Lane to the right. Follow the road for three or four miles. Road D follows Roads A, B, and C. Surprise. For more information, a detailed pamphlet is available at the **Chamber of Commerce,** 76 Main St. (☎631-283-0402, ext. 21. Open Su-Th 10am-4pm; F-Sa 11am-4pm).

Back in town, at the corner of Main and Meeting House Ln. is the **Southampton Historical Museum,** where you'll find a collection of buildings and exhibits set up to replicate an 1800s main street with a school-house, carpentry, cobbler, apothecary and blacksmith. (☎631-283-2494. Open June 12-Sept. 15 Tu-Su 11am-5pm; by appointment in winter. $3; students & seniors $2; children 6-12 $1; under 6 free.) The Venetian-style **Parrish Art Museum** is on the other side of Main Street. Here, a modern gallery houses a contemporary collection concentrating on American artists, particularly those (like William Merritt Chase and Fairfield Porter) who lived and worked near Southampton. The Parrish is surrounded by a garden showcasing reproduced Roman busts. (☎631-283-2118. Open June-Sept. M-Sa 11am-5pm, Su 1-5pm. Suggested donation $2, seniors $1, students free. Wheelchair accessible.)

Amidst the expensive boutiques and eateries, an inexpensive meal can be found at **Sip and Soda,** a restaurant with refreshing diner food and homemade ice cream.

Just outside Southampton at the intersection of Hwy. 27 and Old Mill Rd., the tiny community of Water Mill hosts the original mill that was built "to supply the necessities of the towne" in 1644. The **Water Mill Museum** has been in its present location since 1726 and is open for tours. (☎631-726-4625. Open late May to late Sept. M-Sa 11am-5pm, Su 1-5pm. $2; seniors $1.50; children free.)

EAST HAMPTON AND AMAGANSETT

From the East Hampton train station: Walk along Newtown Lane into town. From the Amagansett train station: Walk along Main St. into town. ***Taxi*** *☎631-668-6600 or 631-324-0077.*

The center of **East Hampton** is home to more art galleries, clothing stores, and colonial memorabilia outlets than one would care to imagine, but the town is great for strolling, window-shopping, and whiling away the hours. Many artists have found inspiration and refuge here—most prominently Jackson Pollock. To get to Main Beach, go down to Main St. and follow it back out of town. But after passing the pond, instead of making a right onto the Montauk Highway, continue straight through the light and drive about three quarters of a mile to the ocean. If hungry, stop in at **Dressen's Excelsior Market,** on Newtown Lane, one of the few remnants of the town's down-to-earth past. Dressen's cooks small lightly-crisped doughnuts (50¢) that put chain-store rivals to shame. For a pricey picnic lunch, try **Barefoot Contessa** across the street, one of many gourmet markets in the area, but one of few in town.

Nearby **Amagansett** is little more than a tiny Main St. If you want to catch a glimpse of some of the larger houses in the area, head south of the highway to Further Lane and examine the estates from the street. Back in town, the **Farmers' Market**, 367 Rte. 27 Main Street, attracts locals and tourists alike to its fresh food sections, coffee shop, and pastries (☎631-267-3894; M-Th 7am-6 pm, F-Sa 8am-9pm, Su 7am-8pm). And although the beaches require permits, a brilliant ploy by many Hamptons' beaches to keep out the plebes, the **Atlantic Avenue Beach** is walkable from the center of town (approx. one mile). In the evening, Amagansett hosts some great live music. **The Stephen Talkhouse,** 161 Main St., hosts performers such as Marianne Faithfull and Judy Collins, as well as lesser-known acts. (☎516-267-3117; www.stephentalkhouse.com. Performances begin at 9pm. Tickets $5-10.)

SAG HARBOR

Directions: *The LIRR does not stop at Sag Harbor, but the town is accessible via Bridgehampton. Take a taxi from the station: Hampton Bays Taxi ☎631-725-8900.*

Sag Harbor sits on the north shore of the South Fork, one of the diamonds in the rough of Long Island. Founded in 1707, this port used to be more important than New York Harbor as its deep waters made for easy navigation. At its peak, the winsome village was the world's fourth-largest whaling port. James Fenimore Cooper began his first novel, *Precaution,* in a Sag Harbor hotel in 1824. During Prohibition, the harbor served as a major meeting place for smugglers and rum-runners from the Caribbean.

SIGHTS

In the past few years, an increasing number of tourists have returned to the quiet, tree-lined streets of salt-box cottages and Greek Revival mansions. Sag Harbor's former grandeur survives in the second-largest collection of Colonial buildings in the

US and in the cemeteries lined with the gravestones of Revolutionary soldiers and sailors. Check out the **Sag Harbor Whaling Museum** in the Masonic Temple at the corner of Main St. and Garden St. A huge whale rib arches over the front door. Note the antique washing machine, made locally in 1864, and the excellent scrimshaw collection. (☎631-725-0770. Open May-Sept. M-Sa 10am-5pm, Su 1-5pm. $3; seniors $2; ages 6-13 $1. Tours by appointment; $2.) The equally intriguing **Custom House,** the authentic 18th Century home across the street, features an extensive collection of period furniture and trivial keepsakes. (☎631-725-0250. Open Jun.-Sept. Sa-Su 10am-5pm; July-Aug. daily 10am-5pm. $3; ages 7-14 and seniors $1.50.) Less than a mile from the wharf is **Haven's Beach,** where it costs $10 to park.

For more information, a large windmill in the center of the town harbors a **Tourist Office** (☎631-725-0011; open Sept-May Sa-Su 10am-5pm; June-Sept. M-Su 10am-5pm).

FOOD

Across the street from the Harbor sits **The Dockside Bar and Grill,** 26 Bay St. Although the fare is pricey (entrees run $11.95-17.95), the outdoor patio is crowded and lively with a nice view (☎631-725-7100; Open Su-Sa 10am-10pm, Bar serves until 12pm). **The Harbor Deli**, 111 Main St. offers a less costly alternative where you can pick up a deli and find your own dockside picnic spot. Sandwiches $3.75-5.50 (617-725-7398; Open Su-Th. 6am-7pm, F-Sa 6am-8pm).

MONTAUK

Directions: *LIRR to Montauk and head to the right out of the train station along the 4-lane road. This is Edgemere Rd., which leads straight to the village green, a 10-15min. walk. M-F the only trains back to the city leave at 10:36pm and 12:52am, Sa-Su there are several afternoon and evening trains; the Hampton Jitney makes a dozen trips daily.*

As the easternmost point of the South Fork, Montauk offers an unobstructed view of the Atlantic Ocean. Despite the slightly commercialized tourist/hotel areas and the three-hour trip, the peaceful salt air is worth the effort.

SIGHTS

The 110-foot **Montauk Point Lighthouse and Museum,** off Rte. 27., was built in 1796 by special order of President George Washington. The first public works project in the newly formed United States, the lighthouse guided many ships into the harbor, including the schooner *La Amistad.* If your lungs are willing, climb the 137 spiraling steps to the top for a view across the Long Island Sound to Connecticut and Rhode Island. (☎631-668-2544. Open Jun.-Sept. M-F and Su 10:30am-6pm, Sa 10:30am-7:30pm; other times call for info. $4; seniors $3.50; under 12 $2.50.)

You too can set out on the open seas. Try a half-day fluke-fishing cruise with **Viking** (☎631-668-5700; $32, children $15, including equipment; departs 8am and 1pm; no reservations necessary) or **Lazybones** (☎631-668-5671; $30, children $15, including equipment; departs 7am and 1pm; reservations required). Viking also runs whale-watching cruises (July-Aug. Th-Su 10:30am; $40, seniors $35, children $20).

Back in town, off the main drag, is an out-of-place high-rise apartment building. Real-estate developer Carl Fischer built this anomaly as part of his attempt to turn Montauk into a Miami Beach of the north. If you look around, you'll see that the plan failed. For more information on things to do and see in Montauk, check out the **Chamber of Commerce,** 742 Montauk Highway, in the center of town (☎631-668-2428. Open M-Sa 10am-5pm, Su 10am-4pm).

FOOD

Seafood is what Montauk does best. **Lunch,** on Hwy. 27 (the Montauk Highway), in the Napeague Stretch, features a lobster roll ($11.75) that is worth every penny. (☎631-267-3740. Open daily 11:30am-10pm.) **Gosman's Clam Bar,** on Flamingo Rd. by the ocean, is a good place to get a plate of mussels ($5.95) or a lobster (market price). (☎631-668-2549. Open Jun.-Sept. M-Su 12pm-9pm, weekends in the fall, weather permitting).

ACCOMMODATIONS

Hither Hills State Park, 4 miles west of Montauk along the highway and accessible from the village green in Montauk via taxi, offers lovely vistas, swimming, campsites

HOW TO BE A BEACH BUM WITHOUT REALLY TRYING

Getting to the beach in the Hamptons is complicated by steep parking fees and resident permits. Driving, therefore, is problematic. A better option may be to take a taxi from the train station or to simply walk. There is no charge to get onto any beach in the Hamptons, so anyone can walk on for free.

A bicycle may be helpful in your travels. While it is difficult to carry a bicycle onto the LIRR (call 718-558-8228 for more information), it is possible to rent a bicycle for the day once in the Hamptons. **Bermuda Bikes Plus** (☎631-324-6688) in East Hampton and **Rotations Bicycle Center** in Southampton (☎631-283-2890) have daily rentals for $30 and $25 respectively.

Beaches that allow non-residents to park (for a fee, of course), include Atlantic Avenue Beach in Amagansett, Mecox Beach in Bridgehampton, Essex Street Beach, Gin Beach, Hither Hills Beach and Kirk Park Beach in Montauk, Fowler Beach in Southampton, Beach Lane Beach in Wainscott.

($24/car), and picnicking spots (☎631-668-2554. Open daily 8am-9pm). While lodging anywhere on the South Fork requires some planning, the **Blue Haven Motel,** 533 W. Lake Ln., offers good clean rooms for comparatively cheap prices: $170 on the weekends but almost $100 less during the week (☎631-668-5943).

FIRE ISLAND

***No cars** are allowed on the island. **By train and ferry: LIRR to Sayville** ($9.50). Take a taxi to the port. **Ferries from Sayville** (☎631-589-0810) go to Sailors' Haven (round-trip $9), Cherry Grove, and Fire Island Pines (round-trip $11, under 11 $5). **LIRR to Bay Shore** ($9.50). The Port is in walking distance down Maple Ave. **Ferries from Bay Shore** (☎516-665-3600) go to Kismet, Saltaire, Fair Harbor, Atlantic, Dunewood, Ocean Beach, Seaview, and Ocean Bay Park (round-trip $11.50, under 12 $5.50). **LIRR to Patchogue** ($10.75). Walk to ferry. **Ferries from Patchogue** (☎516-475-1665) go to Davis Park and Watch Hill (round-trip $11, under 12 $4.25). To **travel between towns,** call one of many water taxi companies. **Water Taxi** ☎516-665-8885. Prices vary.*

Pristine, quiet towns dot Fire Island, southern Long Island's barrier against the temperamental Atlantic. Residents have done much to fend off the bright lights of the tourist industry, even as property values have soared. Some towns retain their original layout of closely packed bungalows without yards. The amazingly influential urban planner Robert Moses himself could not build a road across the island because citizens fought so fiercely to retain their quiet plots of land. Since then, the state has protected most areas of Fire Island by declaring them either state parks or federal "wilderness areas." This lack of infrastructure insures both peace and inconvenience; visitors must often take water taxis to travel between towns. Seventeen summer communities have managed to forge distinct niches on Fire Island. The separation has made the towns diverse—providing homes for middle-class clusters, openly gay communities (see **Gay New York,** p. 198), and pockets of vacationing Hollywood stars.

SIGHTS

The **Fire Island National Seashore** (☎516-289-4810 for the headquarters in Patchogue) is the official moniker for the stretches of coastline that hug the island. This is Fire Island's biggest draw and the daytime hotspot for summertime fishing, clamming, and guided nature walks. The **Fire Island Lighthouse Visitor Center** (☎631-661-4876; small museum open daily 9:30am-5pm) houses the only monument on the isle. The facilities at **Sailor's Haven** (just west of the Cherry Grove community) include a marina, a nature trail, and a famous beach. Similar facilities at **Watch Hill** (☎631-597-6455) include a 26-unit campground, where reservations are required.

The **Sunken Forest,** so called because of its location behind the dunes, is another of the island's natural wonders. Located directly west of Sailor's Haven, its soil supports an unusual and attractive combination of gnarled holly, sassafras, and poison ivy. Some of the forest's specimens are over 200 years old. From the summit of the dunes, you can see the forest's trees laced together in a hulking, uninterrupted mesh.

The largest community on Fire Island, **Ocean Beach** is naturally the most publicly accessible. Just make sure you show some respect: signs warn visitors: no drinking in public; no walking around town without a shirt; and no "discourteous" public displays. Ocean Beach's main street is lined with gray shingled buildings, restaurants, small groceries, and beachwear shops.

Take any side street (perpendicular to the main drag) all the way across the island to arrive at miles and miles of coastline. Once there, you can walk along the shore to see the beachfront homes that grow larger as you travel either way down the beach. The largest homes are located about two miles away in posh **Saltaire** (a completely residential community), followed closely by the up-and-coming town of **Fair Harbor.** If you walk in the other direction just over 2½ mi., you will arrive at the private bungalows and raised boardwalks of **Cherry Grove** and the colossal homes of **Fire Island Pines,** two predominantly gay communities (for more see **Gay New York,** p. 198).

FOOD AND NIGHTLIFE

While dining on Fire Island is often exorbitantly priced, you can grab a delightful bite to eat at **Michael's Pizzeria** (☎631-583-7858. Heroes $8.50, pizza and pasta $14-18; open M-W 11:30am-midnight, Th-Sa 11am-4am, Su 1-11pm), or you can make your own lunch at the **Ocean Beach Trading Co.** (☎631-583-8440; open M-Th 7am-6pm, F 7am-10:30pm, Sa 7am-9:30pm), one of three grocery stores on the strip. Here, you can also pick up a list of services and phone numbers, a map, and a brief history of the island in the *Fire Island News* or the *Fire Island Tide*. Save enough money for a soft, chewy oatmeal raisin cookie ($2), one of many gigantic desserts from **Rachel's Bakeshop** (☎631-583-9552. Open daily 7am-10pm). **The Alligator** is a barely adorned bar that concentrates instead on drinks ($2-5) and a big-screen TV (☎631-583-8896; Sa cover $5; open M-F 4pm-4am and Sa-Su noon-4am).

Those in the know travel by water taxi to nearby **Ocean Bay Park,** a community that grew tired of the restrictions in nearby Ocean Beach and founded this haven for rule-bending renogades. **Flynns** serves lunch and dinner nightly, while rocking the island every weekend. (☎631-583-5000. Open off-season F-Sa noon-2am, after June 31 Su-Th noon-11pm.)

ACCOMMODATIONS

Ferries run late into the night, but if you want to spend the night, shack up at Clegg's Hotel (☎631-583-5399), which has clean rooms and a friendly, knowledgeable staff. Room prices vary according to season, number of vacancies, and days of the week. Doubles can cost anywhere from $80 on a weekday to $300 for a two-night stay during a peak-season weekend.

HUDSON VALLEY

TARRYTOWN AND SLEEPY HOLLOW

By car: take the New York State Thruway (I-87) to Exit 9 (Tarrytown), and take Route 9 into town. By train: from Grand Central Station, 60-min. ride on Metro North Hudson Line (☎212-532-4900. Trains run 6:30am-1:20am, $5.50 off peak, $7.50 rush hour).

Less than thirty miles north of the big city, the bucolic towns of Tarrytown and Sleepy Hollow capture the landscape and legends of 19th Century American Romanticism in historical mansions, estates, farms, and churches.

SIGHTS

The Tarrytown area provided the inspiration for 19th century author Washington Irving's tales—most famously *The Legend of Sleepy Hollow*. Also an amateur landscape artist with an interest in architecture, Irving transformed a two-story Dutch cottage into his magnificent home **Sunnyside,** West Sunnyside Lane off Rte. 9. While the house offers a fascinating glimpse into Irving's life, the manicured grounds alone are worth the visit. Summer and special events include jazz festivals and candle-lit tours (☎914-591-8763; $8, seniors $7, students 12-17 $4; 5 and under free. Grounds open Mar.-Dec. daily 10am-5pm; Cottage open M and W-Su 10am-5pm).

A few miles north along Rte. 9 lies **Lyndhurst,** 635 S. Broadway, a Gothic Revival palace acquired by railroad tycoon Jay Gould in 1880. Stately grounds ensconce the 19th Century mansion with rose and fern gardens, a carriage house, and the remains of what was once considered to be the largest and finest private conservatory in the nation. The intricate rooms are interesting, but the gardens are the main draw. (☎914-631-4481. Open Apr.-Oct. Tu-Su 10am-5pm; Nov.-Mar. Sa-Su 10am-4pm. $10, seniors $9, children 12-17 $4, under 12 free; grounds alone $4.)

Approximately ten miles north of Tarrytown, Sleepy Hollow boasts the **Union Church of Pocantico Hills,** 3 miles on Rte. 114 off Rte. 9. Nine vibrant stained-glass windows by Marc Chagall adorn the walls in this small church. In addition, Henri Matisse's last completed work, "Rose Window," hangs high above the altar. (☎914-631-2069. Open Apr.-Dec. M-F 11am-5pm, Sa 10am-2pm, Su 2pm-5pm. Suggested donation $3.) Farther north along Rte. 9 lies **Phillipsburg Manor,** a 17th-century working farm and living history venue with rare breeds of cattle and sheep, costumed guides, and a working mill wheel. (☎914-631-3992. Open Apr.-Dec. M and W-Su 10am-5pm, but last admission is 4pm. $8, seniors $7, children 5-17 $4.) Running out of Phillipsburg Manor are tours to **Kykuit,** the Rockefeller Estate. Tours are pricey ($20 for all visitors under 65) and long (approx. 2.25 hours), but the lecture tour explains the mansion's original art, sculpture, and furniture and promises exquisite views.

FOOD

If the various admissions fees have left you pinching pennies while you look to dine, stop in at **Lefteris Gyro,** 1 North Main Street, for authentic Greek food—the small Greek salad is gigantic for $5.25, and hamburgers are a mere $2.95. (☎914-524-9687. Open daily 11am-10pm.)

WEST POINT

By car: from NYC take I-87. Once over the Tappan Zee Bridge, take exit 13N onto the Palisades Interstate Parkway heading north. Take the PIP north to its end (Bear Mountain traffic circle). Follow signs for Route 9W north (3d exit off traffic circle). Exit 9W via West Point exit, Stony Lonesome exit, or Route 293 exit. By bus: Short Line Bus from the New York Port Authority (roundtrip $26.05). The bus only runs a few times a day, so call ahead and plan accordingly. (☎800-631-8405.)

History buffs, military zealots, and anyone fascinated by the prim, proper and powerful should consider exploring West Point, America's oldest and most famous service academy. The academy is carved into the cliffs the Hudson Highlands, the foothills of the Catskills. In addition to the Revolutionary War sights, the imposing gothic buildings, and majestic vistas that comprise the immense campus, West Point boasts an illustrious lists of graduates including Grant, Lee, MacArthur and Eisenhower.

SIGHTS

The expansive and pristine **Visitors Center,** located just below **Thayer Gate,** is a good starting place for a tour. (☎845-938-2638. Open daily 9am-4:45 pm.) The center provides pamphlets and walking and driving tour maps and displays a brief instructional video, various army memorabilia, and a replica of a cadet's room complete with replicated wax cadets. Just behind the Visitors Center lies the **West Point Museum.** (☎914-938-2203. Open daily 10:30am-4:15 pm.) The gothic building houses one of the largest and oldest collections of military memorabilia in America, with weapons and uniforms dating back to colonial times.

The campus itself is home to two Revolutionary War sites—**Fort Clinton** and **Fort Putnam**, the latter originally under the command of George Washington. Also of interest is the assortment of war monuments, particularly **Trophy Point,** the store house for many intriguing US war relics, and the **Battle Monument,** rumored to be the largest polished granite shaft in the Western hemisphere (in case you were wondering where the defense budget went). Other popular sites include the **Cadet Chapel,** which contains the world's largest organ, and **The Plain,** the famous West

Point parade ground. It's approximately a five-mile walk through the sights, so driving maps and guided bus tours provide an alternative option at the Visitors Center. The guided bus tours run two hours and begin twice a day, 11:15 am and 1:15 pm. (☎914-446-4724. $8, children $5.)

FOOD

Find refuge and food at **Schades,** 457 Highland Falls, for a pizza ($5.95-$14.95) or a burger ($4.75-5.95). (☎845-446-2626. Open Su-Th 11am-9pm; F-Sa 11am-10pm.)

THE CATSKILLS

WOODSTOCK

By car, take I-87 to Exit 19 (Rte. 28 W to Rte. 375 N) or Exit 20 (Rte. 32 to Rte. 212). By bus, ***Adirondack Trailways*** *(☎800-225-6815) leaves from the Port Authority and travels directly to Woodstock (2.5 hrs.; round trip $42, one-day round trip Tu-Th $27.50).*

Amidst the Catskills' purple haze lies Woodstock, a colony of the Arts and the alleged home of the 1969 music festival that actually took place in nearby Bethel. Founded in 1902 as a utopian community, Woodstock followed an artistic bent through the expressionist 50s and the music revolution of the 60s. Now, its quaint Main Street is lined with art galleries, craft stores, and a medley of New Age boutiques that come alive on the weekends.

SIGHTS

A hip pastiche of local and international, contemporary and creative, **The Center for Photography,** 59 Tinker St., is Woodstock at its finest. The two-room gallery offers a lecture series, exhibitions, and workshops. (☎845-679-9957. Open W-Su, noon-5pm.) The **F-Stop Cafe,** inside the gallery, serves hot coffee and tea to live music. Also in town, the **Byrdcliffe Arts Colony,** 34 Tinker St., the first American utopian arts and crafts colony, has country pathways meandering around the rustic buildings on 300 wooded acres. (☎845-679-2079. Open F-Su noon-5pm.) Check out the pyrotechnic displays of an award-winning glass blower at **Woodstock Glass Works,** 70 Rock City Rd. (☎845-679-5575.) If it isn't *kunst* but karma that pulls you upstate, the **Zen Monastery's** meditation retreats promise respite and relaxation, if not enlightenment (S. Planck Rd. ☎845-688-2228). For further guidance, an information hut, run by the Chamber of Commerce sits in the center of town (☎845-679-6234. Open Th-Su 11:30- 6:30).

FOOD AND ENTERTAINMENT

Taco Juan's, 31 Tinker St., is famous for cheap but sumptuous eats. Juan's has sass and unbeatable burritos—$3.25 for a baby, $5.50 for a large (☎845-679-9673). For a quick bite to eat, The Catskill Mountain Pizza Company, 51 Mill Hill Rd., serves pizza by the slice ($1.60). (☎845-246-8334. Open M-Th 11am-10 pm, F-Sa 11am-11pm, midnight in the summer.) While Landau Grill, 17 Mill Hill Rd., is more expensive, the restaurant offers a full raw bar ($8-16) in addition to regular fare and a large patio for outdoor dining (☎845-679-8937). Also more upscale is Joshua's, a Middle Eastern restaurant with gazpacho and baked brie as otherworldly as the stores surrounding it ($4.95-9.00).

In the evenings, Woodstock hosts a vast array of entertainment. Started by writer and poet Hervey White 80 years ago, **Maverick Concert Series** hosts an eclectic mix of world-famous musicians in a barn-like structure set in the woods (www.maverickconcerts.org; ☎845-679-8217 or 845-679-8556). For the latest independent films, check out **Tinker Cinema,** 132 Tinker St. (☎845-679-6608.)

ACCOMMODATIONS

Hotels often require a two-night minimum and a reservation during the summer, so it is imperative to call ahead. Eight miles outside the center of Woodstock, **Rip Van Winkle Campground,** 149 Blue Mountain Rd., is a large, family-run campsite, that grants access to trout fishing and swimming in the Plattekill Creek. The campground's facilities include playgrounds and basketball courts. Rates from $23.50 a day with no hookups to $31.90 with a 50 amp full hookup (☎845-246-8334. Reservations ☎800-724-1239. Open May-Oct.).

Twin Gables Guest House, 73 Tinker St., is a good bet in the center of town. The nine-room guest house is clean and cozy, even if the decor is a little outdated, with guest rooms to accommodate various budgets. Singles with a hall bathroom run $59 and doubles with a private bath start at $99 (☎845-679-9479). At the **Woodstock Inn,** 48 Tannery Brook Rd., along the millstream, charming meets affordable. All rooms have a private bath, Reservations necessary. Standard rooms for two $99, efficiencies with kitchen $139, and two-room apartments $159. All include an extensive continental breakfast. (☎845-679-8211.)

BEAR MOUNTAIN STATE PARK

Located at the intersection of the Palisades Parkway and Route 9W 50 miles north of the city. Short Line Buses run from Port Authority to the park and take about an hour (☎800-631-8405. Round trip $21). By train, Metro North runs trains to Peekskill and Garrison, from where you can take a $25 cab to the park.

Bear Mountain includes over 80 square miles of wilderness and 140 miles of marked trails, and boasts some of the taller Catskill Mountains; the expansive, sparkling Hessian Lake; a section of the Hudson River; and an enormous swimming pool. The main attraction, other than the land and the lake itself, is the **Trailside Museum and Zoo,** the oldest of its kind in the US. The zoo, with several meandering paths, allows visitors to safely view some of the region's more ferocious wildlife, such as bobcat, coyote, and two black bears. The museum focuses on the park's history. (☎845-786-2701. Museum/zoo open daily summer 9am-5pm, winter 9am-4:30pm; $1, 5-13 $.50, under 5 free, $5 to park.) Also scattered through the park are statues, such as one of **Walt Whitman.** His stance, "afoot and lighthearted," is meant to evoke his poem "Song of the Open Road." Replete with historical significance, the park also contains the earliest part of the Appalachian Trail and stars in a song by Bob Dylan about a picnic gone horribly wrong: the "Talkin' Bear Mountain Picnic Massacre Blues." For further park information call the Park Visitor Center (☎845-786-5003. Open Apr.-Oct. 8am-6pm, Nov.-Mar. 8am-5pm.)

Located in the center of the park stands the **Bear Mountain Inn,** designed in Swiss Chalet Style. Although the standard rooms are not very large, they run relatively cheap ($89/double). The inn also provides quieter, more remote lodges ($99/double). Reservations are strongly suggested (☎845-786-2731). Nestled into the enormous yet strangely cozy second floor lodge in the Main Inn is a restaurant with an outdoor patio. But the fare is pricey ($9.95-17.95 for dinner), and a picnic might accord better with the change book (restaurant open for lunch daily 11:30am-4pm, and dinner Su-Th 5-9pm, F-Sa 5-10pm).

NEW JERSEY

HOBOKEN

*Take **subway** lines B, D, F, N, Q, or R to 34th St., then take the **PATH train** ($1) to the first stop in Hoboken. The PATH train also leaves from the F stations at 23rd and 14th Sts., and the PATH stations at 9th St./Sixth Ave., Christopher St./Greenwich Ave., and the World Trade Center. To get to Hoboken's main drag, **Washington St.,** walk along Hudson Pl. from the PATH station to Hudson St., make a right, walk one block to Newark St., turn left, walk two blocks to Washington St.*

Across the Hudson River from downtown Manhattan, Hoboken is the mythical birthplace of baseball (1846) and Frank Sinatra (1917). In 1642 the town became the home to the first brewery in the New World. Today Hoboken continues to reign as a bastion of brew as bars drunkenly trip over each other on the sidewalks. But before getting caught up in the alcoholic frenzy of Hoboken nightlife, you may want to indulge in charms not served in a frosty mug.

SIGHTS

Hoboken's greatest attraction may be its location, placing it in ideal position for a glimpse of the city you've recently escaped. Walking uphill on the far eastern side of

8th St. and across the grass until reaching a cannon, you will reach **Castle Point,** which offers a spectacular vista of Manhattan's West Side. In the summer, Hoboken hosts the **Movies under the Stars** festival, on Hudson Pl.. In front of the NJ Transit train terminal, is **Erie-Lackawanna Train Plaza** (☎201-420-2207 for schedule. W at dusk).

FOOD

Restaurants in Hoboken cater to the town's burgeoning yuppie population. **The Hoboken Gourmet Company,** 423 Washington St., serves healthy salads and fresh sandwiches ($5-6). A young local crowd enjoys breakfast until 2pm. (☎201-795-0110. Open M-F 6:30am-9pm, Sa-Su 6:30am-7pm.) **La Isla,** 104 Washington St., is a charming take-out-turned-sit-down Cuban restaurant. Daily lunch specials range from $5-9, dinner entrees from $10-16. (☎201-659-8197. Open M-Sa 7am-10pm, Su brunch 11am-4pm.) Slightly more elegant, **Amanda's,** 908 Washington St., features New American fare at reasonable prices. The regular menu starts around $16 for an entree, but the bargain is the early dinner special ($20 for 2 or $10 per person). (☎201-798-0101. Open M-Th 5-10pm, F-Sa 5-11pm, Su 5-9pm; Sa-Su brunch 11am-3pm; early dinner special M-Sa 5-6pm.)

NIGHTLIFE

Before or after dinner, you can attack the Hoboken bar scene. The **8th Street Tavern,** 800 Washington St., is an old standby. One of Hoboken's "original bars," this tavern boasts friendly clientele and inexpensive beer (Coors $2.50). The bartender Frank, a fixture since 1942, says "We've no phone, we like people to drop in." (Open M-Th 10am-2am, F-Sa 10am-3am). The atmosphere of the bars in Hoboken is reminiscent of a college fraternity party. If you're looking for something slightly different, try **Maxwell's,** 1039 Washington St., a restaurant/bar which is also home to all-age underground musical acts with a cover up to $18 (average $6-8). Shows occasionally sell out, so get tickets in advance from Maxwell's or Ticketmaster (☎201-507-8900 or 212-307-7171. Open Tu-Su 5pm-late).

ATLANTIC CITY

Atlantic City lies halfway down New Jersey's eastern seashore, accessible via the ***Garden State Pkwy.*** *and the* ***Atlantic City Expwy. Buses: Greyhound*** *(☎609-340-2000). Buses travel every 30min. between Port Authority (NYC) and most major casinos (2½hr., casino drop-off rates $30 round-trip). Many casinos, in addition to the round-trip discounts, will give gamblers between $15 and $20 in coins upon arrival. (Trump Plaza offers $20 for starting your gambling spree at their casino.)* ***New Jersey Transit*** *(☎215-569-3752 or 800-582-5946) offers hourly service between NYC and the transit station on Atlantic Ave. between Michigan and Ohio St. ($25, seniors $11 each way).* ***Gray Line Tours*** *(☎800-669-0051) offers several daytrips to Atlantic City (3hr.; $22 on weekdays, $24 on weekends). Don't pitch your ticket receipt, which is redeemable for cash, chips, or food from casinos when you arrive. Tropicana and the Sands offer $20 per person. The bus drops riders at the casino and picks you up later the same day. Call for nearest NYC bus pick-up locations. Call ☎800-995-8898 for info about economical overnight packages. Terminal open 24hr.* ***Visitor Information: Atlantic City Convention Center and Visitors Bureau,*** *2314 Pacific Ave. (☎888-228-4748). Open daily 11am-7pm. A new Visitors Center has also been built on the Atlantic Expressway approximately 1 mi. after the Pleasantville Toll Plaza. Open daily 9am-5pm.*

The geography of Atlantic City is subconsciously implanted into the minds of generations of Americans. For over 50 years, board-gaming strategists have been passing "Go" to collect their $200 and buying properties in efforts to control this coastal city as reincarnated on the *Monopoly* board. The opulence of Boardwalk and Park Place gradually faded into neglect, still visible in decrepit streets and alleys, and then into a megadollar tackiness. Casinos rose from the rubble of the boardwalk in the 1970s, and these days, Atlantic City's beachside hot-spot status is assured by the waves of urban professionals looking for a fast buck, quick tan, and maybe even a loose romance. Velvet-lined temples of glitter (each with a dozen restaurants and big-name entertainment) overlook the beach and draw all kinds, from international princes to local paupers.

$IGHT$ AND CAINO

Attractions cluster on and around the Boardwalk, which runs east-west along the Atlantic Ocean. Running parallel to the Boardwalk, Pacific and Atlantic Ave. offer

cheap restaurants, hotels, and convenience stores. *Atlantic Ave. can be dangerous after dark, and any street farther out can be dangerous even by day.* Getting around is easy on foot and more pleasant on the boardwalk than in the neighborhoods. **Parking** at the Sands Hotel is free, but "for patrons only," so spend a dollar at the slots. Lots near the boards run $3-7.

All casinos on the Boardwalk fall within a dice toss of one another. The farthest south is **The Hilton** (☎609-347-7111), between Providence and Voston Ave., and the farthest north is **Showboat** (☎609-343-4000), at Delaware Ave. and Boardwalk. If you liked *Aladdin*, you'll love the **Taj Mahal,** 1000 Boardwalk (☎609-449-1000). Donald Trump's cartoonesque glittering castle is too ostentatious to be missed—it was neglected payments on this tasteless tallboy that cast the financier into his billion dollar tailspin. Speaking of *Monopoly*, Trump owns three other hotel casinos in the city: **Trump Plaza** (☎609-441-6000) and **Trump World's Fair** (☎609-344-6000) on the Boardwalk and **Trump Castle** (☎609-441-2000) at the Marina. The **Sands** (☎609-441-4000), at Indiana Ave., stands tall and flashy with its pink-and-green seashell motif. And, as if you couldn't guess, all are open 24hr.

There's something for everyone in Atlantic City, thanks to the Boardwalk. Those under 21 (or those tired of the endless cycle of winning and losing) **gamble for prizes** at one of the many arcades that line the Boardwalk. It feels like real gambling, but the teddy bear in the window is easier to win than the convertible on display at Caesar's. The **Steel Pier,** an extension in front of the Taj Mahal, juts into the coastal waters with a ferris wheel that spins riders over the Atlantic. It also offers the rest of the usual amusement park suspects: roller coaster, tilt-a-whirl, carousel, kiddie rides, and many a game of "skill." Rides cost $2-5 each. (Open daily noon-midnight; call the Taj Mahal for winter hrs.) When you tire of spending money, check out the **beach,** although **Ventnor City,** just west of Atlantic City, offers more tranquil shores.

ACCOMMODATIONS

Large, red-carpeted beachfront hotels have bumped smaller operators a few streets back to **Pacific Ave.,** one block from the Boardwalk. Reserve ahead, especially on weekends, or face the plight of forking over all your blackjack earnings and then some for mediocre lodging. Many hotels lower their rates mid-week and in winter, when water temperature and gambling fervor drop significantly. If you have a car, it pays to stay in **Absecon,** about 8 mi. from Atlantic City; Exit 40 from the Garden State Pkwy. leads to Rte. 30 and cheap rooms.

In Atlantic City proper, try the **Inn of the Irish Pub,** 164 St. James Pl., near the Ramada Tower just off the boardwalk. These are the best budget accommodations in town. Doubles with shared bath $53-65, with private bath $75-85; quad with shared bath $85-89 (☎609-344-9963). The **Comfort Inn,** 154 South Kentucky Ave., near the Sands, is another good choice. Basic rooms with king size or 2 queen size beds and, true to Atlantic City swank, a jacuzzi. Breakfast, free parking, and a heated pool. Sept.-May $59, June $69-79, July $89, Aug. $99, early Sept. $69.

FOOD

Atlantic City's most affordable eats are a mere flight of stairs away from the otherwise pricey town's cheapest beds. At one of the few Atlantic City spots where locals rule, the **Inn of the Irish Pub,** 164 St. James Pl., no item on the menu exceeds $6. The lunch special (M-F 11:30am-2pm) includes a pre-selected sandwich and a cup of soup for $2. Domestic drafts are $1. (☎345-9613. Open 24hr.) **Pacific Ave.** is cramped with steak, sub, and pizza shops. There's never a dull moment at the vibrant **White House Sub Shop,** 2301 Arctic Ave., which plays host to more celebrities than its national capital namesake, such as the late Frank Sinatra. Ol' Blue Eyes was rumored to have had these immense subs ($4-9) flown to him while he was on tour. (☎345-1564 or 345-8599. Open M-Th 10am-midnight, F-Sa 10am-1am, Su 11am-11pm.) For a complete rundown of local dining, pick up a copy of *Shorecast Insider's Guide At the Shore* or *Whoot* (both free) from a hotel lobby, restaurant, or a local store.

Planning Your Trip

DOCUMENTS & FORMALITIES

US EMBASSIES AND CONSULATES ABROAD

Contact the nearest embassy or consulate to obtain information regarding visas and permits to the United States. Offices are only open limited hours, so call well before you depart. The US **State Department** provides contact information for US diplomatic missions on the Internet at http://foia.state.gov/keyofficers.asp. Foreign embassies in the US are located in Washington, D.C., but there are consulates in New York City (see **Service Directory: Consulates and Embassies,** p. 280) that can be helpful in an emergency. For a more extensive list of embassies and consulates in the US, consult the web site www.embassy.org.

AUSTRALIA. Embassy and Consulate: Moonah Pl., Yarralmula **(Canberra),** ACT 2600 (☎02 6214 5600; American Citizens Services fax 6214 5970,www.usis-australia.gov/embassy). **Other Consulates:** MLC Centre, Level 59, 19-29 Martin Pl., **Sydney,** NSW 2000 (☎61-2 9373 9200; fax 9373 9125); 553 St. Kilda Rd., **Melbourne,** VIC 3004 (☎03 9526 5900; fax 9525 0769); 16 St. George's Terr., 13th fl., **Perth,** WA 6000 (☎08 9202 1224; fax 9231 9444).

CANADA. Embassy and Consulate: 490 Sussex Dr., **Ottawa,** ON K1N 1G8 (☎613-238-5335; fax 688-3101; www.usembassycanada.gov). **Other Consulates:** 615 Macleod Trail SE, **Calgary,** AB T2G 4T8 (☎403-266-8962; fax 264-6630); 2000 Barrington St., Cogswell Tower, suite 910, **Halifax,** NS B3J 3K1 (☎902-429-2485; fax 423-6861); 1155 St. Alexandre St., **Montréal,** QC H2Z 1Z2 (mailing address: P.O. Box 65, Station Desjardins, **Montréal,** QC H5B 1G1); (☎514-398-9695; fax 398-9748); 2 Place Terrasse Dufferin, C.P. 939, **Québec City,** QC G1R 4T9 (☎418-692-2095; fax 692-4640); 360 University Ave., **Toronto,** ON M5G 1S4 (☎416-595-1700; fax 595-0051); 1095 West Pender St., **Vancouver,** BC V6E 2M6 (☎604-685-4311; fax 685-5285).

IRELAND. Embassy and Consulate: 42 Elgin Rd., **Dublin** 4 (☎01 668 8777/668 7122; fax 668 9946; www.usembassy.ie).

NEW ZEALAND. Embassy and Consulate: 29 Fitzherbert Terr. (or P.O. Box 1190), Thorndon, **Wellington** (☎04 472 2068; fax 471 2380; http://usembassy.state.gov/wellington). **Other Consulate:** Yorkshire General Bldg., 4th fl., 29 Shortland St., **Auckland** (☎09 303 2724; fax 366 0870).

SOUTH AFRICA. Embassy and Consulate: P.O. Box 9536, Pretoria 0001, 877 Pretorius St., **Pretoria** (☎27-12 342-1048; fax 342-2244; http://usembassy.state.gov/pretoria). **Other Consulates:** 7th Fl., Monte Carlo Building, Heerengracht, Foreshore (mailing address: P.O. Box 6773, Roggebaai, 8012), **Cape Town** (☎021 421-4351; fax 425-3014); 2901 Durban Bay Building, 333 Smith St., **Durban** (☎031 304-4737; fax 301-0265); 1 River St., Killarney (mailing address: P.O. Box 1762, Houghton, 2041), **Johannesburg** (☎011 644-8000; fax 646-6916; visa helpline 011 646-6916).

UK. Embassy and Consulate: 24 Grosvenor Sq., **London** W1A 2LQ (☎20 7499 9000; fax 7495 5012; www.usembassy.org.uk). **Other Consulates:** Queen's House, 14 Queen St., **Belfast,** N. Ireland BT1 6EQ (☎028 9032 8239; fax 9024 8482); 3 Regent Terr., **Edinburgh,** Scotland EH7 5BW (☎0131 556 8315; fax 557 6023).

PASSPORTS

REQUIREMENTS

All foreign visitors except Canadians need valid passports to enter the United States and to re-enter their own country. The US does not allow entrance if the holder's passport expires in under six months; returning home with an expired passport is often illegal, and may result in a fine. Canadians need to demonstrate proof of Canadian citizenship, such as a citizenship card with photo ID.

PHOTOCOPIES

Be sure to photocopy the page of your passport with your photo, **passport number,** and other identifying information, as well as any **visas, travel insurance policies, plane tickets,** or **traveler's check serial numbers.** Carry one set of copies in a safe place, apart from the originals, and leave another set at home. Consulates also recommend that you carry an **expired passport** or an official copy of your **birth certificate** in a part of your baggage separate from other documents.

LOST PASSPORTS

If you lose your passport, immediately notify the local police and the consulate of your home government. To expedite its replacement, it helps to have a photocopy of the passport to show as ID and to provide proof of citizenship. In some cases, a replacement may take weeks to process, and it may be valid only for a limited time. Any **visas** stamped in your old passport will be irretrievably lost. In an emergency, ask for immediate **temporary traveling papers** that will permit you to re-enter your home country. Your passport is a public document belonging to your nation's government. You may have to surrender it to a US government official, but if you do not get it back in a reasonable amount of time, inform the nearest mission of your home country.

NEW PASSPORTS

File any new passport or renewal applications (usually available at post offices, passport offices, or courts of law) well in advance of your departure date. Most passport offices offer rush services for a steep fee. Citizens living abroad who need a passport or renewal should contact the nearest consular service of their home country.

Australia: Info ☎131 232; passports.australia@dfat.gov.au; www.dfat.gov.au/passports. Hours: M-F 8am-8pm, Sa-Su 8.30am-5.15pm. Apply for a passport at a post office, passport office (in Adelaide, Brisbane, Canberra, Darwin, Hobart, Melbourne, Newcastle, Perth, or Sydney), or overseas diplomatic or consular mission.

Ireland: Applications available at a *Garda* station or post office which provides Passport Express service. The completed application should be sent to either the Passport Office at Setanta Centre, Molesworth Street, Dublin 2 (☎01 671 1633; fax 671 1092; www.irlgov.ie/iveagh), or, if a resident in the Munster counties of Clare, Cork, Kerry, Limerick, Tipperary, or Waterford, to the Passport Office, Irish Life Building, 1A South Mall, Cork (☎021 272 525/276 964).

New Zealand: Applications available free of charge by contacting the New Zealand Passport Office (☎0800 22 50 50 or 4 474 8100; fax 4 474 8010), downloading it from the web site (www.passports.govt.nz), or for a fee at most travel agencies. Send completed applications to the New Zealand Passport Office, Department of International Affairs, P.O. Box 10-526, Wellington, New Zealand.

South Africa: Passports issued only in Pretoria, but all applications must still be submitted or forwarded to the nearest South African consulate. Processing time is 3 months or more. For more information, see http://usaembassy.southafrica.net/VisaForms/Passport/Passport2000.html.

UK: Info ☎0870 521 0410; www.ukpa.gov.uk. Applications available from passport office, main post office, travel agent, or online (for UK residents only) at www.ukpa.gov.uk/forms/f_app_pack.htm. Apply by mail or in person at a passport office. The wait is about 4 weeks.

VISAS AND PERMITS

VISAS

Citizens of South Africa and some other countries need a visa—a stamp, sticker, or insert in your passport specifying the purpose of your travel and the permitted duration of your stay—in addition to a valid passport for entrance to the US. See http://travel.state.gov/visa_services.html for more information. To obtain a visa, contact a US embassy or consulate.

Citizens of most European countries, Australia, New Zealand, and Ireland can waive US visas through the **Visa Waiver Program.** Visitors qualify if they are traveling only for business or pleasure (*not* work or study), are staying for fewer than **90 days,** have proof of intent to leave (e.g. a return plane ticket), possess an I-94W form (arrival/departure certificate attached to their visa upon arrival), and are traveling on particular air or sea carriers. See http://travel.state.gov/vwp.html for more information.

If you lose your I-94 form, you can replace it by filling out form I-102, although it's very unlikely that the form will be replaced within the time of your stay. The form is available at the nearest **Immigration and Naturalization Service (INS)** office (☎800-375-5283; www.ins.usdoj.gov), through the forms request line (☎800-870-3676) or online (www.ins.usdoj.gov/graphics/formsfee/forms/i-102.htm). Mail completed forms to an INS office. See www.ins.usdoj.gov/graphics/howdoi/arrdepart.htm for more information. **Visa extensions** are sometimes granted with a completed I-539 form; call the forms request line (☎800-870-3676) or get it online at www.ins.usdoj.gov/graphics/formsfee/forms/i-539.htm.

All travelers, except Canadians, planning a stay of more than 90 days also need to obtain a visa. For more information, see **Living in the City,** p. 269.

WORK AND STUDY PERMITS

Admission as a visitor does not include the right to **work,** which is authorized only by a work permit. Entering the US to **study** also requires a special visa. For more information, see **Living in the City** (see p. 270) and http://travel.state.gov.

IDENTIFICATION

For more information on all the forms of identification listed below, contact the organization that provides the service, the **International Student Travel Confederation (ISTC),** Herengracht 479, 1017 BS Amsterdam, Netherlands (☎+31 20 421 2800; fax 421 2810; www.istc.org).

STUDENT AND TEACHER IDENTIFICATION

The **International Student Identity Card (ISIC),** the most widely accepted form of student identification, provides discounts on sights, accommodations, and airfare.

Institution-specific IDs from the US are equally effective in New York, but for international travelers the ISIC is preferable. In addition to identification, all ISIC cardholders have access to a 24-hour **emergency helpline** for medical, legal, and financial emergencies (☎877-370-ISIC in North America, elsewhere call US collect ☎1-715-345-0505), and US cardholders are also eligible for insurance benefits. Many student travel agencies issue ISICs, including: STA Travel in Australia, the UK, the US, and New Zealand; Travel CUTS in Canada; usit in the Republic of Ireland and Northern Ireland; SASTS in South Africa; Campus Travel in the UK; Council Travel in the US. The card is valid from September of one year to December of the following year and costs US$22. Applicants must be degree-seeking students of a secondary or post-secondary school and must be at least 12 years of age. Because of the proliferation of fake ISICs, some services (particularly airlines) require additional proof of student identity, such as a school ID or a letter attesting to your student status, signed by your registrar and stamped with your school seal. The **International Teacher Identity Card (ITIC)** offers the same insurance coverage as well as similar but limited discounts. The fee is US$22.

YOUTH IDENTIFICATION

The ISTC issues a discount card to travelers who are 26 years old or under, but are not students. This one-year **International Youth Travel Card** (**IYTC;** formerly the **GO 25** Card) offers many of the same benefits as the ISIC. Most organizations that sell the ISIC also sell the IYTC (US$22).

CUSTOMS

ENTERING THE US

Upon entering the United States, international travelers must declare certain items from abroad and pay a duty on the value of those articles that exceeds the allowance established by the United States customs service. Most tourists are unlikely to have anything to declare upon entering the US. You must be 21 years old to bring alcohol into the US. See www.customs.gov/travel/travel.htm for more information.

LEAVING THE US

Upon exiting the United States, international travelers must declare all articles acquired in the US and pay a **duty** on the value of articles in excess of your home country's allowance. See www.embassy.org/embassies for specific countries' allowances. In order to expedite your return, keep receipts for all goods acquired on your travels. Note that goods and gifts purchased at **duty-free** shops in the US are not exempt from duty or sales tax at your point of return and thus must be declared; "duty-free" merely means that you need not pay a tax in the country of purchase.

FURTHER RESOURCES

Australia: Australian Customs National Information Line (in Australia call 01 300 363 263, from elsewhere call +61 2 6275 6666; www.customs.gov.au).

Canada: Canadian Customs, 2265 St. Laurent Blvd., Ottawa, ON K1G 4K3 (☎800-461-9999 within Canada (24hr.), 613-993-0534 from elsewhere; www.revcan.ca).

Ireland: Customs Information Office, Irish Life Centre, Lower Abbey St., Dublin 1 (☎01 878 8811; fax 878 0836; ceadmin@revenue.iol.ie; www.revenue.ie).

New Zealand: New Zealand Customhouse, 17-21 Whitmore St., Box 2218, Wellington (☎04 473 6099; fax 473 7370; www.customs.govt.nz).

South Africa: Commissioner for Customs and Excise, Private Bag X47, Pretoria 0001 (☎012 314 9911; fax 328 6478; www.gov.za).

UK: Her Majesty's Customs and Excise, Passenger Enquiry Team, Wayfarer House, Great South West Rd., Feltham, Middlesex TW14 8NP (☎(020) 7202 4227; fax 7202 4216; www.hmce.gov.uk).

US: US Customs Service, 1330 Pennsylvania Ave. NW, Washington, D.C. 20229 (☎(202) 354-1000; www.customs.gov).

PACKING

CONVERTERS AND ADAPTERS. In the US and Canada, electricity is 110V; 220V electrical appliances don't like 110V current. Visit a hardware store for an adapter (changes the shape of the plug) and a converter (changes the voltage). Don't make the mistake of using only an adapter (unless appliance instructions explicitly state otherwise).

FILM. Despite disclaimers, airport security X-rays *can* fog film, so if you're bringing film with speeds over 800, the best idea is to either buy a lead-lined pouch, sold at camera stores, or ask the security to hand inspect it. Always pack it in your carry-on luggage, since higher-intensity X-rays are used on checked luggage. All types of film for all types of cameras are available in NYC, but 35mm is the most prevalent.

MONEY MATTERS

CURRENCY AND EXCHANGE

The main unit of currency in the US is the **dollar** (represented by the symbol $ which precedes the numeral), which is divided into 100 **cents** (represented by the symbol ¢, which follows the numeral). Currency in the US celebrates the nation's political icons. Founding father George Washington presides on the front of the $1 bill, Abraham Lincoln the $5, original Treasury Secretary Alexander Hamilton the $10, rough and tumble President Andrew Jackson the $20, Civil War general Ulysses Grant the $50, and inventor and diplomat Benjamin Franklin the $100. Coins are 1¢ (penny), 5¢ (nickel), 10¢ (dime), 25¢ (quarter). Recently, the US has also introduced a $1 gold-colored coin (made out of copper) with the intention of phasing out the $1 bill.

The currency chart below is based on August 2001 exchange rates between US dollars ($), Australian dollars (A$), Canadian dollars (CDN$), British pounds (UK£), Irish pounds (IR£), New Zealand dollars (NZ$), South African rand (ZAR), and European Union euros (EUR€). Check the currency converter on the *Let's Go* homepage (www.letsgo.com/Thumb), any major newspaper, or the web (e.g. www.cnnfn.com or www.bloomberg.com) for the latest exchange rates.

THE GREENBACK (THE US DOLLAR)

CURRENCY

AUS$1 = $0.52	US$1 = AUS$1.92
CDN$1 = $0.66	US$1 = CDN$1.51
IR£1 = $1.07	US$1 = IR£0.93
NZ$1 = $0.42	US$1 = NZ$2.38
ZAR1 = $0.12	US$1 = ZAR8.14
UK£1 = $1.40	US$1 = UK£0.71
EUR€1 = $0.84	US$1 = EUR€1.19

Convert your currency infrequently and in large amounts to minimize exorbitant exchange fees. As a general rule, it is cheaper to convert money once you arrive in New York than in your home country. Try to buy traveler's checks in US dollars so that you will not have to exchange currency in the process of cashing them. A good rule of thumb is to exchange money where the margin between their buy and sell prices is no more than 5%. Most banks will not cash personal checks unless you open an account with them, a time-consuming affair (see **Service Directory: Currency Exchange,** p. 280).

GETTING MONEY FROM HOME

AMERICAN EXPRESS. Cardholders can withdraw cash from their checking accounts at any of AmEx's major offices and many representative offices (up to $1000 every 21 days; no service charge, no interest). AmEx "Express Cash" withdrawals from the AmEx ATMs are automatically debited from the cardholder's checking account or line of credit. Green card holders may withdraw up to US$1000 in any seven-day period (2% transaction fee; min. US$2.50, max. US$20). To enroll in Express Cash, card members may call 800-227-4669 in the US; elsewhere call the US collect +1 336-393-1111.

WESTERN UNION. Travelers from most of the world can wire money to and from their home country or state through Western Union's money transfer services. In the US, call 800-325-6000; in Canada, 800-235-0000; in the UK, 0800 83 38 33. To wire money within the US using a credit card (D/MC/V), call 800-CALL-CASH. The rates for sending cash are generally $10-11 cheaper than with a credit card, and the money is usually available at the place you're sending it to within an hour. To find the nearest Western Union location, consult www.westernunion.com.

TRAVELERS CHECKS

Travelers checks are sold at banks and other money-related agencies for a small commission. Each agency provides refunds if your checks are lost or stolen, and many provide additional services, such as toll-free refund hotlines abroad, emergency message services, and stolen credit card assistance. Use travelers checks like cash at most hotels and large businesses, or cash them commission-free at a branch of the agency or at banks.

American Express, Call 800 251 902 in Australia; in New Zealand 0800 441 068; in the UK 0800 521 313; in the US and Canada 800-221-7282; elsewhere call US collect +1 801-964-6665; see web site (www.aexp.com) for locations. Available in US dollars at 1-4% commission at AmEx offices, banks, AAA offices, and on the American Express web site. *Cheques for Two* can be signed by either of 2 people traveling together.

Citicorp: In the US and Canada call 800-645-6556; elsewhere call US collect +1 813-623-1709. Traveler's checks (available only in US dollars, British pounds, and German marks) at 1-2% commission. Call 24hr.

Thomas Cook MasterCard: In the US and Canada call 800-223-7373; in the UK call 0800 62 21 01; elsewhere call UK collect +44 1733 31 89 50. Checks available in 13 currencies at 2% commission. See www.thomascook.com for more information.

Visa: In the US call 800-227-6811; in the UK call ☎0800 89 50 78; elsewhere call UK collect +44 (1733) 31 89 49. See www.visa.com/pd/cheq/main.html for more information.

CREDIT CARDS

Few establishments in the city reject all major cards, but you'll probably come across at least one establishment that only takes cold, hard cash. However, credit cards are invaluable in an emergency—an unexpected hospital bill or the loss of traveler's checks—which may leave you temporarily without other resources. Major credit cards such as **MasterCard** and **Visa** can be used to extract cash advances in dollars from associated banks and teller machines throughout NYC for favorable exchange rates. **American Express** cards also work in some ATMs, as well as at AmEx offices and major airports. All such machines require a **Personal Identification Number (PIN).** Ask your credit card company for a PIN before you leave; without it, you will be unable to withdraw cash with your credit card outside your home country. If you already have a PIN, make sure it will work in the US. Credit cards often offer an array of other services, from insurance to emergency assistance; check with your company. **Visa** (☎800-336-8472), **MasterCard** (☎800-307-7309), **American Express** (☎800-843-2273), and the **Discover Card** (☎800-347-2683; outside US 1-801-902-3100) are all widely recognized in the US.

CASH CARDS (ATM CARDS)

Cash machines—or Automated Teller Machines (ATMs)—are everywhere in NYC. ATMs get the same wholesale exchange rate as credit cards, but there is often a limit on the amount of money you can withdraw per day (around US$500). There is also typically a surcharge of US$1-2 per withdrawal. The two major international money networks are **Cirrus** (US ☎800-424-7787) and **PLUS** (US ☎800-843-7587). **NYCE** is a major US network.

Visa TravelMoney allows you to access money from any ATM that accepts Visa cards. (For local customer assistance in the US, call 800-847-2399.) Obtain a card by either visiting a nearby Thomas Cook or Citicorp office, by calling toll-free in the US 877-394-2247, or checking with your local bank to see if it issues TravelMoney cards. **Road Cash** (☎877-762-3227; www.roadcash.com) issues cards in the US with a minimum US$300 deposit.

COSTS

Accommodations in NYC start around $22 for dorm-style living and $60 for a hotel single. A satisfying sit-down meal can be had for around $8, and some museums offer discounts for students and seniors. There are certainly deals and freebies out there, but the streets are not lined with gold. With NYC's exciting activities, plan on spending a minimum of $70-120 per day. No matter how cheap you are, you will not be able to carry all your cash with you, and keeping large sums in a money belt is risky and ill-advised. Non-cash reserves are a necessary precaution in the big bad city. Unfortunately, out-of-state personal checks are not readily accepted in NYC, even at banks.

HEALTH

For lists of doctors, hospitals, pharmacies, and emergency numbers, see **Service Directory,** p. 282.

MEDICAL ASSISTANCE ON THE ROAD

New York has a slew of excellent hospitals, both public and private. If you are concerned about being able to access medical support while traveling, there are special support services you may employ. The *MedPass* from **GlobalCare, Inc.,** 2001 Westside Pkwy., #120, Alpharetta, GA 30004, USA (☎800-860-1111; fax 770-475-0058; www.globalems.com), provides 24hr. international medical assistance. The **International Association for Medical Assistance to Travelers** (**IAMAT;** US ☎716-754-4883, Canada ☎416-652-0137, New Zealand ☎03 352 20 53; www.sentex.net/~iamat) has free membership, lists English-speaking doctors worldwide, and offers detailed info on immunization requirements and sanitation. If your regular **insurance** policy does not cover travel abroad, you may wish to purchase additional coverage.

Those with medical conditions (diabetes, allergies to antibiotics, epilepsy, heart conditions) may want to obtain a stainless-steel **Medic Alert** ID tag (first year US$35, annually thereafter US$20), which identifies one's condition and gives a 24-hour collect-call number. Contact the Medic Alert Foundation, 2323 Colorado Ave, Turlock, CA 95382, USA (☎888-633-4298; www.medicalert.org).

AIDS AND HIV

In December 1998, it was estimated that out of every 100,000 people in NY State, almost 50 have **Acquired Immune Deficiency Syndrome (AIDS)**. That rate was noticeably higher in New York City. The easiest mode of HIV transmission is direct blood-to-blood contact with an HIV-positive person; *never* share intravenous drug, tattooing, or other needles. The most common mode of transmission is sexual intercourse. **Use latex condoms in all sexual encounters**—these are readily available everywhere; see Women's Health, below.

If you are **HIV positive,** contact the Bureau of Consular Affairs, #4811, Department of State, Washington, D.C. 20520 (☎202-647-1488; fax 647-3000; http://travel.state.gov). According to US law, **HIV-positive persons are not permitted to enter the US.** However, HIV testing is required only for those planning to immigrate permanently. Travelers from areas with particularly high concentrations of HIV positive persons or persons with AIDS may be required to provide more information when applying.

For more information on AIDS, call the **US Centers for Disease Control** 24-hour hotline at 800-342-2437, or contact the **Joint United Nations Programme on HIV/AIDS**

(UNAIDS), 20 av. Appia 20, CH-1211 Geneva 27, Switzerland (☎+41 22 791 36 66; fax 791 41 87). Council Travel's brochure, *Travel Safe: AIDS and International Travel,* is available at their offices and on their web site (www.ciee.org/Isp/safety/travelsafe.htm).

WOMEN'S HEALTH

Abortion is legal in New York state; if you are in the New York area and need an abortion, contact the **National Abortion Federation,** a professional association of abortion providers. Call its toll-free hotline for information, counseling, and the names of qualified medical professionals in the area. (☎800-772-9100. Open M-F 9am-7pm.) The NAF has informational publications for individuals and health-care clinics alike. Clinics they recommend must maintain certain safety and operational standards. In New York, the NAF will refer you to the Planned Parenthood clinics (or call directly 212-274-7200).

Although reliable contraception is easily obtainable in New York City, women taking **birth control pills** should bring enough to allow for extended stays and should bring a copy of their prescription, since forms of the pill vary a good deal. **Condoms** can be found in any pharmacy, either behind the main counter or right on the shelves. Many of the city's pharmacies, conveniently, stay open all night, and every corner grocery and 24-hour store will be sure to have condoms near the cashier.

INSURANCE

Travel insurance generally covers four basic areas: medical/health problems, property loss, trip cancellation/interruption, and emergency evacuation. Although your regular insurance policies may well extend to travel-related accidents, you may consider purchasing travel insurance if the cost of potential trip cancellation/interruption is greater than you can absorb. Prices for travel insurance purchased separately generally run about US$50 per week for full coverage, while trip cancellation/interruption may be purchased separately at a rate of about US$5.50 per US$100 of coverage.

Medical insurance (especially university policies) often covers costs incurred abroad; check with your provider. **Canadians** are protected by their home province's health insurance plan for up to 90 days after leaving the country; check with the provincial Ministry of Health or Health Plan Headquarters for details. **Homeowners' insurance** (or your family's coverage) often covers theft during travel and loss of travel documents (passport, plane ticket, railpass, etc.) up to US$500.

ISIC and **ITIC** provide basic insurance benefits, including US$100 per day of in-hospital sickness for up to 60 days, US$3000 of accident-related medical reimbursement, and US$25,000 for emergency medical transport. Cardholders have access to a toll-free 24-hour helpline for medical, legal, and financial emergencies overseas (US and Canada ☎800-626-2427, elsewhere call US collect +1 713-267-2525). **American Express** (US ☎800-528-4800) grants most cardholders automatic car rental insurance (collision and theft, but not liability) and ground travel accident coverage of US$100,000 on flight purchases made with the card.

INSURANCE PROVIDERS. Council and **STA** (see p. 241) offer a range of plans that can supplement your basic coverage. Other private insurance providers in the US and Canada include: **Access America** (☎800-284-8300); **Berkely Group/Carefree Travel Insurance** (☎800-323-3149; www.berkely.com); **Globalcare Travel Insurance** (☎800-821-2488; www.globalcare-cocco.com); and **Travel Assistance International** (☎800-821-2828; www.worldwide-assistance.com). Providers in the **UK** include **Campus Travel** (☎01865 25 80 00) and **Columbus Travel Insurance** (☎020 7375 0011). In **Australia,** try **CIC Insurance** (☎9202 8000).

USEFUL ORGANIZATIONS & PUBLICATIONS

The US **Centers for Disease Control and Prevention** (**CDC;** ☎877-FYI-TRIP; www.cdc.gov/travel) provides information for travelers and maintains an international fax information service. The CDC's comprehensive booklet *Health Information for International Travel,* an annual rundown of disease, immunization, and general health advice, is free online or US$25 via the Public Health Foundation (☎877-252-1200). Consult the appropriate government agency of your home country for consular information sheets on health, entry requirements, and other issues for various countries. For quick information on health and other travel warnings, call the **Overseas Citizens Services** (☎202-647-5225; after-hours 202-647-4000), contact a passport agency or an embassy or consulate abroad. For information on medical evacuation services and travel insurance firms, see the US government's web site at http://travel.state.gov/medical.html or the **British Foreign and Commonwealth Office** (www.fco.gov.uk).

For detailed information on travel health, including a country-by-country overview of diseases and a list of travel clinics, try the **International Travel Health Guide,** Stuart Rose, MD (Travel Medicine, US$24.95; www.travmed.com). For general health info, contact the **American Red Cross** (☎800-564-1234).

GETTING TO NEW YORK

BY PLANE

If you're planning to fly into New York, you will have to choose not only a carrier but an airport as well. Three airports serve the New York metropolitan region. The largest, **John F. Kennedy Airport,** or JFK (☎718-244-4444), is 12 miles from midtown Manhattan in southern Queens and handles most international flights. **LaGuardia Airport** (☎718-533-3400), 6 miles from midtown in northern Queens, is the smallest, offering domestic flights as well as hourly shuttles to and from Boston and Washington, D.C. **Newark International Airport** (☎973-961-6000), 12 miles from midtown in Newark, NJ, offers both domestic and international flights at budget fares often not available at the other airports (although getting to and from Newark can be expensive).

DETAILS AND TIPS

Timing: Airfares to the US peak mid-June to early September; holidays are also expensive times to travel. Midweek (M-Th morning) round-trip flights run $40-50 cheaper than weekend flights, but the latter are generally less crowded and more likely to permit frequent-flier upgrades. Return-date flexibility is usually not an option for the budget traveler; traveling with an "open return" ticket can be pricier than fixing a return date when buying the ticket and paying later to change it.

Commuter Shuttles: The Delta Shuttle and the US Airways Shuttle are a relatively inexpensive mode of transportation between Washington D.C., Boston, and NYC (in any variation). The USAir Shuttle, which leaves every hour on the hour, is slightly cheaper than the Delta Shuttle, which leaves every hour on the half hour, under most circumstances. The cheapest fare offered by USAirways is a $85 one-way weekend fare. For both airlines, look for youth or student fares when buying more than one round-trip.

BUDGET & STUDENT TRAVEL AGENCIES

While knowledgeable agents specializing in flights to the US can make your life easy and help you save, they may not spend the time to find you the lowest possible fare—they get paid on commission. Travelers holding **ISIC** and **IYTC cards** qualify for discounts from student travel agencies. Most flights from budget agencies are on major airlines, but in peak season some may sell seats on less reliable chartered aircraft.

usit world (www.usitworld.com). Over 50 **usit campus** branches in the UK (www.usitcampus.co.uk), including 52 Grosvenor Gardens, **London** SW1W 0AG (☎0870 240 10 10); **Manchester** (☎0161 273 1880); and **Edinburgh** (☎0131 668 3303). Nearly 20 **usit NOW** offices in Ireland, including 19-21 Aston Quay, O'Connell Bridge, **Dublin** 2 (☎01 602 1600; www.usitnow.ie), and **Belfast** (☎02 890 327 111; www.usitnow.com). Offices in Athens, Auckland, Brussels, Frankfurt, Johannesburg, Lisbon, Luxembourg, Madrid, Paris, Sofia, and Warsaw.

Council Travel (www.counciltravel.com). Countless US offices, including branches in Atlanta, Boston, Chicago, L.A., New York, San Francisco, Seattle, and Washington, D.C. Check the web site or call 800-2-COUNCIL (226-8624) for the office nearest you. Also an office at 28A Poland St. (Oxford Circus), **London,** W1V 3DB (☎0207 437 77 67).

CTS Travel, 44 Goodge St., **London** W1T 2AD (☎0207 636 0031; fax 0207 637 5328; ctsinfo@ctstravel.co.uk).

STA Travel, 7890 S Hardy Dr., Ste. 110, Tempe AZ 85284 (24hr. reservations and info ☎800-777-0112; fax 480-592-0876; www.sta-travel.com). A student and youth travel organization with over 150 offices worldwide (check their web site for a listing of all their offices), including US offices in Boston, Chicago, L.A., New York, San Francisco, Seattle, and Washington, D.C. Ticket booking, travel insurance, railpasses, and more. In the UK, walk-in office 11 Goodge St., **London** W1T 2PF or call 0870-160-6070. In New Zealand, 10 High St., **Auckland** (☎09 309 0458). In Australia, 366 Lygon St., **Melbourne** Vic 3053 (☎03 9349 4344).

Travel CUTS (Canadian Universities Travel Services Limited), 187 College St., **Toronto,** ON M5T 1P7 (☎416-979-2406; fax 979-8167; www.travelcuts.com). 60 offices across Canada. Also in the UK, 295-A Regent St., **London** W1R 7YA (☎0207-255-1944).

COMMERCIAL AIRLINES

Commercial airlines' lowest regular offer is the **APEX** (Advance Purchase Excursion) fare. Generally, reservations must be made seven to 21 days ahead of departure, with seven to 14-day minimum-stay and up to 90-day maximum-stay restrictions. These fares carry hefty cancellation and change penalties (fees rise in summer). Book peak-season APEX fares early; by May you will have a hard time getting your desired departure date. For phone numbers of popular carriers to New York City, see **Service Directory** (p. 279).

STANDBY FLIGHTS

Traveling standby requires considerable flexibility in arrival and departure dates and cities. Companies dealing in standby flights sell vouchers rather than tickets, along with the promise to get to your destination (or near your destination) within a certain window of time (typically 1-5 days). You call in before your specific window of time to hear your flight options and the probability that you will be able to board each flight. You can then decide which flights you want to try to make, show up at the appropriate airport at the appropriate time, present your voucher, and board if space is available. Vouchers can usually be bought for both one-way and round-trip travel. You may receive a monetary refund only if every available flight within your date range is full; if you opt not to take an available (but perhaps less convenient) flight, you can only get credit toward future travel. Carefully read agreements with any company offering standby flights as tricky fine print can leave you in a lurch. To check on a company's service record in the US, call the Better Business Bureau (☎212-533-6200). It is difficult to receive refunds, and clients' vouchers will not be honored when an airline fails to receive payment in time.

TICKET CONSOLIDATORS

Ticket consolidators, or **"bucket shops,"** buy unsold tickets in bulk from commercial airlines and sell them at discounted rates. The best place to look is in the Sunday travel section of any major newspaper where many bucket shops place tiny ads. Call quickly, as availability is typically extremely limited. Not all bucket shops are reliable, so insist on a receipt that gives full details of restrictions, refunds, and tickets, and pay by credit card (2-5% fee) so you can stop payment if you never receive tickets. For more, see www.travel-library.com/air-travel/consolidators.html.

TRAVELING WITHIN THE US AND CANADA. Travel Avenue (☎800-333-3335; www.travelavenue.com) rebates commercial fares to or from the US (5% for over US$550) and will search for cheap flights from anywhere for a fee. **NOW Voyager,** 74 Varick St., Ste. 307, New York, NY 10013 (☎212-431-1616; fax 219-1793; www.nowvoyagertravel.com) arranges discounted flights both within the US and internationally. Other consolidators worth trying: **Airfare Busters** (☎800-232-8783; www.af.busters.com); **Interworld** (☎305-443-4929; fax 443-0351); **Pennsylvania Travel** (☎800-331-0947); **Rebel** (☎800-227-3235; travel@rebeltours.com; www.rebeltours.com); **Cheap Tickets** (☎800-377-1000; www.cheaptickets.com); **Student Universe** (272-9676; www.studentuniverse.com) and **Travac** (☎800-872-8800; fax 212-714-9063; www.travac.com). Yet more consolidators on the web include the **Internet Travel Network** (www.itn.com); **Travel Information Services** (www.tiss.com); **TravelHUB**

(www.travelhub.com); and **The Travel Site** (www.thetravelsite.com). Keep in mind that these are just suggestions to get you started in your research; *Let's Go* does not endorse any of these agencies. As always, be cautious, and research companies before you hand over your credit card number.

TRAVELING FROM THE UK. In London, the **Air Travel Advisory Bureau** (☎0207 636 5000; www.atab.co.uk) can provide names of reliable consolidators and discount flight specialists.

BY BUS

Getting in and out of New York can be less expensive and more scenic by bus or train than by plane. The hub of the Northeast bus network, New York's **Port Authority Terminal,** 41st St. and Eighth Ave., is a huge modern facility with labyrinthine bus terminals (☎212-435-7000; Subway: A, C, E to 42nd St.-Port Authority). The Port Authority has good information and security services, but the surrounding neighborhood is somewhat deserted at night, and it pays to be wary of pickpockets and call a cab. Exercise caution in the terminal's bathrooms.

Greyhound (☎800-231-2222; www.greyhound.com) operates the largest number of lines, departing from **Boston** (4½hr.; $42, $84 round-trip), **Philadelphia** (2hr.; $21, $42 round-trip), **Washington, D.C.** (4½hr.; $42, $84 round-trip), and **Montreal** (8hr.; $70, $109 round-trip). The fares listed require no advance purchase, but discounts can be had by purchasing tickets 14 days in advance. Ask about the three-day advance purchase two-for-one deal. A number of **discounts** are available on Greyhound's standard-fare tickets: students ride for 15% off with the Student Advantage Card (☎800-333-2920, www.studentadvantage.com to purchase the $20 card), senior citizens ride for 10 percent off, children under 11 ride for half-fare, and children under two ride for free in the lap of an adult (one per adult). A traveler with a physical disability may bring along a companion for free after clearing them by calling 800-752-4841.

Those looking for cheap trips to other major urban centers on the Eastern Seaboard can try asking around the ticket stalls of the bus companies that congregate around **Division St.,** at Forsyth St. in Chinatown near the Manhattan Bridge. While you may have to decipher the Chinese-language signs, the buses are often proper coaches, and the fares are a substantial savings (New York to Boston buses, for instance, are $15-25 one-way).

BY TRAIN

You can save money by purchasing your tickets in advance, so plan ahead. **Amtrak** (☎800-USA-RAIL/872-7245; www.amtrak.com) is the only provider of intercity passenger train service in the US. The web page lists up-to-date schedules, fares, and arrival and departure info. Many qualify for discounts: senior citizens (10 percent off); students (15 percent off) with a Student Advantage Card (see **By Bus** for how to purchase); travelers with disabilities (15% off); children 2-15 accompanied by a parent (50% off); children under age two (free); current members of the US armed forces, active-duty veterans, and their dependents (25% off). "Rail SALE" offers online discounts of up to 90%; visit the Amtrak web site for details and reservations.

Amtrak's trains connect NYC to most other parts of the country through **Penn Station,** 33rd St. and Eighth Ave. (Subway: 1, 2, 3, 9, A, C, E to 34th St.-Penn Station). From Boston 4-6hr., $50-120 one-way; from Washington, D.C., 3-4½hr., $67-118 one-way; from Philadelphia 1½hr., $43-77 one-way. **Long Island Railroad** (see **Daytripping,** p. 217) and the **New Jersey Transit** both run out of Penn Station.

BY CAR

There are several major paths leading to New York. From New Jersey there are three choices, each costing $6. The **Holland Tunnel** connects to lower Manhattan, exiting into the SoHo area. From the New Jersey Turnpike you'll probably end up at the **Lincoln Tunnel,** which exits in Midtown in the West 40s. The third, and arguably easiest, option is the **George Washington Bridge,** which crosses the Hudson River into northern Manhattan, offering access to either Harlem River Drive or the West Side Highway. From New England or Connecticut, from I-87 or I-95 follow signs for the **Willis Avenue Bridge** (toll-free) or the **Triboro Bridge** ($3.50). From there get onto the FDR Drive, which runs along the east side of Manhattan and exits onto city streets every 10 blocks or so. The **speed limit** in New York State, as in most other states, is 55 miles per hour. As in most other states, wearing a seat belt is required by law. For information on renting a car, see **Service Directory,** (p. 279).

SPECIFIC CONCERNS

OLDER TRAVELERS

Senior citizens are eligible for a wide range of discounts on transportation, museums, movies, theaters, concerts, restaurants, and accommodations throughout New York City. If you don't see a senior citizen price listed, it's certainly worth it to ask—the discount may be 15% or more.

DISABLED TRAVELERS

The city's **buses** all have excellent wheelchair access. Call the Transit Authority Access (☎718-596-8585) for information on public transit accessibility. Access-A-Ride door-to-door service is available for some; call to apply (see number above). In general it is advisable to inform airlines and hotels in advance of a disability when making arrangements for travel; some time may be needed to prepare special accommodations.

Arrange transportation well in advance to ensure a smooth trip. Hertz, Avis, and National **car rental agencies** have hand-controlled vehicles at some locations. In the US, both **Amtrak** and major airlines will accommodate disabled passengers if notified at least 72 hours in advance. Hearing-impaired travelers may contact Amtrak using teletype printers (☎800-872-7245). **Greyhound** buses will provide free travel for a companion; if you are without a fellow traveler, call Greyhound (☎800-752-4841) at least 48 hours before you leave and they will make arrangements for you.

Elevators and escalator accessibility hotline: ☎1-800-734-6772, 24hr.

Access-A-Ride: ☎1-877-337-2017. (For public transportation.)

USEFUL RESOURCES

Society for the Advancement of Travel for the Handicapped (SATH), 347 Fifth Ave., #610, New York, NY 10016, (☎212-447-7284; www.sath.org). An advocacy group that publishes the quarterly travel magazine *OPEN WORLD* (free for members, US$13 for nonmembers). Also publishes a wide range of info sheets on disability travel facilitation and destinations. Annual membership US$45, students and seniors US$30.

TOUR AGENCIES

Directions Unlimited, 123 Green Ln., Bedford Hills, NY 10507, USA (☎914-241-1700 or 800-533-5343; www.travel-cruises.com). Specializes in arranging individual and group vacations, tours, and cruises for the physically disabled.

The Guided Tour Inc., 7900 Old York Rd., #114B, Elkins Park, PA 19027, USA (☎800-783-5841 or 215-782-1370; www.guidedtour.com). Organizes travel programs for persons with developmental and physical challenges around the US.

DIETARY CONCERNS

Vegetarians won't have any problem eating cheap and well in New York. Excellent vegetarian restaurants abound, and almost every non-vegetarian place offers non-meat options (see **Food,** p. 129). For information about vegetarian travel, contact the **North American Vegetarian Society,** P.O. Box 72, Dolgeville, NY 13329, (☎518-568-7970; www.navs-online.org), publishes information about vegetarian travel, including *Transformative Adventures, a Guide to Vacations and Retreats* (US$15), and the *Vegetarian Journal's Guide to Natural Food Restaurants in the US and Canada* (US$12).

Travelers who keep **kosher** should call a New York synagogue for information (your own synagogue or college Hillel office should have lists of NYC Jewish institutions). ChaBad houses (centers for Lubavitch Hassidim and outreach) should also be able to either provide kosher food or direct you to it. NYU's ChaBad is located at 566 La Guardia #715 (☎212-998-4945), and the Upper East Side's ChaBad *shuckles* is at 311 E. 83rd St., Suite. B (☎212-717-4613). They also provide general information, help, classes, and matchmaking for religious visitors.

INTERNET RESOURCES

American Automobile Association (AAA) Travel Related Services (www.aaa.com). Provides maps and guides free to members. Offers emergency road and travel services and auto insurance (for members). For emergency road services or to become a member, call ☎800-222-4357.

Big World Magazine (www.bigworld.com). A budnget travel 'zine with a web page with great links to travel pages.

Expedia (www.expedia.com). Everything budget for trips.

Let's Go (www.letsgo.com). Find our newsletter, information about our books, travel, and other fun stuff. There's also a message board and forum for talking about your journeys and for asking questions.

New York Today (www.newyorktoday.com). The New York Times provides webcrawlers with in-depth entertainment info daily; also Food, Accommodations, and every other category of info.

TravelHUB (www.travelhub.com). A great site for cheap travel deals.

Travelocity (www.travelocity.com). More marvelous travel info and deals.

Village Voice (www.villagevoice.com). Known citywide for its lengthy real estate listings–the place to find apartment swaps, sublets, and rentals.

ESSENTIAL INFORMATION

FLIGHT PLANNING ON THE INTERNET

The Web is a great place to look for travel bargains–it's fast, it's convenient, and you can spend as long as you like exploring options without driving your travel agent insane.

Many airline sites offer special last-minute deals on the Web. Other sites do the legwork and compile the deals for you–try www.bestfares.com, www.onetravel.com, www.lowestfare.com, and www.travelzoo.com.

STA (www.sta-travel.com) and **Council** (www.counciltravel.com) provide quotes on student tickets.

Expedia (msn.expedia.com) and **Travelocity** (www.travelocity.com) offer full travel services.

Priceline (www.priceline.com) allows you to specify a price, and obligates you to buy any ticket that meets or beats it; be prepared for antisocial hours and odd routes.

Skyauction (www.skyauction.com) allows you to bid on both last-minute and advance-purchase tickets, but you may not get your first-choice dates.

Just one last note–to protect yourself, make sure that the site uses a secure server before handing over any credit card details. Happy hunting!

Accommodations

If you know someone who knows someone who lives in New York, get that person's phone number and ask to stay with them. The cost of living in New York can rip the seams out of your wallet. At true full-service establishments, a night will cost at least $125, with an additional hotel tax of 13.4%. Many reasonable choices are available for about $70 a night, but it depends on your priorities. People traveling alone may want to spend more to stay in a safer neighborhood. The young and the outgoing may prefer a budget-style place crowded with students; honeymooning couples may not.

Hostels offer fewer amenities than hotels, yet manage to preserve a greater feeling of camaraderie. Cheap YMCAs and YWCAs offer another budget option, but young backpackers may miss the intimacy and social life a hostel can offer. All of these places advise you to reserve in advance. Budget hotels are concentrated around Times Square, the lower part of Midtown, and the Upper West Side.

Crime-free neighborhoods in the city exist only in dreams; never leave anything of value in your room if you are staying in budget accommodations. Many places have safes or lockers available, some for an extra fee. Don't sleep in your car, and never, ever sleep outdoors anywhere in New York. The city has a hard enough time protecting its homeless population—tourists simply would not stand a chance.

The internet often expedites finding New York accommodations. Many of the accommodations listed below have websites and some offer discounts for internet reservations—ask when calling. There are also a number of online sites that list accommodations such as **New York City Reference** (www.panix.com/clay/nyc/query.cgi?H3), the **Hotel Guide** (www.HOTELGUIDE.com), **New York citysearch.com** (www.newyork.citysearch.com/), and **New York Today** (www.nytoday.com). For long-term accommodations, see **Living in the City**, p. 274.

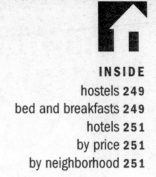

HOSTELS

Hostels are generally dorm-style accommodations where the sexes sleep apart in large rooms with bunk beds or on the floor. Because most hostelers don't place a huge premium on luxury or privacy, hostel beds can cost as little as $14 per night. As a trade-off, expect few frills. Guests must often rent or bring their own sheets or "sleep sacks" (two sheets sewn together); sleeping bags are usually not allowed. Many hostels make kitchens and utensils available for their guests, and some provide storage areas and laundry facilities. In most hostels, you can get a room with fewer occupants and more conveniences for a little more money. Most guests are students or of student age, often from outside the US, but the clientele can be surprisingly mixed.

If you're going to travel extensively in the rest of the US or Canada, you should consider joining **Hostelling International-American Youth Hostels (HI-AYH),** the leading organization of US hostels. There are over 300 HI-AYH-affiliated hostels throughout North America; these are usually kept up to a higher standard than most private hostels, although they tend to be more strict and institutional. HI-AYH runs an excellent hostel in New York, with much space and many amenities (see p. 263). Yearly **HI-AYH membership** is $25 for adults, $10 for those under 18, $35 for families, and $15 for those over 54. **Nonmembers** who wish to stay at an HI-AYH hostel usually pay $3 extra, which can be applied toward membership. For more information, contact HI-AYH, 733 15th St. NW, #840, Washington, D.C. 20005 (☎202-783-6161; fax 202-783-6171; www.hiayh.org) or inquire at any HI-affiliated hostel.

Although you might not be as enthusiastic as the Village People, don't overlook the **Young Men's Christian Association (YMCA)** or the **Young Women's Christian Association (YWCA),** which have seven branches in New York City: three in Manhattan, two in Queens, and two in Brooklyn. Slightly more expensive than hostels but usually much more uniform and cleaner; singles average $45-61 per night, and rooms include use of a library, pool, and other facilities. However, you may have to share a room and use a communal bath or shower. Some YMCAs in New York (listed below) accept women and families as well as men. Reserve at least two weeks in advance and expect to pay a refundable key deposit of about $10. For information and reservations, write or call **The Y's Way,** 224 E. 47th St., New York, NY 10017 (☎212-308-2899; http://ymcanyc.org).

A very friendly alternative to hostels is **Homestay New York,** 630 E. 19th St., Brooklyn (☎718-434-2071; helayne@homestayny.com; www.homestayny.com). Travelers are placed in homes of New York City residents, mostly in outer boroughs but all within 30min. of Manhattan. Rates from $90 per day for a standard single to $130 for a deluxe double and include some meals, a Metrocard, and a phone card. Call or email for reservations at least 10 days ahead.

BED AND BREAKFASTS

Bed and Breakfasts (private homes that rent out one or more spare rooms to travelers) are a great alternative to impersonal hotel and motel rooms. They're hardly your stereotypical B&Bs—no sleepy New England village squares or big front porches—but Manhattan does have a wide selection. Many don't have phones, TVs, or showers with their rooms. Reservations should be made a few weeks in advance, usually with a deposit. Most apartments listed have two-night minimums. Some B&B's are "hosted," while others are "unhosted," meaning that the people renting you the room will not be there. Most B&B agencies list accommodations in boroughs other than Manhattan; these can be an excellent budget alternative. Prices vary according to borough, neighborhood, and accommodation size (but generally run singles $70-100; doubles $80-135), so call for specifics with a neighborhood and price range in mind. **Urban Ventures** (☎594-5650; fax 947-9320; www.urbanventures.com) is the oldest and most established agency in the city, with a whopping 900 listings covering Manhattan, plus additional listings for Brooklyn and Queens. **New World Bed and Breakfast** (☎675-5600 or toll-free from within the U.S. and Canada, ☎800-443-3800) specializes in short-term furnished apartments, and **Bed and Breakfast of New York** (☎645-8134) offers weekly and monthly rates.

HOTELS

A single in a cheap hotel can be had for as little as $60-85. Don't expect a large room, however. Most hotel rooms should be reserved in advance. Ask the hotel owner if you can see a room before you pay for it. You should be told in advance whether the bathroom is communal or private. Most hotels require a key deposit when you register. Check-in usually takes place between 11am and 6pm; check-out before 11am. You may be able to store your gear for the day even after vacating your room and returning the key, but many proprietors will not take responsibility for the safety of your belongings. Some hotels require a *non-refundable* deposit for reservations. However, the hotel may allow you to use your deposit on a future stay at the hotel.

ACCOMMODATIONS BY PRICE

Hotel prices vary by season and by room. The price ranges listed below are by no means exact.

$40 AND UNDER				
Aladdin Hotel	(260)		West End Studios	(265)
Big Apple Hostel	(260)		YMCA-Vanderbilt	(259)
Central Park Hostel	(263)		**$81-100**	
Chelsea Center Hotel	(255)		Americana Inn	(259)
Chelsea International Hostel	(256)		Chelsea Inn	(255)
Chelsea Star Hotel	(256)		Herald Square Hotel	(257)
International Student Center	(263)		Madison Hotel	(255)
International Student Hospice	(255)		New York Inn	(259)
Jazz on the Park	(263)		St. Mark's Hotel	(253)
Manhattan Youth Castle	(260)		**$101-120**	
New York Int'l HI-AYH Hostel	(263)		Best Western President Hotel	(259)
Sugar Hill International House	(266)		Broadway Inn	(259)
Uptown Hostel	(266)		Chelsea Savoy Hotel	(256)
$41-60			Gershwin Hotel	(253)
YMCA-Flushing	(267)		Hotel Belleclaire	(261)
$61-80			Hotel Grand Union	(255)
The Amsterdam Inn	(261)		Hotel Wolcott	(257)
Carlton Arms Hotel	(255)		Skyline Hotel	(259)
Chelsea Star Hotel	(256)		**$121 AND UP**	
Crystal's Castle Bed and Breakfast	(265)		Akwaaba Mansion	(266)
Hayden Hall	(261)		Bed and Breakfast on the Park	(267)
Hotel 17	(255)		Chelsea Hotel	(255)
Larchmont Hotel	(253)		Hotel Olcott	(260)
Malibu Studios Hotel	(260)		Hotel Stanford	(257)
Murray Hill Inn	(255)		Hudson Hotel	(259)
New York Bed and Breakfast	(265)		Milford Plaza	(260)
Pickwick Arms Hotel	(259)		Quality Hotel and Suites	(257)
Pioneer Hotel	(253)		Sheraton LaGuardia East Hotel	(267)
Portland Square Hotel	(259)		ThirtyThirty	(255)
West Side Inn	(261)		Union Square Inn	(255)
West Side YMCA	(261)		Washington Square Hotel	(253)

ACCOMMODATIONS BY NEIGHBORHOOD

Let's Go lists prices excluding tax, unless otherwise noted. The following accommodations are the best hostels, YMCA/YWCAs, hotels, and B&Bs in New York; all are ranked according to quality, value, price, safety, and location.

HOTEL
IN
NY
Shared Accommodations (with bath) starting from $29.99 + taxes.
Private Rooms (with bath) starting from $99.00 + taxes
Internet/ Fax Service
Open 24 hours
Roof-Top Terrace
Clubroom & Social Lounge
Unbeatable Location convenient to Midtown, Times Square, Chelsea & Greenwich Village
Hostel rooms available
RATES DEPEND UPON AVAILABILITY
INTERCLUB
The Gershwin Hotel
New York
7 East 27th Street, New York, NY 10016
Tel: 212-545-8000 Fax: 212-684-5546
Special Events: 212-447-6466

LITTLE ITALY

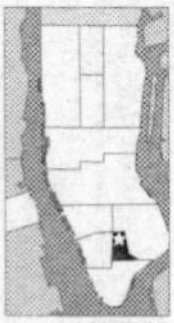

see map pp. 312-313

Pioneer Hotel, 341 Broome St. between Elizabeth St. and the Bowery. (☎226-1482; fax 266-3525). Subway: J, M to Bowery; B, D, Q to Grand St. In a 100-year-old building, the Pioneer is a good, no-frills place to stay if you want to be close to the addictive nightlife of SoHo and the East Village. All rooms have TV, sinks, and ceiling fans. Rooms with private bath have A/C. Check-out 11am. Reservations recommended at least 6 weeks in advance during peak season. Singles $69; doubles $89, with bath $99. AmEx/D/DC/MC/V.

GREENWICH VILLAGE

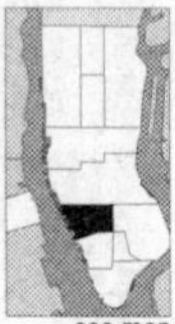

see map pp. 316-317

Washington Square Hotel, 103 Waverly Pl., at MacDougal St. (☎777-9515 or 800-222-0418; fax 979-8373). Subway: A, B, C, D, E, F, Q to W. 4th St. The lobby's marble and brass match the fantastic location. A/C, cable TV, key-card entry to rooms. Clean and comfortable rooms all have private bath. Friendly, multilingual staff. C3 is the hotel's trendy restaurant/bar. 24hr. exercise room. 10% ISIC discount. Continental breakfast included. Reserve 2 months or more in advance for weekend, 1 month for weekdays. Singles $126-145; doubles $148-160; queen-size bed or two twins $160-180; quads $181-190. Roll-away bed $20. AmEx/JCB/MC/V.

Larchmont Hotel, 27 W. 11th St. between Fifth and Sixth Aves. (☎989-9333; fax 989-9496). Subway: N, R, L, 4, 5, 6 to 14th St./Union Sq. Spacious, clean rooms in a white-washed brownstone on a quiet block. A/C, TV, desks, closets, and wash basins in all rooms. Shared bath. Continental breakfast included. Reserve 5-6 weeks in advance. Singles $70-95; doubles $90-115; queen-size bed $109-125. AmEx/MC/V.

DORMITORIES

New York University, 14a Washington Pl. (☎998-4621; www.nyu.edu/housing/summer). You do not have to be enrolled in NYU summer school to get housing, but summer school students get priority and lower rates, and housing is only available for individuals, not families or couples. Housing options in the East, Greenwich, and West Villages as well as near South Street Seaport. Min. age of 17, unless an approved summer school student. Max. stay 11-12 weeks. Min. stay 3 consecutive weeks. Reception M-Tu 9am-5pm, W-Th 9am-7pm, Su 9am-2pm. Call for prices.

EAST VILLAGE

see map pp. 320-321

St. Mark's Hotel, 2 St. Mark's Pl., at Third Ave. (☎674-2192; fax 420-0854). Subway: 6 to Astor Pl. Functional, clean rooms, in perhaps the most exciting location in the city. Call ahead for reservations. All rooms with private bath and cable TV. Rooms with a full bed $99.07, with a queen-size bed $108.61, with 2 twin beds $113.02, with two full-size beds $130.67. Cash and travelers checks only.

Chelsea Center Hostel (East Village branch), on 12th St. between First Ave. and Avenue A. Run by the Chelsea Center Hostel (p. 256)—call them for details.

UNION SQUARE, GRAMERCY, AND MURRAY HILL

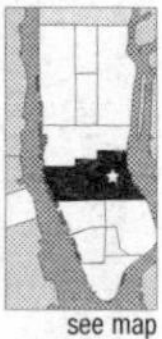

see map pp. 322-323

Gershwin Hotel, 7 E. 27th St. between Madison and Fifth Aves. (☎545-8000; fax 684-5546; reservations@gershwinhotel.com; www.gershwinhotel.com). Subway: 6, N, R to 28th St. This funky, chic hotel full of pop art, modern furniture, and artsy twenty-somethings seems like a set from Alice in Wonderland—MTV-style. The pristine hotel offers spaces for poetry, comedy, concerts, and open-mic nights and even has its own art gallery. Private rooms come with bathrooms, cable TV, A/C, and phones. Internet $1 per 4min. Reception 24hr. Check-out 11am. Economy rooms (single or double occupancy only) $99, standard rooms (single or double occupancy only) $169, superior rooms $199, family rooms $269, one-bedroom suites $299; triples and quads add $10 per person. $15 extra for Th to Sa. Dorm rooms also available: 8-12 bed dorms $30 per bed. AmEx/MC/V.

Carlton Arms Hotel, 160 E. 25th St. between Third and Lexington Aves. (☎679-0680; www.carltonarms.com). Subway: 6 to 23rd St. Each room is decorated by a different artist. 11C is the "good daughter/bad daughter" room—half the room is festooned in teenybopper posters, the other half in horror-movie pics. A black line marks the divide. The rooms (54 in total) are spacious, although summer travelers should note that there is no A/C. Check-out 11:30am. Reserve for summer 2 months in advance; confirm 10 days in advance. Singles $70, with bath $85; doubles $90, $100; triples $110, 120; quads $105, $117. $5-11 discounts for students and foreign travelers. Pay for 7 or more nights up front and get a 10% discount. MC/V.

ThirtyThirty, 30 E. 30th St. between Park Ave. South and Madison Aves. (☎689-1900 or 800-804-4480; fax 689-0023; info@thirtythirtynyc.com; www.thirtythirty-nyc.com). A sleek, modern hotel in a prime location at relatively budget prices. All rooms have cable TV, A/C, iron, hair dryer, and phones with voicemail. Singles $125; doubles $165; suites $245.

Hotel Grand Union, 34 E. 32nd St. between Park Ave. South and Madison Ave. (☎683-5890; fax 689-7397; grandunionhotel@aol.com; www.hotelgrandunion.com). Subway: 6 to 33rd St. This centrally-located hotel offers fairly spacious rooms with cable TV, phone and voicemail, A/C, mini-fridge, and bathroom. 24hr. security. Wheelchair accessible. Singles and doubles $116; triples $132; quads $158. AmEx/D/DC/JCB/MC/V.

Murray Hill Inn, 143 E. 30th St. between Third and Lexington Aves. (☎683-6900 or 888-996-6376; fax 545-0103; murhillinn@aol.com; www.murrayhillinn.com). Subway: 6 to 28th St. Floral-print, simple rooms at reasonable prices. 5 floors—no elevator. All rooms have A/C, cable TV, and phone. 21-day max. stay. Check-in 2pm. Check-out noon. Singles $75, private bath $115; doubles $95, private bath $125.

Hotel 17, 225 E. 17th St. between Second and Third Aves. (☎475-2845; fax 677-8178; hotel17@worldnet.att.net; http://hotel17.citysearch.com). This historic 120-room hotel served as the setting for Woody Allen's *Manhattan Murder Mystery;* Madonna even had her portrait done in these eccentric accommodations. The mostly foreign crowd enjoys high-ceilinged rooms with A/C and cable TV. Some rooms have fireplaces (good); many have frankly disastrous wallpaper. Check-in 2pm. Check-out noon. No children under 18 accepted. Singles $70-75; doubles $80-95; triples $140-150. Weekly rates: singles $425; doubles $600. No credit cards.

Union Square Inn, 209 E. 14th St. between Second and Third Aves. (☎614-0500; fax 614-0512; www.unionsquareinn.com). Subway: 4, 5, 6, N, R to 14th St./Union Sq. or L to 3rd Ave. A 5-floor walk-up promises 40 renovated rooms, all with cable TV and A/C. Reception 24hr. Check-in 2pm. Check-out noon. Singles and doubles $139-169, depending on room size; triples and quads add $20 per person.

Madison Hotel, 21 E. 27th St., at Madison Ave. (☎532-7373 or 800-9MADISON; fax 686-0092; madihotel@aol.com; www.madison-hotel.com). Subway: 6, N, R to 28th St. With its tiny lobby and small rooms, the Madison isn't much in terms of atmosphere, but the rooms are well-priced: cable TV, A/C, and private bath. Breakfast included. $5 cable deposit; $40 phone deposit. Check-in noon. Check-out 11am. Singles $99; doubles $121; rooms for 2-4 with 2 double beds $145. AmEx/D/MC/V.

HOSTELS

International Student Hospice, 154 E. 33rd St. between Lexington and Third Aves. (☎228-7470; fax 228-4689). Subway: 6 to 33rd St. Up a flight of stairs in a brownstone with a brass plaque saying "I.S.H." This non-profit hostel better resembles a house full of bric-a-brac than a hostel. Rooms for 1-4 people; tiny hall bathroom. Call ahead. $28 per night including tax; $20 per night if you pay for a week up front.

CHELSEA

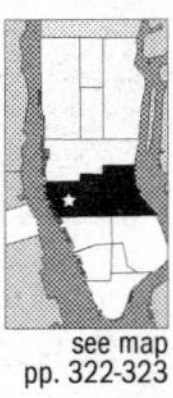
see map pp. 322-323

Chelsea Hotel, 222 W. 23rd St. (☎243-3700). Subway: 1, 9 to 23rd St. The grand old dame of bohemian hotels is about as story-filled as it gets. Plaques outside commemorate artists who've stayed here (Thomas Wolfe and Dylan Thomas among them), and the lobby is decorated with artwork. Most rooms with A/C and private bathrooms. Many rooms with kitchens. Doubles $165-265. Triples $235-265. Suites $325-385. Call for long-term stay rates.

Chelsea Inn, 46 W. 17th St., between Fifth and Sixth Aves., (☎645-8989 or 800-640-6469; fax 645-1903; chelseainn@earthlink.net; www.chelseainn.com). Subway: F to 14th St. or 1, 9 to 18th St. Charmingly mismatched antiques in spacious rooms. All rooms with A/C, cable TV, phone, fridge, safe, and coffee makers. Reception M-Sa 9am-11pm, Su 9am-9pm. Check-in 3pm. Check-out noon. Reservations recommended. Guest rooms with shared bath $89-129; studios $129-169; 1-bedroom suites $169-199; 2-bedroom suites $179-259.

Chelsea Savoy Hotel, 204 W. 23rd St., at Seventh Ave., (☎929-9353; fax 741-6309; www.chelseasavoynyc.com). Subway: 1, 9, C, E to 23rd St. Clean, functional, welcoming rooms. All with private bath, cable TV, A/C, irons, and hair dryers. Reception 24hr. Group rates available. Check-in 3pm. Check-out 11am. Reservations recommended. Wheelchair accessible. Singles $99-115; doubles $125-155; quad $145-185.

Chelsea Star Hotel, 300 W. 30th St., at Eighth Ave. (☎244-7827; fax 279-9018; www.starhotelny.com). Subway: A, C, E to 34th St.-Penn Station. Stay in one of the theme rooms where Madonna reportedly lived when she was a struggling artist. Clean and coveted. On the second and third floors. Reception daily 8am-midnight. Residents get keys. Safe deposit box $5. Max. stay 21 days. Check-in noon. Check-out 11am. Reserve at least one month in advance. No wheelchair access. All rooms with shared bathrooms (20 rooms, 4 per bath). Dorms $30; single $79; double $99; triple $119; quad $129.

HOSTELS

Chelsea Center Hostel, 313 W. 29th St. between Eighth and Ninth Aves. (☎643-0214; fax 473-3945; www.chelseacenterhostel.com). Subway: 1, 2, 3, 9, A, C, E to 34th St. To enter, ring the labeled buzzer at the door. Gregarious, knowledgable, multilingual staff will help you out with New York tips. Room for 20 guests in this quiet residential-home-turned-hostel. 15 stay in a spacious basement room with a summer camp feel; the rest in a bedroom on the main floor. A lovely garden adds to the charm. 2 showers. Light breakfast included. Linen provided. Check-in 8:30am-10:45pm. Flexible lockout 11am-5pm. Cash and traveler's checks only. Dorm beds $30.

Chelsea International Hostel, 251 W. 20th St. between Seventh and Eighth Aves., in Chelsea (☎647-0010; fax 727-7289; www.chelseahostel.com). Subway: 1, 9, C, E to 23rd St. Scandinavians and other Europeans make up the bulk of the clientele of this enclosed hostel with funky youth travelers. The congenial staff offers pizza Wednesday night. There's a backyard garden, but the smallish rooms themselves are merely utilitarian. Kitchens, laundry room, TV rooms. Internet access ($0.19 per minute). Key deposit $10. Check-in 8am-6pm. Reservations recommended. 4- and 6-person dorms $27; private rooms $65. AmEx/MC/V.

HERALD SQUARE

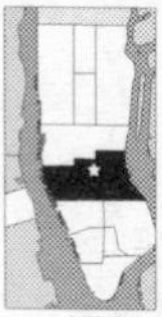
see map pp. 322-323

Hotel Stanford, 43 W. 32nd St. between Fifth Ave. and Broadway (☎563-1500 or 800-365-1114; fax 629-0043; stanfordny@aol.com; www.hotelstanford.citysearch.com). Subway: B, D, F, N, Q, R to 34th St. This Korean District hotel's lobby glitters with sparkling ceiling lights and a polished marble floor. Rooms are impeccably clean, with firm mattresses, plush carpeting, private bathrooms, cable TV, phones, A/C, refrigerators. Continental breakfast included. Check-in 3pm. Check-out noon. Reservations recommended. Singles $120-150; doubles and twins $150-180; suites $200-250. AmEx/D/JCB/MC/V.

Herald Square Hotel, 19 W. 31st St., between Fifth Ave. and Broadway (☎279-4017 or 800-727-1888; fax 643-9208; www.heraldsquarehotel.com). Subway: B, D, F, N, R to 34th St. In the Beaux-Arts home of the original *Life* magazine and they won't let you forget it. *Life* covers grace the hallways and the small, pleasant rooms. Rooms include cable TV, safe, phone, voicemail, and A/C; most have private bathrooms. Reserve 2-3 weeks in advance. 10% discount for ISIC card holders. Singles $85 (shared bathroom singles $65); doubles $125; twins $140; triples $150; quads $160. AmEx/D/JCB/MC/V.

Hotel Wolcott, 4 W. 31st St. between Fifth Ave. and Broadway (☎268-2900; fax 563-0096; sales@wolcott.com; www.wolcott.com). Subway: B, D, F, N, R to 34th St. An unexpectedly ornate lobby. The building boasts a history as rich as its decor: here, in the early 1900s, Titanic survivors wrote letters and, decades later, 50s rock-and-roll legend Buddy Holly recorded two hit albums in now-defunct studios upstairs. The rooms are less grand but include bathrooms, A/C, cable TV, phones, voicemail, and even Nintendo (although you'll have to pay for the last one). In-room Internet $9.95 per 12 hours. Safe deposit boxes. Self-service laundry. Singles and doubles $99-140; triples $115-160; suites for 3 $150-190. AmEx/JCB/MC/V.

MIDTOWN

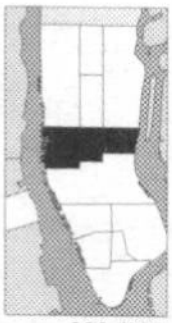
see map pp. 326-327

Quality Hotel and Suites, 59 W. 46th St. between Fifth and Sixth Aves. (☎719-2300, 800-567-7720 for reservations). Subway: B, D, F to Rockefeller Center. Located in the heart of midtown a few yards from Rockefeller Center. Classy but subdued rooms. Health facility downstairs. Complimentary breakfast, complimentary phone calls, in room safes, color TVs. The 193 rooms have been recently renovated, and are each equipped with private bath, A/C and TV. Regular room with double bed averages $179, depending on availability. During sales, a regular room can be as low as $89. All major credit cards.

Carlton Arms Hotel

Home Away From Home

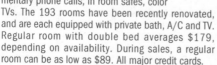

Algonquin Hotel

the chelsea star
NEW YORK'S MOST EXCITING
THEME HOTEL
• Centrally located, across from Penn Station/Madison Square Garden
• Walking distance to Time Square, Empire State, 5th Avenue Shopping
• Roof top summer garden; laundry; internet kiosk
• Dorms from $30 per night (all rooms air conditioned)
• Private rooms with shared bathroom from $75 per night
• Luxury, en suite apartments from $140 per night, weekly rates available
toll • free
www.chelseastar.com
877·827·NYNY
voice (212) 244·7827 email reservations@starhotelny.com fax (212) 279·9018
300 West 30th Street at 8th Avenue New York•NY 10001

Pickwick Arms Hotel, 230 E. 51st St. between Second and Third Aves. (☎355-0300 or 800-742-5945). Subway: 6 to 51st St.; E, F to 53rd St.-Lexington Ave. Business types congregate in this well-priced, mid-sized hotel. Chandeliered marble lobby contrasts with tiny rooms and tinier hall bathrooms. Roof garden and airport service available. A/C, cable TV, phones, and voicemail in all rooms. Check-in 2pm. Check-out 1pm. Singles $75-115; doubles with bath $140-150; studios with double bed and sofa for 2 people $215, but no elevator access. Additional person in room $20. Credit card necessary to guarantee room. AmEx/D/MC/V.

YMCA-Vanderbilt, 224 E. 47th St. between Second and Third Aves. (☎756-9600; fax 752-0210). Subway: 6 to 51st St.; E, F to 53rd St.-Lexington Ave. Convenient, with reasonable security. Clean, brightly lit lobby bustles with international visitors. Small rooms have A/C and cable TV; usually enough bathrooms to go around. Free use of well-equipped gym and safe-deposit boxes. Five shuttles per day to the airports. No key deposit. 25-night max. stay. Check-in 3pm. Check-out 11am. Luggage storage until departure $1 per bag. Make reservations 2-3 weeks in advance and guarantee with a credit card. Singles $85; twin bunk $95. AmEx/MC/V.

Americana Inn, 69 W. 38th St. (☎840-2019). Subway: N, R to 34th St., B, D, Q, and F to 42nd St. Great location makes up for the drab exterior. Each of the 50 clean, simple rooms is equipped with a TV, sink, and A/C. Five shared baths on each floor. Internet access $1 per 6min. No smoking. Singles $85-95; doubles $95-105; triples $105-115. AmEx/MC/V.

TIMES SQUARE AND THEATER DISTRICT

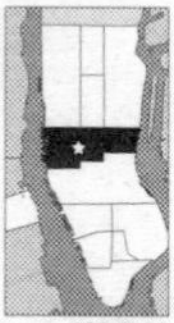

see map pp. 326-327

Hudson Hotel, 356 W. 58th St. between Eighth and Ninth Aves. (☎554-6000). Subway: A, C, B, D, 1, 9 to 59th St. If you are looking for a full-service hotel, this is as chic and swank as it gets. The luxuries don't stop at this new hotel: customized greenhouses, utopian garden courtyard, super-popular bar, yoga studio, an Olympic size swimming pool, etc. The decadent rooms contain down comforters, oak walls, rotating art exhibits, mood-lighting as well as an ultra-modern bathroom. Standard rooms run $155-$255, with suites as high as $500, but there is an occasional $95 special that is worth looking into. All major credit cards.

Best Western President Hotel, 234 W. 48th St. between Broadway and Eighth Ave. (☎246-8800). Subway: 1, 9, C, E to 50th St. This chain hotel offers yet another full-service lodging option. The 16 floors contain 350 tastefully decorated rooms. The friendly staff, comfortable lounge, and two restaurants make this an attractive choice. A pool and gym are available for an additional $20/day. Reserve as soon as possible. Room with a double bed $109-169. All major credit cards.

Skyline Hotel, 725 Tenth Ave., at 49th St. (☎586-3400). Subway: C, E to 50th St. Large, well-kept rooms with full amenities. Pool with panoramic view of the city, restaurant and free storage parking. Farther away from Times Square than other hotels, which allows more space for less money, and still a stone's throw from the theatre district. Make reservations as early as possible, though walk-ins are welcome depending on space. Rooms with double beds run $99-169, subject to availability. AmEx/D/DC/MC/V.

Broadway Inn, 264 W. 46th St., at Eighth Ave. (☎997-9200 or 800-826-6300; fax 768-2807). Subway: 1, 2, 3, 9, 7, N, R, S to 42nd St.-Times Square. These quiet, clean rooms have the dignity of a European B&B. The helpful staff and cozy common room/lobby contribute to the friendly and quaint atmosphere. TV, data port jack, private bath, and A/C in all rooms. Continental breakfast included. No wheelchair access. Singles $110-145; doubles $140-160 (high-end includes jacuzzi); suites (for 2 adults and 2 children 6-12 or 3 adults) $185-205. AmEx/D/DC/MC/V.

New York Inn, 765 Eighth Ave. between 46th and 47th Sts. (☎247-5400). Subway: C, E to 50th St. Not luxurious, but the rooms are clean, well-kept, and equipped with a private bath, A/C and a TV. Frequented by a strongly South American and European crowd. Continental breakfast included. Call two weeks ahead of time for reservations. Singles $89; Doubles $99-115, equipped with two double beds $130. AmEx/MC/V.

Portland Square Hotel, 132 W. 47th St. between Sixth and Seventh Aves. (☎382-0600 or 800-388-8988). Subway: 1, 2, 3, 9, A, C, E, N, R to 42nd St.-Times Square. A self-proclaimed "theater hotel," this pretty building has been lodging theatergoers since 1904. The rooms are institutional but clean and offer a variety of options for the budget-minded. All rooms have A/C and a TV. Small singles and doubles with shared bath $65-75. A double with a private bath offers more space for $125. AmEx/MC/V.

Milford Plaza, 270 W. 45th St. between Broadway and Eighth Ave. (☎869-3600). Subway: 1, 2, 3, 9, A, C, E, N, R to 42nd St.-Times Sq. One of Midtown's enormous full-service hotels. The hotel contains 1300 large classy rooms that fill with families and tourists from all over the world. Complimentary gym facilities and game room. Maximum stay 14 days. Hotel restaurant and lounge. Rooms $129-225 for one person, $134-240 for two persons, and $15 for each additional person with a maximum of three to a room. All major credit cards.

HOSTELS

Big Apple Hostel, 119 W. 45th St. between Sixth and Seventh Aves. (☎302-2603; fax 302-2605; www.bigapplehostel.com). Subway: 1, 2, 3, 9, A, C, E, N, R to 42nd St.-Times Sq. Centrally located, this hostel has clean, carpeted rooms, kitchen with refrigerator, luggage room, big back deck (closed 2-6am) with grill, common rooms, and laundry facilities. Americans accepted with out-of-state photo ID or other convincing proof that they're tourists. Reception 24hr. Safe deposit available at reception (25¢). Internet access $1 per 5min. No reservations accepted Aug.-Sept. except through website or by fax—send your credit card number. No curfew. No wheelchair access. Bunk in dorm-style room with shared bath $36; singles and doubles $90. MC/V.

Aladdin Hotel, 317 W. 45th St. between Eighth and Ninth Aves. (☎246-8580; fax 246-6036). Subway: 1, 2, 3, 9, A, C, E, N, R to 42nd St.-Times Square. The multi-variegated decor makes the lobby and common room/smoking lounge look like a circus. Although rooms are cramped and without fans, the hotel is abuzz with international travelers who appreciate the low prices. A rooftop garden adds a nice touch. Internet access $1 per 10min. Lockers of various size $3-5. Laundry facilities. Reserve at least one week in advance. Out of state ID or passport required. No wheelchair access. 4-bed dorms $35 per bed; singles and doubles with shared bath $87-99. AmEx/D/DC/JBC/MC/V.

UPPER EAST SIDE

see map pp. 328-329

Manhattan Youth Castle, 1596 Lexington Ave. between 101st and 102nd Sts. (☎831-4440; fax 722-55746). Subway: 6 to 103rd St. Small and affordable accommodation in the friendly and unique environment bordering Spanish Harlem and the Upper East Side. Helpful staff offers special themed tours of the city. 3-week max. stay. Reservations recommended. Call two months in advance for summer, otherwise 2 weeks is sufficient. Passport ID required. Key deposit $5. $30 per person per day; $200 per person per week. AmEx/MC/V.

De Hirsch Residence, 1395 Lexington Ave., at 92nd St. (☎415-5650 or 800-858-4692; fax 415-5578). Subway: 6 to 96th St. Affiliated with the 92nd St. YMHA/YWHA, De Hirsch has some of the larger, cleaner, and more convenient hostel housing in the city. Rooms near huge hall bathrooms, kitchens, and laundry machines on (at least) every other floor. Single-sex floors, strictly enforced. 24hr. access and security. Discounted access to the many facilities of the 92nd St. Y ($89 per month) and reduced rates for concerts. Organized activities such as walking tours of New York. All have A/C. Rents only on monthly basis. Wheelchair accessible. Single $995 per month; shared room $690-805 per person per month.

UPPER WEST SIDE

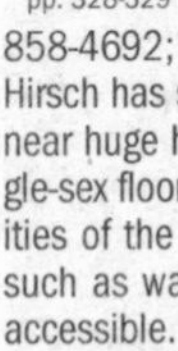

see map pp. 332-333

Malibu Studios Hotel, 2688 Broadway, at 103rd St. (☎222-2954 or 800-647-2227; fax 678-6842; rooms@malibuhotel.com; www.malibuhotelnyc.com). Subway: 1, 9 to 103rd St. Clean rooms, done up in a black and white motif. Standard rooms have sinks, shared baths, and TV; deluxe rooms include private bath, phones, A/C, and TV. Reception 24hr. Reservations required. No wheelchair access. Singles/doubles $79; triples/quads (two double beds) $89. Deluxe singles and doubles $129; triples/quads $149.

Hotel Olcott, 27 W. 72nd St. between Central Park West and Columbus Ave. (☎877-4200; fax 580-0511; www.hotelolcott.com). Subway: B, C to 72nd St. Just off Central Park, with a lobby that wouldn't be out of place in some of the neighborhood's grander buildings. Rooms are large, and feature A/C, cable TV, and kitchenettes. Internet access ($1 per 4 min.). One night's deposit required (checks or money orders). 1-2 person studios $130 (weekly $840); 1-2 person suites $150 (weekly $980); $15 per extra person (weekly $70). MC/V.

Hotel Belleclaire, 250 W. 77th St., at Broadway. (☎362-7700; 877-468-3522; fax 362-1004). Subway: 1, 9 to 79th St. In a landmark building with marble staircases. Renovations were finished in 2001, which means everything looks spanking new. Scandinavian furnishings and fluffy comforters make for comfortable stays. Gym and room service. All 170 rooms come with A/C, cable TV, and fridge. Check-in 3pm. Check-out noon. Economy room (shared bath) $99-129. Special rate for *Let's Go* readers $119. Other rooms $159-229.

The Amsterdam Inn, 340 Amsterdam Ave., at 76th St. (☎579-7500; fax 579-6127; www.amsterdaminn.com). Subway: 1, 9 to 79th St. The 25 rooms are small but renovated and clean. Two-floor walk up to the lobby. All rooms have A/C and color TV. Check-in 3pm. Check-out 11am. Singles $75; doubles $95; with private bath $125. Cash only.

Hotel Hayden Hall, 117 W. 79th St., at Columbus Ave. (☎787-4900; fax 496-3975; reservations@haydenhall.com; www.haydenhall.com). Subway: B, C to 81st St. Great location, but the grey paint on the walls isn't the greatest of decor schemes. Rooms come with fridge and phone, but no A/C. Good weekly rates. Reservations recommended. Singles and doubles with shared bath $65; 2- to 3-person room with private bath $90; 4-person room $100; 2-room suite for up to 4 $125.

West Side Inn, 237 W. 107th St. between Broadway and Amsterdam Ave. (☎866-0061 or 866-0062; fax 866-0062; westsideinn@aol.com; www.westsideinn.com). Subway: 1, 9 to 110th St. Decent and clean private rooms with shared kitchenettes and bathrooms on each floor. Rooms with TV, A/C, and fridge. Check-in 3pm. Check-out 11am. Internet access $1 per 4min. Call 2-3 weeks in advance. Prices $65-100, depending on number of people in room; call for off-season rates.

West Side YMCA, 5 W. 63rd St., at Central Park W. (☎875-4273 or 875-4173; fax 875-1334; wsguestrooms@ymcanyc.org; www.ymcanyc.org). Subway: A, B, C, D, 1, 9 to 59th St./ Columbus Circle. Behind the Y's impressive Moorish façade stand 482 basic, small rooms. No beautiful decor here, but there is free access to facilities (including 2 pools and a very well-equipped fitness center). All rooms have A/C and cable TV. Check-in 2:30pm. Check-out noon. 25-day max. stay. Wheelchair access. Singles $65-90, with bath $110-130; doubles (bunk beds) $95-105, with bath (double bed) $120-150.

West End Studios, 850 West End Ave. between 101st and 102nd Sts. (☎749-7104; fax 865-5130). Subway: 1, 9 to 103rd St. If all you want in a hotel room is a bed to sleep on, you got it. Rooms are lacking in decor, but all have A/C, refrigerator, and TV. Shared bathrooms only. Reserve at least 3 weeks in advance. Check-in 3pm. Check-out noon. Internet access $1 per 5min. Single bed $69; double bed $89; triples $109; two double beds $119.

RATES FROM $19.99 AND UP

HOSTELS

Jazz on the Park, 36 W. 106th St. (aka Duke Ellington Blvd.), at Central Park West (☎932-1600; fax 932-1700; jazzonpark@aol.com; www.jazzhostel.com). Subway: B, C to 103rd St. The Jazz riffs to the tune of clean, brightly-colored hostel-dom. Chic, modern decor. Lockers and A/C make you a real cool cat. Enough activities that you might not actually leave the hostel—live jazz in the downstairs lounge; all-you-can-eat BBQs on the terrace on W and Su in summer ($5); and Sunday gospel brunches. Internet access $1 per 5min. 210 beds. Linen, towels, and breakfast included. Check-out 11am. No curfew. No wheelchair access. Reservations essential June-Oct. 12- to 14-bed dorms $30; 6- to 8-bed dorms $32; 4-bed dorms $34; private rooms (full or bunk beds) $88; prices include tax.

New York International HI-AYH Hostel, 891 Amsterdam Ave., at 103rd St. (☎932-2300; fax 932-2574; reserve@hinewyork.org; www.hinewyork.org). Subway: 1, 9, B, C to 103rd St. In a block-long landmark building resides the mother of all youth hostels—the largest in the US, with 90 dorm-style rooms and 624 beds. Soft carpets and spotless bathrooms. The A/C is a welcome touch in summer. Kitchens and dining rooms, communal TV lounges, and a large outdoor garden. Internet access. Linen and towels included. 29-night max. stay, 7-nights in summer. Credit card reservations a must. Check-in any time. Check-out 11am (late check-out fee $5). No curfew. Nov.-Apr.: 10- to 12-bed dorms $27; 6- to 8-bed dorms $30; 4-bed dorms $33. May-Oct. dorms $2 more. Non-members $3 more. Groups of 4-9 may get private rooms with bathroom ($120); groups of 10 or more definitely will.

Central Park Hostel, 19 W. 103rd St. between Manhattan Ave. and Central Park West. (☎678-0491; fax 678-0453; www.centralparkhostel.com). Subway: B, C to 103rd St. Clean, air-conditioned rooms. Shared bathrooms. Linen/towels provided. Lockers available. 13-day max. stay. No curfew. Key deposit $2. Dorm $25; private double $75.

International Student Center, 38 W. 88th St. between Central Park W. and Columbus Ave. (☎787-7706). Subway: B, C to 86th St. Open only to foreigners aged 18-30; you must show a foreign passport or valid visa. An aging brownstone on a tree-lined street noted for frequent celebrity sightings. No-frills, livable dorms include showers and linens. Single and mixed-sex rooms available. Large basement TV lounge with kitchen, fridge, and affable atmosphere. Key deposit $10. 7-night max. stay (14 days in winter). No curfew. Reception daily 8am-11pm. No reservations, and generally full in summer, but call after 10:30am on the day you wish to stay to check for availability. No wheelchair access; lots of stairs. 8- to 10-bed dorms $15. Cash or travelers checks only.

DORMITORIES

Columbia University, 1230 Amsterdam Ave., at 120th St. (☎678-3235; fax 678-3222). Subway: 1, 9 to 116th St. Whittier Hall sets aside 10 rooms year-round, all equipped with full beds. Rooms are clean, max. 4 people. Generally tight 24hr. security. Not the safest neighborhood, but well-populated until fairly late at night. Singles $55; doubles with A/C and bath (some with kitchen) $75. Reserve in Mar. for May-Aug., in July for Sept.-Dec. 1-week max. stay. Credit card deposit required. AmEx/D/MC/V.

HARLEM

see map pp. 334-335

As you hunt down lodging in Harlem, don't be alarmed that none of the listed accommodations have very large signs. Signs are often difficult to see from the street so following the numbers might be easier. The lack of a bold marking does not necessarily imply ill repute. Conversely, not all signless accommodations ensure a safe lodging experience, so check with a guide or hosteling book first.

BED AND BREAKFASTS

New York Bed and Breakfast, 134 W. 119th St. between Lenox and Adam Clayton Powell Aves. (☎666-0559; fax 663-5000). Subway: 2, 3 to 116th St. or 125th St. Run by Gisèle of the Uptown Hostel (see below), this B&B features a double and single bed in every airy room, coffee, juice, and danish for breakfast, and an aloof black cat, Harlem. 2-night min. stay. Check-in 1-7pm. Summer reserve 1 month in advance. Next door, Gisèle also owns **another B&B** featuring essentially the same rates and conditions—five dollars less, but no breakfast or pets. Jun.-Aug. doubles $75, triples $105 all with shared baths. Expect about $10 less off-peak season.

Crystal's Castle Bed & Breakfast, 119 W. 119th St. between Lenox Ave. and Adam Clayton Powell Blvd. (☎865-5522; fax 280-2061). Subway: 2, 3 to 125th St. In the center of the lively Mount Morris Historic district, this green and white brown stone has two clean rooms. Continental breakfast included. 25% deposit required. Check-out 1pm. Call at least 2 months in advance in summer; 1 month ahead in off-season. 1-week cancellation notice required. Single $76; double $97; both $409 per week (plus tax). About $20 less off peak. MC/V.

HOSTELS

Sugar Hill International House, 722 St. Nicholas Ave., at 146th St. (☎926-7030). Subway: A, B, C, D to 145th St. Across from subway, in lively Sugar Hill. Brownstone with large and spacious rooms (25-30 beds total), a quiet family feel, garden out back, and an adorable but spoiled dog. Friendly staff is a living library of Harlem history and entertainment. Rooms for 2-10 people. All-female room available. Internet access $1 per 10min. Facilities include kitchens, stereo, and library. Rooms $25-30. Key deposit $10. 2-week max. stay. Check-in 9am-10pm. Check-out 11am. Call 1 month in advance during off-season. No reservations accepted Jul.-Sept., so call in the morning. Passport ID required. No smoking.

Uptown Hostel, 239 Lenox Ave., at 122nd St. (☎666-0559; fax 663-5000). Subway: 2, 3 to 125th St. Also run by the knowledgeable Gisèle, who knows the neighborhood well and helps long-term travelers find apartments and temporary jobs. Bunk beds in clean, comfy rooms. Spacious hall bathrooms. Wonderful new common room and kitchen add to the family atmosphere. Key deposit $10. Check-in 11am-8pm. Lockout (i.e. you need to leave) June-Aug. 11am-4pm. Call as far in advance as possible in summer, 2 days in advance the rest of the year. Sept.-May singles $20, doubles $25; June-Aug. singles $22, doubles $30.

BROOKLYN

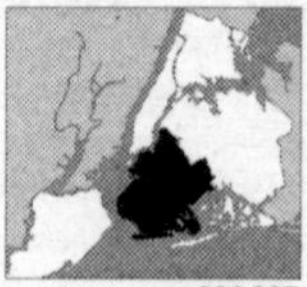

see map pp. 336-337

Akwaaba Mansion, 347 MacDonough St., in Bedford-Stuyvesant. (☎718-455-5958; fax 718-774-1744). Subway: A, C to Utica Ave.; turn to Stuyvesant Ave., make a left, and walk four blocks to MacDonough St. The B&B won an award from the New York Landmarks Preservation Society, and photographers come here to do fashion and advertising shoots. Each of the 18 rooms has its own theme; all are decorated in African cultural decor. Library, TV room, tree-shaded patio, wrap-around sun porch, and breakfast in an elegant dining room. Rooms comfortably accommodate 2. All include private bath and A/C. Check-in 4-7pm. Check-out 11am. F jazz and Su brunch with Southern/African cuisine ($10). Call at least a month in advance to reserve a room. Rooms $120-135; weekends $135-150. MC/V

Bed & Breakfast on the Park, 113 Prospect Park W., between 6th and 7th Sts., in Prospect Park (☎718-499-6115; fax 718-499-1385). Subway: F to Seventh Ave./Park Slope; then 2 blocks east and 2 blocks north. Perfect for putting up nervous parents who doubt the city's safety (or beauty). A magnificently restored brownstone jam-packed with Victoriana, this decadent, aromatic opiate of a hotel lacks only adequate horse stables and gas lighting. Classy furnishings (rococo armoires, oriental carpets, damask) are museum-quality, but you can touch and even fall asleep on them. Gourmet breakfast in sumptuous (not-so) common room. 8 doubles (2 with shared bath), each in a different style, $125-300.

QUEENS

see map pp. 340-341

Sheraton LaGuardia East Hotel, 135-20 39th Ave., off Main St., Flushing (☎718-460-6666 or 888-268-0717; fax 718-445-2655). Yes, it's another link in a big hotel chain, but if you've got to be in Queens, there's not much in terms of accommodations options. Cable TV, A/C, phone. Continental breakfast included. Doubles $230-245.

YMCA-Flushing, 138-46 Northern Blvd. between Union and Bowne Sts., in Flushing (☎718-961-6880; fax 718-461-4691). Subway: 7 to Flushing-Main St.; from there walk 10min. north on Main St. and turn right onto Northern Blvd. The area between the Y and Flushing's nearby shopping district is lively and well populated, but the neighborhood deteriorates north of Northern Blvd. Carpeted, small, clean rooms with cable TV and A/C; shared bathrooms only. Access to all Y facilities (including gym, squash courts, and swimming pools) included. 25-night max. stay. Key deposit $10. Reserve at least a month in advance for summer, one week otherwise. Singles $50; doubles $70; triples $80. AmEx/MC/V.

INSIDE

Living in NYC

These little town blues, they're melting away.
I'm gonna make a brand new start of it, in Old New York.
If you can make it there, you'll make it anywhere,
It's up to you, New York, New York.
-Fred Ebb

Long after the days when the Statue of Liberty ushered hopeful immigrants into the land of opportunity, foreigners and US citizens alike continue to flood the streets of NYC, looking for fame and fortune. The Big Apple is the center of many industries, from business to publishing, Broadway to Lincoln Center. Every year thousands of college grads swarm to Wall St., millions of actors come to wait tables, and packs of well-dressed beautiful people fight over Diana Vreeland and Donna Karan's legacy. Welcome to the center of it all; you'll get all the immediate excitement and opportunity you're looking for, and you may even find that this city is the place for you.

VISAS AND WORK PERMITS

LONG-TERM VISAS

All travelers planning to stay more than 90 days (180 days for Canadians) need to obtain either a non-immigrant (for temporary stay) or immigrant (for permanent stay) visa. Most travelers need a **B-2,** or "pleasure tourist," visa. Those planning to travel to the US for a different purpose—such as students or temporary workers—must apply for a different visa in the appropriate category (see **Study and Work Visas,** below). Be sure to double-check entrance requirements at the nearest US embassy or consulate, or consult the **Bureau of Consular Affairs** web page (http://travel.state.gov/visa_services.html#niv).

SIX-MONTH TOURIST VISAS. Visa applications should generally be processed through the American embassy or consulate in the country of your residence (see **Planning Your Trip,** p. 233). Or, the **Center for International Business and Travel (CIBT),** 23201 New Mexico Ave. NW #210, Washington, D.C. 20016 (☎202-244-9500 or 800-925-2428), can secure B-2 visas to and from all possible countries for a variable service charge (6-month visa around $45). If you lose your I-94 form, you can replace it at the nearest **Immigration and Naturalization Service (INS)** office (☎800-375-5283; www.ins.usdoj.gov), although it's unlikely that the form will be replaced during your stay. **Visa extensions** are sometimes attainable with a completed I-539 form; call the forms request line (☎800-870-3676). HIV-positive individuals cannot get a visa to enter the US. B-2 applicants must prove that they do not intend to immigrate by demonstrating that the purpose of their trip is for business, pleasure, or medical treatment; that they plan to remain for a limited period; and that they have a residence outside the US.

STUDY AND WORK VISAS

Working and studying are the only means of staying in the US for longer than six months. Unfortunately, separate visas are required for both. Holders of B-2 visas and those who have entered the US visa-free under the Visa Waiver Pilot Program cannot enter into full-time study or paid employment.

STUDY VISAS. Two types of study visas are available: the **F-1,** for **academic studies** (including language school), and the **M-1,** for **non-academic and vocational studies.** In order to secure a study visa, you must already be accepted into a full course of study at an educational institution approved by the Immigration and Naturalization Services (INS). F-1 applicants must also prove they have enough readily-available funds to meet all expenses for the first year of study; M-1 applicants must have evidence that sufficient funds are immediately available to pay all tuition and living costs for the entire period of intended stay. Applications should be processed through the American embassy or consulate in your country of residence (see **Planning Your Trip,** p. 235).

WORK PERMITS. In typical bureaucratic style, there are dozens of employment visas, most of which are nearly impossible to get. There are three general categories of work visas/permits: **employment-based visas,** generally issued to skilled or highly educated workers that already have a job offer in the US; **temporary worker visas,** which have fixed time limits and very specific classifications (for instance, "artists or entertainers who perform under a program that is culturally unique" or "persons who have practical training in the education of handicapped children"); and **cultural exchange visas,** which allow for employment by participants in either fellowships or reciprocal work programs with the aim of promoting cultural and historical exchange. For more on the requirements for each type of visa, visit http://travel.state.gov/visa_services.html#niv. While the chances of getting a work visa may seem next to impossible, there is hope: the **Council on International Educational Exchange (CIEE)** facilitates a **work/study/intern exchange** program between the US and citizens of Australia, China, France, Germany, Italy, Japan, Spain, Taiwan, and the UK. For a fee, CIEE will guide university students and recent graduates through the red tape of the visa application process; once in the US, they can also help you find employment (see **Finding Work,** p. 270). For more information, contact your local Council Travel office or visit the CIEE web site (www.ciee.org).

FINDING WORK

Minimum wage in NYC is very low ($5.15 per hr.) considering the exorbitant cost of living. In order to afford life as a New Yorker, you'll need to make at least $10 an hour, and even then, you'll still only be gazing longingly at most of the city's restaurants, shops, and clubs. When you are hired you will have to fill out **W-2 and I-9 tax forms** that authorize the government to take out state, federal, and Social Security taxes from your paycheck; in addition, New Yorkers pay city income tax (living outside the five boroughs, however, eliminates city tax). The combined income taxes in New York can be anywhere from 20 to 60%, so plan accordingly when budgeting your pay. Paycheck withholdings do not include government **health insurance;** only full-time, year-round jobs provide insurance, and then it is through a private provider. The standard work week is 40 hours; if you work more than this, you are entitled to **overtime pay,** usually 150% of your hourly wage. In an eight-hour workday, most jobs allow you to take a lunch break, although whether it is paid or unpaid varies.

RESOURCES

When finding a job in New York, the **Internet** will be your best friend; numerous web sites are devoted to placing folks like you in swank joints throughout the city (see **Job Hunting on the Internet,** right). While technology has eliminated some of the pavement-pounding, many jobs are still found only through old-fashioned leg work. Check the **classifieds** of New York's newspapers, particularly in the *Village Voice*, *New York Press*, and the Sunday edition of the *New York Times*. Also check **bulletin boards** in local coffee shops, markets, libraries, and community centers for help wanted posters (for a list of community centers, see **Community Resources,** p. 276). In addition, all of New York's colleges and universities have **career and employment offices;** even if you can't get into the office itself (some may require a school ID to enter), most have bulletin boards outside (for a list of colleges and universities in New York, see **Studying in New York,** p. 273). Sometimes a restaurant or store will post a sign in the window—keep your eyes peeled. As a last resort, it can be fruitful to **go door-to-door with your resume** and a cover letter, particularly if you're targeting a type of establishment that is concentrated in a given area (this works well in an area like SoHo, for example, for someone interested in finding work at a gallery).

ESSENTIAL INFORMATION

JOB HUNTING ON THE INTERNET

Putting the keywords "New York" and "jobs" into any good search engine yields hundreds of thousands of results. Here are a few that stand out.

www.careerbuilder.com
allows a search of more than 70 sites leading the user to a possible job matchup.

www.ci.nyc.ny.us/html/filmcom/pdf/tech.pdf
gives info on productions being filmed in NY on a weekly basis.

www.freelancers.com
specializes in "creative" jobs in design, photo, illustration, and fine arts.

www.monster.com
helps find jobs and internships through the help of trendy cartoon icon Thwacker. Very comprehensive.

newyorkjobs.net
specializes in high-tech, high-power jobs. Allows you to post your resume free of charge.

newyork.preferredjobs.com
is similar to a recruitment firm—they match applicants with potential employers. You can also post a resume, search listings, and read company profiles.

www.summerjobs.com
is a great site for finding, oddly enough, a summer job. Links to a varied, if small, selection of quality jobs in NYC and Long Island.

OPTIONS FOR WORK

CHILDCARE

Childcare can be a lucrative field, as babysitters and nannies are always in demand. Make sure you know what you're getting into, though, as some parents think you should also do housework. If you go through an agency, make sure you research the company thoroughly, as many of them make a killing on fees while providing little service or support to you (some also have a limit on what you can be paid by the family, and some don't do the background checks on the families that they claim to do).

FOOD SERVICE

The highest-paid food service employees are generally **waiters** and waitresses. Waitstaff make less than minimum wage, but their salary is supplemented with **tips,** which can average upwards of $15 per hour. Since tipping is 15-20% of the bill, the more expensive the restaurant, the more tips for the waitstaff (although higher-class restaurants want experienced staff). If you are working as a **cashier** or

host, you won't make much in tips and your salary will be close to minimum wage. **Bartenders** make great tips, but they work late and usually need certification and previous experience.

HEAD HUNTERS

The following agencies work to find that special employee for companies, and that special job for you. These are *not* temp agencies: companies and employees should both be looking for a long-term match.

Seven Staffing, 36 E. 12th St. (☎254-8600; fax 358-7524; www.sevenstaffing.com). Places proud computer geeks in choice jobs.

Wall Street Services, 11 Broadway, Ste. 930 (☎509-7200; fax 509-1673; www.wallstservice.com). Finds opportunities in the financial sector.

INTERNSHIPS AND VOLUNTEERING

New York City headquarters just about every industry and nonprofit sector imaginable, with the exception of government (and even then, there's the high-profile Mayor's Office and City Hall). In particular, NYC is the primary American home for publishing, advertising, theater, television, finance, fashion, and museum curating; it also houses offices for most international and nationwide nonprofit organizations. In other words, if you want it, it's here. While it's difficult to get paying, short-term positions at these offices, most are eager for interns; however, even interning and volunteering in the Big Apple is fiercely competitive. Be sure to contact your organization of choice early (around three to six months before you plan to arrive) and be prepared for an extensive application process. Manhattan College (see **Colleges and Universities,** p. 273) sponsors an internship program for foreign students.

TEMPORARY WORK

One of the easiest (and most mindless) ways to earn money is as a temp worker. Offices often hire employees for short periods (anywhere from a few days to several months) through temp agencies, massive clearinghouses of unemployed but oh-so-skilled workers. Most jobs are secretarial in nature: data entry, filing, answering phones, etc. Agencies may be able to place you in full-time work after only a few weeks; if they do, health insurance is often included.

National Association of Temporary Staffing Services, New York Chapter (☎646-435-6350; www.natss.org/ny). Large organization with branches in NYC, Westchester, and Long Island.

Oliver Staffing Inc., 350 Lexington Ave. (☎634-1234). Temporary employment agency serving the gay and lesbian business community.

Paladin Staffing Services, 270 Madison Ave. (☎545-7850; fax 689-0881; newyork-recruiter@paladinstaff.com; www.paladinstaff.com). Specializing in marketing, advertising, communications, and creative temporary placements.

STUDYING IN NEW YORK

The following is a select list of colleges, universities, and specialty schools in New York. For a complete list of academic institutions in the city, visit the official New York City web site at www.ci.nyc.ny.us.

COLLEGES AND UNIVERSITIES

Barnard College, Columbia University, Office of Admissions, 3009 Broadway, New York, NY 10027 (☎854-2014; fax 854-6220; admissions@barnard.edu; www.barnard.columbia.edu). Hosts a pre-college summer program for high school girls. Office of Pre-College Programs, Barnard College, Columbia University, 3009 Broadway, New York, NY 10027 (☎854-8866; fax 854-8867; pcp@barnard.edu; www.barnard.edu/pcp/).

City University of New York (CUNY), Office of Admissions, 1114 Ave. of the Americas, 15th Fl., New York, NY 10036 (☎997-2869; www.cuny.edu). Serves all CUNY campuses, including community colleges throughout the city, and Brooklyn College, City College, Hunter College, John Jay College, and Queens College.

Columbia University, Student Services, 203 Lewisohn Hall, Mail Code 4111, 2970 Broadway, New York, NY 10027; Office of Admissions, 3009 Broadway, New York, NY 10027. (Services: ☎854-2820; fax 854-7400; summersession@columbia.edu; www.columbia.edu. Admissions: ☎854-2014; fax 854-6220.) School of Continuing Education includes a high school program, summer school, visiting students program, and special courses, including creative writing.

Fordham University, Office of Undergraduate Admission, Thebaud Hall, 441 East Fordham Rd., New York, NY 10458 (☎800-FORDHAM, Rose Hill campus 718-817-4000, Lincoln Center campus 636-6710; fax 718-367-9404 to Rose Hill, 636-7002 to Lincoln Center; enroll@fordham.edu; www.fordham.edu). Campuses in the Bronx (Rose Hill) and Manhattan (Lincoln Center). Summer programs for undergraduate and graduate students.

Joggers in Central Park

Chinatown Grocery Shopping

Snowy Brooklyn Brownstones

Manhattan College, Office of Admissions, Manhattan College Parkway, Riverdale, New York 10471 (☎800-MC2-XCEL or 718-862-7200; fax 718-862-8019; admit@manhattan.edu; www.manhattan.edu). Sponsors the New York City Semester for college students; contact Susan Hannon, the program coordinator (☎718-862-7476; shannon@manhattan.edu).

New School University, Office of Admissions and Student Services, 66 W. 12th St., New York, NY 10011 (☎229-5600; www.newschool.edu). This avant-garde and intellectually rigorous university has over 20,000 continuing education students enrolled in everything from its Educated Citizen Project to the Dial Cyberspace Campus.

New York University, Office of Summer Sessions, 7 E. 12th St., 6th Fl., New York, NY 10003 (☎998-1212; fax 995-4103; www.nyu.edu/summer). Welcomes visiting students to its massive summer school.

SPECIALTY SCHOOLS

The Cooper Union for the Advancement of Science and Art, Cooper Square, New York, NY 10003 (general info ☎353-4000, adult education 353-4195; www.cooper.edu). Large, inexpensive adult education program in architecture, art, and engineering.

Fashion Institute of Technology, Office of Admissions, Room C139, Seventh Ave. at 27th St., New York, NY 10001 (☎217-7775; www.fitnyc.suny.edu). Offers extremely competitive programs for visiting students.

French Culinary Institute, Office of Admissions, 462 Broadway, New York, NY 10013 (☎219-8890 and 888-FCI-CHEF; fax 431-3054; www.frenchculinary.com). Very expensive courses (2-9 months) for serious amateurs and career chefs.

The Juilliard School, Evening Division, 60 Lincoln Center Plaza, New York, NY 10023 (☎799-5040; juilliardatnight@juilliard.edu; www.juilliard.edu). Evening programs for adults aged 18-88, with or without artistic talent. Intensive summer courses also available.

LONG-TERM ACCOMMODATIONS

So you're one of millions looking for an apartment in NYC (competition is so fierce that city slickers joke about scouring *NYTimes* obituaries); the market is extremely tight, rents are high, brokerage fees exorbitant, and most landlords will not rent without a guarantor on the lease and all potential tenants present when the decision to rent is made. However, this isn't the impossible dream (although you'll probably need a cell phone, call waiting, and eight hours a day to make this dream reality); like everything else here, finding housing is possible with a little perseverance, ingenuity, and luck.

APARTMENTS

TIPS. Unless you are planning on permanently relocating to New York, **subletting** an apartment for a limited period of time is your best bet. When New Yorkers feel the need to escape, they will rent out their (usually furnished) apartments for a month or more. For longer stays, it is easier to become a **roommate** in someone's apartment than to find your own lease. When apartment hunting in NYC, **act fast.** If you find something suitable (but perhaps not your dream apartment), take it immediately; it *will* be gone when you call back, and you're *not* going to find your dream place. However, do not rush your search: always thoroughly investigate the apartment and surrounding neighborhood to make sure you feel comfortable living there. Finding an apartment in Brooklyn or Queens will be **cheaper and less competitive** than Manhattan, and not that inconvenient. Hoboken, West New York, and Weehawken, across the Hudson, also offer more for your money, a view of the Manhattan skyline, and a quick $1 (cheaper than the subway) commute to the center of everything.

RESOURCES. **Word of mouth** can be the best way to find a place in NYC. Ask friends if they know of vacancies; ask your friends' friends if they know of vacancies. If you are staying at the **Uptown Hostel** (see **Accommodations,** p. 266), Gisèle will often help you find a cheap apartment. Check the **Village Voice** for listings early Wednesday mornings (the day it comes to press). Their web site (www.villagevoice.com) is another resource that can get the information to you a night before those poor, misguided seekers who wait in line on Astor Pl. the next morning for a hard copy. The **New York Times** also has a helpful classified section with real estate options (online at www.nytimes.com). There are also myriad **web sites** devoted to finding roommates, subletters, and apartments throughout the city; type "New York" and "apartments" in and watch your search engine go crazy. And, seriously: check the **NYTimes obituary** section. If your search is too frustrating and exhausting, turn to a **realtor.** Be warned, however, that brokerage fees are extremely high. For realtors and web sites listing sublets and rentals, see **Room for Rent,** opposite page.

OTHER OPTIONS

DORMS

Many universities in New York rent out their vacant dorms to summer visitors. The length of stay varies depending on the school, but often you can stay for the entire summer. The two largest dormitory options are at **New York University** (see **Accommodations,** p. 253) and at **Long Island University,** Brooklyn Campus, 1 University Plaza, Brooklyn, New York 11201 (Main ☎718-488-1011; Resident Hall Director 780-1552), in downtown Brooklyn. Rates at LIU average $50 per night, but vary depending on your length of stay. For a more complete list of colleges and universities in New York, see **Studying in New York,** p. 273, or www.ci.nyc.ny.us.

HOME EXCHANGE AND RENTAL

For shorter stays, home exchange and rental can be cost-effective options, particularly for families with children. Home rentals, as opposed to exchanges, are much more expensive, although they are remarkably cheaper than an extended stay at a comparably serviced hotel. In New York, most home exchanges and rentals come with kitchen, cleaning lady, telephones, and TV. Unfortunately, it can be difficult to arrange an exchange or rental for more than one month. Both rentals and exchanges are organized by the following services. A great web site listing many other home exchange companies is at www.aitec.edu.au/~bwechner/Documents/Travel/Lists/Home ExchangeClubs.html.

ESSENTIAL INFORMATION

ROOM FOR RENT!

Gamut Realty Group, 301 E. 78th St. (☎879-4229; fax 517-5356). Assists in finding sublets and short- and long-term rooms and apartments. Open M-F 9am-6pm, Sa-Su 10am-4pm.

Gay Roommate Information Network (☎627-4242) matches gay roommates.

Manhattan Lodgings (☎677-7616) is a network that puts visitors in contact with New York apartment tenants who want to rent out their respective pads for a few days or weeks.

New York Habitat, 307 Seventh Ave., Ste. 306 (☎255-8018; fax 627-1416; rent@nyhabitat.com; www.nyhabitat.com). Finds sublets (www.nyhabitat-sublet.com), roommates (www.nyhabitat-roommate.com), and apartment rentals.

WEB SITES LISTING SUBLETS, RENTALS, AND SWAPS:

www.relocationcentral.com helps with everything from apartment hunting to renting a moving van.

www.roomiematch.com is a "quick and amusing" search engine that helps young New Yorkers find flatmates.

www.summerexchange.com is a list of summer housing offers. Find a space or post your own.

HomeExchange.com, P.O. Box 30085, Santa Barbara, CA 93130 (☎805-898-9660; admin@HomeExchange.com; www.homeexchange.com).

The Invented City: International Home Exchange, 41 Sutter St., Ste. 1090, San Francisco, CA 94104 (☎800-788-2489 in the US, 415-252-1141 elsewhere; invented@aol.com; www.invented-city.com). For $75, your offer is listed in a catalog and you have access to a database of thousands of homes for exchange.

HOSTELS

Although many of New York's hostels have maximum stay limits, some do allow long-term stays. If a hostel doesn't have a maximum stay limit, ask, and perhaps you shall receive. Otherwise, hostels that do have limits usually hover between 25 and 30 days; for a two- or three-month stay, it's always possible to stay at two or three different hostels, in singles, for the duration of your trip. For a list of hostels, see **Accommodations By Neighborhood,** p. 251. The **DeHirsch Residence,** on the Upper East Side, rents rooms by the month (see p. 260). In addition, **YMCA-Flushing** allows long-term stays with advance notice (see p. 267).

MONEY MATTERS

BANKING

If you don't have an account at one of the city's mega-banks, it might be worth your while to open a new checking account. New York is expensive and you'll be withdrawing money frequently; unfortunately, ATM fees are as expensive as everything else in NYC. The largest banks are **Citibank** (☎800-627-3999), **Chase Manhattan** (☎800-935-9935), and the **Bank of New York** (☎888-LINK-BNY). These three clamor over one another to have an ATM on every corner. While this makes ATM withdrawals inexpensive, those savings are often made up for by expensive monthly account fees. Smaller, local banks might be cheaper and friendlier, albeit less ATM convenient.

To open a checking account, you'll need a social security number, local address, and minimum deposit (for the cheapest accounts, it's usually around $100-200). Foreign visitors will find it nearly impossible to open a checking account; consider opening a savings account instead. Call your bank of choice about their requirements for foreign account holders; usually, you will need to register for a social security number first.

CUTTING CORNERS

It may seem impossible to live on a budget in the Big Apple, but with planning and self-restraint, it can happen. The largest expense is undoubtedly housing. The cheapest option is to live in Hoboken or other nearby areas of NJ, where rent is cheap and commuting costs negligible ($1 to Midtown). The outer boroughs also have less expensive rents, and are much, much cooler than NJ, but cheap housing in Queens or Brooklyn may be in less safe neighborhoods. City transportation is very expensive ($1.50 per ride), especially if you need to commute to work/school/play every day. Buying a 30-day unlimited-ride MetroCard ($63) is by far the cheapest option, because cars are either too expensive, too inconvenient, or both. What will *really* hurt your finances quickly—without you noticing—is entertainment. The city abounds with tempting concerts, shows, good restaurants, bars, and clubs. Most of these things are worth the splurge, but there are ways of getting around high prices if you know where to look. Free events happen all the time, and, especially during the summertime, extremely famous DJs, bands, theater groups, and dance companies offer free entertainment. If you skim the *NYTimes*, *Village Voice*, or *New York* every now and then, you should have plenty of cheap options.

COMMUNITY RESOURCES

COMMUNITY CENTERS

The following are umbrella organizations for community centers throughout the five boroughs. Contact them for a list of centers in your neighborhood.

United Neighborhood Houses of New York (UNH), 70 W. 36th St., 5th Fl. (☎967-0322; fax 967-0792; www.unhny.org). Partnerships with community centers throughout the 5 boroughs; check their web page for a complete list.

United Community Centers, 613 New Lots Ave., Brooklyn (☎718-649-7979). Similar to UNH.

ETHNIC RESOURCES

For more resources, see **Cultural Institutes,** p. 175.

Chinese American Planning Council, 150 Elizabeth St. (☎941-0925).

Jewish Community Center, 15 W. 65th St., 8th Fl. (☎580-0099; fax 799-0254; www.jccny.org).

Instituto Cervantes, 122 E. 42nd St., Ste. 807 (☎689-4232; fax 545-8837). A cultural center for Spanish-speakers.

Schomburg Center for Research in Black Culture, 515 Malcolm X Blvd. (☎491-2200; www.nypl.org/research/sc.sc.html). Has information on African, African-American, and West Indian community and cultural centers.

WOMEN'S RESOURCES

Barnard College/Columbia University Women's Center, 3009 Broadway (☎854-4907).

Brooklyn College Women's Center, 227 New Ingersoll Hall, Brooklyn (☎718-780-5777).

Hunter College Women's Center, 695 Park Ave., Box 368.

National Organization for Women, (☎627-9895).

NYU Women's Center, 21 Washington Pl., Box #179.

WORKING OUT

Membership at most of NYC's swank gyms is high-priced. Cheaper alternatives include public fitness centers and YMCA/YWCAs. **Public fitness centers,** or recreation centers, are run by the city government and feature most of the amenities, classes, and equipment of the brand-name gyms. Membership is an astounding $10-25 per *year* and there are over 30 branches throughout the city. In Manhattan, gyms include Asser Levy, E. 23rd St. (☎447-2020), between 1st and FDR Dr.; Carmine (☎242-5228), on 7th Ave. at Clarkson St.; East 54th St., 358 E. 54th St. (☎397-3154); and West 59th St. (☎317-3159), at 10th Ave. and 59th St. Another affordable option are the city's **YMCAs, YWCAs, and YM-YWHAs.** Facilities at the following locations are high quality (call the Vanderbilt Y for other locations): Vanderbilt YMCA, 224 E. 47th St. (☎756-9600); 92nd St. YM-YWHA, 1395 Lexington Ave. (☎415-5729), at 92nd St.; and YWCA, 610 Lexington Ave. (☎735-9753), at 53rd St.

9026
DRIVERS WANTED
212-957-4646
1N83

Service Directory

ACCOMMODATION AGENCIES

See also ***Realtors****, p. 282.*
Homestay New York, 630 E. 19th St., Brooklyn (☎718-434-2071).
YMCA, 224 E. 47th St. (☎212-308-2899).

AIRLINES

Major airlines have numerous Manhattan offices; call for the closest location.
American, ☎800-433-7300.
Continental, ☎800-525-0280.
Delta, ☎800-221-1212.
Northwest, ☎800-225-2525
TWA, ☎800-221-2000.
United, ☎800-241-6522.
US Airways, ☎800-428-4322.

AIRPORTS

John F. Kennedy Airport (JFK), ☎718-244-4444. In Queens.
LaGuardia Airport, ☎718-533-3400. In Queens.
Newark Int'l Airport, ☎973-961-6000. In NJ.

AIRPORT TRANSPORT

Gray Line Air Shuttle, ☎800-451-0455. Serves JFK, LaGuardia, and Newark.
New York Airport Service. ☎212-875-8200.Serves JFK and LaGardia.
Olympia Trails Coach, ☎212-964-6233. Serves Newark.
SuperShuttle, ☎212-258-3826. Serves JFK, LaGuardia, and Newark.

AUTO RENTAL

AAMCAR Rent-a-Car, 315 W. 96th St., between West End Ave. and Riverside Dr. (☎212-222-8500). Open M-F 7:30am-7:30pm, Sa 9am-5pm, Su 9am-7pm.
Avis, 800-831-2847.
Dollar: at JFK ☎718-656-2400; at LaGuardia ☎718-779-5600 , 800-800-4000.
Enterprise, ☎800-736-8222.
Hertz, 800-831-2847.
Nationwide, 241 W. 40th St., between Seventh and Eighth Ave. (☎212-867-1234). Open M-F 7:30am-6:30pm.

BICYCLE RENTAL

Pedal Pushers, 1306 Second Ave. between 68th and 69th Sts. (☎288-5592). 3-speeds $4 per hr., $10 per day, $12 overnight; 10-speeds $5 per hr., $14 per day, $14 overnight; mountain bikes $6 per hr., $17 per day, $25 overnight. Overnight rentals require $150 deposit on a major credit card, regular rentals only need major credit card, passport, or a NY state driver's license deposit. Open F-M 10am-6pm, W 10am-7pm, Th 10am-8pm. Helmet extra $2 per day.

Loeb Boathouse, mid-park at 75th St., in Central Park (☎861-4137; 717-9048). 3-speeds $8 per hr., 10-speeds $10, tandems $15. Valid ID and $100 cash or credit card deposit required. Open Apr.-Sept. daily 10am-5pm, weather permitting.

Metro Bicycle Stores, 113 Lexington Ave. at 88th St. (☎427-4450). Seven convenient locations throughout the city. $7 per hr., $35 per day, $45 overnight. Daily rentals due back 30min. before store closes and overnight rentals next day at 10am. $250 cash or credit card deposit and valid ID required. Helmet rental $2.50 per bike. Open F-W 9:30am-6:30pm, Th 9:30am-7:30pm.

BUDGET TRAVEL AGENCIES

Council Travel, 254 Greene St. (☎212-254-2525; www.counciltravel.com).

STA Travel, 10 Downing St. (☎212-627-3111).

BUSES

*See also **Metro Transit,** p. 282.*

Green Bus Lines, ☎718-995-4700. Serves Jamaica and central Queens.

Greyhound, ☎800-231-2222.

Jamaica Buses, Inc., ☎718-526-0800. Serves Jamaica and Rockaway.

Liberty Lines Express, ☎718-652-8400. Serves the Bronx.

MTA/Long Island Bus, ☎516-766-6722.

New York Bus Service, ☎718-994-5500. Serves the Bronx.

Port Authority Terminal, ☎212-435-7000.

Queens Surface Corp., ☎718-445-3100.

TriBoro Coach Corp., ☎718-335-1000. Serves Forest Hills, Ridgewood, Jackson Hts., and Midtown.

CONSULATES

Australia, 150 E. 42nd St., 34th Fl. (☎212-351-6500). No visa services.

British Commonwealth, 800 Second Ave (☎212-599-8478).

Canada, Main Concourse Level, 1251 Avenue Of The Americas (☎212-596-1700).

German, 871 UN Plaza, 49th St.(☎212-610-9700).

France, 934 Fifth Ave. (☎212-606-3600). Visa services, 10 E. 74th St. (☎212-472-8110).

Ireland, 345 Park Ave. (☎212-319-2555).

Israel, 800 Second Ave. (☎212-499-5000).

New Zealand, 780 Third Ave., Suite 1904 (☎212-832-4038).

South Africa, 333 E. 38th St., 9th Fl. (☎212-213-4880).

UK, 845 Third Ave. (☎212-745-0200).

CRISIS AND HELP LINES

*See also **Emergency,** p. 281; **Hospitals,** p. 281; **Medical Clinics,** p. 282; and **Women's Health,** p. 283.*

AIDS Information, ☎212-807-6655. Open M-F 10am-9pm, Sa noon-3pm.

AIDS Hotline, ☎212-447-8200. Open daily 9am-9pm; 24hr. recording.

Alcohol and Substance Abuse Info Line, ☎800-274-2042. 24hr. info and referrals.

Crime Victims' Hotline, ☎212-577-7777. 24hr. counseling and referrals.

Gay and Lesbian Switchboard, ☎989-0999; glnh.@glnh.org. Open M-F 4-8pm, Sa noon-5pm. 24hr. recording.

Help Line, ☎212-532-2400. Crisis counseling and referrals. Open daily 9am-10:30pm.

National Abortion Federation, ☎800-772-9100. Open M-F 9am-10pm, Sa-Su 9am-5pm.

Poison Control Center, ☎212-764-7667. Open 24hr.

Roosevelt Hospital Rape Crisis Center, ☎212-523-4728. M-F 9am-5pm.

Samaritans, ☎212-673-3000. Suicide prevention. Open 24hr.

Sex Crimes Report Line, ☎212-267-7273. NYPD-related. 24hr. information and referrals.

Venereal Disease Information, ☎212-788-4415. Open M-F 9am-5pm.

CURRENCY EXCHANGE

American Express, American Express Tower, 200 Vesey St. (☎212-640-2000), near the World Financial Center. Open M-F 8:30am-5:30pm. Other branches include:

Macy's Herald Square, 151 W. 34th St. (☎212-695-8075), at Seventh Ave., on Macy's balcony level. Open M-Sa 10am-6pm.

420 Lexington Ave. (☎212-687-3700), at 43rd St. Open M-F 9am-6pm.

822 Lexington Ave. (☎212-758-6510), near 63rd St. Open M-F 9am-6pm, Sa 10am-4pm.

374 Park Ave. and 53rd St. (☎212-421-8240). Open M-F 9am-5:30pm.

1185 Sixth Ave. and 47th St. (☎212-398-8585). Open M-F 9am-6pm.

111 Broadway (☎212-693-1100), near Pine St. Open M-F 8:30am-5:30pm.

200 Fifth Ave. (☎212-691-9797), at 23rd St. Open M-F 8:30am-5:30pm and Sa 10am-4pm.

Bank Leumi, 579 Fifth Ave. (☎917-542-2343), at 47th St. Open M-F 9am-3pm.

Cheque Point USA, 1568 Broadway (☎212-750-2400), at 47th St. Other branches throughout the city; call for locations. Open daily 8am-7pm.

Thomas Cooke, 29 Broadway (☎800-287-7362), at Morris St. Open M-F 8:30am-4:30pm.

DENTISTS

Emergency Dental Associates, ☎800-439-9299. 24hr.

NYU College of Dentistry, ☎212-998-9800. Open M-Th 8:30am-6:45pm, F 8:30am-4pm.

DISABLED RESOURCES

Access-A-Ride, ☎646-252-5252. 337-2017. For public transport.

Directions Unlimited, 123 Green Ln., Bedford Hills (☎914-241-1700, 800-533-5343).

Elevators and Escalator Accessibility, ☎800-734-6772. 24hr.

Moss Rehab Hospital Travel Information Service, ☎ 800-CALL-MOSS.

Society for the Advancement of Travel for the Handicapped (SATH), 347 Fifth Ave., #610, (☎212-447-7284).

Transit Authority Access, ☎718-596-8585.

DRY CLEANERS

Midnight Express Cleaners, ☎212-921-0111. Open M-F 8am-8pm, Sa 9am-1pm; closed Sa July-Aug. Picks up laundry.

EMERGENCY

In an emergency, ***dial 911.*** *See also* ***Crisis and Help Lines,*** *p. 281;* ***Hospitals,*** *p. 281;* ***Medical Clinics,*** *p. 282; and* ***Women's Health,*** *p. 283.*

Ambulance: ☎212-988-8800.

Fire: ☎212-999-2222.

Police (non-emergency): ☎212-374-5000.

ENTERTAINMENT INFO

See also ***Ticket Services,*** *p. 283.*

Parks & Recreation Special Events Hotline, ☎212-360-3456. 24hr.

MoviePhone, ☎777-FILM/3456.

NYC/ON STAGE Hotline, ☎212-768-1818.

HOSPITALS

See also ***Crisis and Help Lines,*** *p. 280;* ***Emergency,*** *p. 281;* ***Medical Clinics,*** *p. 282; and* ***Women's Health,*** *p. 283.*

Bellevue Hospital Center, 462 First Ave. (☎212-562-4141), at 27th. St. Adult ER ☎562-3015; pediatric ER ☎562-3025.

Beth Israel Medical Center, First Ave. at E. 16th St. (☎212-420-2000). Adult ER ☎420-2840; pediatric ER ☎420-2860.

Bronx-Lebanon Hospital Center, 1650 Grand Concord (☎718-590-1800). 2 ERs: 1650 Grand Concord (☎718-518-5120), 1276 Fulton Ave. (☎718-960-8700).

Brooklyn Hospital Center, 121 DeKalb Ave. (☎718-250-8000). ER ☎718-250-8075.

Columbia-Presbyterian Medical Center, 622 W. 168th St. (☎212-305-2500). ER ☎305-6204.

Interfaith Medical Center, 555 Prospect Pl., near Franklin St., Brooklyn (☎718-935-7000). 2 ERs: St. Marks (☎718-935-7110), Atlantic Ave. (☎718-604-6110).

Jacobi Medical Center, 1400 Pelham Parkway South, Bronx. ER ☎718-918-5000.

Jamaica Hospital Medical Center, 8900 Van Wyck Expressway (☎718-206-6000), in Jamaica, Queens. ER ☎718-206-6066.

Mount Sinai Medical Center, Fifth Ave. and 100th St. (☎212-241-6500). ER ☎241-7171.

New York University Medical Center, 560 First Ave., between 32nd and 33rd St. (☎212-263-7300). ER ☎263-5550.

New York University Downtown Hospital, 170 William St., between Spruce and Beekman Sts. (☎212-312-5000).

IN-LINE SKATE RENTAL

Blades, 428 Chambers St., and eight stores in the Metropolitan area (☎212-96491944). Open M-Sa 10am-9pm, Su 11am-7pm.

Peck and Goodie Skates, 917 Eighth Ave., between 54th and 55th St. (☎212-246-6123). Open M-F 11am-8pm, Sa 10am-8pm, Su 11am-7pm.

INTERNET ACCESS

Canal Jean Co., 504 Broadway, between Spring and Broome St. (☎212-226-3663), in SoHo. Free. Open daily 9:30am-9pm.

alt.coffee, 139 Ave. A, between 8th and 9th St. (☎212-529-2233). Open M-F 7:30-1:30am, Sa-Su 10-2am.

Cybercafe, 273 Lafayette St. (☎212-334-5140), at the corner of Prince St. Open M-F 9am-10pm, Sa-Su 11am-10pm.

Kinko's. Over 30 locations; call ☎800-254-6567 for the one you want. Open 24hr.

LIBRARIES

Bronx Reference Center, 2556 Bainbridge Ave. (☎718-579-4200). Open M and W 10am-8pm; Tu and Th 10am-6pm; F noon-6pm, Sa 10am-5pm.

Brooklyn Public Library, Grand Army Plaza, Brooklyn (☎718-230-2100). Open M-Th 9am-8pm, F-Sa 9am-6pm.

Donnell Library Center, 20 W. 53rd St., between Fifth and Sixth Ave. (☎212-621-0618). Across the street from the Museum of Modern Art. Open M, W, and F 10am-6pm, Tu and Th 10am-8pm, Sa 10am-5pm.

Mid-Manhattan Library, 455 Fifth Ave. (☎212-340-0849), at 40th St. Open M, W, and Th 9am-9pm, Tu 11am-7pm, F-Sa 10am-6pm.

New York Public Library, 11 W. 40th St. (☎212-930-0830, 869-8089), entrance on Fifth Ave. at 42nd St. Open M and Th-Sa 10am-6pm, Tu-W 11am-7:30pm.

New York Public Library for the Performing Arts (☎212-870-1630). Relocated to Mid-Manhattan Library until Feb. 2001; at Lincoln Center after Feb. 2001.

Queensborough Public Library, 89-11 Merrick Blvd., Jamaica, Queens (☎718-990-0700). Open M-F, 10am-9pm, Sa 10am-5:30pm.

Schomburg Center for Research in Black Culture, 515 Lenox Ave./Malcolm X Blvd. (☎212-491-2200), on the corner of 135th St. Library open M-W noon-8pm, Th-Sa 10am-6pm; archives open M-W noon-5pm and Th-Sa 10am-5pm.

St. George Library Center, 5 Central Ave., Staten Island (☎718-442-8560). M and Th, noon-8pm, Tu-W 10am-6pm, F noon-6pm, and Sa 10am-5pm.

MEDICAL CLINICS

See also ***Crisis and Help Lines,*** *p. 280;* ***Dentists,*** *p. 281;* ***Emergency,*** *p. 281;* ***Hospitals,*** *p. 281;* ***Pharmacies,*** *p. 282; and* ***Women's Health,*** *p. 283.*

Callen-Lorde Community Health Center, 356 W. 18th St., between Eighth and Ninth Aves. (☎212-271-7200). Serves the queer community. Open M 12:30-8pm, Tu and Th-F 9am-4:30pm, W 8:30am-1pm and 3-8pm.

D*O*C*S, 55 E. 34th St. (☎212-252-6000), at Park and Madison Aves. Also at: 1555 Third Ave. (☎212-828-2300), at 88th St.; 202 W. 23rd St. (☎212-352-2600). Open M-Th 8am-8pm, F 8am-7pm, Sa 9am-3pm, Su 9am-2pm.

Doctors Walk-in Clinic, 55 E. 34th St., between Park and Madison Ave. (☎212-252-6001, ext. 2). Open M-Th 8am-8pm, F 8am-7pm, Sa 9am-3pm, Su 9am-2pm.

Gay Men's Health Crisis-Geffen Clinic, 119 W. 24th St., between Sixth and Seventh Aves. (☎212-367-1100). Open Tu and Th 1-8pm, W and F noon-8pm, Sa 10am-6pm.

METRO TRANSIT

See also ***Airport Transport,*** *p. 279;* ***Buses,*** *p. 280; and* ***Trains,*** *p. 283.*

Bus Info, ☎516-766-6722.

General Info, ☎718-330-1234 in English, ☎718-330-4847 for other languages.

MetroCard Info, ☎800-638-7622, ☎212-638-7622.

Reduced Fare Info, ☎718-243-2999, ☎718-878-0165 TDD.

PHARMACIES

See also ***Medical Clinics,*** *p. 282.*

Duane Reade, 224 57th St., at Broadway (☎212-541-9708). Open 24hr. Other locations: 2465 Broadway, at 91st St. (☎212-799-3172); 1279 Third Ave., at 74th St. (☎212-744-2668); 378 Sixth Ave., at Waverly Pl. (☎212-674-5357).

CVS, ☎800-746-7287.

Rite-Aid, ☎800-748-3243.

POSTAL SERVICES

US Postal Service Customer Service Assistance Center, ☎212-967-8585 (M-F 8:30am-6pm), ☎800-725-2161 (24hr.).

Central Post Office, 0421 Eighth Ave. (☎212-330-3601), occupying the block

REALTORS

See also ***Accommodation Agencies,*** *p. 282.*

DG Neary Realty, 57 W. 16th St., on the corner of Sixth Ave. (☎633-2727; fax 989-1207). Open Su-F 10am-6pm, Sa 10am-4pm.

Gamut Realty Group, 301 E. 78th St. (☎212-879-4229). Open M-F 9am-6pm, Sa-Su 10am-4pm.

Manhattan Lodgings, ☎212-677-7616.

New York Habitat, 307 Seventh Ave., Ste. 306 (☎212-255-8018).

Rainbow Roommates, 268 W. 22nd St., near Eighth Ave. (☎627-8612; www.rainbowroommates.com). Open Tu-Sa noon-6pm.

SALONS

Astor Place Hair Designers, 2 Astor Pl., at Broadway (☎212-475-9854). Open M-Sa 8am-8pm, Su 9am-6pm. Cuts start at $14.

Ginger Rose on Bleecker, 154 Bleecker St., between Thompson St. and LaGuardia Pl. (☎212-677-6511). Open M-Sa 10am-8pm, Su noon-6pm. Cuts start at $20.50.

Jean Louis David, 1180 Sixth Ave., at 46th St. (☎212-944-7389). Open M-F 10am-7pm, Th 10am-8pm. Cuts around $23.50.

TAXIS

All City Taxis, ☎718-402-2323.

Bell Radio Taxi, ☎212-206-1700.

Tri-State, ☎212-777-7171.

Tel Aviv, ☎212-777-7777.

Taxi Commission, 40 Rector St. (☎212-221-8294). Open M-F 9am-5pm.

TICKET SERVICES

*See also **Entertainment Info,** p. 281.*

Discount Tickets, ☎212-221-0885.

Tele-Charge, ☎212-239-6200 (24hr.).

Ticket Central, ☎212-279-4200. Daily 1-8pm.

Ticketmaster, ☎212-307-4100.

TKTS, ☎212-768-1818.

TOURIST INFORMATION

*See also **Accommodation Agencies,** p. 282.*

New York Convention and Visitors Bureau, 810 Seventh Ave., at 53rd St. (☎212-484-1222). Open M-F 8:30am-5pm, Sa-Su 9am-5pm.

New York State Department of Economic Development, 633 Third Ave., between 40th and 41th St. (☎212-803-2200, 800-CALL-NYS). Open M-F 9am-5:30pm.

Staten Island Chamber of Commerce, 130 Bay St. (☎718-727-1900.) Open M-F 9am-5pm.

Ti-mes Square Visitors Center, 1560 Broadway, between 46th and 47th St. (☎212-768-1560; fax 997-4021). Open daily 9am-6pm. Other locations: Grand Central terminal, south side of the main concourse; Penn Station terminal, south side of the Amtrak rotunda; at 34th St., between Seventh and Eighth Ave.; Manhattan Mall info booth at 33rd and 6th St.

Lower East Side Visitors Center, 261 Broome St., between Orchard and Allen (☎266-9010). Open Su-F 10am-4pm.

Tavelers' Aid of NY & NJ, at JFK Airport (☎718-656-4870), in Terminal 4W. Open daily 9am-8pm.

TRAINS

*See also **Metro Transit,** p. 282.*

Amtrak, ☎800-872-7245.

Grand Central Station, ☎212-340-3000.

Long Island Railroad (LIRR), ☎718-217-5477, 516-822-5477.

NJ Transit, ☎973-762-5100, 800-772-2222 in NJ.

PATH, ☎800-234-7284.

Metro-North Commuter Lines, ☎800-638-7646.

WOMEN'S HEALTH

*See also **Crisis and Help Lines,** p. 280; **Hospitals,** p. 281; and **Medical Clinics,** p. 282.*

Eastern Women's Center, 44 E. 30th St. (☎212-686-6066), between Park and Madison Ave. Exams by appointment only; walk-in pregnancy testing.

Planned Parenthood, Margaret Sanger Center, 26 Bleecker St. (☎212-274-7200). Also in Brooklyn, 44 Court St., and the Bronx, 349 E. 149th St. and Cortland St.

Women's Health Line, New York City Department of Health (☎212-230-1111). Open M-F 8am-6pm.

DISCOUNT CARD

10%

off on direct reservations at either hotel.

The HERALD SQUARE HOTEL
19 West 31st Street NY. NY 10001
(212) 279 - 4017 1 (800) 727 -1888

The PORTLAND SQUARE HOTEL
132 West 47th Street NY NY 10036
(212) 382-0600 1 (800) 388-8988

Card must be presented upon check in.
Valid until 12/31/02

Index

#

A

B

C

D

E

F

G

H

L

M

O

P

Q

T

U

V

W

X

Y

Z

Maps

INSIDE

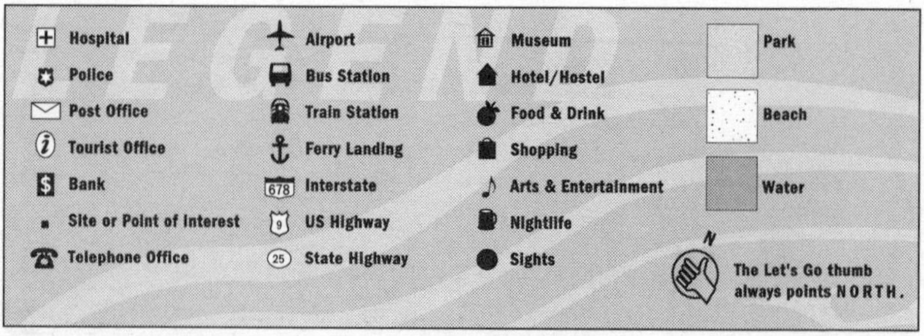

LEGEND
Hospital
Police
Post Office
Tourist Office
Bank
Site or Point of Interest
Telephone Office
Airport
Bus Station
Train Station
Ferry Landing
678
Interstate
9
US Highway
25
State Highway
Museum
Hotel/Hostel
Food & Drink
Shopping
Arts & Entertainment
Nightlife
Sights
Park
Beach
Water
N
The Let's Go thumb always points NORTH.

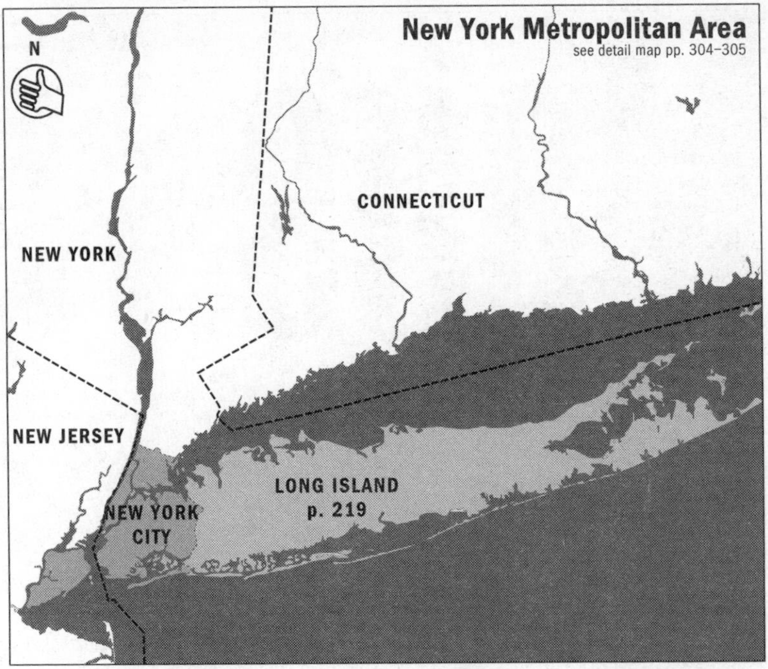
New York Metropolitan Area
see detail map pp. 304–305
N
CONNECTICUT
NEW YORK
NEW JERSEY
LONG ISLAND
p. 219
NEW YORK
CITY

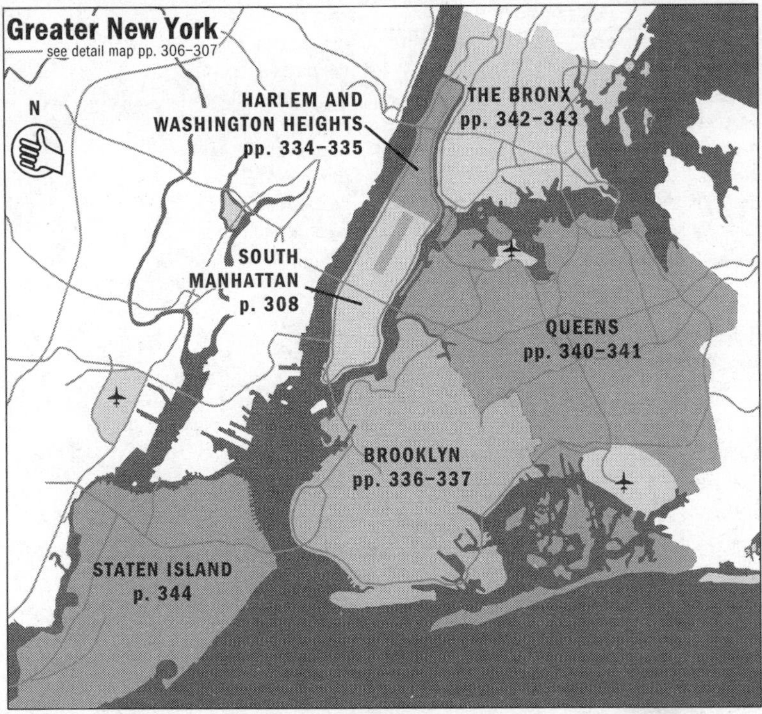
Greater New York
see detail map pp. 306–307
N
HARLEM AND
WASHINGTON HEIGHTS
pp. 334–335
THE BRONX
pp. 342–343
SOUTH
MANHATTAN
p. 308
QUEENS
pp. 340–341
BROOKLYN
pp. 336–337
STATEN ISLAND
p. 344

Ashokan Reservoir
Kingston
Rhinebeck
Falls Village
Hyde Park
Vanderbilt Mansion
FDR Home
Cornwall Bridge
New Paltz
Litchfield
Poughkeepsie
Vassar College
New Preston
Housatonic River
NEW YORK
New Milford
Lake Candlewood
Newburgh
Fahnestock State Park
State Pkwy.
State Thruway
West Point
Brewster
Danbury
Bethel
Peekskill
Warwick
New York
Bear Mountain State Park
Taconic
Ridgefield
Harriman State Park
Hudson River
Van Cortlandt Manor
Stratford
Greenwood Lake
Pywy.
Saw Mill
Norwalk
Bridgeport
Suffern
Tarrytown
American Shakespeare Theatre
Stamford
NEW JERSEY
Greenwich
Paramus
Rye
Paterson
Yonkers
Bayville
Sunken Meadow State Park
Passaic
Huntington
Newark
Hicksville
Long Island
LaGuardia Airport
Levittown
Newark International Airport
NEW YORK CITY
JFK Airport
Bay Shore
Garden State Pkwy.
Jersey Tnpk.
Freeport
Sunrise Hwy.
Long Beach
Jones Beach State Park
Robert Moses State Park
New York Bay
Sandy Hook
Gateway National Recreation Area
0
10 miles
0
10 kilometers
87
9
9W
55
44
7
202
22
84
6
17
684
15
1
95
287
80
280
9A
495
78
27
278

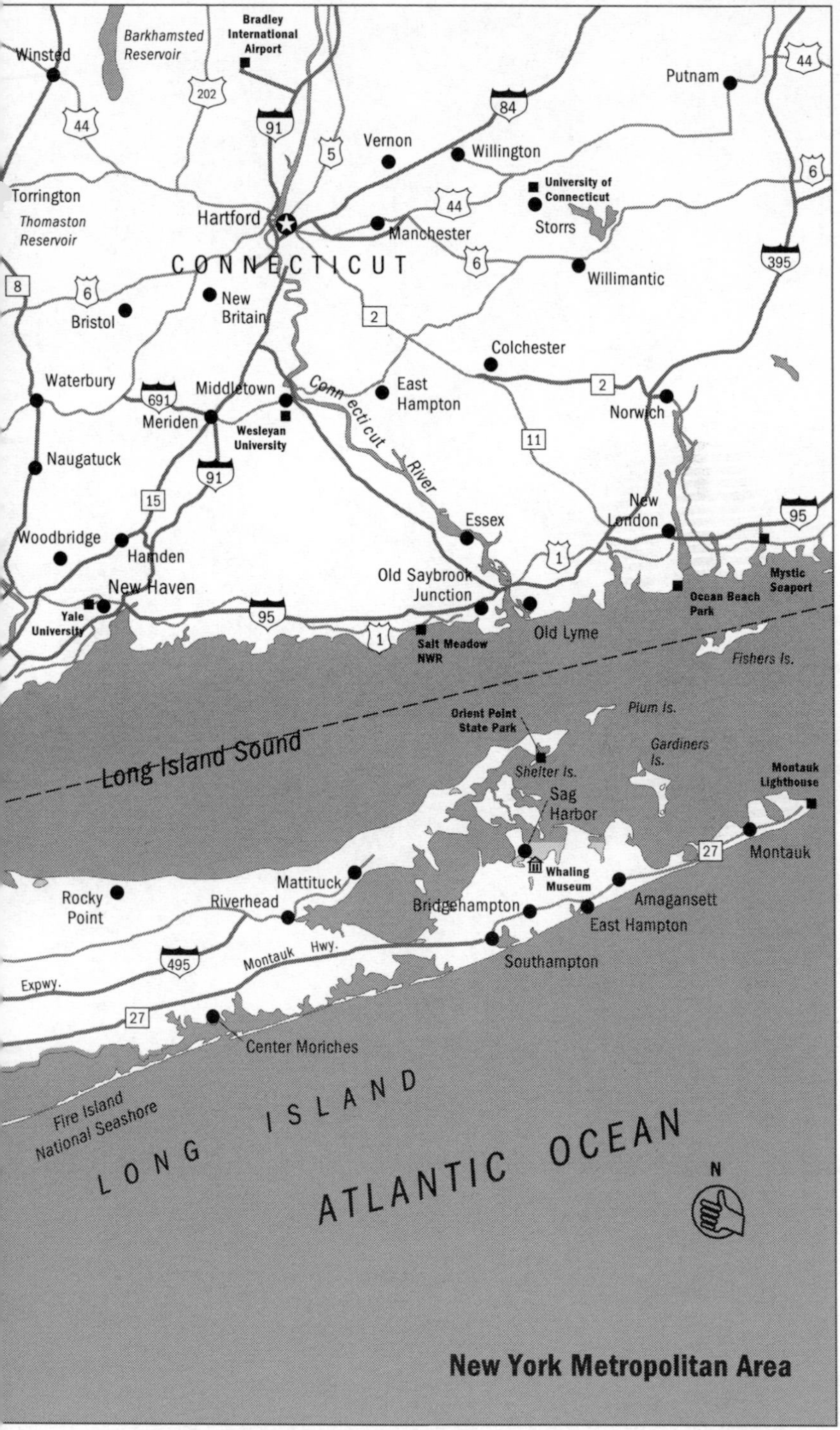
Winsted
Barkhamsted Reservoir
Bradley International Airport
202
91
84
44
Putnam
5
Vernon
Willington
6
University of Connecticut
Storrs
Torrington
Thomaston Reservoir
Hartford
Manchester
CONNECTICUT
Willimantic
395
8
Bristol
New Britain
2
Colchester
Waterbury
691
Middletown
East Hampton
Meriden
Wesleyan University
Norwich
11
Naugatuck
Connecticut River
15
Essex
New London
95
Woodbridge
Hamden
Old Saybrook Junction
New Haven
Yale University
1
Salt Meadow NWR
Old Lyme
Ocean Beach Park
Mystic Seaport
Fishers Is.
Plum Is.
Orient Point State Park
Long Island Sound
Gardiners Is.
Shelter Is.
Sag Harbor
Montauk Lighthouse
Montauk
27
Whaling Museum
Mattituck
Rocky Point
Riverhead
Bridgehampton
Amagansett
East Hampton
Southampton
495
Montauk Hwy.
Expwy.
Center Moriches
Fire Island National Seashore
LONG ISLAND
ATLANTIC OCEAN
N
New York Metropolitan Area

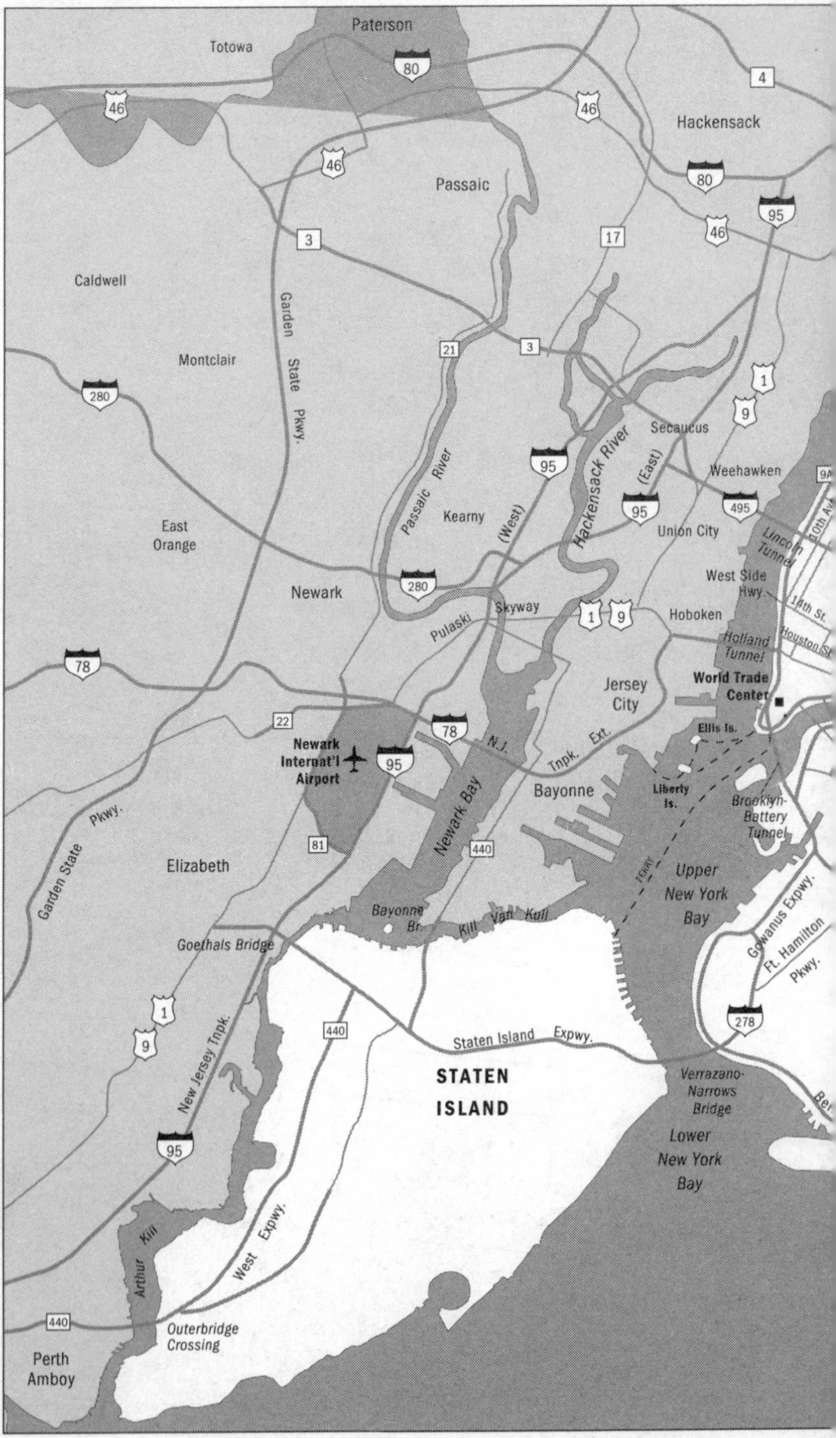
Paterson
Totowa
Hackensack
Passaic
Caldwell
Garden State Pkwy.
Montclair
Secaucus
Weehawken
Passaic River
Kearny
Hackensack River
(West)
(East)
Union City
East Orange
Lincoln Tunnel
West Side Hwy.
Newark
Pulaski Skyway
Hoboken
14th St.
Houston St.
Holland Tunnel
World Trade Center
Jersey City
Ellis Is.
N.J. Tnpk. Ext.
Newark Internat'l Airport
Bayonne
Liberty Is.
Brooklyn-Battery Tunnel
Newark Bay
Elizabeth
Ferry
Upper New York Bay
Gowanus Expwy.
Ft. Hamilton Pkwy.
Bayonne Br.
Kill Van Kull
Goethals Bridge
Staten Island Expwy.
STATEN ISLAND
New Jersey Tnpk.
Verrazano-Narrows Bridge
Lower New York Bay
West Expwy.
Arthur Kill
Outerbridge Crossing
Perth Amboy

Greater New York

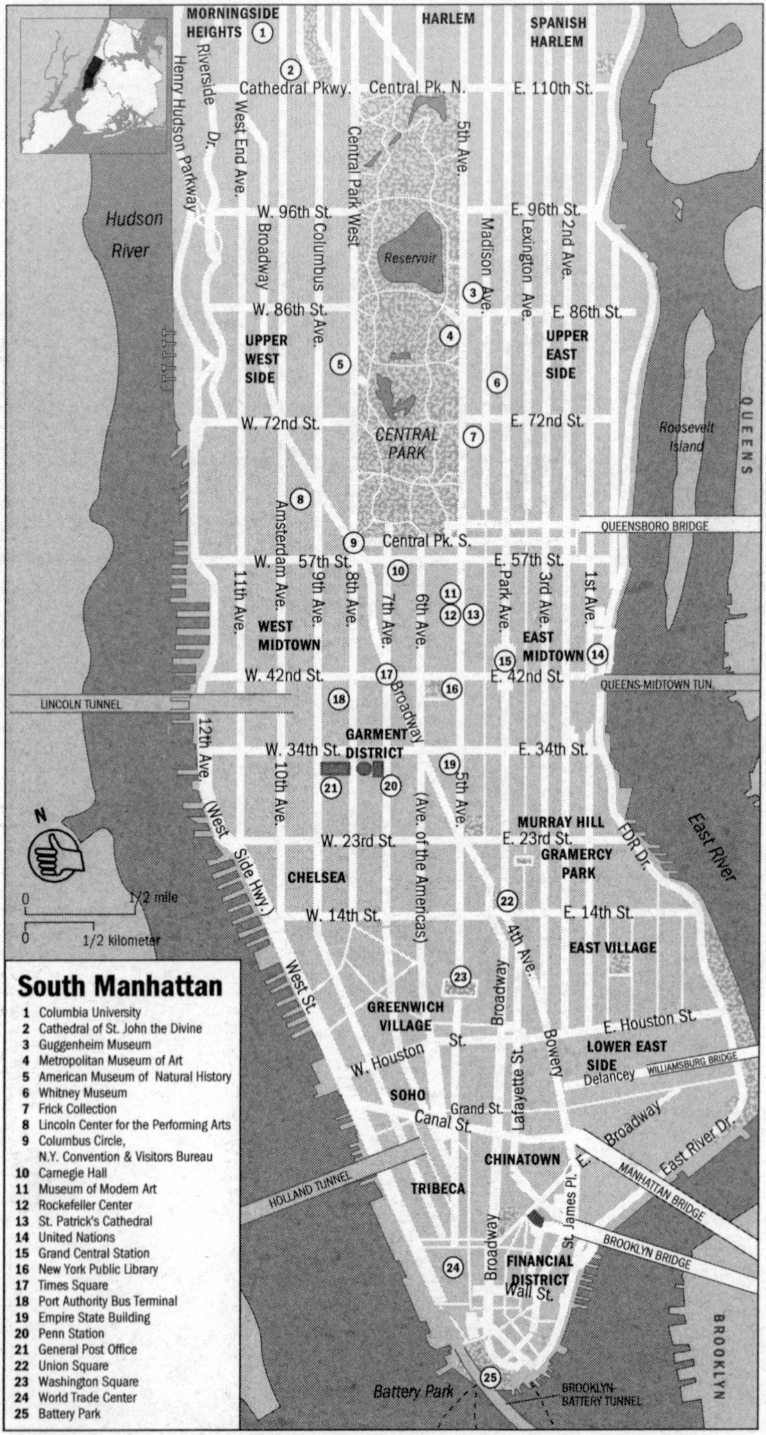
South Manhattan
1 Columbia University
2 Cathedral of St. John the Divine
3 Guggenheim Museum
4 Metropolitan Museum of Art
5 American Museum of Natural History
6 Whitney Museum
7 Frick Collection
8 Lincoln Center for the Performing Arts
9 Columbus Circle, N.Y. Convention & Visitors Bureau
10 Carnegie Hall
11 Museum of Modern Art
12 Rockefeller Center
13 St. Patrick's Cathedral
14 United Nations
15 Grand Central Station
16 New York Public Library
17 Times Square
18 Port Authority Bus Terminal
19 Empire State Building
20 Penn Station
21 General Post Office
22 Union Square
23 Washington Square
24 World Trade Center
25 Battery Park
MORNINGSIDE HEIGHTS
HARLEM
SPANISH HARLEM
Cathedral Pkwy.
Central Pk. N.
E. 110th St.
Riverside Dr.
Henry Hudson Parkway
West End Ave.
Central Park West
5th Ave.
Hudson River
W. 96th St.
E. 96th St.
Broadway
Columbus Ave.
Reservoir
Madison Ave.
Lexington Ave.
2nd Ave.
W. 86th St.
E. 86th St.
UPPER WEST SIDE
UPPER EAST SIDE
W. 72nd St.
E. 72nd St.
CENTRAL PARK
Roosevelt Island
QUEENS
Amsterdam Ave.
QUEENSBORO BRIDGE
Central Pk. S.
W. 57th St.
E. 57th St.
11th Ave.
9th Ave.
8th Ave.
7th Ave.
6th Ave.
Park Ave.
3rd Ave.
1st Ave.
WEST MIDTOWN
EAST MIDTOWN
W. 42nd St.
E. 42nd St.
QUEENS-MIDTOWN TUN.
LINCOLN TUNNEL
12th Ave.
GARMENT DISTRICT
W. 34th St.
E. 34th St.
10th Ave.
(Ave. of the Americas)
N
(West Side Hwy.)
MURRAY HILL
W. 23rd St.
E. 23rd St.
FDR Dr.
East River
GRAMERCY PARK
CHELSEA
0 1/2 mile
0 1/2 kilometer
W. 14th St.
E. 14th St.
4th Ave.
EAST VILLAGE
West St.
GREENWICH VILLAGE
E. Houston St.
W. Houston St.
LOWER EAST SIDE
Delancey
WILLIAMSBURG BRIDGE
Bowery
Lafayette St.
SOHO
Grand St.
Canal St.
E. Broadway
East River Dr.
CHINATOWN
HOLLAND TUNNEL
TRIBECA
MANHATTAN BRIDGE
St. James Pl.
BROOKLYN BRIDGE
FINANCIAL DISTRICT
Wall St.
BROOKLYN
Battery Park
BROOKLYN-BATTERY TUNNEL

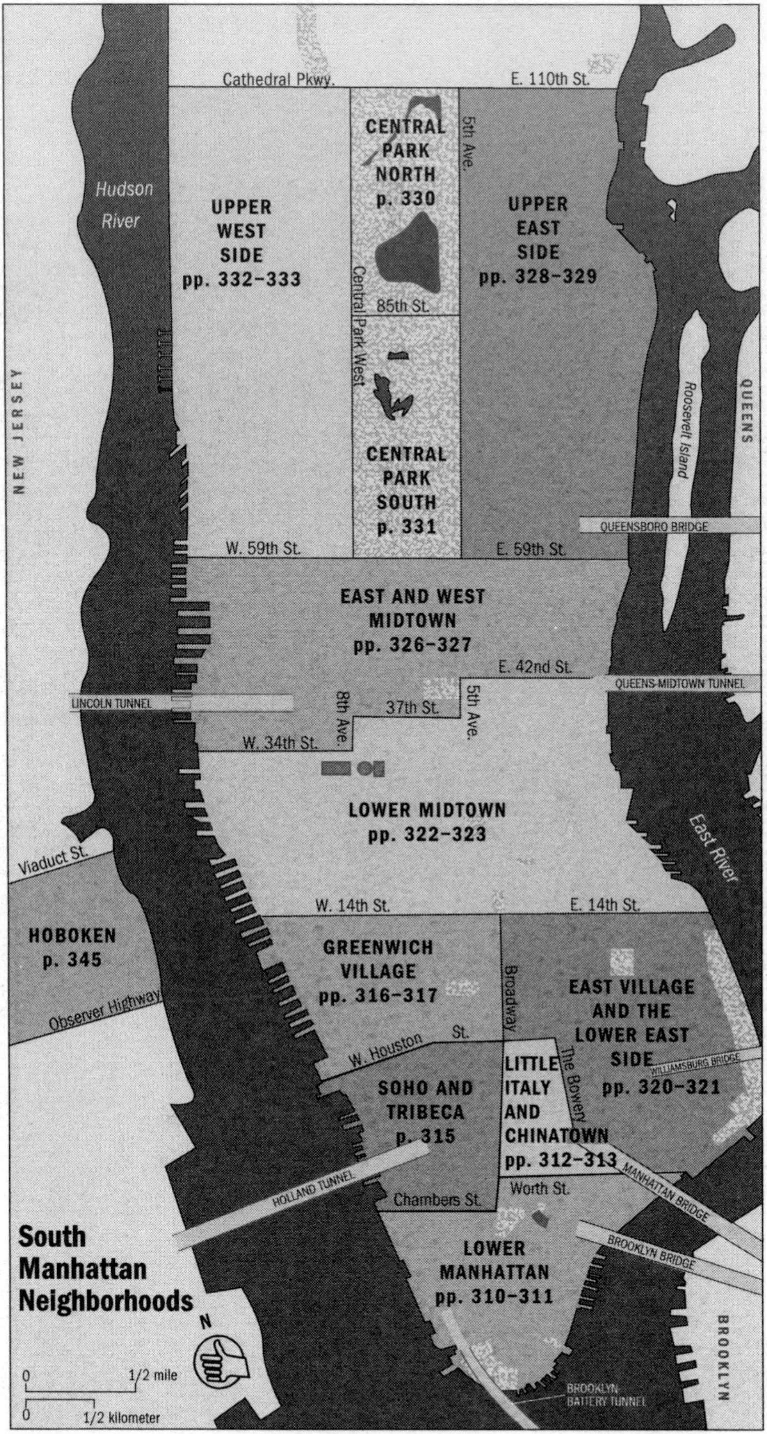
Cathedral Pkwy.
E. 110th St.
Hudson River
UPPER WEST SIDE pp. 332–333
CENTRAL PARK NORTH p. 330
5th Ave.
UPPER EAST SIDE pp. 328–329
85th St.
Central Park West
NEW JERSEY
QUEENS
Roosevelt Island
CENTRAL PARK SOUTH p. 331
QUEENSBORO BRIDGE
W. 59th St.
E. 59th St.
EAST AND WEST MIDTOWN pp. 326–327
E. 42nd St.
QUEENS-MIDTOWN TUNNEL
LINCOLN TUNNEL
8th Ave.
37th St.
5th Ave.
W. 34th St.
LOWER MIDTOWN pp. 322–323
East River
Viaduct St.
W. 14th St.
E. 14th St.
HOBOKEN p. 345
GREENWICH VILLAGE pp. 316–317
Broadway
EAST VILLAGE AND THE LOWER EAST SIDE pp. 320–321
Observer Highway
W. Houston St.
LITTLE ITALY AND CHINATOWN pp. 312–313
The Bowery
WILLIAMSBURG BRIDGE
SOHO AND TRIBECA p. 315
MANHATTAN BRIDGE
HOLLAND TUNNEL
Chambers St.
Worth St.
BROOKLYN BRIDGE
South Manhattan Neighborhoods
LOWER MANHATTAN pp. 310–311
N
BROOKLYN
0 1/2 mile
0 1/2 kilometer
BROOKLYN-BATTERY TUNNEL

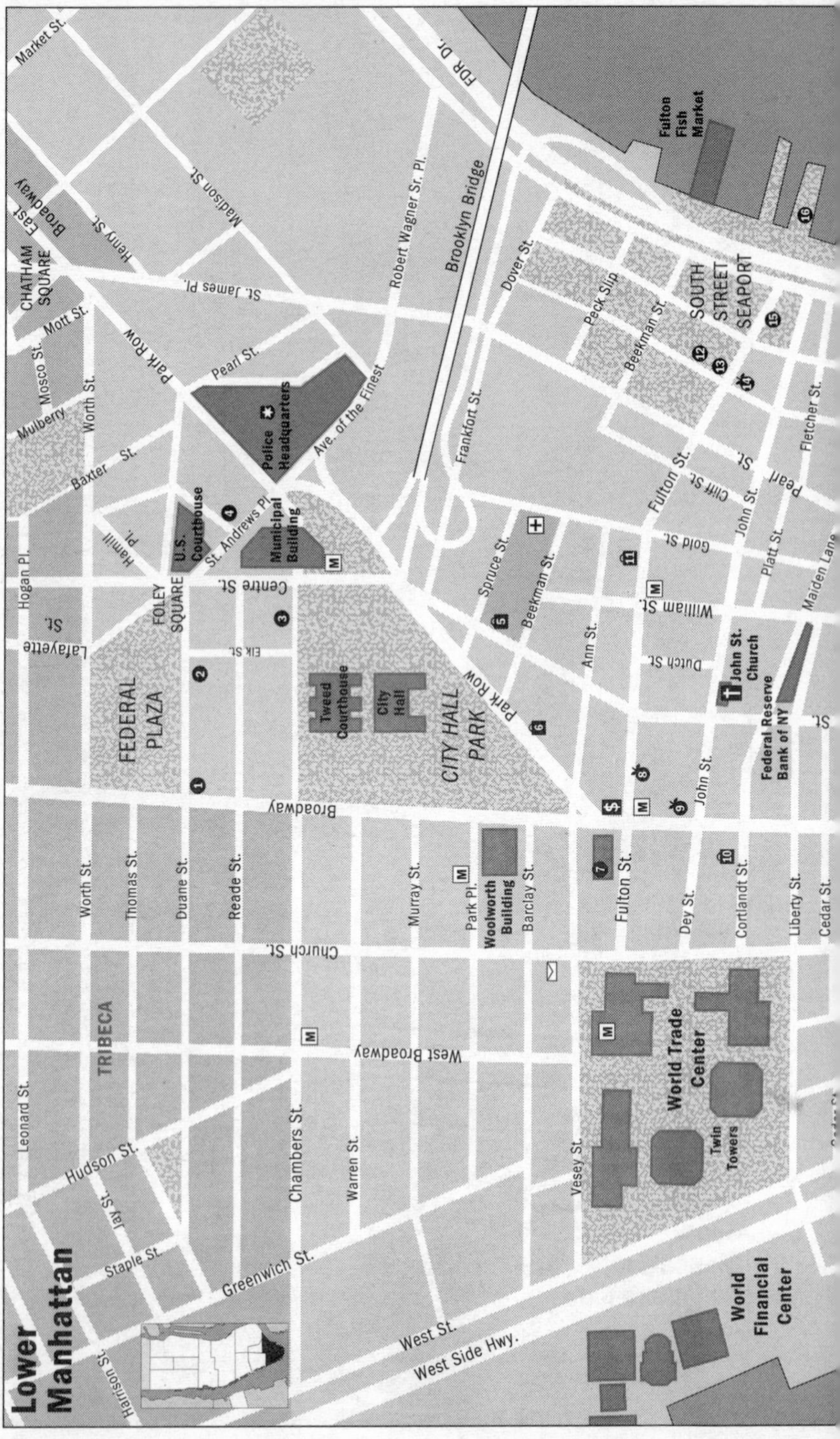
Lower Manhattan
Market St.
FDR Dr.
Madison St.
Robert Wagner Sr. Pl.
Brooklyn Bridge
Fulton Fish Market
East Broadway
Henry St.
CHATHAM SQUARE
St. James Pl.
Dover St.
Peck Slip
Beekman St.
SOUTH STREET SEAPORT
Mott St.
Mosco St.
Mulberry
Worth St.
Park Row
Pearl St.
Police Headquarters
Ave. of the Finest
Frankfort St.
Fletcher St.
Baxter St.
Hamill Pl.
U.S. Courthouse
St. Andrews Pl.
Municipal Building
Fulton St.
Cliff St.
Pearl St.
John St.
Gold St.
Platt St.
Maiden Lane
Spruce St.
Beekman St.
Hogan Pl.
Lafayette St.
FOLEY SQUARE
Centre St.
William St.
Elk St.
Dutch St.
Ann St.
John St. Church
FEDERAL PLAZA
Tweed Courthouse
City Hall
CITY HALL PARK
Park Row
Federal Reserve Bank of NY
John St.
Broadway
Worth St.
Thomas St.
Duane St.
Reade St.
Murray St.
Park Pl.
Woolworth Building
Barclay St.
Fulton St.
Dey St.
Cortlandt St.
Liberty St.
Cedar St.
Church St.
TRIBECA
West Broadway
World Trade Center
Twin Towers
Leonard St.
Hudson St.
Jay St.
Chambers St.
Warren St.
Vesey St.
Staple St.
Greenwich St.
West St.
West Side Hwy.
World Financial Center
Harrison St.

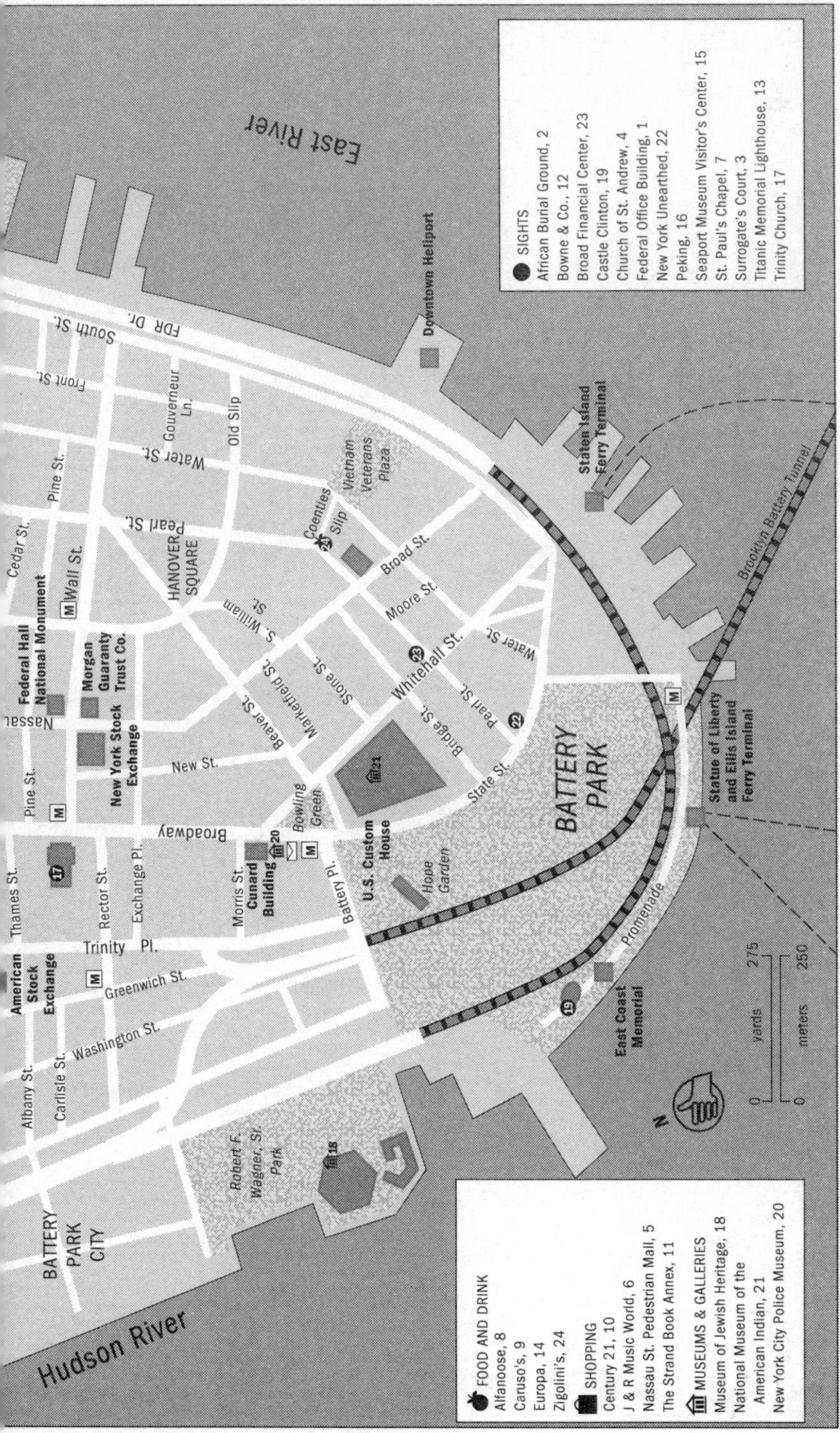
SIGHTS
African Burial Ground, 2
Bowne & Co., 12
Broad Financial Center, 23
Castle Clinton, 19
Church of St. Andrew, 4
Federal Office Building, 1
New York Unearthed, 22
Peking, 16
Seaport Museum Visitor's Center, 15
St. Paul's Chapel, 7
Surrogate's Court, 3
Titanic Memorial Lighthouse, 13
Trinity Church, 17
FOOD AND DRINK
Alfanoose, 8
Caruso's, 9
Europa, 14
Zigolini's, 24
SHOPPING
Century 21, 10
J & R Music World, 6
Nassau St. Pedestrian Mall, 5
The Strand Book Annex, 11
MUSEUMS & GALLERIES
Museum of Jewish Heritage, 18
National Museum of the
American Indian, 21
New York City Police Museum, 20
East River
Hudson River
BATTERY PARK
BATTERY PARK CITY
Robert F. Wagner, Sr. Park
Downtown Heliport
Staten Island Ferry Terminal
Statue of Liberty and Ellis Island Ferry Terminal
Brooklyn Battery Tunnel
East Coast Memorial
Promenade
Hope Garden
U.S. Custom House
Bowling Green
Cunard Building
New York Stock Exchange
Federal Hall National Monument
Morgan Guaranty Trust Co.
American Stock Exchange
HANOVER SQUARE
Vietnam Veterans Plaza
Coenties Slip
FDR Dr.
South St.
Front St.
Water St.
Pearl St.
Gouverneur Ln.
Old Slip
Pine St.
Cedar St.
Wall St.
Nassau
Broad St.
Moore St.
Whitehall St.
S. William St.
Stone St.
Marketfield St.
Beaver St.
Bridge St.
State St.
New St.
Broadway
Battery Pl.
Morris St.
Exchange Pl.
Rector St.
Thames St.
Trinity Pl.
Greenwich St.
Washington St.
Carlisle St.
Albany St.
yards 0 275
meters 0 250
N

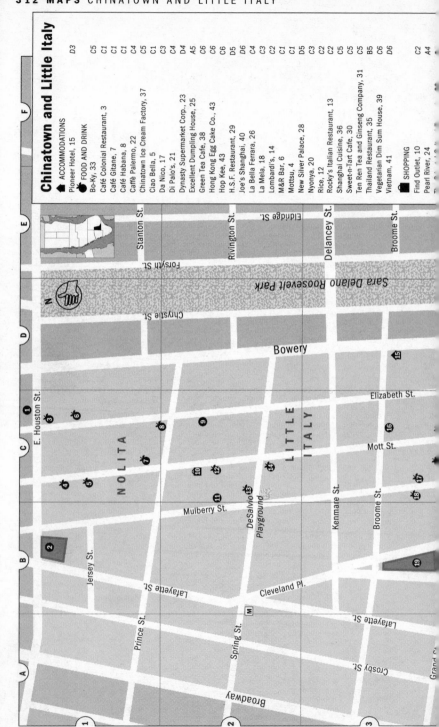

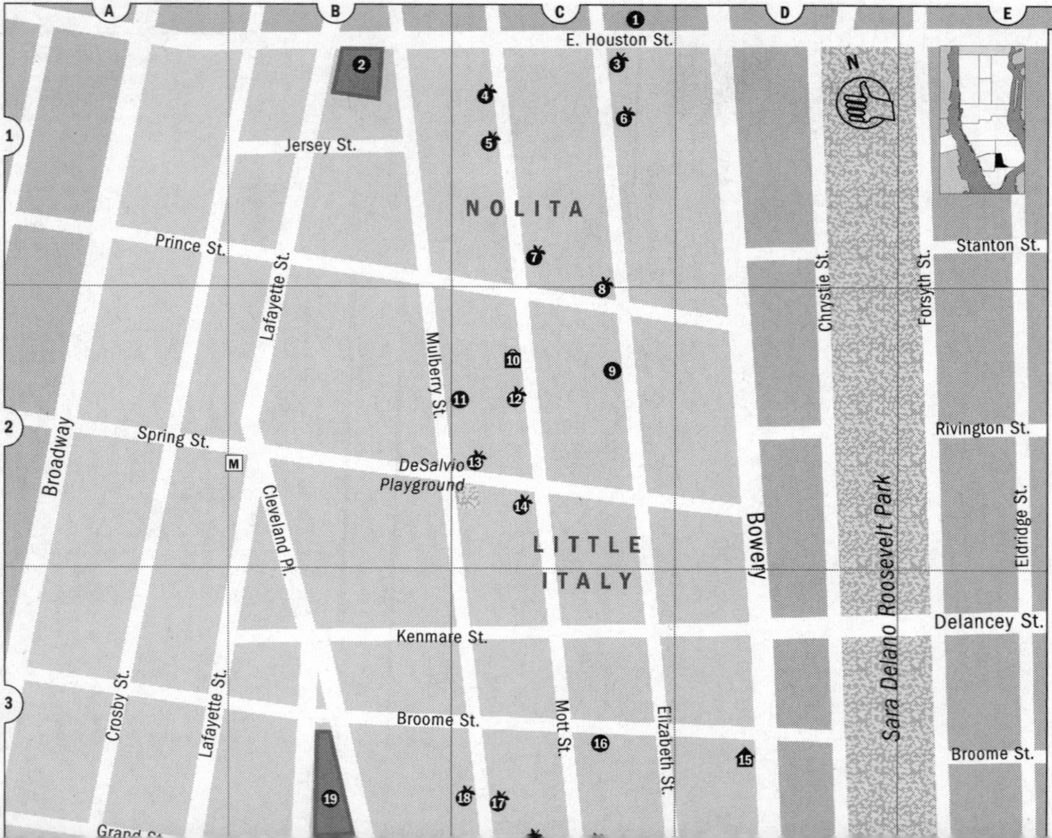

Chinatown and Little Italy

ACCOMMODATIONS

Pioneer Hotel, 15	D3

FOOD AND DRINK

Bo-Ky, 33	C5
Café Colonial Restaurant, 3	C1
Café Gitane, 7	C1
Café Habana, 8	C1
Caffè Palermo, 22	C4
Chinatown Ice Cream Factory, 37	C5
Ciao Bella, 5	C1
Da Nico, 17	C3
Di Palo's, 21	C4
Dynasty Supermarket Corp., 23	D4
Excellent Dumpling House, 25	A5
Green Tea Cafe, 38	C6
Hong Kong Egg Cake Co., 43	C6
Hop Kee, 43	C6
H.S.F. Restaurant, 29	D5
Joe's Shanghai, 40	D6
La Bella Ferrara, 26	C4
La Mela, 18	C3
Lombardi's, 14	C2
M&R Bar, 6	C1
Mottsu, 4	C1
New Silver Palace, 28	D5
Nyonya, 20	C3
Rice, 12	C2
Rocky's Italian Restaurant, 13	C2
Shanghai Cuisine, 36	C5
Sweet-n-Tart Cafe, 30	C5
Ten Ren Tea and Ginseng Company, 31	C5
Thailand Restaurant, 35	B5
Vegetarian Dim Sum House, 39	C6
Vietnam, 41	D6

SHOPPING

Find Outlet, 10	C2
Pearl River, 24	A4

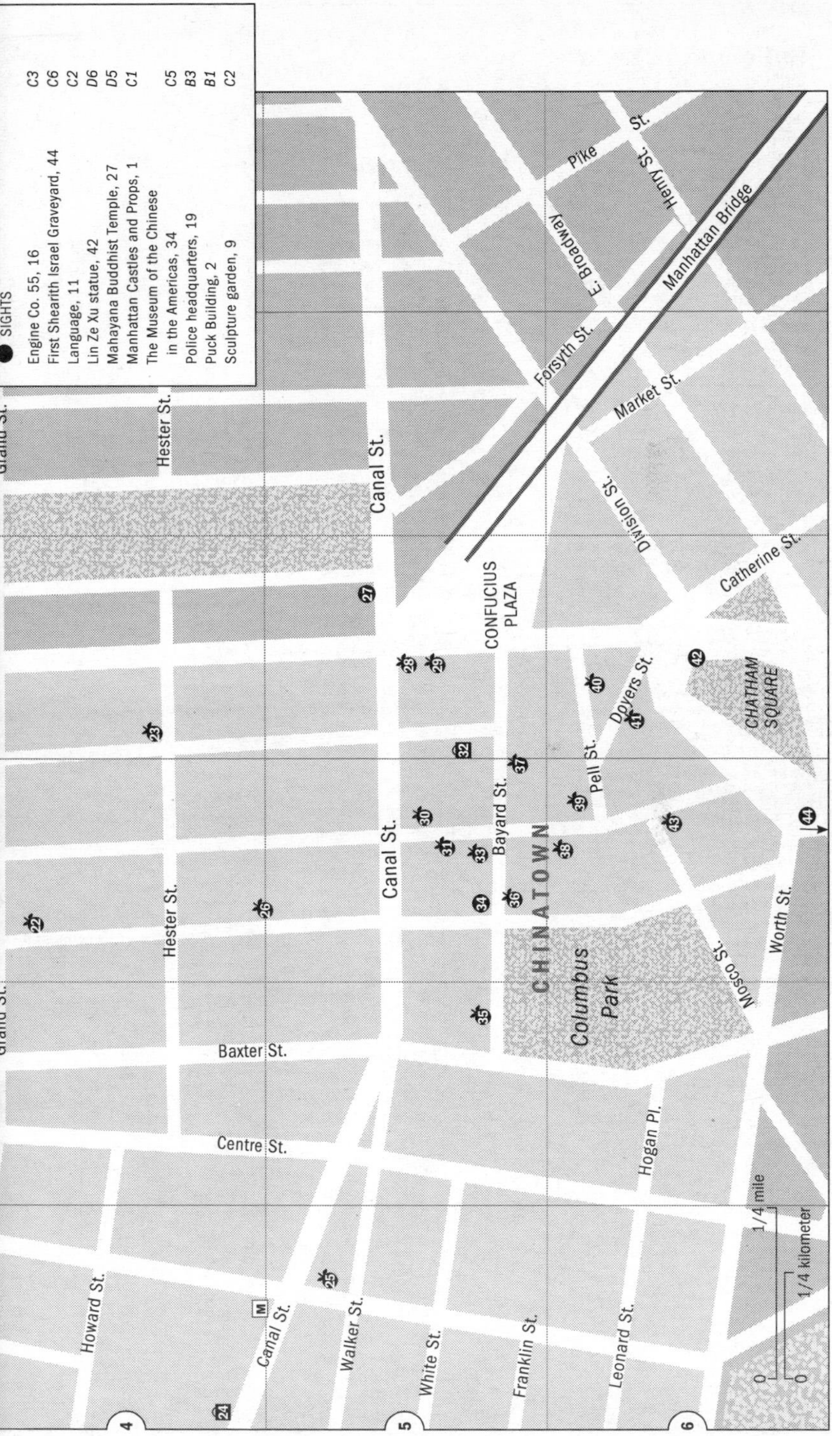
SIGHTS
Engine Co. 55, 16 C3
First Shearith Israel Graveyard, 44 C6
Language, 11 C2
Lin Ze Xu statue, 42 D6
Mahayana Buddhist Temple, 27 D5
Manhattan Castles and Props, 1 C1
The Museum of the Chinese in the Americas, 34 C5
Police headquarters, 19 B3
Puck Building, 2 B1
Sculpture garden, 9 C2
Hester St.
Canal St.
Pike St.
E. Broadway
Henry St.
Manhattan Bridge
Forsyth St.
Market St.
Division St.
Catherine St.
CONFUCIUS PLAZA
CHATHAM SQUARE
Doyers St.
Pell St.
Bayard St.
CHINATOWN
Columbus Park
Mosco St.
Worth St.
Baxter St.
Centre St.
Hogan Pl.
Howard St.
Walker St.
White St.
Franklin St.
Leonard St.
1/4 mile
1/4 kilometer
4
5
6

SoHo and TriBeCa

FOOD AND DRINK

Bouley Bakery, 63	*B7*
Brisas del Caribe, 40	*D3*
Bubby's, 60	*B5*
Dean and Deluca, 16	*D2*
El Teddy's, 59	*C5*
Jerry's, 24	*D2*
Kelley and Ping Asian Grocery and Noodle Shop, 7	*C1*
Le Gamin Cafe, 2	*B1*
Lucky's Juice Joint, 5	*C1*
Lupe's East L.A. Kitchen, 53	*B3*
Pakistan Tea House, 64	*C7*
Penang, 22	*D2*
Space Untitled, 8	*C1*
Yaffa's Tea Room, 62	*A6*

SHOPPING

Agnès B., 26	*C2*
Anna Sui, 25	*C2*
Armani, 15	*D2*
Canal Jean Co, 39	*D3*
Cynthia Rowley, 27	*C2*
Girlprops.com, 29	*C2*
INA, 14	
Joseph, 25	*C2*
K. Trimming, 38	*D3*
Sephora, 17	*D2*
Universal News and Cafe Corp, 42	*C1*
Untitled, 30	*C2*

ARTS & ENTERTAINMENT

Angelika Film Center, 10	*D1*
Film Forum, 1	*A1*
Knitting Factory, 58	*C6*
SoHo Repertory Theater, 56	*C5*
SoHo Think Tank Theater, 36	*C3*
Wetlands Preserve, 55	*A5*

MUSEUMS & GALLERIES

Artists Space, 46	*C3*
David Zuirner, 45	*C3*
Deitch Projects, 47	*C3*
Dia Center for the Arts, 6	*C1*
Drawing Center, 48	*C3*
Exit Art/The First World, 19	*D2*
Guggenheim Museum SoHo, 13	*D2*
Illustration House, 21	*D2*
Museum for African Art, 11	*D1*
New Museum of Contemporary Art, 12	*D2*
New York City Fire Museum, 33	*A3*
The Painting Center, 44	*C3*
POP International Galleries, 4	*C1*
Shakespeare's Fulcrum, 54	*A4*
Staley-Wise, 17	*D2*
Thread Waxing Space, 43	*D3*
Tony Shafrazi, 28	*C2*
The Work Space, 20	*D2*

SIGHTS

Haughwout Building, 41	*D3*
TriBeCa Grill, 61	*A6*

NIGHTLIFE

Bar 89, 37	*D3*
Cafe Noir, 51	*B4*
Circa Tabac, 52	*B3*
Denizen, 34	*B3*
Fanelli's, 23	*D2*
Kilimanjaro, 57	*D6*
Lucky Strike, 49	*C4*
MercBar, 9	*D1*
Milady's, 31	*B2*
Naked Lunch Bar and Lounge, 50	*B4*
NV and 289 Lounge, 32	*A3*
Scharmann's, 35	*C3*
X-R Bar, 3	*B1*

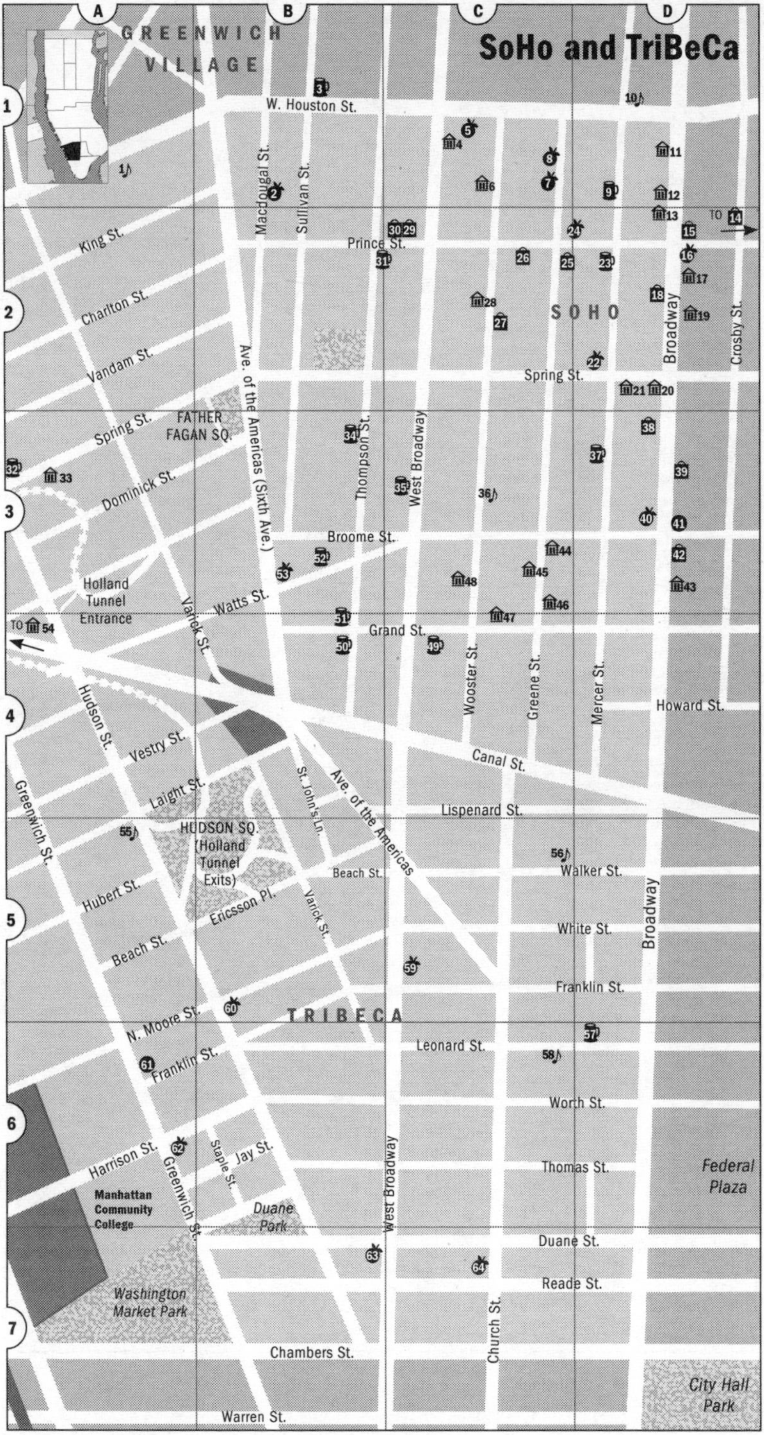
SoHo and TriBeCa
A
B
C
D
1
2
3
4
5
6
7
GREENWICH VILLAGE
W. Houston St.
Macdougal St.
Sullivan St.
King St.
Prince St.
Charlton St.
SOHO
Vandam St.
Spring St.
Broadway
Crosby St.
Ave. of the Americas (Sixth Ave.)
FATHER FAGAN SQ.
Thompson St.
West Broadway
Dominick St.
Broome St.
Holland Tunnel Entrance
Watts St.
Varick St.
Grand St.
TO
Wooster St.
Greene St.
Mercer St.
Howard St.
Hudson St.
Canal St.
Vestry St.
Laight St.
St. John's Ln.
Ave. of the Americas
Lispenard St.
Greenwich St.
HUDSON SQ. (Holland Tunnel Exits)
Beach St.
Walker St.
Hubert St.
Ericsson Pl.
White St.
Franklin St.
N. Moore St.
TRIBECA
Leonard St.
Worth St.
Harrison St.
Staple St.
Jay St.
Thomas St.
Federal Plaza
Manhattan Community College
Duane Park
Duane St.
Reade St.
Church St.
Washington Market Park
Chambers St.
City Hall Park
Warren St.

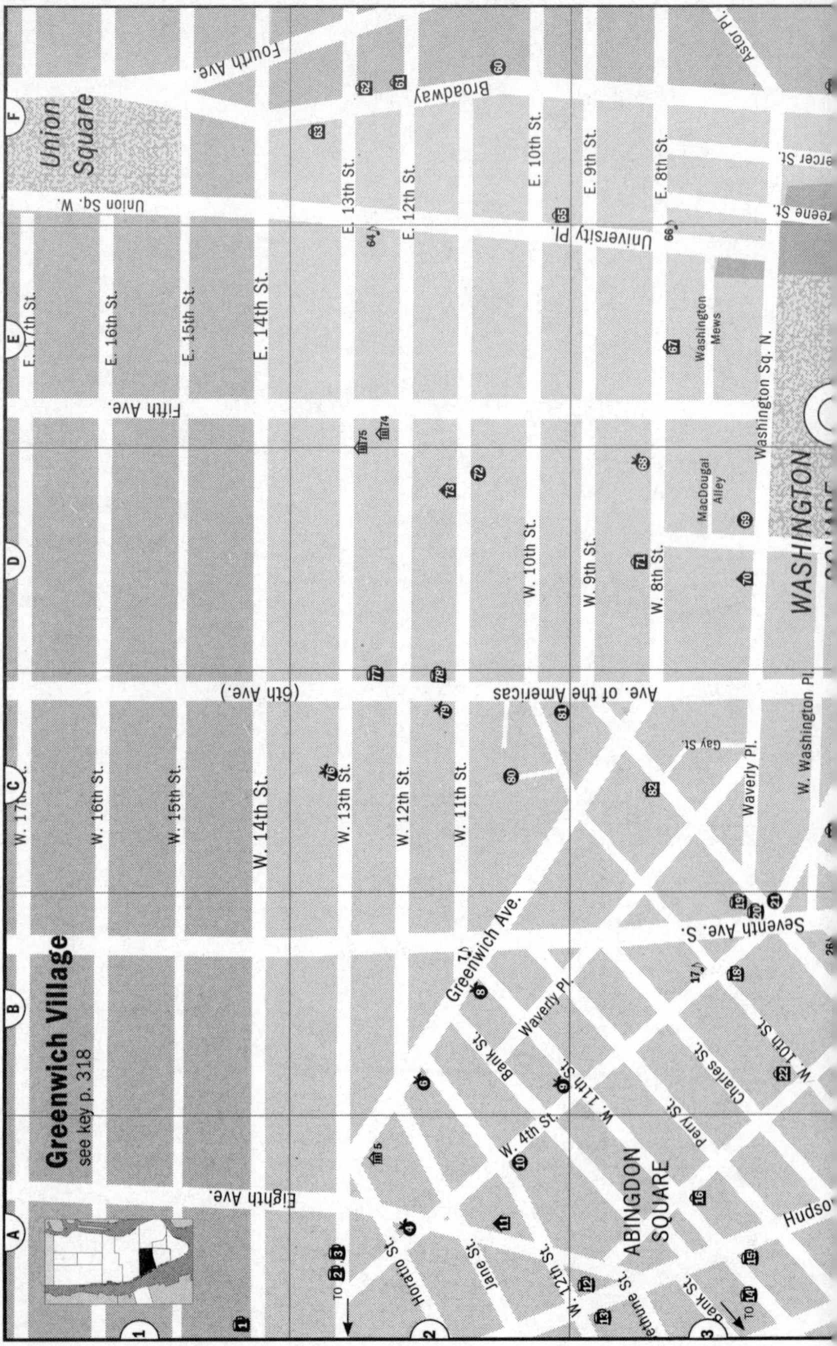

Greenwich Village
see key p. 318
Union Square
Union Sq. W.
Fourth Ave.
Broadway
Astor Pl.
E. 17th St.
E. 16th St.
E. 15th St.
E. 14th St.
E. 13th St.
E. 12th St.
E. 10th St.
E. 9th St.
E. 8th St.
University Pl.
Washington Mews
Washington Sq. N.
Fifth Ave.
MacDougal Alley
W. 10th St.
W. 9th St.
W. 8th St.
WASHINGTON
(6th Ave.)
Ave. of the Americas
Gay St.
Waverly Pl.
W. Washington Pl.
W. 17th St.
W. 16th St.
W. 15th St.
W. 14th St.
W. 13th St.
W. 12th St.
W. 11th St.
Greenwich Ave.
Seventh Ave. S.
Bank St.
W. 4th St.
W. 11th St.
Perry St.
Charles St.
W. 10th St.
Eighth Ave.
Horatio St.
Jane St.
W. 12th St.
Bethune St.
ABINGDON SQUARE
Hudson
TO

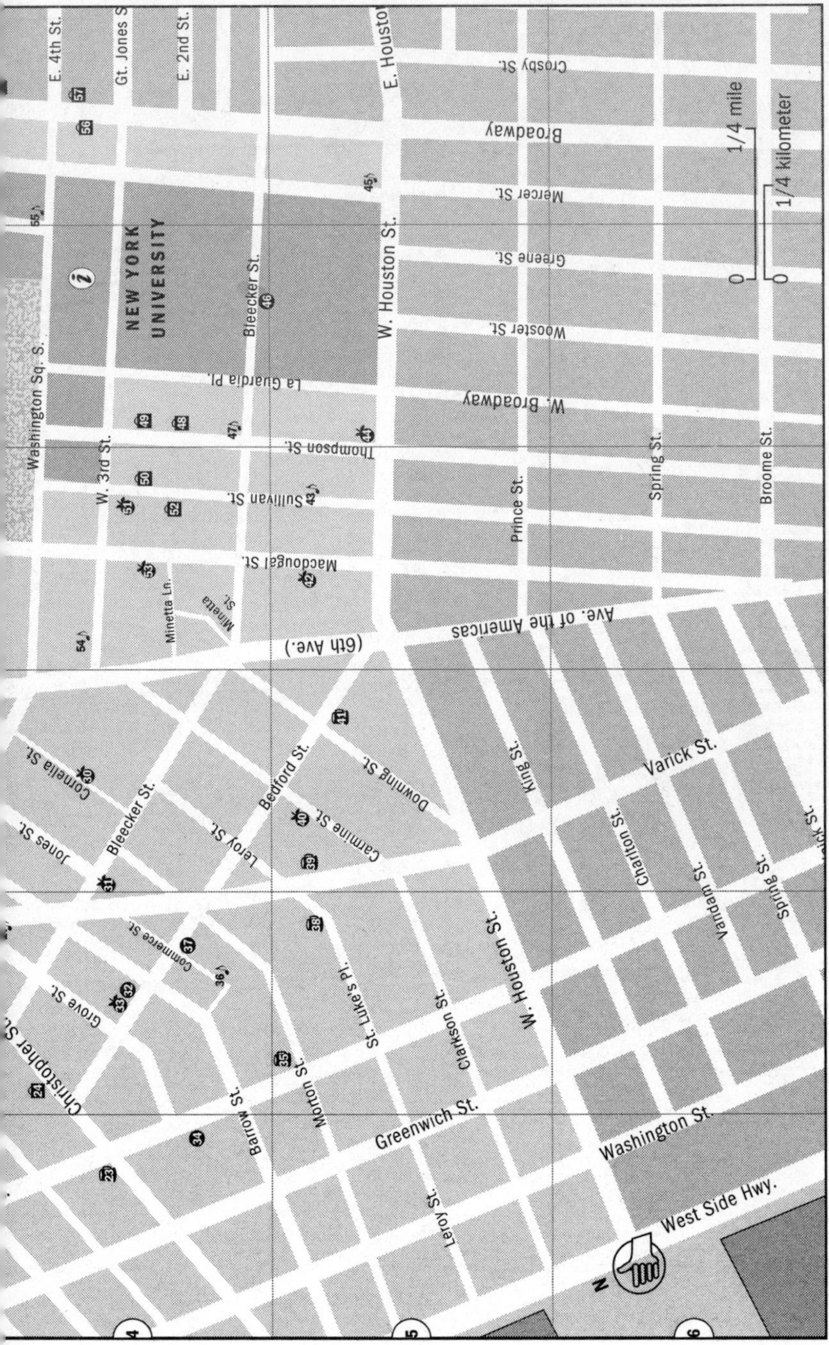
E. 4th St.
Gt. Jones St.
E. 2nd St.
E. Houston St.
Crosby St.
Broadway
Mercer St.
Greene St.
Wooster St.
W. Broadway
1/4 mile
1/4 kilometer
0
NEW YORK UNIVERSITY
Washington Sq. S.
Bleecker St.
W. Houston St.
La Guardia Pl.
W. 3rd St.
Thompson St.
Sullivan St.
Macdougal St.
Minetta Ln.
Minetta St.
Prince St.
Spring St.
Broome St.
Ave. of the Americas
(6th Ave.)
Cornelia St.
Bleecker St.
Jones St.
Leroy St.
Bedford St.
Downing St.
Carmine St.
King St.
Varick St.
Charlton St.
Vandam St.
Spring St.
Commerce St.
Grove St.
Christopher St.
Barrow St.
Morton St.
St. Luke's Pl.
Clarkson St.
W. Houston St.
Greenwich St.
Washington St.
Leroy St.
West Side Hwy.
N
4
5
6

Greenwich Village

see map pp. 316–317

ACCOMMODATIONS

Incentra Village House, 11	*A2*
Larchmont Hotel, 73	*D3*
Washington Square Hotel, 76	*D2*

FOOD AND DRINK

Arturo's Pizza, 44	*E5*
Caffè Dante, 41	*D5*
Caffè Mona Lisa, 31	*C4*
Chez Brigitte, 8	*B2*
Corner Bistro, 4	*A2*
Day-O, 6	*B2*
Eva's, 68	*D3*
Grey Dog Cafe, 40	*C5*
John's Pizzeria, 31	*C4*
Moustache, 30	*C4*
Olive Tree Cafe, 53	*D4*
Peanut Butter & Co., 51	*D4*
Ray's Pizza, 79	*C2*
Spain, 76	*C2*
Tartine, 9	*B2*

SHOPPING

Andy's Chee-pee's, 56	*D3*
Antique Boutique, 58	*F4*
Biography Bookstore, 16	*A3*
Cheap Jack's, 63	*F2*
Condomania, 22	*B3*
Disc-O-Rama, 28	*C3*
Forbidden Planet, 62	*F2*
Generation Records, 48	*E4*
La Petite Coquette, 65	*F2*
The Leather Man, 24	*E3*
Oscar Wilde Bookstore, 82	*C3*
Patricia Field, 67	*F2*
Second Coming Records, 50	*D4*
Shakespeare and Company, 59	*F3*
Strand, 61	*F2*
Tower Records, 57	*F4*
Uncle Sam's Army Navy, 71	*D3*
Village Chess Shop, 49	*E4*
Village Comics, 52	*D4*

MUSEUMS

Forbes Magazine Galleries, 74	*E2*
Parson's Exhibition Center, 75	*D2*
National Museum and Archive of Lesbian and Gay History, 5	*A2*

ARTS & ENTERTAINMENT

Actors Playhouse, 27	*B4*
Angelika Film Center, 45	*F5*
Arthur's Tavern, 26	*B3*
The Bitter End, 47	*E4*
Blue Note, 54	*D4*
Bottom Line, 55	*F4*
Bowlmor Lanes, 64	*E2*
Cherry Lane, 36	*B4*
Iris & B. Gerald Cantor Film Center, 66	*F3*
Small's, 17	*B3*
Sullivan St. Playhouse, 43	*D5*
Village Vanguard, 7	*B2*

SIGHTS

75½ Bedford street, 37	*B4*
Chumley's, 32	*B4*
Church of St. Luke's in the Fields, 34	*A4*
Grace Church, 60	*F2*
Jefferson Market Library, 81	*C2*
Patchin Place, 80	*C2*
Picasso, 46	*E4*
The Row, 69	*D3*
Sheridan Square, 21	*B3*
The New School, 10	*A2*
Weatherman, 72	*D2*

NIGHTLIFE

Absolutely 4th, 18	*B3*
Automatic Slims, 14	*A3*
Bar d'O, 41	*C5*
Bar 6, 77	*C2*
Chi Chiz, 23	*B4*
Crazy Nanny's, 39	*C5*
The Cubbyhole, 12	*A3*
The Duplex, 20	*B3*
Hell, 2	*A2*
Henrietta Hudson, 35	*B5*
Kava Lounge, 13	*A3*
Lure, 3	*A2*
Panache Brasserie, 78	*C2*
Rose's Turn, 25	*B3*
The Slaughtered Lamb Pub, 29	*C3*
Stonewall, 19	*B3*
The Village Idiot, 1	*A1*
The Whitehorse Tavern, 15	*A3*
Guilty Pleasure and Living Legends, 38	*B5*

East Village and Lower East Side

see map pp. 320–321

ACCOMMODATIONS

St. Mark's Hotel, 21	*B2*

FOOD AND DRINK

2nd Ave. Delicatessen, 32	*C2*
Alt. Coffee, 50	*D2*
Bulgin' Waffles Café, 71	*D3*
Casa Mexicana, 108	*D5*
Cucina di Pesce, 82	*C3*
Dojo Restaurant, 20	*C2*
Economy Candy, 107	*D4*
El Sombrero, 103	*D4*
Elvie's Turo-Turo, 3	*D1*
Flor's Kitchen, 39	*D2*
Frank, 79	*C3*
Grilled Cheese, 99	*D4*
Guss Lower East Side Pickle Corp., 113	*D6*
Kate's Joint, 58	*E3*
Katz's Delicatessen, 96	*D4*
La Focacceria, 42	*D2*
Mama's Food Shop, 62	*E3*
Max, 59	*E3*
Moishe's Bake Shop, 27	*C2*
National Café, 3	*D1*
Rivingdon 99 Café, 108	*D5*
Sentosa, 116	*D6*
Something Sweet, 37	*C1*
St. Dymphna's, 45	*D2*
Step Mama's, 61	*E3*
Tiengarden, 102	*D4*
Two Boots Restaurant, 63, 64	*D3*
Veniero's, 4	*C1*
Veselka, 31	*C2*
Whole Earth Bakery and Kitchen, 45	*D2*
Yaffa Café, 46	*D2*
Yakitori Taisho, 20	*C2*
Yonah Schimmel Knishery, 92	*C4*

SHOPPING

Adorned, 75	C3
JBJ Discount Pet Shop, 93	C4
CD & Cassette Annex, 22	B2
Downtown Music Gallery, 80	C3
Honeymoon, 54	E3
House of Trance, 47	D2
It's a Mod, Mod World, 70	D3
Jammyland, 72	C3
Kim's Video and Audio, 22	B2
Kiehl's, 8	*B1*
Las Venus Lounge, 104	D4
Lot 76 NYC, 89	C4
Love Saves the Day, 26	C2
Lucky Wang, 100	D4
Manhattan Portage, 36	C2
Metropolis, 18	B2
Miracle on St. Mark's, 47	D2
NYC Mart, 25	C2
Physical Graffiti, 47	D2
Religious Sex, 44	D2
Rags-A-Gogo, 41	C2
See Hear, 28	C2
Shoshana's Place, 36	C2
Sounds, 22	B2
St. Mark's Bookshop, 17	B2
Starfish & Jelli, 47	D2
Tatiana, 47	D2
Zao, 92	D4

MUSEUMS & GALLERIES

Lower East Side Tenement Museum, 112	*D5*
Ukranian Museum, 6	*C1*
Merchant's House Museum, 86	*B3*

ARTS & ENTERTAINMENT

Anthology Film Archives, 74	*C3*
Astor Place Theater, 14	*B2*
CBGB, 84	*C3*
Cinema Village, 11	*A1*
Continental, 19	*B2*
Detour, 5	*C1*
Fez, 87	*B3*
Mercury Lounge, 97	*D4*
Millennium Film Workshop, 81	*C3*
NY Theatre Workshop, 78	*C3*
Orpheum, 29	*C2*
Theater for the New City, 40	*D2*
Tonic, 110	*E5*

SIGHTS

6th St. and Ave. B Garden, 57	*E3*
10th St. Garden, 52	*E2*
Abe. Lebewohl Park, 33	*C2*
Colonnade Row, 12	*B2*
Community Garden, 53	*E2*
Congregation Anshe Chesed, 105	*D4*
Cooper Union, 16	*B2*
The Cube, 13	*B2*
The Eldridge St. Synagogue, 114	*D6*
Joseph Papp Public Theater, 15	*B2*
Liz Christy Bowery-Houston Garden, 88	*C4*
Lower East Side Visitors Center, 111	*D5*
Miracle Garden, 60	*E3*
New York Marble Cemeteries, 74, 78	*C3*
Space 2B, 65	*D3*
St. George Ukrainian Catholic Church, 24	*C2*
St. Mark's in the Bowery Church, 34	*C2*

NIGHTLIFE

The Anyway Café, 76	*C3*
The Bar, 51	*D2*
Barmacy, 1	*D1*
Bbar (Bowery Bar), 85	*B3*
BC No Rio, 106	*E4*
Beauty Bar, 7	*C2*
bOb Bar, 91	*C4*
Coup, 55	*D3*
Coyote Ugly, 49	*D2*
d.b.a., 69	*D3*
Fun, 115	*C6*
Idlewild, 90	*C4*
Izzy Bar, 38	*D2*
Joe's Bar, 56	*D3*
Joe's Pub, 15	*B2*
KGB, 83	*B3*
Korova Milk Bar, 2	*D3*
La Linea, 67	*D4*
Lucky Cheng's, 66	*D3*
Max Fish, 98	*D4*
McSorley's, 23	*B2*
Motor City Bar, 109	*D5*
Open Air, 48	*D2*
Orchard Bar, 95	*D4*
The Patio, 68	*D3*
Rivertown Lounge, 94	*D4*
Sake Bar Decibel, 30	C2
The Slipper Room, 101	*D4*
Spa, 10	*A1*
Tenth St. Lounge, 35	*C2*
Tribe, 43	*D2*
Webster Hall, 9	B1

East Village and Lower East Side
see key p. 319
200 yards
200 meters
N
Szold Pl.
Avenue D
Avenue C
Avenue B
Avenue A
First Avenue
Second Avenue
Third Avenue
Fourth Ave.
Lafayette St.
E. 15th St.
E. 14th St.
E. 13th St.
E. 12th St.
E. 11th St.
E. 10th St.
E. 9th St.
E. 8th St.
St. Mark's Pl.
E. 7th St.
E. 6th St.
E. 5th St.
E. 4th St.
E. 3rd St.
E. 2nd St.
Stuyvesant St.
Tompkins Square Park
ALPHABET CITY
EAST VILLAGE
COOPER SQUARE
Cooper Union
NOHO
Gt. Jones St.
Bond St.
Astor Pl.
Wanamaker Pl.
Waverly Pl.
University Pl.
New York University
W. 4th St.
W. 3rd St.
Shinbone
UNION SQUARE

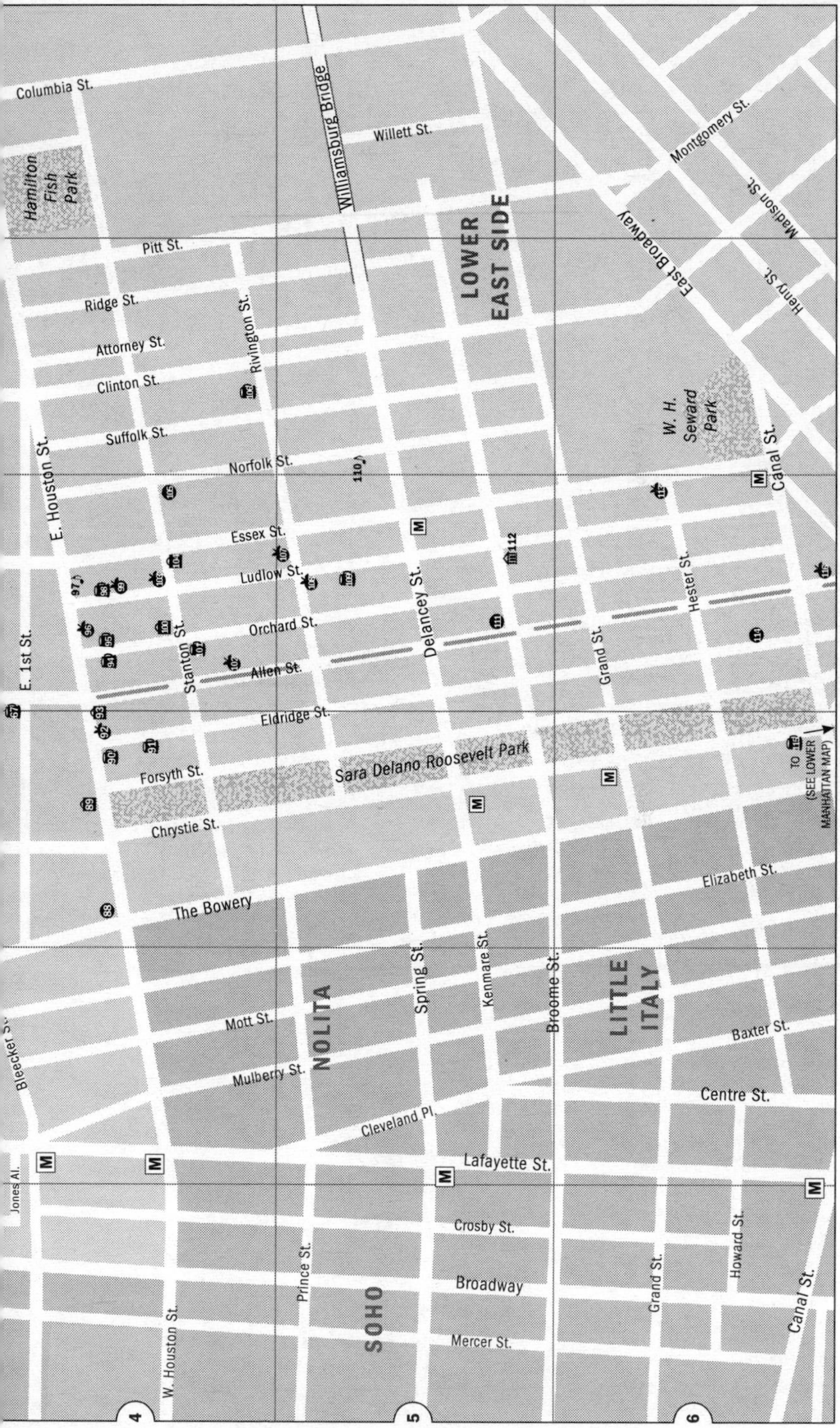
Columbia St.
Willett St.
Williamsburg Bridge
Montgomery St.
Madison St.
Hamilton Fish Park
LOWER EAST SIDE
East Broadway
Pitt St.
Henry St.
Ridge St.
Rivington St.
Attorney St.
Clinton St.
W. H. Seward Park
Suffolk St.
E. Houston St.
Canal St.
Norfolk St.
Essex St.
Ludlow St.
Delancey St.
Hester St.
Orchard St.
E. 1st St.
Stanton St.
Grand St.
Allen St.
Eldridge St.
Sara Delano Roosevelt Park
Forsyth St.
TO (SEE LOWER MANHATTAN MAP)
Chrystie St.
Elizabeth St.
The Bowery
Spring St.
Kenmare St.
Broome St.
LITTLE ITALY
NOLITA
Mott St.
Bleecker St.
Baxter St.
Mulberry St.
Centre St.
Cleveland Pl.
Lafayette St.
Jones Al.
Crosby St.
Prince St.
Howard St.
Broadway
SOHO
Mercer St.
W. Houston St.
4
5
6

Lower Midtown
see key p. 324
A
B
C
1
2
3
4
5
6
W. 42nd St.
W. 41st St.
W. 40th St.
W. 39th St.
W. 38th St.
W. 37th St.
W. 36th St.
W. 35th St.
W. 34th St.
W.33rd St.
W. 32nd St.
W. 31st St.
W. 30th St.
W. 29th St.
W. 28th St.
W. 27th St.
W. 26th St.
W. 25th St.
W. 24th St.
W. 23rd St.
W. 22nd St.
W. 21st St.
W. 20th St.
W. 19th St.
W. 18th St.
W. 17th St.
W. 16th St.
W. 15th St.
W. 14th St.
Port Authority Bus Terminal
Lincoln Tunnel
Jacob K. Javits Convention Center
GARMENT
DISTRICT
Macy's
HERALD
SQUARE
General Post Office
Madison Square Garden
Penn Station
Chelsea Park
CHELSEA
Eleventh Ave.
Tenth Ave.
Ninth Ave.
Eighth Ave.
Seventh Ave.
West Side Hwy.
Eleventh Ave.
TO 94
TO 96
97
0
550 yards
0
500 meters
N

D
E
F
Bryant Park
New York Public Library
American Standard Building
MURRAY HILL
(VEHICULAR TUNNEL BELOW STREET)
E. 42nd St.
E. 41st St.
E. 40th St.
E. 39th St.
E. 38th St.
E. 37th St.
E. 36th St.
E. 35th St.
E. 34th St.
E. 33rd St.
E. 32nd St.
E. 31st St.
E. 30th St.
E. 29th St.
E. 28th St.
E. 27th St.
E. 26th St.
E. 25th St.
E. 24th St.
E. 23rd St.
E. 22nd St.
E. 21st St.
E. 20th St.
E. 19th St.
E. 18th St.
E. 17th St.
E. 16th St.
E. 15th St.
E. 14th St.
E. 13th St.
W. 13th St.
Madison Ave.
Park Ave.
Lexington Ave.
Third Ave.
Second Ave.
First Ave.
FDR Dr.
Empire State Building
Broadway
Fifth Ave.
Avenue of the Americas (Sixth Ave.)
Madison Square
Park Ave. S.
GRAMERCY PARK
Gramercy Park
FLATIRON DISTRICT
Union Square
Irving Pl.
Stuyvesant Square

Lower Midtown

see map pp. 322–323

ACCOMMODATIONS

Carlton Arms Hotel, 29	E4
Chelsea Center Hostel, 93	B3
Chelsea Inn, 61	D5
Chelsea International Hostel, 73	C5
Chelsea Savoy Hotel, 74	C4
Gershwin Hotel, 20	D4
Herald Square Hotel, 10	D3
Hotel 17, 32	F5
Hotel Chelsea, 75	C4
Hotel Grand Union, 19	E3
Hotel Stanford, 9	D3
Hotel Wolcott, 11	D3
International Student Hospice, 24	E3
Madison Hotel, 21	E4
Murray Hill Inn, 25	E3
Senton Hotel, 15	D4
ThirtyThirty, 17	D3
Union Square Inn, 34	F6

FOOD AND DRINK

71 Irving Place, 42	E5
Bendix Diner, 80	B5
Blue Moon Mexican Café, 82	B5
Chat 'n' Chew, 53	D5
Coffee Shop Bar, 50	E5
Curry in a Hurry, 23	E3
F & B, 77	C4
Jai-Ya, 27	E3
Kitchen, 79	B5
Little Pie Co., 88	B6
Mary Ann's, 83	C6
Minar, 12	D3
Molly's, 30	F5
Negril, 92	B4
Pete's Tavern, 41	E5
Republic, 51	E6
Spring Joy, 81	B5
Sunburst Espresso Bar, 31	E5
Tibetan Kitchen, 26	E3
Zen Palate, 37	E6

SHOPPING

Books of Wonder, 60	D5
The Complete Traveller Bookstore, 4	E2
H & M, 5	D2
Kikko Import, Inc., 14	D3
Lord and Taylor, 1	D1
Manhattan Mall, 7	C3
Midnight Records, 78	C4
Nobody Beats the Wiz, 8	D3
Reminiscence, 67	D4
Revolution Books, 62	D5
Rock and Soul, 6	C2
Throb, 33	F6
Weiss and Mahoney, 54	D5

SIGHTS

69th Regiment Armory, 28	E4
American Academy of Dramatic Arts, 18	E3
Chelsea Market, 87	B6
Church of the Incarnation, 3	E2
Church of the Transfiguration, 16	D3
Cushman Row, 86	B5
Flatiron Building, 56	D4
Flower District, 13	C3
General Theological Seminary, 91	B5
Hotel Chelsea, 76	C4
Metropolitan Life Insurance Tower, 45	E4
National Arts Club, 44	E5
New York Life Insurance Building, 22	E4
Pierpont Morgan Library, 2	E2
The Player's Club, 43	E5
St. Peter's Church, 85	B5
The Theodore Roosevelt Birthplace, 46	E5
Union Square Savings Bank, 38	E6

NIGHTLIFE

B.M.W. Bar, 69	C5
Billiard Club, 72	C5
Centrofly, 63	D5
Cheetah, 58	D5
Chelsea Bar and Billiards, 59	D5
Gotham Comedy Club, 65	D4
Heartland Brewery, 49	E5
Lemon, 48	E5
Lola, 66	D4
Metronome Club, 55	D5
Ohm, 57	D4
Old Town Bar and Grill, 47	E5
Passerby, 90	B6
Peter McManus, 70	C5
Tramps, 64	D5
Tunnel, 94	A3
Upright Citizens Brigade Theater, 68	C4
Wild Lily Tea Room, 95	A5

ARTS & ENTERTAINMENT

Bowlmor, 52	E6
Chelsea Piers, 96	A5
The Cooler, 89	B6
Dance Theater Workshop, 71	C5
De La Guarda, 39	E6
Irving Plaza, 35	E6
Joyce Theater, 84	B5
The Kitchen, 97	A5
Union Square Theater, 40	E5
Vineyard Theater Company's Dimson Theater, 36	E6

Midtown

see map pp. 326-327

ACCOMMODATIONS

Aladdin Hotel, 64	*B4*
Americana Inn, 43	*D5*
Best Western President Hotel, 60	*C3*
Big Apple Hostel, 50	*C4*
Broadway Inn, 59	*F3*
Hudson Hotel, 2	*B2*
Milford Plaza, 58	*C4*
New York Inn, 61	*B4*
Pickwick Arms Hotel, 28	*C3*
Portland Square Hotel, 48	*C3*
Quality Hotel and Suites, 41	*D4*
Skyline Hotel, 68	*A3*
YMCA–Vanderbilt, 30	*F3*

FOOD AND DRINK

Aureole, 24	*E1*
Becco, 66	*B4*
Dishes, 32	*E4*
Fresco by Scotto, on the go, 34	*E3*
Hourglass Tavern, 67	*B4*
Le Beaujolais, 66	*B4*
Manganaro's, 72	*B5*
Mangia, 36	*D3*
Original Fresco Tortillas, 70	*B5*
Sapporo, 51	*C3*
Sardi's, 55	*C4*
Teuscher Chocolatier, 38	*D3*

NIGHTLIFE

Chase, 3	*C2*
La Nueva Escuelita, 71	*B5*

SHOPPING

Bergdorff-Goodman, 17	*D2*
The Counter Spy Shop, 35	*D3*
The Drama Book Shop, 52	*C3*
F.A.O. Schwarz, 16	*D2*
Fine Line, 26	*E2*
Gotham Book Mart, 40	*D3*
Hacker Art Books, 14	*D2*
Hammacher Schlemmer, 25	*E2*
Saks Fifth Avenue, 37	*D3*
Tiffany & Co., 20	*D2*

ARTS & ENTERTAINMENT

Birdland, 62	*B4*
Carnegie Hall, 6	*C2*
City Center, 7	*C2*
Lamb's, 49	*C4*
Late Show with David Letterman, 4	*C2*
Manhattan Theater Club, 9	*C2*
NBC Studios, 46	*D3*
Playwrights Horizons, 69	*B4*
Primary Stages, 63	*B4*
Roseland, 5	*C3*
Samuel Beckett Theater, 69	*B4*
Shubert Theater, 57	*C4*
Swing 46, 65	*B4*
Ziegfeld, 8	*C2*

SIGHTS

The Algonquin Hotel, 42	*D4*
Citigroup Center, 27	*E2*
City Center Theater, 10	*C2*
Crown Building, 18	*D2*
The Dramatists Guild, 53	*C4*
GE Building, 45	*D3*
John Jay College of Criminal Justice, 1	*A2*
The New York Times, 54	*C4*
Pulitzer Fountain, 15	*D1*
Radio City Music Hall, 47	*D3*
Schubert Alley, 56	*C4*
Sony Plaza, 21	*D2*
St. Bartholomew's Church, 33	*E3*
Trump Tower, 19	*D2*
Unicef House, 31	*F4*
University Club, 13	*D2*

MUSEUMS & GALLERIES

American Craft Museum, 11	*D3*
Christie's, 39	*D3*
Fuller Building, 23	*E2*
International Center of Photography, 44	*D4*
Japan Society, 29	*F3*
Museum of Modern Art	*D2*
Museum of Television and Radio, 12	*D3*
Pace Gallery, 22	*E2*

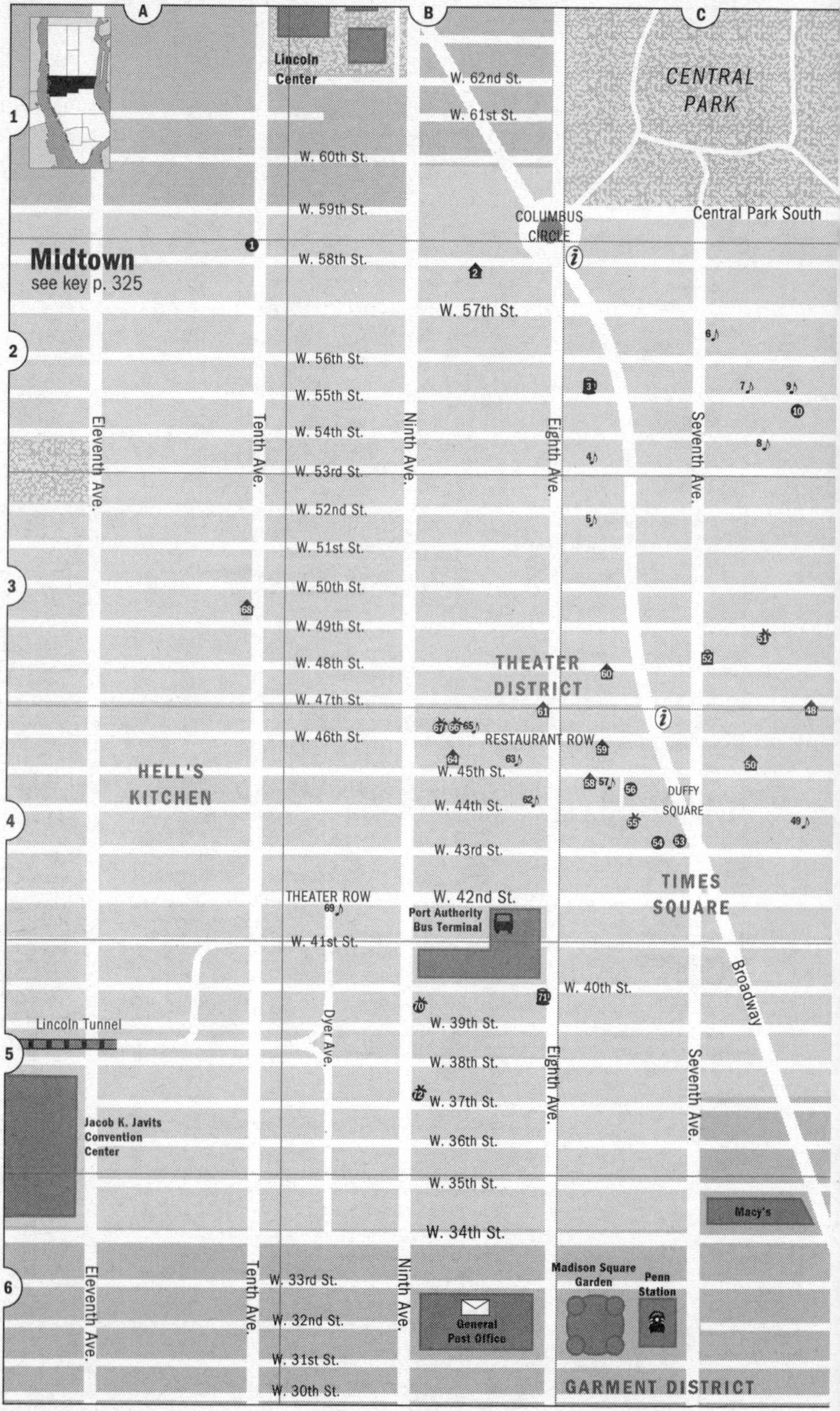
Midtown
see key p. 325
A
B
C
1
2
3
4
5
6
Lincoln Center
CENTRAL PARK
W. 62nd St.
W. 61st St.
W. 60th St.
W. 59th St.
COLUMBUS CIRCLE
Central Park South
W. 58th St.
W. 57th St.
W. 56th St.
W. 55th St.
W. 54th St.
W. 53rd St.
W. 52nd St.
W. 51st St.
W. 50th St.
W. 49th St.
W. 48th St.
W. 47th St.
W. 46th St.
W. 45th St.
W. 44th St.
W. 43rd St.
W. 42nd St.
W. 41st St.
W. 40th St.
W. 39th St.
W. 38th St.
W. 37th St.
W. 36th St.
W. 35th St.
W. 34th St.
W. 33rd St.
W. 32nd St.
W. 31st St.
W. 30th St.
Eleventh Ave.
Tenth Ave.
Ninth Ave.
Eighth Ave.
Seventh Ave.
Broadway
Dyer Ave.
THEATER DISTRICT
RESTAURANT ROW
HELL'S KITCHEN
DUFFY SQUARE
TIMES SQUARE
THEATER ROW
Port Authority Bus Terminal
Lincoln Tunnel
Jacob K. Javits Convention Center
Macy's
Madison Square Garden
Penn Station
General Post Office
GARMENT DISTRICT

D
E
F
E. 62nd St.
E. 61st St.
E. 60th St.
Queensboro Bridge.
Grand Army Plaza
Bloomingdale's
E. 59th St.
Plaza Hotel
E. 58th St.
E. 57th St.
Sutton Pl.
Ave. of the Americas
Fifth Ave.
E. 56th St.
E. 55th St.
E. 54th St.
Madison Ave.
Second Ave.
First Ave.
Museum of Modern Art
E. 53rd St.
E. 52nd St.
E. 51st St.
St. Patrick's Cathedral
Third Ave.
Beekman Pl.
E. 50th St.
Rockefeller Center
Park Ave.
Waldorf Astoria
Lexington Ave.
E. 49th St.
(VEHICULAR TUNNEL BELOW STREET)
E. 48th St.
DIAMOND ROW
E. 47th St.
United Nations
E. 46th St.
E. 45th St.
(Sixth Ave.)
Vanderbilt Ave.
Metlife Building
E. 44th St.
First Ave.
Grand Central Terminal
Chrysler Building
E. 43rd St.
E. 42nd St.
Tudor City Pl.
BRYANT PARK
New York Public Library
Madison Ave.
E. 41st St.
E. 40th St.
(VEHICULAR TUNNEL BELOW STREET)
Park Ave.
E. 39th St.
American Standard Building
FDR Dr.
Queens-Midtown Tunnel
MURRAY HILL
E. 38th St.
Fifth Ave.
E. 37th St.
Pierpont Morgan Library
Lexington Ave.
E. 36th St.
Tunnel Entrance St.
E. 35th St.
Empire State Building
HERALD SQUARE
E. 34th St.
E. 33rd St.
E. 32nd St.
E. 31st St.
E. 30th St.
0 yards 275
0 meters 250
N

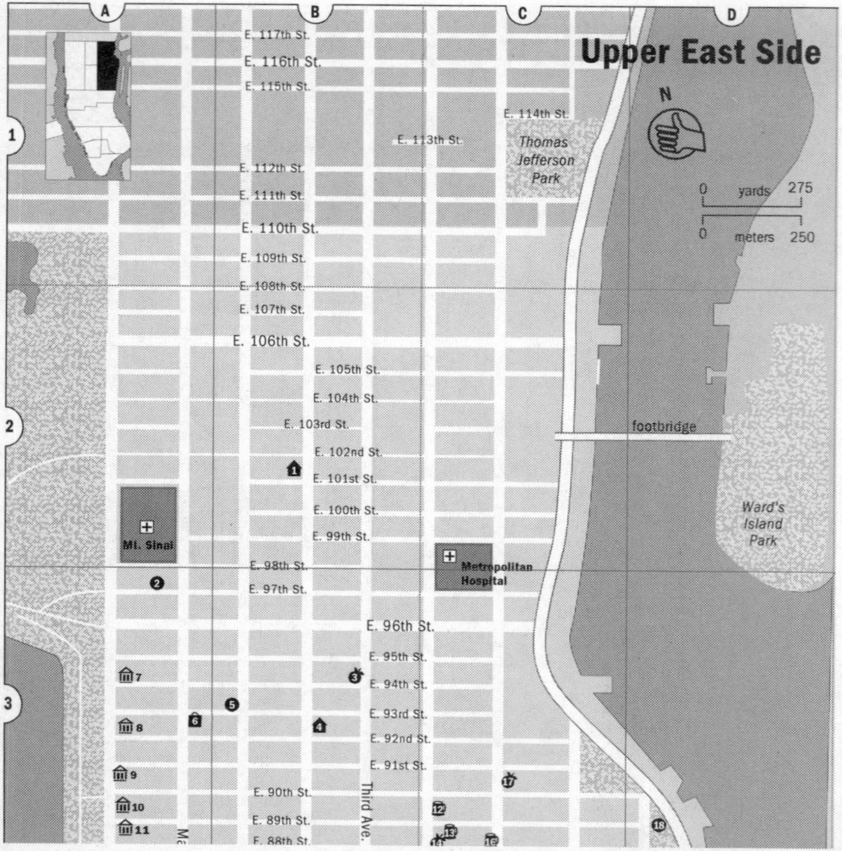

Upper East Side

ACCOMMODATIONS

DeHirsch Residence, 4	B3
Manhattan Youth Castle, 1	B2

FOOD AND DRINK

Barking Dog Luncheonette, 3	B3
Dallas BBQ, 37	B5
Candle Café, 32	B5
EJ's Luncheonette, 36	B5
El Pollo, 17	C3
Grace's Marketplace, 38	B5
Jackson Hole, 61	B6
Le Pain Quotidia, 23	A4
Papaya King, 21	B4
Saigon Grill, 14	C3
Tony's di Napoli, 20	C4
Viand, 52	A6

SHOPPING

Argosy Bookstore, 56	B5
Barneys NY, 51	A6
Bloomingdale's, 57	B6
Chick Darrow's Fun Antiques & Collectibles, 62	C6
Corner Bookstore, 6	A3
Encore, 24	A4
HMV, 22	B4
Michael's, 27	A4
Rita Ford Music Boxes, 48	A6
Tender Buttons, 58	B6

MUSEUMS

Asia Society, 39	B5
Cooper-Hewitt, 9	A3
Frick Collection, 40	A5
Guggenheim Museum, 11	A3
International Center of Photography, 7	A3
Jewish Museum, 8	A3
Metropolitan Museum of Art, 26	A4

ARTS & ENTERTAINMENT

Dicapo Opera Theater, 33	B5
Cultural Institutes:	
Alliance Française, 55	B6
Americas Society, 43	B6
China Institute, 60	B6
Goethe Institute, 25	A4
Italian Cultural Institute, 41	B5
Spanish Institute, 42	B5

SIGHTS

Gracie Mansion, 18	D3
Grolier Club, 54	B6
Henderson Place Historic District, 19	D4
Hunter College, 45	B6
Holy Trinity, 15	C4
Knickerbocker Club, 49	A6
Lotos Club, 46	A6
The Metropolitan Club, 50	A6
Russian Orthodox Church, 5	B3
St. Jean Baptiste, 34	B5
St. Nicholas Russian Orthodox Cathedral, 2	A3
Temple Emanu-El, 47	A6
Union Club, 44	B5

NIGHTLIFE

American Trash, 29	C5
Auction House, 13	C3
Brother Jimmy's Carolina Kitchen BBQ, 30	C5
Comic Strip Live, 28	B4
Dangerfield's, 63	C6
Match Uptown, 53	A6
Mo's Caribbean Bar and Grille, 31	C5
Ozone, 12	C3
Spancill Hill, 16	C3

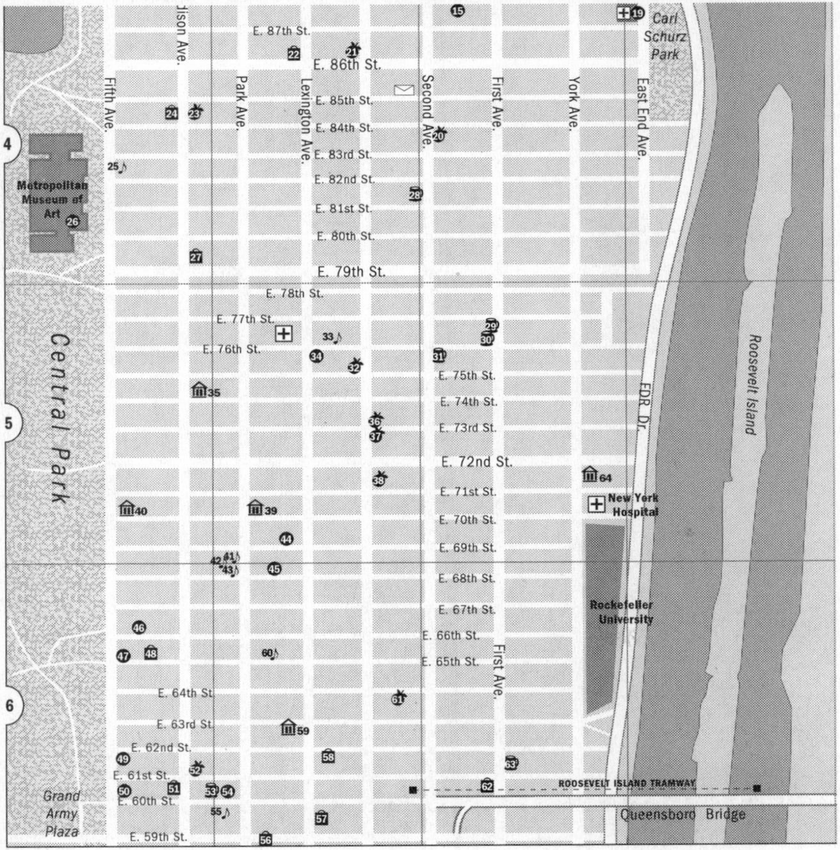

Museum of American Illustration, 59 — B6
National Academy Museum, 10 — A3
Sotheby's. 64 — C5
Whitney Museum, 35 — A5

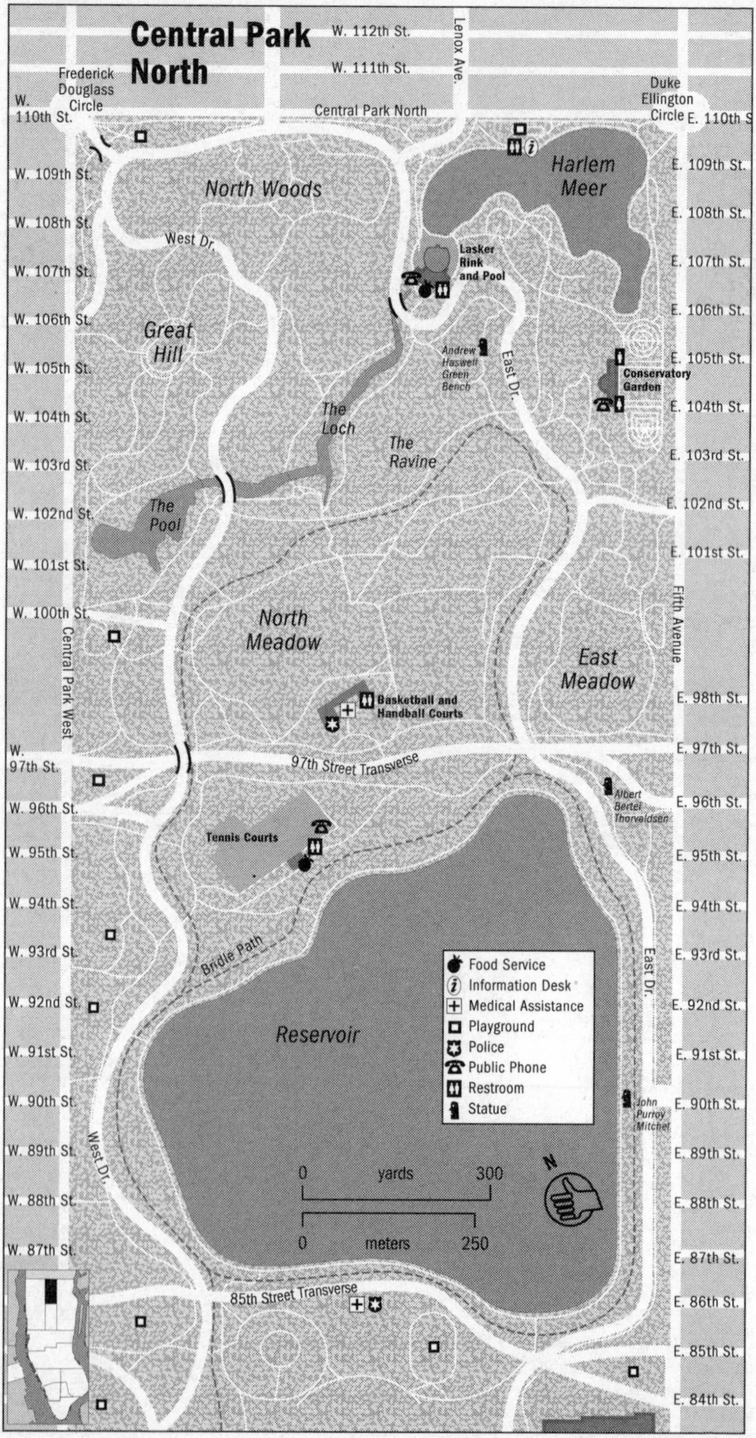
Central Park North
W. 112th St.
W. 111th St.
Lenox Ave.
Frederick Douglass Circle
W. 110th St.
Central Park North
Duke Ellington Circle
E. 110th St.
North Woods
Harlem Meer
W. 109th St.
E. 109th St.
W. 108th St.
E. 108th St.
West Dr.
Lasker Rink and Pool
W. 107th St.
E. 107th St.
W. 106th St.
E. 106th St.
Great Hill
Andrew Haswell Green Bench
East Dr.
W. 105th St.
E. 105th St.
Conservatory Garden
The Loch
W. 104th St.
E. 104th St.
The Ravine
W. 103rd St.
E. 103rd St.
The Pool
W. 102nd St.
E. 102nd St.
W. 101st St.
E. 101st St.
Fifth Avenue
W. 100th St.
North Meadow
Central Park West
East Meadow
Basketball and Handball Courts
E. 98th St.
W. 97th St.
97th Street Transverse
E. 97th St.
Albert Bertel Thorvaldsen
W. 96th St.
E. 96th St.
Tennis Courts
W. 95th St.
E. 95th St.
W. 94th St.
E. 94th St.
W. 93rd St.
Bridle Path
East Dr.
E. 93rd St.
Food Service
Information Desk
Medical Assistance
Playground
Police
Public Phone
Restroom
Statue
W. 92nd St.
E. 92nd St.
Reservoir
W. 91st St.
E. 91st St.
John Purroy Mitchel
W. 90th St.
E. 90th St.
W. 89th St.
West Dr.
E. 89th St.
0 yards 300
0 meters 250
N
W. 88th St.
E. 88th St.
W. 87th St.
E. 87th St.
85th Street Transverse
E. 86th St.
E. 85th St.
E. 84th St.

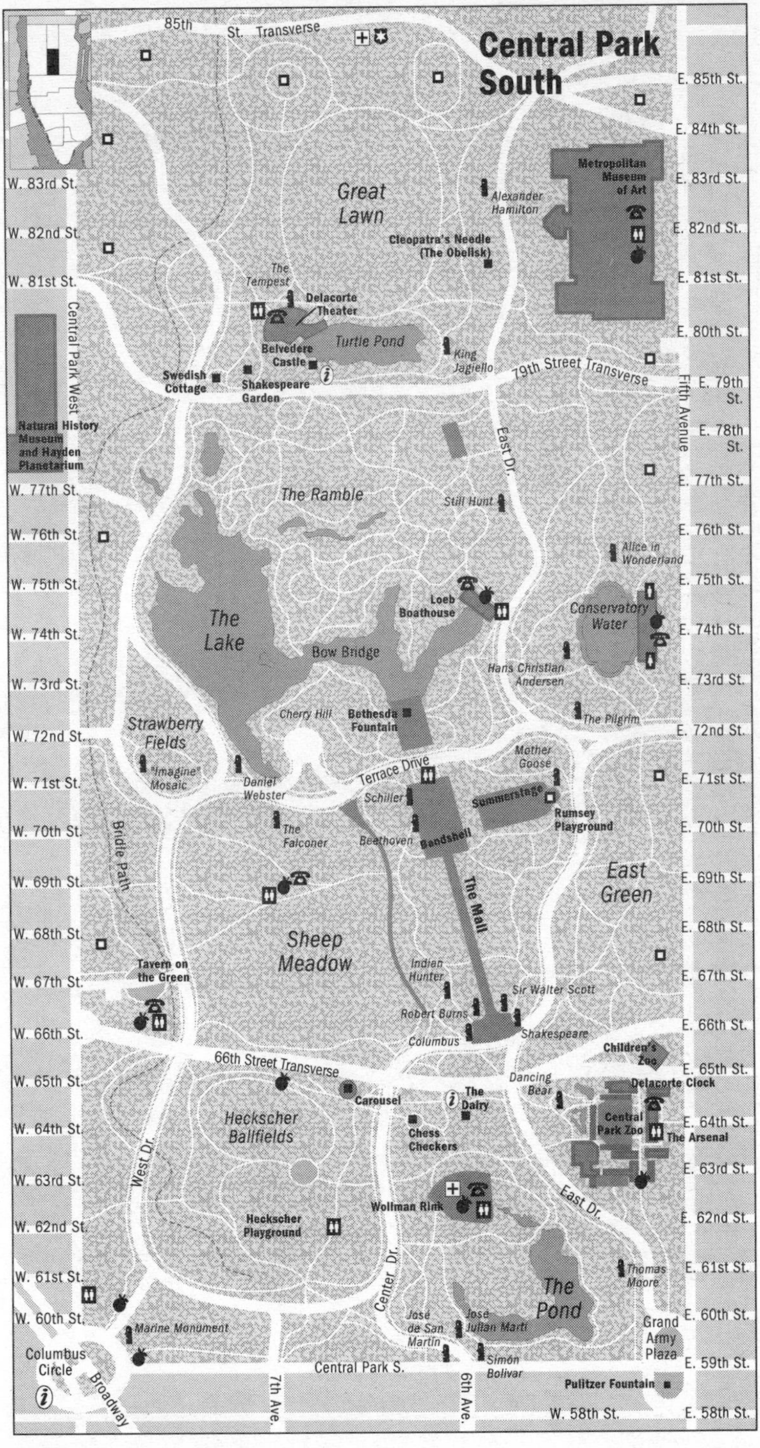
Central Park South
85th St. Transverse
Great Lawn
Metropolitan Museum of Art
Alexander Hamilton
Cleopatra's Needle (The Obelisk)
The Tempest
Delacorte Theater
Turtle Pond
Belvedere Castle
King Jagiello
79th Street Transverse
Swedish Cottage
Shakespeare Garden
Central Park West
Natural History Museum and Hayden Planetarium
East Dr.
Fifth Avenue
The Ramble
Still Hunt
Alice in Wonderland
Loeb Boathouse
Conservatory Water
The Lake
Bow Bridge
Hans Christian Andersen
Cherry Hill
Bethesda Fountain
The Pilgrim
Strawberry Fields
"Imagine" Mosaic
Daniel Webster
Terrace Drive
Mother Goose
Schiller
Summerstage
Rumsey Playground
The Falconer
Beethoven
Bandshell
Bridle Path
East Green
The Mall
Sheep Meadow
Tavern on the Green
Indian Hunter
Sir Walter Scott
Robert Burns
Shakespeare
Columbus
66th Street Transverse
Children's Zoo
Delacorte Clock
Dancing Bear
Carousel
The Dairy
Heckscher Ballfields
Chess Checkers
Central Park Zoo
The Arsenal
West Dr.
Wollman Rink
East Dr.
Heckscher Playground
Center Dr.
Thomas Moore
The Pond
Marine Monument
José de San Martín
José Julián Martí
Grand Army Plaza
Columbus Circle
Broadway
Central Park S.
Simón Bolívar
Pulitzer Fountain
7th Ave.
6th Ave.
W. 58th St.
W. 83rd St.
W. 82nd St.
W. 81st St.
W. 77th St.
W. 76th St.
W. 75th St.
W. 74th St.
W. 73rd St.
W. 72nd St.
W. 71st St.
W. 70th St.
W. 69th St.
W. 68th St.
W. 67th St.
W. 66th St.
W. 65th St.
W. 64th St.
W. 63rd St.
W. 62nd St.
W. 61st St.
W. 60th St.
E. 85th St.
E. 84th St.
E. 83rd St.
E. 82nd St.
E. 81st St.
E. 80th St.
E. 79th St.
E. 78th St.
E. 77th St.
E. 76th St.
E. 75th St.
E. 74th St.
E. 73rd St.
E. 72nd St.
E. 71st St.
E. 70th St.
E. 69th St.
E. 68th St.
E. 67th St.
E. 66th St.
E. 65th St.
E. 64th St.
E. 63rd St.
E. 62nd St.
E. 61st St.
E. 60th St.
E. 59th St.
E. 58th St.

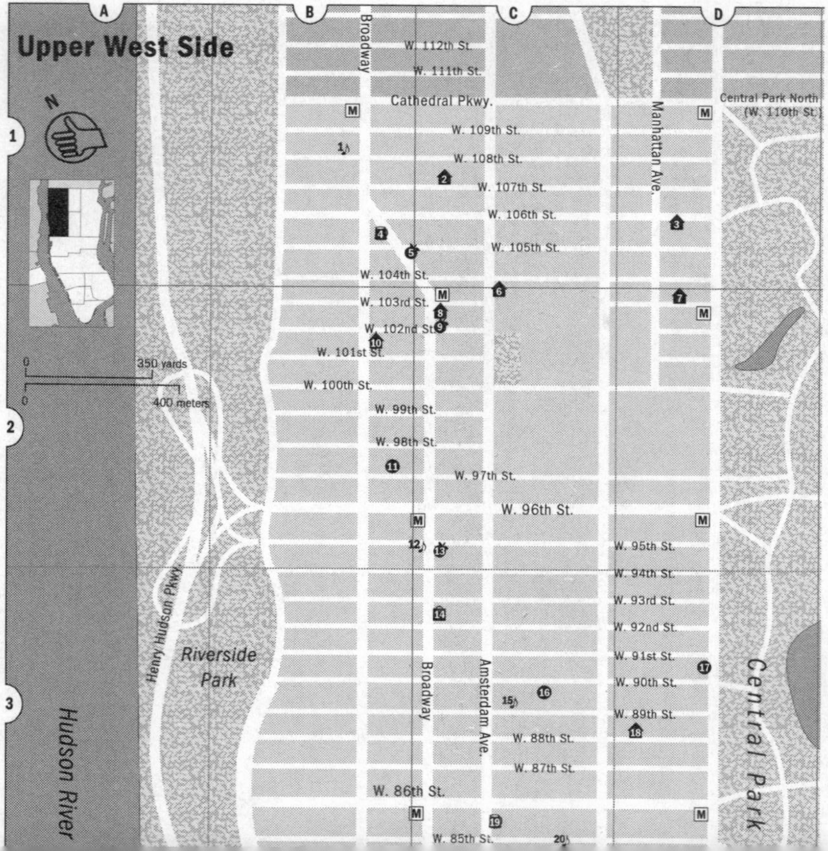

Upper West Side

ACCOMMODATIONS	
The Amsterdam Inn, 38	C4
Central Park Hostel, 7	D2
Hotel Hayden Hall, 31	C4
Hotel Belleclaire, 37	C4
Hotel Olcott, 49	D5
International Student Center, 18	D3
Jazz on the Park, 3	D1
Malibu Studios Hotel, 8	C2
New York International HI-AYH Hostel, 6	C2
West End Studios, 10	B2
West Side Inn, 2	C1
West Side YMCA, 64	D6
FOOD AND DRINK	
Big Nick's Pizza and Burger Joint, 36	C4
Brother Jimmy's, 26	C4
Café La Fortuna, 47	D5
Café Lalo, 22	C4
Café Mozart, 51	C5
Good Enough to Eat, 21	C4
Gray's Papaya, 45	C5
H&H Bagels, 29	C4
Henry's, 5	B1
Hi-Life Bar and Grill, 24	C4
Ivy's Cafe, 46	C5
La Caridad 78 Restaurant, 35	C4
The Lemongrass Grill, 13	C2
Mama Mexico, 9	C2
Ollie's, 52	C5
Zabar's, 28	C4
SHOPPING	
Allan and Suzi, 30	C4
Applause Theater and Cinema Books, 44	C5
Gryphon Bookshops, 27	C4
Gryphon Record Shop, 43	C5
Maxilla & Mandible, 25	C4
Murder Ink, 14	C3
Ordning & Reda, 48	D5

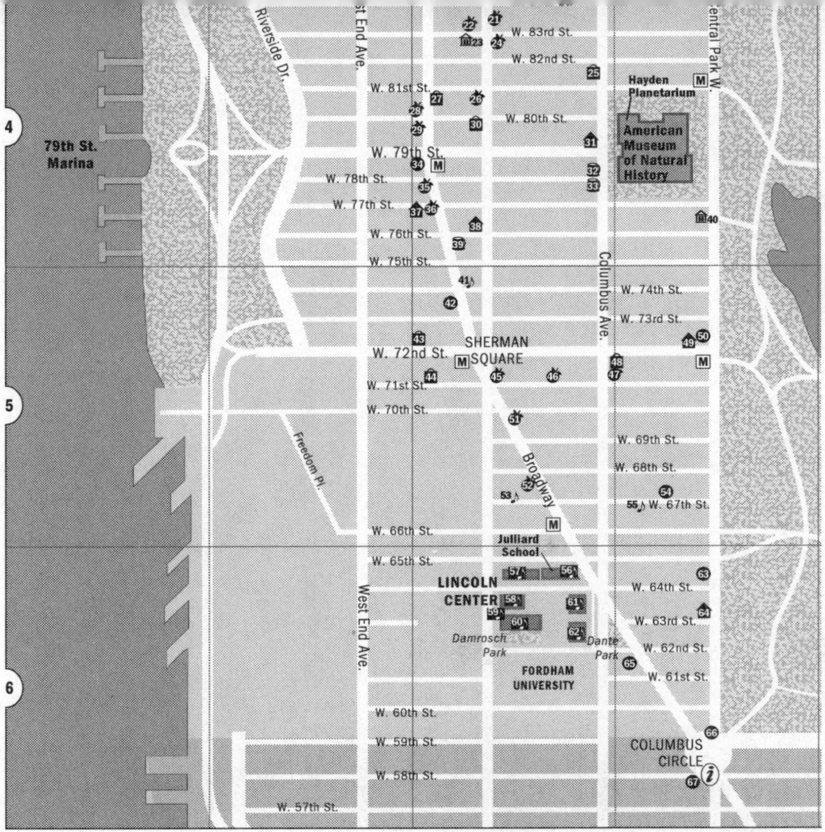

American Museum of Natural History	D4
The Children's Museum of Manhattan, 23	C4
New York Historical Society, 40	D4

♪ ARTS & ENTERTAINMENT

Beacon Theatre, 41	C5
Bloomingdale School of Music, 1	B1
Claremont Stables, 15	C3
Live with Regis (WABC), 55	D5
Mannes College of Music, 20	C3
Merkin Concert Hall, 53	C5
Symphony Space, 12	C2
at Lincoln Center:	
Alice Tully Hall, 56	C6
Avery Fisher Hall, 61	C6
Metropolitan Opera House, 60	C6
New York Public Library for the Performing Arts, 59	C6
New York State Theater, 62	C6
Vivian Beaumont Theater, 58	C6
Walter E. Reade Theater, 57	C6

SIGHTS

Ansonia Hotel, 42	C5
Apthorp Apartments, 34	C4
American Bible Society, 65	D6
Dakota Apartments, 50	D5
El Dorado Apartments, 17	D3
Hotel des Artistes, 54	D5
Lotus Garden, 11	B2
New York Convention Center and Visitors Bureau, 67	D6
New York Society for Ethical Culture, 63	D6
Trump International Hotel and Towers, 66	D6
West Side Community Garden, 16	C3

NIGHTLIFE

Evelyn Lounge, 32	C4
Merchants, 19	C3
Potion Lounge, 33	C4
Smoke, 4	B1
Yogi's, 39	C4

Harlem and Washington Heights

ACCOMMODATIONS

Crystal's Castle Bed & Breakfast, 35	*E6*
New York Bed and Breakfast, 34	*E6*
Sugar Hill International House, 8	*D4*
Uptown Hostel, 41	*E6*

FOOD AND DRINK

Amir's Falafel, 27	*C7*
Copeland's, 10	*C4*
Fairway, 19	*C5*
Gary's Jamaican Hot Pot, 18	*D5*
The Hungarian Pastry Shop, 30	*C7*
Koronet Pizza, 29	*C7*
La Marmite, 36	*D6*
Manna's Too!!, 16	*E5*
Massawa, 26	*D6*
Obaa Koryoe, 22	*C6*
Sisters, 44	*E6*
Sylvia's, 43	*E5*
Toast, 21	*C5*
Tom's Restaurant, 28	*C7*

SHOPPING

Liberation Bookstore, 17	*E5*
Sugar Hill Thrift Shop, 9	*D4*

MUSEUMS & GALLERIES

Audubon Terrace Museum Group, 6	*C3*
City Museum of New York, 32	*E7*
Cloisters, 1	*A2*
Museo El Barrio, 33	*E7*
Studio Museum, 40	*E6*

ARTS & ENTERTAINMENT

Apollo Theatre, 38	*D5*
Cotton Club, 20	*C5*
Lenox Lounge, 42	*E6*
Londel's, 13	*D4*
Showman's Café, 37	*D6*
St. Nick's Pub, 7	*D3*

SIGHTS

The Abyssinian Baptist Church, 14	*E4*
Audubon Ballroom, 4	*C2*
Cathedral of St. John the Divine, 31	*D7*
City College, 12	*D4*
Grant's Tomb, 24	*C6*
Hamilton Grange, 11	*D4*
Little Red Lighthouse, 2	*A3*
Morris-Jumel Mansion, 5	*D2*
Riverside Church, 25	*C6*
The Schomburg Center for Research in Black Culture, 15	*E5*
Teresa Hotel, 39	D6
Yeshiva University, 3	*B3*

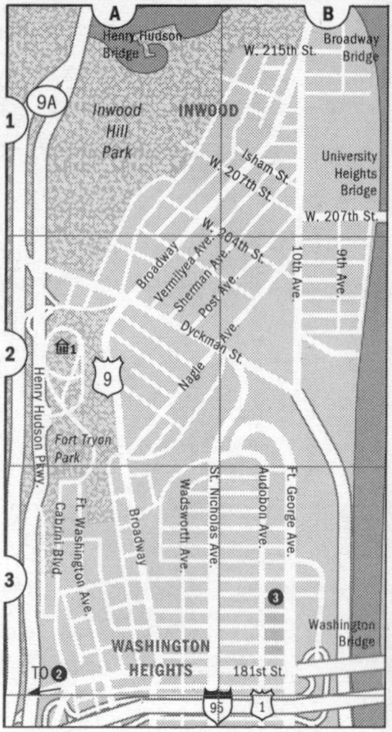

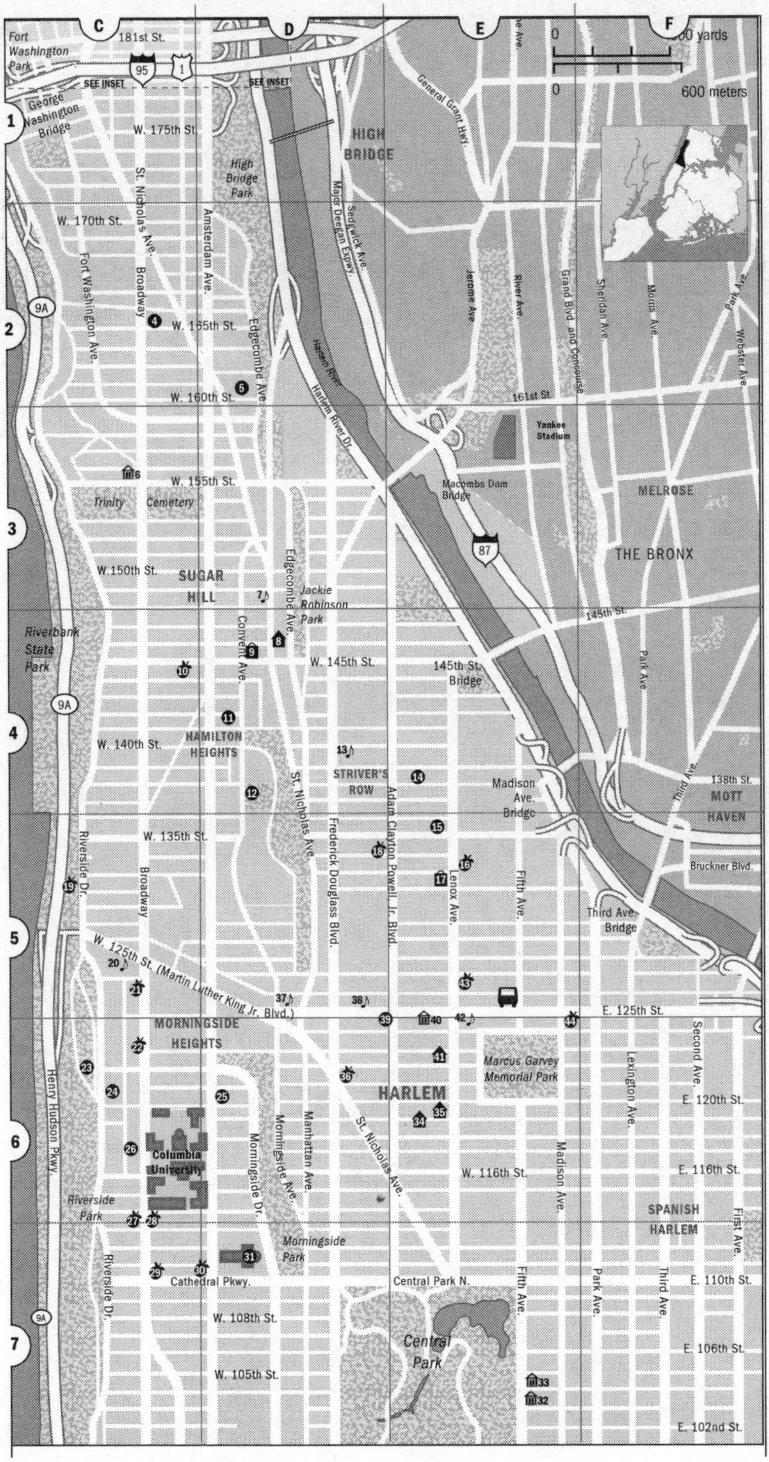
C
D
E
F
1
2
3
4
5
6
7
0
600 yards
0
600 meters
Fort Washington Park
181st St.
SEE INSET
SEE INSET
George Washington Bridge
W. 175th St.
High Bridge Park
HIGH BRIDGE
General Grant Hwy.
W. 170th St.
St. Nicholas Ave.
Amsterdam Ave.
Broadway
Fort Washington Ave.
W. 165th St.
Edgecombe Ave.
Major Deegan Expwy.
Sedgwick Ave.
Harlem River
Harlem River Dr.
Jerome Ave.
River Ave.
Grand Blvd. and Concourse
Sheridan Ave.
Morris Ave.
Park Ave.
Webster Ave.
W. 160th St.
161st St.
Yankee Stadium
W. 155th St.
Trinity Cemetery
Macombs Dam Bridge
MELROSE
THE BRONX
W.150th St.
SUGAR HILL
Jackie Robinson Park
145th St.
Riverbank State Park
Convent Ave.
W. 145th St.
145th St. Bridge
HAMILTON HEIGHTS
W. 140th St.
STRIVER'S ROW
St. Nicholas Ave.
Frederick Douglass Blvd.
Adam Clayton Powell, Jr. Blvd.
Madison Ave. Bridge
138th St.
MOTT HAVEN
Third Ave.
W. 135th St.
Riverside Dr.
Lenox Ave.
Fifth Ave.
Bruckner Blvd.
Third Ave. Bridge
W. 125th St. (Martin Luther King Jr. Blvd.)
E. 125th St.
MORNINGSIDE HEIGHTS
Marcus Garvey Memorial Park
HARLEM
Lexington Ave.
Second Ave.
E. 120th St.
Henry Hudson Pkwy.
Columbia University
Morningside Dr.
Morningside Ave.
Manhattan Ave.
Madison Ave.
W. 116th St.
E. 116th St.
Riverside Park
SPANISH HARLEM
First Ave.
Morningside Park
Cathedral Pkwy.
Central Park N.
Park Ave.
E. 110th St.
W. 108th St.
Central Park
E. 106th St.
W. 105th St.
E. 102nd St.
9A
95
1
87

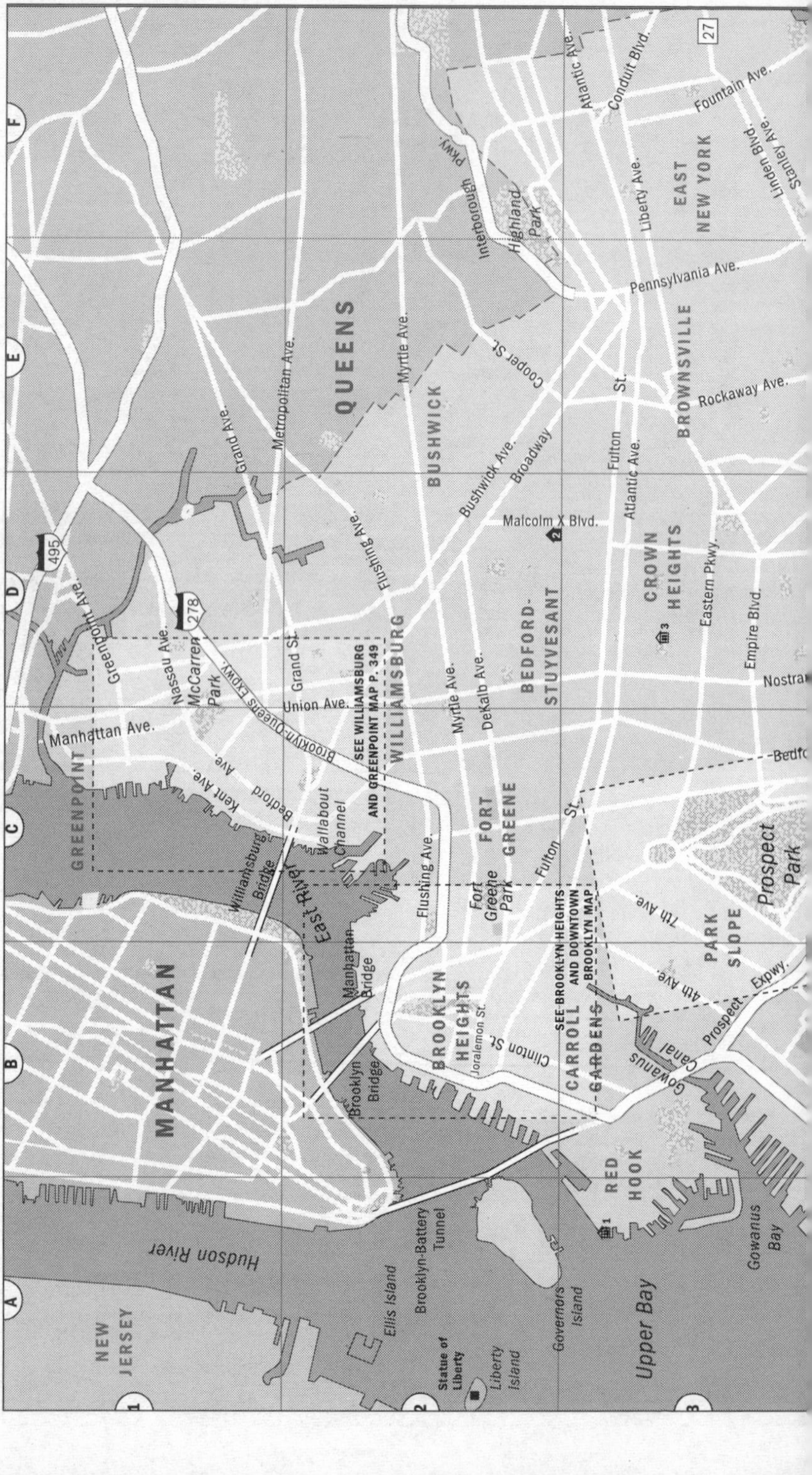

QUEENS
BUSHWICK
WILLIAMSBURG
GREENPOINT
BEDFORD-STUYVESANT
CROWN HEIGHTS
EAST NEW YORK
BROWNSVILLE
FORT GREENE
BROOKLYN HEIGHTS
CARROLL GARDENS
PARK SLOPE
RED HOOK
MANHATTAN
NEW JERSEY
Prospect Park
Highland Park
McCarren Park
Fort Greene Park
Hudson River
East River
Upper Bay
Gowanus Bay
Gowanus Canal
Wallabout Channel
Ellis Island
Liberty Island
Statue of Liberty
Governors Island
Brooklyn-Battery Tunnel
Brooklyn Bridge
Manhattan Bridge
Williamsburg Bridge
SEE WILLIAMSBURG AND GREENPOINT MAP P. 349
SEE BROOKLYN HEIGHTS AND DOWNTOWN BROOKLYN MAP
Brooklyn-Queens Expwy.
Prospect Expwy.
Interborough Pkwy.
Atlantic Ave.
Conduit Blvd.
Fountain Ave.
Linden Blvd.
Stanley Ave.
Liberty Ave.
Pennsylvania Ave.
Rockaway Ave.
Cooper St.
Myrtle Ave.
Metropolitan Ave.
Grand Ave.
Flushing Ave.
Bushwick Ave.
Broadway
Malcolm X Blvd.
Fulton St.
Eastern Pkwy.
Empire Blvd.
Nostra
Bedfo
Grand St.
Union Ave.
Nassau Ave.
Greenpoint Ave.
Manhattan Ave.
Kent Ave.
Bedford Ave.
DeKalb Ave.
7th Ave.
4th Ave.
Joralemon St.
Clinton St.
495
278
27
A
B
C
D
E
F
1
2
3

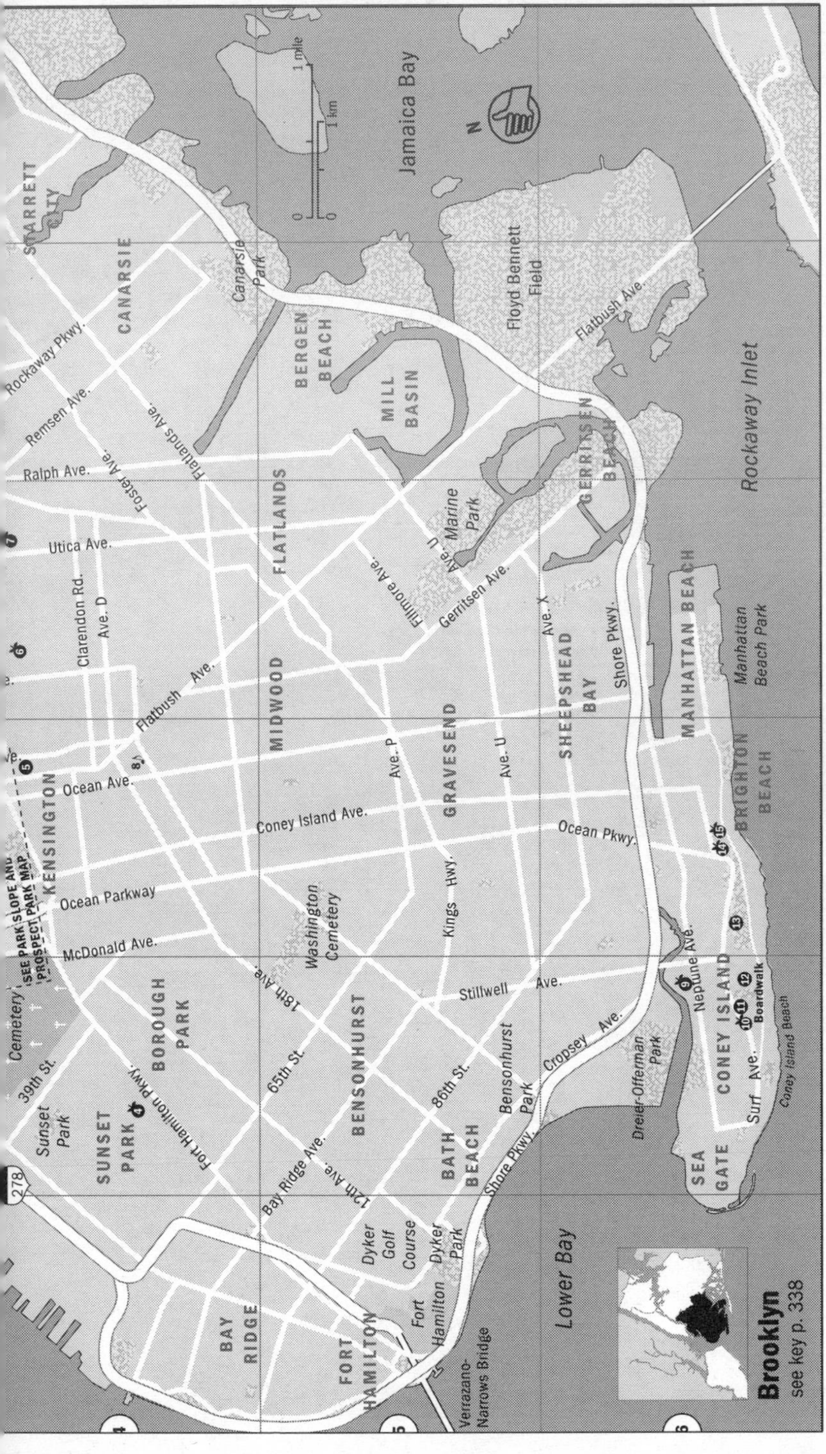

Brooklyn
see key p. 338
Jamaica Bay
Lower Bay
Rockaway Inlet
0
1 mile
1 km
N
STARRETT CITY
CANARSIE
Canarsie Park
BERGEN BEACH
MILL BASIN
Floyd Bennett Field
FLATLANDS
Marine Park
GERRITSEN BEACH
MANHATTAN BEACH
Manhattan Beach Park
BRIGHTON BEACH
CONEY ISLAND
Coney Island Beach
Boardwalk
SEA GATE
Dreier-Offerman Park
SHEEPSHEAD BAY
GRAVESEND
MIDWOOD
KENSINGTON
Washington Cemetery
BENSONHURST
Bensonhurst Park
BATH BEACH
BOROUGH PARK
SUNSET PARK
Sunset Park
Cemetery
SEE PARK SLOPE AND PROSPECT PARK MAP
BAY RIDGE
FORT HAMILTON
Fort Hamilton
Dyker Golf Course
Dyker Park
Verrazano-Narrows Bridge
Rockaway Pkwy.
Remsen Ave.
Ralph Ave.
Flatlands Ave.
Foster Ave.
Utica Ave.
Clarendon Rd.
Ave. D
Flatbush Ave.
Ocean Ave.
Coney Island Ave.
Ocean Parkway
McDonald Ave.
18th Ave.
39th St.
Fort Hamilton Pkwy.
65th St.
Bay Ridge Ave.
12th Ave.
86th St.
Shore Pkwy.
Cropsey Ave.
Stillwell Ave.
Kings Hwy.
Ave. P
Ave. U
Ave. X
Shore Pkwy.
Ocean Pkwy.
Neptune Ave.
Surf Ave.
Gerritsen Ave.
Fillmore Ave.
Ave. U
278
4
5
6
7
8
9
10
11
12
13
14
15

Brooklyn

see map pp. 336–337

ACCOMMODATIONS

Akwaaba Mansion, 2	*D2*

FOOD AND DRINK

Gia Lam, 4	*B4*
Hammond's Finger Lickin' Bakery, 7	*D4*
Nathan's, 10	*B6*
Primorski Restaurant, 14	*C6*
Roy's Jerk Chicken, 6	*D4*
Sea Lane Bakery, 15	*C6*
Totonno Pizzeria Napolitano, 9	*C2*

MUSEUMS & GALLERIES

Brooklyn Children's Museum, 3	*D3*
Waterfront Museum, 1	*A3*

ARTS & ENTERTAINMENT

Brooklyn Center for Performing Arts, 8	*C4*

SIGHTS

Coney Island Amusement Parks, Circus Sideshow, Museum, 11	*B6*
Erasmus Hall Academy, 5	*C4*
Keyspan Park, 12	*B4*
New York Aquarium, 13	*C6*

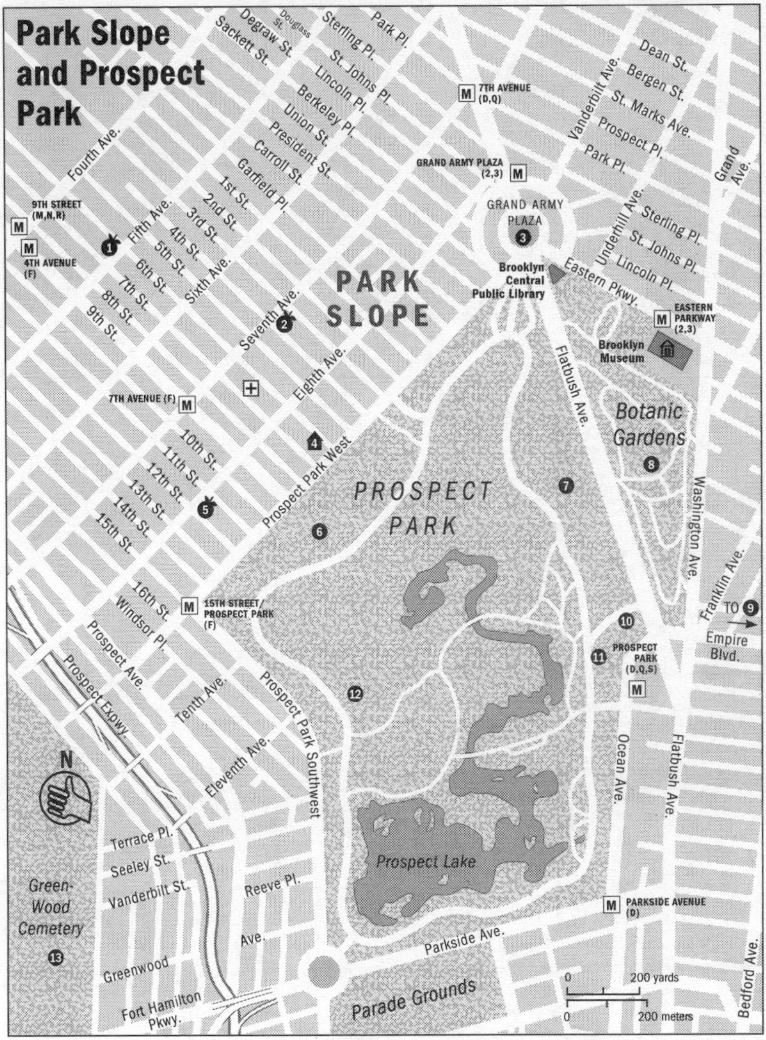

ACCOMMODATIONS

Bed & Breakfast on the Park, 4

FOOD

12th Street Bar and Grill, 5
Coco Roco, 1
Sotto Voce, 2

SIGHTS

Bandshell, 6
Botanic Gardens, 8
Carousel, 11
Ebbets Field, 9
Friends Cemetary, 12
Greenwood Cemetery, 13
Leffert's Homestead, 10
Memorial Arch, 3
Prospect Park Wildlife Center, 7

Queens

ACCOMMODATIONS

YMCA-Flushing, 21	D1

FOOD AND DRINK

Anand Bhavan, 14	B2
Eddie's Sweet Shop, 38	C3
Elias Corner, 4	B1
Flushing Noodle, 25	D1
Galaxy Pastry Shop, 6	B1
Jackson Diner, 15	B2
Jai-Ya, 16	B2
Joe's Shanghai, 20	D1
Kum Gang San, 24	D1
The Lemon Ice King of Corona, 29	C2
Nick's Pizza, 39	C2
Penang, 17	B2
Più Bello, 37	C2
Uncle George's, 7	A1
Rincon Salvadoreño, 41	D3

MUSEUMS & GALLERIES

American Museum of the Moving Image, 9	A2
Holocenter, 11	A2
Isamu Noguchi Garden Museum, 3	A1
Jamaica Arts Center, 43	D3
MOMA Queens, 12	A2
New York Center for Media Arts, 11	A2
Phun Phactory, 11	A2
PS1 Contemporary Art Center, 11	A2

ARTS & ENTERTAINMENT

Colden Center for the Performing Arts, 33	D2
Queens Theater in the Park, 34	C2
Thalia Spanish Theater, 13	A2

SIGHTS

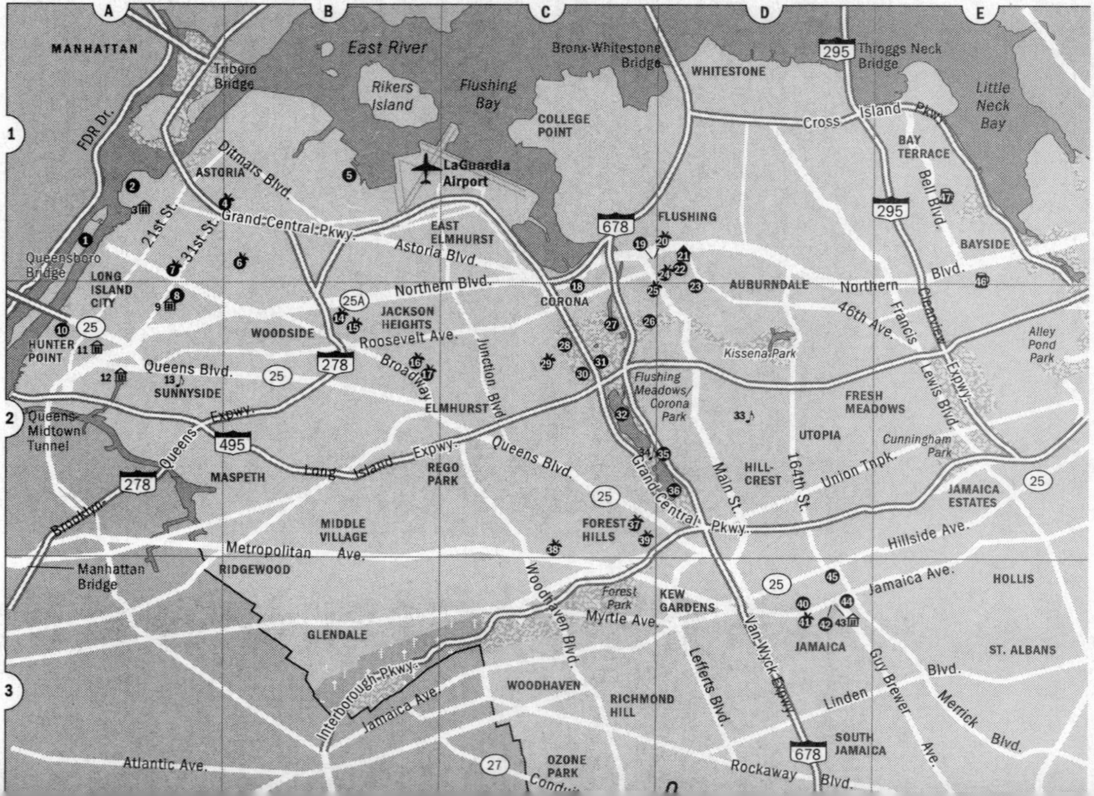

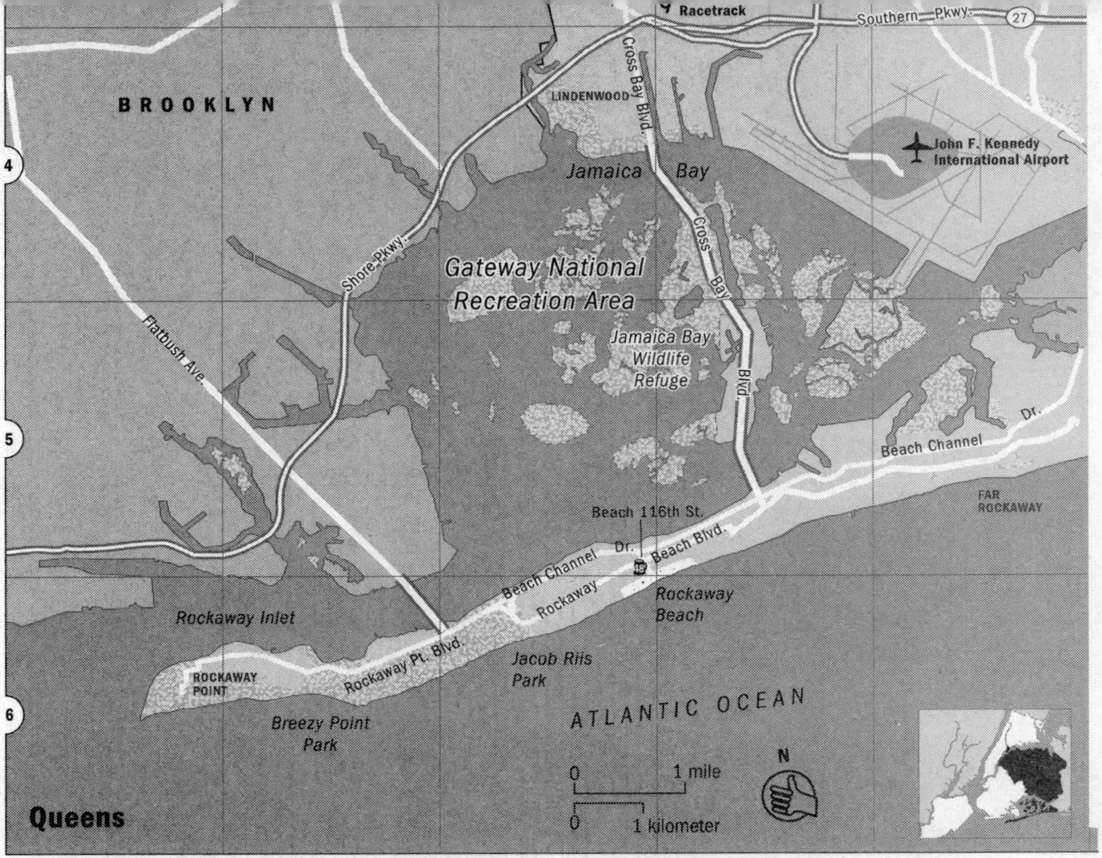

Racetrack
Southern Pkwy.
27
BROOKLYN
LINDENWOOD
Cross Bay Blvd.
John F. Kennedy International Airport
4
Jamaica Bay
Shore Pkwy.
Gateway National Recreation Area
Jamaica Bay Wildlife Refuge
Flatbush Ave.
5
Beach Channel Dr.
FAR ROCKAWAY
Beach 116th St.
Rockaway Beach Blvd.
48
Rockaway Inlet
Rockaway Beach
Rockaway Pt. Blvd.
Jacob Riis Park
ROCKAWAY POINT
6
Breezy Point Park
ATLANTIC OCEAN
N
0
1 mile
0
1 kilometer
Queens

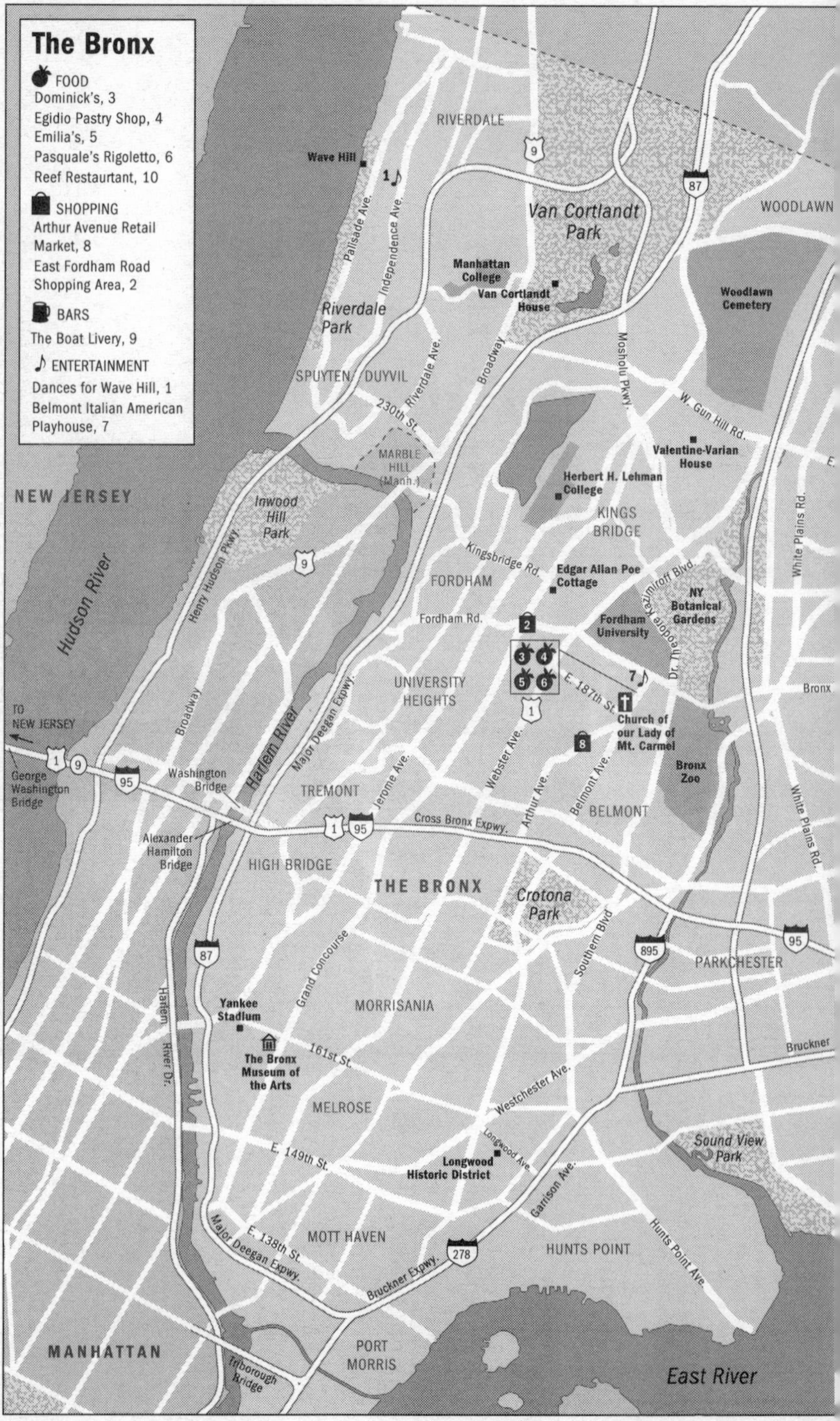
The Bronx
FOOD
Dominick's, 3
Egidio Pastry Shop, 4
Emilia's, 5
Pasquale's Rigoletto, 6
Reef Restaurant, 10
SHOPPING
Arthur Avenue Retail Market, 8
East Fordham Road Shopping Area, 2
BARS
The Boat Livery, 9
ENTERTAINMENT
Dances for Wave Hill, 1
Belmont Italian American Playhouse, 7
RIVERDALE
Wave Hill
Van Cortlandt Park
WOODLAWN
Manhattan College
Van Cortlandt House
Woodlawn Cemetery
Palisade Ave.
Independence Ave.
Riverdale Park
Riverdale Ave.
Broadway
Mosholu Pkwy.
SPUYTEN DUYVIL
230th St.
W. Gun Hill Rd.
MARBLE HILL (Manh.)
Valentine-Varian House
Herbert H. Lehman College
NEW JERSEY
Inwood Hill Park
KINGS BRIDGE
Kingsbridge Rd.
Edgar Allan Poe Cottage
Henry Hudson Pkwy.
Hudson River
FORDHAM
Fordham Rd.
Dr. Theodore Kazimiroff Blvd.
NY Botanical Gardens
Fordham University
White Plains Rd.
UNIVERSITY HEIGHTS
E. 187th St.
Major Deegan Expwy.
Church of our Lady of Mt. Carmel
Bronx
TO NEW JERSEY
Broadway
Harlem River
Webster Ave.
Arthur Ave.
Belmont Ave.
Bronx Zoo
George Washington Bridge
Washington Bridge
Jerome Ave.
TREMONT
BELMONT
Cross Bronx Expwy.
Alexander Hamilton Bridge
HIGH BRIDGE
THE BRONX
Crotona Park
Southern Blvd
PARKCHESTER
Grand Concourse
MORRISANIA
Harlem River Dr.
Yankee Stadium
The Bronx Museum of the Arts
161st St.
Bruckner
Westchester Ave.
MELROSE
Sound View Park
Longwood Ave.
E. 149th St.
Longwood Historic District
Garrison Ave.
Hunts Point Ave.
MOTT HAVEN
E. 138th St.
Major Deegan Expwy.
HUNTS POINT
Bruckner Expwy.
MANHATTAN
PORT MORRIS
Triborough Bridge
East River

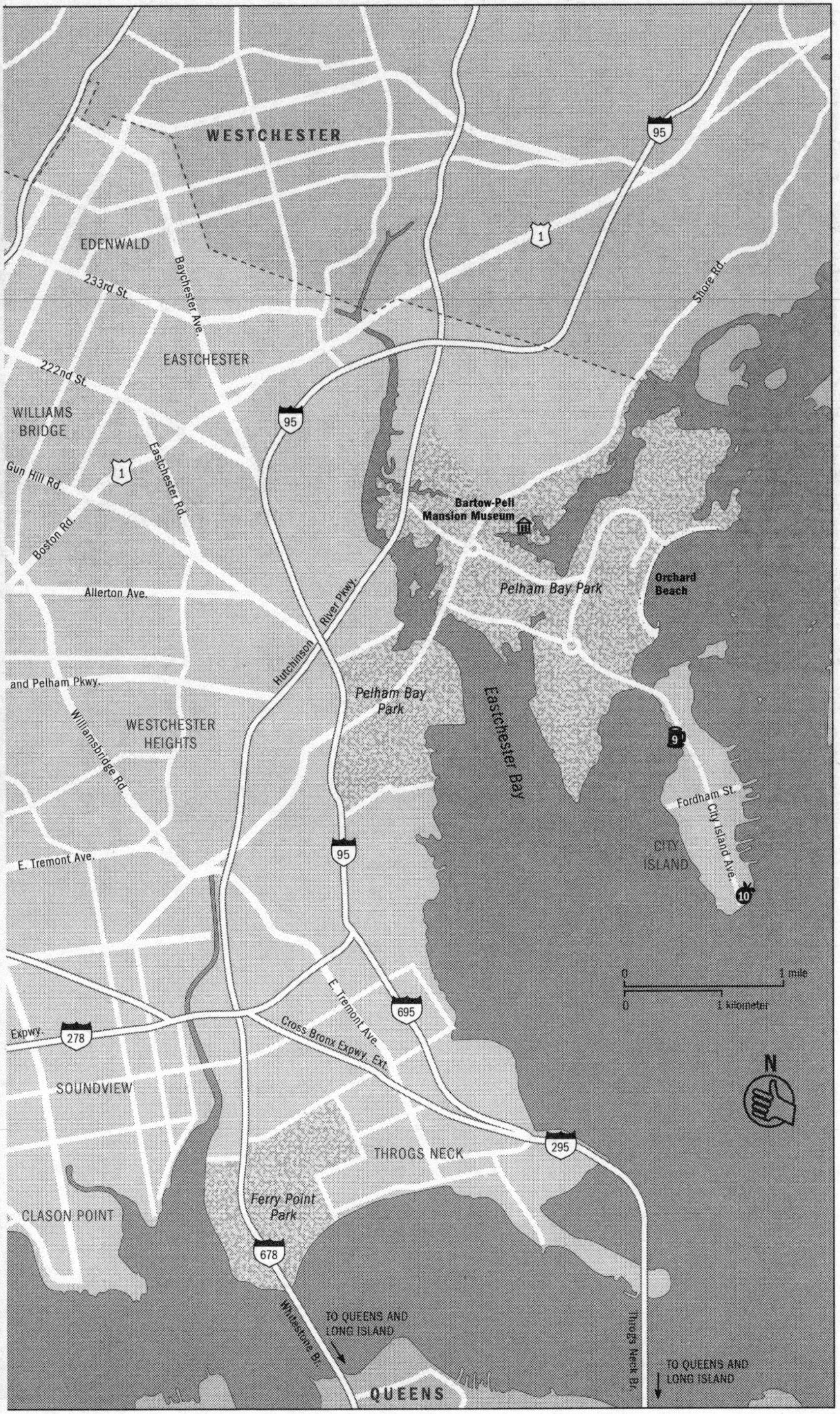
WESTCHESTER
95
1
EDENWALD
233rd St.
Baychester Ave.
EASTCHESTER
Shore Rd.
222nd St.
WILLIAMS
BRIDGE
95
Eastchester Rd.
Gun Hill Rd.
1
Boston Rd.
Bartow-Pell
Mansion Museum
Orchard
Beach
Pelham Bay Park
Allerton Ave.
Hutchinson River Pkwy.
and Pelham Pkwy.
Pelham Bay
Park
Eastchester Bay
WESTCHESTER
HEIGHTS
Williamsbridge Rd.
9
Fordham St.
City Island Ave.
CITY
ISLAND
10
E. Tremont Ave.
95
0
1 mile
0
1 kilometer
695
Expwy.
278
E. Tremont Ave.
Cross Bronx Expwy. Ext.
N
SOUNDVIEW
295
THROGS NECK
Ferry Point
Park
CLASON POINT
678
Whitestone Br.
TO QUEENS AND
LONG ISLAND
Throgs Neck Br.
TO QUEENS AND
LONG ISLAND
QUEENS

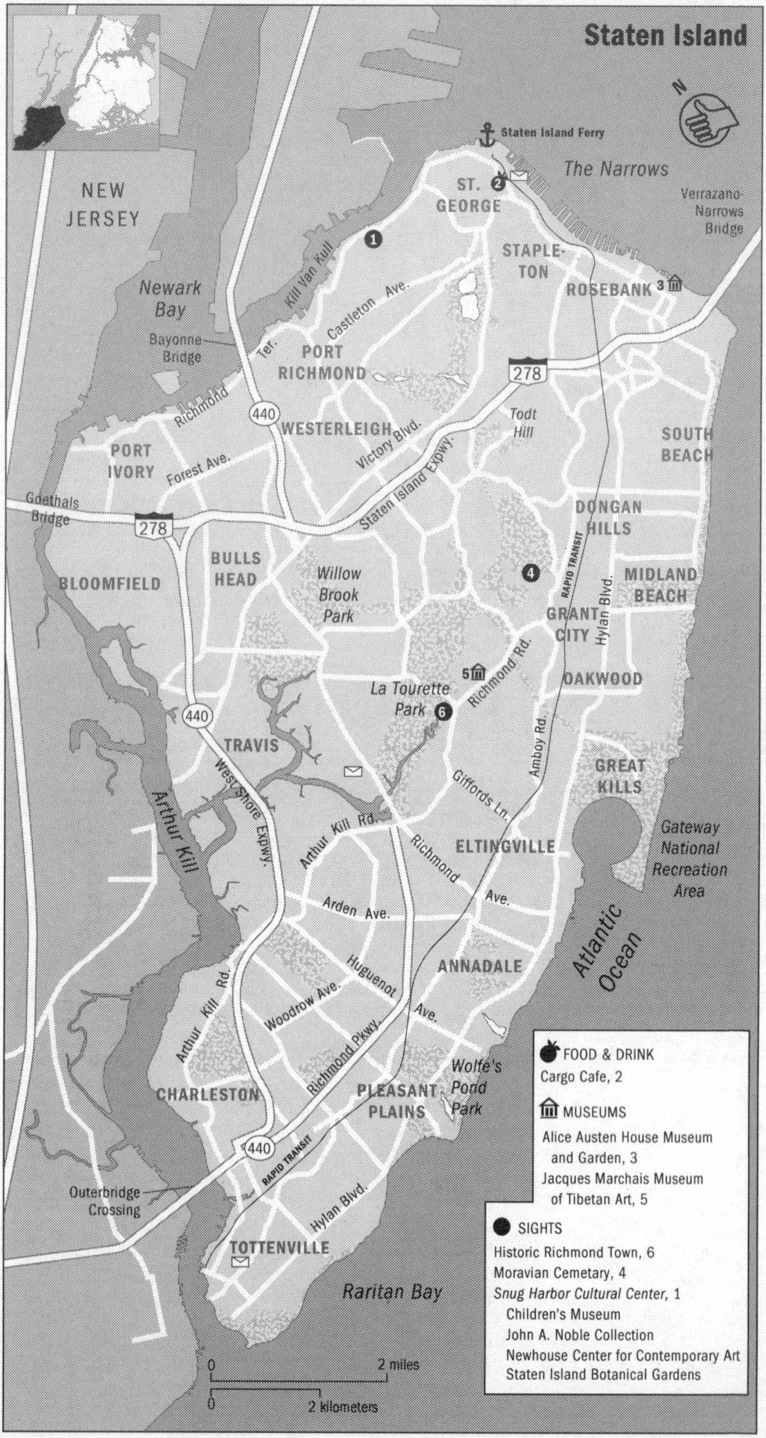
Staten Island
Staten Island Ferry
The Narrows
Verrazano-Narrows Bridge
ST. GEORGE
STAPLETON
ROSEBANK
NEW JERSEY
Newark Bay
Bayonne Bridge
Kill Van Kull
Castleton Ave.
Richmond Ter.
PORT RICHMOND
WESTERLEIGH
Victory Blvd.
Todt Hill
SOUTH BEACH
PORT IVORY
Forest Ave.
Goethals Bridge
Staten Island Expwy.
DONGAN HILLS
BULLS HEAD
BLOOMFIELD
Willow Brook Park
RAPID TRANSIT
MIDLAND BEACH
GRANT CITY
Hylan Blvd.
Richmond Rd.
OAKWOOD
La Tourette Park
TRAVIS
Amboy Rd.
GREAT KILLS
West Shore Expwy.
Arthur Kill
Gifford's Ln.
Arthur Kill Rd.
ELTINGVILLE
Richmond Ave.
Gateway National Recreation Area
Arden Ave.
Atlantic Ocean
ANNADALE
Huguenot Ave.
Arthur Kill Rd.
Woodrow Ave.
Richmond Pkwy.
Wolfe's Pond Park
CHARLESTON
PLEASANT PLAINS
RAPID TRANSIT
Outerbridge Crossing
Hylan Blvd.
TOTTENVILLE
Raritan Bay
0 2 miles
0 2 kilometers
FOOD & DRINK
Cargo Cafe, 2
MUSEUMS
Alice Austen House Museum and Garden, 3
Jacques Marchais Museum of Tibetan Art, 5
SIGHTS
Historic Richmond Town, 6
Moravian Cemetary, 4
Snug Harbor Cultural Center, 1
Children's Museum
John A. Noble Collection
Newhouse Center for Contemporary Art
Staten Island Botanical Gardens

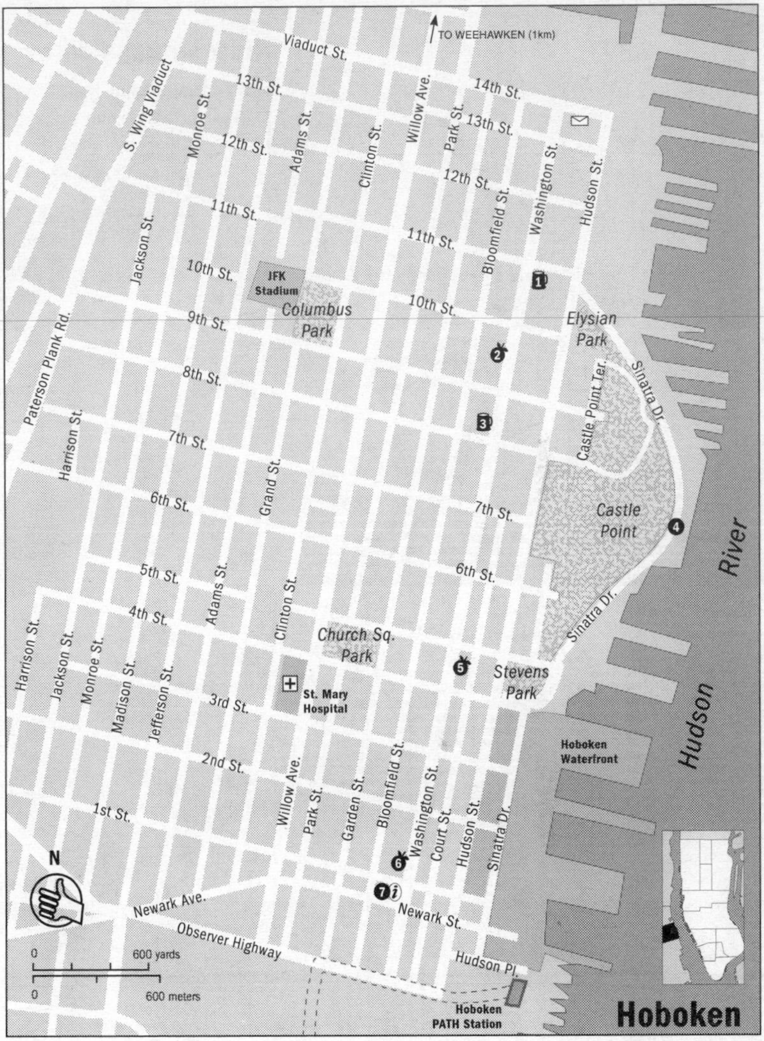

FOOD AND DRINK
Amanda's, 2
The Hoboken Gourmet Company, 5
La Isla, 6

SIGHTS
City Hall, 7
Overlook Point, 4

NIGHTLIFE
8th Street Tavern, 3
Maxwell's, 1

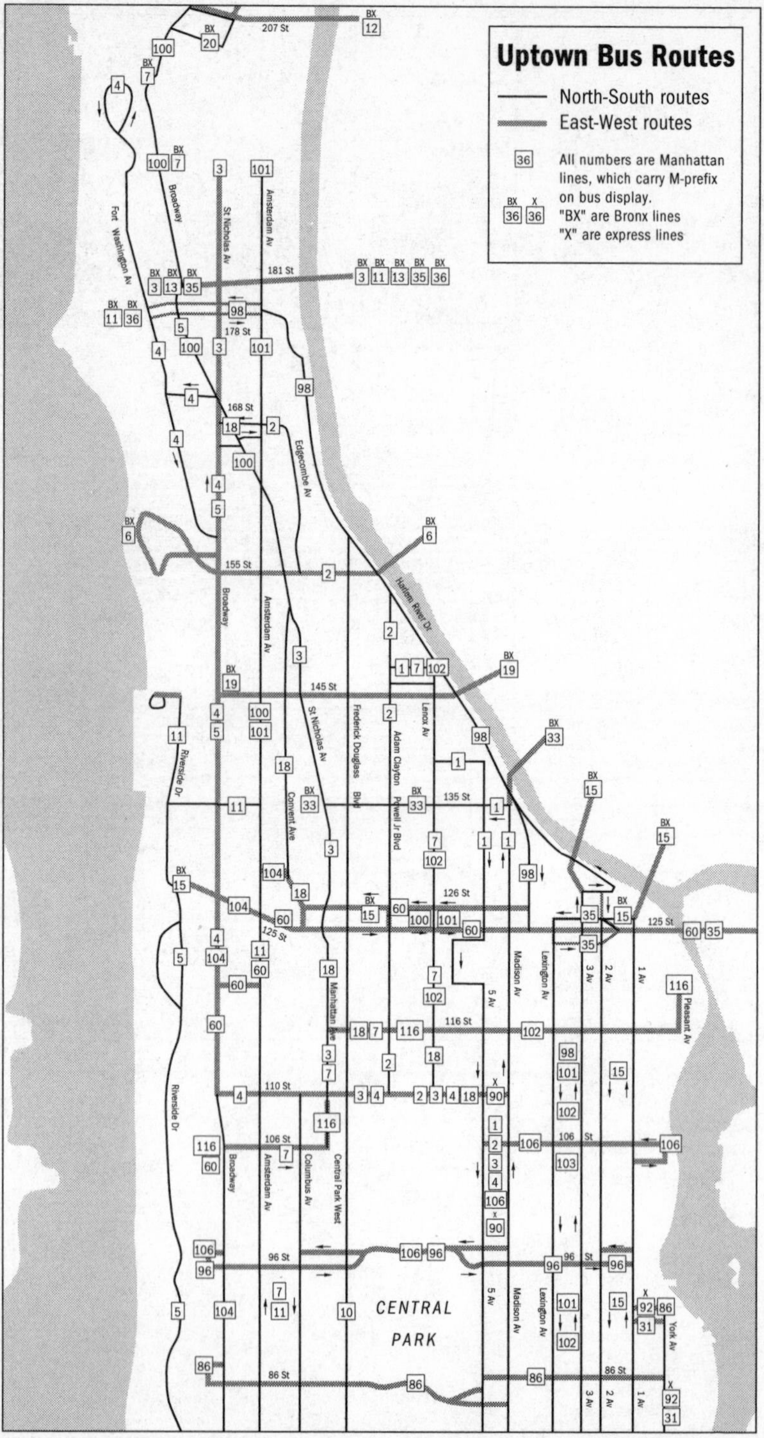
Uptown Bus Routes
North-South routes
East-West routes
All numbers are Manhattan lines, which carry M-prefix on bus display.
"BX" are Bronx lines
"X" are express lines
207 St
181 St
178 St
168 St
155 St
145 St
135 St
126 St
125 St
116 St
110 St
106 St
96 St
86 St
Fort Washington Av
Broadway
St Nicholas Av
Amsterdam Av
Edgecombe Av
Harlem River Dr
Riverside Dr
Convent Ave
Frederick Douglass Blvd
Adam Clayton Powell Jr Blvd
Lenox Av
Manhattan Ave
Columbus Av
Central Park West
5 Av
Madison Av
Lexington Av
3 Av
2 Av
1 Av
Pleasant Av
York Av
CENTRAL PARK

Downtown Bus Routes
North-South routes
East-West routes
All numbers are Manhattan lines, which carry M-prefix on bus display.
"Q" are Queens lines;
"B" are Brooklyn lines
"X" are express lines
CENTRAL PARK
Riverside Dr
Broadway
81 St
79 St
Columbus Av
Central Park West
5 Av
Lexington Av
3 Av
2 Av
1 Av
York Av
72 St
68 St
67 St
66 St
65 St
Madison Av
Amsterdam Av
West End Av
60 St
59 St
57 St
50 St
49 St
10 Av
9 Av
8 Av
7 Av
6 Av
42 St
12 Av
Park Av S
34 St
11 Av
23 St
20 St
14 St
Av A
Av B
Av C
Av D
Greenwich St
9 St
8 St
10 St
Lafayette St
Christopher
Houston St
Bowery
West St
Hudson St
Varick St
Canal St
E Broadway
Madison St
Worth St
Chambers St
Trinity Pl
Manhattan Br

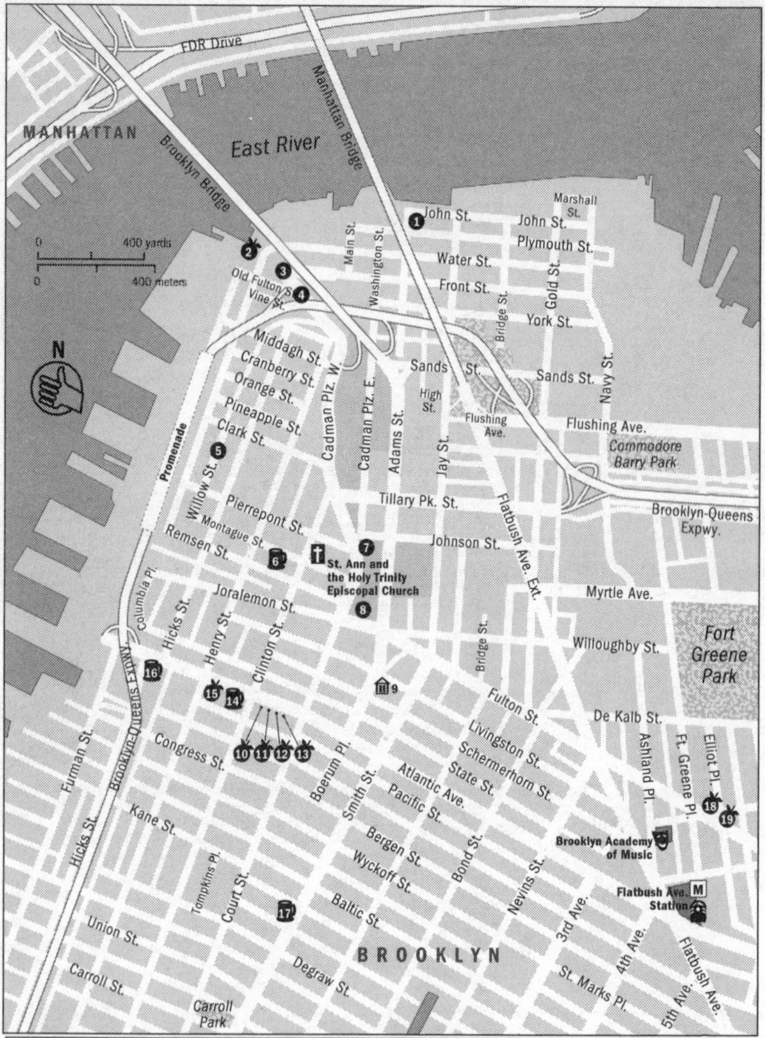

Brooklyn Heights and Downtown Brooklyn

FOOD
Brooklyn Moon, 19
Caravan, 11
Damascus Bakery, 10
Fountain Cafe, 13
Grimaldi's, 2
Keur N'Deye, 18
Petite Crevette, 15
Sahadi Importing Company, 12

NIGHTLIFE
Halcyon, 17
Montague Street Saloon, 6
Montero's Bar & Grill, 16
Waterfront Ale House, 14

SIGHTS
135 Plymouth St., 1
Borough Hall, 8
Brooklyn Bridge, Anchorage, 4
Brooklyn Historical Society, 7
The Eagle Warehouse and Storage Co., 3
Willow Street, 5

MUSEUMS
New York Transit Museum, 9

Williamsburg and Greenpoint

FOOD

Bliss, 9
L Cafe, 8
Miyako, 11
Oznot's Dish, 2
Phoebe's, 24
Planet Thailand, 5
The Read Cafe and Bookshop, 6
Stylowa Restaurant, 1
Vera Cruz, 10

SHOPPING

Clovis Press, 16
Domsey's, 20
Girdle Factory, 15
Ugly Luggage, 14

MUSEUMS AND GALLERIES

Arena@Feed, 17
Lunar Base, 18
Pierogi 2000, 7
Rome, 22
The Williamsburg Art and Historical Center, 21

NIGHTLIFE

Brooklyn Ale House, 4
Galapagos, 13
Pete's Candy Store, 23
Teddy's, 3
Yabby's, 19

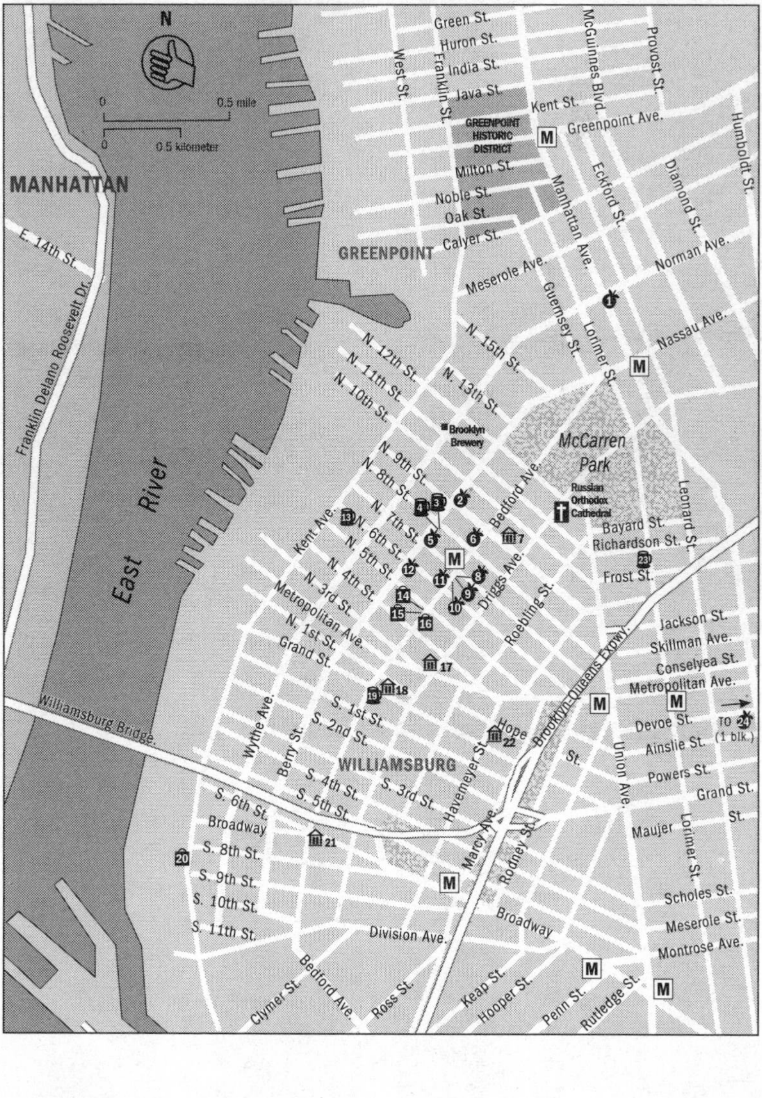

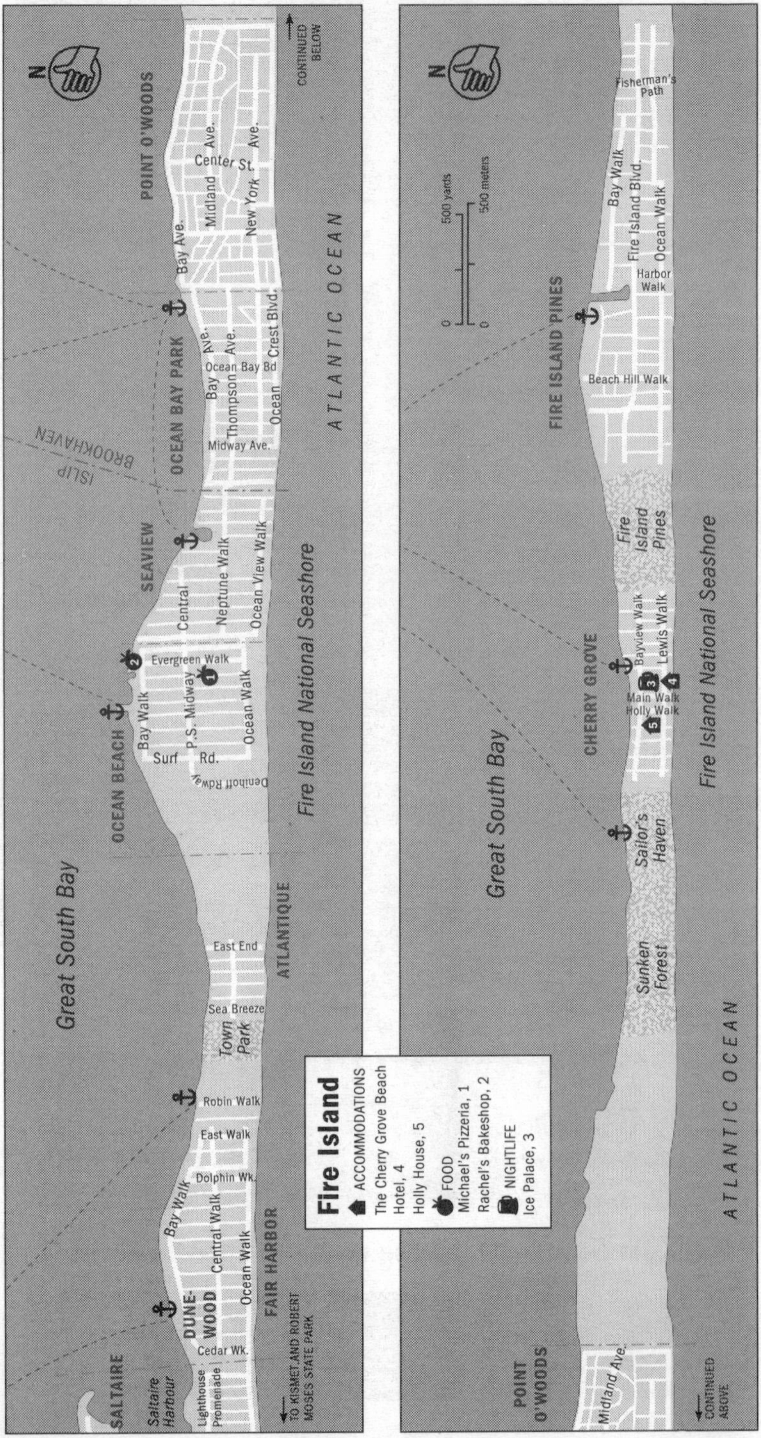
Fire Island
ACCOMMODATIONS
The Cherry Grove Beach Hotel, 4
Holly House, 5
FOOD
Michael's Pizzeria, 1
Rachel's Bakeshop, 2
NIGHTLIFE
Ice Palace, 3
Great South Bay
ATLANTIC OCEAN
Fire Island National Seashore
POINT O'WOODS
OCEAN BAY PARK
SEAVIEW
OCEAN BEACH
ATLANTIQUE
FAIR HARBOR
DUNE-WOOD
SALTAIRE
Saltaire Harbour
Lighthouse Promenade
ISLIP
BROOKHAVEN
Bay Ave.
Midland Ave.
Center St.
New York Ave.
Crest Blvd.
Ocean Bay Bd
Thompson Ave.
Midway Ave.
Ocean
Central
Neptune Walk
Ocean View Walk
Evergreen Walk
Bay Walk
P.S. Midway
Ocean Walk
Surf Rd.
Denihoff Rdway
East End
Sea Breeze
Town Park
Robin Walk
East Walk
Dolphin Wk.
Central Walk
Cedar Wk.
CONTINUED BELOW
TO KISMET AND ROBERT MOSES STATE PARK
500 yards
500 meters
FIRE ISLAND PINES
Fisherman's Path
Bay Walk
Fire Island Blvd.
Ocean Walk
Harbor Walk
Beach Hill Walk
Fire Island Pines
CHERRY GROVE
Bayview Walk
Lewis Walk
Main Walk
Holly Walk
Sailor's Haven
Sunken Forest
POINT O'WOODS
Midland Ave.
CONTINUED ABOVE

Moooore Room.
Real American Airlines deals for students and faculty, online at StudentUniverse. Earn AAdvantage miles and enjoy *more room throughout Coach only on American**.
StudentUniverse.com
featuring
AmericanAirlines
800.272.9676
RESTRICTIONS: A portion of or all travel may be on American Eagle, American's regional airline affiliate. American Airlines, American Eagle and AAdvantage are marks of American Airlines, Inc. American Airlines reserves the right to change AAdvantage program rules, regulations, travel awards and special offers at any time without notice, and to end the AAdvantage program with six months notice. American Airlines is not responsible for products or services by other participating companies. *Only American has removed rows of seats throughout Coach to provide more room for more Coach passengers than any other airline. Now available on all two-class aircraft; three-class aircraft reconfiguration in progress; not available on American Eagle.

Travel Cheep.
Visit StudentUniverse for real deals on student and faculty airline tickets, rail passes, and hostel memberships.
StudentUniverse.com
Real Travel Deals
800.272.9676

Will you have enough stories to tell your grandchildren?
Yahoo! Travel
Do You Yahoo!?

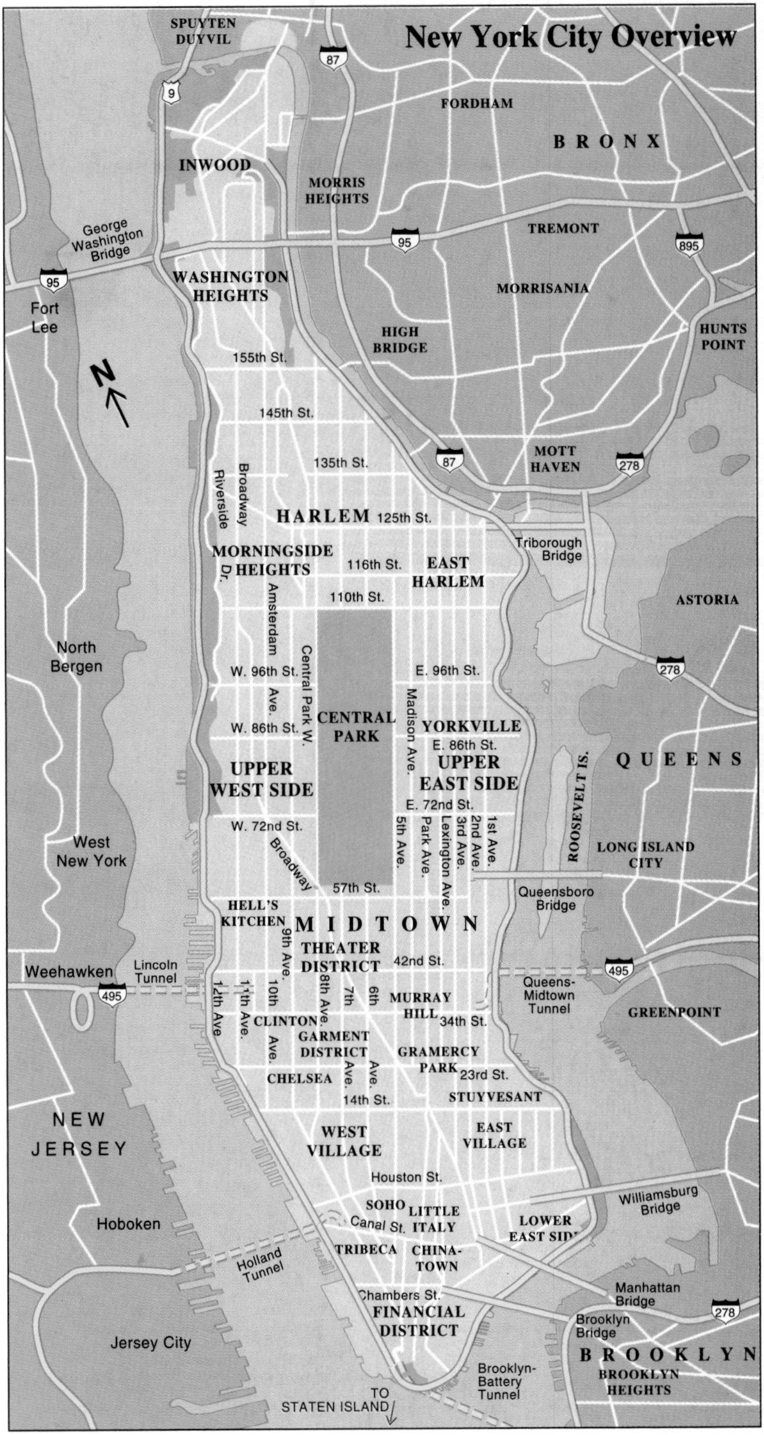
New York City Overview
SPUYTEN DUYVIL
87
9
FORDHAM
BRONX
INWOOD
MORRIS HEIGHTS
George Washington Bridge
95
TREMONT
895
95
Fort Lee
WASHINGTON HEIGHTS
MORRISANIA
HIGH BRIDGE
HUNTS POINT
155th St.
N
145th St.
135th St.
87
MOTT HAVEN
278
Riverside Dr.
Broadway
HARLEM
125th St.
Triborough Bridge
MORNINGSIDE HEIGHTS
116th St.
EAST HARLEM
110th St.
Amsterdam Ave.
ASTORIA
North Bergen
Central Park W.
W. 96th St.
E. 96th St.
278
Madison Ave.
CENTRAL PARK
W. 86th St.
YORKVILLE
E. 86th St.
UPPER EAST SIDE
QUEENS
UPPER WEST SIDE
ROOSEVELT IS.
E. 72nd St.
W. 72nd St.
5th Ave.
Park Ave.
Lexington Ave.
3rd Ave.
2nd Ave.
1st Ave.
West New York
Broadway
LONG ISLAND CITY
57th St.
Queensboro Bridge
HELL'S KITCHEN
MIDTOWN
9th Ave.
THEATER DISTRICT
42nd St.
495
Weehawken
Lincoln Tunnel
495
Queens-Midtown Tunnel
12th Ave.
11th Ave.
10th Ave.
8th Ave.
7th Ave.
6th Ave.
MURRAY HILL
34th St.
GREENPOINT
CLINTON
GARMENT DISTRICT
GRAMERCY PARK
23rd St.
CHELSEA
14th St.
STUYVESANT
NEW JERSEY
WEST VILLAGE
EAST VILLAGE
Houston St.
Williamsburg Bridge
SOHO
LITTLE ITALY
Canal St.
Hoboken
LOWER EAST SIDE
TRIBECA
CHINA-TOWN
Holland Tunnel
Chambers St.
Manhattan Bridge
FINANCIAL DISTRICT
Brooklyn Bridge
278
Jersey City
BROOKLYN
Brooklyn-Battery Tunnel
BROOKLYN HEIGHTS
TO STATEN ISLAND

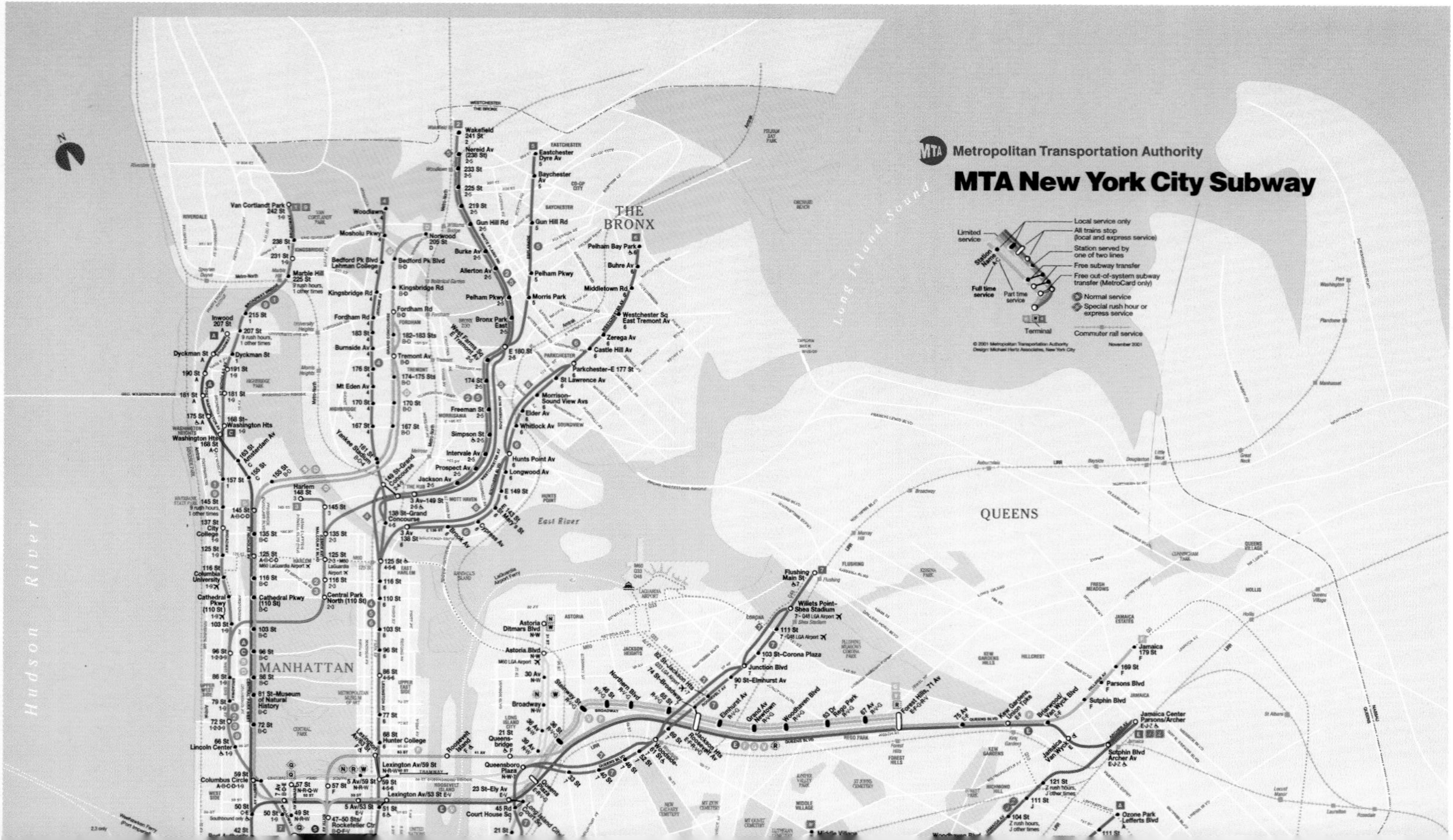
Metropolitan Transportation Authority
MTA New York City Subway
Local service only
All trains stop (local and express service)
Station served by one of two lines
Free subway transfer
Free out-of-system subway transfer (MetroCard only)
Normal service
Special rush hour or express service
Commuter rail service
Limited service
Full time service
Part time service
Terminal
© 2001 Metropolitan Transportation Authority
November 2001
THE BRONX
MANHATTAN
QUEENS
Long Island Sound
East River
Hudson River

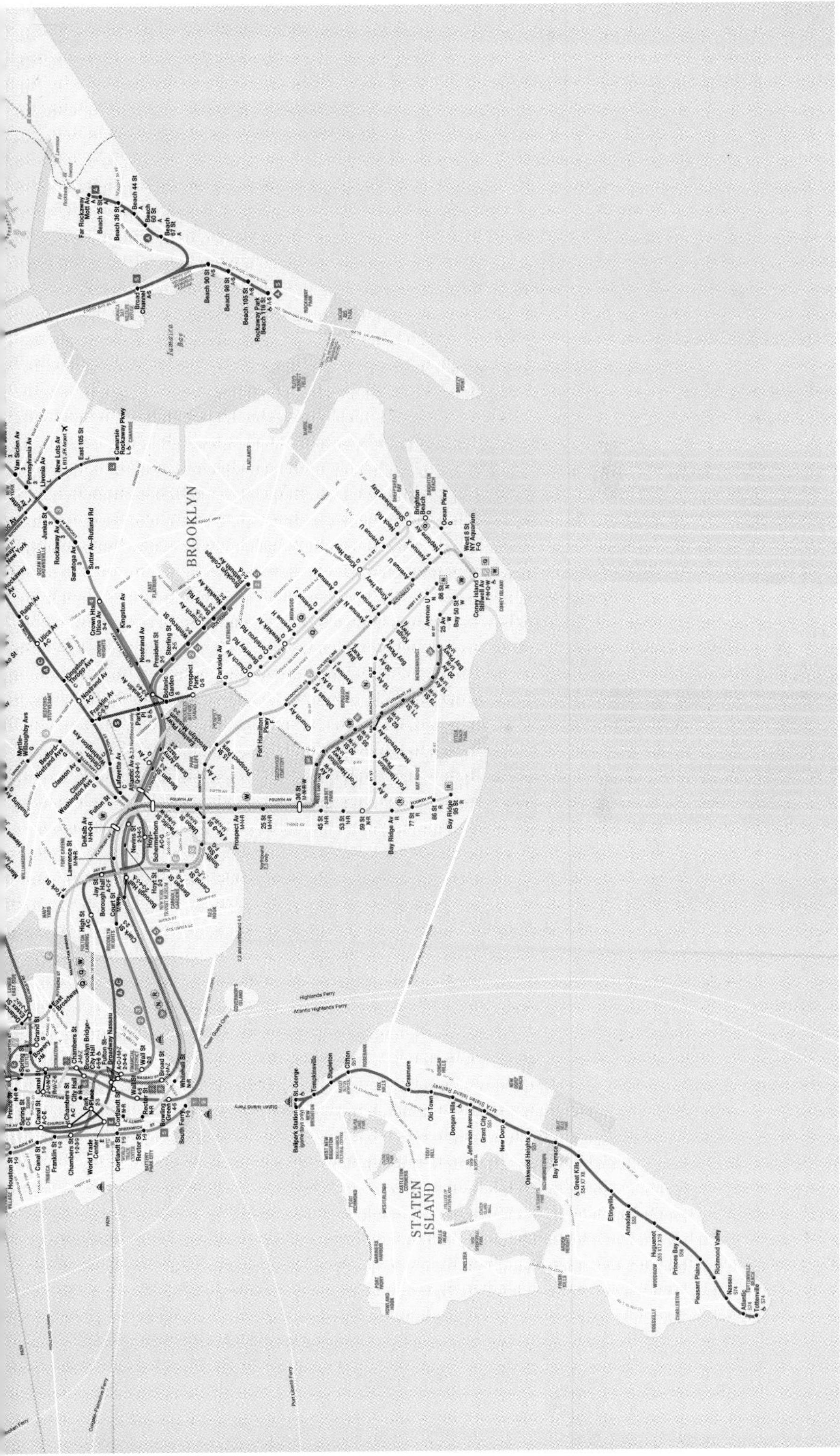
BROOKLYN
STATEN ISLAND
Jamaica Bay
Far Rockaway Mott Av
Beach 25 St
Beach 36 St
Beach 44 St
Beach 60 St
Beach 67 St
Broad Channel
Beach 90 St
Beach 98 St
Beach 105 St
Rockaway Park Beach 116 St
Canarsie Rockaway Pkwy
East 105 St
New Lots Av
Van Siclen Av
Pennsylvania Av
Livonia Av
Junius St
Rockaway Av
Saratoga Av
Sutter Av-Rutland Rd
Brooklyn College Flatbush Av
Kingston Av
Nostrand Av
Crown Hts-Utica Av
Utica Av
Ralph Av
Rockaway Av
Kingston-Throop Avs
Nostrand Av
Franklin Av
Botanic Garden
Prospect Park
Parkside Av
Church Av
Beverly Rd
Cortelyou Rd
Newkirk Av
Avenue H
Avenue J
Avenue M
Kings Hwy
Avenue U
Neck Rd
Sheepshead Bay
Brighton Beach
Ocean Pkwy
West 8 St NY Aquarium
Coney Island Stillwell Av
Bay 50 St
25 Av
86 St
Avenue U
Kings Hwy
Bay Pkwy
20 Av
18 Av
New Utrecht Av
Fort Hamilton Pkwy
Bay Ridge 95 St
86 St
77 St
Bay Ridge Av
59 St
53 St
45 St
36 St
25 St
Prospect Av
Fort Hamilton Pkwy
Church Av
Ditmas Av
18 Av
Avenue I
Bay Pkwy
Avenue N
Avenue P
Avenue X
Atlantic Av
Lafayette Av
Fulton St
Clinton-Washington Avs
Classon Av
Bedford-Nostrand Avs
Myrtle-Willoughby Avs
DeKalb Av
Nevins St
Hoyt-Schermerhorn
Hoyt St
Borough Hall
Court St
Jay St
High St
York St
Clark St
Bergen St
Carroll St
Smith-9 Sts
4 Av-9 St
7 Av
15 St
Grand Army Plaza
Union St
Whitehall St
South Ferry
Bowling Green
Wall St
Broad St
Fulton St
Rector St
Cortlandt St
World Trade Center
Chambers St
City Hall
Brooklyn Bridge-City Hall
Canal St
Spring St
Houston St
Franklin St
East Broadway
Grand St
Bowery
St. George
Tompkinsville
Stapleton
Clifton
Grasmere
Old Town
Dongan Hills
Jefferson Avenue
Grant City
New Dorp
Oakwood Heights
Bay Terrace
Great Kills
Eltingville
Annadale
Huguenot
Princes Bay
Pleasant Plains
Richmond Valley
Nassau
Atlantic
Tottenville
Ballpark Station (game days only)
MTA Staten Island Railway
Staten Island Ferry
Highlands Ferry
Atlantic Highlands Ferry
Port Liberte Ferry

Downtown Manhattan

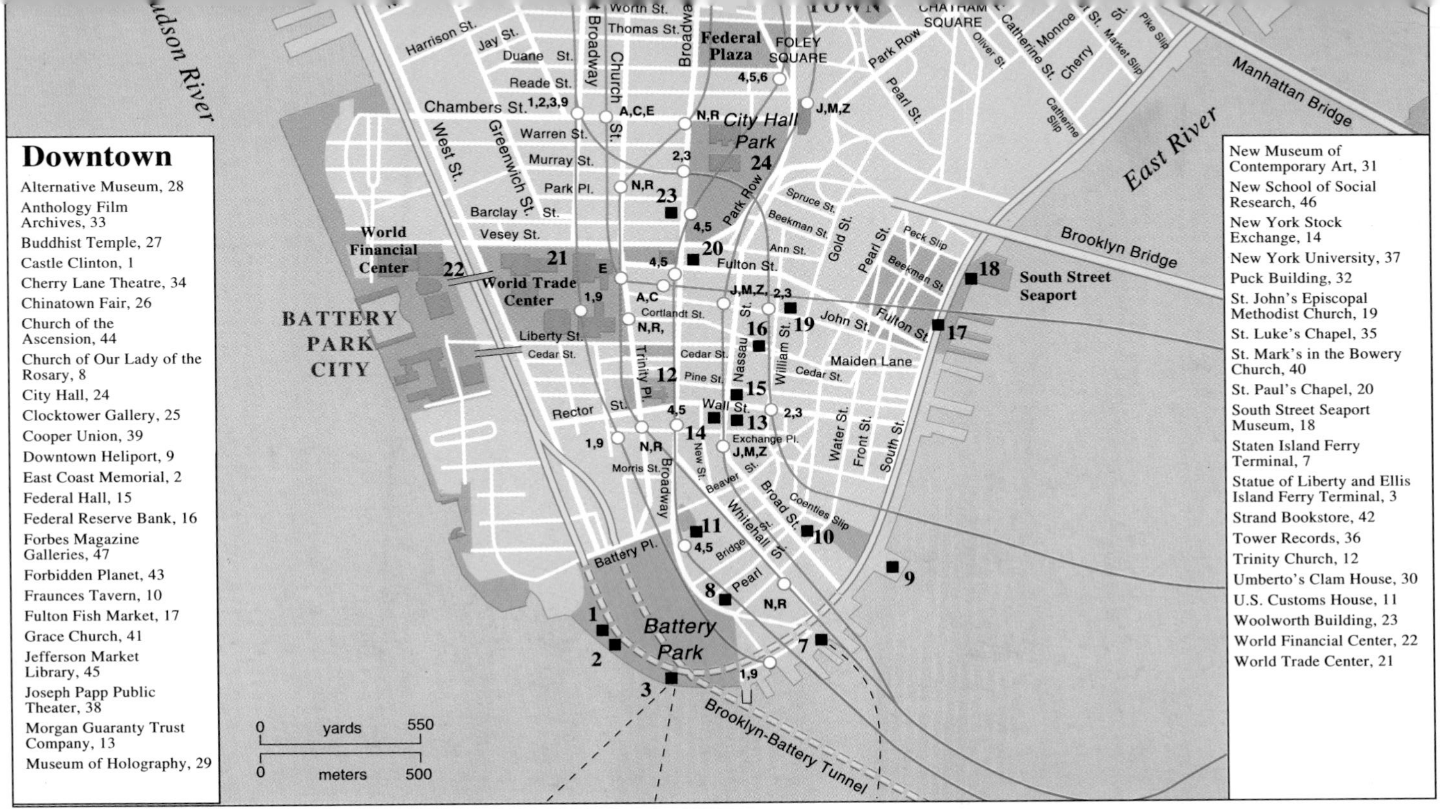

Downtown

Alternative Museum, 28
Anthology Film Archives, 33
Buddhist Temple, 27
Castle Clinton, 1
Cherry Lane Theatre, 34
Chinatown Fair, 26
Church of the Ascension, 44
Church of Our Lady of the Rosary, 8
City Hall, 24
Clocktower Gallery, 25
Cooper Union, 39
Downtown Heliport, 9
East Coast Memorial, 2
Federal Hall, 15
Federal Reserve Bank, 16
Forbes Magazine Galleries, 47
Forbidden Planet, 43
Fraunces Tavern, 10
Fulton Fish Market, 17
Grace Church, 41
Jefferson Market Library, 45
Joseph Papp Public Theater, 38
Morgan Guaranty Trust Company, 13
Museum of Holography, 29
New Museum of Contemporary Art, 31
New School of Social Research, 46
New York Stock Exchange, 14
New York University, 37
Puck Building, 32
St. John's Episcopal Methodist Church, 19
St. Luke's Chapel, 35
St. Mark's in the Bowery Church, 40
St. Paul's Chapel, 20
South Street Seaport Museum, 18
Staten Island Ferry Terminal, 7
Statue of Liberty and Ellis Island Ferry Terminal, 3
Strand Bookstore, 42
Tower Records, 36
Trinity Church, 12
Umberto's Clam House, 30
U.S. Customs House, 11
Woolworth Building, 23
World Financial Center, 22
World Trade Center, 21

Midtown Manhattan

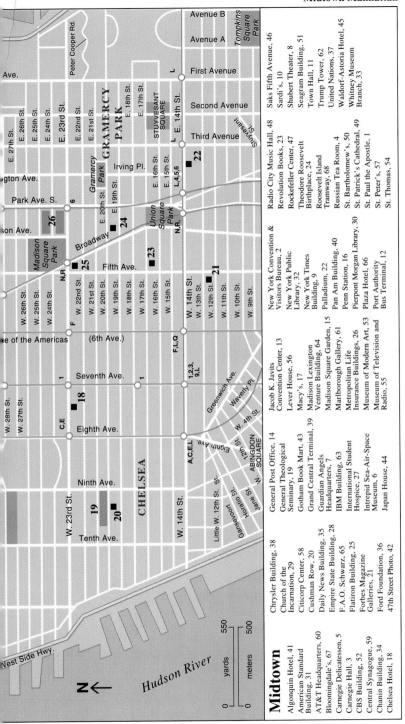

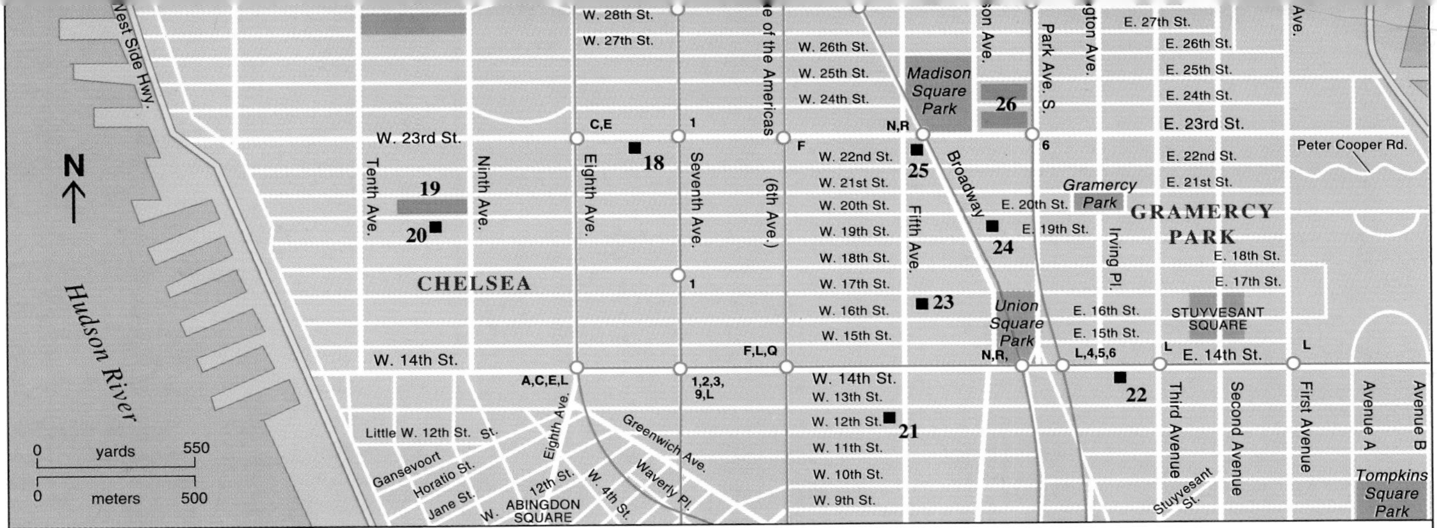

Midtown

- Algonquin Hotel, 41
- American Standard Building, 31
- AT&T Headquarters, 60
- Bloomingdale's, 67
- Carnegie Delicatessen, 5
- Carnegie Hall, 3
- CBS Building, 52
- Central Synagogue, 59
- Chanin Building, 34
- Chelsea Hotel, 18
- Chrysler Building, 38
- Church of the Incarnation, 29
- Citicorp Center, 58
- Cushman Row, 20
- Daily News Building, 35
- Empire State Building, 28
- F.A.O. Schwarz, 65
- Flatiron Building, 25
- Forbes Magazine Galleries, 21
- Ford Foundation, 36
- 47th Street Photo, 42
- General Post Office, 14
- General Theological Seminary, 19
- Gotham Book Mart, 43
- Grand Central Terminal, 39
- Guardian Angels Headquarters, 7
- IBM Building, 63
- International Student Hospice, 27
- Intrepid Sea-Air-Space Museum, 6
- Japan House, 44
- Jacob K. Javits Convention Center, 13
- Lever House, 56
- Macy's, 17
- Madison Lexington Venture Building, 64
- Madison Square Garden, 15
- Marlborough Gallery, 61
- Metropolitan Life Insurance Buildings, 26
- Museum of Modern Art, 53
- Museum of Television and Radio, 55
- New York Convention & Visitors Bureau, 2
- New York Public Library, 32
- New York Times Building, 9
- Palladium, 22
- Pan Am Building, 40
- Penn Station, 16
- Pierpont Morgan Library, 30
- Plaza Hotel, 66
- Port Authority Bus Terminal, 12
- Radio City Music Hall, 48
- Revolution Books, 23
- Rockefeller Center, 47
- Theodore Roosevelt Birthplace, 24
- Roosevelt Island Tramway, 68
- Russian Tea Room, 4
- St. Bartholomew's, 50
- St. Patrick's Cathedral, 49
- St. Paul the Apostle, 1
- St. Peter's, 57
- St. Thomas, 54
- Saks Fifth Avenue, 46
- Sardi's, 10
- Shubert Theater, 8
- Seagram Building, 51
- Town Hall, 11
- Trump Tower, 62
- United Nations, 37
- Waldorf-Astoria Hotel, 45
- Whitney Museum Branch, 33

Uptown Manhattan

Uptown

- American Museum of Natural History, 53
- The Ansonia, 55
- The Arsenal, 25
- Asia Society, 14
- Belvedere Castle, 36
- Bethesda Fountain, 33
- Blockhouse No. 1, 42
- Bloomingdale's, 22
- Bridle Path, 30
- Cathedral of St. John the Divine, 47
- Central Park Zoo, 24
- Chess and Checkers House, 28
- Children's Museum of Manhattan, 51
- Children's Zoo, 26
- China House, 19
- Cleopatra's Needle, 38
- Columbia University, 46
- Conservatory Garden, 2
- Cooper-Hewitt Museum, 7
- The Dairy, 27
- Dakota Apartments, 56
- Delacorte Theater, 37
- El Museo del Barrio, 1
- Fordham University, 60
- Frick Museum, 13
- Gracie Mansion, 10
- Grant's Tomb, 45
- Great Lawn, 39
- Guggenheim Museum, 9
- Hayden Planetarium (at the American Museum of Natural History), 53
- Hector Memorial, 50
- Hotel des Artistes, 57
- Hunter College, 16
- International Center of Photography, 5
- Jewish Museum, 6
- The Juilliard School (at Lincoln Center), 59
- Lincoln Center, 59
- Loeb Boathouse, 34
- Masjid Malcolm Shabazz , 43
- Metropolitan Museum of Art, 11
- Mt. Sinai Hospital, 4
- Museum of American Folk Art, 58
- Museum of American Illustration, 21
- Museum of the City of New York, 3
- National Academy of Design, 8
- New York Convention & Visitors Bureau, 61
- New York Historical Society, 54
- New York Hospital, 15
- Plaza Hotel, 23
- Police Station (Central Park), 40
- Rockefeller University, 20
- 7th Regiment Armory, 17
- Shakespeare Garden, 35
- Soldiers and Sailors Monument, 49
- Strawberry Fields, 32
- Studio Museum in Harlem, 44
- Symphony Space, 48
- Tavern on the Green, 31
- Temple Emanu-El, 18
- Tennis Courts, 41
- Whitney Museum of American Art, 12
- Wollman Rink, 29
- Zabar's, 52

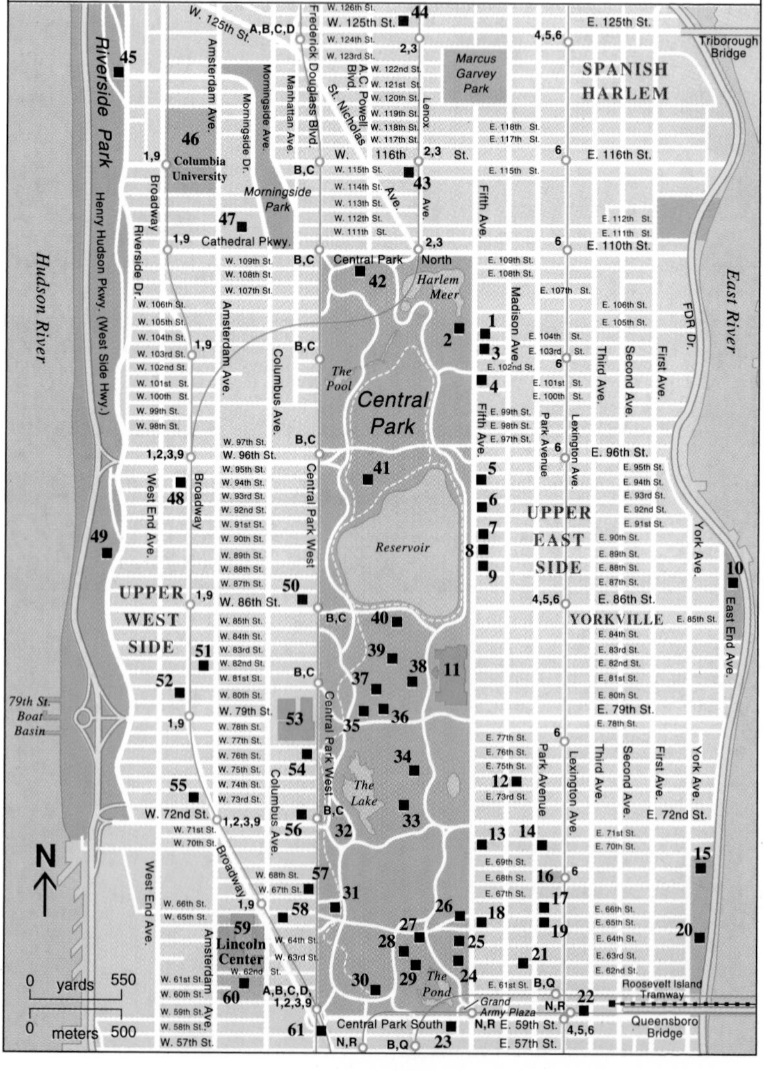